# A WRITER'S READER

# A WRITER'S READER

## NINTH EDITION

**Donald Hall**

**D. L. Emblen**
*Santa Rosa Junior College*

New York  San Francisco  Boston
London  Toronto  Sydney  Tokyo  Singapore  Madrid
Mexico City  Munich  Paris  Cape Town  Hong Kong  Montreal

Editor-in-Chief: Joseph Terry
Acquisitions Editor: Lynn M. Huddon
Executive Marketing Manager: Carlise Paulson
Supplements Editor: Donna Campion
Production Manager: Donna DeBenedictis
Project Coordination, Text Design, and Electronic Page Makeup: The Clarinda
    Company
Senior Cover Designer/Manager: Nancy Danahy
Cover Illustration: © Connie Hayes/Stock Illustration Source, Inc.
Manufacturing Buyer: Lucy Hebard
Printer and Binder: The Maple-Vail Book Manufacturing Group
Cover Printer: John P. Pow Company, Inc.

Library of Congress Cataloging-in-Publication Data

A writer's reader / [edited by] Donald Hall, D. L. Emblen.—9th ed.
        p. cm.
    Includes index.
    ISBN 0-321-08748-8 (pbk.)
    1. College readers.   2. Report writing—Problems, exercises, etc.   3. English
language—Rhetoric—Problems, exercises, etc.   I. Hall, Donald, 1928–
II. Emblen, D. L. (Donald Lewis), 1918–

PE1417.W67 2002
808'.0427—cd21

                                                                        2001020415

Please visit our website at http://www.ablongman.com

ISBN 0-321-08748-8

1 2 3 4 5 6 7 8 9 10—MA—04 03 02 01

For William R. Booth

# Contents

# Preface

Reading well precedes writing well. Of all the ancestors claimed by a fine piece of prose, the most important is the prose from which the writer learned his craft. Writers learn craft not by memorizing rules about restrictive clauses, but by striving to equal a standard formed from reading.

A composition course, then, must be two courses: one in reading, another in writing. If students lack practice in writing, they are usually unpracticed readers as well. Most students lack quality of reading as well as quantity; and if we assert that good models help us, we admit that bad models hurt us. People who read bad prose twelve hours a week—newspapers, popular fiction, textbooks—are as ill served as people who read nothing at all. Surely most textbooks, from freshman handbooks through the text for Psych 101, encourage the illusion that words merely stand in for ideas, or carry information on their backs—that words exist for the convenience of thinking, much as turnpikes exist for the sake of automobiles.

This barbarism underlies the vogue of speed reading, which urges us to scan lines for comprehension, ignoring syntax and metaphor, ignoring image and feeling and sound. If we are to grow and to learn—and surely if we are to write well—we must learn to read slowly and intimately, and to read good writing. We must learn to read actively, even aggressively, without the passivity derived from watching television. The active reader questions as he reads, subjects each author's ideas to skeptical scrutiny, and engages the writer in dialog as part of the reading process.

For language embodies the human psyche. Learning to read—that privilege so recently extended to the ancestors of most of us—allows us to enter human history. In books, we perceive the gesture, the pulse, the heartbeat, the pallor, the eye movement, the pitch, and the tone of people who lived before us, or who live now in other places, in other skins, in other habits, customs, beliefs, and ideas.

Language *embodies* the human psyche, which includes ideas and the feelings that properly accompany ideas. There is no sleight-of-mind by which the idea may be separated from its body and remain alive. The body of good writing is rhythm and image, metaphor and syntax, order of phrase and order of paragraph.

## A NOTE TO LATER EDITIONS

Many teachers have helped us prepare the many editions of *A Writer's Reader*—in letters, in conversations at colleges all over the country, in responses to the publisher's survey of users. We thank more people than we can list.

We have added considerable material, and we are pleased with the result. We believe that we have made a representative sampling of good prose. We like some pieces more than others, heaven knows, but we believe that all of them provide something to learn from. We have included a wide variety of prose, mostly contemporary but also historical. We hope that young Americans will attach themselves to the body of our history by immersion in its significant utterances.

We have numbered paragraphs for ease of reference. Although *A Writer's Reader* is a collection of essays, we have again violated coherence by including fiction, feeling that the contrast afforded by a few short stories among the essays was useful and refreshing. We have also included several poems, for the same reason. Perhaps we should make an argument for including poems—but let us just say that we enjoy them, and we hope you do, too. To satisfy students' curiosity, we have included headnotes to the poems; but we have stopped short of suggesting questions after them, lest we seem to surround a landscape garden with a hundred-foot-high concrete wall.

We have chosen to arrange our essays, stories, and poems alphabetically by author. This arrangement makes for random juxtaposition, irrational sequence, and no sense at all—which is why we chose it. We expect no one to teach these pieces in alphabetical order. We expect teachers to find their own order—which they would do whatever order we attempted to impose. In our first edition, we struggled to make a stylistic organization, listing some essays as examples of "Sentences," others as examples of "Paragraphs." For the editors themselves, a year after deciding on our organization, it was no longer clear why essay X was to be studied for its sentences and essay Y for its paragraphs. With a rhetorical organization, one runs into another sort of problem. Although an essay may contain Division, or Process Analysis, or an example of Example, the same essay is likely to use three or four other patterns as well. No piece of real prose is ever so pure as our systems of classification. Thematic organizations, which have their attractions, have similar flaws; is E. B. White's theme in "Once More to the Lake" Mortality? Aging? Youth and Age? Or How I Spent My Summer Vacation?

Our arrangement is more arbitrary than an arrangement by style or rhetoric or theme, and presents itself only to be ignored. At the same time, there are dozens of ways in which these essays (and poems and stories) can be used together. Our Instructor's Manual suggests several combinations. Our Rhetorical Index is printed as an appendix to the text itself and we hope that students will find it useful. Freshmen who return to their rooms from class, set to write a paper using Comparison and Contrast, sometimes find themselves in need of a concrete example of the assigned pattern to imitate. We have also added a Thematic Index.

Thus, we have tried to supply some useful maps to go with our arbitrary arrangement. Following suggestions from several teachers, we have chosen to represent a few authors by small clusters of their work. We have expanded our representation of writing by scientists. In response to many suggestions, we have looked for short, complete essays in exposition and argument on a variety of topics.

In the ninth edition, in response to the suggestions of several readers, we have included additional fine essays by American writers of various ethnic backgrounds—Asian, Hispanic, Native American, and African American. We want *A Writer's Reader* to embody the cultural manyness of the American classroom.

If you miss essays or authors that we eliminated in this edition, please let us know. If there are authors we overlook, whom you would recommend, we solicit your help. Although we intend to remain alert to good prose and to the needs of the classroom, we need help from the outside.

## ACKNOWLEDGMENTS

We thank the following users of earlier editions for their helpful comments: Louise Ackley, Maureen Andrews, Tony Ardizzone, Jo Ann Asbury, Ann Avery, Tom Barnwell, Will Baty, Conrad S. Bayley, Jane Berk, Meredith Berman, Dennis Berthold, Barbara Blaha, C. Bogarad, Charles E. Bolton, Charles Bressler, Patrick Broderick, Otis Bronson, Laurel Broughton, Ingrid Brunner, Ed Buckley, Sandra Burns, Jon Burton, Ann Cameron, Marti Carpenter, Richard Cloyed, Randy Conine, Steven Connelly, Roger Conner, Rebecca Coogan, Charles L. Cornwell, Valecia Crisafulli, Garber Davidson, Virginia de Araujo, Loretta Denner, Robert Duxbury, Cirre Emblen, Clovis Emblen, Linda Schafer Emblen, Lee Engdahl, Elizabeth Failla, Ralph Farve, Gala Fitzgerald, Jerome T. Ford, Frances B. Foreman, Susan Forrest, David S. Gadziola, Peggy Gledhill, Joyce Griffin, Ronald Gurney, David Haakensen, Barbara Hamilton, Bill Harby, Bill Harrison, Walter Harrison, Lowell Hawk, Carol T. Hayes, Peter Heitkamp, Allan Hirsh, Art Hofmann, Samuel G. Hornsby Jr., Nancy Hunt, John Huntington, C. S. Joyce, Donald Kansch, Gregory Keeler, Jeff Kluewer, Deborah Lambert, John Larner, Karen LeFerre, Kennedy P. Leisch, Richard H. Lerner, Opal A. Lovett, Neillie McCrory, Sherry McGuire, Andrew Makarushka, Steven J. Masello, Kenneth Maue, Richard Maxwell, Deanne Milan, Molly Moore-Kehler, Harriet Napierkowski, John Necker, Wayne Neel, Jean O'Donnell, Barbara Olive, Stephen O'Neil, Beverly Palmer, John V. Pastoor, Gerrye Payne, Roscoe Poland, Muriel Rada, Jane McBurney Racine, Martha Rainbolt, Shari Rambo, Dennison G. Rice, James Rosen, Harriet Susskind Rosenblum,

Robert Schwegler, Terry Shelton, Marvin and Helen Sherak, James Shokoff, Donald K. Skiles, Thomas Skmetzo, Marilyn Smith, Arnold Solkov, Andrew Solomon, Richard Speakes, David A. Spurr, Helen Stauffer, Calvin Steever, Art Suchoki, Bernard Sugarman, Kathleen Sullivan, Ron Taylor, Jane Bamblin Thomas, Richard Tubbs, E. Guy Turcotte, Darlene Unrue, Peter Valenti, Sara Varhus, Craig Watson, Richard Webster, Richard Welin, Dorothy Wells, Joseph F. Whelan, Roberta White, Shirley and Russell White, Edith Wiard, Richard A. Widmayer, Gary Williams, J. J. Wilson, Suzanne Wilson, George Wymer, B. Yu, and Robert Lee Zimmerman.

We would like to thank the following people for their help in preparing the current edition: Peter Balbert, Trinity University; Melissa Bernstein, University of Rochester; Rebecca Brittenham, Indiana University; Patsy Callaghan, Central Washington University; Vincent Casaregola, Saint Louis University; Frank R. Cunnigham, University of South Dakota; Charles Harrison, San Jacinto College South; Maura Ives, Texas A&M University; Rodney Keller, Ricks College; C. Susan Kraegel, University of North Florida; Priscilla Orr, Sussex County Community College; Thomas Palakeel, Bradley University; Twila Yates Papay, Rollins College; Deborah K. Richey, Owens Community College; Rick Van Noy, Radford University; and Lynn West, Spokane Community College.

Donald Hall
D. L. Emblen

*Shirley Abbott (b. 1934) was born in Hot Springs, Arkansas. After
she graduated from Texas State College for Women, she won a
Fulbright to study in France. She has worked as an editor, has
written essays for magazines, and produced her first book,* The Art
of Food, *in 1977. In 1983 she produced* Womenfolks: Growing Up
Down South, *which appeared in 1985.*

*She is mistress of tone, her irony largely gentle and in the
service of her ideas. She can define a term, necessary for her
argument, while she amuses us. "The unified field theory of the
science, briefly stated, is that the first step in managing men is to
be a belle." From time to time, her language drops its ironical tone
and becomes fierce.*

— 1 —————————————————————————————————————

# SHIRLEY ABBOTT
## *The Importance of Dissimulation*

———————————————————————————————————————————

### A Footnote on Southern Belles

Of all the skills a Southern woman is supposed to master, managing    1
men is the most important. She can dispense with all others if necessary.
The unified field theory of the science, briefly stated, is that the first step
in managing men is to be a belle. Having captured and married the man
of her choice, the belle then turns into a lady. The difference between a
lady and a belle is that the former has a multitude of responsibilities and
hence a more solid power base, while the belle thinks only of herself.
Some women become ladies without ever having been belles; some remain belles all their lives, though not always successfully. A belle, unlike a lady, however, can operate part time.

The ground rules for playing the belle were invented, or at least    2
elaborated, in the drawing rooms and on the verandas of the old plantation South, but the belle's role, like the lady's, received a particularly
thick coat of lacquer in the last part of the nineteenth century. About
that time reinventing the Old South took on the status of a pagan ritual,

and everybody's grandmother, no matter how plain and shy she may actually have been, was declared to have been "the belle of three counties." Thomas Nelson Page, whose *Social Life in Old Virginia* set out the qualifications for Southern lady, did not forget to describe the old-time belle: "She was exquisite, fine, beautiful; a creature of peach blossom and snow; languid; delicate, saucy; now imperious, now melting, always bewitching. She was not versed in the ways of the world, but she had no need to be; she was better than that; she was well bred. She had not to learn to be a lady, because she was born one . . . She lived in an atmosphere created for her—the pure, clean, sweet atmosphere of her country home . . . Truly she was a strange being. In her muslin and lawn; with her delicious, low, slow musical speech; accustomed to be waited on at every turn, with servants to do her every bidding; unhabituated often even to putting on her dainty slippers or combing her soft hair, she possessed a reserve force which was astounding. She was accustomed to have her wishes obeyed as commands."

3      Venus on Olympus could hardly have outdone her, at least as Mr. Page described her. Even the daughters of the Czar or the King of France knew how to put on their own shoes. I wonder whether Thomas Nelson Page ever saw such a person or whether he was just trying to play a little joke on his gullible Yankee readers. In any case, he got some of the paraphernalia right, even if he completely missed the point. As a period creation, the belle should by all logic have died out by now: not many young women still lurk around the Corinthian columns flirting their fans and waiting for their beaus to call or lounging at their dressing tables waiting for Mammy to do up the buttons on their kidskin boots. And yet the Southern belle has survived. Not because Southern society is unchanging but because the managerial techniques devised by the belle have proved sound. One of the inexplicable peculiarities of the human species is that females usually outnumber males and must chase them down, whereas among most other animals males invariably outnumber females and must therefore exert themselves to find a mate, usually against rough and even deadly competition.

4      And thus even now, all over the South, belles thrive. They turn out in the hundreds to be presented at debutante balls and grand assemblies and cotillions as authorized, anointed belles. Anointed or not, they inhabit every college campus and sorority house and the corridors of every high school. They roam up and down in their pretty little dresses or maybe their neatly ironed jeans. They look shy. They pull mirrors out of their purses and pat their hair. They do whatever else they can do to attract attention without seeming forward. They speak softly, do not express any but admiring opinions about any given subject, smile. Money and social position are the least of the qualifications for being a belle. It requires instead a natural theatricality, a talent for taking on a special role in a comedy of manners that will apparently run forever, no matter how transparent its characters and aims.

Belles are not hard to recognize, though it is more than the accent  5
that gives them away. Young women from Michigan and Idaho can be
just as beautiful and studiedly feminized when they want to, but they
don't go about things in quite the same way as a Southerner—or if they
do, that makes them Southern belles. Southern girls invariably, at an
early age, catch on to the idea that being honest with men is a basic tac-
tical error. You cannot judge a Southern belle by what you see. She is
likely to be ostentatiously charming, polite, enthusiastic, sincere, and
soft-headed. That's the standard model, but there are all styles: wise-
cracking, predatory, corruptible. It takes a keen eye to know what the
performance conceals. Sometimes, of course, it is merely vapidity masking vapidity.

What the belle is after is not love but power—using the prettiest  6
possible weapons, she is fighting a guerrilla war. Beauty is a valuable asset in the game but not a necessity. Brains also help, although any form
of intellectuality will have to be muted or even totally concealed, depending on the situation. As in any underground operation, guile is helpful, as are a cool head and a tough hide. But it is most essential that she
remember she is engaged in a covert activity, and the penalty for tipping
one's hand is losing the game. This is why Scarlett O'Hara, who is so often cited as the model of the Southern belle, was not a very successful
practitioner of the art. Her creator never even intended her to be. From
the start, Margaret Mitchell tells us that Scarlett was incapable of keeping her feelings under wraps: "But for all the modesty of her spreading
skirts, the demureness of hair netted smoothly into a chignon and the
quietness of small white hands, her true self was poorly concealed. The
green eyes in the carefully sweet face were turbulent, willful, lusty with
life, distinctly at variance with her decorous demeanor." Scarlett is too
terrifying to be a belle. I have seen sixteen-year-old amateurs in east
Texas in 1979 who could out-belle Scarlett.

Being a belle has its risks, the worst of which is that she may be per-  7
manently seduced by her own propaganda. She may end up believing that
she really is helpless and dumb and dependent, in which case she will
cease to be a belle and become a victim. The literature of the South is
piled high with the battered corpses of belles, for their strategic and evasive game has tragic potential. Of all the women Tennessee Williams has
created, his failed belles are the most vivid. There is Amanda, the
mother of Laura and Tom in *The Glass Menagerie*. In her Chicago tene-
ment she is pathetic and crazy and broke; her son hates her, her daughter
is lame and shy. Amanda lives on her recollection of an afternoon in Blue
Mountain, her probably fictitious Southern manse, when seventeen gentlemen callers arrived all at once, and there weren't enough chairs to sit
them down in. She keens their wonderful Mississippi names, "Young
Champ Laughlin, Hadley Stevenson who was drowned in Moon Lake,
the Cutrere brothers Wesley and Blake, that beautiful young Fitzhugh
boy from Green County, that wild Wainwright boy."

8        Blanche du Bois from *Streetcar Named Desire* is the archetype of all failed beauties, dreaming of lost and supposedly better days, recollecting which fraternity pin it was that she wore in her senior year at the university, mourning over her lost manor house. Her delusions and evasions, like Amanda's, are too feeble to serve against the misery of her life. Like the South, she nourishes herself on false memories. But she is one of the most touching madwomen ever invented, and even as she is led offstage to the madhouse, she takes the arm of the doctor and remarks, "I have always depended upon the kindness of strangers."

9        Zelda Sayre Fitzgerald was another belle who ended her days in a madhouse. As F. Scott Fitzgerald's wife, she has turned up in so many memoirs of the 1920's as to have taken on the identity of a fictional heroine. In her photographs with her husband, she might have been some Jazz Age movie queen or a character out of one of his novels. But she was no work of fiction. She came from Montgomery, Alabama, an authentic belle by all accounts, in the wild and reckless mode. If there had been no such thing as a belle, she would have invented it, and she captured a talented, handsome Northerner who could be counted on to provide one thing that all belles crave—glamour.

10        But in Nancy Milford's splendid biography of Zelda, another woman emerges besides the Alabama flapper and the chic young wife in her fur coat, posing with her husband on some Paris sidewalk. Scott and Zelda, two perfectly matched people—as Nancy Milford observes, they even looked alike—were to unhinge one another. They got married in 1920, and in ten years Scott had become an alcoholic, and Zelda had begun to go incurably insane. There is, of course, no simple explanation for her madness, but one thread of it was surely her Southern origins. She was playing an ancient female role perfectly, and was an even greater success in New York and Paris than she had been in Montgomery. But along the way she discovered that she had ambitions of her own. She was a writer herself, and she showed real promise as a ballet dancer. She began to realize, apparently, that she could not exist as the adjunct of even the most successful writer in America. Glamour suddenly ceased to suffice. For a Southern belle, this must have been the most self-destructive of insights. And so she lost her mind, dying at last in a fire in a mental hospital in 1948. Not a dancer, not a writer, not a wife, not a belle.

11        Most belles don't come to a tragic end. In an article in *Playboy* in 1972, Marshall Frady described some of his own skirmishes, as he called them, with the ladies of the magnolia, by which he clearly meant not ladies but belles. He was out to sink the notion that belles were either adorable or desirable. Having encountered a number of them, he had observed that the greater their beauty, the greater their stupidity, self-centeredness, and manipulative tendencies. Moreover, he learned that their skills were passed on like some invidious, hemophiliac gene from mother to daughter: among their other tenacious qualities, belles are intent on replicating themselves, and they usually do. What astonished Mr.

Frady most was that the classic Southern belle, in all her silky allure, believes that men exist only to serve her purposes. It is hard to believe this came as news to a reporter so perceptive as he or to the editors of *Playboy*, however accustomed they may be to marketing the reverse idea.

Belles can indeed be lethal. Not only to the men they attract or to themselves but to other women. A teacher I know in an integrated Arkansas high school described the teenaged white belle as the most seriously disruptive force in a student body that had barely managed, over the past eight years, to maintain an uneasy peace. This is a newly consolidated high school of about 1,000 students, equipped with every kind of sports facility, gymnasium, and athletic coach imaginable for the boys and the expectable number of pep squads, bands, and cheerleading teams for the nonathletes, including the girls. 12

As often happens, the black boys were stronger, taller, more skillful than their white teammates, and soon every varsity squad and track team was filled with black players. This, according to the teacher, had worked out splendidly. The black kids had an instant path to achievement, and the white boys had been able to take the competition in a gentlemanly way. In fact, to everyone's delight, the football team began winning championships. The blacks' edge in sports also gave them a political weapon. One year the football players brought an entire season to a halt by striking for better black representation in student government. They won, too. 13

But, my informant continued, for girls of either race high school is the time to forget other kinds of achievements and start competing for boys. What matters is getting elected homecoming queen or being invited to parties, buying pretty clothes. Obviously, in all such endeavors, the white girls were ahead of the blacks. They were more likely to be categorized as pretty, to have money for clothes and jewelry and hairdos, to have pleasant homes and parents who could afford to give them cars, more likely to have their families behind them with the effort it takes to get elected homecoming queen or chief cheerleader and to have the money for uniforms and long dresses and out-of-town trips. Furthermore—just as their granddaddies had feared—the white girls were, in an unadmitted way, attracting the black boys. Why not? The white girls were all well-dressed and comparatively rich and smooth. There had been no interracial dating, needless to say, but the thought had crossed a few minds. The black girls, though the teacher didn't say so, were simply being outgunned in the belle department. Hence racial animosities among the girls had become an intractable problem, with both camps attacking and retaliating and even occasionally growing violent. In an incident last winter, she said, a black girl had literally jumped on a white one in the corridor and pulled out a handful of her well-coiffed blond hair. I tried to look appropriately shocked, but I understood too well how the attacker felt. 14

15     I never made any attempt at becoming a belle, having realized in early adolescence that I had almost none of the qualifications. But I grew up watching some virtuosos. In a corner of the South as remote as Arkansas, with no particular connection to any Tidewater *beau idéal*, and in a little town such as I came from, which hardly even existed before 1880, it is a miracle that anybody had ever heard of the idea anyway. There are, after all, plenty of other ways to find a man. And yet the old notions hung as heavy in the air as the fume of Blue Waltz cologne around the cosmetic counters at the Kress store. No matter how lowly your origins or plain your person, you were expected to be a belle.

16     There was a nucleus of girls who scarcely needed any training, among them a natural talent named Margaret Anne. She was a glorious gold-hued redhead, tending to rotundity at the bottom unless she kept to a strict diet, but brown-eyed and agreeably diminutive. Brought up in a rather splendid home (or so it seemed to her friends), an only child with indulgent and adoring parents, she had already begun to plot by the age of thirteen how to capture a husband and remove herself from this paradise. Her mother, Lula, had been married at fifteen, and Margaret Anne had come along, as they put it, before Lula's sixteenth birthday, so the two of them enjoyed their adolescence together, scheming about bridal gowns and whom to pick as bridesmaids, though the prospective bridegrooms had barely begun to shave. What Margaret Anne wanted was not so much a husband, however, or even a lot of dance dresses and corsages or a sexual partner—though she did want all those—but independence. Some control over her own affairs. Marriage may seem an odd means to that end, but not the way Margaret Anne figured it. She knew who the boss of her house was going to be and who was going to have the fun of spending the money.

17     As she set out, she had the first necessity of her trade well in hand—not her beauty, which was marginal, but the understanding that her first job in life was to attract boys. Second, although she was not stupid, neither was she excessively troubled by her own intelligence or cultural yearnings, which were nil, and she knew better than to display the slightest proficiency at anything. Third, she had the quality of being unattainable, of coming from that "pure, clean, sweet atmosphere" described by Mr. Page. Fourth, she had something Page completely forgot to mention: she was pious, or appeared to be. That is the herbal bouquet for the sauce and an excellent mask for all the calculated moves that a belle has to make.

18     Margaret Anne never missed a Sunday at the Baptist church and following her mother's advice, she sang in the choir. It was a good way to cultivate an otherworldly image as well as to display oneself and to flirt a little tiny bit with the boys in the pews. (In addition to all these benefits, Margaret Anne naturally expected a gold star to be stuck down in the Books Above.) Her silky hair looked very nice against the navy-blue choir robe with its starched white collar. During the preaching, she kept

her great serious brown eyes mostly upon the swirling locks and the flapping coattails of the preacher. When the invitation came, and the piano played "Just as I Am," and the stray lambs walked up the aisle to Jesus, her face would glow like an archangel's, and tears would gleam in her eyes. It was worth sitting through church for.

On Saturdays she used to drive around town, ostensibly doing errands with her mama, but in fact making herself visible, as she did later by herself, when she had her own car. She always knew where to find the boys, recognized every one of their old Pontiacs and Fords, knew exactly who was at basketball practice or football scrimmage and when, could have told the whereabouts of any one of fifteen boys at any time you asked her, as well as the name of every girl any particular boy had dated over the past year and where they had all gone on the date. She herself was usually going steady, but now and then she broke away. She could hug and kiss and loll and fondle in the back seat of a car for hours, but she had no difficulty controlling herself, and she only fondled the steadies. Her mother had directed her to go to her marriage bed intact, and she did. 19

Approaching eighteen, she decided to go after the captain of the football team, a massive, handsome, slow-witted blond named Billy Ray who liked to drink beer and go out with his buddies on weekends stealing hubcaps and drag racing. Margaret Anne naturally disapproved of his mischief-making, but she didn't frown too much. His mischief was her means of controlling him. She let him know just how much beer he could drink and how much devilment he could get into without actually provoking her to return his ponderous class ring, which was adjusted to her finger by means of a pad of adhesive tape. (She did return it, two or three times, just to teach her boy a lesson.) But though Jesus had saved her soul, she intended to save her football captain's soul only so far as she chose. What she wanted for a husband was a bad little boy—not too bad, of course—but flawed enough to be unable to do without her, someone with a dependable need to be forgiven. She understood, and gently caused him to understand, just what the trade-offs were going to be. 20

So they were married, and Billy Ray gave up beer for bourbon before switching to vodka. He quenched his passion for cars by taking over the local Mercury dealership, and he prospered as a salesman because he gave his customers the impression of being too simple-minded to be dishonest. For the same reason, he has made some profitable deals in real estate. He somehow got in on some Title One housing money and contracted to build a series of small-scale high-rises for poor tenants, all of them black and none with any wish to live in an apartment. He now sits on the boards of two banks and is working on a deal to develop some prime lake-shore property. In every respect, he behaves as a man of his station should—he is a grateful husband, a cheerful companion to his friends, a generous if not very interested father, and a heavy drinker who never quite goes over the edge. 21

22        Margaret Anne, now quite fat but still redheaded, has remained a belle in spite of the arrival of three children. In fact, I have seldom seen so perfect a belle as she has become in middle age. She is always "fixed up," goes twice a week to the hairdresser, and wears plenty of nail polish. (She has seventy-five pairs of shoes—and handbags to match—all lined up in a special closet which she showed me the last time I visited her. When the heels need new tips, she gives the shoes and the matching handbag to the maid.) Fat or not, she wears tight clothes, but her favorite outfits are a demure suit with a frothy blouse for day and a pastel chiffon gown for evening.

23        She gives elaborate, noisy parties (catered) where all the men get drunk. She claims to be a dedicated boozer, but she drinks very little in public or, I suspect, in private. She moves about these massive brawls like a queen at a garden party. I have never heard her discuss any abstract subject with anyone, except that occasionally she will talk politics with the men. When she does, she takes care to display irrationality and passion. In his position, Billy Ray has had to get quite close to local politics and sometimes even woo a congressman or senator. Margaret Anne's political acumen consists, therefore, in admiring the men whose favor her husband is currently courting. Her husband's friends, including the politicians, are all as wild about her as if she were still sixteen. Most of them have tried to "get friendly with her," as she calls it, but she tells me that she just gives them a little pat on the arm, tells them they are the sweetest, dearest, best of things, and then reminds them as gently as possible that she loves Billy Ray. She is not interested in middle-aged men, nor reckless enough to sin with her husband's colleagues.

24        Her fascination, whatever it is composed of, certainly does not consist of wit. But she is amusing—she has raised calculated silliness to the level of an art. She never misses a chance to tell you how scatterbrained she is or that she is taking lessons in disco dancing or that she still has all her pink angora sweaters from high school. She dislikes cooking, but when she does cook, she makes silly things: salads with canned fruit and miniature marshmallows and shredded coconut in them; things consisting of canned beans and mushroom soup mixed together and topped off with another can of French-fried onions; green and purple jello in layers; unidentifiable mixtures baked in fish-shaped molds and decorated with pimento and green olives; pies concocted from cracker crumbs and frozen lemonade mixes and aerosol whipped cream. Her basic principle is that nothing should look like what it is, and the compliment she most wants to hear is that "it looks too pretty to eat." Billy Ray used to loathe this sort of stuff but was too intimidated to say so. Now he has grown used to it, and in any case they have a cook six days out of seven.

25        She appears to have gotten everything she wanted out of her marriage: several furs (in a subtropical climate), white wall-to-wall carpet in every room, and a succession of casual daytime lovers not chosen from among her husband's acquaintances or his age group. One of these young

men, she confided to me, was the father of her third child. She speaks of her love affairs with giggles of innocence, for she is as indestructible a virgin as she ever was, and I am sure she fantasizes that she and her "baby boys," as she calls them with a little smile and shiver, are merely hugging and kissing in the back seat. Her eldest child is a redheaded daughter who of course sings in the choir at the Baptist church and last autumn, though a mere sophomore, was chosen homecoming queen.

## CONSIDERATIONS

1. Point out a few specific words or phrases in Abbott's paragraph 1 that establish the tongue-in-cheek tone of her essay.

2. What is especially appropriate in Abbott's use of fictional characters, such as Scarlett O'Hara, from *Gone with the Wind,* and Amanda and Blanche du Bois, from Tennessee Williams's plays, to describe and explain the Southern belle?

3. How did the popularity of belles in an integrated high school contribute to racial strife?

4. Find an example of Abbott's use of irony and explain how it contributes to her effort to strip romanticism from her account of Margaret Anne.

5. What is Abbott's point, if any, in closing her essay with a brief account of Margaret Anne's eldest child?

6. Some readers say Abbott's portrait of Margaret Anne is merely a caricature; others argue that it Is a biography. What points in the essay could you use to support your view of the matter?

*Diane Ackerman (b. 1948) was born in Waukegan, Illinois, attended Penn State, and did graduate work at Cornell University. Her many books of poems are represented in* Jaguar of Sweet Laughter: New and Selected Poems *(1991). She has received grants from the National Endowment for the Arts and the Rockefeller Foundation, and has written many essays for the* New Yorker. *Her books of nonfiction include* On Extended Wings *(1985), her memoir of flying, and* A Natural History of the Senses *(1990), from which we take this sensuous essay. She develops notions of touching and moves smoothly through extended examples—often in long paragraphs—by means of internal transitions. Using a digest of research papers, she makes an essay that is itself a sensuous object. We usually think of images as visual. Examine Ackerman's tactile images, images of touch.*

— 2 ————————————————————————

# DIANE ACKERMAN
## *The Importance of Touch*

—————————————————————————————

1    Language is steeped in metaphors of touch. We call our emotions feelings, and we care most deeply when something "touches" us. Problems can be thorny, ticklish, sticky, or need to be handled with kid gloves. Touchy people, especially if they're coarse, really get on our nerves. *Noli me tangere*, legal Latin for "don't meddle or interfere," translates literally as "Don't touch me," and it was what Christ said to Mary Magdalen after the Resurrection. But it's also one term for the disease lupus, presumably because of the disfiguring skin ulcerations characteristic of that illness. A toccata in music is a composition for organ or other keyboard instrument in a free style. It was originally a piece intended to show touch technique, and the word comes from the feminine past participle of *toccare*, to touch. Music teachers often chide students for having "no sense of touch," by which they mean an indefinable delicacy of execution. In fencing, saying *touché* means that you have been touched by the foil and are conceding to your opponent, although, of

course, we also say it when we think we have been foiled because someone's argumentative point is well made. A touchstone is a standard. Originally, touchstones were hard black stones like jasper or basalt, used to test the quality of gold or silver by comparing the streaks they left on the stone with those of an alloy. "The touchstone of an art is its precision," Ezra Pound once said. D. H. Lawrence's use of the word touch isn't epidermal but a profound penetration into the core of someone's being. So much of twentieth-century popular dancing is simultaneous solo gyration that when people returned to dancing closely with partners again a couple of years ago, we had to call it something different—"touch dancing." "For a while there, it was touch and go," we say of a crisis or precarious situation, not realizing that the expression goes back to horse-and-carriage days, when the wheels of two coaches glanced off each other as they passed, but didn't snag; a modern version would be when two swerving cars brush fenders. What seems real we call "tangible," as if it were a fruit whose rind we could feel. When we die, loved ones swaddle us in heavily padded coffins, making us infants again, lying in our mother's arms before returning to the womb of the earth, ceremonially unborn. As Frederick Sachs writes in *The Sciences*, "The first sense to ignite, touch is often the last to burn out: long after our eyes betray us, our hands remain faithful to the world. . . . in describing such final departures, we often talk of losing touch."

Although I am not a portly middle-aged gentleman with nothing else to do, I am massaging a tiny baby in a hospital in Miami. Often male retirees volunteer to enter preemie wards late at night, when other people have families to tend or a nine-to-five job to sleep toward. The babies don't care about the gender of those who cosset and cuddle them. They soak it up like the manna it is in their wilderness of uncertainty. This baby's arms feel limp, like vinyl. Still too weak to roll over by itself, it can flail and fuss so well the nurses have laid soft bolsters on its bed, to keep it from accidentally wriggling into a corner. Its torso looks as small as a deck of cards. That this is a baby boy lying on his tummy, who will one day play basketball in the summer Olympics, or raise children of his own, or become a heliarc welder, or book passage on a low-orbital plane to Japan for a business meeting, is barely believable. The small life form with a big head, on which veins stand out like river systems, looks so fragile, feels so temporary. Lying in his incubator, or "Isolette," as it's called, emphasizing the isolation of his life, he wears a plumage of wires—electrodes to chart his progress and sound an alarm if need be. Reaching carefully scrubbed, disinfected, warmed hands through the portholes of the incubator with pangs of protectiveness, I touch him; it is like reaching into a chrysalis. First I stroke his head and face very slowly, six times for ten seconds each time, then his neck and shoulders six times. I slide my hands down his back and massage it in long sweeping motions six times, and caress his arms and legs six times. The touching can't be light, or it will tickle him, nor rough, or it will agitate him, but

2

firm and steady, as if one were smoothing a crease from heavy fabric. On a nearby monitor, two turquoise EKG and breath waves flutter across a radiant screen, one of them short and saw-toothed, the other leaping high and dropping low in its own improvisatory dance. His heartbeat reads 153, aerobic peak during a stiff workout for me, but calm for him, because babies have higher normal heart beats than adults. We turn him over on his back and, though asleep, he scrunches up his face in displeasure. In less than a minute, he runs a parade of expressions by us, all of them perfectly readable thanks to the semaphore of the eyebrows, the twisted code of the forehead, the eloquent India rubber of the mouth and chin: irritation, calm, puzzled, happy, mad. . . . Then his face goes slack and his eyelids twitch as he drifts into REM sleep, the blackboard of dreams. Some nurses refer to the tiny preemies, sleeping their sleep of the womb, as fetuses on the outside. What does a fetus dream? Gently, I move his limbs in a mini-exercise routine, stretching out an arm and bending the elbow tight, opening the legs and bending the knees to the chest. Peaceful but alert; he seems to be enjoying it. We turn him onto his tummy once more, and again I begin caressing his head and shoulders. This is the first of three daily touch sessions for him—it may seem a shame to interrupt his thick, druglike sleep, but just by stroking him I am performing a life-giving act.

3      Massaged babies gain weight as much as 50 percent faster than unmassaged babies. They're more active, alert, and responsive, more aware of their surroundings, better able to tolerate noise, and they orient themselves faster and are emotionally more in control. "Less likely to cry one minute, then fall asleep the next minute," as a psychologist, detailing the results of one experiment, explained in *Science News* in 1985, they're "better able to calm and console themselves." In a follow-up examination, eight months later, the massaged preemies were found to be bigger in general, with larger heads and fewer physical problems. Some doctors in California have even been putting preterms on small waterbeds that sway gently, and this experiment has produced infants who are less irritable, sleep better, and have fewer apneas. The touched infants, in these studies and in others, cried less, had better temperaments, and so were more appealing to their parents, which is important because the 7 percent of babies born prematurely figure disproportionately among those who are victims of child abuse. Children who are difficult to raise get abused more often. And people who aren't touched much as children don't touch much as adults, so the cycle continues.

4      A 1988 *New York Times* article on the critical role of touch in child development reported "psychological and physical stunting of infants deprived of physical contact, although otherwise fed and cared for . . . ," which was revealed by one researcher working with primates and others working with World War II orphans. "Premature infants who were massaged for 15 minutes three times a day gained weight 47 percent faster than others who were left alone in their incubators . . . the massaged in-

fants also showed signs that the nervous system was maturing more rapidly: they became more active . . . and more responsive to such things as a face or a rattle . . . infants who were massaged were discharged from the hospital an average of six days earlier." Eight months later, the massaged infants did better in tests of mental and motor ability than the ones who were not.

At the University of Miami Medical School, Dr. Tiffany Field, a child psychologist, has been studying a group of babies admitted to the intensive care unit of its hospital for various reasons. With 13,000 to 15,000 births a year at the hospital, she never lacks for a steady supply of babies. Some are receiving caffeine for bradycardia and apnea problems, one is hydroencephalic, some are the children of diabetic mothers who must be carefully monitored. At one Isolette, a young mother sits on a black kitchen chair by her baby, reaches a hand in and gently strokes, whispering motherly nothings into its ear. Inside another Isolette, a baby girl wearing a white nightie with pink hearts bursts into a classic textbook wail that rises and pulses and sets off the alarm on her monitor. Across the room, a male doctor sits quietly beside a preemie, holding a two-pronged plastic stopper close to her nostrils, trying to teach her to breathe. Next to him, a nurse turns a baby girl onto her tummy and begins a "stim," as they call the massage, shorthand for stimulation. They use the word interchangeably as a verb or a noun. What old faces the preemies have! Changing expressions as they sleep, they seem to be rehearsing emotions. The nurse follows her massage schedule, stroking each part of the preemie six times for ten seconds. The stimulation hasn't changed the baby's sleep patterns, but she's been gaining thirty grams more a day and will soon be going home, almost a week ahead of what one would expect. "There's nothing extra going into the babies," Field explains, "yet they're more active, gain weight faster; and they become more efficient. It's amazing," she continues, "how much information is communicable in a touch. Every other sense has an organ you can focus on, but touch is everywhere."

Saul Schanberg, a neurologist who experiments with rats at Duke University, has found that licking and grooming by the mother rat actually produced chemical changes in the pup; when the pup was taken away from the mother, its growth hormones decreased. ODC (the "now" enzyme that signals it is time for certain chemical changes to begin) dropped in every cell in the body, and protein synthesis fell. Growth began again only when the pup was returned to the mother. When experimenters tried to reverse the bad effects without the mother, they discovered that gentle stroking wouldn't work, only very heavy stroking with a paintbrush that simulated the mother's tongue; after that the pup developed normally. Regardless of whether the deprived rats were returned to their mothers or stroked with paintbrushes by experimenters, they overreacted and required a great deal of touching, far more than they usually do, to respond normally.

7       Schanberg first began his rat experiments as a result of his work in pediatrics; he was especially interested in psychosocial dwarfism. Some children who live in emotionally destructive homes just stop growing. Schanberg found that even growth-hormone injections couldn't prompt the stunted bodies of such children to grow again, but tender loving care did. The affection they received from the nurses when they were admitted to a hospital was often enough to get them back on the right track. What's amazing is that the process is reversible at all. When Schanberg's experiments with infant rats produced identical results, he began to think about human preemies, who are typically isolated and spend much of their early life without human contact. Animals depend on being close to their mothers for basic survival. If the mother's touch is removed (for as little as forty-five minutes in rats), the infant lowers its need for food to keep itself alive until the mother returns. This works out well if the mother is away only briefly, but if she never comes back, then the slower metabolism results in stunted growth. Touch reassures an infant that it's safe; it seems to give the body a go-ahead to develop normally. In many experiments conducted all over the country, babies who were held more became more alert and developed better cognitive abilities years later. It's a little like the strategy one adopts on a sinking ship: First you get into a life raft and call for help. Baby animals call their mothers with a high-pitched cry. Then you take stock of your water and food, and try to conserve energy by cutting down on high-energy activities—growth, for instance.

8       At the University of Colorado School of Medicine, researchers conducted a separation experiment with monkeys, in which they removed the mother. The infant showed signs of helplessness, confusion, and depression, and only the return of its mother and continuous holding for a few days would help it return to normal. During separation, changes occurred in the heart rate, body temperature, brain-wave patterns, sleep patterns, and immune system function. Electronic monitoring of deprived infants showed that touch deprivation caused physical and psychological disturbances. But when the mother was put back, only the psychological disturbances seemed to disappear; true, the infant's behavior reverted to normal, but the physical distresses—susceptibility to disease, and so on—persisted. Among this experiment's implications is that damage is not reversible, and that the lack of maternal contact may lead to possible long-term damage.

9       Another separation study with monkeys took place at the University of Wisconsin, where researchers separated an infant from its mother by a glass screen. They could still see, hear, and smell each other, only touch was missing, but that created a void so serious that the baby cried steadily and paced frantically. In another group, the dividing screen had holes, so the mother and baby could touch through it, which was apparently sufficient because the infants didn't develop serious behavior problems. Those infants who suffered short-term deprivation became adolescents who clung to one another obsessively instead of developing

into independent, confident individuals. When they suffered long-term deprivation, they avoided one another and became aggressive when they did come in contact, violent loners who didn't form good relationships.

In University of Illinois primate experiments, researchers found that a lack of touch produced brain damage. They posed three situations: (1) touch was not possible, but all other contact was, (2) for four hours out of twenty-four the glass divider was removed so the monkeys could interact, and (3) total isolation. Autopsies of the cerebellum showed that those monkeys who were totally isolated had brain damage; the same was true of the partially separated animals. The untampered-with natural colony remained undamaged. Shocking though it sounds, a relatively small amount of touch deprivation alone caused brain damage, which was often displayed in the monkeys as aberrant behavior.

As I rearrange the preemie in his glass home, I notice that on the walls a bright circus design shows clowns, a merry-go-round, tents, balloons, and a repeat banner that says "Wheel of Fortune." "Touch is far more essential than our other sense," I recall Saul Schanberg saying when we spoke, on Key Biscayne, at Johnson & Johnson's extraordinary conference on touch in spring, 1989, a three-day exchange of ideas that brought together neurophysiologists, pediatricians, anthropologists, sociologists, psychologists, and others interested in how touch and touch deprivation affect the mind and body. In many ways, touch is difficult to research. Every other sense has a key organ to study; for touch that organ is the skin, and it stretches over the whole body. Every sense has at least one key research center, except touch. Touch is a sensory system, the influence of which is hard to isolate or eliminate. Scientists can study people who are blind to learn more about vision, and people who are deaf or anosmic to learn more about hearing or smell, but this is virtually impossible to do with touch. They also can't experiment with people who are born without the sense, as they often do with the deaf or blind. Touch is a sense with unique functions and qualities, but it also frequently combines with other senses. Touch affects the whole organism, as well as its culture and the individuals it comes into contact with. "It's ten times stronger than verbal or emotional contact," Schanberg explained, "and it affects damn near everything we do. No other sense can arouse you like touch; we always knew that, but we never realized it had a biological basis."

"You mean how adaptive it is?"

"Yes. If touch didn't feel good, there'd be no species, parenthood, or survival. A mother wouldn't touch her baby in the right way unless the mother felt pleasure doing it. If we didn't like the feel of touching and patting one another, we wouldn't have had sex. Those animals who did more touching instinctively produced offspring which survived, and their genes were passed on and the tendency to touch became even stronger. We forget that touch is not only basic to our species, but the key to it."

14    As a fetus grows in the womb, surrounded by amniotic fluid, it feels liquid warmth, the heartbeat, the inner surf of the mother, and floats in a wonderful hammock that rocks gently as she walks. Birth must be a rude shock after such serenity, and a mother re-creates the womb comfort in various ways (swaddling, cradling, pressing the baby against the left side of her body where her heart is). Right after birth, human (and monkey) mothers hold their babies very close to their bodies. In primitive cultures, a mother keeps her baby close day and night. A baby born to one of the Pygmies of Zaire is in physical contact with someone at least 50 percent of the time, and is constantly being stroked or played with by other members of the tribe. A Kung! mother carries her baby in a *curass*, a sling that holds it upright at her side so that it can nurse, play with her bead necklaces, or interact with others. Kung! infants are in touch with others about 90 percent of the time, whereas our culture believes in exiling babies to cribs, baby carriages, or travel seats, keeping them at arm's length and out of the way.

15    An odd feature of touch is that it doesn't always have to be performed by another person, or even by a living thing. Maternity Hospital in Cambridge, England, discovered that if a premature baby were just placed on a lamb's-wool blanket for a day it would gain an average of fifteen grams more than usual. This was not due to additional heat from the blanket, since the ward was kept warm, but more akin to the tradition of "swaddling" infants, which increases tactile stimulation, decreases stress, and makes them feel lightly cuddled. In other experiments, snug-fitting blankets or clothes reduced the infants' heart rate, relaxed them; they slept more often in their womblike bindings.

16    All animals respond to being touched, stroked, poked in some way, and, in any case, life itself could not have evolved at all without touch—that is, without chemicals touching one another and forming liaisons. In the absence of touching and being touched, people of all ages can sicken and grow touch-starved.* In fetuses, touch is the first sense to develop, and in newborns it's automatic before the eyes open or the baby begins to make sense of the world. Soon after we're born, though we can't see or speak, we instinctively begin touching. Touch cells in the lips make nursing possible, clutch mechanisms in the hands begin to reach out for warmth. Among other things, touch teaches us the difference between *I* and *other*, that there can be someone outside of ourselves, the mother. Mothers and infants do an enormous amount of touching. The first emotional comfort, touching and being touched by our mother, remains the ultimate memory of selfless love, which stays with us life long.

---

*What a curious and deprived life the Dionne quints lived. Born in Ontario, Canada, they were seized by the government and put in a kind of zoo. So they lived in a sterile room behind bars. At one point their mother, who wasn't allowed to touch them, stood in line with the other paying viewers. Only after a lawsuit was she able to get her children back. None of them grew up normally.

The little three-pound universe named Geoffrey, which I am    17
stroking in long gentle caresses, has idly twisted his mouth and just as
quickly untwisted it again. In other incubators around the room, other
lives are stirring, other volunteers continue reaching in through portholes to help the infants begin to make sense of the world. The head research nurse of the ward, a graduate student in neonatal care, gives the
Brazelton sensory test to a baby boy, who responds to a bright-red egg-
rattle. Picking the baby up, she swings it gently around and its eyes go in
the direction of the spin, as they should, then return to the midline.
Next she rings a small schoolbell for ten seconds at each side, and repeats this four times. It is a very Buddhist scene. In a nearby crib, a preemie who is having his hearing tested wears a headset that makes him
look like a telegraph operator. The policy with premature babies used to
be not to disturb them any more than necessary, and they lived in a kind
of isolation booth, but now the evidence about touch is so plentiful and
eloquent that many hospitals encourage touching. "Did you hug your
child today?" asks the bumper sticker. As it turns out, this is more than
a casual question. Touch seems to be as essential as sunlight.

## CONSIDERATIONS

1. Study the differences in Ackerman's style between paragraph 1 and paragraph
2. What are the prominent features of each?

2. Compare the length of Ackerman's paragraphs, especially 1, 2, 5, 7, and 11,
with that of other writers in the text, and comment on your findings.

3. "Reaching . . . through the portholes of the incubator . . . is like reaching
into a chrysalis," writes Ackerman in paragraph 2. Look up the word "chrysalis" to
make sure you understand it. Do the same for the word "simile." Then explain why
Ackerman's use of a figure of speech here is more effective than a literal description
would be. Identify other uses of figurative language by this writer.

4. Inevitably, in a report of this sort, Ackerman uses a number of technical terms,
some of which she explains and some she doesn't: aerobic, apnea, bradycardia, "stim,"
ODC, REM, EKG, anosmic, neonatal, preterms, "preemie." Which of these are explained, more or less, by the context?

5. In several places, but particularly in paragraph 11, Ackerman says, in effect,
that touch is the most important of all the senses. If you doubt her, write an essay that
shows the preeminence of a different sense. If you agree with her, build an essay
around a specific experience of your own or of someone you know.

6. Ackerman is primarily interested in touch as it affects babies born prematurely. If you think touch is important to people of all ages, develop an expository essay
around that idea. It might be helpful to think how touch might have made an important
difference in other essays in your text, such as Maxine Hong Kingston's "Silence" (page
361), John Daniel's "Looking After" (page 152), and Lillian Hellman's "Runaway" (page
285), or in Ernest Hemingway's short story, "Hills Like White Elephants" (page 292).

*Julia Alvarez (b. 1950) at the age of ten emigrated with her parents from the Dominican Republic to the United States. She has written three books of poetry, four novels, and a collection of essays. "A White Woman of Color" first appeared in the* Hungry Mind Review *in 1998 and later in an anthology,* Monkey in the Middle: Writers Growing Up Biracial and Bicultural. *Formerly a professor at Middlebury College, she now lives in Vermont and writes full time.*

*Alvarez's essay begins in the rhetorical mode of comparison and contrast. "The oldest sister had the darkest coloring. . . ." But human life is seldom so simple, and as she continues her narrative, the contrasts of the first paragraphs set themselves against other contrasts. Remark how she builds her narrative into her argument with a mixture of story and interpretation.*

— 3 —————————————————————————————

# JULIA ALVAREZ
## *A White Woman of Color*

———————————————————————————————

1    Growing up in the Dominican Republic, I experienced racism within my own family—though I didn't think of it as racism. But there was definitely a hierarchy of beauty, which was the main currency in our family of daughters. It was not until years later, from the vantage point of the United States and an American education, that I realized that this hierarchy of beauty was dictated by our coloring. We were a progression of whitening, as if my mother were slowly bleaching the color out of her children.

2    The oldest sister had the darkest coloring with very curly hair and "coarse" features. She looked the most like Papa's side of the family and was considered the least pretty. I came next, with "good hair," and skin that back then was a deep olive, for I was a tomboy—another dark mark against me—who would not stay out of the sun. The sister right after me had my skin color, but she was a good girl who stayed indoors, so she

was much paler, her hair a golden brown. But the pride and joy of the family was the baby. She made heads turn—strangers approached asking to feel her silken hair. She was white white—an adjective which was repeated in describing her color as if to deepen the shade of white. Her eyes were brown but her hair was an unaccountable towheaded blond. Because of her coloring, my father was teased that there must have been a German milkman in our neighborhood. How could *she* be *his* daughter? It was clear that this youngest child resembled Mami's side of the family.

Mami's family were *really* white, both in terms of race, and also of     3
class. From them came the Spanish surnames, the pale skin, the lank hair. Her brothers and uncles went to schools abroad and had important businesses in the country. They also emulated the manners and habits of North Americans. Growing up, I remember arguments at the supper table about whether it was proper to tie one's napkin around one's neck or not, how much of one's arm one could properly lay on the table, and whether spaghetti could be eaten with the help of a spoon. My mother, of course, insisted on all the protocol of knives and forks and on eating a little portion of everything served; my father, on the other hand, defended our eating whatever we wanted, with our hands if need be, so we could "have fun" with our food. My mother would snap back that we looked like *jibaritas* who should be living out in the country. Of course, that was precisely where my father's family came from.

Not that Papi's family weren't smart and enterprising, all twenty-     4
five brothers and sisters. (The size of the family in and of itself was considered very country by some members of Mami's family.) Many of Papi's brothers had gone to the university and become professionals. But their education was totally island—no fancy degrees from Andover, Cornell, or Yale, no summer camps or school songs in another language. Papi's family still lived in the interior rather than the capital, in old-fashioned houses, which were decorated in ways that my mother's family would have considered, well, tasteless. I remember antimacassars on the backs of rocking chairs, garish paintings of flamboyant trees, ceramic planters with plastic flowers in bloom. Papi's family were *criollos*—creoles, expansive, proud, colorful—rather than cosmopolitans. (Some members had a sixth finger on their right—or was it their left?—hands.) Their money, kept in a wad in their back pockets, still had the smell of the earth on it, whereas my mother's family had money in Chase Manhattan Bank, most of it with George Washington's picture on it, not Juan Pablo Duarte's.

It was clear to us growing up then that lighter was better, but there     5
was no question of discriminating against someone because he or she was dark-skinned. Everyone's family, even an elite one like Mami's, had darker-skinned members. All Dominicans, as the saying goes, have a little black behind the ears. To separate oneself from those who were darker would have been to divide *una familia*—a sacrosanct entity in our

culture. Neither was white blood necessarily a sign of moral, intellectual, or political superiority. All one has to do is page through a
Dominican history book and look at the number of dark-skinned presidents, dictators, generals, and entrepreneurs to see that power has not
resided exclusively or primarily among the whites on the island. The
leadership of our country historically has been "colored."

6       But being black was something else. A black Dominican was referred to as a "dark indian" (*indio oscuro*)—unless you wanted to come
to blows with him, that is. The real blacks were the Haitians who lived
next door and who occupied the Dominican Republic for twenty years,
from 1822–1844, a fact that can still so inflame the Dominican populace
you'd think it had happened last year. The denial of the Afro-Dominican
part of our culture reached its climax during the dictatorship of Trujillo,
whose own maternal grandmother was Haitian. To protect Dominican
race purity, Trujillo ordered the overnight slaughter of thousands (figures
range from 20,000 to 40,000) of Haitians by his military, who committed
this atrocity using only machetes and knives in order to make this
planned extermination look like a "spontaneous" border skirmish. He
also had the Dominican Republic declared a white nation despite the evidence of the mulatto senators who were forced to pass this ridiculous
measure.

7       So, black was not so good, kinky hair was not so good, thick lips
were not so good. But even if you were *indio oscuro con pelo malo y una
bemba de aquá a Baní*, you could still sit in the front of the bus and order
at the lunch counter—or the equivalent thereof. There was no segregation of races in the halls of power. But in the aesthetic arena—the ones to
which we girls were relegated as females—lighter was better. Lank hair
and pale skin and small, fine features were better. All I had to do was stay
out of the sun and behave myself, and I could pass as a pretty white girl.

8       Another aspect of my growing up also greatly influenced my thinking on race. Although I was raised in the heart of a large family, my day-to-
day caretakers were the maids. Most of these women were dark-skinned,
some of Haitian background. One of them, Misiá had been spared the machetes of the 1937 massacre when she was taken in by our family and hidden from the prowling *guardias*. We children spent most of the day with
these women. They tended to us, nursed us when we were sick, cradled us
when we fell down and scraped an elbow or knee (as a tomboy, there was a
lot of this scraping for me), and most important, they told us stories of *los
santos* and *el barón del cementerio*, of *el cuco* and *las ciguapas*, beautiful
dark-skinned creatures, who escaped capture because their feet were
turned backwards, and so they left behind a false set of footprints. These
women spread the wings of our imaginations and connected us deeply to
the land we came from. They were the ones with the stories that had
power over us.

9       We arrived in Nueva York in 1960, before the large waves of
Caribbean immigrants created little Habanas, Santo Domingos, and San

Juans in the boroughs of the city. Here we encountered a whole new kettle of wax—as my malapropping Mami might have said. People of color
were treated as if they were inferior, prone to violence, uneducated, untrustworthy, lazy—all the "bad" adjectives we were learning in our new
language. Our dark-skinned aunt, Tía Ana, who had lived in New York
for several decades and so was the authority in these matters, recounted
stories of discrimination on buses and subways. These Americans were
so blind! One drop of black and you were black. Everyone back home
would have known that Tía Ana was not black; she had "good hair" and
her skin color was a light *indio.* All week, she worked in a *factoría* in the
Bronx, and when she came to visit us on Saturdays to sew our school
clothes, she had to take three trains to our nice neighborhood where the
darkest face on the street was usually her own.

　　We were lucky to be white Dominicans. But white as we were, we　10
still encountered prejudice. We found that our accents, our habits and
smells added "color" to our complexions. Had we been darker, we certainly could not have bought our mock Tudor house in Jamaica Estates.
In fact, the African American family who moved in across the street several years later needed police protection because of threats. Even so, at
the local school, we endured the bullying of classmates. "Go back to
where you came from!" they yelled at my sisters and me on the playground. When some of them started throwing stones, my mother made
up her mind that we were not safe and began applying to boarding
schools where privilege transformed prejudice into patronage.

　　"So where are you from?" our classmates would ask.　11

　　"Jamaica Estates," I'd say, an edge of belligerence to my voice. It　12
was obvious from my accent, if not my looks, that I was not from there
in the way they meant being from somewhere.

　　"I mean *originally.*"　13

　　And then it would come out, the color, the accent, the cousins with　14
six fingers, the smell of garlic.

　　By the time I went off to college, a great explosion of American cul-　15
ture was taking place on campuses across the country. The Civil Rights
movement, the Vietnam War and subsequent peace movement, and the
women's movement were transforming traditional definitions of
American identity. Ethnicity was in: my classmates wore long braids
like Native Americans, peasant blouses from Mexico, long diaphanous
skirts and dangly earrings from India. Suddenly my foreignness was being celebrated. This reversal felt affirming but also disturbing. As *hui-
pils, serapes,* and embroidered dresses proliferated about me, I had the
feeling that my ethnicity had become a commodity. I resented it.

　　When I began looking for a job after college, I discovered that being　16
a white Latina made me a nonthreatening minority in the eyes of these
employers. My color was a question *only* of culture—and if I kept my
cultural color to myself, I was "no problem." Each time I was hired for
one of my countless visiting appointments to teach creative writing,

freshman English, introductory survey courses—never permanent "invitations," mind you—the inevitable questionnaire would accompany my contract, in which I was to check my race: Caucasian, Black, Native American, Asian, Hispanic, Other. How could a Dominican divide herself in this way? Or was I really a Dominican anymore? And what was Hispanic? A census creation—there is no such culture—how could it define who I was at all? Given this set of options, the truest answer might have been to check Other.

17        Adrift from any Latino community in this country, my culture had become an internal homeland, periodically replenished by trips back "home." But as a professional woman on my own, I felt less and less at home on the island. My values, the loss of my Catholic faith, my wardrobe, my hippy ways, and my feminist ideas separated me from my native culture. I did not subscribe to many of the mores and constraints that seemed to be an intrinsic part of that culture. And since my culture had always been my "color," by rejecting these mores, I had become not only Americanized, but whiter.

18        If I could have been a part of a Latino community in the United States, the struggle might have been if not easier, less private and, therefore, less isolating. These issues of acculturation and ethnicity would have been struggles to share with others like me. But all my North American life I had lived in shifting academic communities—going to boarding schools, then college, and later teaching wherever I could get those yearly appointments—and these communities reflected the dearth of Latinos in the profession. Except for friends in Spanish departments, who tended to have come from their countries of origin to teach rather than being raised in this country as I was, I had very little daily contact with Latinos.

19        I looked for company where I had always found it since coming to this country—in books. At first, the texts that I read and taught were the canonical works that formed the context of the bread-and-butter courses, which as a "visiting instructor," I was hired to teach. These texts were mostly written by white male writers from Britain and the United States, with a few women thrown in, and no Latinos. Thank goodness for the occasional creative writing workshop where I could bring in the multicultural authors I wanted. But since I had been formed in this very academy, I was clueless about where to start. I began to educate myself by reading, and that is when I discovered that there were others out there like me, hybrids who came in a variety of colors and whose ethnicity and race were an evolving process, not a rigid paradigm or a list of boxes, one of which you checked off.

20        This discovery of my ethnicity in books was like a rebirth. I had been going through a pretty bad writer's block: the white page seemed to resist whatever it was I had in me to say. But listening to authors like Maxine Hong Kingston, Toni Morrison, Gwendolyn Brooks, Langston Hughes, Maya Angelou, June Jordan, and to that first wave of Latino writers—Lorna Dee Cervantes, Piri Thomas, Rudolfo Anaya, Edward

Rivera, Ernesto Galarza—I began to hear the language "in color," to see that literature could reflect the otherness I was feeling. A story could allow for the competing claims of different parts of ourselves and where we came from.

Ironically, it was through my own stories and poems that I finally     21
made contact with Latino communities in this country. As I published more, I was invited to read at community centers and bilingual programs. Latino students, who began attending colleges in larger numbers in the late seventies and eighties, sought me out as a writer and teacher "of color." After the publication of *How the Garcia Girls Lost Their Accents*, I found that I had become a sort of spokesperson for Dominicans in this country, a role I had neither sought nor accepted. Of course, some Dominicans refused to grant me any status as a "real" Dominican because I was white. With the color word was also a suggestion of class. My family had not been among the waves of economic immigrants who left the island in the seventies, a generally darker-skinned, working-class group, who might have been the maids and workers in my mother's family house. We had come in 1960, political refugees, with no money but with "prospects": Papi had a friend who was the doctor at the Waldorf-Astoria and who helped him get a job; Mami's family had money in the Chase Manhattan Bank that they could loan us. We changed classes in America—from Mami's elite family to middle-class spics—but our background, education, and most especially our pale skin had made mobility easier for us here. We had not undergone the same kind of race struggles as other Dominicans; therefore, we could not be "real Dominicans."

What I came to understand and accept and ultimately fight for with     22
my writing is the reality that ethnicity and race are not fixed constructs or measurable quantities. What constitutes our ethnicity and our race evolves as we seek to define and redefine ourselves in new contexts. My Latinness is not something someone could take away from me, or leave me out of, with a definition. It is in my blood: it comes from that mixture of biology, culture, native language, and experience that make me a different American from one whose family comes from Ireland or Poland or Italy. My Latinness is also a political choice. I am choosing to hold on to my ethnicity and native language even if I can "pass." I am choosing to color my Americanness with my Dominicanness even if it comes in a light shade of skin color.

As we Latinos redefine ourselves in America, making ourselves up     23
and making ourselves over, we have to be careful in taking up the promises of America not to adopt its limiting racial paradigms. Many of us have shed customs and prejudices that oppressed our gender, race, or class on our native islands and in our native countries. We should not replace these with modes of thinking that are divisive and oppressive of our rich diversity. Maybe as a group that embraces many races and differences, we Latinos can provide a positive multicultural, multiracial model to a divided America.

## CONSIDERATIONS

1. A writer's sense of a particular audience often tells us something of the focus of his or her work. Does Alvarez address her essay to any identifiable group of readers? Support your answer by pointing out what you consider to be substantiating passages.

2. Given the importance that the Dominican Republic plays in Alvarez's family, her history, her ideas about racism, and her sense of self, an interested reader would profit from doing a little research on that small country. Find out where it is, for starters, then continue your exploration.

3. In paragraph 8, Alvarez credits the Haitian servants who took care of her when she was a child with giving her a strong sense of place: "These women [and their stories] spread the wings of our imaginations and connected us deeply to the land we came from." In paragraph 19, "I looked for company where I had always found it since coming to this country—in books." This reliance on stories and books sounds something like Kyoko Mori's "Coming Home to Books" (page 427). Read that essay, think about your own experience, and write your own account of the importance of imagination and books in the forming of your own sense of place.

4. Alvarez moves easily from English to Spanish or some combination of the two— "Nueva York," for instance. A good question for a class discussion might well be, What are non-Spanish readers to do with the non-English words Alvarez uses? Ignore them? Learn Spanish? Rely on the English context for clues? In earlier times, the same problem arose with writers who used Latin terms or, more commonly, French expressions.

5. Alvarez's English vocabulary includes many words that many students find unfamiliar—for example: "antimacassars," in paragraph 4; "sacrosanct," in paragraph 5; "malapropping," in paragraph 9; "diaphanous," in paragraph 15; "mores," in paragraph 17; "acculturation" and "dearth," in paragraph 18; "paradigm," in paragraph 19; and "spics," in paragraph 21. Regular use of a good collegiate dictionary helps. So does learning new words by thinking about their context.

6. Alvarez talks about two kinds of racism. How does she distinguish one from another?

7. In paragraph 16, Alvarez rejects the term "Hispanic." She calls it merely "a census creation." Elsewhere, she uses "Latino." What's the difference?

*Maya Angelou (b. 1928) told an interviewer, "One would say of my life—born loser—had to be; from a broken family, raped at eight, unwed mother at sixteen . . . it's a fact, but it's not the truth."*

*When she grew up, Maya Angelou became an actress, a singer, a dancer, a songwriter, a teacher, an editor, and a poet. She sang and danced professionally in* Porgy *and* Bess *with a company that traveled through twenty-two countries of Europe and Asia. She wrote for the* Ghana Times *and she taught modern dance in Rome and in Tel Aviv. After reading a poem at the inauguration of President Clinton, in 1993, she reached new audiences with all her work. In the same year, she published her most recent prose volume,* Wouldn't Take Nothing for My Journey Now. *The* Complete Collected Poems of Maya Angelou *appeared in 1994.*

*In 1969 she began her autobiography,* I Know Why the Caged Bird Sings, *which was an immediate success. As she says, "I speak to the black experience, but I am always talking about the human condition." The book recounts her early life, with realism and with joy. This selection describes a masterful black con man, skillful at turning white bigotry into black profits.*

---

— **4** ————————————————————————————

# MAYA ANGELOU
## *Mr. Red Leg*

---

Our house was a fourteen-room typical San Franciscan post-    1
Earthquake affair. We had a succession of roomers, bringing and taking
their different accents, and personalities and foods. Shipyard workers
clanked up the stairs (we all slept on the second floor except Mother and
Daddy Clidell) in their steel-tipped boots and metal hats, and gave way
to much-powdered prostitutes, who giggled through their makeup and
hung their wigs on the doorknobs. One couple (they were college graduates) held long adult conversations with me in the big kitchen downstairs, until the husband went off to war. Then the wife who had been so
charming and ready to smile changed into a silent shadow that played

---

infrequently along the walls. An older couple lived with us for a year or so. They owned a restaurant and had no personality to enchant or interest a teenager, except that the husband was called Uncle Jim, and the wife Aunt Boy. I never figured that out.

2    The quality of strength lined with tenderness is an unbeatable combination, as are intelligence and necessity when unblunted by formal education. I was prepared to accept Daddy Clidell as one more faceless name added to Mother's roster of conquests. I had trained myself so successfully through the years to display interest, or at least attention, while my mind skipped free on other subjects that I could have lived in his house without ever seeing him and without his becoming the wiser. But his character beckoned and elicited admiration. He was a simple man who had no inferiority complex about his lack of education and, even more amazing, no superiority complex because he had succeeded despite that lack. He would say often, "I had been to school three years in my life. In Slaten, Texas, times was hard, and I had to help my daddy on the farm."

3    No recriminations lay hidden under the plain statement, nor was there boasting when he said, "If I'm living a little better now, it's because I treats everybody right."

4    He owned apartment buildings and, later, pool halls, and was famous for being that rarity, "a man of honor." He didn't suffer, as many "honest men" do, from the detestable righteousness that diminishes their virtue. He knew cards and men's hearts. So during the age when Mother was exposing us to certain facts of life, like personal hygiene, proper posture, table manners, good restaurants and tipping practices, Daddy Clidell taught me to play poker, blackjack, tonk and high, low, Jick, Jack and the Game. He wore expensive tailored suits and a large yellow diamond stickpin. Except for the jewelry, he was a conservative dresser and carried himself with the unconscious pomp of a man of secure means. Unexpectedly, I resembled him, and when he, Mother and I walked down the street his friends often said, "Clidell, that's sure your daughter. Ain't no way you can deny her."

5    Proud laughter followed those declarations, for he had never had children. Because of his late-arriving but intense paternal sense, I was introduced to the most colorful characters in the Black underground. One afternoon, I was invited into our smoke-filled dining room to make the acquaintance of Stonewall Jimmy, Just Black, Cool Clyde, Tight Coat and Red Leg. Daddy Clidell explained to me that they were the most successful con men in the world, and they were going to tell me about some games so that I would never be "anybody's mark."

6    To begin, one man warned me, "There ain't never been a mark yet that didn't want something for nothing." Then they took turns showing me their tricks, how they chose their victims (marks) from the wealthy bigoted whites and in every case how they used the victims' prejudice against them.

Some of the tales were funny, a few were pathetic, but all were    7
amusing or gratifying to me, for the Black man, the con man who could
act the most stupid, won out every time over the powerful, arrogant
white.

I remember Mr. Red Leg's story like a favorite melody.    8

"Anything that works against you can also work for you once you    9
understand the Principle of Reverse.

"There was a cracker in Tulsa who bilked so many Negroes he    10
could set up a Negro Bilking Company. Naturally he got to thinking,
Black Skin means Damn Fool. Just Black and I went to Tulsa to check
him out. Come to find out, he's a perfect mark. His momma must have
been scared in an Indian massacre in Africa. He hated Negroes only a little more than he despised Indians. And he was greedy.

"Black and I studied him and decided he was worth setting up    11
against the store. That means we were ready to put out a few thousand
dollars in preparation. We pulled in a white boy from New York, a good
con artist, and had him open an office in Tulsa. He was supposed to be a
Northern real estate agent trying to buy up valuable land in Oklahoma.
We investigated a piece of land near Tulsa that had a toll bridge crossing
it. It used to be part of an Indian reservation but had been taken over by
the state.

"Just Black was laid out as the decoy, and I was going to be the fool.    12
After our friend from New York hired a secretary and had his cards
printed, Black approached the mark with a proposition. He told him that
he had heard that our mark was the only white man colored people could
trust. He named some of the poor fools that had been taken by that
crook. It just goes to show you how white folks can be deceived by their
own deception. The mark believed Black.

"Black told him about his friend who was half Indian and half col-    13
ored and how some Northern white real estate agent had found out that
he was the sole owner of a piece of valuable land and the Northerner
wanted to buy it. At first the man acted like he smelled a rat, but from
the way he gobbled up the proposition, turns out what he thought he
smelled was some nigger money on his top lip.

"He asked the whereabouts of the land but Black put him off. He    14
told this cracker that he just wanted to make sure that he would be interested. The mark allowed how he was being interested, so Black said
he would tell his friend and they'd get in touch with him. Black met the
mark for about three weeks in cars and in alleys and kept putting him off
until the white man was almost crazy with anxiety and greed and then
accidentally it seemed Black let drop the name of the Northern real estate agent who wanted the property. From that moment on we knew we
had the big fish on the line and all we had to do was to pull him in.

"We expected him to try to contact our store, which he did. That    15
cracker went to our setup and counted on his whiteness to ally him with
Spots, our white boy, but Spots refused to talk about the deal except to

say the land had been thoroughly investigated by the biggest real estate concern in the South and that if our mark did not go around raising dust he would make sure that there would be a nice piece of money in it for him. Any obvious inquiries as to the rightful ownership of the land could alert the state and they would surely push through a law prohibiting the sale. Spots told the mark he would keep in touch with him. The mark went back to the store three or four times but to no avail, then just before we knew he would crack, Black brought me to see him. That fool was as happy as a sissy in a C.C.C. camp. You would have thought my neck was in a noose and he was about to light the fire under my feet. I never enjoyed taking anybody so much.

16      "Anyhow, I played scary at first but Just Black told me that this was one white man that our people could trust. I said I did not trust no white man because all they wanted was a chance to kill a Black man legally and get his wife in the bed. (I'm sorry, Clidell.) The mark assured me that he was the only white man who did not feel like that. Some of his best friends were colored people. In fact, if I didn't know it, the woman who raised him was a colored woman and he still sees her to this day. I let myself be convinced and then the mark began to drag the Northern whites. He told me that they made Negroes sleep in the street in the North and that they had to clean out toilets with their hands in the North and even things worse than that. I was shocked and said, 'Then I don't want to sell my land to that white man who offered seventy-five thousand dollars for it.' Just Black said, 'I wouldn't know what to do with that kind of money,' and I said that all I wanted was to have enough money to buy a home for my old mom, to buy a business and to make one trip to Harlem. The mark asked how much would that cost and I said I reckoned I could do it on fifty thousand dollars.

17      "The mark told me no Negro was safe with that kind of money. That white folks would take it from him. I said I knew it but I had to have at least forty thousand dollars. He agreed. We shook hands. I said it would do my heart good to see the mean Yankee go down on some of 'our land.' We met the next morning and I signed the deed in his car and he gave me the cash.

18      "Black and I had kept most of our things in a hotel over in Hot Springs, Arkansas. When the deal was closed we walked to our car, drove across the state line and on to Hot Springs.

19      "That's all there was to it."

20      When he finished, more triumphant stories rainbowed around the room riding the shoulders of laughter. By all accounts those storytellers, born Black and male before the turn of the twentieth century, should have been ground into useless dust. Instead they used their intelligence to pry open the door of rejection and not only became wealthy but got some revenge in the bargain.

21      It wasn't possible for me to regard them as criminals or be anything but proud of their achievements.

The needs of a society determine its ethics, and in the Black    22
American ghettos the hero is that man who is offered only the crumbs
from his country's table but by ingenuity and courage is able to take for
himself a Lucullan feast. Hence the janitor who lives in one room but
sports a robin's-egg-blue Cadillac is not laughed at but admired, and the
domestic who buys forty-dollar shoes is not criticized but is appreciated.
We know that they have put to use their full mental and physical powers. Each single gain feeds into the gains of the body collective.

Stories of law violations are weighed on a different set of scales in    23
the Black mind than in the white. Petty crimes embarrass the community and many people wistfully wonder why Negroes don't rob more
banks, embezzle more funds and employ graft in the unions. "We are the
victims of the world's most comprehensive robbery. Life demands a balance. It's all right if we do a little robbing now." This belief appeals particularly to one who is unable to compete legally with his fellow
citizens.

My education and that of my Black associates were quite different    24
from the education of our white schoolmates. In the classroom we all
learned past participles, but in the streets and in our homes the Blacks
learned to drop s's from plurals and suffixes from past-tense verbs. We
were alert to the gap separating the written word from the colloquial. We
learned to slide out of one language and into another without being conscious of the effort. At school, in a given situation, we might respond
with "That's not unusual." But in the street, meeting the same situation,
we easily said, "It be's like that sometimes."

## CONSIDERATIONS

1. Most of Angelou's essay is devoted to Mr. Red Leg telling a story. Notice how
close to pure narration that story is. Compare it with the selections in this book by
Wallace Stegner, George Orwell, or Richard Wright, and contrast the amount of description and narration in Mr. Red Leg's story with that in one of the others.

2. Compare Angelou's essay with that of Frank Conroy, who also emphasizes
memorable characters. How do the two authors differ in their reasons for devoting so
much space to Mr. Red Leg and to Ramos and Ricardo, respectively?

3. At the end of her essay, Angelou sets out an important linguistic principle.
Paraphrase that idea and provide examples from your own experience or research.

4. "Stories of law violations are weighed on a different set of scales in the Black
mind than in the white." Does a similar difference occur in the minds of two generations? Discuss relative justice versus absolute law.

5. Angelou demonstrates her versatility as a writer throughout this essay by managing two voices. Find examples and discuss.

6. From what you learn of Angelou's upbringing in the essay, compile a *negative
report* by a social worker on Angelou's childhood. Are there positive details in the essay
that would allow you to refute a negative report?

*Margaret Atwood (b. 1939) is a Canadian novelist and poet. Born in Ottawa, she now lives in Toronto with her husband and daughter. Her novels include* The Edible Woman *(1969),* Surfacing *(1972),* Lady Oracle *(1976),* Life before Man *(1979),* Bodily Harm *(1982),* The Handmaid's Tale *(1986),* Cat's Eye *(1989),* Wilderness Tips *(1992), and* Good Bones and Simple Murders *(1994). Her original* Selected Poems *came out in 1976, and a second volume in 1987. In 1978 she issued a collection of short stories,* Dancing Girls, *and in 1986 published* Bluebeard's Egg and Other Stories.

*Although she is largely known for her novels, Margaret Atwood has published much nonfiction, including literary criticism as well as topical essays such as this one. This essay is argument that begins with personal anecdote, the voice of one woman examining, defining, proposing, finding analogies, deciding. See how, telling anecdotes out of her own experience, she uses them to refine feelings and beliefs.*

— 5 —————————————

# MARGARET ATWOOD
## *Pornography*

———————————————————

1     When I was in Finland a few years ago for an international writers' conference, I had occasion to say a few paragraphs in public on the subject of pornography. The context was a discussion of political repression, and I was suggesting the possibility of a link between the two. The immediate result was that a male journalist took several large bites out of me. Prudery and pornography are two halves of the same coin, said he, and I was clearly a prude. What could you expect from an Anglo-Canadian? Afterward, a couple of pleasant Scandinavian men asked me what I had been so worked up about. All 'pornography' means, they said, is graphic depictions of whores, and what was the harm in that?

2     Not until then did it strike me that the male journalist and I had two entirely different things in mind. By "pornography," he meant naked bodies and sex. I, on the other hand, had recently been doing the research for my novel *Bodily Harm*, and was still in a state of shock from some of

the material I had seen, including the Ontario Board of Film Censors' "outtakes." By "pornography," I meant women getting their nipples snipped off with garden shears, having meat hooks stuck into their vaginas, being disemboweled; little girls being raped; men (yes, there are some men) being smashed to a pulp and forcibly sodomized. The cutting edge of pornography, as far as I could see, was no longer simple old copulation, hanging from the chandelier or otherwise; it was death, messy, explicit and highly sadistic. I explained this to the nice Scandinavian men. "Oh, but that's just the United States," they said. "Everyone knows they're sick." In their country, they said, violent "pornography" of that kind was not permitted on television or in movies; indeed, excessive violence of any kind was not permitted. They had drawn a clear line between erotica, which earlier studies had shown did not incite men to more aggressive and brutal behavior toward women, and violence, which later studies indicated did.

Some time after that I was in Saskatchewan, where, because of the scenes in *Bodily Harm*, I found myself on an open-line radio show answering questions about "pornography." Almost no one who phoned in was in favor of it, but again they weren't talking about the same stuff I was, because they hadn't seen it. Some of them were all set to stamp out bathing suits and negligees, and, if possible, any depictions of the female body whatsoever. God, it was implied, did not approve of female bodies, and sex of any kind, including that practised by bumblebees, should be shoved back into the dark, where it belonged. I had more than a suspicion that *Lady Chatterley's Lover*, Margaret Laurence's *The Diviners*, and indeed most books by most serious modern authors would have ended up as confetti if left in the hands of these callers.

For me, these two experiences illustrate the two poles of the emotionally heated debate that is now thundering around this issue. They also underline the desirability and even the necessity of defining the terms. "Pornography" is now one of those catchalls, like "Marxism" and "feminism," that have become so broad they can mean almost anything, ranging from certain verses in the Bible, ads for skin lotion and sex texts for children to the contents of *Penthouse*, Naughty '90s postcards and films with titles containing the word *Nazi* that show vicious scenes of torture and killing. It's easy to say that sensible people can tell the difference. Unfortunately, opinions on what constitutes a sensible person vary.

But even sensible people tend to lose their cool when they start talking about this subject. They soon stop talking and start yelling, and the name-calling begins. Those in favor of censorship (which may include groups not noticeably in agreement on other issues, such as some feminists and religious fundamentalists) accuse the others of exploiting women through the use of degrading images, contributing to the corruption of children, and adding to the general climate of violence and threat in which both women and children live in this society; or, though they may not give much of a hoot about actual women and children, they invoke moral standards and God's supposed aversion to "filth," "smut" and deviated *preversion*, which may mean ankles.

6      The camp in favor of total "freedom of expression" often comes out howling as loud as the Romans would have if told they could no longer have innocent fun watching the lions eat up Christians. It too may include segments of the population who are not natural bedfellows: those who proclaim their God-given right to freedom, including the freedom to tote guns, drive when drunk, drool over chicken porn and get off on videotapes of women being raped and beaten, may be waving the same anticensorship banner as responsible liberals who fear the return of Mrs. Grundy, or gay groups for whom sexual emancipation involves the concept of "sexual theater." *Whatever turns you on* is a handy motto, as is *A man's home is his castle* (and if it includes a dungeon with beautiful maidens strung up in chains and bleeding from every pore, that's his business).

7      Meanwhile, theoreticians theorize and speculators speculate. Is today's pornography yet another indication of the hatred of the body, the deep mind–body split, which is supposed to pervade Western Christian society? Is it a backlash against the women's movement by men who are threatened by uppity female behavior in real life, so like to fantasize about women done up like outsize parcels, being turned into hamburger, kneeling at their feet in slavelike adoration or sucking off guns? Is it a sign of collective impotence, of a generation of men who can't relate to real women at all but have to make do with bits of celluloid and paper? Is the current flood just a result of smart marketing and aggressive promotion by the money men in what has now become a multibillion-dollar industry? If they were selling movies about men getting their testicles stuck full of knitting needles by women with swastikas on their sleeves, would they do as well, or is this penchant somehow peculiarly male? If so, why? Is pornography a power trip rather than a sex one? Some say that those ropes, chains, muzzles and other restraining devices are an argument for the immense power female sexuality still wields in the male imagination: you don't put these things on dogs unless you're afraid of them. Others, more literary, wonder about the shift from the 19th-century Magic Woman or Femme Fatale image to the lollipop-licker, airhead or turkey-carcass treatment of women in porn today. The proporners don't care much about theory: they merely demand product. The antiporners don't care about it in the final analysis either: there's dirt on the street, and they want it cleaned up, now.

8      It seems to me that this conversation, with its *You're-a-prude/You're-a-pervert* dialect, will never get anywhere as long as we continue to think of this material as just "entertainment." Possibly we're deluded by the packaging, the format: magazine, book, movie, theatrical presentation. We're used to thinking of these things as part of the "entertainment industry," and we're used to thinking of ourselves as free adult people who ought to be able to see any kind of "entertainment" we

want to. That was what the First Choice pay-TV debate was all about. After all, it's only entertainment, right? Entertainment means fun, and only a killjoy would be antifun. What's the harm?

This is obviously the central question: *What's the harm?* If there isn't any real harm to any real people, then the antiporners can tsk-tsk and/or throw up as much as they like, but they can't rightfully expect more legal controls or sanctions. However, the no-harm position is far from being proven.

(For instance, there's a clear-cut case for banning—as the federal government has proposed—movies, photos and videos that depict children engaging in sex with adults: real children are used to make the movies, and hardly anybody thinks this is ethical. The possibilities for coercion are too great.)

To shift the viewpoint, I'd like to suggest three other models for looking at "pornography"—and here I mean the violent kind.

Those who find the idea of regulating pornographic materials repugnant because they think it's Fascist or Communist or otherwise not in accordance with the principles of an open democratic society should consider that Canada has made it illegal to disseminate material that may lead to hatred toward any group because of race or religion. I suggest that if pornography of the violent kind depicted these acts being done predominantly to Chinese, to blacks, to Catholics, it would be off the market immediately, under the present laws. Why is hate literature illegal? Because whoever made the law thought that such material might incite real people to do real awful things to other real people. The human brain is to a certain extent a computer: garbage in, garbage out. We only hear about the extreme cases (like that of American multimurderer Ted Bundy) in which pornography has contributed to the death and/or mutilation of women and/or men. Although pornography is not the only factor involved in the creation of such deviance, it certainly has upped the ante by suggesting both a variety of techniques and the social acceptability of such actions. Nobody knows yet what effect this stuff is having on the less psychotic.

Studies have shown that a large part of the market for all kinds of porn, soft and hard, is drawn from the 16-to-21-year-old population of young men. Boys used to learn about sex on the street, or (in Italy, according to Fellini movies) from friendly whores, or, in more general surroundings, from girls, their parents, or, once upon a time, in school, more or less. Now porn has been added, and sex education in the schools is rapidly being phased out. The buck has been passed, and boys are being taught that all women secretly like to be raped and that real men get high on scooping out women's digestive tracts.

Boys learn their concept of masculinity from other men: is this what most men want them to be learning? If word gets around that rapists are "normal" and even admirable men, will boys feel that in order to be normal, admirable and masculine they will have to be rapists?

Human beings are enormously flexible, and how they turn out depends a lot on how they're educated, by the society in which they're immersed as well as by their teachers. In a society that advertises and glorifies rape or even implicitly condones it, more women get raped. It becomes socially acceptable. And at a time when men and the traditional male role have taken a lot of flak and men are confused and casting around for an acceptable way of being male (and, in some cases, not getting much comfort from women on that score), this must be at times a pleasing thought.

15     It would be naïve to think of violent pornography as just harmless entertainment. It's also an educational tool and a powerful propaganda device. What happens when boy educated on porn meets girl brought up on Harlequin romances? The clash of expectations can be heard around the block. She wants him to get down on his knees with a ring, he wants her to get down on all fours with a ring in her nose. Can this marriage be saved?

16     Pornography has certain things in common with such addictive substances as alcohol and drugs: for some, though by no means for all, it induces chemical changes in the body, which the user finds exciting and pleasurable. It also appears to attract a "hard core" of habitual users and a penumbra of those who use it occasionally but aren't dependent on it in any way. There are also significant numbers of men who aren't much interested in it, not because they're undersexed but because real life is satisfying their needs, which may not require as many appliances as those of users.

17     For the "hard core," pornography may function as alcohol does for the alcoholic: tolerance develops, and a little is no longer enough. This may account for the short viewing time and fast turnover in porn theatres. Mary Brown, chairwoman of the Ontario Board of Film Censors, estimates that for every one mainstream movie requesting entrance to Ontario, there is one porno flick. Not only the quantity consumed but the quality of explicitness must escalate, which may account for the growing violence: once the big deal was breasts, then it was genitals, then copulation, then that was no longer enough and the hard users had to have more. The ultimate kick is death, and after that, as the Marquis de Sade so boringly demonstrated, multiple death.

18     The existence of alcoholism has not led us to ban social drinking. On the other hand, we do have laws about drinking and driving, excessive drunkenness and other abuses of alcohol that may result in injury or death to others.

19     This leads us back to the key question: what's the harm? Nobody knows, but this society should find out fast, before the saturation point is reached. The Scandinavian studies that showed a connection between depictions of sexual violence and increased impulse toward it on the part of male viewers would be a starting point, but many more questions remain to be raised as well as answered. What, for instance, is the crucial difference between men who are users and men who are not? Does using

affect a man's relationship with actual women, and, if so, adversely? Is there a clear line between erotica and violent pornography, or are they on an escalating continuum? Is this a "men versus women" issue, with all men secretly siding with the proporners and all women secretly siding against? (I think not; there are lots of men who don't think that running their true love through the Cuisinart is the best way they can think of to spend a Saturday night, and they're just as nauseated by films of someone else doing it as women are.) Is pornography merely an expression of the sexual confusion of this age or an active contributor to it?

Nobody wants to go back to the age of official repression, when 20 even piano legs were referred to as "limbs" and had to wear pantaloons to be decent. Neither do we want to end up in George Orwell's *1984*, in which pornography is turned out by the State to keep the proles in a state of torpor, sex itself is considered dirty and the approved practice is only for reproduction. But Rome under the emperors isn't such a good model either.

If all men and women respected each other, if sex were considered 21 joyful and life-enhancing instead of a wallow in germ-filled glop, if everyone were in love all the time, if, in other words, many people's lives were more satisfactory for them than they appear to be now, pornography might just go away on its own. But since this is obviously not happening, we as a society are going to have to make some informed and responsible decisions about how to deal with it.

## CONSIDERATIONS

1. In explaining that "pornography" means different things to different people, Atwood separates "erotica" from *her* definition of "pornography." How does she make that distinction and, more important, why?

2. Paragraph 7 consists largely of questions. Are they real questions or rhetorical questions? Explain the difference.

3. According to Atwood, what is the central question in the debate about pornography?

4. What is Atwood's strategy as demonstrated in paragraph 11? What does she hope to accomplish using it?

5. In paragraph 6, Atwood refers to "the return of Mrs. Grundy." Who was Mrs. Grundy, and why does her name pop up in so many discussions of pornography, sexual values, and the like?

6. Librarians (and others) struggle with a dilemma: whether or not to install pornography filters on public computer terminals. What are the principal elements that make the decision so difficult? Where would Atwood stand on the question? Where do you stand? And why?

*In 1994, the* Michigan Quarterly Review *published an issue devoted to the male body, to which Margaret Atwood contributed "Alien Territory." See page 640 for John Updike's "The Disposible Rocket," from the same issue of the magazine.*

*Only a novelist might have written this essay, with its inventions, with its statements embodied in imagined scenes. From numbered section to section, she changes her tone or method of attack. Finally, she has her topic surrounded.*

— 6

# MARGARET ATWOOD
## *Alien Territory*

### 1

1      He conceives himself in alien territory. Not his turf—alien! Listen! The rushing of the red rivers, the rustling of the fresh leaves in the dusk, always in the dusk, under the dark stars, and the wish-wash of the heavy soothing sea, which becomes—yes!—the drums of the natives, beating, beating, louder, faster, lower, slower. Are they hostile? Who knows, because they're invisible.

2      He sleeps and wakes, wakes and sleeps, and suddenly all is movement and suffering and terror and he is shot out gasping for breath into blinding light and a place that's even more dangerous, where food is scarce and two enormous giants stand guard over his wooden prison. Shout as he might, rattle the bars, nobody comes to let him out. One of the giants is boisterous and hair-covered, with a big stick; the other walks more softly but has two enormous bulgy comforts which she selfishly refuses to detach and give away, to him. Neither of them looks anything like him, and their language is incomprehensible.

3      Aliens! What can he do? And to make it worse, they surround him with animals—bears, rabbits, cats, giraffes—each one of them stuffed and, evidently, castrated, because although he looks and looks, all they have at best is a tail. Is this the fate the aliens have in store for him, as well?

*Where did I come from?* he asks, for what will not be the first time.  4
*Out of me,* the bulgy one says fondly, as if he should be pleased. Out of
*where?* Out of *what?* He covers his ears, shutting out the untruth, the
shame, the pulpy horror. It is not to be thought, it is not to be borne!

No wonder that at the first opportunity he climbs out of the win-  5
dow and joins a gang of other explorers, each one of them an exile, an immigrant, like himself. Together they set out on their solitary journeys.

What are they searching for? Their homeland. Their true country.  6
The place they came from, which can't possibly be here.

## 2

All men are created equal, as someone said who was either very  7
hopeful or very mischievous. What a lot of anxiety could have been
avoided if he'd only kept his mouth shut.

Sigmund was wrong about the primal scene: Mom and Dad, key-  8
hole version. That might be upsetting, true, but there's another one:

Five guys standing outside, pissing into a snowbank, a river, the un-  9
derbrush, pretending not to look down. Or maybe *not* looking down: gazing upward, at the stars, which gives us the origin of astronomy. Anything
to avoid comparisons, which aren't so much odious as intimidating.

And not only astronomy: quantum physics, engineering, laser tech-  10
nology, all numeration between zero and infinity. Something safely abstract, detached from you; a transfer of the obsession with size to
anything at all. Lord, Lord, they measure everything: the height of the
Great Pyramids, the rate of fingernail growth, the multiplication of
viruses, the sands of the sea, the number of angels that can dance on the
head of a pin. And then it's only a short step to proving that God is a
mathematical equation. Not a person. Not a body, Heaven forbid. Not one
like yours. Not an earthbound one, not one with size and therefore pain.

When you're feeling blue, just keep on whistling. Just keep on mea-  11
suring. Just don't look down.

## 3

The history of war is a history of killed bodies. That's what war is:  12
bodies killing other bodies, bodies being killed.

Some of the killed bodies are those of women and children, as a side  13
effect you might say. Fallout, shrapnel, napalm, rape and skewering, anti-
personnel devices. But most of the killed bodies are men. So are most of
those doing the killing.

Why do men want to kill the bodies of other men? Women don't  14
want to kill the bodies of other women. By and large. As far as we know.

Here are some traditional reasons: Loot. Territory. Lust for power.  15
Hormones. Adrenaline high. Rage. God. Flag. Honor. Righteous anger.
Revenge. Oppression. Slavery. Starvation. Defense of one's life. Love; or,

a desire to protect the women and children. From what? From the bodies of other men.

16    What men are most afraid of is not lions, not snakes, not the dark, not women. Not any more. What men are most afraid of is the body of another man.

17    Men's bodies are the most dangerous things on earth.


### 4

18    On the other hand, it could be argued that men don't have any bodies at all. Look at the magazines! Magazines for women have women's bodies on the covers, magazines for men have women's bodies on the covers. When men appear on the covers of magazines, it's magazines about money, or about world news. Invasions, rocket launches, political coups, interest rates, elections, medical breakthroughs. *Reality.* Not *entertainment.* Such magazines show only the heads, the unsmiling heads, the talking heads, the decision-making heads, and maybe a little glimpse, a coy flash of suit. How do we know there's a body, under all that discreet pinstriped tailoring? We don't, and maybe there isn't.

19    What does this lead us to suppose? That women are bodies with heads attached, and men are heads with bodies attached? Or not, depending.

20    You can have a body, though, if you're a rock star, an athlete, or a gay model. As I said, *entertainment.* Having a body is not altogether serious.


### 5

21    Or else too serious for words.

22    The thing is: Men's bodies aren't dependable. Now it does, now it doesn't, and so much for the triumph of the will. A man is the puppet of his body, or vice versa. He and it make tomfools of each other: It lets him down. Or up, at the wrong moment. Just stare hard out the schoolroom window and recite the multiplication tables and pretend this isn't happening! Your face at least can be immobile. Easier to have a trained dog, which will do what you want it to, nine times out of ten.

23    The other thing is: Men's bodies are detachable. Consider the history of statuary: The definitive bits get knocked off so easily, through revolution or prudery or simple transportation, with leaves stuck on for substitutes, fig or grape; or in more northern climates, maple. A man and his body are soon parted.

24    In the old old days, you became a man through blood. Through incisions, tattoos, splinters of wood; through an intimate wound, and the refusal to flinch. Through being beaten by older boys, in the dormitory, with a wooden paddle you were forced to carve yourself. The torments varied, but they were all torments. *It's a boy,* they cry with joy. *Let's cut some off!*

Every morning I get down on my knees and thank God for not cre-   25
ating me a man. A man so chained to unpredictability. A man so much at
the mercy of himself. A man so prone to sadness. A man who has to take
it like a man. A man, who can't fake it.

In the gap between desire and enactment, noun and verb, intention   26
and infliction, *want* and *have*, compassion begins.


## 6

Bluebeard ran off with the third sister, intelligent though beautiful,   27
and shut her up in his palace. *Everything here is yours, my dear*, he said
to her. *Just don't open the small door. I will give you the key; however I
expect you not to use it.*

Believe it or not, this sister was in love with him, even though she   28
knew he was a serial killer. She roamed over the whole palace, ignoring
the jewels and the silk dresses and the piles of gold. Instead she went
through the medicine cabinet and the kitchen drawers, looking for clues
to his uniqueness. Because she loved him, she wanted to understand
him. She also wanted to cure him. She thought she had the healing
touch.

But she didn't find out a lot. In his closet there were suits and ties   29
and matching shoes and casual wear, some golf outfits and a tennis rac-
quet, and some jeans for when he wanted to rake up the leaves. Nothing
unusual, nothing kinky, nothing sinister. She had to admit to being a little disappointed.

She found his previous women quite easily. They were in the linen   30
closet, neatly cut up and ironed flat and folded, stored in mothballs and
lavender. Bachelors acquire such domestic skills. The women didn't
make much of an impression on her, except the one who looked like his
mother. That one she took out with rubber gloves on and slipped into the
incinerator in the garden. *Maybe it was his mother*, she thought. *If so,
good riddance.*

She read through his large collection of cookbooks, and prepared   31
the dishes on the most-thumbed pages. At dinner he was politeness itself, pulling out her chair and offering more wine and leading the conversation around to topics of the day. She said gently that she wished he
would talk more about his feelings. He said that if she had his feelings,
she wouldn't want to talk about them either. This intrigued her. She was
now more in love with him and more curious than ever.

*Well*, she thought, *I've tried everything else; it's the small door or*   32
*nothing. Anyway, he gave me the key.* She waited until he had gone to
the office or wherever it was he went, and made straight for the small
door. When she opened it, what should be inside but a dead child. A
small dead child with its eyes wide open.

*It's mine*, he said, coming up behind her. *I gave birth to it. I warned*   33
*you. Weren't you happy with me?*

34     *It looks like you,* she said, not turning around, not knowing what to say. She realized now that he was not sane in any known sense of the word, but she still hoped to talk her way out of it. She could feel the love seeping out of her. Her heart was dry ice.

35     *It is me,* he said sadly. *Don't be afraid.*

36     *Where are we going?* she said, because it was getting dark, and there was suddenly no floor.

37     *Deeper,* he said.

## 7

38     Those ones. Why do women like them? They have nothing to offer, none of the usual things. They have short attention spans, falling-apart clothes, old beat-up cars, if any. The cars break down, and they try to fix them, and don't succeed, and give up. They go on long walks, from which they forget to return. They prefer weeds to flowers. They tell trivial fibs. They perform clumsy tricks with oranges and pieces of string, hoping desperately that someone will laugh. They don't put food on the table. They don't make money. Don't, can't, won't.

39     They offer nothing. They offer the great clean sweep of nothing, the unseen sky during a blizzard, the dark pause between moon and moon. They offer their poverty, an empty wooden bowl; the bowl of a beggar, whose gift is to ask. Look into it, look down deep, where potential coils like smoke, and you might hear anything. Nothing has yet been said.

40     They have bodies, however, Their bodies are unlike the bodies of other men. Their bodies are verbalized. *Mouth, eye, hand, foot,* they say. Their bodies have weight, and move over the ground, step by step, like yours. Like you they roll in the hot mud of the sunlight, like you they are amazed by morning, like you they can taste the wind, like you they sing. *Love,* they say, and at the time they always mean it, as you do also. They can say *lust* as well, and *disgust;* you wouldn't trust them otherwise. They say the worst things you have ever dreamed. They open locked doors. All this is given to them for nothing.

41     They have their angers. They have their despair, which washes over them like gray ink, blanking them out, leaving them immobile, in metal kitchen chairs, beside closed windows, looking out at the brick walls of deserted factories, for years and years. Yet nothing is with them; it keeps faith with them, and from it they bring back messages.

42     *Hurt,* they say and suddenly their bodies hurt again, like real bodies. *Death,* they say, making the word sound like the backwash of a wave. Their bodies die, and waver, and turn to mist. And yet they can exist in two worlds at once: lost in earth or eaten by flames, and here. In this room, when you re-say them, in their own words.

43     But why do women like them? Not *like,* I mean to say: *adore.* (Remember, that despite everything, despite all I have told you, the

rusted cars, the greasy wardrobes, the lack of breakfasts, the hopelessness, remain the same.)

Because if they can say their own bodies, they could say yours also.   44
Because they could say *skin* as if it meant something, not only to them
but to you. Because one night, when the snow is falling and the moon is
blotted out, they could put their empty hands, their hands filled with
poverty, their beggar's hands, on your body, and bless it, and tell you it is
made of light.

## CONSIDERATIONS

1. Which of these authors in your text—Ackerman, Hegland, Early—might be
helpful in understanding the first few paragraphs of Atwood's essay? Explain.

2. In paragraph 10, deploring our tendency to quantify whatever crosses our
path, Atwood cries out, "Lord, Lord, they measure everything." In what way, as a student, are you all too familiar with that tendency to reduce reality to numbers?

3. The obvious companion piece in this text for Atwood's "Alien Territory" is
Updike's "The Disposable Rocket," page 640. Point out and discuss some of the differences and/or similarities.

4. How do you account for the apparent disconnectedness of Atwood's essay—
separate sentences or even fragments presented as though they were paragraphs?

5. Given the fact that much of Atwood's reputation derives from aggressive and
unyielding feminist writings, are any of her statements in "Alien Territory" surprising?

6. Paragraph 23 ends with a statement that probably sounds familiar: "A man
and his body are soon parted." Something you've heard before? Atwood's use of it
demonstrates a useful device for a writer. Explain.

7. Atwood divides her essay into seven numbered sections. What do those section breaks do that the breaks between paragraphs don't? What is her strategy in dividing the essay so?

*Wendell Berry (b. 1934), essayist, novelist, and poet, was born and educated in Kentucky. He left home to teach in New York and California, and eventually returned to his "native hill." In 1986 his first collection of short stories,* The Wild Birds, *was published by North Point Press, which had also reissued his earlier novels,* A Place on Earth *and* Nathan Coulter. *In 1992 he brought out a second story collection,* Fidelity. *Among his many volumes of poetry are* Collected Poems: 1957–1982 *(1987) and* Sabbaths *(1987). His essay collections include* Recollected Essays *(1981),* The Gift of Good Land *(1981),* Standing by Words *(1984), and* Standing on Earth *(1991). While he continues to farm his Kentucky acreage, he harvests literature in three genres: in 1994 he cropped one book of poetry,* Entries, *and one of fiction,* Watch with Me; *in 1995 he collected new essays,* Another Turn of the Crank. *In 2000 he published a long essay,* Life Is a Miracle—*subtitled* An Essay against Modern Superstition—*and a novel,* Jayber Crow.

*Wendell Berry writes an essay—or a novel or a poem—with the same diligence and thoroughness with which he ploughs a field. Here, he uses closeness of description, in personal narrative, to arrive at judgment. In his essay, he shows the abilities that provide character in his novels and images in his poems.*

— 7

# WENDELL BERRY
## *A Native Hill*

1    I start down from one of the heights of the upland, the town of Port Royal at my back. It is a winter day, overcast and still, and the town is closed in itself, humming and muttering a little, like a winter beehive.

2    The dog runs ahead, prancing and looking back, knowing the way we are about to go. This is a walk well established with us—a route in our minds as well as on the ground. There is a sort of mystery in the establishment of these ways. Any time one crosses a given stretch of country with some frequency, no matter how wanderingly one begins, the

tendency is always toward habit. By the third or fourth trip, without realizing it, one is following a fixed path, going the way one went before.
After that, one may still wander, but only by deliberation, and when
there is reason to hurry, or when the mind wanders rather than the feet,
one returns to the old route. Familiarity has begun. One has made a relationship with the landscape, and the form and the symbol and the enactment of the relationship is the path. These paths of mine are seldom
worn on the ground. They are habits of mind, directions, and turns. They
are as personal as old shoes. My feet are comfortable in them.

From the height I can see far out over the country, the long open  3
ridges of the farmland, the wooded notches of the streams, the valley of the
river opening beyond, and then more ridges and hollows of the same kind.

Underlying this country, nine hundred feet below the highest  4
ridgetops, more than four hundred feet below the surface of the river, is sea
level. We seldom think of it here; we are a long way from the coast and the
sea is alien to us. And yet the attraction of sea level dwells in this country
as an ideal dwells in a man's mind. All our rains go in search of it and, de-
parting, they have carved the land in a shape that is fluent and falling. The
streams branch like vines, and between the branches the land rises steeply
and then rounds and gentles into the long narrowing fingers of ridgeland.
Near the heads of the streams even the steepest land was not too long ago
farmed and kept cleared. But now it has been given up and the woods is returning. The wild is flowing back like a tide. The arable ridgetops reach
out above the gathered trees like headlands into the sea, bearing their human burdens of fences and houses and barns, crops and roads.

Looking out over the country, one gets a sense of the whole of it:  5
the ridges and hollows, the clustered buildings of the farms, the open
fields, the woods, the stock ponds set like coins into the slopes. But this
is a surface sense, an exterior sense, such as you get from looking down
on the roof of a house. The height is a threshold from which to step down
into the wooded folds of the land, the interior, under the trees and along
the branching streams.

I pass through a pasture gate on a deep-worn path that grows shal-  6
low a little way beyond and then disappears altogether into the grass.
The gate has gathered thousands of passings to and fro, that have divided
like the slats of a fan on either side of it. It is like a fist holding together
the strands of a net.

Beyond the gate the land leans always more steeply toward the  7
branch. I follow it down, and then bear left along the crease at the bottom
of the slope. I have entered the downflow of the land. The way I am going
is the way the water goes. There is something comfortable and fit-feeling
in this, something free in this yielding to gravity and taking the shortest
way down. The mind moves through the watershed as the water moves.

As the hollow deepens into the hill, before it has yet entered the  8
woods, the grassy crease becomes a raw gulley, and along the steepening
slopes on either side I can see the old scars of erosion, places where the

earth is gone clear to the rock. My people's errors have become the features of my country.

9      It occurs to me that it is no longer possible to imagine how this country looked in the beginning, before the white people drove their plows into it. It is not possible to know what was the shape of the land here in this hollow when it was first cleared. Too much of it is gone, loosened by the plows and washed away by the rain. I am walking the route of the departure of the virgin soil of the hill. I am not looking at the same land the first-comers saw. The original surface of the hill is as extinct as the passenger pigeon. The pristine America that the first white men saw is a lost continent, sunk like Atlantis in the sea. The thought of what was here once and is gone forever will not leave me as long as I live. It is as though I walk knee-deep in its absence.

10      The slopes along the hollow steepen still more and I go in under the trees. I pass beneath the surface. I am enclosed, and my sense, my interior sense, of the country becomes intricate. There is no longer the possibility of seeing very far. The distances are closed off by the trees and the steepening walls of the hollow. One cannot grow familiar here by sitting and looking as one can up in the open on the ridge. Here the eyes become dependent on the feet. To see the woods from the inside one must look and move and look again. It is inexhaustible in its standpoints. A lifetime will not be enough to experience it all.

11      Not far from the beginning of the woods, and set deep in the earth in the bottom of the hollow, is a rock-walled pool not a lot bigger than a bathtub. The wall is still nearly as straight and tight as when it was built. It makes a neatly turned narrow horseshoe, the open end downstream. This is a historical ruin, dug here either to catch and hold the water of the little branch, or to collect the water of a spring whose vein broke to the surface here—it is probably no longer possible to know which. The pool is filled with earth now, and grass grows in it. And the branch bends around it, cut down to the bare rock, a torrent after heavy rain, other times bone dry. All that is certain is that when the pool was dug and walled there was deep topsoil on the hill to gather and hold the water. And this high up, at least, the bottom of the hollow, instead of the present raw notch of the streambed, wore the same mantle of soil as the slopes, and the stream was a steady seep or trickle, running most or all of the year. This tiny pool no doubt once furnished water for a considerable number of stock through the hot summers. And now it is only a lost souvenir, archaic and useless, except for the bitter intelligence there is in it. It is one of the monuments to what is lost.

12      Like the pasture gates, the streams are great collectors of comings and goings. The streams go down, and paths always go down beside the streams. For a while I walk along an old wagon road that is buried in leaves—a fragment, beginningless and endless as the middle of a sentence on some scrap of papyrus. There is a cedar whose branches reach over this road, and under the branches I find the leavings of two kills of

some bird of prey. The most recent is a pile of blue jay feathers. The other has been rained on and is not identifiable. How little we know. How little of this was intended or expected by any man. The road that has become the grave of men's passages has led to the life of the woods.

> And I say to myself: Here is your road
> without beginning or end, appearing
> out of the earth and ending in it, bearing
> no load but the hawk's kill, and the leaves
> building earth on it, something more
> to be borne. Tracks fill with earth
> and return to absence. The road was worn
> by men bearing earth along it. They have come
> to endlessness. In their passing
> they could not stay in, trees have risen
> and stand still. It is leading to the dark,
> to morning where you are not. Here
> is your road, beginningless and endless as God.

Now I have come down within the sound of the water. The winter 13 has been rainy, and the hill is full of dark seeps and trickles, gathering fi nally, along these creases, into flowing streams. The sound of them is one of the elements, and defines a zone. When their voices return to the hill after their absence during summer and autumn, it is a better place to be. A thirst in the mind is quenched.

I have already passed the place where water began to flow in the lit- 14 tle stream bed I am following. It broke into the light from beneath a rock ledge, a thin glittering stream. It lies beside me as I walk, overtaking me and going by, yet not moving, a thread of light and sound. And now from below comes the steady tumble and rush of the water of Camp Branch— whose nameless camp was it named for?—and gradually as I descend the sound of the smaller stream is lost in the sound of the larger.

The two hollows join, the line of the meeting of the two spaces ob- 15 scured even in winter by the trees. But the two streams meet precisely as two roads. That is, the stream *beds* do; the one ends in the other. As for the meeting of the waters, there is no looking at that. The one flow does not end in the other, but continues in it, one with it, two clarities merged without a shadow.

All waters are one. This is a reach of the sea, flung like a net over 16 the hill, and now drawn back to the sea. And as the sea is never raised in the earthly nets of fishermen, so the hill is never caught and pulled down by the watery net of the sea. But always a little of it is. Each of the gathering strands of the net carries back some of the hill melted in it. Sometimes, as now, it carries so little that the water seems to flow clear; sometimes it carries a lot and is brown and heavy with it. Whenever greedy or thoughtless men have lived on it, the hill has literally flowed out of their tracks into the bottom of the sea.

17       There appears to be a law that when creatures have reached the level of consciousness, as men have, they must become conscious of the creation; they must learn how they fit into it and what its needs are and what it requires of them, or else pay a terrible penalty: the spirit of the creation will go out of them, and they will become destructive. The very earth will depart from them and go where they cannot follow.

18       My mind is never empty or idle at the joinings of streams. Here is the work of the world going on. The creation is felt, alive, and intent on its materials, in such places. In the angle of the meeting of the two streams stands the steep wooded point of the ridge, like the prow of an upturned boat—finished, as it was a thousand years ago, as it will be in a thousand years. Its becoming is only incidental to its being. It will be because it is. It has no aim or end except to be. By being it is growing and wearing into what it will be. The fork of the stream lies at the foot of the slope like hammer and chisel laid down at the foot of a finished sculpture. But the stream is no dead tool; it is alive, it is still at its work. Put your hand to it to learn the health of this part of the world. It is the wrist of the hill.

19       Perhaps it is to prepare to hear some day the music of the spheres that I am always turning my ears to the music of streams. There is indeed a music in streams, but it is not for the hurried. It has to be loitered by and imagined. Or imagined *toward*, for it is hardly for men at all. Nature has a patient ear. To her the slowest funeral march sounds like a jig. She is satisfied to have the notes drawn out to the lengths of days or weeks or months. Small variations are acceptable to her, modulations as leisurely as the opening of a flower.

20       The stream is full of stops and gates. Here it has piled up rocks in its path, and pours over them into a tiny pool it has scooped at the foot of its fall. Here it has been dammed by a mat of leaves caught behind a fallen limb. Here it must force a narrow passage, here a wider one. Tomorrow the flow may increase or slacken, and the tone will shift. In an hour or a week that rock may give way, and the composition will advance by another note. Some idea of it may be got by walking slowly along and noting the changes as one passes from one little fall or rapid to another. But this is a highly simplified and diluted version of the real thing, which is too complex and widespread ever to be actually heard by us. The ear must imagine an impossible patience in order to grasp even the unimaginableness of such music.

21       But the creation is musical, and this is a part of its music, as birdsong is, or the words of poets. The music of the streams is the music of the shaping of the earth, by which the rocks are pushed and shifted downward toward the level of the sea.

22       And now I find lying in the path an empty beer can. This is the track of the ubiquitous man Friday of all our woods. In my walks I never fail to discover some sign that he has preceded me. I find his empty shotgun shells, his empty cans and bottles, his sandwich wrappings. In

wooded places along roadsides one is apt to find, as well, his overtravelled bedsprings, his outcast refrigerator, and heaps of the imperishable refuse of his modern kitchen. A year ago, almost in this same place where I have found his beer can, I found a possum that he had shot dead and left lying, in celebration of his manhood. He is the true American pioneer, perfectly at rest in his assumption that he is the first and the last whose inheritance and fate this place will ever be. Going forth, as he may think, to sow, he only broadcasts his effects.

As I go down the path alongside Camp Branch, I walk by the edge of    23
croplands abandoned only within my own lifetime. On my left are south slopes where the woods are old, long undisturbed. On my right, the more fertile north slopes are covered with patches of briars and sumacs and a lot of young walnut trees. Tobacco of an extraordinary quality was once grown here, and then the soil wore thin, and these places were given up for the more accessible ridges that were not so steep, where row-cropping made better sense anyway. But now, under the thicket growth, a mat of bluegrass has grown to testify to the good nature of this ground. It was fine dirt that lay here once, and I am far from being able to say that I could have resisted the temptation to plow it. My understanding of what is best for it is the tragic understanding of hindsight, the awareness that I have been taught what was here to be lost by the loss of it.

We have lived by the assumption that what was good for us would    24
be good for the world. And this has been based on the even flimsier assumption that we could know with any certainty what was good even for us. We have fulfilled the danger of this by making our personal pride and greed the standard of our behavior toward the world—to the incalculable disadvantage of the world and every living thing in it. And now, perhaps very close to too late, our great error has become clear. It is not only our own creativity—our own capacity for life—that is stifled by our arrogant assumption; the creation itself is stifled.

We have been wrong. We must change our lives, so that it will be    25
possible to live by the contrary assumption that what is good for the world will be good for us. And that requires that we make the effort to *know* the world and to learn what is good for it. We must learn to cooperate in its processes, and to yield to its limits. But even more important, we must learn to acknowledge that the creation is full of mystery; we will never entirely understand it. We must abandon arrogance and stand in awe. We must recover the sense of the majesty of creation, and the ability to be worshipful in its presence. For I do not doubt that it is only on the condition of humility and reverence before the world that our species will be able to remain in it.

Standing in the presence of these worn and abandoned fields, where    26
the creation has begun its healing without the hindrance or the help of man, with the voice of the stream in the air and the woods standing in silence on all the slopes around me, I am deep in the interior not only of my place in the world, but of my own life, its sources and searches and

concerns. I first came into these places following the men to work when I was a child. I knew the men who took their lives from such fields as these, and their lives to a considerable extent made my life what it is. In what came to me from them there was both wealth and poverty, and I have been a long time discovering which was which.

27   It was in the woods here along Camp Branch that Bill White, my grandfather's hired hand, taught me to hunt squirrels. Bill lived in a little tin-roofed house on up nearer the head of the hollow. And this was, I suppose more than any other place, his hunting ground. It was the place of his freedom, where he could move without subservience, without considering who he was or who anybody else was. On late summer mornings, when it was too wet to work, I would follow him into the woods. As soon as we stepped in under the trees he would become silent, and absolutely attentive to the life of the place. He was a good teacher and an exacting one. The rule seemed to be that if I wanted to stay with him, I had to make it possible for him to forget I was there. I was to make no noise. If I did he would look back and make a downward emphatic gesture with his hand, as explicit as writing: Be quiet, or go home. He would see a squirrel crouched in a fork or lying along the top of a branch, and indicate with a grin and a small jerk of his head where I should look; and then wait, while I, conscious of being watched and demanded upon, searched it out for myself. He taught me to look and to listen and to be quiet. I wonder if he knew the value of such teaching or the rarity of such a teacher.

28   In the years that followed I hunted often here alone. And later in these same woods I experienced my first obscure dissatisfactions with hunting. Though I could not have put it into words then, the sense had come to me that hunting as I knew it—the eagerness to kill something I did not need to eat—was an artificial relation to the place, when what I was beginning to need, just as inarticulately then, was a relation that would be deeply natural and meaningful. That was a time of great uneasiness and restlessness for me. It would be the fall of the year, the leaves would be turning, and ahead of me would be another year of school. There would be confusions about girls and ambitions, the wordless hurried feeling that time and events and my own nature were pushing me toward what I was going to be—and I had no notion what it was, or how to prepare.

29   And then there were years when I did not come here at all—when these places and their history were in my mind, and part of me, in places thousands of miles away. And now I am here again, changed from what I was, and still changing. The future is no more certain to me now than it ever was, though its risks are clearer, and so are my own desires. I am the father of two young children whose lives are hostages given to the future. Because of them and because of events in the world, life seems more fearful and difficult to me now than ever before; but it is also more inviting, and I am constantly aware of its nearness to joy. Much of the interest and excitement that I have in my life now has come from the deepening, in

the years since my return here, of my relation to this countryside that is my native place. For in spite of all that has happened to me in other places, the great change and the great possibility of change in my life has been in my sense of this place. The major difference is perhaps only that I have grown able to be wholeheartedly present here. I am able to sit and be quiet at the foot of some tree here in this woods along Camp Branch, and feel a deep peace, both in the place and in my awareness of it, that not too long ago I was not conscious of the possibility of. This peace is partly in being free of the suspicion that pursued me for most of my life, no matter where I was, that there was perhaps another place I *should* be, or would be happier or better in; it is partly in the increasingly articulate consciousness of being here, and of the significance and importance of being here.

After more than thirty years I have at last arrived at the candor nec-  30
essary to stand on this part of the earth that is so full of my own history and so much damaged by it, and ask: What *is* this place? What is in it? What is its nature? How should men live in it? What must I do?

I have not found the answers, though I believe that in partial and  31
fragmentary ways they have begun to come to me. But the questions are more important than their answers. In the final sense they *have* no an-swers. They are like the questions—they are perhaps the same ques-tions—that were the discipline of Job. They are part of the necessary enactment of humility, teaching a man what his importance is, what his responsibility is, and what his place is, both on the earth and in the order of things. And though the answers must always come obscurely and in fragments, the questions must be persistently asked. They are fertile questions. In their implications and effects, they are moral and esthetic and, in the best and fullest sense, practical. They promise a relationship to the world that is decent and preserving.

They are also, both in origin and effect, religious. I am uneasy with  32
the term, for such religion as has been openly practiced in this part of the world has promoted and fed upon a destructive schism between body and soul, heaven and earth. It has encouraged people to believe that the world is of no importance, and that their only obligation in it is to sub-mit to certain churchly formulas in order to get to heaven. And so the people who might have been expected to care most selflessly for the world have had their minds turned elsewhere—to a pursuit of "salva-tion" that was really only another form of gluttony and self-love, the de-sire to perpetuate their own small lives beyond the life of the world. The heaven-bent have abused the earth thoughtlessly, by inattention, and their negligence has permitted and encouraged others to abuse it deliber-ately. Once the creator was removed from the creation, divinity became only a remote abstraction, a social weapon in the hands of the religious institutions. This split in public values produced or was accompanied by, as it was bound to be, an equally artificial and ugly division in people's lives, so that a man, while pursuing heaven with the sublime appetite he

thought of as his soul, could turn his heart against his neighbors and his hands against the world. For these reasons, though I know that my questions *are* religious, I dislike having to *say* that they are.

33       But when I ask them my aim is not primarily to get to heaven. Though heaven is certainly more important than the earth if all they say about it is true, it is still morally incidental to it and dependent on it, and I can only imagine it and desire it in terms of which I know of the earth. And so my questions do not aspire beyond the earth. They aspire *toward* it and *into* it. Perhaps they aspire *through* it. They are religious because they are asked at the limit of what I know; they acknowledge mystery and honor its presence in the creation; they are spoken in reverence for the order and grace that I see, and that I trust beyond my power to see.

34       The stream has led me down to an old barn built deep in the hollow to house the tobacco once grown on those abandoned fields. Now it is surrounded by the trees that have come back on every side—a relic, a fragment of another time, strayed out of its meaning. This is the last of my historical landmarks. To here, my walk has had insistent overtones of memory and history. It has been a movement of consciousness through knowledge, eroding and shaping, adding and wearing away. I have descended like the water of the stream through what I know of myself, and now that I have there is a little more to know. But here at the barn, the old roads and the cow paths—the formal connections with civilization—come to an end.

35       I stoop between the strands of a barbed wire fence, and in that movement I go out of time into timelessness. I come into a wild place. I walk along the foot of a slope that was once cut bare of trees, like all the slopes of this part of the country—but long ago; and now the woods is established again, the ground healed, the trees grown big, their trunks rising clean, free of undergrowth. The place has a serenity and dignity that one feels immediately; the creation is whole in it and unobstructed. It is free of the strivings and dissatisfactions, the partialities and imperfections of places under the mechanical dominance of men. Here, what to a housekeeper's eye might seem disorderly is nonetheless orderly and within order; what might seem arbitrary or accidental is included in the design of the whole as if by intention; what might seem evil or violent is a comfortable member of the household. Where the creation is whole nothing is extraneous. The presence of the creation here makes this a holy place, and it is as a pilgrim that I have come—to give the homage of awe and love, to submit to mystification. It is the creation that has attracted me, its perfect interfusion of life and design. I have made myself its follower and its apprentice.

36       One early morning last spring, I came and found the woods floor strewn with bluebells. In the cool sunlight and the lacy shadows of the spring woods the blueness of those flowers, their elegant shape, their delicate fresh scent kept me standing and looking. I found a rich delight in them that I cannot describe and that I will never forget. Though I had

been familiar for years with most of the spring woods flowers, I had never seen these and had not known they grew here. Looking at them, I felt a strange feeling of loss and sorrow that I had never seen them before. But I was also exultant that I saw them now—that they were here.

For me, in the thought of them will always be the sense of the joy-  37
ful surprise with which I found them—the sense that came suddenly to me then that the world is blessed beyond my understanding, more abundantly than I will ever know. What lives are still ahead of me here to be discovered and exulted in, tomorrow, or in twenty years? What wonder will be found here on the morning after my death? Though as a man I inherit great evils and the possibility of great loss and suffering, I know that my life is blessed and graced by the yearly flowering of the bluebells. How perfect they are! In their presence I am humble and joyful. If I were given all the learning and all the methods of my race I could not make one of them, or even imagine one. Solomon in all his glory was not arrayed like one of these. It is the privilege and the labor of the apprentice of creation to come with his imagination into the unimaginable, and with his speech into the unspeakable.

## CONSIDERATIONS

1. To think of habits as paths worn in the mind is no very original metaphor. How does Berry distinguish this image as he works it into the essay?

2. Berry's essay, like the walk he is reporting, is a leisurely experience that should be taken in an unhurried manner. Much of this easy pace is due to his style: he makes an observation, then pauses to reflect on it and related things, then moves along to another observation, and another reflective pause, and so on. The result is a pleasing, thoughtful mix of the factual and the insightful. Try writing a short, descriptive essay in this style.

3. "Nature has a patient ear," writes Berry in paragraph 19, using a literary technique called personification. Look for examples of personification in the works of other writers, or make up several yourself (e.g., "the blindness of the night," "the laughter of the wind," "the soul of the abandoned house"). Then explain the meaning of personification and its value to a writer like Berry.

4. Assuming paragraph 30 is an explicit pronouncement of his thesis, what varied means does Berry use to embody these ideas?

5. In paragraph 22, Berry finds "the track of the ubiquitous man Friday." Who is this, and why "Friday"? One bit of evidence that Friday had been there was "a possum that he had shot dead and left lying, in celebration of his manhood." The tone of "in celebration of his manhood" is different from that of the rest of the essay. Explain.

6. Throughout his essay, Berry works to evoke a sense of place—that hill where he grew up and to which he now returns. Yet he also thinks on a wider scale—the state of the nation, and even the world. Is he successful in fusing the various planes? If so, how does he manage it? If not, why not?

7. The questions Berry asks in paragraph 30 are similar to those asked by Margaret Atwood in paragraph 4 of her "Alien Territory," yet the effects they have and the writer's strategies in asking them are entirely different. Explain in a short essay.

*Ambrose Bierce (1842–1914?) was born in a log cabin on Horse Cave Creek in Ohio. He educated himself by reading the books in his father's small library and as a young man served in the army during the Civil War. Starting as a journalist in California, he made himself an elegant writer of short stories, which were often supernatural or macabre in theme. Because he was writing in the primitive West, in a country still generally primitive, his serious work went largely unrecognized. Melancholy deepened into misanthropy. The definitions in* The Devil's Dictionary *(1906) are funny indeed—but the humor is serious, and the wit is bitter.*

*In 1913, Bierce put his affairs in order and went to Mexico, which was in the midst of a civil war. He wrote a friend as he left, ". . . if you hear of my being stood up against a Mexican stone wall and shot to rags please know that I think it a pretty good way to depart this life. It beats old age, disease, or falling down a flight of stairs." He was never heard from again.*

— **8** —

# AMBROSE BIERCE
## *Some Devil's Definitions*

1    *Belladonna, n.* In Italian a beautiful lady; in English a deadly poison. A striking example of the essential identity of the two tongues.

2    *Bigot, n.* One who is obstinately and zealously attached to an opinion that you do not entertain.

3    *Bore, n.* A person who talks when you wish him to listen.

4    *Brute, n. See* HUSBAND.

5    *Cabbage, n.* A familiar kitchen-garden vegetable about as large and wise as a man's head.

6    *Calamity, n.* A more than commonly plain and unmistakable reminder that the affairs of this life are not of our own ordering. Calamities are of two kinds: misfortune to ourselves, and good fortune to others.

7    *Cannibal, n.* A gastronome of the old school who preserves the simple tastes and adheres to the natural diet of the pre-pork period.

8    *Cannon, n.* An instrument employed in the rectification of national boundaries.

*Cat, n.* A soft, indestructible automaton provided by nature to be kicked when things go wrong in the domestic circle.   9

*Christian, n.* One who believes that the New Testament is a divinely inspired book admirably suited to the spiritual needs of his neighbor. One who follows the teachings of Christ in so far as they are not inconsistent with a life of sin.   10

*Clairvoyant, n.* A person, commonly a woman, who has the power of seeing that which is invisible to her patron—namely, that he is a blockhead.   11

*Commerce, n.* A kind of transaction in which A plunders from B the goods of C, and for compensation B picks the pocket of D of money belonging to E.   12

*Compromise, n.* Such an adjustment of conflicting interests as gives each adversary the satisfaction of thinking he has got what he ought not to have, and is deprived of nothing except what was justly his due.   13

*Compulsion, n.* The eloquence of power.   14

*Congratulation, n.* The civility of envy.   15

*Conservative, n.* A statesman who is enamored of existing evils, as distinguished from the Liberal, who wishes to replace them with others.   16

*Consul, n.* In American politics, a person who having failed to secure an office from the people is given one by the Administration on condition that he leave the country.   17

*Consult, v.t.* To seek another's approval of a course already decided on.   18

*Corsair, n.* A politician of the seas.   19

*Coward, n.* One who in a perilous emergency thinks with his legs.   20

*Curiosity, n.* An objectionable quality of the female mind. The desire to know whether or not a woman is cursed with curiosity is one of the most active and insatiable passions of the masculine soul.   21

*Cynic, n.* A blackguard whose faulty vision sees things as they are, not as they ought to be. Hence the custom among the Scythians of plucking out a cynic's eyes to improve his vision.   22

*Dance, v.i.* To leap about to the sound of tittering music, preferably with arms about your neighbor's wife or daughter. There are many kinds of dances, but all those requiring the participation of the two sexes have two characteristics in common: they are conspicuously innocent, and warmly loved by the vicious.   23

*Debauchee, n.* One who has so earnestly pursued pleasure that he has had the misfortune to overtake it.   24

*Decalogue, n.* A series of commandments, ten in number—just enough to permit an intelligent selection for observance, but not enough to embarrass the choice.   25

*Defame, v.t.* To lie about another. To tell the truth about another.   26

*Dentist, n.* A prestidigitator who, putting metal in your mouth, pulls coins out of your pocket.   27

28   *Die, n.* The singular of "dice." We seldom hear the word, because there is a prohibitory proverb, "Never say die."

29   *Discussion, n.* A method of confirming others in their errors.

30   *Distance, n.* The only thing that the rich are willing for the poor to call theirs, and keep.

31   *Duel, n.* A formal ceremony preliminary to the reconciliation of two enemies. Great skill is necessary to its satisfactory observance; if awkwardly performed the most unexpected and deplorable consequences sometimes ensue. A long time ago a man lost his life in a duel.

32   *Eccentricity, n.* A method of distinction so cheap that fools employ it to accentuate their incapacity.

33   *Edible, adj.* Good to eat, and wholesome to digest, as a worm to a toad, a toad to a snake, a snake to a pig, a pig to a man, and a man to a worm.

34   *Education, n.* That which discloses to the wise and disguises from the foolish their lack of understanding.

35   *Effect, n.* The second of two phenomena which always occur together in the same order. The first, called a Cause, is said to generate the other—which is no more sensible than it would be for one who has never seen a dog except in pursuit of a rabbit to declare the rabbit the cause of the dog.

36   *Egotist, n.* A person of low taste, more interested in himself than in me.

37   *Erudition, n.* Dust shaken out of a book into an empty skull.

38   *Eulogy, n.* Praise of a person who has either the advantages of wealth and power, or the consideration to be dead.

39   *Female, n.* One of the opposing, or unfair, sex.

40   *Fib, n.* A lie that has not cut its teeth. A habitual liar's nearest approach to truth: the perigee of his eccentric orbit.

41   *Fiddle, n.* An instrument to tickle human ears by friction of a horse's tail on the entrails of a cat.

42   *Friendship, n.* A ship big enough to carry two in fair weather, but only one in foul.

43   *Garter, n.* An elastic band intended to keep a woman from coming out of her stockings and desolating the country.

44   *Ghost, n.* The outward and visible sign of an inward fear.

45   *Glutton, n.* A person who escapes the evils of moderation by committing dyspepsia.

46   *Gout, n.* A physician's name for the rheumatism of a rich patient.

47   *Grammar, n.* A system of pitfalls thoughtfully prepared for the feet of the self-made man, along the path by which he advances to distinction.

48   *Guillotine, n.* A machine which makes a Frenchman shrug his shoulders with good reason.

## CONSIDERATIONS

1. To appreciate the humor in some of Bierce's definitions, you may have to look up in your dictionary some of the words found here, such as "gastronome," "zealously," "adversary," "civility," "insatiable," "prestidigitator," "perigee," "dyspepsia." How do you add words to your working vocabulary?

2. *The Devil's Dictionary* was first published in 1906. Judging from the definitions here, would you say that Bierce's book is dated? Which items strike you as most relevant to our times? Which are least relevant? Why?

3. Do you find a consistent tone or attitude in Bierce's dictionary? Explain and provide ample evidence.

4. Who among these authors would most appreciate Bierce's brand of humor: Frederick Douglass ("Plantation Life"), James Thurber ("Which"), Margaret Atwood ("Alien Territory"), Flannery O'Connor ("A Good Man Is Hard to Find"), or George Orwell ("A Hanging")? Explain, making comparisons.

5. Compose a page of definitions for your own Devil's Dictionary, perhaps concentrating on words currently popular.

*Sven Birkerts (b. 1951) was awarded the National Book Critics Circle Citation for Excellence in Reviewing in 1986, and in 1991 he received a Lila Wallace–Reader's Digest Award. His books of essays include* An Artificial Wilderness *(1987),* The Electric Life *(1989),* American Energies *(1992),* Gutenberg Elegies *(1994), and* Readings *(1999). Birkerts frequently reviews contemporary fiction and poetry, publishing in the* New Republic, Mirabella, *and the* Atlantic, *among other magazines. In addition, he writes essays that observe American culture with an eye both critical and shrewd. Birkerts teaches in the Bennington College MFA Program and collaborates with Donald Hall on* Writing Well.

*For "word processor," read "computer" throughout. Birkerts, who still uses a typewriter, started publication as a literary critic. He continues to review and to evaluate books, and has extended himself into memoir, but he has also become a prophet attacking the deprivations of technology as it takes over the act of writing. He attacks with argumentative assertion; he attacks with irony.*

*"I've heard it said that now* everyone *can become a writer.*

*"Hot dog."*

— 9 —

# SVEN BIRKERTS
## *Objections Noted: Word Processing*

1    People ask me why I refuse to use a word processor. I tell them because it feels like a typewriter with a condom over it. The very sight of one of those sculpted plastic instruments with its pert ticket-counter "everything's under control" screen depresses me beyond measure. It makes me feel how close the final victory of technology over spirit really is. Hell, it *is* the victory of technology over spirit.

2    Neither can I bear the chirping good humor with which owners talk about their disks and programs.

The word-processor argument. Most people, I'm sure, maintain   3
that there *is* no word-processor argument. Indeed, I hardly ever meet
anyone who writes who isn't using one—a few poets, maybe . . . Louis
Simpson . . .

Lemmings!   4
Literature has got lightweight and modular enough without writers   5
all shifting their idly fluffed-together paragraphs around. If you can't organize it in your head, it's not ready to be organized.
The WP is a death-ray directed at the last remnants of the   6
prophetic soul.

The word processor is just a tool, they say. Just a tool. Just a tool.   7
Never mind that it's an ugly tool, utterly alien from anything relating to
spirit. (Would you paint with a steel-handled brush?) Never mind that
the machine you work on changes the compositional process, changes
you. It's just a tool.
Like any tool, the WP came into being to meet a need. Writers were   8
tired of wadding up sheets of paper, of playing cut and paste with paragraphs, of drawing lines to bridge one part of a text to another. The technology was there to bring the material/production side of writing in line
with the rest of the twentieth century. The quasi-"intelligence" of the
computer was put into the service of the infinitely complex intellec-
tual/psychological operation of writing.
Given that so many writers profess themselves to be iconoclasts,   9
sturdy individualists, etc., the rate of defection from paper and metal to
plastic and electricity is nothing short of astonishing.
These are the same people who love the old game of baseball and   10
scream at any move to modernize or streamline its immemorial rituals.
But the lemmings did line up to leap. Why?   11

They say it's because the user can *quickly* make changes, correc-   12
tions, erasures, rearrangements. Because he can try things out and then
get rid of them. Because he has more access to his text, more control, a
sense of mastery. Because the WP vanquishes fear, eliminates the block-
inducing threat that the white page seems to hold.
I've heard it said that now *everyone* can become a writer.   13
Hot dog.   14
I think the real reason for the rush to molded plastic, the deep-down   15
unacknowledged reason, is that the apparatus confers a feeling of power,
of being plugged in to something. For we all know, in that same deep-
down place, that the writer, the thinker, the person who would speak up
for spirit, has never had less power. Ever. Has never been such a zero.
Why not a humming bright unit that allows the user to say, "I, too, belong to the modern world. You can see screens just like this at the airport, on Wall Street, in the offices on Madison Avenue."

16      The word processor has, among other things, made the word more susceptible to the directives of the will. The ruling paradigm is now one of change, of changeability. The writer says, with Valéry, that the work is never finished. Clearly demarcated draft stages have been superseded by a single stage—the unstable, open, "in-process" stage. Writing is closer to becoming that unfixed play of signifiers celebrated by French literary theoreticians. Literary morticians. Indeed: writing has been brought many steps closer to resembling the mutability of thought itself—which never rests, except in the crystallizations of written language.

17      The stability of the word—epitomized by the independent, fixed, *printed* sign—has been correspondingly undermined.

18      Writing on the word processor: It's like eating those force-fed new chickens that have never seen sunlight. Like eating fish bred in indoor pools.

19      Word "processing": In the sixties the word "processed" was a term of fierce derision. Blacks called a brother "processed" when they wanted to mark him as a "Tom."

20      The shift from manual writing to the typewriter to the word processor roughly corresponds to the shift from walking to riding in a carriage to riding in a car. In both cases, the progression is toward ease and facilitation. But, we might ask, what has become of our ancient relationship to land, to sky, to time itself?

21      A flat, opaque two-sided sheet of paper is replaced by an electronic screen of indeterminate depth. Where a black mark was conspicuously *imposed* upon the white surface, we now find a green mark elicited from the humming green screen. The broken-up left-to-right linearity is replaced, for the writer, by what *feels* like an unbroken continuity (the apparatus does the lineation). The static character of the typed sign gives way to the fluid, provisional character of the processed sign. The composition blocks—sentences, paragraphs—are no less fluid.

22      If the movement from speech to writing was, in part, an attempt to impose fixity upon the fleeting, then might we not in some sense be moving back toward the laxity of the impromptu—at least on the level of conception, where everything exists under the aspect of replaceability?

23      Writing on a word processor: the principle of Don Juanism projected upon the sentence. The writer is more likely to be haunted by the thought that there is a better word than this, a better sentence, a more interesting ordering of paragraphs.

24      Writing by hand, even typewriter, inevitably results in visible corrections, in drafts. These are, in effect, the record of the evolution of the

thought and its expression. The WP handily eliminates every trace. The writer never has to look over his shoulder and see what a botch he's made of things. Less conscience, less sense of consequence.

As Louis Simpson wrote: "If I think I can easily change the next     25
word and there's nothing final about what I'm writing, then the nature of my writing changes."
How would you live if you knew you could live forever?     26
The ideal of *le mot juste* is vaporized; the new ideals are of plurality     27
and provisionality.

I've noticed that I read a word-processed page differently—more     28
casually—than a typewritten page. Could the mode of writing significantly influence the mode of reading? Maybe. When everybody becomes a writer, no one will read.
The difference between seeing your words drawn forth from the     29
depths of a screen versus seeing them planted on the page through the mechanical action of a key is enormous. The screen, with its electrical "live" humming and its impatiently pulsing cursor, represents (much like TV) a quasi-consciousness. Does the writer feel just the slightest bit less responsible?

Speaking for myself: writing is very much a matter of drafts, *dis-*     30
*tinct* written drafts. I believe that prose is produced as much by the body, the rhythmic sense, as it is by intellect and verbal imagination. It wants to build up a certain musculature on the page. The instant correctability afforded by the WP allows for cosmetic alterations that are often quite adequate. But *merely* adequate. My experience has shown me that the best writing comes when I am forced to type over something that I've already deemed to be finished. My impatience—not to mention the new rhythmic state I'm in—forces me to push the language further. In the process of retyping the text, I reach more deeply into it. Later, the words give me the impression of having been handled, worn smooth.
Even simple mistakes can be read as signs, parapraxias signaling the     31
incompleteness of an expression. When a page of prose is done, I no longer make typos.

Already it's getting hard to find ribbons. The people who used to re-     32
pair typewriters are retiring, dying off. The day will come—soon—when journals will accept only disk submissions.

There . . . I've succeeded in depressing myself. All of a sudden my     33
desk looks like a museum: the beautiful pencil, the sharpener, the pens, the stack of paper like a street of dreams. The Olivetti clattering as I type this: sad hoofbeats of a retreating army. . . .

## CONSIDERATIONS

1. Would you say that Birkerts presents a well-organized argument against the writer's use of word processors? Explain.

2. Why, in paragraph 3, does Birkerts select Louis Simpson as his example of a poet who does not use a word processor?

3. Birkerts uses two methods of dividing his essay into units. One of them is the conventional paragraph break. What is the other, and what effect does it have on the whole essay?

4. With what kind of voice are we supposed to read paragraph 14, which consists solely of "Hot dog"?

5. To understand the gist of Birkert's paragraphs 25, 26, and 27, one must understand the French phrase he uses in 27. Explain.

6. See Michael Booth's essay, page 72, for additional comments on technological progress.

*Louise Bogan (1897–1970)—poet, and critic of poetry in her quarterly reviews of "Verse" for the* New Yorker—*was born in Maine and spent her adult life in New York City. Her poetry, criticism, and letters have been collected in many volumes.* Journey around My Room *(1980), from which we take "Miss Cooper and Me," is subtitled* The Autobiography of Louise Bogan. *It was edited by Ruth Limmer, after Bogan's death, from the poet's notebooks and private papers.*

*Louise Bogan makes an analogy without presenting it as an analogy. She describes the contrasting appearances of her suburb and of Boston's "highly civilized nucleus." Study how she uses this comparison to embody the social difference, as observed in Miss Cooper.*

## — 10 —

# LOUISE BOGAN
## *Miss Cooper and Me*

Boston was a city that possessed a highly civilized nucleus com- 1
posed of buildings built around a square. These buildings were copies of palaces in Italy, churches in England, and residences in Munich. The square's centre was occupied by a triangular plot of grass, garnished at its three corners by large palms growing in tubs. The streetcars rattled by these. Perhaps, too, a bed of begonias and coleuses pleased the eye with some simple horticultural pattern. I can't remember clearly. It was the architecture which warmed my heart. The sight of imitation true Gothic, imitation true Italian Renaissance, and imitation false Gothic revival often gave me that sensation in the pit of the stomach which heralds both love and an intense aesthetic experience. And to this day I have never been able to extirpate from my taste a thorough affection for potted palms.

Harold Street, on the other hand, had not emerged from the brain of 2
an architect of any period. It was a street not only in a suburb but on the edge of a suburb, and it was a carpenter's dull skill with pine planks and

**61**

millwork in general that could be thanked for the houses' general design. Our house, built to accommodate three families, one to a floor, was perhaps two years old. Carpenters hammered new three-family houses together continually, on all sides of it. For several of my adolescent years, until the street was finally given up as completed, I watched and heard the construction of these houses. Even when finished, they had an extremely provisional look, as though a breath of wind could blow them away.

3      Sometimes I think that, between us, my mother and I must have invented Miss Cooper; this is impossible, however, because of our splendid ignorance of the materials of which Miss Cooper was composed. We both lighted upon her simultaneously through the commendation of the drawing teacher in my school, who thought I was Talented, and Should Have Further Instruction. I was, it is true, thrown into a high state of nervous tension at the sight of a drawing board. This state passed for talent at the time. It must have been something else, since nothing ever came of it.

4      Miss Cooper lived in the Hotel Oxford, and I lived on Harold Street, and a whole world, a whole civilization, or, if you will, the lack of a whole world, of a whole civilization, lay between.

5      The Hotel Oxford stood a few yards up one street leading to the remarkable square. A fair-sized section of quarry had gone into its manufacture. And within it was heavily weighted down with good, solid woodwork, mahogany in color; with statues, large and small, of bronze and of marble, representing draped winged creatures which, although caught in attitudes of listening or looking or touching, gave the impression of deafness, blindness, and insensibility. (I thought these quite pretty at the time.) It was weighted with plush draperies, with gilt picture frames half a foot broad, with a heavy, well-fed, well-mustached staff of clerks. The little elevator, manned by a decrepit old boy in a toupee, sighed up through floors heavily carpeted in discreet magenta. Miss Cooper's studio was at the top of the building. It had no skylight and it looked out onto the railway yards, but it was directly under the roof; it had that distinction.

6      The big room looked as though, at some time in the past, the great conflagration of art had passed over it, charring the walls, the floor, and the ceiling, together with the objects they contained. Everything looked burned and tarnished: the brown pongee curtains; the dull bronze, brass, and copper; the black, twisted wrought iron; the cracked and carved wood of the Spanish chairs. Or perhaps it was the wave of art that had once washed briefly against it, leaving pale casts of the human hand and foot, life and death masks, a little replica of the Leaning Tower of Pisa, a tiny marble bowl surmounted by alabaster doves (the litter of art-form bric-a-brac) in its wake. In any case, there it was, and I had never seen anything like it before, and had it been Michelangelo's own workroom, it could not have been more remarkable to me.

Against this sombre background, Miss Cooper stood out like porce-   7
lain. She was smaller at sixty than myself at thirteen. Her white hair,
combed into a series of delicate loops over her forehead, resembled the
round feathers that sometimes seep out of pillows. Her white teeth, solid
and young, made her smile a delightful surprise. She dressed in the loose
Liberty silks which constituted a uniform for the artistic women of the
period; around her neck hung several chains of Florentine silver. Personal
distinction, in those days, to me meant undoubted nobility of soul.
Distinguished physical traits went right through to the back, as it were,
indelibly staining mind and spirit. And Miss Cooper, being stamped all
over with the color and designs of art as well as by the traits of gentility,
made double claims upon my respect and imagination.

It is difficult to put down coldly the terrific excitement engendered   8
in my breast by those Saturday afternoons. I would come in, unpin my
hat, lay off my coat, and there was the still life, freshly fitted into chalk
marks, on the low table, and there was the leather stool on which I sat,
and there was the charcoal paper pinned to its board, and the array of
wonderful materials: sticks of charcoal, beautifully black, slender, and
brittle; pastels, running through shade after delicate shade in a shallow
wooden box; the fixative; the kneaded rubber. And there was Miss
Cooper, the adept at these mysteries. Sometimes in the autumn
evenings, after the lesson was finished, she lighted candles and made me
tea. That is, she brought in from a kitchen as big as a closet, off the hall,
a tray on which sat two cups and two saucers of Italian pottery, and a
plate of what I called cookies and she called biscuits. Many times, after a
cup of this tea, I staggered out into a world in which everything seemed
suspended in the twilight, floating in mid-air, as in a mirage. I waited for
the trolley car which would take me back to Harold Street in a daze, full
of enough romantic nonsense to poison ten lives at their root.

Sometimes I wondered about Miss Cooper's own work in the field   9
of graphic art. Pictures produced by her hand—pastels and water colors,
all very accurate and bright—hung on the walls. But there was never anything on drawing board or easel. Every summer she disappeared into that
fabulous region known as "abroad"; she did not bring back portfolios full
of sketches, but only another assortment of small objects: carved wood
from Oberammergau, Tanagra figurines, Florentine leather boxes, and
strings of gold-flecked beads from Venice. These joined the artistic litter
in the studio.

The enchantment worked for two years. In the autumn of the third,   10
something had changed. In a pupil, the abstracted look in Miss Cooper's
eye could have been put down to loss of interest; in a teacher, I could not
account for it. Miss Cooper lived in my mind at a continual point of perfection; she was like a picture: she existed, but not in any degree did she
live or change. She existed beyond simple human needs, beyond hunger

and thirst, beyond loneliness, weariness, below the heights of joy and despair. She could not quarrel and she could not sigh. I had assigned to her the words and the smile by which I first knew her, and I refused to believe her capable of any others. But now, behind my shoulder, those October afternoons, I often heard her sigh, and she spent more time in the closet-like kitchen, rattling china and spoons, than she spent in the studio itself. I knew that she was having a cup of tea alone, while I worked in the fading light. She was still gentle, still kind. But she was not wholly there. I had lost her.

11     It is always ourselves that we blame for such losses, when we are young. For weeks I went about inventing reasons for Miss Cooper's defection; I clung to some and rejected others. When we are young, we are proud; we say nothing; we are silent and we watch. My ears became sharpened to every tired tone in her voice, to every clink of china and spoon, to every long period of her silence. One afternoon she came out of the kitchen and stood behind me. She had something in her hand that crackled like paper, and when she spoke she mumbled as though her mouth were full. I turned and looked at her; she was standing with a greasy paper bag in one hand and a half-eaten doughnut in the other. Her hair was still beautifully arranged; she still wore the silver and fire-opal ring on the little finger of her right hand. But in that moment she died for me. She died and the room died and the still life died a second death. She had betrayed me. She had betrayed the Hotel Oxford and the replica of the Leaning Tower of Pisa and the whole world of romantic notions built up around her. She had let me down; she had appeared as she was: a tired old woman who fed herself for comfort. With perfect ruthlessness I rejected her utterly. And for weeks, at night, in the bedroom of the frame house in Harold Street, I shed tears that rose from anger as much as disappointment, from disillusion and from dismay. I can't remember that for one moment I entertained pity for her. It was for myself that I kept that tender and cleansing emotion. Yes, it was for myself and for dignity and gentility soiled and broken that I shed those tears. At fifteen and for a long time thereafter, it is a monstrous thing, the heart.

## CONSIDERATIONS

1. Why, in this account of an individual, does Bogan open her essay with two paragraphs about architecture?

2. What's the point, in paragraph 3, of capitalizing "Talented" and "Should Have Further Instruction"?

3. What are some examples of the way Bogan re-creates her girlhood experience as though we were seeing it through the girl's eyes?

4. What do you make of the curious phrase, ". . . it is a monstrous thing, the heart"?

5. If you have had a disillusioning experience, build it into a personal essay, making use of "Miss Cooper and Me."

*Daniel J. Boorstin (b. 1914) attended Oxford University as a Rhodes Scholar after graduating from Harvard University. He was admitted to the bar, taught history for twenty-five years at the University of Chicago, and served as Librarian of Congress from 1975 to 1987. He has written many books: his* The Americans: The Colonial Experience *won the Bancroft Award in 1959;* The Americans: The National Experience *won the Francis Parkman Prize in 1966;* The Americans: The Democratic Experience *won the Pulitzer Prize in 1974.* The Discoverers, *subtitled* A History of Man's Search to Know His World and Himself, *appeared in 1983 and* The Creators *in 1992. Most recently, Boorstin collected* Cleopatra's Nose: Essays on the Unexpected *(1994).* Random House published The Daniel J. Boorstin Reader *in 1995.*

*Boorstin's clearly written and organized prose presents the author's ideas by way of supposition as well as through knowledge of history. He also supplies appropriate information from observation. Think of how the pseudo-event has come to dominate politics. This is our culture, in which celebrities are people who are famous for being famous.*

— 11 ——————————————————————————

# DANIEL J. BOORSTIN
## *The Pseudo-Event*

————————————————————————————————

Admiring Friend: "My, that's a beautiful baby you have there!"
Mother: "Oh, that's nothing—you should see his photograph!"

The simplest of our extravagant expectations concerns the amount      1
of novelty in the world. There was a time when the reader of an unexcit-
ing newspaper would remark, "How dull is the world today!" Nowadays
he says, "What a dull newspaper!" When the first American newspaper,
Benjamin Harris' *Publick Occurrences Both Forreign and Domestick*,
appeared in Boston on September 25, 1690, it promised to furnish news
regularly once a month. But, the editor explained, it might appear oftener

"if any Glut of Occurrences happen." The responsibility for making news was entirely God's—or the Devil's. The newsman's task was only to give "an Account of such considerable things as have arrived unto our Notice."

2  Although the theology behind this way of looking at events soon dissolved, this view of the news lasted longer. "The skilled and faithful journalist," James Parton observed in 1866, "recording with exactness and power the thing that has come to pass, is Providence addressing men." The story is told of a Southern Baptist clergyman before the Civil War who used to say, when a newspaper was brought in the room, "Be kind enough to let me have it a few minutes, till I see how the Supreme Being is governing the world." Charles A. Dana, one of the great American editors of the nineteenth century, once defended his extensive reporting of crime in the New York *Sun* by saying, "I have always felt that whatever the Divine Providence permitted to occur I was not too proud to report."

3  Of course, this is now a very old-fashioned way of thinking. Our current point of view is better expressed in the definition by Arthur MacEwen, whom William Randolph Hearst made his first editor of the San Francisco *Examiner*: "News is anything that makes a reader say, 'Gee whiz!' " Or, put more soberly, "News is whatever a good editor chooses to print."

4  We need not be theologians to see that we have shifted responsibility for making the world interesting from God to the newspaperman. We used to believe there were only so many "events" in the world. If there were not many intriguing or startling occurrences, it was no fault of the reporter. He could not be expected to report what did not exist.

5  Within the last hundred years, however, and especially in the twentieth century, all this has changed. We expect the papers to be full of news. If there is no news visible to the naked eye, or to the average citizen, we still expect it to be there for the enterprising newsman. The successful reporter is one who can find a story, even if there is no earthquake or assassination or civil war. If he cannot find a story, then he must make one—by the questions he asks of public figures, by the surprising human interest he unfolds from some commonplace event, or by "the news behind the news." If all this fails, then he must give us a "think piece"—an embroidering of well-known facts, or a speculation about startling things to come.

6  This change in our attitude toward "news" is not merely a basic fact about the history of American newspapers. It is a symptom of a revolutionary change in our attitude toward what happens in the world, how much of it is new, and surprising, and important. Toward how life can be enlivened, toward our power and the power of those who inform and educate and guide us, to provide synthetic happenings to make up for the lack of spontaneous events. Demanding more than the world can give us, we require that something be fabricated to make up for the world's deficiency. This is only one example of our demand for illusions.

Many historical forces help explain how we have come to our pres-   7
ent immoderate hopes. But there can be no doubt about what we now expect, nor that it is immoderate. Every American knows the anticipation
with which he picks up his morning newspaper at breakfast or opens his
evening paper before dinner, or listens to the newscasts every hour on
the hour as he drives across country, or watches his favorite commentator on television interpret the events of the day. Many enterprising
Americans are now at work to help us satisfy these expectations. Many
might be put out of work if we should suddenly moderate our expectations. But it is we who keep them in business and demand that they fill
our consciousness with novelties, that they play God for us.

The new kind of synthetic novelty which has flooded our experi-   8
ence I will call "pseudo-events." The common prefix "pseudo" comes
from the Greek word meaning false, or intended to deceive. Before I recall the historical forces which have made these pseudo-events possible,
have increased the supply of them and the demand for them, I will give a
commonplace example.

The owners of a hotel, in an illustration offered by Edward L.   9
Bernays in his pioneer *Crystallizing Public Opinion* (1923), consult a
public relations counsel. They ask how to increase their hotel's prestige
and so improve their business. In less sophisticated times, the answer
might have been to hire a new chef, to improve the plumbing, to paint
the rooms, or to install a crystal chandelier in the lobby. The public relations counsel's technique is more indirect. He proposes that the management stage a celebration of the hotel's thirtieth anniversary. A
committee is formed, including a prominent banker, a leading society
matron, a well-known lawyer, an influential preacher, and an "event" is
planned (say a banquet) to call attention to the distinguished service the
hotel has been rendering the community. The celebration is held, photographs are taken, the occasion is widely reported, and the object is accomplished. Now this occasion is a pseudo-event, and will illustrate all
the essential features of pseudo-events.

This celebration, we can see at the outset, is somewhat—but not   10
entirely—misleading. Presumably the public relations counsel would not
have been able to form his committee of prominent citizens if the hotel
had not actually been rendering service to the community. On the other
hand, if the hotel's services had been all that important, instigation by
public relations counsel might not have been necessary. Once the celebration has been held, the celebration itself becomes evidence that the
hotel really is a distinguished institution. The occasion actually gives
the hotel the prestige to which it is pretending.

It is obvious, too, that the value of such a celebration to the owners   11
depends on its being photographed and reported in newspapers, magazines, newsreels, on radio, and over television. It is the report that gives
the event its force in the minds of potential customers. The power to
make a reportable event is thus the power to make experience. One is reminded of Napoleon's apocryphal reply to his general, who objected that

circumstances were unfavorable to a proposed campaign: "Bah, I make circumstances!" The modern public relations counsel—and he is, of course, only one of many twentieth-century creators of pseudo-events— has come close to fulfilling Napoleon's idle boast. "The counsel on public relations," Mr. Bernays explains, "not only knows what news value is, but knowing it, he is in a position to *make news happen*. He is a creator of events."

12     The intriguing feature of the modern situation, however, comes precisely from the fact that the modern news makers are not God. The news they make happen, the events they create, are somehow not quite real. There remains a tantalizing difference between man-made and God-made events.

13     A pseudo-event, then, is a happening that possesses the following characteristics:

*1:* It is not spontaneous, but comes about because someone has planned, planted, or incited it. Typically, it is not a train wreck or an earthquake, but an interview.

*2:* It is planted primarily (not always exclusively) for the immediate purpose of being reported or reproduced. Therefore, its occurrence is arranged for the convenience of the reporting or reproducing media. Its success is measured by how widely it is reported. Time relations in it are commonly fictitious or factitious; the announcement is given out in advance "for future release" and written as if the event had occurred in the past. The question, "Is it real?" is less important than, "Is it newsworthy?"

*3:* Its relation to the underlying reality of the situation is ambiguous. Its interest arises largely from this very ambiguity. Concerning a pseudo-event the question, "What does it mean?" has a new dimension. While the news interest in a train wreck is in *what* happened and in the real consequences, the interest in an interview is always, in a sense, in *whether* it really happened and in what might have been the motives. Did the statement really mean what it said? Without some of this ambiguity a pseudo-event cannot be very interesting.

*4:* Usually it is intended to be a self-fulfilling prophecy. The hotel's thirtieth-anniversary celebration, by saying that the hotel is a distinguished institution, actually makes it one.

14     A perfect example of how pseudo-events can dominate is the recent popularity of the quiz show format. Its original appeal came less from the fact that such shows were tests of intelligence (or of dissimulation) than from the fact that the situations were elaborately contrived—with isolation booths, armed bank guards, and all the rest—and they purported to inform the public.

15     The application of the quiz show format to the so-called "Great Debates" between Presidential candidates in the election of 1960 is only another example. These four campaign programs, pompously and self-

righteously advertised by the broadcasting networks, were remarkably successful in reducing great national issues to trivial dimensions. With appropriate vulgarity, they might have been called the $400,000 Question (Prize: a $100,000-a-year job for four years). They were a clinical example of the pseudo-event, of how it is made, why it appeals, and of its consequences for democracy in America.

In origin the Great Debates were confusedly collaborative between   16
politicians and news makers. Public interest centered around the pseudo-event itself: the lighting, make-up, ground rules, whether notes would be allowed, etc. Far more interest was shown in the performance than in what was said. The pseudo-events spawned in turn by the Great Debates were numberless. People who had seen the shows read about them the more avidly, and listened eagerly for interpretations by news commentators. Representatives of both parties made "statements" on the probable effects of the debates. Numerous interviews and discussion programs were broadcast exploring their meaning. Opinion polls kept us informed on the nuances of our own and other people's reactions. Topics of speculation multiplied. Even the question whether there should be a fifth debate became for a while a lively "issue."

The drama of the situation was mostly specious, or at least had an   17
extremely ambiguous relevance to the main (but forgotten) issue: which participant was better qualified for the Presidency. Of course, a man's ability, while standing under klieg lights, without notes, to answer in two and a half minutes a question kept secret until that moment, had only the most dubious relevance—if any at all—to his real qualifications to make deliberate Presidential decisions on long-standing public questions after being instructed by a corps of advisers. The great Presidents in our history (with the possible exception of F.D.R.) would have done miserably; but our most notorious demagogues would have shone. A number of exciting pseudo-events were created—for example, the Quemoy-Matsu issue.* But that, too, was a good example of a pseudo-event: it was created to be reported, it concerned a then-quiescent problem, and it put into the most factitious and trivial terms the great and real issue of our relation to Communist China.

The television medium shapes this new kind of political quiz-show   18
spectacular in many crucial ways. Theodore H. White has proven this with copious detail in his *The Making of the President: 1960* (1961). All the circumstances of this particular competition for votes were far more novel than the old word "debate" and the comparisons with the Lincoln-Douglas Debates suggested. Kennedy's great strength in the critical first debate, according to White, was that he was in fact not "debating" at all, but was seizing the opportunity to address the whole nation; while Nixon stuck close to the issues raised by his opponent, rebutting them

---

*Hotly debated by Kennedy and Nixon in 1960: should these islands off the Chinese mainland be defended by the United States as part of Nationalist China's territory?

one by one. Nixon, moreover, suffered a handicap that was serious only on television: he has a light, naturally transparent skin. On an ordinary camera that takes pictures by optical projection, this skin photographs well. But a television camera projects electronically, by an "image-orthicon tube" which has an x-ray effect. This camera penetrates Nixon's transparent skin and brings out (even just after a shave) the tiniest hair growing in the follicles beneath the surface. For the decisive first program Nixon wore a make-up called "Lazy Shave" which was ineffective under these conditions. He therefore looked haggard and heavy-bearded by contrast to Kennedy, who looked pert and clean-cut.

19    This greatest opportunity in American history to educate the voters by debating the large issues of the campaign failed. The main reason, as White points out, was the compulsions of the medium. "The nature of both TV and radio is that they abhor silence and 'dead time.' All TV and radio discussion programs are compelled to snap question and answer back and forth as if the contestants were adversaries in an intellectual tennis match. Although every experienced newspaperman and inquirer knows that the most thoughtful and responsive answers to any difficult question come after long pause, and that the longer the pause the more illuminating the thought that follows it, nonetheless the electronic media cannot bear to suffer a pause of more than five seconds; a pause of thirty seconds of dead time on air seems interminable. Thus, snapping their two-and-a-half-minute answers back and forth, both candidates could only react for the cameras and the people, they could not think." Whenever either candidate found himself touching a thought too large for two-minute exploration, he quickly retreated. Finally the television-watching voter was left to judge, not on issues explored by thoughtful men, but on the relative capacity of the two candidates to perform under television stress.

20    Pseudo-events thus lead to emphasis on pseudo-qualifications. Again the self-fulfilling prophecy. If we test Presidential candidates by their talents on TV quiz performances, we will, of course, choose presidents for precisely these qualifications. In a democracy, reality tends to conform to the pseudo-event. Nature imitates art.

21    We are frustrated by our very efforts publicly to unmask the pseudo-event. Whenever we describe the lighting, the make-up, the studio setting, the rehearsals, etc., we simply arouse more interest. One newsman's interpretation makes us more eager to hear another's. One commentator's speculation that the debates may have little significance makes us curious to hear whether another commentator disagrees.

22    Pseudo-events do, of course, increase our illusion of grasp on the world, what some have called the American illusion of omnipotence. Perhaps, we come to think, the world's problems can really be settled by "statements," by "Summit" meetings, by a competition of "prestige," by overshadowing images, and by political quiz shows.

Once we have tasted the charm of pseudo-events, we are tempted to     23
believe they are the only important events. Our progress poisons the
sources of our experience. And the poison tastes so sweet that it spoils
our appetite for plain fact. Our seeming ability to satisfy our exaggerated
expectations makes us forget that they are exaggerated.

## CONSIDERATIONS

1. "VIKING PROMOTION HITS TOWN THIS WEEK"—banner headline on page
1 of the *Park Rapids* (Minnesota) *Enterprise*, July 30, 1986. Hard news or pseudo-event?
Explain. See also newspaper coverage of Microsoft's "Windows 95," on August 24,
1995. Which seemed to be more important: the new product itself or the publicity
campaign promoting it?

2. Boorstin, a professor of history, distinguishes between spontaneous events and
events that are staged to advance a position or to promote a person or an institution. He
argues that there "remains a tantalizing difference between man-made and God-made
events." In what sense is that difference "tantalizing"?

3. Use Boorstin's criteria to find an example of a pseudo-event in a newspaper or
a newsmagazine. Analyze the piece to determine if it possesses the characteristics he
lists. Does it, for example, contain ambiguities?

4. Why, according to Boorstin, are pseudo events harmful? Do you agree? Will
the baby in Boorstin's epigraph ever measure up to the photograph?

5. Through the first three paragraphs of his essay, Boorstin makes extensive use
of short quotations carefully chosen to illustrate his point. Is there a limit to the number
of quotations a given essay can employ effectively? Explain. Where might you find several quotations on a particular subject?

6. Study Boorstin's essay as an example of argument. Which of his techniques reveal the argumentative nature of his writing? (Don't ignore the epigraph that precedes
his first paragraph.)

*Michael Booth (b. 1965) is a staff writer for the* Denver Post. *Since growing up in northern Minnesota and attending Macalester College in St. Paul, he has worked for the* Washington Post *Foreign Desk and as a freelance writer. His articles and essays have appeared in the* New York Times, *the* Minnesota Monthly, *and* Sojourners. *This commentary on the information superhighway first appeared in the* Sunday Perspective *of the* Denver Post.

*Articles written for Sunday supplements tend to be punchy, with brief paragraphs, in an informal style. "That dispute was not a fluke, it was a wake-up call." Booth's breezy language allows him to combine dense argument with the look of lightness.*

## — 12

# MICHAEL BOOTH
## *Watch Out for Traffic Jams on the Information Highway*

1    Fifty-three years ago, essayist E. B. White, who tended to carry the weight of the world's future on his shoulders, added a new worry to his long list of forebodings. It was 1938, and he had recently seen television for the first time.

2    "I believe television is going to be the test of the modern world, and that in this new opportunity to see beyond the range of our vision we shall discover either a new and unbearable disturbance of the general peace or a saving radiance in the sky," White wrote, in his column, "One Man's Meat."

3    "We shall stand or fall by television—of that I am quite sure."

4    White's words are not only remarkable because the past five decades have proven them to be dead-on prophecy. They are stunning because we may repeat them today and see that the next test of the modern world is likely to be the hottest concept in popular culture: "The Information Superhighway."

Last spring the news magazines and science writers couldn't say    5
enough about the glorious revolution that fiber optic cable would bring
into our homes. This fall, the business pages are full of speculation about
possible mergers among Paramount, Viacom and cable giant TCI Inc.,
with journalists buying wholesale the claims of financial analysts that
such mega-combinations will create exciting synergies of programming,
technology and marketing.

Put simply, the information superhighway means that every con-    6
ceivable function of computers, telephones, stereos and video will be
combined onto a television screen. We will be able to order any movie
ever made, at any time. Or call the boss from the home computer, watch
him pitch a new idea to the sales staff on our video screen, and fax him a
summary. Or pick out a new coffee pot on the Sears Shopping Channel
and charge it electronically.

Amid the pro-technology hype whipped up by a media frenzy, we    7
hear over and over that the information superhighway will fundamentally transform our lives. The gurus of the information age, whether in
the words of cable czar John Malone or of Vice President Al Gore, chant
the mantra that the changes will free our minds. As with all new waves
of technology, we assume the transformation will be for the better.

You would think we might have learned by now.    8

The simple point that seems to be lost, perhaps because it is so sim-    9
ple, is that what we are talking about here is television. Each of the wonderful new powers we will have, whatever their other value, will mean
spending more time shackled before the television, the same box that
brought us "Three's Company"; the same box that tries to sell Thigh-
masters to Americans and Greater Serbia to Yugoslavians; the same box
that hails "Seinfeld," a shallow satire of such minutiae as frequent flyer
miles and handicapped parking spaces, as its greatest triumph in recent
years.

Why is it even necessary to point out the absurdity of television    10
people, who tell us, "Yes, you're right, we can't create anything worth
watching on 80 channels right now, but just watch what we can do on
500." The new programming will be different, they tell us, because it
won't be the same old sitcoms and formula cop dramas; the new programs will be service-oriented. We will have the Macy's Channel, and the
Hotel Channel, and channels that allow us to walk through the Library
of Congress and pick out what we want without leaving the La-Z-Boy.

Again it's a simple question: Why do we want that? Even in-person    11
shopping at Macy's is neither a happy nor uplifting experience. It means
shopping at a mall, even the best of which are merely artificial catacombs of consumption. Then remove the experience to yet another level
of artificiality, television, and you have eliminated the only remotely re-
deeming element of shopping: human contact.

Fine, the TV gurus will say, but how can you criticize the concept    12
of the Library Channel? Imagine all that information at our fingertips.

Every written fact or opinion known to mankind will be contained in the television.

13      But what's wrong with getting into the car, or, god forbid, walking down to the local public library, asking someone at the counter for help (or better yet looking it up for ourselves), walking up the musty back stairway past the posters of upcoming author readings and paintings of ships at sea, and hunkering down at the end of a dimly lit row to browse through a hand-stitched clothbound copy of "The Caine Mutiny," and in the process discovering three other Herman Wouk novels that we'd like to read someday?

14      Not everyone can get to the library, they will say; to oppose change is elitist, a roadblock to progress for the masses of people who see television as their friend. In that case, the cable moguls should provide their electronic miracle free of charge to every disabled American, and also wire the homes of every single parent or elderly shut-in or high school dropout stuck in a blighted neighborhood, and tutor them in how to use it, and leave the rest of us alone to live our lives that are too busy, too complicated and too humane to settle for virtual reality.

15      E. B. White knew what trouble would come from man's preference for the artful copy over the original. Television, White wrote 53 years ago, "will insist that we forget the primary and the near in favor of the secondary and remote. . . . In sufficient accumulation, radio sounds and television sights may become more familiar to us than their originals."

16      Let's ask one more question that seems to concern so few who have jumped on the technology bullet train. Is it the primary intent of cable executives like John Malone or Ted Turner to provide for the spiritual enlightenment of the world? Or is their first goal to make as much money as humanly possible for themselves and their shareholders? Certainly there's nothing wrong with making money, but there is also nothing heroic about it. Remember that it is not Mahatma Gandhi, Albert Einstein and Martin Luther King, Jr. asking the world to welcome the information superhighway. It is Time-Warner, AT&T and the Cartoon Channel.

17      Forget the new programming we may or may not see, which may or may not change our lives. Think about how this new technology may change for the worse what we already have, as these things tend to do. The true genius of the superhighway may just be that the television folks will get us to pay for things in the future that we currently enjoy free. The executive mind looks at it this way: Broadcast TV channels are free. Public libraries, bottomless wells of information, all free. For a nominal, fixed charge, access to local phone service is unlimited. What a waste.

18      The solution? Run every TV program and information service through a fiber optic cable and a "smart box" in every home, an innovation which, of course, is far too expensive and progressive to be offered free. Add a video picture to the telephone, so that callers can see each other and pay for the privilege. If people don't want to see each other, they may have to pay not to.

Perhaps that sounds too much like a conspiracy. Until we recall   19
that our benevolent neighborhood phone company, the same one now
forging billion-dollar alliances with cable TV firms, recently offered us a
new service dubbed "Caller ID," allowing us to see the phone number
and name of an incoming call before we pick up the phone. It soon followed that if we didn't want the new service, we would have to pay a
"blocking fee."

That dispute was not a fluke, it was a wake-up call. The American   20
psyche is not rooted in information and education; it is rooted in salesmanship. And the first tenet of salesmanship is to convince customers
they can't live without your product; the second tenet is that if the first
tenet fails, create a monopoly so that they have to buy it.

No doubt any hope for a massive popular resistance to all the new   21
information technology is fleeting.

We demanded and got cable television reform and regulation long   22
before we demanded health-care reform, and that fact alone offers insight
into the state of our culture. But let us at least learn to question those who
claim they will bring a revolution to our lives through the 20-inch screen.

We owe that to someone like E. B. White, who was worried about   23
us and television long before we thought to worry for ourselves.

"When I was a child people simply looked about them and were   24
moderately happy," White wrote in his closing thoughts on television.
"Today they peer beyond the seven seas, bury themselves deep in tidings,
and by and large what they see and hear makes them unutterably sad."

I hope that decades from now, I will stumble across White's words   25
again as I scroll through the electronic library stored conveniently in my
television set. And I hope that as the digitized letters float across the
screen, I will reach for my remote control, and turn the television off.

## CONSIDERATIONS

1. Summarize Booth's objections to the heralding of the "information superhighway."

2. If you disagree with Booth's position on the "superhighway," what are some
questions you might put to him?

3. In an essay, describe and evaluate your own present sources of information.
That is, discuss the relative importance to you of teachers, books, magazines, newspapers, radio, TV, the Internet.

4. "The changes will free our minds" is a claim often made by proponents of the
new communication technology. Free them from what?

5. In paragraph 15, following E. B. White's lead, Booth envisions a future in which
we value image over reality. Read the two-line dialog Daniel Boorstin uses as an epigraph for his essay "The Pseudo-Event" (page 65), written nearly two generations ago.
Discuss your notions of the impact of electronic information on our perception of reality.

6. Consider Booth's use of the term "catacombs" in paragraph 11. Would "halls" or
"palaces" work as well? Think about the nature of connotations as opposed to denotations.

*Gwendolyn Brooks (b. 1917) grew up in Chicago. She lives there still and has been Poet Laureate of Illinois since 1968. Her books of poems began with* A Street in Brownsville *(1945);* Annie Allen *(1949) won the Pulitzer Prize. "The Bean Eaters" was the title poem of a volume published in 1960. She has written autobiography and works for children. In 1986 Brooks was named Consultant in Poetry at the Library of Congress. Congress has renamed the position, and now the consultant is called the Poet Laureate.*

— **13** ——————————————————————————————

# GWENDOLYN BROOKS
## *The Bean Eaters*

---

They eat beans mostly, this old yellow pair.
Dinner is a casual affair.
Plain chipware on a plain and creaking wood,
Tin flatware.

5     Two who are Mostly Good.
Two who have lived their day,
But keep on putting on their clothes
And putting things away.

And remembering . . .
10    Remembering, with twinklings and twinges,
As they lean over the beans in their rented back room
     that is full of beads and receipts and dolls and clothes,
     tobacco crumbs, vases and fringes.

*Raymond Carver (1938–88) grew up in California, studied writing at the University of Iowa, and lived a life for many years dominated by alcohol. His disability limited the number of his good stories and poems. He was almost forty when he stopped drinking and concentrated on literary work. Shortly after he turned sober, he fell in love with poet Tess Gallagher, whom he married on his deathbed. In the ten years until he died at fifty, Carver wrote his best stories, essays, and poems. He was called a minimalist because of the spare style of his short fiction. His prose was almost grudging, as if he spoke from a mouth that scarcely opened. His dialog is relentlessly accurate.*

*At a time when American readers had been paying little attention to the short story, Raymond Carver's books of stories became best sellers and were translated into many languages. The ambiance of most of his stories—motels and trailer parks, poverty and alcoholism—fits perfectly with the restraint of his minimalism. One of Carver's later stories, "A Small, Good Thing," differs from earlier Carver in its milieu and in the hopefulness of its final episode. The prose remains spare.*

— **14** —

# RAYMOND CARVER
## *A Small, Good Thing*

Saturday afternoon she drove to the bakery in the shopping center. 1
After looking through a loose-leaf binder with photographs of cakes taped onto the pages, she ordered chocolate, the child's favorite. The cake she chose was decorated with a space ship and launching pad under a sprinkling of white stars, and a planet made of red frosting at the other end. His name, SCOTTY, would be in green letters beneath the planet. The baker, who was an older man with a thick neck, listened without saying anything when she told him the child would be eight years old next Monday. The baker wore a white apron that looked like a smock. Straps cut under his arms, went around in back and then to the front again,

where they were secured under his heavy waist. He wiped his hands on his apron as he listened to her. He kept his eyes down on the photographs and let her talk. He let her take her time. He'd just come to work and he'd be there all night, baking, and he was in no real hurry.

2    She gave the baker her name, Ann Weiss, and her telephone number. The cake would be ready on Monday morning, just out of the oven, in plenty of time for the child's party that afternoon. The baker was not jolly. There were no pleasantries between them, just the minimum exchange of words, the necessary information. He made her feel uncomfortable, and she didn't like that. While he was bent over the counter with the pencil in his hand, she studied his coarse features and wondered if he'd ever done anything else with his life besides be a baker. She was a mother and thirty-three years old, and it seemed to her that everyone, especially someone the baker's age—a man old enough to be her father—must have children who'd gone through this special time of cakes and birthday parties. There must be that between them, she thought. But he was abrupt with her—not rude, just abrupt. She gave up trying to make friends with him. She looked into the back of the bakery and could see a long, heavy wooden table with aluminum pie pans stacked at one end; and beside the table a metal container filled with empty racks. There was an enormous oven. A radio was playing country-Western music.

3    The baker finished printing the information on the special order card and closed up the binder. He looked at her and said, "Monday morning." She thanked him and drove home.

4    On Monday morning, the birthday boy was walking to school with another boy. They were passing a bag of potato chips back and forth and the birthday boy was trying to find out what his friend intended to give him for his birthday that afternoon. Without looking, the birthday boy stepped off the curb at an intersection and was immediately knocked down by a car. He fell on his side with his head in the gutter and his legs out in the road. His eyes were closed, but his legs moved back and forth as if he were trying to climb over something. His friend dropped the potato chips and started to cry. The car had gone a hundred feet or so and stopped in the middle of the road. The man in the driver's seat looked back over his shoulder. He waited until the boy got unsteadily to his feet. The boy wobbled a little. He looked dazed, but okay. The driver put the car into gear and drove away.

5    The birthday boy didn't cry, but he didn't have anything to say about anything either. He wouldn't answer when his friend asked him what it felt like to be hit by a car. He walked home, and his friend went on to school. But after the birthday boy was inside his house and was telling his mother about it—she sitting beside him on the sofa, holding his hands in her lap, saying, "Scotty, honey, are you sure you feel all right, baby?" thinking she would call the doctor anyway—he suddenly

lay back on the sofa, closed his eyes, and went limp. When she couldn't wake him up, she hurried to the telephone and called her husband at work. Howard told her to remain calm, remain calm, and then he called an ambulance for the child and left for the hospital himself.

Of course, the birthday party was canceled. The child was in the hospital with a mild concussion and suffering from shock. There'd been vomiting, and his lungs had taken in fluid which needed pumping out that afternoon. Now he simply seemed to be in a very deep sleep—but no coma, Dr. Francis had emphasized, no coma, when he saw the alarm in the parents' eyes. At eleven o'clock that night, when the boy seemed to be resting comfortably enough after the many X-rays and the lab work, and it was just a matter of his waking up and coming around, Howard left the hospital. He and Ann had been at the hospital with the child since that afternoon, and he was going home for a short while to bathe and change clothes. "I'll be back in an hour," he said. She nodded. "It's fine," she said. "I'll be right here." He kissed her on the forehead, and they touched hands. She sat in the chair beside the bed and looked at the child. She was waiting for him to wake up and be all right. Then she could begin to relax.

Howard drove home from the hospital. He took the wet, dark streets very fast, then caught himself and slowed down. Until now, his life had gone smoothly and to his satisfaction—college, marriage, another year of college for the advanced degree in business, a junior partnership in an investment firm. Fatherhood. He was happy and, so far, lucky—he knew that. His parents were still living, his brothers and his sister were established, his friends from college had gone out to take their places in the world. So far, he had kept away from any real harm, from those forces he knew existed and that could cripple or bring down a man if the luck went bad, if things suddenly turned. He pulled into the driveway and parked. His left leg began to tremble. He sat in the car for a minute and tried to deal with the present situation in a rational manner. Scotty had been hit by a car and was in the hospital, but he was going to be all right. Howard closed his eyes and ran his hand over his face. He got out of the car and went up to the front door. The dog was barking inside the house. The telephone rang and rang while he unlocked the door and fumbled for the light switch. He shouldn't have left the hospital, he shouldn't have. "Goddamn it!" he said. He picked up the receiver and said, "I just walked in the door!"

"There's a cake here that wasn't picked up," the voice on the other end of the line said.

"What are you saying?" Howard asked.

"A cake," the voice said. "A sixteen-dollar cake."

Howard held the receiver against his ear, trying to understand. "I don't know anything about a cake," he said. "Jesus, what are you talking about?"

"Don't hand me that," the voice said.

13    Howard hung up the telephone. He went into the kitchen and poured himself some whiskey. He called the hospital. But the child's condition remained the same; he was still sleeping and nothing had changed there. While water poured into the tub, Howard lathered his face and shaved. He'd just stretched out in the tub and closed his eyes when the telephone rang again. He hauled himself out, grabbed a towel, and hurried through the house, saying, "Stupid, stupid," for having left the hospital. But when he picked up the receiver and shouted, "Hello!" there was no sound at the other end of the line. Then the caller hung up.

14    He arrived back at the hospital a little after midnight. Ann still sat in the chair beside the bed. She looked up at Howard, and then she looked back at the child. The child's eyes stayed closed, the head was still wrapped in bandages. His breathing was quiet and regular. From an apparatus over the bed hung a bottle of glucose with a tube running from the bottle to the boy's arm.

15    "How is he?" Howard said. "What's all this?" waving at the glucose and the tube.

16    "Dr. Francis's orders," she said. "He needs nourishment. He needs to keep up his strength. Why doesn't he wake up, Howard? I don't understand, if he's all right."

17    Howard put his hand against the back of her head. He ran his fingers through her hair. "He's going to be all right. He'll wake up in a little while. Dr. Francis knows what's what."

18    After a time, he said, "Maybe you should go home and get some rest. I'll stay here. Just don't put up with this creep who keeps calling. Hang up right away."

19    "Who's calling?" she asked.

20    "I don't know who, just somebody with nothing better to do than call up people. You go on now."

21    She shook her head. "No," she said, "I'm fine."

22    "Really," he said. "Go home for a while, and then come back and spell me in the morning. It'll be all right. What did Dr. Francis say? He said Scotty's going to be all right. We don't have to worry. He's just sleeping now, that's all."

23    A nurse pushed the door open. She nodded at them as she went to the bedside. She took the left arm out from under the covers and put her fingers on the wrist, found the pulse, then consulted her watch. In a little while, she put the arm back under the covers and moved to the foot of the bed, where she wrote something on a clipboard attached to the bed.

24    "How is he?" Ann said. Howard's hand was a weight on her shoulder. She was aware of the pressure from his fingers.

25    "He's stable," the nurse said. Then she said, "Doctor will be in again shortly. Doctor's back in the hospital. He's making rounds right now."

26    "I was saying maybe she'd want to go home and get a little rest," Howard said. "After the doctor comes," he said.

"She could do that," the nurse said. "I think you should both feel free to do that, if you wish." The nurse was a big Scandinavian woman with blond hair. There was the trace of an accent in her speech. 27

"We'll see what the doctor says," Ann said. "I want to talk to the doctor. I don't think he should keep sleeping like this. I don't think that's a good sign." She brought her hand up to her eyes and let her head come forward a little. Howard's grip tightened on her shoulder, and then his hand moved up to her neck, where his fingers began to knead the muscles there. 28

"Dr. Francis will be here in a few minutes," the nurse said. Then she left the room. 29

Howard gazed at his son for a time, the small chest quietly rising and falling under the covers. For the first time since the terrible minutes after Ann's telephone call to him at his office, he felt a genuine fear starting in his limbs. He began shaking his head. Scotty was fine, but instead of sleeping at home in his own bed, he was in a hospital bed with bandages around his head and a tube in his arm. But this help was what he needed right now. 30

Dr. Francis came in and shook hands with Howard, though they'd just seen each other a few hours before. Ann got up from the chair. "Doctor?" 31

"Ann," he said and nodded. "Let's just first see how he's doing," the doctor said. He moved to the side of the bed and took the boy's pulse. He peeled back one eyelid and then the other. Howard and Ann stood beside the doctor and watched. Then the doctor turned back the covers and listened to the boy's heart and lungs with his stethoscope. He pressed his fingers here and there on the abdomen. When he was finished, he went to the end of the bed and studied the chart. He noted the time, scribbled something on the chart, and then looked at Howard and Ann. 32

"Doctor, how is he?" Howard said. "What's the matter with him exactly?" 33

"Why doesn't he wake up?" Ann said. 34

The doctor was a handsome, big-shouldered man with a tanned face. He wore a three-piece blue suit, a striped tie, and ivory cufflinks. His gray hair was combed along the sides of his head, and he looked as if he had just come from a concert. "He's all right," the doctor said. "Nothing to shout about, he could be better, I think. But he's all right. Still, I wish he'd wake up. He should wake up pretty soon." The doctor looked at the boy again. "We'll know some more in a couple of hours, after the results of a few more tests are in. But he's all right, believe me, except for the hairline fracture of the skull. He does have that." 35

"Oh, no," Ann said. 36

"And a bit of concussion, as I said before. Of course, you know he's in shock," the doctor said. "Sometimes you see this in shock cases. This sleeping." 37

38      "But he's out of any real danger?" Howard said. "You said before he's not in a coma. You wouldn't call this a coma, then—would you, doctor?" Howard waited. He looked at the doctor.

39      "No, I don't want to call it a coma," the doctor said and glanced over at the boy once more. "He's just in a very deep sleep. It's a restorative measure the body is taking on its own. He's out of any real danger, I'd say that for certain, yes. But we'll know more when he wakes up and the other tests are in," the doctor said.

40      "It's a coma," Ann said. "Of sorts."

41      "It's not a coma yet, not exactly," the doctor said. "I wouldn't want to call it coma. Not yet, anyway. He's suffered shock. In shock cases, this kind of reaction is common enough; it's a temporary reaction to bodily trauma. Coma. Well, coma is a deep, prolonged unconsciousness, something that could go on for days, or weeks even. Scotty's not in that area, not as far as we can tell. I'm certain his condition will show improvement by morning. I'm betting that it will. We'll know more when he wakes up, which shouldn't be long now. Of course, you may do as you like, stay here or go home for a time. But by all means feel free to leave the hospital for a while if you want. This is not easy, I know." The doctor gazed at the boy again, watching him, and then he turned to Ann and said, "You try not to worry, little mother. Believe me, we're doing all that can be done. It's just a question of a little more time now." He nodded at her, shook hands with Howard again, and then he left the room.

42      Ann put her hand over the child's forehead. "At least he doesn't have a fever," she said. Then she said, "My God, he feels so cold, though. Howard? Is he supposed to feel like this? Feel his head."

43      Howard touched the child's temples. His own breathing had slowed. "I think he's supposed to feel this way right now," he said. "He's in shock, remember? That's what the doctor said. The doctor was just in here. He would have said something if Scotty wasn't okay."

44      Ann stood there a while longer, working her lip with her teeth. Then she moved over to her chair and sat down.

45      Howard sat in the chair next to her chair. They looked at each other. He wanted to say something else and reassure her, but he was afraid, too. He took her hand and put it in his lap, and this made him feel better, her hand being there. He picked up her hand and squeezed it. Then he just held her hand. They sat like that for a while, watching the boy and not talking. From time to time, he squeezed her hand. Finally, she took her hand away.

46      "I've been praying," she said.

47      He nodded.

48      She said, "I almost thought I'd forgotten how, but it came back to me. All I had to do was close my eyes and say, 'Please God, help us—help Scotty,' and then the rest was easy. The words were right there. Maybe if you prayed, too," she said to him.

"I've already prayed," he said. "I prayed this afternoon—yesterday   49
afternoon, I mean—after you called, while I was driving to the hospital.
I've been praying," he said.

"That's good," she said. For the first time, she felt they were to-   50
gether in it, this trouble. She realized with a start that, until now, it had
only been happening to her and to Scotty. She hadn't let Howard into it,
though he was there and needed all along. She felt glad to be his wife.

The same nurse came in and took the boy's pulse again and checked   51
the flow from the bottle hanging above the bed.

In an hour, another doctor came in. He said his name was Parsons,   52
from Radiology. He had a bushy mustache. He was wearing loafers, a
Western shirt, and a pair of jeans.

"We're going to take him downstairs for more pictures," he told   53
them. "We need to do some more pictures, and we want to do a scan."

"What's that?" Ann said. "A scan?" She stood between this new   54
doctor and the bed. "I thought you'd already taken all your X-rays."

"I'm afraid we need some more," he said. "Nothing to be alarmed   55
about. We just need some more pictures, and we want to do a brain scan
on him."

"My God," Ann said.   56

"It's perfectly normal procedure in cases like this," this new doctor   57
said. "We just need to find out for sure why he isn't back awake yet. It's
normal medical procedure, and nothing to be alarmed about. We'll be
taking him down in a few minutes," this doctor said.

In a little while, two orderlies came into the room with a gurney.   58
They were black-haired, dark-complexioned men in white uniforms, and
they said a few words to each other in a foreign tongue as they unhooked
the boy from the tube and moved him from his bed to the gurney. Then
they wheeled him from the room. Howard and Ann got on the same elevator. Ann gazed at the child. She closed her eyes as the elevator began
its descent. The orderlies stood at either end of the gurney without saying anything, though once one of the men made a comment to the other
in their own language, and the other man nodded slowly in response.

Later that morning, just as the sun was beginning to lighten the   59
windows in the waiting room outside the X-ray department, they
brought the boy out and moved him back up to his room. Howard and
Ann rode up on the elevator with him once more, and once more they
took up their places beside the bed.

They waited all day, but still the boy did not wake up. Occasionally,   60
one of them would leave the room to go downstairs to the cafeteria to
drink coffee and then, as if suddenly remembering and feeling guilty, get
up from the table and hurry back to the room. Dr. Francis came again
that afternoon and examined the boy once more and then left after
telling them he was coming along and could wake up at any minute now.

Nurses, different nurses from the night before, came in from time to time. Then a young woman from the lab knocked and entered the room. She wore white slacks and a white blouse and carried a little tray of things which she put on the stand beside the bed. Without a word to them, she took blood from the boy's arm. Howard closed his eyes as the woman found the right place on the boy's arm and pushed the needle in.

61    "I don't understand this," Ann said to the woman.

62    "Doctor's orders," the young woman said. "I do what I'm told. They say draw that one, I draw. What's wrong with him, anyway?" she said. "He's a sweetie."

63    "He was hit by a car," Howard said. "A hit-and-run."

64    The young woman shook her head and looked again at the boy. Then she took her tray and left the room.

65    "Why won't he wake up?" Ann said. "Howard? I want some answers from these people."

66    Howard didn't say anything. He sat down again in the chair and crossed one leg over the other. He rubbed his face. He looked at his son and then he settled back in the chair, closed his eyes, and went to sleep.

67    Ann walked to the window and looked out at the parking lot. It was night, and cars were driving into and out of the parking lot with their lights on. She stood at the window with her hands gripping the sill, and knew in her heart that they were into something now, something hard. She was afraid, and her teeth began to chatter until she tightened her jaws. She saw a big car stop in front of the hospital and someone, a woman in a long coat, get into the car. She wished she were that woman and somebody, anybody, was driving her away from here to somewhere else, a place where she would find Scotty waiting for her when she stepped out of the car, ready to say *Mom* and let her gather him in her arms.

68    In a little while, Howard woke up. He looked at the boy again. Then he got up from the chair, stretched, and went over to stand beside her at the window. They both stared out at the parking lot. They didn't say anything. But they seemed to feel each other's insides now, as though the worry had made them transparent in a perfectly natural way.

69    The door opened and Dr. Francis came in. He was wearing a different suit and tie this time. His gray hair was combed along the sides of his head, and he looked as if he had just shaved. He went straight to the bed and examined the boy. "He ought to have come around by now. There's just no good reason for this," he said. "But I can tell you we're all convinced he's out of any danger. We'll just feel better when he wakes up. There's no reason, absolutely none, why he shouldn't come around. Very soon. Oh, he'll have himself a dilly of a headache when he does, you can count on that. But all of his signs are fine. They're as normal as can be."

70    "It is a coma, then?" Ann said.

71    The doctor rubbed his smooth cheek. "We'll call it that for the time being, until he wakes up. But you must be worn out. This is hard. I know this is hard. Feel free to go out for a bite," he said. "It would do you good.

I'll put a nurse in here while you're gone if you'll feel better about going. Go and have yourselves something to eat."

"I couldn't eat anything," Ann said.                                                                72

"Do what you need to do, of course," the doctor said. "Anyway, I    73
wanted to tell you that all the signs are good, the tests are negative, nothing showed up at all, and just as soon as he wakes up he'll be over the hill."

"Thank you, doctor," Howard said. He shook hands with the doctor    74
again. The doctor patted Howard's shoulder and went out.

"I suppose one of us should go home and check on things," Howard    75
said. "Slug needs to be fed, for one thing."

"Call one of the neighbors," Ann said. "Call the Morgans. Anyone    76
will feed a dog if you ask them to."

"All right," Howard said. After a while, he said, "Honey, why don't    77
*you* do it? Why don't you go home and check on things, and then come back? It'll do you good. I'll be right here with him. Seriously," he said. "We need to keep up our strength on this. We'll want to be here for a while even after he wakes up."

"Why don't *you* go?" she said. "Feed Slug. Feed yourself."         78

"I already went," he said. "I was gone for exactly an hour and fif-    79
teen minutes. You go home for an hour and freshen up. Then come back."

She tried to think about it, but she was too tired. She closed her    80
eyes and tried to think about it again. After a time, she said, "Maybe I *will* go home for a few minutes. Maybe if I'm not just sitting right here watching him every second, he'll wake up and be all right. You know? Maybe he'll wake up if I'm not here. I'll go home and take a bath and put on clean clothes. I'll feed Slug. Then I'll come back."

"I'll be right here," he said. "You go on home, honey. I'll keep an    81
eye on things here." His eyes were bloodshot and small, as if he'd been drinking for a long time. His clothes were rumpled. His beard had come out again. She touched his face, and then she took her hand back. She understood he wanted to be by himself for a while, not have to talk or share his worry for a time. She picked her purse up from the nightstand, and he helped her into her coat.

"I won't be gone long," she said.                                    82

"Just sit and rest for a little while when you get home," he said.    83
"Eat something. Take a bath. After you get out of the bath, just sit for a while and rest. It'll do you a world of good, you'll see. Then come back," he said. "Let's try not to worry. You heard what Dr. Francis said."

She stood in her coat for a minute trying to recall the doctor's exact    84
words, looking for any nuances, any hint of something behind his words other than what he had said. She tried to remember if his expression had changed any when he bent over to examine the child. She remembered the way his features had composed themselves as he rolled back the child's eyelids and then listened to his breathing.

85   She went to the door, where she turned and looked back. She looked at the child, and then she looked at the father. Howard nodded. She stepped out of the room and pulled the door closed behind her.

86   She went past the nurses' station and down to the end of the corridor, looking for the elevator. At the end of the corridor, she turned to her right and entered a little waiting room where a Negro family sat in wicker chairs. There was a middle-aged man in a khaki shirt and pants, a baseball cap pushed back on his head. A large woman wearing a housedress and slippers was slumped in one of the chairs. A teenaged girl in jeans, hair done in dozens of little braids, lay stretched out in one of the chairs smoking a cigarette, her legs crossed at the ankles. The family swung their eyes to Ann as she entered the room. The little table was littered with hamburger wrappers and Styrofoam cups.

87   "Franklin," the large woman said as she roused herself. "Is it about Franklin?" Her eyes widened. "Tell me now, lady," the woman said. "Is it about Franklin?" She was trying to rise from her chair, but the man had closed his hand over her arm.

88   "Here, here," he said. "Evelyn."

89   "I'm sorry," Ann said. "I'm looking for the elevator. My son is in the hospital, and now I can't find the elevator."

90   "Elevator is down that way, turn left," the man said as he aimed a finger.

91   The girl drew on her cigarette and stared at Ann. Her eyes were narrowed to slits, and her broad lips parted slowly as she let the smoke escape. The Negro woman let her head fall on her shoulder and looked away from Ann, no longer interested.

92   "My son was hit by a car," Ann said to the man. She seemed to need to explain herself. "He has a concussion and a little skull fracture, but he's going to be all right. He's in shock now, but it might be some kind of coma, too. That's what really worries us, the coma part. I'm going out for a little while, but my husband is with him. Maybe he'll wake up while I'm gone."

93   "That's too bad," the man said and shifted in the chair. He shook his head. He looked down at the table, and then he looked back at Ann. She was still standing there. He said, "Our Franklin, he's on the operating table. Somebody cut him. Tried to kill him. There was a fight where he was at. At this party. They say he was just standing and watching. Not bothering nobody. But that don't mean nothing these days. Now he's on the operating table. We're just hoping and praying, that's all we can do now." He gazed at her steadily.

94   Ann looked at the girl again, who was still watching her, and at the older woman, who kept her head down, but whose eyes were now closed. Ann saw the lips moving silently, making words. She had an urge to ask what those words were. She wanted to talk more with these people who were in the same kind of waiting she was in. She was afraid, and they were afraid. They had that in common. She would have liked to have

said something else about the accident, told them more about Scotty, that it had happened on the day of his birthday, Monday, and that he was still unconscious. Yet she didn't know how to begin. She stood looking at them without saying anything more.

She went down the corridor the man had indicated and found the    95
elevator. She waited a minute in front of the closed doors, still wondering if she was doing the right thing. Then she put out her finger and touched the button.

She pulled into the driveway and cut the engine. She closed her    96
eyes and leaned her head against the wheel for a minute. She listened to the ticking sounds the engine made as it began to cool. Then she got out of the car. She could hear the dog barking inside the house. She went to the front door, which was unlocked. She went inside and turned on lights and put on a kettle of water for tea. She opened some dogfood and fed Slug on the back porch. The dog ate in hungry little smacks. It kept running into the kitchen to see that she was going to stay. As she sat down on the sofa with her tea, the telephone rang.

"Yes!" she said as she answered. "Hello!"    97

"Mrs. Weiss," a man's voice said. It was five o'clock in the morn-    98
ing, and she thought she could hear machinery or equipment of some kind in the background.

"Yes, yes! What is it?" she said. "This is Mrs. Weiss. This is she.    99
What is it, please?" She listened to whatever it was in the background. "Is it Scotty, for Christ's sake?"

"Scotty," the man's voice said. "It's about Scotty, yes. It has to do    100
with Scotty, that problem. Have you forgotten about Scotty?" the man said. Then he hung up.

She dialed the hospital's number and asked for the third floor. She    101
demanded information about her son from the nurse who answered the telephone. Then she asked to speak to her husband. It was, she said, an emergency.

She waited, turning the telephone cord in her fingers. She closed    102
her eyes and felt sick at her stomach. She would have to make herself eat. Slug came in from the back porch and lay down near her feet. He wagged his tail. She pulled at his ear while he licked her fingers. Howard was on the line.

"Somebody just called here," she said. She twisted the telephone    103
cord. "He said it was about Scotty," she cried.

"Scotty's fine," Howard told her. "I mean, he's still sleeping.    104
There's been no change. The nurse has been in twice since you've been gone. A nurse or else a doctor. He's all right."

"This man called. He said it was about Scotty," she told him.    105

"Honey, you rest for a little while, you need the rest. It must be that    106
same caller I had. Just forget it. Come back down here after you've rested. Then we'll have breakfast or something."

107    "Breakfast," she said. "I don't want any breakfast."

108    "You know what I mean," he said. "Juice, something. I don't know. I don't know anything, Ann. Jesus, I'm not hungry, either. Ann, it's hard to talk now. I'm standing here at the desk. Dr. Francis is coming again at eight o'clock this morning. He's going to have something to tell us then, something more definite. That's what one of the nurses said. She didn't know any more than that. Ann? Honey, maybe we'll know something more then. At eight o'clock. Come back here before eight. Meanwhile, I'm right here and Scotty's all right. He's still the same," he added.

109    "I was drinking a cup of tea," she said, "when the telephone rang. They said it was about Scotty. There was a noise in the background. Was there a noise in the background on that call you had, Howard?"

110    "I don't remember," he said. "Maybe the driver of the car, maybe he's a psychopath and found out about Scotty somehow. But I'm here with him. Just rest like you were going to do. Take a bath and come back by seven or so, and we'll talk to the doctor together when he gets here. It's going to be all right, honey. I'm here, and there are doctors and nurses around. They say his condition is stable."

111    "I'm scared to death," she said.

112    She ran water, undressed, and got into the tub. She washed and dried quickly, not taking the time to wash her hair. She put on clean underwear, wool slacks, and a sweater. She went into the living room, where the dog looked up at her and let its tail thump once against the floor. It was just starting to get light outside when she went out to the car.

113    She drove into the parking lot of the hospital and found a space close to the front door. She felt she was in some obscure way responsible for what had happened to the child. She let her thoughts move to the Negro family. She remembered the name Franklin and the table that was covered with hamburger papers, and the teenaged girl staring at her as she drew on her cigarette. "Don't have children," she told the girl's image as she entered the front door of the hospital. "For God's sake, don't."

114    She took the elevator up to the third floor with two nurses who were just going on duty. It was Wednesday morning, a few minutes before seven. There was a page for a Dr. Madison as the elevator doors slid open on the third floor. She got off behind the nurses, who turned in the other direction and continued the conversation she had interrupted when she'd gotten into the elevator. She walked down the corridor to the little alcove where the Negro family had been waiting. They were gone now, but the chairs were scattered in such a way that it looked as if people had just jumped up from them the minute before. The tabletop was cluttered with the same cups and papers, the ashtray was filled with cigarette butts.

115    She stopped at the nurses' station. A nurse was standing behind the counter, brushing her hair and yawning.

"There was a Negro boy in surgery last night," Ann said. "Franklin   116
was his name. His family was in the waiting room. I'd like to inquire
about his condition."

A nurse who was sitting at a desk behind the counter looked up   117
from a chart in front of her. The telephone buzzed and she picked up the
receiver, but she kept her eyes on Ann.

"He passed away," said the nurse at the counter. The nurse held the   118
hairbrush and kept looking at her. "Are you a friend of the family or
what?"

"I met the family last night," Ann said. "My own son is in the hos-   119
pital. I guess he's in shock. We don't know for sure what's wrong. I just
wondered about Franklin, that's all. Thank you." She moved down the
corridor. Elevator doors the same color as the walls slid open and a gaunt,
bald man in white pants and white canvas shoes pulled a heavy cart off
the elevator. She hadn't noticed these doors last night. The man wheeled
the cart out into the corridor and stopped in front of the room nearest the
elevator and consulted a clipboard. Then he reached down and slid a tray
out of the cart. He rapped lightly on the door and entered the room. She
could smell the unpleasant odors of warm food as she passed the cart.
She hurried on without looking at any of the nurses and pushed open the
door to the child's room.

Howard was standing at the window with his hands behind his   120
back. He turned around as she came in.

"How is he?" she said. She went over to the bed. She dropped her   121
purse on the floor beside the nightstand. It seemed to her she had been
gone a long time. She touched the child's face. "Howard?"

"Dr. Francis was here a little while ago," Howard said. She looked   122
at him closely and thought his shoulders were bunched a little.

"I thought he wasn't coming until eight o'clock this morning," she   123
said quickly.

"There was another doctor with him. A neurologist."   124

"A neurologist," she said.   125

Howard nodded. His shoulders were bunching, she could see that.   126
"What'd they say, Howard? For Christ's sake, what'd they say? What is it?"

"They said they're going to take him down and run more tests on   127
him, Ann. They think they're going to operate, honey. Honey, they *are*
going to operate. They can't figure out why he won't wake up. It's more
than just shock or concussion, they know that much now. It's in his
skull, the fracture, it has something, something to do with that, they
think. So they're going to operate. I tried to call you, but I guess you'd already left the house."

"Oh, God," she said. "Oh, please, Howard, please," she said, taking   128
his arms.

"Look!" Howard said. "Scotty! Look, Ann!" He turned her toward   129
the bed.

130    The boy had opened his eyes, then closed them. He opened them again now. The eyes stared straight ahead for a minute, then moved slowly in his head until they rested on Howard and Ann, then traveled away again.

131    "Scotty," his mother said, moving to the bed.

132    "Hey, Scott," his father said. "Hey, son."

133    They leaned over the bed. Howard took the child's hand in his hands and began to pat and squeeze the hand. Ann bent over the boy and kissed his forehead again and again. She put her hands on either side of his face. "Scotty, honey, it's Mommy and Daddy," she said. "Scotty?"

134    The boy looked at them, but without any sign of recognition. Then his mouth opened, his eyes scrunched closed, and he howled until he had no more air in his lungs. His face seemed to relax and soften then. His lips parted as his last breath was puffed through his throat and exhaled gently through the clenched teeth.

135    The doctors called it a hidden occlusion and said it was a one-in-a-million circumstance. Maybe if it could have been detected somehow and surgery undertaken immediately, they could have saved him. But more than likely not. In any case, what would they have been looking for? Nothing had shown up in the tests or in the X-rays.

136    Dr. Francis was shaken. "I can't tell you how badly I feel. I'm so very sorry, I can't tell you," he said as he led them into the doctors' lounge. There was a doctor sitting in a chair with his legs hooked over the back of another chair, watching an early-morning TV show. He was wearing a green delivery-room outfit, loose green pants and green blouse, and a green cap that covered his hair. He looked at Howard and Ann and then looked at Dr. Francis. He got to his feet and turned off the set and went out of the room. Dr. Francis guided Ann to the sofa, sat down beside her, and began to talk in a low, consoling voice. At one point, he leaned over and embraced her. She could feel his chest rising and falling evenly against her shoulder. She kept her eyes open and let him hold her. Howard went into the bathroom, but he left the door open. After a violent fit of weeping, he ran water and washed his face. Then he came out and sat down at the little table that held a telephone. He looked at the telephone as though deciding what to do first. He made some calls. After a time, Dr. Francis used the telephone.

137    "Is there anything else I can do for the moment?" he asked them.

138    Howard shook his head. Ann stared at Dr. Francis as if unable to comprehend his words.

139    The doctor walked them to the hospital's front door. People were entering and leaving the hospital. It was eleven o'clock in the morning. Ann was aware of how slowly, almost reluctantly, she moved her feet. It seemed to her that Dr. Francis was making them leave when she felt they should stay, when it would be more the right thing to do to stay. She gazed out into the parking lot and then turned around and looked back at

the front of the hospital. She began shaking her head. "No, no," she said. "I can't leave him here, no." She heard herself say that and thought how unfair it was that the only words that came out were the sort of words used on TV shows where people were stunned by violent or sudden deaths. She wanted her words to be her own. "No," she said, and for some reason the memory of the Negro woman's head lolling on the woman's shoulder came to her. "No," she said again.

"I'll be talking to you later in the day," the doctor was saying to   140
Howard. "There are still some things that have to be done, things that have to be cleared up to our satisfaction. Some things that need explaining."

"An autopsy," Howard said.   141

Dr. Francis nodded.   142

"I understand," Howard said. Then he said, "Oh, Jesus. No, I don't   143
understand, doctor. I can't, I can't. I just can't."

Dr. Francis put his arm around Howard's shoulders. "I'm sorry.   144
God, how I'm sorry." He let go of Howard's shoulders and held out his hand. Howard looked at the hand, and then he took it. Dr. Francis put his arms around Ann once more. He seemed full of some goodness she didn't understand. She let her head rest on his shoulder, but her eyes stayed open. She kept looking at the hospital. As they drove out of the parking lot, she looked back at the hospital.

At home, she sat on the sofa with her hands in her coat pockets.   145
Howard closed the door to the child's room. He got the coffee-maker going and then he found an empty box. He had thought to pick up some of the child's things that were scattered around the living room. But instead he sat down beside her on the sofa, pushed the box to one side, and leaned forward, arms between his knees. He began to weep. She pulled his head over into her lap and patted his shoulder. "He's gone," she said. She kept patting his shoulder. Over his sobs, she could hear the coffee-maker hissing in the kitchen. "There, there," she said tenderly. "Howard, he's gone. He's gone and now we'll have to get used to that. To being alone."

In a little while, Howard got up and began moving aimlessly around   146
the room with the box, not putting anything into it, but collecting some things together on the floor at one end of the sofa. She continued to sit with her hands in her coat pockets. Howard put the box down and brought coffee into the living room. Later, Ann made calls to relatives. After each call had been placed and the party had answered, Ann would blurt out a few words and cry for a minute. Then she would quietly explain, in a measured voice, what had happened and tell them about arrangements. Howard took the box out to the garage, where he saw the child's bicycle. He dropped the box and sat down on the pavement beside the bicycle. He took hold of the bicycle awkwardly so that it leaned against his chest. He held it, the rubber pedal sticking into his chest. He gave the wheel a turn.

147         Ann hung up the telephone after talking to her sister. She was looking up another number when the telephone rang. She picked it up on the
first ring.

148         "Hello," she said, and she heard something in the background, a
humming noise. "Hello!" she said. "For God's sake," she said. "Who is
this? What is it you want?"

149         "Your Scotty, I got him ready for you," the man's voice said. "Did
you forget him?"

150         "You evil bastard!" she shouted into the receiver. "How can you do
this, you evil son of a bitch?"

151         "Scotty," the man said. "Have you forgotten about Scotty?" Then
the man hung up on her.

152         Howard heard the shouting and came in to find her with her head
on her arms over the table, weeping. He picked up the receiver and listened to the dial tone.

153         Much later, just before midnight, after they had dealt with many
things, the telephone rang again.

154         "You answer it," she said. "Howard, it's him, I know." They were
sitting at the kitchen table with coffee in front of them. Howard had a
small glass of whiskey beside his cup. He answered on the third ring.

155         "Hello," he said. "Who is this? Hello! Hello!" The line went dead.
"He hung up," Howard said. "Whoever it was."

156         "It was him," she said. "That bastard. I'd like to kill him," she said.
"I'd like to shoot him and watch him kick," she said.

157         "Ann, my God," he said.

158         "Could you hear anything?" she said. "In the background? A noise,
machinery, something humming?"

159         "Nothing, really. Nothing like that," he said. "There wasn't much
time. I think there was some radio music. Yes, there was a radio going,
that's all I could tell. I don't know what in God's name is going on," he said.

160         She shook her head. "If I could, could get my hands on him." It
came to her then. She knew who it was. Scotty, the cake, the telephone
number. She pushed the chair away from the table and got up. "Drive me
down to the shopping center," she said. "Howard."

161         "What are you saying?"

162         "The shopping center. I know who it is who's calling. I know who it
is. It's the baker, the son-of-a-bitching baker, Howard. I had him bake a
cake for Scotty's birthday. That's who's calling. That's who has the number and keeps calling us. To harass us about that cake. The baker, that
bastard."

163         They drove down to the shopping center. The sky was clear and
stars were out. It was cold, and they ran the heater in the car. They
parked in front of the bakery. All of the shops and stores were closed, but
there were cars at the far end of the lot in front of the movie theater. The

bakery windows were dark, but when they looked through the glass they could see a light in the back room and, now and then, a big man in an apron moving in and out of the white, even light. Through the glass, she could see the display cases and some little tables with chairs. She tried the door. She rapped on the glass. But if the baker heard them, he gave no sign. He didn't look in their direction.

They drove around behind the bakery and parked. They got out of the car. There was a lighted window too high up for them to see inside. A sign near the back door said THE PANTRY BAKERY, SPECIAL ORDERS. She could hear faintly a radio playing inside and something creak—an oven door as it was pulled down? She knocked on the door and waited. Then she knocked again, louder. The radio was turned down and there was a scraping sound now, the distinct sound of something, a drawer, being pulled open and then closed. 164

Someone unlocked the door and opened it. The baker stood in the light and peered out at them. "I'm closed for business," he said. "What do you want at this hour? It's midnight. Are you drunk or something?" 165

She stepped into the light that fell through the open door. He blinked his heavy eyelids as he recognized her. "It's you," he said. 166

"It's me," she said. "Scotty's mother. This is Scotty's father. We'd like to come in " 167

The baker said, "I'm busy now. I have work to do." 168

She had stepped inside the doorway anyway. Howard came in behind her. The baker moved back. "It smells like a bakery in here. Doesn't it smell like a bakery in here, Howard?" 169

"What do you want?" the baker said. "Maybe you want your cake? That's it, you decided you want your cake. You ordered a cake, didn't you?" 170

"You're pretty smart for a baker," she said. "Howard, this is the man who's been calling us." She clenched her fists. She stared at him fiercely. There was a deep burning inside her, an anger that made her feel larger than herself, larger than either of these men. 171

"Just a minute here," the baker said. "You want to pick up your three-day-old cake? That it? I don't want to argue with you, lady. There it sits over there, getting stale. I'll give it to you for half of what I quoted you. No. You want it? You can have it. It's no good to me, no good to anyone now. It cost me time and money to make that cake. If you want it, okay, if you don't, that's okay, too. I have to get back to work." He looked at them and rolled his tongue behind his teeth. 172

"More cakes," she said. She knew she was in control of it, of what was increasing in her. She was calm. 173

"Lady, I work sixteen hours a day in this place to earn a living," the baker said. He wiped his hands on his apron. "I work night and day in here, trying to make ends meet." A look crossed Ann's face that made the baker move back and say, "No trouble, now." He reached to the counter and picked up a rolling pin with his right hand and began to tap it against the palm of his other hand. "You want the cake or not? I have 174 to get back to work. Bakers work at night," he said again. His eyes were small, mean-looking, she thought, nearly lost in the bristly flesh around his cheeks. His neck was thick with fat.

175    "I know bakers work at night," Ann said. "They make phone calls at night, too. You bastard," she said.

176    The baker continued to tap the rolling pin against his hand. He glanced at Howard. "Careful, careful," he said to Howard.

177    "My son's dead," she said with a cold, even finality. "He was hit by a car Monday morning. We've been waiting with him until he died. But, of course, you couldn't be expected to know that, could you? Bakers can't know everything—can they, Mr. Baker? But he's dead. He's dead, you bastard!" Just as suddenly as it had welled in her, the anger dwindled, gave way to something else, a dizzy feeling of nausea. She leaned against the wooden table that was sprinkled with flour, put her hands over her face, and began to cry, her shoulders rocking back and forth. "It isn't fair," she said. "It isn't, isn't fair."

178    Howard put his hand at the small of her back and looked at the baker. "Shame on you," Howard said to him. "Shame."

179    The baker put the rolling pin back on the counter. He undid his apron and threw it on the counter. He looked at them, and then he shook his head slowly. He pulled a chair out from under the card table that held papers and receipts, an adding machine, and a telephone directory. "Please sit down," he said. "Let me get you a chair," he said to Howard. "Sit down now, please." The baker went into the front of the shop and returned with two little wrought-iron chairs. "Please sit down, you people."

180    Ann wiped her eyes and looked at the baker. "I wanted to kill you," she said. "I wanted you dead."

181    The baker had cleared a space for them at the table. He shoved the adding machine to one side, along with the stacks of notepaper and receipts. He pushed the telephone directory onto the floor, where it landed with a thud. Howard and Ann sat down and pulled their chairs up to the table. The baker sat down, too.

182    "Let me say how sorry I am," the baker said, putting his elbows on the table. "God alone knows how sorry. Listen to me. I'm just a baker. I don't claim to be anything else. Maybe once, maybe years ago, I was a different kind of human being. I've forgotten, I don't know for sure. But I'm not any longer, if I ever was. Now I'm just a baker. That don't excuse my doing what I did, I know. But I'm deeply sorry. I'm sorry for your son, and sorry for my part in this," the baker said. He spread his hands out on the table and turned them over to reveal his palms. "I don't have any children myself, so I can only imagine what you must be feeling. All I can say to you now is that I'm sorry. Forgive me, if you can," the baker said. "I'm not an evil man, I don't think. Not evil, like you said on the phone. You got to understand what it comes down to is I don't know how to act anymore, it would seem. Please," the man said, "let me ask you if you can find it in your hearts to forgive me?"

It was warm inside the bakery. Howard stood up from the table and 183
took off his coat. He helped Ann from her coat. The baker looked at
them for a minute and then nodded and got up from the table. He went
to the oven and turned off some switches. He found cups and poured coffee from an electric coffee-maker. He put a carton of cream on the table,
and a bowl of sugar.

"You probably need to eat something," the baker said. "I hope 184
you'll eat some of my hot rolls. You have to eat and keep going. Eating is
a small, good thing in a time like this," he said.

He served them warm cinnamon rolls just out of the oven, the icing 185
still runny. He put butter on the table and knives to spread the butter.
Then the baker sat down at the table with them. He waited. He waited
until they each took a roll from the platter and began to eat. "It's good to
eat something," he said, watching them. "There's more. Eat up. Eat all
you want. There's all the rolls in the world in here."

They ate rolls and drank coffee. Ann was suddenly hungry, and the 186
rolls were warm and sweet. She ate three of them, which pleased the
baker. Then he began to talk. They listened carefully. Although they
were tired and in anguish, they listened to what the baker had to say.
They nodded when the baker began to speak of loneliness, and of the
sense of doubt and limitation that had come to him in his middle years.
He told them what it was like to be childless all these years. To repeat
the days with the ovens endlessly full and endlessly empty. The party
food, the celebrations he'd worked over. Icing knuckle-deep. The tiny
wedding couples stuck into cakes. Hundreds of them, no, thousands by
now. Birthdays. Just imagine all those candles burning. He had a necessary trade. He was a baker. He was glad he wasn't a florist. It was better
to be feeding people. This was a better smell anytime than flowers.

"Smell this," the baker said, breaking open a dark loaf. "It's a heavy 187
bread, but rich." They smelled it, then he had them taste it. It had the
taste of molasses and coarse grains. They listened to him. They ate what
they could. They swallowed the dark bread. It was like daylight under
the fluorescent trays of light. They talked on into the early morning, the
high, pale cast of light in the windows, and they did not think of leaving.

## CONSIDERATIONS

1. Note the straightforward, matter-of-fact way Carver gives us the details of a
calamity breaking into the hitherto orderly lives of a middle-class family. Compare this
with the technique of Ernest Hemingway in his short story "Hills Like White Elephants,"
page 292. What is the most obvious difference in the way they tell their stories? Does
that make any difference in the effect the stories have on the reader? Explain.

2. How do the parents' repeated questions about a coma affect the reader? How
much time is covered by the story?

3. What is the point, if any, of bringing Franklin's family into the story?

4. Discuss Carver's use of very detailed observations. Focus on one part of the story in which such details are noticeable.

5. It is the characters—not Carver—who say how terrible the boy's death was. Study paragraph 134, and then comment on why the author does not express *his* feelings.

6. How does Carver's work of fiction differ from a strictly factual report, say that of Martin Gansberg's newspaper account, "38 Who Saw Murder Didn't Call the Police," page 228, or the autobiographical narration of Lillian Hellman in "Runaway," page 285, or that of Carver's "My Father's Life," page 97.

*Raymond Carver's essay "My Father's Life" begins with the duplication of names and continues with a moment of mistaken identity. The reader of Carver's stories will notice resemblances between father and son, and respond to Carver's close-mouthed compassion for his father's unhappy life. The flatness of Carver's language is appropriate to his subject and becomes an illustration of his subject.*

# — 15 —

# RAYMOND CARVER
## *My Father's Life*

My dad's name was Clevie Raymond Carver. His family called him Raymond and friends called him C. R. I was named Raymond Clevie Carver, Jr. I hated the "Junior" part. When I was little my dad called me Frog, which was okay. But later, like everybody else in the family, he began calling me Junior. He went on calling me this until I was thirteen or fourteen and announced that I wouldn't answer to that name any longer. So he began calling me Doc. From then until his death, on June 17, 1967, he called me Doc, or else Son. 1

When he died, my mother telephoned my wife with the news. I was away from my family at the time, between lives, trying to enroll in the School of Library Science at the University of Iowa. When my wife answered the phone, my mother blurted out, "Raymond's dead!" For a moment, my wife thought my mother was telling her that I was dead. Then my mother made it clear *which* Raymond she was talking about and my wife said, "Thank God. I thought you meant *my* Raymond." 2

My dad walked, hitched rides, and rode in empty boxcars when he went from Arkansas to Washington State in 1934, looking for work. I don't know whether he was pursuing a dream when he went out to Washington. I doubt it. I don't think he dreamed much. I believe he was simply looking for steady work at decent pay. Steady work was meaningful work. He picked apples for a time and then landed a construction laborer's job on the Grand Coulee Dam. After he'd put aside a little money, 3 he bought a car and drove back to Arkansas to help his folks, my grand-parents, pack up for the move west. He said later that they were about to starve down there, and this wasn't meant as a figure of speech. It was during that short while in Arkansas, in a town called Leola, that my mother met my dad on the sidewalk as he came out of a tavern.

4      "He was drunk," she said. "I don't know why I let him talk to me. His eyes were glittery. I wish I'd had a crystal ball." They'd met once, a year or so before, at a dance. He'd had girlfriends before her, my mother told me. "Your dad always had a girlfriend, even after we married. He was my first and last. I never had another man. But I didn't miss anything."

5      They were married by a justice of the peace on the day they left for Washington, this big, tall country girl and a farmhand-turned-construction worker. My mother spent her wedding night with my dad and his folks, all of them camped beside the road in Arkansas.

6      In Omak, Washington, my dad and mother lived in a little place not much bigger than a cabin. My grandparents lived next door. My dad was still working on the dam, and later, with the huge turbines producing electricity and the water backed up for a hundred miles into Canada, he stood in the crowd and heard Franklin D. Roosevelt when he spoke at the construction site. "He never mentioned those guys who died building that dam," my dad said. Some of his friends had died there, men from Arkansas, Oklahoma, and Missouri.

7      He then took a job in a sawmill in Clatskanie, Oregon, a little town alongside the Columbia River. I was born there, and my mother has a pic-ture of my dad standing in front of the gate to the mill, proudly holding me up to face the camera. My bonnet is on crooked and about to come untied. His hat is pushed back on his forehead, and he's wearing a big grin. Was he going in to work or just finishing his shift? It doesn't matter. In either case, he had a job and a family. These were his salad days.

8      In 1941 we moved to Yakima, Washington, where my dad went to work as a saw filer, a skilled trade he'd learned in Clatskanie. When war broke out, he was given a deferment because his work was considered nec-essary to the war effort. Finished lumber was in demand by the armed ser-vices, and he kept his saws so sharp they could shave the hair off your arm.

9      After my dad had moved us to Yakima, he moved his folks into the same neighborhood. By the mid-1940s the rest of my dad's family—his brother, his sister, and her husband, as well as uncles, cousins, nephews, and most of their extended family and friends—had come out from Arkansas. All because my dad came out first. The men went to work at Boise Cascade, where my dad worked, and the women packed apples in the canneries. And in just a little while, it seemed—according to my mother—everybody was better off than my dad. "Your dad couldn't keep money," my mother said. "Money burned a hole in his pocket. He was always doing for others."

10     The first house I clearly remember living in, at 1515 South Fifteenth Street, in Yakima, had an outdoor toilet. On Halloween night, or just any night, for the hell of it, neighbor kids, kids in their early

teens, would carry our toilet away and leave it next to the road. My dad would have to get somebody to help him bring it home. Or these kids would take the toilet and stand it in somebody else's backyard. Once they actually set it on fire. But ours wasn't the only house that had an outdoor toilet. When I was old enough to know what I was doing, I threw rocks at the other toilets when I'd see someone go inside. This was called bombing the toilets. After a while, though, everyone went to indoor plumbing until, suddenly, our toilet was the last outdoor one in the neighborhood. I remember the shame I felt when my third-grade teacher, Mr. Wise, drove me home from school one day. I asked him to stop at the house just before ours, claiming I lived there.

I can recall what happened one night when my dad came home late   11
to find that my mother had locked all the doors on him from the inside. He was drunk, and we could feel the house shudder as he rattled the door. When he'd managed to force open a window, she hit him between the eyes with a colander and knocked him out. We could see him down there on the grass. For years afterward, I used to pick up this colander—it was as heavy as a rolling pin—and imagine what it would feel like to be hit in the head with something like that.

It was during this period that I remember my dad taking me into   12
the bedroom, sitting me down on the bed, and telling me that I might have to go live with my Aunt LaVon for a while. I couldn't understand what I'd done that meant I'd have to go away from home to live. But this, too—whatever prompted it—must have blown over, more or less, anyway, because we stayed together, and I didn't have to go live with her or anyone else.

I remember my mother pouring his whiskey down the sink.   13
Sometimes she'd pour it all out and sometimes, if she was afraid of getting caught, she'd only pour half of it out and then add water to the rest. I tasted some of his whiskey once myself. It was terrible stuff, and I don't see how anybody could drink it.

After a long time without one, we finally got a car, in 1949 or 1950,   14
a 1938 Ford. But it threw a rod the first week we had it, and my dad had to have the motor rebuilt.

"We drove the oldest car in town," my mother said. "We could have   15
had a Cadillac for all he spent on car repairs." One time she found someone else's tube of lipstick on the floorboard, along with a lacy handkerchief. "See this?" she said to me. "Some floozy left this in the car."

Once I saw her take a pan of warm water into the bedroom where   16
my dad was sleeping. She took his hand from under the covers and held it in the water. I stood in the doorway and watched. I wanted to know what was going on. This would make him talk in his sleep, she told me. There were things she needed to know, things she was sure he was keeping from her.

Every year or so, when I was little, we would take the North Coast   17
Limited across the Cascade Range from Yakima to Seattle and stay in the Vance Hotel and eat, I remember, at a place called the Dinner Bell Cafe.

Once we went to Ivar's Acres of Clams and drank glasses of warm clam broth.

18        In 1956, the year I was to graduate from high school, my dad quit his job at the mill in Yakima and took a job in Chester, a little sawmill town in northern California. The reasons given at the time for his taking the job had to do with a higher hourly wage and the vague promise that he might, in a few years' time, succeed to the job of head filer in this new mill. But I think, in the main, that my dad had grown restless and simply wanted to try his luck elsewhere. Things had gotten a little too predictable for him in Yakima. Also, the year before, there had been the deaths, within six months of each other, of both his parents.

19        But just a few days after graduation, when my mother and I were packed to move to Chester, my dad penciled a letter to say he'd been sick for a while. He didn't want us to worry, he said, but he'd cut himself on a saw. Maybe he'd got a tiny sliver of steel in his blood. Anyway, something had happened and he'd had to miss work, he said. In the same mail was an unsigned postcard from somebody down there telling my mother that my dad was about to die and that he was drinking "raw whiskey."

20        When we arrived in Chester, my dad was living in a trailer that belonged to the company. I didn't recognize him immediately. I guess for a moment I didn't want to recognize him. He was skinny and pale and looked bewildered. His pants wouldn't stay up. He didn't look like my dad. My mother began to cry. My dad put his arm around her and patted her shoulder vaguely, like he didn't know what this was all about, either. The three of us took up life together in the trailer, and we looked after him as best we could. But my dad was sick, and he couldn't get any better. I worked with him in the mill that summer and part of the fall. We'd get up in the mornings and eat eggs and toast while we listened to the radio, and then go out the door with our lunch pails. We'd pass through the gate together at eight in the morning, and I wouldn't see him again until quitting time. In November I went back to Yakima to be closer to my girlfriend, the girl I'd made up my mind I was going to marry.

21        He worked at the mill in Chester until the following February, when he collapsed on the job and was taken to the hospital. My mother asked if I would come down there and help. I caught a bus from Yakima to Chester, intending to drive them back to Yakima. But now, in addition to being physically sick, my dad was in the midst of a nervous breakdown, though none of us knew to call it that at the time. During the entire trip back to Yakima, he didn't speak, not even when asked a direct question. ("How do you feel, Raymond?" "You okay, Dad?") He'd communicate, if he communicated at all, by moving his head or by turning his palms up as if to say he didn't know or care. The only time he said anything on the trip, and for nearly a month afterward, was when I was speeding down a gravel road in Oregon and the car muffler came loose. "You were going too fast," he said.

22        Back in Yakima a doctor saw to it that my dad went to a psychiatrist. My mother and dad had to go on relief, as it was called, and the

county paid for the psychiatrist. The psychiatrist asked my dad, "Who is the President?" He'd had a question put to him that he could answer. "Ike," my dad said. Nevertheless, they put him on the fifth floor of Valley Memorial Hospital and began giving him electroshock treatment. I was married by then and about to start my own family. My dad was still locked up when my wife went into this same hospital, just one floor down, to have our first baby. After she had delivered, I went upstairs to give my dad the news. They let me in through a steel door and showed me where I could find him. He was sitting on a couch with a blanket over his lap. *Hey,* I thought. *What in hell is happening to my dad?* I sat down next to him and told him he was a grandfather. He waited a minute and then he said, "I feel like a grandfather." That's all he said. He didn't smile or move. He was in a big room with a lot of other people. Then I hugged him, and he began to cry.

Somehow he got out of there. But now came the years when he 23 couldn't work and just sat around the house trying to figure what next and what he'd done wrong in his life that he'd wound up like this. My mother went from job to crummy job. Much later she referred to that time he was in the hospital, and those years just afterward, as "when Raymond was sick." The word *sick* was never the same for me again.

In 1964, through the help of a friend, he was lucky enough to be 24 hired on at a mill in Klamath, California. He moved down there by himself to see if he could hack it. He lived not far from the mill, in a one-room cabin not much different from the place he and my mother had started out living in when they went west. He scrawled letters to my mother, and if I called she'd read them aloud to me over the phone. In the letters, he said it was touch and go. Every day that he went to work, he felt like it was the most important day of his life. But every day, he told her, made the next day that much easier. He said for her to tell me he said hello. If he couldn't sleep at night, he said, he thought about me and the good times we used to have. Finally, after a couple of months, he regained some of his confidence. He could do the work and didn't think he had to worry that he'd let anybody down ever again. When he was sure, he sent for my mother.

He'd been off from work for six years and had lost everything in 25 that time—home, car, furniture, and appliances, including the big freezer that had been my mother's pride and joy. He'd lost his good name too—Raymond Carver was someone who couldn't pay his bills—and his self-respect was gone. He'd even lost his virility. My mother told my wife, "All during that time Raymond was sick we slept together in the same bed, but we didn't have relations. He wanted to a few times, but nothing happened. I didn't miss it, but I think he wanted to, you know."

During those years I was trying to raise my own family and earn a 26 living. But, one thing and another, we found ourselves having to move a lot. I couldn't keep track of what was going down in my dad's life. But I did have a chance one Christmas to tell him I wanted to be a writer. I might as well have told him I wanted to become a plastic surgeon. "What are you going to write about?" he wanted to know. Then, as if to help me out, he said, "Write about stuff you know about. Write about some of those fishing trips we took." I said I would, but I knew I wouldn't. "Send me what you write," he said. I said I'd do that, but then I didn't. I wasn't writing anything about fishing, and I didn't think he'd particularly care about, or even necessarily understand, what I was writing in those days. Besides, he wasn't a reader. Not the sort, anyway, I imagined I was writing for.

27      Then he died. I was a long way off, in Iowa City, with things still to say to him. I didn't have the chance to tell him goodbye, or that I thought he was doing great at his new job. That I was proud of him for making a comeback.

28      My mother said he came in from work that night and ate a big supper. Then he sat at the table by himself and finished what was left of a bottle of whiskey, a bottle she found hidden in the bottom of the garbage under some coffee grounds a day or so later. Then he got up and went to bed, where my mother joined him a little later. But in the night she had to get up and make a bed for herself on the couch. "He was snoring so loud I couldn't sleep," she said. The next morning when she looked in on him, he was on his back with his mouth open, his cheeks caved in. *Graylooking*, she said. She knew he was dead—she didn't need a doctor to tell her that. But she called one anyway, and then she called my wife.

29      Among the pictures my mother kept of my dad and herself during those early days in Washington was a photograph of him standing in front of a car, holding a beer and a stringer of fish. In the photograph he is wearing his hat back on his forehead and has this awkward grin on his face. I asked her for it and she gave it to me, along with some others. I put it up on my wall, and each time we moved, I took the picture along and put it up on another wall. I looked at it carefully from time to time, trying to figure out some things about my dad, and maybe myself in the process. But I couldn't. My dad just kept moving further and further away from me and back into time. Finally, in the course of another move, I lost the photograph. It was then that I tried to recall it, and at the same time make an attempt to say something about my dad, and how I thought that in some important ways we might be alike. I wrote the poem when I was living in an apartment house in an urban area south of San Francisco, at a time when I found myself, like my dad, having trouble with alcohol. The poem was a way of trying to connect up with him.

PHOTOGRAPH OF MY FATHER IN HIS TWENTY-SECOND YEAR

*October.* Here in this dank, unfamiliar kitchen
I study my father's embarrassed young man's face.
Sheepish grin, he holds in one hand a string
of spiny yellow perch, in the other
a bottle of Carlsberg beer.

In jeans and flannel shirt, he leans
against the front fender of a 1934 Ford.
He would like to pose brave and hearty for his posterity,
wear his old hat cocked over his ear
All his life my father wanted to be bold.

But the eyes give him away, and the hands
that limply offer the string of dead perch
and the bottle of beer. Father, I love you,
yet how can I say thank you, I who can't hold my liquor either
and don't even know the places to fish.

The poem is true in its particulars, except that my dad died in June   30
and not October, as the first word of the poem says. I wanted a word with
more than one syllable to it to make it linger a little. But more than that,
I wanted a month appropriate to what I felt at the time I wrote the
poem—a month of short days and failing light, smoke in the air, things
perishing. June was summer nights and days, graduations, my wedding
anniversary, the birthday of one of my children. June wasn't a month
your father died in.

After the service at the funeral home, after we had moved outside, a   31
woman I didn't know came over to me and said, "He's happier where he
is now." I stared at this woman until she moved away. I still remember
the little knob of a hat she was wearing. Then one of my dad's cousins—
I didn't know the man's name—reached out and took my hand. "We all
miss him," he said, and I knew he wasn't saying it just to be polite.

I began to weep for the first time since receiving the news. I hadn't   32
been able to before. I hadn't had the time, for one thing. Now, suddenly, I
couldn't stop. I held my wife and wept while she said and did what she
could do to comfort me there in the middle of that summer afternoon.

I listened to people say consoling things to my mother, and I was   33
glad that my dad's family had turned up, had come to where he was. I
thought I'd remember everything that was said and done that day and
maybe find a way to tell it sometime. But I didn't. I forgot it all, or nearly.
What I do remember is that I heard our name used a lot that afternoon,
my dad's name and mine. But I knew they were talking about my dad.
*Raymond*, these people kept saying in their beautiful voices out of my
childhood. *Raymond*.

## CONSIDERATIONS

1. In paragraph 26, Carver's father expresses an interest in his son's announcement that he wanted to be a writer. "Send me what you write," says the father. "I said I'd
do that, but then I didn't." Why didn't he? Build your answer into a short essay about
what you know of father-son relationships.

2. At the end of paragraph 7, the writer decides, with respect to his father, that "These were his salad days." It's an old expression, dating back to Shakespeare, but not often used these days. Basing your conclusion on the rest of the paragraph, what do you think it means?

3. To what extent is Carver's biographical essay about his father also autobiographical? Would that be true of any writer of a biography?

4. Bearing in mind that Raymond Carver Sr., and subsequently his family, moved to the Northwest in the midthirties, explain how that move was, in miniature, exemplary of a large-scale migration that changed the demographic make-up of the far western states.

5. In a different essay, "On Writing," Carver says, "Writers don't need tricks or gimmicks or even necessarily to be the smartest fellows on the block. At the risk of appearing foolish, a writer sometimes needs to be able to just stand and gape at this or that thing—a sunset or an old shoe—in absolute and simple amazement." What do you find in "My Father's Life," or in Carver's two short stories, "A Small, Good Thing" and "Errand," that points up his statement about writers?

6. "June wasn't a month your father died in." What has that to do with dating the poem Carver wrote about his father?

*"Errand," Carver's story out of the life of Anton Chekhov (the great Russian playwright and author of short stories), comes from the last book of stories he published before his death. Carver and his wife planned a trip to Russia, largely to see Chekhov's grave, but he died before they could take the trip. In obituaries, Carver was called "The American Chekhov," and "America's Chekhov."*

— 16

# RAYMOND CARVER
## *Errand*

Chekhov. On the evening of March 22, 1897, he went to dinner in     1
Moscow with his friend and confidant Alexei Suvorin. This Suvorin was
a very rich newspaper and book publisher, a reactionary, a self-made man
whose father was a private at the battle of Borodino. Like Chekhov, he
was the grandson of a serf. They had that in common: each had peasant's
blood in his veins. Otherwise, politically and temperamentally, they
were miles apart. Nevertheless, Suvorin was one of Chekhov's few inti-
mates, and Chekhov enjoyed his company.

Naturally, they went to the best restaurant in the city, a former     2
town house called the Hermitage—a place where it could take hours,
half the night even, to get through a ten-course meal that would, of
course, include several wines, liqueurs, and coffee. Chekhov was impec-
cably dressed, as always—a dark suit and waistcoat, his usual pince-nez.
He looked that night very much as he looks in the photographs taken of
him during this period. He was relaxed, jovial. He shook hands with the
maître d', and with a glance took in the large dining room. It was brilliantly illuminated by ornate chandeliers, the tables occupied by elegantly dressed men and women. Waiters came and went ceaselessly. He
had just been seated across the table from Suvorin when suddenly, without warning, blood began gushing from his mouth. Suvorin and two
waiters helped him to the gentlemen's room and tried to stanch the flow
of blood with ice packs. Suvorin saw him back to his own hotel and had a
bed prepared for Chekhov in one of the rooms of the suite. Later, after

another hemorrhage, Chekhov allowed himself to be moved to a clinic that specialized in the treatment of tuberculosis and related respiratory infections. When Suvorin visited him there, Chekhov apologized for the "scandal" at the restaurant three nights earlier but continued to insist there was nothing seriously wrong. "He laughed and jested as usual," Suvorin noted in his diary, "while spitting blood into a large vessel."

3      Maria Chekhov, his younger sister, visited Chekhov in the clinic during the last days of March. The weather was miserable; a sleet storm was in progress, and frozen heaps of snow lay everywhere. It was hard for her to wave down a carriage to take her to the hospital. By the time she arrived she was filled with dread and anxiety.

4      "Anton Pavlovich lay on his back," Maria wrote in her *Memoirs*. "He was not allowed to speak. After greeting him, I went over to the table to hide my emotions." There, among bottles of champagne, jars of caviar, bouquets of flowers from well-wishers, she saw something that terrified her: a freehand drawing, obviously done by a specialist in these matters, of Chekhov's lungs. It was the kind of sketch a doctor often makes in order to show his patient what he thinks is taking place. The lungs were outlined in blue, but the upper parts were filled in with red. "I realized they were diseased," Maria wrote.

5      Leo Tolstoy was another visitor. The hospital staff were awed to find themselves in the presence of the country's greatest writer. The most famous man in Russia? Of course they had to let him in to see Chekhov, even though "nonessential" visitors were forbidden. With much obsequiousness on the part of the nurses and resident doctors, the bearded, fierce-looking old man was shown into Chekhov's room. Despite his low opinion of Chekhov's abilities as a playwright (Tolstoy felt the plays were static and lacking in any moral vision. "Where do your characters take you?" he once demanded of Chekhov. "From the sofa to the junk room and back"), Tolstoy liked Chekhov's short stories. Furthermore, and quite simply, he loved the man. He told Gorky, "What a beautiful, magnificent man: modest and quiet, like a girl. He even walks like a girl. He's simply wonderful." And Tolstoy wrote in his journal (everyone kept a journal or a diary in those days), "I am glad I love . . . Chekhov."

6      Tolstoy removed his woollen scarf and bearskin coat, then lowered himself into a chair next to Chekhov's bed. Never mind that Chekhov was taking medication and not permitted to talk, much less carry on a conversation. He had to listen, amazedly, as the Count began to discourse on his theories of the immortality of the soul. Concerning that visit, Chekhov later wrote, "Tolstoy assumes that all of us (humans and animals alike) will live on in a principle (such as reason or love) the essence and goals of which are a mystery to us. . . . I have no use for that kind of immortality. I don't understand it, and Lev Nikolayevich was astonished I didn't."

Nevertheless, Chekhov was impressed with the solicitude shown 7
by Tolstoy's visit. But, unlike Tolstoy, Chekhov didn't believe in an af-
terlife and never had. He didn't believe in anything that couldn't be ap-
prehended by one or more of his five senses. And as far as his outlook on
life and writing went, he once told someone that he lacked "a political,
religious, and philosophical world view. I change it every month, so I'll
have to limit myself to the description of how my heroes love, marry,
give birth, die, and how they speak."

Earlier, before his t.b. was diagnosed, Chekhov had remarked, 8
"When a peasant has consumption, he says, 'There's nothing I can do. I'll
go off in the spring with the melting of the snows.' " (Chekhov himself
died in the summer, during a heat wave.) But once Chekhov's own tuberculosis was discovered he continually tried to minimize the seriousness
of his condition. To all appearances, it was as if he felt, right up to the
end, that he might be able to throw off the disease as he would a lingering catarrh. Well into his final days, he spoke with seeming conviction of
the possibility of an improvement. In fact, in a letter written shortly before his end, he went so far as to tell his sister that he was "getting fat"
and felt much better now that he was in Badenweiler.

Badenweiler is a spa and resort city in the western area of the Black 9
Forest, not far from Basel. The Vosges are visible from nearly anywhere
in the city, and in those days the air was pure and invigorating. Russians
had been going there for years to soak in the hot mineral baths and prom-
enade on the boulevards. In June, 1904, Chekhov went there to die.

Earlier that month, he'd made a difficult journey by train from 10
Moscow to Berlin. He traveled with his wife, the actress Olga Knipper, a
woman he'd met in 1898 during rehearsals for "The Seagull." Her contemporaries describe her as an excellent actress. She was talented, pretty,
and almost ten years younger than the playwright. Chekhov had been
immediately attracted to her, but was slow to act on his feelings. As always, he preferred a flirtation to marriage. Finally, after a three-year
courtship involving many separations, letters, and the inevitable misun-
derstandings, they were at last married, in a private ceremony in
Moscow, on May 25, 1901. Chekhov was enormously happy. He called
Olga his "pony," and sometimes "dog" or "puppy." He was also fond of
addressing her as "little turkey" or simply as "my joy."

In Berlin, Chekhov consulted with a renowned specialist in pul- 11
monary disorders, a Dr. Karl Ewald. But, according to an eyewitness, after the doctor examined Chekhov he threw up his hands and left the
room without a word. Chekhov was too far gone for help: this Dr. Ewald
was furious with himself for not being able to work miracles, and with
Chekhov for being so ill.

A Russian journalist happened to visit the Chekhovs at their hotel 12
and sent back this dispatch to his editor: "Chekhov's days are numbered.

He seems mortally ill, is terribly thin, coughs all the time, gasps for breath at the slightest movement, and is running a high temperature." This same journalist saw the Chekhovs off at Potsdam Station when they boarded their train for Badenweiler. According to his account, "Chekhov had trouble making his way up the small staircase at the station. He had to sit down for several minutes to catch his breath." In fact, it was painful for Chekhov to move: his legs ached continually and his insides hurt. The disease had attacked his intestines and spinal cord. At this point he had less than a month to live. When Chekhov spoke of his condition now, it was, according to Olga, "with an almost reckless indifference."

13      Dr. Schwöhrer was one of the many Badenweiler physicians who earned a good living by treating the well-to-do who came to the spa seeking relief from various maladies. Some of his patients were ill and infirm, others simply old and hypochondriacal. But Chekhov's was a special case: he was clearly beyond help and in his last days. He was also very famous. Even Dr. Schwöhrer knew his name: he'd read some of Chekhov's stories in a German magazine. When he examined the writer early in June, he voiced his appreciation of Chekhov's art but kept his medical opinions to himself. Instead, he prescribed a diet of cocoa, oatmeal drenched in butter, and strawberry tea. This last was supposed to help Chekhov sleep at night.

14      On June 13, less than three weeks before he died, Chekhov wrote a letter to his mother in which he told her his health was on the mend. In it he said, "It's likely that I'll be completely cured in a week." Who knows why he said this? What could he have been thinking? He was a doctor himself, and he knew better. He was dying, it was as simple and as unavoidable as that. Nevertheless, he sat out on the balcony of his hotel room and read railway timetables. He asked for information on sailings of boats bound for Odessa from Marseilles. But he *knew*. At this stage he had to have known. Yet in one of the last letters he ever wrote he told his sister he was growing stronger by the day.

15      He no longer had any appetite for literary work, and hadn't for a long time. In fact, he had very nearly failed to complete *The Cherry Orchard* the year before. Writing that play was the hardest thing he'd ever done in his life. Toward the end, he was able to manage only six or seven lines a day. "I've started losing heart," he wrote Olga. "I feel I'm finished as a writer, and every sentence strikes me as worthless and of no use whatever." But he didn't stop. He finished his play in October, 1903. It was the last thing he ever wrote, except for letters and a few entries in his notebook.

16      A little after midnight on July 2, 1904, Olga sent someone to fetch Dr. Schwöhrer. It was an emergency: Chekhov was delirious. Two young Russians on holiday happened to have the adjacent room, and Olga hurried next door to explain what was happening. One of the youths was in his bed asleep, but the other was still awake, smoking and reading. He left the hotel at a run to find Dr. Schwöhrer. "I can still hear the sound of

the gravel under his shoes in the silence of that stifling July night," Olga wrote later on in her memoirs. Chekhov was hallucinating, talking about sailors, and there were snatches of something about the Japanese. "You don't put ice on an empty stomach," he said when she tried to place an ice pack on his chest.

Dr. Schwöhrer arrived and unpacked his bag, all the while keeping    17
his gaze fastened on Chekhov, who lay gasping in the bed. The sick man's pupils were dilated and his temples glistened with sweat. Dr. Schwöhrer's face didn't register anything. He was not an emotional man, but he knew Chekhov's end was near. Still, he was a doctor, sworn to do his utmost, and Chekhov held on to life, however tenuously. Dr. Schwöhrer prepared a hypodermic and administered an injection of camphor, something that was supposed to speed up the heart. But the injection didn't help—nothing, of course, could have helped. Nevertheless, the doctor made known to Olga his intention of sending for oxygen. Suddenly, Chekhov roused himself, became lucid, and said quietly, "What's the use? Before it arrives I'll be a corpse."

Dr. Schwöhrer pulled on his big moustache and stared at Chekhov.    18
The writer's cheeks were sunken and gray, his complexion waxen; his breath was raspy. Dr. Schwöhrer knew the time could be reckoned in minutes. Without a word, without conferring with Olga, he went over to an alcove where there was a telephone on the wall. He read the instructions for using the device. If he activated it by holding his finger on a button and turning a handle on the side of the phone, he could reach the lower regions of the hotel—the kitchen. He picked up the receiver, held it to his ear, and did as the instructions told him. When someone finally answered, Dr. Schwöhrer ordered a bottle of the hotel's best champagne. "How many glasses?" he was asked. "Three glasses!" the doctor shouted into the mouthpiece. "And hurry, do you hear?" It was one of those rare moments of inspiration that can easily enough be overlooked later on, because the action is so entirely appropriate it seems inevitable.

The champagne was brought to the door by a tired-looking young    19
man whose blond hair was standing up. The trousers of his uniform were wrinkled, the creases gone, and in his haste he'd missed a loop while buttoning his jacket. His appearance was that of someone who'd been resting (slumped in a chair, say, dozing a little), when off in the distance the phone had clamored in the early-morning hours—great God in Heaven!—and the next thing he knew he was being shaken awake by a superior and told to deliver a bottle of Moët to Room 211. "And hurry, do you hear?"

The young man entered the room carrying a silver ice bucket with    20
the champagne in it and a silver tray with three cut-crystal glasses. He found a place on the table for the bucket and glasses, all the while craning his neck, trying to see into the other room, where someone panted ferociously for breath. It was a dreadful, harrowing sound, and the young

man lowered his chin into his collar and turned away as the ratchety breathing worsened. Forgetting himself, he stared out the open window toward the darkened city. Then this big imposing man with a thick moustache pressed some coins into his hand—a large tip, by the feel of it—and suddenly the young man saw the door open. He took some steps and found himself on the landing, where he opened his hand and looked at the coins in amazement.

21      Methodically, the way he did everything, the doctor went about the business of working the cork out of the bottle. He did it in such a way as to minimize, as much as possible, the festive explosion. He poured three glasses and, out of habit, pushed the cork back into the neck of the bottle. He then took the glasses of champagne over to the bed. Olga momentarily released her grip on Chekhov's hand—a hand, she said later, that burned her fingers. She arranged another pillow behind his head. Then she put the cool glass of champagne against Chekhov's palm and made sure his fingers closed around the stem. They exchanged looks—Chekhov, Olga, Dr. Schwöhrer. They didn't touch glasses. There was no toast. What on earth was there to drink to? To death? Chekhov summoned his remaining strength and said, "It's been so long since I've had champagne." He brought the glass to his lips and drank. In a minute or two Olga took the empty glass from his hand and set it on the nightstand. Then Chekhov turned onto his side. He closed his eyes and sighed. A minute later, his breathing stopped.

22      Dr. Schwöhrer picked up Chekhov's hand from the bedsheet. He held his fingers to Chekhov's wrist and drew a gold watch from his vest pocket, opening the lid of the watch as he did so. The second hand on the watch moved slowly, very slowly. He let it move around the face of the watch three times while he waited for signs of a pulse. It was three o'clock in the morning and still sultry in the room. Badenweiler was in the grip of its worst heat wave in years. All the windows in both rooms stood open, but there was no sign of a breeze. A large, black-winged moth flew through a window and banged wildly against the electric lamp. Dr. Schwöhrer let go of Chekhov's wrist. "It's over," he said. He closed the lid of his watch and returned it to his vest pocket.

23      At once Olga dried her eyes and set about composing herself. She thanked the doctor for coming. He asked if she wanted some medication—laudanum, perhaps, or a few drops of valerian. She shook her head. She did have one request, though: before the authorities were notified and the newspapers found out, before the time came when Chekhov was no longer in her keeping, she wanted to be alone with him for a while. Could the doctor help with this? Could he withhold, for a while anyway, news of what had just occurred?

24      Dr. Schwöhrer stroked his moustache with the back of a finger. Why not? After all, what difference would it make to anyone whether this matter became known now or a few hours from now? The only detail that remained was to fill out a death certificate, and this could be

done at his office later on in the morning, after he'd slept a few hours. Dr. Schwöhrer nodded his agreement and prepared to leave. He murmured a few words of condolence. Olga inclined her head. "An honor," Dr. Schwöhrer said. He picked up his bag and left the room and, for that matter, history.

It was at this moment that the cork popped out of the champagne bottle; foam spilled down onto the table. Olga went back to Chekhov's bedside. She sat on a footstool, holding his hand, from time to time stroking his face. "There were no human voices, no everyday sounds," she wrote. "There was only beauty, peace, and the grandeur of death." 25

She stayed with Chekhov until daybreak, when thrushes began to call from the garden below. Then came the sound of tables and chairs being moved about down there. Before long, voices carried up to her. It was then a knock sounded at the door. Of course she thought it must be an official of some sort—the medical examiner, say, or someone from the police who had questions to ask and forms for her to fill out, or maybe, just maybe, it could be Dr. Schwöhrer returning with a mortician to render assistance in embalming and transporting Chekhov's remains back to Russia. 26

But, instead, it was the same blond young man who'd brought the champagne a few hours earlier. This time, however, his uniform trousers were neatly pressed, with stiff creases in front, and every button on his snug green jacket was fastened. He seemed quite another person. Not only was he wide awake but his plump cheeks were smooth-shaven, his hair was in place, and he appeared anxious to please. He was holding a porcelain vase with three long-stemmed yellow roses. He presented these to Olga with a smart click of his heels. She stepped back and let him into the room. He was there, he said, to collect the glasses, ice bucket, and tray, yes. But he also wanted to say that, because of the extreme heat, breakfast would be served in the garden this morning. He hoped this weather wasn't too bothersome; he apologized for it. 27

The woman seemed distracted. While he talked, she turned her eyes away and looked down at something in the carpet. She crossed her arms and held her elbows. Meanwhile, still holding his vase, waiting for a sign, the young man took in the details of the room. Bright sunlight flooded through the open windows. The room was tidy and seemed undisturbed, almost untouched. No garments were flung over chairs, no shoes, stockings, braces, or stays were in evidence, no open suitcases. In short, there was no clutter, nothing but the usual heavy pieces of hotel-room furniture. Then, because the woman was still looking down, he looked down, too, and at once spied a cork near the toe of his shoe. The woman did not see it—she was looking somewhere else. The young man wanted to bend over and pick up the cork, but he was still holding the roses and was afraid of seeming to intrude even more by drawing any further attention to himself. Reluctantly, he left the cork where it was and 28 raised his eyes. Everything was in order except for the uncorked, half-empty bottle of champagne that stood alongside two crystal glasses over on the little table. He cast his gaze about once more. Through an open door he saw that the third glass was in the bedroom, on the nightstand. But someone still occupied the bed! He couldn't see a face, but the figure under the covers lay perfectly motionless and quiet. He noted the figure and looked elsewhere. Then, for a reason he couldn't understand, a feeling of uneasiness took hold of him. He cleared his throat and moved his weight to the other leg. The woman still didn't look up or break her silence. The young man felt his cheeks grow warm. It occurred to him, quite without his having thought it through, that he should perhaps suggest an alternative to breakfast in the garden. He coughed, hoping to focus the woman's attention, but she didn't look at him. The distinguished foreign guests could, he said, take breakfast in their rooms this morning if they wished. The young man (his name hasn't survived, and it's likely he perished in the Great War) said he would be happy to bring up a tray. Two trays, he added, glancing uncertainly once again in the direction of the bedroom.

29       He fell silent and ran a finger around the inside of his collar. He didn't understand. He wasn't even sure the woman had been listening. He didn't know what else to do now; he was still holding the vase. The sweet odor of the roses filled his nostrils and inexplicably caused a pang of regret. The entire time he'd been waiting, the woman had apparently been lost in thought. It was as if all the while he'd been standing there, talking, shifting his weight, holding his flowers, she had been someplace else, somewhere far from Badenweiler. But now she came back to herself, and her face assumed another expression. She raised her eyes, looked at him, and then shook her head. She seemed to be struggling to understand what on earth this young man could be doing there in the room holding a vase with three yellow roses. Flowers? She hadn't ordered flowers.

30       The moment passed. She went over to her handbag and scooped up some coins. She drew out a number of banknotes as well. The young man touched his lips with his tongue; another large tip was forthcoming, but for what? What did she want him to do? He'd never before waited on such guests. He cleared his throat once more.

31       No breakfast, the woman said. Not yet, at any rate. Breakfast wasn't the important thing this morning. She required something else. She needed him to go out and bring back a mortician. Did he understand her? Herr Chekhov was dead, you see. *Comprenez-vous?* Young man? Anton Chekhov was dead. Now listen carefully to me, she said. She wanted him to go downstairs and ask someone at the front desk where he could go to find the most respected mortician in the city. Someone reliable, who took great pains in his work and whose manner was appropriately reserved. A mortician, in short, worthy of a great artist. Here, she said, and pressed the money on him. Tell them downstairs that I have

specifically requested you to perform this duty for me. Are you listening? Do you understand what I'm saying to you?

The young man grappled to take in what she was saying. He chose      32
not to look again in the direction of the other room. He had sensed that something was not right. He became aware of his heart beating rapidly under his jacket, and he felt perspiration break out on his forehead. He didn't know where he should turn his eyes. He wanted to put the vase down.

Please do this for me, the woman said. I'll remember you with grat-      33
itude. Tell them downstairs that I insist. Say that. But don't call any unnecessary attention to yourself or to the situation. Just say that this is necessary, that I request it—and that's all. Do you hear me? Nod if you understand. Above all, don't raise an alarm. Everything else, all the rest, the commotion—that'll come soon enough. The worst is over. Do we understand each other?

The young man's face had grown pale. He stood rigid, clasping the      34
vase. He managed to nod his head.

After securing permission to leave the hotel he was to proceed qui-      35
etly and resolutely, though without any unbecoming haste, to the mortician's. He was to behave exactly as if he were engaged on a very important errand, nothing more. He *was* engaged on an important errand, she said. And if it would help keep his movements purposeful he should imagine himself as someone moving down the busy sidewalk carrying in his arms a porcelain vase of roses that he had to deliver to an important man. (She spoke quietly, almost confidentially, as if to a relative or a friend.) He could even tell himself that the man he was going to see was expecting him, was perhaps impatient for him to arrive with his flowers. Nevertheless, the young man was not to become excited and run, or otherwise break his stride. Remember the vase he was carrying! He was to walk briskly, comporting himself at all times in as dignified a manner as possible. He should keep walking until he came to the mortician's house and stood before the door. He would then raise the brass knocker and let it fall, once, twice, three times. In a minute the mortician himself would answer.

This mortician would be in his forties, no doubt, or maybe early      36
fifties—bald, solidly built, wearing steel-frame spectacles set very low on his nose. He would be modest, unassuming, a man who would ask only the most direct and necessary questions. An apron. Probably he would be wearing an apron. He might even be wiping his hands on a dark towel while he listened to what was being said. There'd be a faint whiff of formaldehyde on his clothes. But it was all right, and the young man shouldn't worry. He was nearly a grown-up now and shouldn't be frightened or repelled by any of this. The mortician would hear him out. He was a man of restraint and bearing, this mortician, someone who could help allay people's fears in this situation, not increase them. Long ago he'd acquainted himself with death in all its various guises and forms;

death held no surprises for him any longer, no hidden secrets. It was this man whose services were required this morning.

37      The mortician takes the vase of roses. Only once while the young man is speaking does the mortician betray the least flicker of interest, or indicate that he's heard anything out of the ordinary. But the one time the young man mentions the name of the deceased, the mortician's eyebrows rise just a little. Chekhov, you say? Just a minute, and I'll be with you.

38      Do you understand what I'm saying, Olga said to the young man. Leave the glasses. Don't worry about them. Forget about crystal wineglasses and such. Leave the room as it is. Everything is ready now. We're ready. Will you go?

39      But at that moment the young man was thinking of the cork still resting near the toe of his shoe. To retrieve it he would have to bend over, still gripping the vase. He would do this. He leaned over. Without looking down, he reached out and closed it into his hand.

## *CONSIDERATIONS*

1. "Errand" is reprinted from a collection of Carver's short stories and would thus be labeled "fiction," yet it is obviously based on accounts of Chekhov's death, including surviving letters of the Russian writer's wife. What does this suggest about the firm line conventionally drawn between fiction and nonfiction? What parts of the story seem to be clearly one or the other?

2. Very much a realist in his own writing, Chekhov once advised a young writer to avoid writing about emotions and to concentrate on perceivable things or events or persons that would evoke those emotions. He would have admired, for example, this eighteenth-century haiku by Yosa Buson:

> The piercing chill I feel:
> My dead wife's comb in our bedroom
> Under my heel.

What do you find in "Errand" or "A Small, Good Thing" that suggests Carver might have learned something from Chekhov? Can you apply the same idea to your own writing?

3. "It was one of those rare moments of inspiration that can easily enough be overlooked later on, because the action is so entirely appropriate it seems inevitable." Why does the writer, in paragraph 18, so obviously admire the sudden action of the doctor?

4. In paragraph 37, "The mortician takes the vase of roses." The last time we saw the roses they were back in Chekhov's room in the hotel. What's going on here?

5. One critic of Chekhov's last and most famous play, *The Cherry Orchard,* complained that "nothing happens in it." Nothing, said Chekhov, but the world changing before your face. The same critic could not say the same thing about "Errand"—after all, a great man dies. But Chekhov himself and certainly Carver might add this: the death is not the point of the story; it is merely the means. The means to what?

6. After reading the story and thinking about it, what reason can you offer for Carver's entitling the story "Errand"?

*Michelle Cliff (b. 1946) was born in Kingston, Jamaica, was educated in New York and London, and lives in California. Her books include prose poems,* Claiming an Identity They Taught Me to Despise *(1980), three novels—*Abeng *(1984),* No Telephone to Heaven *(1987), and* Free Enterprise *(1993)—and a book of short stories,* Bodies of Water *(1990). In 1990 she won the James Baldwin Award of the Oakland Black Writers Guild and International Black Writers Association.*

*Michelle Cliff's memory and imagination, locating detail by means of imagery, escort the reader into complexities of race and colonialism. Notice how her memoir of ethnicity and emigration uses personal narrative, interrupted by snatches of objective fact and stories gathered from the lives of others.*

## — 17 —

# MICHELLE CLIFF
### *If I Could Write This in Fire,*
### *I Would Write This in Fire*

### I

We were standing under the waterfall at the top of Orange River. 1
Our chests were just beginning to mound—slight hills on either side. In the center of each were our nipples, which were losing their sideways look and rounding into perceptible buttons of dark flesh. Too fast it seemed. We touched each other, then, quickly and almost simultaneously, raised our arms to examine the hairs growing underneath. Another sign. Mine was wispy and light-brown. My friend Zoe had dark hair curled up tight. In each little patch the riverwater caught the sun so we glistened.

The waterfall had come about when my uncles dammed up the 2
river to bring power to the sugar mill. Usually, when I say "sugar mill" to anyone not familiar with the Jamaican countryside or for that matter my family, I can tell their minds cast an image of tall smokestacks,

**115**

enormous copper cauldrons, a man in a broad-brimmed hat with a whip, and several dozens of slaves—that is, if they have any idea of how large sugar mills once operated. It's a grandiose expression—like plantation, verandah, out-building. (Try substituting farm, porch, outside toilet.) To some people it even sounds romantic.

3    Our sugar mill was little more than a round-roofed shed, which contained a wheel and woodfire. We paid an old man to run it, tend the fire, and then either bartered or gave the sugar away, after my grandmother had taken what she needed. Our canefield was about two acres of flat land next to the river. My grandmother had six acres in all—one donkey, a mule, two cows, some chickens, a few pigs, and stray dogs and cats who had taken up residence in the yard.

4    Her house had four rooms, no electricity, no running water. The kitchen was a shed in the back with a small pot-bellied stove. Across from the stove was a mahogany counter, which had a white enamel basin set into it. The only light source was a window, a small space covered partly by a wooden shutter. We washed our faces and hands in enamel bowls with cold water carried in kerosene tins from the river and poured from enamel pitchers. Our chamber pots were enamel also, and in the morning we carefully placed them on the steps at the side of the house where my grandmother collected them and disposed of their contents. The outhouse was about thirty yards from the back door—a "closet" as we called it—infested with lizards capable of changing color. When the door was shut it was totally dark, and the lizards made their presence known by the noise of their scurrying through the torn newspaper, or the soft shudder when they dropped from the walls. I remember most clearly the stench of the toilet, which seemed to hang in the air in that climate.

5    But because every little piece of reality exists in relation to another little piece, our situation was not that simple. It was to our yard that people came with news first. It was in my grandmother's parlor that the Disciples of Christ held their meetings. Zoe lived with her mother and sister on borrowed ground in a place called Breezy Hill. She and I saw each other almost every day on our school vacations over a period of three years. Each morning early—as I sat on the cement porch with my coffee cut with condensed milk—she appeared: in her straw hat, school tunic faded from blue to gray, white blouse, sneakers hanging around her neck. We had coffee together, and a piece of hard-dough bread with butter and cheese, waited a bit and headed for the river. At first we were shy with each other. We did not start from the same place.

6    There was land. My grandparents' farm. And there was color.

7    (My family was called *red*. A term which signified a degree of whiteness. "We's just a flock of red people," a cousin of mine said once.) In the hierarchy of shades I was considered among the lightest. The countrywomen who visited my grandmother commented on my "tall" hair—meaning long. Wavy, not curly.

8    I had spent the years from three to ten in New York and spoke—at first—like an American. I wore American clothes: shorts, slacks, bathing

suit. Because of my American past I was looked upon as the creator of games. Cowboys and Indians. Cops and Robbers. Peter Pan.

(While the primary colonial identification for Jamaicans was    9
English, American colonialism was a strong force in my childhood—and of course continues today. We were sent American movies and American music. American aluminum companies had already discovered bauxite on the island and were shipping the ore to their mainland. United Fruit bought our bananas. White Americans came to Montego Bay, Ocho Rios, and Kingston for their vacations and their cruise ships docked in Port Antonio and other places. In some ways America was seen as a better place than England by many Jamaicans. The farm laborers sent to work in American agribusiness came home with dollars and gifts and new clothes; there were few who mentioned American racism. Many of the middle class who emigrated to Brooklyn or Staten Island or Manhattan were able to pass into the white American world—saving their blackness for other Jamaicans or for trips home; in some cases, forgetting it altogether. Those middle-class Jamaicans who could not pass for white managed differently—not unlike the Bajans in Paule Marshall's *Brown Girl, Brownstones*—saving, working, investing, buying property. Completely separate in most cases from Black Americans.)

I was someone who had experience with the place that sent us    10
triple features of B-grade western and gangster movies. And I had tall hair and light skin. And I was the granddaughter of my grandmother. So I had power. I was the cowboy, Zoe was my sidekick, the boys we knew were Indians. I was the detective, Zoe was my "girl," the boys were the robbers. I was Peter Pan, Zoe was Wendy Darling, the boys were the lost boys. And the terrain around the river—jungled and dark green—was Tombstone, or Chicago, or Never-Never Land.

This place and my friendship with Zoe never touched my life in    11
Kingston. We did not correspond with each other when I left my grandmother's home.

I never visited Zoe's home the entire time I knew her. It was a    12
given: never suggested, never raised.

Zoe went to a state school held in a country church in Red Hills. It    13
had been my mother's school. I went to a private all-girls school where I was taught by white Englishwomen and pale Jamaicans. In her school the students were caned as punishment. In mine the harshest punishment I remember was being sent to sit under the *lignum vitae* to "commune with nature." Some of the girls were out-and-out white (English and American), the rest of us were colored—only a few were dark. Our uniforms were blood-red gabardine, heavy and hot. Classes were held in buildings meant to re-create England: damp with stone floors, facing onto a cloister, or quad as they called it. We began each day with the headmistress leading us in English hymns. The entire school stood for an hour in the zinc-roofed gymnasium.

Occasionally a girl fainted, or threw up. Once, a girl had a grand mal    14
seizure. To any such disturbance the response was always "keep

singing." While she flailed on the stone floor, I wondered what the mistresses would do. We sang "Faith of Our Fathers," and watched our classmate as her eyes rolled back in her head. I thought of people swallowing their tongues. This student was dark—here on a scholarship—and the only woman who came forward to help her was the gamesmistress, the only dark teacher. She kneeled beside the girl and slid the white web belt from her tennis shorts, clamping it between the girl's teeth. When the seizure was over, she carried the girl to a tumbling mat in a corner of the gym and covered her so she wouldn't get chilled.

15   Were the other women unable to touch this girl because of her darkness? I think that now. Her darkness and her scholarship. She lived on Windward Road with her grandmother; her mother was a maid. But darkness is usually enough for women like those to hold back. Then, we usually excused that kind of behavior by saying they were "ladies." (We were constantly being told we should be ladies also. One teacher went so far as to tell us many people thought Jamaicans lived in trees and we had to show these people they were mistaken.) In short, we felt insufficient to judge the behavior of these women. The English ones (who had the corner on power in the school) had come all this way to teach us. Shouldn't we treat them as the missionaries they were certain they were? The creole Jamaicans had a different role: they were passing on to those of us who were light-skinned the creole heritage of collaboration, assimilation, loyalty to our betters. We were expected to be willing subjects in this outpost of civilization.

16   The girl left school that day and never returned.

17   After prayers we filed into our classrooms. After classes we had games: tennis, field hockey, rounders (what the English call baseball), netball (what the English call basketball). For games we were divided into "houses"—groups named for Joan of Arc, Edith Cavell, Florence Nightingale, Jane Austen. Four white heroines. Two martyrs. One saint. Two nurses. (None of us knew then that there were Black women with Nightingale at Scutari.) One novelist. Three involved in white men's wars. Two dead in white men's wars. *Pride and Prejudice.*

18   Those of us in Cavell wore red badges and recited her last words before a firing squad in W. W. I: "Patriotism is not enough. I must have no hatred or bitterness toward anyone."

19   *Sorry to say I grew up to have exactly that.*

20   *Looking back:* To try and see when the background changed places with the foreground. To try and locate the vanishing point: where the lines of perspective converge and disappear. Lines of color and class. Lines of history and social context. Lines of denial and rejection. When did *we* (the light-skinned middle-class Jamaicans) take over for *them* as oppressors? I need to see when and how this happened. When what should have been reality was overtaken by what was surely unreality. When the house nigger became master.

21   "What's the matter with you? You think you're white or something?"

"Child, what you want to know 'bout Garvey for? The man was    22
nothing but a damn fool."

"They not our kind of people."    23

Why did we wear wide-brimmed hats and try to get into Oxford?    24
Why did we not return?

*Great Expectations:* a novel about origins and denial, about the fu-    25
tility and tragedy of that denial, about attempting assimilation. We
learned this novel from a light-skinned Jamaican woman—she concentrated on what she called the "love affair" between Pip and Estella.

*Looking back:* Through the last page of *Sula.* "And the loss pressed    26
down on her chest and came up into her throat. 'We was girls together,'
she said as though explaining something." It was Zoe, and Zoe alone, I
thought of. She snapped into my mind and I remembered no one else.
Through the greens and blues of the riverbank. The flame of red hibiscus
in front of my grandmother's house. The cracked grave of a former
landowner. The fruit of the ackee which poisons those who don't know
how to prepare it.

*"What is to become of us?"*    27

We borrowed a baby from a woman and used her as our dolly.    28
Dressed and undressed her. Dipped her in the riverwater. Fed her with
the milk her mother had left with us, and giggled because we knew
where the milk had come from.

*A letter:* "I am desperate. I need to get away. I beg you one fifty-dollar."    29

I send the money because this is what she asks for. I visit her on a    30
trip back home. Her front teeth are gone. Her husband beats her and she
suffers blackouts. I sit on her chair. She is given birth control pills which
aggravate her "condition." We boil up sorrel and ginger. She is being
taught by Peace Corps volunteers to embroider linen mats with little
lambs on them and gives me one as a keepsake. We cool off the sorrel
with a block of ice brought from the shop nearby. The shopkeeper immediately recognizes me as my grandmother's granddaughter and refuses to
sell me cigarettes. (I am twenty-seven.) We sit in the doorway of her
house, pushing back the colored plastic strands which form a curtain,
and talk about Babylon and Dred. About Manley and what he's doing for
Jamaica. About how hard it is. We walk along the railway tracks—no
longer used—to Crooked River and the post office. Her little daughter
walks beside us and we recite a poem for her: "Mornin' buddy/Me no
buddy fe wunna/Who den, den I saw?" and on and on.

I can come and go. And I leave. To complete my education in    31
London.

## II

Their goddam kings and their goddam queens. Grandmotherly    32
Victoria spreading herself thin across the globe. Elizabeth II on our TV
screens. We stop what we are doing. We quiet down. We pay our respects.

33     1981: In Massachusetts I get up at 5 A.M. to watch the royal wedding. I tell myself maybe the IRA will intervene. It's got to be better than starving themselves to death. Better to be a kamikaze in St. Paul's Cathedral than a hostage in Ulster. And last week Black and white people smashed storefronts all over the United Kingdom. But I really don't believe we'll see royal blood on TV. I watch because they once ruled us. In the back of the cathedral a Maori woman sings an aria from Handel, and I notice that she is surrounded by the colored subjects.

34     To those of us in the commonwealth the royal family was the perfect symbol of hegemony. To those of us who were dark in the dark nations, the prime minister, the parliament barely existed. We believed in royalty—we were convinced in this belief. Maybe it played on some ancestral memories of West Africa—where other kings and queens had been. Altars and castles and magic.

35     The faces of our new rulers were everywhere in my childhood. Calendars, newsreels, magazines. Their presences were often among us. Attending test matches between the West Indians and South Africans. They were our landlords. Not always absentee. And no matter what Black leader we might elect—were we to choose independence—we would be losing something almost holy in our impudence.

36     WE ARE HERE BECAUSE YOU WERE THERE BLACK PEOPLE AGAINST STATE BRUTALITY BLACK WOMEN WILL NOT BE INTIMIDATED WELCOME TO BRITAIN . . . WELCOME TO SECOND-CLASS CITIZENSHIP (slogans of the Black movement in Britain)

37     Indian women cleaning the toilets in Heathrow airport. This is the first thing I notice. Dark women in saris trudging buckets back and forth as other dark women in saris—some covered by loosefitting winter coats—form a line to have their passports stamped.

38     The triangle trade: molasses/rum/slaves. Robinson Crusoe was on a slave-trading journey. Robert Browning was a mulatto. Holding pens. Jamaica was a seasoning station. Split tongues. Sliced ears. Whipped bodies. The constant pretense of civility against rape. Still. Iron collars. Tinplate masks. The latter a precaution: to stop the slaves from eating the sugar cane.

39     A pregnant woman is to be whipped—they dig a hole to accommodate her belly and place her face down on the ground. Many of us became light-skinned very fast. Traced ourselves through bastard lines to reach the duke of Devonshire. The earl of Cornwall. The lord of this and the lord of that. Our mothers' rapes were the things unspoken.

40     You say: But Britain freed her slaves in 1833. Yes.

41     Tea plantations in India and Ceylon. Mines in Africa. The Cape-to-Cairo Railroad. Rhodes scholars. Suez Crisis. The white man's bloody burden. Boer War. Bantustans. Sitting in a theatre in London in the seventies. A play called *West of Suez*. A lousy play about British colonials. The finale comes when several well-known white actors are machine-gunned by several lesser-known Black actors. (As Nina

Simone says: "This is a show tune but the show hasn't been written for it yet.")

The red empire of geography classes. "The sun never sets on the   42
British empire and you can't trust it in the dark." Or with the dark peoples. "Because of the Industrial Revolution European countries went in search of markets and raw materials." Another geography (or was it a history) lesson.

Their bloody kings and their bloody queens. Their bloody peers.   43
Their bloody generals. Admirals. Explorers. Livingstone. Hillary. Kitchener. All the bwanas. And all their beaters, porters, sherpas. Who found the source of the Nile. Victoria Falls. The tops of mountains. Their so-called discoveries reek of untruth. How many dark people died so they could misname the physical features in their blasted gazetteer. A statistic we shall never know. Dr. Livingstone, I presume you are here to rape our land and enslave our people.

There are statues of these dead white men all over London.   44

An interesting fact: The swear word "bloody" is a contraction of   45
"by my lady"—a reference to the Virgin Mary. They do tend to use their ladies. Name ages for them. Places for them. Use them as screens, inspirations, symbols. And many of the ladies comply. While the national martyr Edith Cavell was being executed by the Germans in 1915 in Belgium (called "poor little Belgium" by the allies in the war), the Belgians were engaged in the exploitation of the land and peoples of the Congo.

And will we ever know how many dark peoples were "imported" to   46
fight in white men's wars. Probably not. Just as we will never know how many hearts were cut from African people so that the Christian doctor might be a success—i.e., extend a white man's life. Our Sister Killjoy observes this from her black-eyed squint.

Dr. Schweitzer—humanitarian, authority on Bach, winner of the   47
Nobel Peace Prize—on the people of Africa: "The Negro is a child, and with children nothing can be done without the use of authority. We must, therefore, so arrange the circumstances of our daily life that my authority can find expression. With regard to Negroes, then, I have coined the formula: 'I am your brother, it is true, but your elder brother.'" (*On the Edge of the Primeval Forest*, 1961)

They like to pretend we didn't fight back. We did: with obeah, poi-   48
son, revolution. It simply was not enough.

"Colonies . . . these places where 'niggers' are cheap and the earth   49
is rich." (W.E.B. DuBois, "The Souls of White Folk")

A cousin is visiting me from Cal Tech where he is getting a degree   50
in engineering. I am learning about the Italian Renaissance. My cousin is recognizably Black and speaks with an accent. I am not and do not—unless I am back home, where the "twang" comes upon me. We sit for some time in a bar in his hotel and are not served. A light-skinned Jamaican comes over to our table. He is an older man—a professor at the

University of London. "Don't bother with it, you hear. They don't serve us in this bar." A run-of-the-mill incident for all recognizably Black people in this city. But for me it is not.

51     Henry's eyes fill up, but he refuses to believe our informant. "No, man, the girl is just busy." (The girl is a fifty-year-old white woman, who may just be following orders. But I do not mention this. I have chosen sides.) All I can manage to say is, "Jesus Christ, I hate the fucking English." Henry looks at me. (In the family I am known as the "lady cousin." It has to do with how I look. And the fact that I am twenty-seven and unmarried—and for all they know, unattached. They do not know that I am really the lesbian cousin.) Our informant says—gently, but with a distinct tone of disappointment—"My dear, is that what you're studying at the university?"

52     You see—the whole business is very complicated.

53     Henry and I leave without drinks and go to meet some of his white colleagues at a restaurant I know near Covent Garden Opera House. The restaurant caters to theatre types and so I hope there won't be a repeat of the bar scene—at least they know how to pretend. Besides, I tell myself, the owners are Italian *and* gay; they *must* be halfway decent. Henry and his colleagues work for an American company which is paying their way through Cal Tech. They mine bauxite from the hills in the middle of the island and send it to the United States. A turnaround occurs at dinner: Henry joins the white men in a sustained mockery of the waiters: their accents and the way they walk. He whispers to me: "Why you want to bring us to a battyman's den, lady?" (*Battyman* = *faggot* in Jamaican.) I keep quiet.

54     We put the white men in a taxi and Henry walks me to the underground station. He asks me to sleep with him. (It wouldn't be incest. His mother was a maid in the house of an uncle and Henry has not seen her since his birth. He was taken into the family. She was let go.) I say that I can't. I plead exams. I can't say that I don't want to. Because I remember what happened in the bar. But I can't say that I'm a lesbian either—even though I want to believe his alliance with the white men at dinner was forced: not really him. He doesn't buy my excuse. "Come on, lady, let's do it. What's the matter, you 'fraid?" I pretend I am back home and start patois to show him somehow I am not afraid, not English, not white. I tell him he's a married man and he tells me he's a ram goat. I take the train to where I am staying and try to forget the whole thing. But I don't. I remember our different skins and our different experiences within them. And I have a hard time realizing that I am angry with Henry. That to him—no use in pretending—a queer is a queer.

55     1981: I hear on the radio that Bob Marley is dead and I drive over the Mohawk Trail listening to a program of his music and I cry and cry and cry. Someone says: "It wasn't the ganja that killed him, it was poverty and working in a steel foundry when he was young."

56     I flash back to my childhood and a young man who worked for an aunt I lived with once. He taught me to smoke ganja behind the house.

And to peel an orange with the tip of a machete without cutting through the skin—"Love" it was called: a necklace of orange rind the result. I think about him because I heard he had become a Rastaman. And then I think about Rastas.

We are sitting on the porch of an uncle's house in Kingston—the    57
family and I—and a Rastaman comes to the gate. We have guns but they are locked behind a false closet. We have dogs but they are tied up. We are Jamaicans and know that Rastas mean no harm. We let him in and he sits on the side of the porch and shows us his brooms and brushes. We buy some to take back to New York. "Peace, missis."

There were many Rastas in my childhood. Walking the roadside    58
with their goods. Sitting outside their shacks in the mountains. The outsides painted bright—sometimes with words. Gathering at Palisadoes Airport to greet the Conquering Lion of Judah. They were considered figures of fun by most middle-class Jamaicans. Harmless—like Marcus Garvey.

Later: white American hippies trying to create the effect of dred in    59
their straight white hair. The ganja joint held between their straight white teeth. "Man, the grass is good." Hanging out by the Sheraton pool. Light-skinned Jamaicans also dredlocked, also assuming the ganja. Both groups moving to the music but not the words. Harmless. "Peace, brother."

## III

My grandmother: "Let us thank God for a fruitful place." My grand-    60
father: "Let us rescue the perishing world."

This evening on the road in western Massachusetts there are pock-    61
ets of fog. Then clear spaces. Across from a pond a dog staggers in front of my headlights. I look closer and see that his mouth is foaming. He stumbles to the side of the road—I go to call the police.

I drive back to the house, radio playing "difficult" piano pieces. And    62
I think about how I need to say all this. This is who I am. I am not what you allow me to be. Whatever you decide me to be. In a bookstore in London I show the woman at the counter my book and she stares at me for a minute, then says: "You're a Jamaican." "Yes." "You're not at all like our Jamaicans."

Encountering the void is nothing more nor less than understanding    63
invisibility. Of being fogbound.

*Then:* It was never a question of passing. It was a question of hiding.    64
Behind Black and white perceptions of who we were—who they thought we were. Tropics. Plantations. Calypso. Cricket. We were the people with the musical voices and the coronation mugs on our parlor tables. I would be whatever figure those foreign imaginations cared for me to be. It would be so simple to let others fill in for me. So easy to startle them with a flash of anger when their visions got out of hand—but never to

sustain the anger for myself. It could become a life lived within myself.
A life cut off. I know who I am but you will never know who I am. I may
in fact lose touch with who I am.

65     I hid from my real sources. But my real sources were also hidden
from me.

66     *Now:* It is not a question of relinquishing privilege. It is a question
of grasping more of myself. I have found that in the real sources are concealed my survival. My speech. My voice. To be colonized is to be rendered insensitive. To have those parts necessary to sustain life numbed.
And this is in some cases—in my case—perceived as privilege. The test of
a colonized person is to walk through a shantytown in Kingston and not
bat an eye. This I cannot do. Because part of me lives there—and as I grasp
more of this part I realize what needs to be done with the rest of my life.

67     Sometimes I used to think we were like the Marranos—the
Sephardic Jews forced to pretend they were Christians. The name was
given to them by the Christians, and meant "pigs." But once out of Spain
and Portugal, they became Jews openly again. Some settled in Jamaica.
They knew who the enemy was and acted for their own survival. But
they remained Jews always.

68     We also knew who the enemy was—I remember jokes about the
English. Saying they stank, saying they were stingy, that they drank too
much and couldn't hold their liquor, that they had bad teeth, were dirty
and dishonest, were limey bastards, and horse-faced bitches. We said the
men only wanted to sleep with Jamaican women. And that the women
made pigs of themselves with Jamaican men.

69     But of course this was seen by us—the light-skinned middle class—
with a double vision. We learned to cherish that part of us that was
them—and to deny the part that was not. Believing in some cases that
the latter part had ceased to exist.

70     None of this is as simple as it may sound. We were colorists and we
aspired to oppressor status. (Of course, almost any aspiration instilled by
Western civilization is to oppressor status: success, for example.) Color
was the symbol of our potential: color taking in hair "quality," skin tone,
freckles, nose-width, eyes. We did not see that color symbolism was a
method of keeping us apart: in the society, in the family, between
friends. Those of us who were light-skinned, straight-haired, etc., were
given to believe that we could actually attain whiteness—or at least
those qualities of the colonizer which made him superior. We were convinced of white supremacy. If we failed, we were not really responsible
for our failures: we had all the advantages—but it was that one persistent
drop of blood, that single rogue gene that made us unable to conceptual-
ize abstract ideas, made us love darkness rather than despise it, which
was to be blamed for our failure. Our dark part had taken over: an inherited imbalance in which the doom of the creole was sealed.

71     I am trying to write this as clearly as possible, but as I write I realize
that what I say may sound fabulous, or even mythic. It is. It is insane.

Under this system of colorism—the system which prevailed in my    72
childhood in Jamaica, and which has carried over to the present—rarely
will dark and light people co-mingle. Rarely will they achieve between
themselves an intimacy informed with identity. (I should say here that I
am using the categories light and dark both literally and symbolically.
There are dark Jamaicans who have achieved lightness and the "advantages" which go with it by their successful pursuit of oppressor status.)

Under this system light and dark people will meet in those ways in    73
which the light-skinned person imitates the oppressor. But imitation
goes only so far: the light-skinned person becomes an oppressor in fact.
He/she will have a dark chauffeur, a dark nanny, a dark maid, and a dark
gardener. These employees will be paid badly. Because of the slave past,
because of their dark skin, the servants of the middle class have been
used according to the traditions of the slavocracy. They are not seen as
workers for their own sake, but for the sake of the family who has employed them. It was not until Michael Manley became prime minister
that a minimum wage for houseworkers was enacted—and the indignation of the middle class was profound.

During Manley's leadership the middle class began to abandon the    74
island in droves. Toronto. Miami. New York. Leaving their houses and
businesses behind and sewing cash into the tops of suitcases. Today—
with a new regime—they are returning: "Come back to the way things
used to be" the tourist advertisement on American TV says. "Make it
Jamaica again. Make it your own."

But let me return to the situation of houseservants as I remember it:    75
They will be paid badly, but they will be "given" room and board.
However, the key to the larder will be kept by the mistress in her dresser
drawer. They will spend Christmas with the family of their employers
and be given a length of English wool for trousers or a few yards of cotton
for dresses. They will see their children on their days off: their extended
family will care for the children the rest of the time. When the employers
visit their relations in the country, the servants may be asked along—oftentimes the servants of the middle class come from the same part of the
countryside their employers have come from. But they will be expected
to work while they are there. Back in town, there are parts of the house
they are allowed to move freely around; other parts they are not allowed
to enter. When the family watches the TV the servant is allowed to
watch also, but only while standing in a doorway. The servant may have
a radio in his/her room, also a dresser and a cot. Perhaps a mirror. There
will usually be one ceiling light. And one small square louvered window.

*A true story:* One middle-class Jamaican woman ordered a Persian    76
rug from Harrod's in London. The day it arrived so did her new maid. She
was going downtown to have her hair touched up, and told the maid to
vacuum the rug. She told the maid she would find the vacuum cleaner in
the same shed as the power mower. And when she returned she found
that the fine nap of her new rug had been removed.

77     The reaction of the mistress was to tell her friends that the "girl" was backward. She did not fire her until she found that the maid had scrubbed the teflon from her new set of pots, saying she thought they were coated with "nastiness."

78     The houseworker/mistress relationship in which one Black woman is the oppressor of another Black woman is a cornerstone of the experience of many Jamaican women.

79     I remember another true story: In a middle-class family's home one Christmas, a relation was visiting from New York. This woman had brought gifts for everybody, including the housemaid. The maid had been released from a mental institution recently, where they had "treated" her for depression. This visiting light-skinned woman had brought the dark woman a bright red rayon blouse and presented it to her in the garden one afternoon, while the family was having tea. The maid thanked her softly, and the other woman moved toward her as if to embrace her. Then she stopped, her face suddenly covered with tears, and ran into the house, saying, "My God, I can't, I can't."

80     We are women who come from a place almost incredible in its beauty. It is a beauty which can mask a great deal and which has been used in that way. But that the beauty is there is a fact. I remember what I thought the freedom of my childhood, in which the fruitful place was something I took for granted. Just as I took for granted Zoe's appearance every morning on my school vacations—in the sense that I knew she would be there. That she would always be the one to visit me. The perishing world of my grandfather's graces at the table, if I ever seriously thought about it, was somewhere else.

81     Our souls were affected by the beauty of Jamaica, as much as they were affected by our fears of darkness.

82     There is no ending to this piece of writing. There is no way to end it. As I read back over it, I see that we/they/I may become confused in the mind of the reader: but these pronouns have always co-existed in my mind. The Rastas talk of the "I and I"—a pronoun in which they combine themselves with Jah. Jah is a contraction of Jahweh and Jehova, but to me always sounds like the beginning of Jamaica. I and Jamaica is who I am. No matter how far I travel—how deep the ambivalence I feel about ever returning. And Jamaica is a place in which we/they/I connect and disconnect—change place.

## CONSIDERATIONS

1. In her last paragraph, Cliff says, "There is no ending to this piece of writing." In paragraph 52: "the whole business is very complicated." In paragraph 70: "None of this is as simple as it may sound." In paragraph 64: "I may in fact lose touch with who I am." In what way might such candid admissions serve the writer or the reader?

2. Which passages seem to be carefully thought out? Which seem to be the most impulsively written?

3. Michelle Cliff writes of the complicating fact of variations of skin color, as does Julia Alvarez, in "A White Woman of Color" (page 18). Write a comparative essay on the two accounts.

4. How does Cliff's childhood friendship with Zoe contribute to the general drift of the essay?

5. Paragraph 40 ends with the word "Yes," punctuated as though it were a sentence. What else does that sentence say besides "Yes"?

6. At the end of the little story Cliff tells in paragraph 79, why did the gift-bearing guest run away from the maid and cry, "My God, I can't, I can't"? What has this to do with Michelle Cliff?

7. Read Jamaica Kincaid's essay "On Seeing England for the First Time" (page 346). Then write an explanation of how Cliff's essay may help one understand Kincaid's hatred of England.

*Judith Ortiz Cofer (b. 1952) came to the United States from Puerto Rico when she was four. She moved back and forth between Puerto Rico and Brooklyn, where her father was stationed in the Brooklyn Navy Yard. The conflict of places was a conflict within her soul. We take this essay from her* Silent Dancing, *subtitled* A Partial Remembrance of a Puerto Rican Childhood.

*Many writers who learn English as a second language seem not handicapped but invigorated by learning to write in a second tongue. Cofer writes, "I never cease to experiment with [language]. . . . It was a challenge, not only to learn English, but to master it enough to teach it and—the ultimate goal—to write poetry in it."*

*Judith Ortiz Cofer's essay is constructed carefully, sometimes by means of images the way a poem is. She interprets these images to give the memoir its impetus. Look at the way, in the beginning, she uses yellow, green, and degrees of skin color. "Everything was color-coded, including the children."*

— **18** —

# JUDITH ORTIZ COFER
## *Primary Lessons*

1    My mother walked me to my first day at school at La Escuela Segundo Ruiz Belvis, named after the Puerto Rican patriot born in our town. I remember yellow cement with green trim. All the classrooms had been painted these colors to identify them as government property. This was true all over the Island. Everything was color-coded, including the children, who wore uniforms from first through twelfth grade. We were a midget army in white and brown, led by the hand to our battleground. From practically every house in our barrio emerged a crisply ironed uniform inhabited by the savage creatures we had become over a summer of running wild in the sun.

2    At my grandmother's house where we were staying until my father returned to Brooklyn Yard in New York and sent for us, it had been complete chaos, with several children to get ready for school. My mother had

"Primary Lessons" by Judith Ortiz Cofer is reprinted with permission from the publisher of *Silent Dancing: A Partial Remembrance of a Puerto Rican Childhood* (Houston: Arte Público Press—University of Houston, 1990).

pulled my hair harder than usual while braiding it, and I had dissolved into a pool of total self-pity. I wanted to stay home with her and Mamá, to continue listening to stories in the late afternoon, to drink *café con leche* with them, and to play rough games with my many cousins. I wanted to continue living the dream of summer afternoons in Puerto Rico, and if I could not have it, then I wanted to go back to Paterson, New Jersey, back to where I imagined our apartment waited, peaceful and cool for the three of us to return to our former lives. Our gypsy lifestyle had convinced me, at age six, that one part of life stops and waits for you while you live another for a while—and if you don't like the present, you can always return to the past. Buttoning me into my stiff blouse while I tried to squirm away from her, my mother attempted to explain to me that I was a big girl now and should try to understand that, like all the other children my age, I had to go to school.

"What about him?" I yelled pointing at my brother who was loung- 3
ing on the tile floor of our bedroom in his pajamas, playing quietly with a toy car.

"He's too young to go to school, you know that. Now stay still." 4
My mother pinned me between her thighs to button my skirt, as she had learned to do from Mamá, from whose grip it was impossible to escape.

"It's not fair, it's not fair. I can't go to school here. I don't speak 5
Spanish." It was my final argument, and it failed miserably because I was shouting my defiance in the language I claimed not to speak. Only I knew what I meant by saying in Spanish that I did not speak Spanish. I had spent my early childhood in the United States, where I lived in a bubble created by my Puerto Rican parents in a home where two cultures and languages became one. I learned to listen to the English from the television with one ear while I heard my mother and father speaking in Spanish with the other. I thought I was an ordinary American kid—like the children on the shows I watched—and that everyone's parents spoke a secret second language at home. When we came to Puerto Rico right before I started first grade, I switched easily to Spanish. It was the language of fun, of summertime games. But school—that was a different matter.

I made one last desperate attempt to make my mother see reason: 6
"Father will be very angry. You know that he wants us to speak good English." My mother, of course, ignored me as she dressed my little brother in his playclothes. I could not believe her indifference to my father's wishes. She was usually so careful about our safety and the many other areas that he was forever reminding her about in his letters. But I was right, and she knew it. Our father spoke to us in English as much as possible, and he corrected my pronunciation constantly—not "jes" but "y-es." Y-es, sir. How could she send me to school to learn Spanish when we would be returning to Paterson in just a few months?

But, of course, what I feared was not language, but loss of freedom. 7
At school there would be no playing, no stories, only lessons. It would

not matter if I did not understand a word, and I would not be allowed to make up my own definitions. I would have to learn silence. I would have to keep my wild imagination in check. Feeling locked into my stiffly starched uniform, I only sensed all this. I guess most children can intuit their loss of childhood's freedom on that first day of school. It is separation anxiety too, but mother is just the guardian of the "playground" of our early childhood.

8      The sight of my cousins in similar straits comforted me. We were marched down the hill of our barrio where Mamá's robin-egg-blue house stood at the top. I must have glanced back at it with yearning. Mamá's house—a place built for children—where anything that could be broken had already been broken by my grandmother's early batch of offspring (they ranged in age from my mother's oldest sisters to my uncle who was six months older than me). Her house had long since been made child-proof. It had been a perfect summer place. And now it was September— the cruelest month for a child.

9      *La Mrs.*, as all the teachers were called, waited for her class of first-graders at the door of the yellow and green classroom. She too wore a uniform: It was a blue skirt and a white blouse. This teacher wore black high heels with her "standard issue." I remember this detail because when we were all seated in rows she called on one little girl and pointed to the back of the room where there were shelves. She told the girl to bring her a shoebox from the bottom shelf. Then, when the box had been placed in her hands, she did something unusual. She had the little girl kneel at her feet and take the pointy high heels off her feet and replace them with a pair of satin slippers from the shoe box. She told the group that every one of us would have a chance to do this if we behaved in her class. Though confused about the prize, I soon felt caught up in the competition to bring *La Mrs.* her slippers in the morning. Children fought over the privilege.

10     Our first lesson was English. In Puerto Rico, every child has to take twelve years of English to graduate from school. It is the law. In my parents' school days, all subjects were taught in English. The U.S. Department of Education had specified that as a U.S. territory, the Island had to be "Americanized," and to accomplish this task, it was necessary for the Spanish language to be replaced in one generation through the teaching of English in all schools. My father began his school day by saluting the flag of the United States and singing "America" and "The Star-Spangled Banner" by rote, without understanding a word of what he was saying. The logic behind this system was that, though the children did not understand the English words, they would remember the rhythms. Even the games the teacher's manuals required them to play became absurd adaptations. "Here We Go Round the Mulberry Bush" became "Here We Go Round the Mango Tree." I have heard about the confusion caused by the use of a primer in which the sounds of animals were featured. The children were forced to accept that a rooster says

*cockadoodledoo,* when they knew perfectly well from hearing their own roosters each morning that in Puerto Rico a rooster says *cocorocó.* Even the vocabulary of their pets was changed; there are still family stories circulating about the bewilderment of a first-grader coming home to try to teach his dog to speak in English. The policy of assimilation by immersion failed on the Island. Teachers adhered to it on paper, substituting their own materials for the texts, but no one took their English home. In due time, the program was minimized to the one class in English per day that I encountered when I took my seat in *La Mrs.'s* first grade class.

Catching us all by surprise, she stood very straight and tall in front of us and began to sing in English:    11

> Pollito  —  Chicken
> Gallina  —  Hen
> Lápiz  —  Pencil
> Y Pluma  —  Pen.

"Repeat after me, children: Pollito—Chicken," she commanded in    12
her heavily accented English that only I understood, being the only child in the room who had ever been exposed to the language. But I too remained silent. No use making waves or showing off. Patiently *La Mrs.* sang her song and gestured for us to join in. At some point it must have dawned on the class that this silly routine was likely to go on all day if we did not "repeat after her." It was not her fault that she had to follow the rule in her teacher's manual stating that she must teach English *in* English, and that she must not translate, but merely repeat her lesson in English until the children "begin to respond" more or less "unconsciously." This was one of the vestiges of the regimen followed by her predecessors in the last generation. To this day I can recite "Pollito—Chicken" mindlessly, never once pausing to visualize chicks, hens, pencils, or pens.

I soon found myself crowned "teacher's pet" without much effort    13
on my part. I was a privileged child in her eyes simply because I lived in "Nueva York," and because my father was in the navy. His name was an old one in our pueblo, associated with once-upon-a-time landed people and long-gone money. Status is judged by unique standards in a culture where, by definition, everyone is a second-class citizen. Remembrance of past glory is as good as titles and money. Old families living in decrepit old houses rank over factory workers living in modern comfort in cement boxes—all the same. The professions raise a person out of the dreaded "sameness" into a niche of status, so that teachers, nurses, and everyone who went to school for a job were given the honorifics of *El Míster* or *La Mrs.* by the common folks, people who were likely to be making more money in American factories than the poorly paid educators and government workers.

14    My first impressions of the hierarchy began with my teacher's shoe-changing ceremony and the exaggerated respect she received from our parents. *La Mrs.* was always right, and adults scrambled to meet her requirements. She wanted all our schoolbooks covered in the brown paper now used for paper bags (used at that time by the grocer to wrap meats and other foods). That first week of school the grocer was swamped with requests for paper which he gave away to the women. That week and the next, he wrapped produce in newspapers. All school projects became family projects. It was considered disrespectful at Mamá's house to do homework in privacy. Between the hours when we came home from school and dinner time, the table was shared by all of us working together with the women hovering in the background. The teachers communicated directly with the mothers, and it was a matriarchy of far-reaching power and influence.

15    There was a black boy in my first-grade classroom who was also the teacher's pet but for a different reason than I: I did not have to do anything to win her favor; he would do anything to win a smile. He was as black as the cauldron that Mamá used for cooking stew and his hair was curled into tight little balls on his head—*pasitas*, like little raisins glued to his skull, my mother had said. There had been some talk at Mamá's house about this boy; Lorenzo was his name. I later gathered that he was the grandson of my father's nanny. Lorenzo lived with Teresa, his grandmother, having been left in her care when his mother took off for "Los Nueva Yores" shortly after his birth. And they were poor. Everyone could see that his pants were too big for him—hand-me-downs—and his shoe soles were as thin as paper. Lorenzo seemed unmindful of the giggles he caused when he jumped up to erase the board for *La Mrs.* and his baggy pants rode down to his thin hips as he strained up to get every stray mark. He seemed to relish playing the little clown when she asked him to come to the front of the room and sing his phonetic version of "o-bootifool, forpashios-keeis," leading the class in our incomprehensible tribute to the American flag. He was a bright, loving child, with a talent for song and mimicry that everyone commented on. He should have been chosen to host the PTA show that year instead of me.

16    At recess one day, I came back to the empty classroom to get something. My cup? My nickel for a drink from the kiosk man? I don't remember. But I remember the conversation my teacher was having with another teacher. I remember because it concerned me, and because I memorized it so that I could ask my mother to explain what it meant.

17    "He is a funny *negrito*, and, like a parrot, he can repeat anything you teach him. But his Mamá must not have the money to buy him a suit."

18    "I kept Rafaelito's First Communion suit; I bet Lorenzo could fit in it. It's white with a bow-tie," the other teacher said.

19    "But, Marisa," laughed my teacher, "in that suit, Lorenzo would look like a fly drowned in a glass of milk."

Both women laughed. They had not seen me crouched at the back   20
of the room, digging into my schoolbag. My name came up then.

"What about the Ortiz girl? They have money."   21

"I'll talk to her mother today. The superintendent, *El Americano*   22
from San Juan, is coming down for the show. How about if we have her
say her lines in both Spanish and English?"

The conversation ends there for me. My mother took me to   23
Mayagüez and bought me a frilly pink dress and two crinoline petticoats
to wear underneath so that I looked like a pink and white parachute with
toothpick legs sticking out. I learned my lines, "Padres, maestros, Mr.
Leonard, bienvenidos/Parents, teachers, Mr. Leonard, welcome. . . ."
My first public appearance. I took no pleasure in it. The words were formal and empty. I had simply memorized them. My dress pinched me at
the neck and arms, and made me itch all over.

I had asked my mother what it meant to be a "mosca en un vaso de   24
leche," a fly in a glass of milk. She had laughed at the image, explaining
that it meant being "different," but that it wasn't something I needed to
worry about.

## CONSIDERATIONS ——

1. Although she was born in Puerto Rico, Judith Cofer objected as strenuously as
she could (she was six at the time) when her mother dressed her for her first day at the
Puerto Rican school. "I can't go to school here," she cried, "I don't speak Spanish."
Why did that argument fail, and what was the child really afraid of? Compare hers with
your own memories of the first day of school.

2. "Everything was color-coded, including the children," writes Cofer in her
opening paragraph. Is that merely an observation, or does it convey a larger implication
about the child's situation?

3. Compare and contrast Cofer's childhood experience with language and that of
Maxine Hong Kingston in "Silence" (page 361).

4. Cofer takes some time in her essay to explain how the children learned that
people were sorted out by their social or political class. Teachers, for example, were
called "La Mrs." What was one dramatic way her teacher taught that lesson? Compare
that with your own experience (or lack thereof) in learning to respect teachers.

5. What did Cofer remember most vividly from the little story of Lorenzo? Why
does she include that story in her essay?

6. The U.S. Department of Education attempted to "Americanize" Puerto Rico by
replacing the Spanish language in one generation through the teaching of English in all
schools. Use this in an argumentative essay setting forth your views on bilingual teaching in the United States.

*Billy Collins (b. 1941) has most recently selected his poems for*
*Sailing Alone around My Room (2001). This book made news in*
*2000 when Random House could not come to an agreement with*
*the University of Pittsburgh Press to reprint Collins's earlier work.*
*Publication was delayed. As Collins remarked, "It's nice to be*
*fought over by a couple of presses. Poets don't usually enjoy this*
*sort of tug-of-war."*

## — 19

# BILLY COLLINS
## *Marginalia*

Sometimes the notes are ferocious,
skirmishes against the author
raging along the borders of every page
in tiny black script.
If I could just get my hands on you,
Kierkegaard, or Conor Cruise O'Brien,
they seem to say,
I would bolt the door and beat some logic into your head.

Other comments are more offhand, dismissive—
"Nonsense." "Please!" "HA!!"—
that kind of thing.
I remember once looking up from my reading,
my thumb as a bookmark,
trying to imagine what the person must look like
who wrote "Don't be a ninny"
alongside a paragraph in *The Life of Emily Dickinson.*

Students are more modest
needing to leave only their splayed footprints
along the shore of the page.
One scrawls "Metaphor" next to a stanza of Eliot's.
Another notes the presence of "Irony"
fifty times outside the paragraphs of *A Modest Proposal.*

Or they are fans who cheer from the empty bleachers,
hands cupped around their mouths.
"Absolutely," they shout                                      25
to Duns Scotus and James Baldwin.
"Yes." "Bull's-eye." "My man!"
Check marks, asterisks, and exclamation points
rain down along the sidelines.

And if you have managed to graduate from college               30
without ever having written "Man vs. Nature"
in a margin, perhaps now
is the time to take one step forward.

We have all seized the white perimeter as our own
and reached for a pen if only to show                          35
we did not just laze in an armchair turning pages;
we pressed a thought into the wayside,
planted an impression along the verge.

Even Irish monks in their cold scriptoria
jotted along the borders of the Gospels                        40
brief asides about the pains of copying,
a bird singing near their window,
or the sunlight that illuminated their page—
anonymous men catching a ride into the future
on a vessel more lasting than themselves.                      45

And you have not read Joshua Reynolds,
they say, until you have read him
enwreathed with Blake's furious scribbling.

Yet the one I think of most often,
the one that dangles from me like a locket,                    50
was written in the copy of *Catcher in the Rye*
I borrowed from the local library
one slow, hot summer.
I was just beginning high school then,
reading books on a davenport in my parents' living room,       55
and I cannot tell you
how vastly my loneliness was deepened,
how poignant and amplified the world before me seemed,
when I found on one page

a few greasy looking smears                                    60
and next to them, written in soft pencil—
by a beautiful girl, I could tell,
whom I would never meet—
"Pardon the egg salad stains, but I'm in love."

*Frank Conroy (b. 1936) grew up in various towns along the eastern seaboard and attended Haverford College in Pennsylvania. He plays jazz piano, was director of the literature program at the National Endowment for the Arts from 1982 to 1987, and now directs the writing program at the University of Iowa. In 1985 he published a collection of short stories called* Midair *and in 1993 his novel* Body and Soul.

*He writes about his early life in* Stop-Time, *from which we take this episode. His prose possesses the qualities that make the best reminiscence: details feel exact and bright, though miniature with distance, like the landscape crafted for background to model trains.*

— **20** ————————————————————————————

# FRANK CONROY
## *A Yo-Yo Going Down*

————————————————————————————

1    The common yo-yo is crudely made, with a thick shank between two widely spaced wooden disks. The string is knotted or stapled to the shank. With such an instrument nothing can be done except the simple up-down movement. My yo-yo, on the other hand, was a perfectly balanced construction of hard wood, slightly weighted, flat, with only a sixteenth of an inch between the halves. The string was not attached to the shank, but looped over it in such a way as to allow the wooden part to spin freely on its own axis. The gyroscopic effect thus created kept the yo-yo stable in all attitudes.

2    I started at the beginning of the book and quickly mastered the novice, intermediate, and advanced stages, practicing all day every day in the woods across the street from my house. Hour after hour of practice, never moving to the next trick until the one at hand was mastered.

3    The string was tied to my middle finger, just behind the nail. As I threw—with your palm up, make a fist; throw down your hand, fingers unfolding, as if you were casting grain—a short bit of string would tighten across the sensitive pad of flesh at the tip of my finger. That was

the critical area. After a number of weeks I could interpret the condition of the string, the presence of any imperfections on the shank, but most importantly the exact amount of spin or inertial energy left in the yo-yo at any given moment—all from that bit of string on my fingertip. As the throwing motion became more and more natural I found I could make the yo-yo "sleep" for an astonishing length of time—fourteen or fifteen seconds—and still have enough spin left to bring it back to my hand. Gradually the basic moves became reflexes. Sleeping, twirling, swinging, and precise aim. Without thinking, without even looking, I could run through trick after trick involving various combinations of the elemental skills, switching from one to the other in a smooth continuous flow. On particularly good days I would hum a tune under my breath and do it all in time to the music.

Flicking the yo-yo expressed something. The sudden, potentially   4
comic extension of one's arm to twice its length. The precise neatness of it, intrinsically soothing, as if relieving an inner tension too slight to be noticeable, the way a man might hitch up his pants simply to enact a re-assuring gesture. It felt good. The comfortable weight in one's hand, the smooth, rapid-descent down the string, ending with a barely audible snap as the yo-yo hung balanced, spinning, pregnant with force and the slave of one's fingertip. That it was vaguely masturbatory seems inescapable. I doubt that half the pubescent boys in America could have been captured by any other means, as, in the heat of the fad, half of them were. A single Loop-the-Loop might represent, in some mysterious way, the act of mas-turbation, but to break down the entire repertoire into the three stages of throw, trick, and return representing erection, climax, and detumescence seems immoderate.

The greatest pleasure in yo-yoing was an abstract pleasure—watch-   5
ing the dramatization of simply physical laws, and realizing they would never fail if a trick was done correctly. The geometric purity of it! The string wasn't just a string, it was a tool in the enactment of theorems. It was a line, an idea. And the top was an entirely different sort of idea, a gyroscope, capable of storing energy and of interacting with the line. I re-member the first time I did a particularly lovely trick, one in which the sleeping yo-yo is swung from right to left while the string is interrupted by an extended index finger. Momentum carries the yo-yo in a circular path around the finger, but instead of completing the arc the yo-yo falls on the taut string between the performer's hands, where it continues to spin in an upright position. My pleasure at that moment was as much from the beauty of the experiment as from pride. Snapping apart my hands I sent the yo-yo into the air above my head, bouncing it off noth-ing, back into my palm.

I practiced the yo-yo because it pleased me to do so, without the   6
slightest application of will power. It wasn't ambition that drove me, but the nature of yo-yoing. The yo-yo represented my first organized attempt to control the outside world. It fascinated me because I could see my

progress in clearly defined stages, and because the intimacy of it, the almost spooky closeness I began to feel with the instrument in my hand, seemed to ensure that nothing irrelevant would interfere. I was, in the language of jazz, "up tight" with my yo-yo, and finally free, in one small area at least, of the paralyzing sloppiness of life in general.

7      The first significant problem arose in the attempt to do fifty consecutive Loop-the-Loops. After ten or fifteen the yo-yo invariably started to lean and the throws became less clean, resulting in loss of control. I almost skipped the whole thing because fifty seemed excessive. Ten made the point. But there it was, written out in the book. To qualify as an expert you had to do fifty, so fifty I would do.

8      It took me two days, and I wouldn't have spent a moment more. All those Loop-the-Loops were hard on the strings. Time after time the shank cut them and the yo-yo went sailing off into the air. It was irritating, not only because of the expense (strings were a nickel each, and fabricating your own was unsatisfactory), but because a random element had been introduced. About the only unforeseeable disaster in yo-yoing was to have your string break, and here was a trick designed to do exactly that. Twenty-five would have been enough. If you could do twenty-five clean Loop-the-Loops you could do fifty or a hundred. I supposed they were simply trying to sell strings and went back to the more interesting tricks.

9      The witty nonsense of Eating Spaghetti, the surprise of The Twirl, the complex neatness of Cannonball, Backwards Round the World, or Halfway Round the World—I could do them all, without false starts or sloppy endings. I could do every trick in the book. Perfectly.

10     The day was marked on the kitchen calendar (God Gave Us Bluebell Natural Bottled Gas). I got on my bike and rode into town. Pedaling along the highway I worked out with the yo-yo to break in a new string. The twins were appearing at the dime store.

11     I could hear the crowd before I turned the corner. Kids were coming on bikes and on foot from every corner of town, rushing down the streets like madmen. Three or four policemen were busy keeping the street clear directly in front of the store, and in a small open space around the doors some of the more adept kids were running through their tricks, showing off to the general audience or stopping to compare notes with their peers. Standing at the edge with my yo-yo safe in my pocket, it didn't take me long to see I had them all covered. A boy in a sailor hat could do some of the harder tricks, but he missed too often to be a serious threat. I went inside.

12     As Ramos and Ricardo performed I watched their hands carefully, noticing little differences in style, and technique. Ricardo was a shade classier, I thought, although Ramos held an edge in the showy two-handed stuff. When they were through we went outside for the contest.

13     "Everybody in the alley!" Ramos shouted, his head bobbing an inch or two above the others. "Contest starting now in the alley!" A hundred

excited children followed the twins into an alley beside the dime store and lined up against the wall.

"Attention all kids!" Ramos yelled, facing us from the middle of the street like a drill sergeant. "To qualify for contest you got to Rock the Cradle. You got to rock yo-yo in cradle four time. Four time! Okay? Three time no good. Okay. Everybody happy?" There were murmurs of disappointment and some of the kids stepped out of line. The rest of us closed ranks. Yo-yos flicked nervously as we waited. "Winner receive grand prize. Special Black Beauty Prize Yo-Yo with Diamonds," said Ramos, gesturing to his brother who smiled and held up the prize, turning it in the air so we could see the four stones set on each side. ("The crowd gasped . . ." I want to write. Of course they didn't. They didn't make a sound, but the impact of the diamond yo-yo was obvious.) We'd never seen anything like it. One imagined how the stones would gleam as it revolved, and how much prettier the tricks would be. The ultimate yo-yo! The only one in town! Who knew what feats were possible with such an instrument? All around me a fierce, nervous resolve was settling into the contestants, suddenly skittish as race-horses.          14

"Ricardo will show trick with Grand Prize Yo-Yo. Rock the Cradle four time!"          15

"One!" cried Ramos.          16

"Two!" the kids joined in.          17

"Three!" It was really beautiful. He did it so slowly you would have thought he had all the time in the world. I counted seconds under my breath to see how long he made it sleep.          18

"Four!" said the crowd.          19

"Thirteen" I said to myself as the yo-yo snapped back into his hand. Thirteen seconds. Excellent time for that particular trick.          20

"Attention all kids!" Ramos announced. "Contest start now at head of line."          21

The first boy did a sloppy job of gathering his string but managed to rock the cradle quickly four times.          22

"Okay." Ramos tapped him on the shoulder and moved to the next boy, who fumbled. "Out." Ricardo followed, doing an occasional Loop-the-Loop with the diamond yo-yo. "Out . . . out . . . okay," said Ramos as he worked down the line.          23

There was something about the man's inexorable advance that unnerved me. His decisions were fast, and there was no appeal. To my surprise I felt my palms begin to sweat. Closer and closer he came, his voice growing louder, and then suddenly he was standing in front of me. Amazed, I stared at him. It was as if he'd appeared out of thin air.          24

"What happen boy, you swarrow bubble gum?"          25

The laughter jolted me out of it. Blushing, I threw down my yo-yo and executed a slow Rock the Cradle, counting the four passes and hesitating a moment at the end so as not to appear rushed.          26

"Okay." He tapped my shoulder. "Good."          27

28    I wiped my hands on my blue jeans and watched him move down the line. "Out . . . out . . . out." He had a large mole on the back of his neck.

29    Seven boys qualified. Coming back, Ramos called out, "Next trick Backward Round the World! Okay? Go!"

30    The first two boys missed, but the third was the kid in the sailor hat. Glancing quickly to see that no one was behind him, he hunched up his shoulder, threw, and just barely made the catch. There was some loose string in his hand, but not enough to disqualify him.

31    Number four missed, as did number five, and it was my turn. I stepped forward, threw the yo-yo almost straight up over my head, and as it began to fall pulled very gently to add some speed. It zipped neatly behind my legs and there was nothing more to do. My head turned to one side, I stood absolutely still and watched the yo-yo come in over my shoulder and slap into my hand. I added a Loop-the-Loop just to show the tightness of the string.

32    "Did you see that?" I heard someone say.

33    Number seven missed, so it was between myself and the boy in the sailor hat. His hair was bleached by the sun and combed up over his forehead in a pompadour, held from behind by the white hat. He was a year or two older than me. Blinking his blue eyes nervously, he adjusted the tension of his string.

34    "Next trick Cannonball! Cannonball! You go first this time," Ramos said to me.

35    Kids had gathered in a circle around us, those in front quiet and attentive, those in back jumping up and down to get a view." "Move back for room," Ricardo said, pushing them back. "More room, please."

36    I stepped into the center and paused, looking down at the ground. It was a difficult trick. The yo-yo had to land exactly on the string and there was a chance I'd miss the first time. I knew I wouldn't miss twice. "Can I have one practice?"

37    Ramos and Ricardo consulted in their mother tongue, and then Ramos held up his hands. "Attention all kids! Each boy have one practice before trick."

38    The crowd was then silent, watching me. I took a deep breath and threw, following the fall of the yo-yo with my eyes, turning slightly, matador-fashion, as it passed me. My finger caught the string, the yo-yo came up and over, and missed. Without pausing I threw again. "Second time," I yelled, so there would be no misunderstanding. The circle had been too big. This time I made it small, sacrificing beauty for security. The yo-yo fell where it belonged and spun for a moment. (A moment I don't rush, my arms widespread, my eyes locked on the spinning toy. The Trick! There it is, brief and magic right before your eyes! My hands are frozen in the middle of a deaf-and-dumb sentence, holding the whole airy, tenuous statement aloft for everyone to see.) With a quick snap I broke up the trick and made my catch.

Ramos nodded. "Okay. Very good. Now next boy." 39

Sailor-hat stepped forward, wiping his nose with the back of his 40
hand. He threw once to clear the string.

"One practice," said Ramos. 41

He nodded. 42

"C'mon Bobby," someone said. "You can do it." 43

Bobby threw the yo-yo out to the side, made his move, and missed. 44
"Damn," he whispered. (He said "dahyum.") The second time he got
half-way through the trick before his yo-yo ran out of gas and fell impo-
tently off the string. He picked it up and walked away, winding slowly.

Ramos came over and held my hand in the air. "The winner!" he 45
yelled. "Grand prize Black Beauty Diamond Yo-Yo will now be
awarded."

Ricardo stood in front of me. "Take off old yo-yo." I loosened the 46
knot and slipped it off. "Put out hand." I held out my hand and he looped
the new string on my finger, just behind the nail, where the mark was.
"You like Black Beauty," he said, smiling as he stepped back. "Diamond
make pretty colors in the sun."

"Thank you," I said. 47

"Very good with yo-yo. Later we have contest for whole town. 48
Winner go to Miami for State Championship. Maybe you win. Okay?"

"Okay." I nodded. "Thank you." 49

A few kids came up to look at Black Beauty. I threw it once or twice 50
to get the feel. It seemed a bit heavier than my old one. Ramos and
Ricardo were surrounded as the kids called out their favorite tricks.

"Do Pickpocket! Pickpocket!" 51

"Do the Double Cannonball!" 52

"Ramos! Ramos! Do the Turkish Army!" 53

Smiling, waving their hands to ward off the barrage of requests, the 54
twins worked their way through the crowd toward the mouth of the alley. I watched them moving away and was immediately struck by a wave
of fierce and irrational panic. "Wait," I yelled, pushing through after
them. "Wait!"

I caught them on the street. 55

"No more today," Ricardo said, and then paused when he saw it 56
was me. "Okay. The champ. What's wrong? Yo-yo no good?"

"No. It's fine." 57

"Good. You take care of it." 58

"I wanted to ask when the contest is. The one where you get to go 59
to Miami."

"Later. After school begins." They began to move away. "We have 60
to go home now."

"Just one more thing," I said, walking after them. "What is the 61
hardest trick you know?"

Ricardo laughed. "Hardest trick is killing flies in air." 62

63    "No, no. I mean a real trick."

64    They stopped and looked at me. "There is a very hard trick," Ricardo said. "I don't do it, but Ramos does. Because you won the contest he will show you. But only once, so watch carefully."

65    We stepped into the lobby of the Sunset Theater. Ramos cleared his string. "Watch," he said, and threw. The trick started out like a Cannonball, and then unexpectedly folded up, opened again, and as I watched breathlessly the entire complex web spun around in the air, propelled by Ramos' two hands making slow circles like a swimmer. The end was like the end of a Cannonball.

66    "That's beautiful," I said, genuinely awed. "What's it called?"

67    "The Universe."

68    "The Universe," I repeated.

69    "Because it goes around and around," said Ramos, "like the planets."

## CONSIDERATIONS

1. List the ways in which Conroy says one can get pleasure from the yo-yo.

2. How much of "performance" is play? Would you use the word "performance" for the work of a painter, an opera singer, a tennis star, a poet? Are professional athletes paid to play? What is the difference between work and play?

3. One respected writer says that "play is the direct opposite of seriousness"; yet writers like Conroy are serious in recalling their childhood play. Can you resolve this apparent contradiction? "I practiced the yo-yo because it pleased me to do so, without the slightest application of will power," Conroy writes. Consider the relevance or irrelevance of will power to pleasure.

4. Conroy's essay might be divided into two major sections. Where would you draw the dividing line? Describe the two sections in terms of the author's intention. In the second section, the author makes constant use of dialogue; in the first, there is none. Why?

5. In paragraph 14, Conroy interrupts his narrative with a parenthetical remark about himself as the writer: "('The crowd gasped . . .' I want to write. Of course they didn't. They didn't make a sound, but the impact of the diamond yo-yo was obvious.)" Are such glimpses of the writer useful or merely distracting? Discuss.

— 21 —

# BERNARD COOPER
## *Burl's*

I

1   I loved the restaurant's name, a compact curve of a word. Its sign, five big letters rimmed in neon, hovered above the roof. I almost never saw the sign with its neon lit; my parents took me there for early summer dinners, and even by the time we left—father cleaning his teeth with a toothpick, mother carrying steak bones in a doggie bag—the sky was still bright. Heat rippled off the cars parked along Hollywood Boulevard, the asphalt gummy from hours of sun.

2   With its sleek architecture, chrome appliances, and arctic temperature, Burl's offered a refuge from the street. We usually sat at one of the booths in front of the plate-glass windows. During our dinner, people came to a halt before the news-vending machine on the corner and burrowed in their pockets and purses for change.

3   The waitresses at Burl's wore brown uniforms edged in checked gingham. From their breast pockets frothed white lace handkerchiefs. In between reconnaissance missions to the table, they busied themselves behind the counter and shouted "Tuna to travel" or "Scorch that patty" to a harried short-order cook who manned the grill. Miniature pitchers of cream and individual pats of butter were extracted from an industrial refrigerator. Coca-Cola shot from a glinting spigot. Waitresses dodged and bumped one another, frantic as atoms.

4      My parents usually lingered after the meal, nursing cups of coffee while I played with the beads of condensation on my glass of ice water, tasted Tabasco sauce, or twisted pieces of my paper napkin into mangled animals. One evening, annoyed with my restlessness, my father gave me a dime and asked me to buy him a *Herald Examiner* from the vending machine in front of the restaurant.

5      Shouldering open the heavy glass door, I was seared by a sudden gust of heat. Traffic roared past me and stirred the air. Walking toward the newspaper machine, I held the dime so tightly it seemed to melt in my palm. Duty made me feel large and important. I inserted the dime and opened the box, yanking a *Herald* from the spring contraption that held it as tight as a mousetrap. When I turned around, paper in hand, I saw two women walking toward me.

6      Their high heels clicked on the sun-baked pavement. They were tall, broad-shouldered women who moved with a mixture of haste and defiance. They'd teased their hair into nearly identical black beehives. Dangling earrings flashed in the sun, brilliant as prisms. Each of them wore the kind of clinging, strapless outfit my mother referred to as a cocktail dress. The silky fabric—one dress was purple, the other pink—accentuated their breasts and hips and rippled with insolent highlights. The dresses exposed their bare arms, the slope of their shoulders, and the smooth, powdered plane of flesh where their cleavage began.

7      I owned at the time a book called *Things for Boys and Girls to Do.* There were pages to color, intricate mazes, and connect-the-dots. But another type of puzzle came to mind as I watched those women walking toward me: What's Wrong With This Picture? Say the drawing of a dining room looked normal at first glance; on closer inspection, a chair was missing its leg and the man who sat atop it wore half a pair of glasses.

8      The women had Adam's apples.

9      The closer they came, the shallower my breathing was. I blocked the sidewalk, an incredulous child stalled in their path. When they saw me staring, they shifted their purses and linked their arms. There was something sisterly and conspiratorial about their sudden closeness. Though their mouths didn't move, I thought they might have been communicating without moving their lips, so telepathic did they seem as they joined arms and pressed together, synchronizing their heavy steps. The pages of the *Herald* fluttered in the wind. I felt them against my arm, light as batted lashes.

10      The woman in pink shot me a haughty glance and yet she seemed pleased that I'd taken notice, hungry to be admired by a man, or even an awestruck eight-year-old boy. She tried to stifle a grin, her red lipstick more voluptuous than the lips it painted. Rouge deepened her cheekbones. Eye shadow dusted her lids, a clumsy abundance of blue. Her face was like a page in *Things for Boys and Girls to Do,* colored by a kid who went outside the lines.

At close range, I saw that her wig was slightly askew. I was certain 11
it was a wig because my mother owned several; three Styrofoam heads
lined a shelf in my mother's closet; upon them were perched a Page-Boy,
an Empress, and a Baby-Doll, all in shades of auburn. The woman in the
pink dress wore her wig like a crown of glory.

But it was the woman in the purple dress who passed nearest me, 12
and I saw that her jaw was heavily powdered, a half-successful attempt
to disguise the tell-tale shadow of a beard. Just as I noticed this, her heel
caught on a crack in the pavement and she reeled on her stilettos. It was
then that I witnessed a rift in her composure, a window through which I
could glimpse the shades of maleness that her dress and wig and makeup
obscured. She shifted her shoulders and threw out her hands like a surfer
riding a curl. The instant she regained her balance, she smoothed her
dress, patted her hair, and sauntered onward.

Any woman might be a man. The fact of it clanged through the 13
chambers of my brain. In broad day, in the midst of traffic, with my parents drinking coffee a few feet away, I felt as if everything I understood,
everything I had taken for granted up to that moment—the curve of the
earth, the heat of the sun, the reliability of my own eyes—had been
squeezed out of me. Who were those men? Did they help each other get
inside those dresses? How many other people and things were not what
they seemed? From the back, the impostors looked like women once
again, slinky and curvaceous, purple and pink. I watched them disappear
into the distance, their disguises so convincing that other people on the
street seemed to take no notice, and for a moment I wondered if I had
imagined the whole encounter, a visitation by two unlikely muses.

Frozen in the middle of the sidewalk, I caught my reflection in the 14
window of Burl's, a silhouette floating between his parents. They faced
one another across a table. Once the solid embodiments of woman and
man, pedestrians and traffic appeared to pass through them.


## II

There were some mornings, seconds before my eyes opened and my 15
senses gathered into consciousness, that the child I was seemed to hover
above the bed, and I couldn't tell what form my waking would take—the
body of a boy or the body of a girl. Finally stirring, I'd blink against the
early light and greet each incarnation as a male with mild surprise. My
sex, in other words, didn't seem to be an absolute fact so much as a pleasant, recurring accident.

By the age of eight, I'd experienced this groggy phenomenon several 16
times. Those ethereal moments above my bed made waking up in the
tangled blankets, a boy steeped in body heat, all the more astonishing.
That this might be an unusual experience never occurred to me; it was
one among a flood of sensations I could neither name nor ignore.

17    And so, shocked as I was when those transvestites passed me in front of Burl's, they confirmed something about which I already had an inkling: the hazy border between the sexes. My father, after all, raised his pinky when he drank from a teacup, and my mother looked as faded and plain as my father until she fixed her hair and painted her face.

18    Like most children, I once thought it possible to divide the world into male and female columns. Blue/Pink. Rooster/Hens. Trousers/ Skirts. Such divisions were easy, not to mention comforting, for they simplified matter into compatible pairs. But there also existed a vast range of things that didn't fit neatly into either camp: clocks, milk, telephones, grass. There were nights I fell into a fitful sleep while trying to sex the world correctly.

19    Nothing typified the realms of male and female as clearly as my parents' walk-in closets. Home alone for any length of time, I always found my way inside them. I could stare at my parents' clothes for hours, grateful for the stillness and silence, haunting the very heart of their privacy.

20    The overhead light in my father's closet was a bare bulb. Whenever I groped for the chain in the dark, it wagged back and forth and resisted my grasp. Once the light clicked on, I saw dozens of ties hanging like stalactites. A monogrammed silk bathrobe sagged from a hook, a gift my father had received on a long-ago birthday and, thinking it fussy, rarely wore. Shirts were cramped together along the length of an aluminum pole, their starched sleeves sticking out as if in a half-hearted gesture of greeting. The medicinal odor of mothballs permeated the boxer shorts that were folded and stacked in a built-in drawer. Immaculate underwear was proof of a tenderness my mother couldn't otherwise express; she may not have touched my father often, but she laundered his boxers with infinite care. Even back then, I suspected that a sense of duty was the final erotic link between them.

21    Sitting in a neat row on the closet floor were my father's boots and slippers and dress shoes. I'd try on his wingtips and clomp around, slipping out of them with every step. My wary, unnatural stride made me all the more desperate to effect some authority. I'd whisper orders to imagined lackeys and take my invisible wife in my arms. But no matter how much I wanted them to fit, those shoes were as cold and hard as marble.

22    My mother's shoes were just as uncomfortable, but a lot more fun. From a brightly colored array of pumps and slingbacks, I'd pick a pair with the glee and deliberation of someone choosing a chocolate. Whatever embarrassment I felt was overwhelmed by the exhilaration of being taller in a pair of high heels. Things will look like this someday, I said to myself, gazing out from my new and improved vantage point as if from a crow's nest. Calves elongated, arms akimbo, I gauged each step so that I didn't fall over and moved with what might have passed for grace had someone seen me, a possibility I scrupulously avoided by locking the door.

23    Back and forth I went. The longer I wore a pair of heels, the better my balance. In the periphery of my vision, the shelf of wigs looked like a

throng of kindly bystanders. Light streamed down from a high window, causing crystal bottles to glitter, the air ripe with perfume. A makeup mirror above the dressing table invited my self-absorption. Sound was muffled. Time slowed. It seemed as if nothing bad could happen as long as I stayed within those walls.

Though I'd never been discovered in my mother's closet, my par-   24 ents knew that I was drawn toward girlish things—dolls and jump rope and jewelry—as well as to the games and preoccupations that were expected of a boy. I'm not sure now if it was my effeminacy itself that bothered them as much as my ability to slide back and forth, without the slightest warning, between male and female mannerisms. After I'd finished building the model of an F-17 bomber, say, I'd sit back to examine my handiwork, pursing my lips in concentration and crossing my legs at the knee.

## III

One day my mother caught me standing in the middle of my bed-   25 room doing an imitation of Mary Injijikian, a dark, overeager Armenian girl with whom I believed myself to be in love, not only because she was pretty but because I wanted to be like her. Collector of effortless A's, Mary seemed to know all the answers in class. Before the teacher had even finished asking a question, Mary would let out a little grunt and practically levitate out of her seat, as if her hand were filled with helium. "Could we please hear from someone else today besides Miss Injijikian," the teacher would say. *Miss Injijikian.* Those were the words I was repeating over and over to myself when my mother caught me. To utter them was rhythmic, delicious, and under their spell I raised my hand and wiggled like Mary. I heard a cough and spun around. My mother froze in the doorway. She clutched the folded sheets to her stomach and turned without saying a word. My sudden flush of shame confused me. Weren't boys supposed to swoon over girls? Hadn't I seen babbling, heartsick men in a dozen movies?

Shortly after the Injijikian incident, my parents decided to send me   26 to gymnastics class at the Los Angeles Athletic Club, a brick relic of a building on Olive Street. One of the oldest establishments of its kind in Los Angeles, the club prohibited women from the premises. My parents didn't have to say it aloud: they hoped a fraternal atmosphere would toughen me up and tilt me toward the male side of my nature.

My father drove me downtown so I could sign up for the class, meet   27 the instructor, and get a tour of the place. On the way there, he reminisced about sports. Since he'd grown up in a rough Philadelphia neighborhood, sports consisted of kick-the-can or rolling a hoop down the street with a stick. The more he talked about his physical prowess, the more convinced I became that my day-dreams and shyness were a disappointment to him.

28    The hushed lobby of the athletic club was paneled in dark wood. A few solitary figures were hidden in wing chairs. My father and I introduced ourselves to a man at the front desk who seemed unimpressed by our presence. His aloofness unnerved me, which wasn't hard considering that no matter how my parents put it, I knew their sending me here was a form of disapproval, a way of banishing the part of me they didn't care to know.

29    A call went out over the intercom for someone to show us around. While we waited, I noticed that the sand in the standing ashtrays had been raked into perfect furrows. The glossy leaves of the potted plants looked as if they'd been polished by hand. The place seemed more like a well-tended hotel than an athletic club. Finally, a stoop-shouldered old man hobbled toward us, his head shrouded in a cloud of white hair. He wore a T-shirt that said "Instructor"; his arms were so wrinkled and anemic, I thought I might have misread it. While we followed him to the elevator, I readjusted my expectations, which had involved fantasies of a hulking drill sergeant barking orders at a flock of scrawny boys.

30    The instructor, mumbling to himself and never turning around to see if we were behind him, showed us where the gymnastics class took place. I'm certain the building was big, but the size of the room must be exaggerated by a trick of memory, because when I envision it, I picture a vast and windowless warehouse. Mats covered the wooden floor. Here and there, in remote and lonely pools of light, stood a pommel horse, a balance beam, and parallel bars. Tiers of bleachers rose into darkness. Unlike the cloistered air of a closet, the room seemed incomplete without a crowd.

31    Next we visited the dressing room, empty except for a naked middle-aged man. He sat on a narrow bench and clipped his formidable toenails. Moles dotted his back. He glistened like a fish.

32    We continued to follow the instructor down an aisle lined with numbered lockers. At the far end, steam billowed from the doorway that led to the showers. Fresh towels stacked on a nearby table made me think of my mother; I knew she liked to have me at home with her—I was often her only companion—and I resented her complicity in the plan to send me here.

33    The tour ended when the instructor gave me a sign-up sheet. Only a few names preceded mine. They were signatures, or so I imagined, of other soft and wayward sons.

## IV

34    When the day of the first gymnastics class arrived, my mother gave me money and a gym bag and sent me to the corner of Hollywood and Western to wait for a bus. The sun was bright, the traffic heavy. While I sat there, an argument raged inside my head, the familiar, battering debate between the wish to be like other boys and the wish to be like my-

self. Why shouldn't I simply get up and go back home, where I'd be left alone to read and think? On the other hand, wouldn't life be easier if I liked athletics, or learned to like them?

No sooner did I steel my resolve to get on the bus than I thought of something better: I could spend the morning wandering through Woolworth's, then tell my parents I'd gone to the class. But would my lie stand up to scrutiny? As I practiced describing phantom gymnastics, I became aware of a car circling the block. It was a large car in whose shaded interior I could barely make out the driver, but I thought it might be the man who owned the local pet store. I'd often gone there on the pretext of looking at the cocker spaniel puppies huddled together in their pen, but I really went to gawk at the owner, whose tan chest, in the V of his shirt, was the place I most wanted to rest my head. Every time the man moved, counting stock or writing a receipt, his shirt parted, my mouth went dry, and I smelled the musk of sawdust and dogs.

I found myself hoping that the driver was the man who ran the pet store. I was thrilled by the unlikely possibility that the sight of me, slumped on a bus bench in my T-shirt and shorts, had caused such a man to circle the block. Up to that point in my life, lovemaking hovered somewhere in the future, an impulse a boy might aspire to but didn't indulge. And there I was, sitting on a bus bench in the middle of the city, dreaming I could seduce an adult. I showered the owner of the pet store with kisses and, as aquariums bubbled, birds sang, and mice raced in a wire wheel, slipped my hand beneath his shirt. The roar of traffic brought me to my senses. I breathed deeply and blinked against the sun. I crossed my legs at the knee in order to hide an erection. My fantasy left me both drained and changed. The continent of sex had drifted closer.

The car made another round. This time the driver leaned across the passenger seat and peered at me through the window. He was a complete stranger, whose gaze filled me with fear. It wasn't the surprise of not recognizing him that frightened me, it was what I did recognize—the unmistakable shame in his expression, and the weary temptation that drove him in circles. Before the car behind him honked, he mouthed "hello" and cocked his head. What now, he seemed to be asking. A bold, unbearable question.

I bolted to my feet, slung the gym bag over my shoulder, and hurried toward home. Now and then I turned around to make sure he wasn't trailing me, both relieved and disappointed when I didn't see his car. Even after I became convinced that he wasn't at my back—my sudden flight had scared him off—I kept turning around to see what was making me so nervous, as if I might spot the source of my discomfort somewhere on the street. I walked faster and faster, trying to outrace myself. Eventually, the bus I was supposed to have taken roared past. Turning the corner, I watched it bob eastward.

Closing the kitchen door behind me, I vowed never to leave home again. I was resolute in this decision without fully understanding why, or what it was I hoped to avoid; I was only aware of the need to hide and a vague notion, fading fast, that my trouble had something to do with sex. Already the mechanism of self-deception was at work. By the time my mother rushed into the kitchen to see why I'd returned so early, the thrill I'd felt while waiting for the bus had given way to indignation.

40      I poured out the story of the man circling the block and protested, with perhaps too great a passion, my own innocence. "I was just sitting there," I said again and again. I was so determined to deflect suspicion away from myself, and to justify my missing the class, that I portrayed the man as a grizzled pervert who drunkenly veered from lane to lane as he followed me halfway home.

41      My mother cinched her housecoat. She seemed moved and shocked by what I told her, if a bit incredulous, which prompted me to be more dramatic. "It wouldn't be safe," I insisted, "for me to wait at the bus stop again."

42      No matter how overwrought my story, I knew my mother wouldn't question it, wouldn't bring the subject up again; sex of any kind, especially sex between a man and a boy, was simply not discussed in our house. The gymnastics class, my parents agreed, was something I could do another time.

43      And so I spent the remainder of that summer at home with my mother, stirring cake batter, holding the dustpan, helping her fold the sheets. For a while I was proud of myself for engineering a reprieve from the athletic club. But as the days wore on, I began to see that my mother had wanted me with her all along, and forcing that to happen wasn't such a feat. Soon a sense of compromise set in; by expressing disgust for the man in the car, I'd expressed disgust for an aspect of myself. Now I had all the time in the world to sit around and contemplate my desire for men. The days grew long and stifling and hot, an endless sentence of self-examination.

44      Only trips to the pet store offered any respite. Every time I went there, I was too electrified with longing to think about longing in the abstract. The bell tinkled above the door, animals stirred within their cages, and the handsome owner glanced up from his work.

## V

45      I handed my father the *Herald.* He opened the paper and disappeared behind it. My mother stirred her coffee and sighed. She gazed at the sweltering passersby and probably thought herself lucky. I slid into the vinyl booth and took my place beside my parents.

46      For a moment, I considered asking them about what had happened on the street, but they would have reacted with censure and alarm, and I sensed there was more to the story than they'd ever be willing to tell me. Men in dresses were only the tip of the iceberg. Who knew what other wonders existed—a boy, for example, who wanted to kiss a man—exceptions the world did its best to keep hidden.

It would be years before I heard the word "transvestite," so I strug-  47
gled to find a word for what I'd seen. "He-she" came to mind, as lilting as
"Injijikian." "Burl's" would have been perfect, like "boys" and "girls"
spliced together, but I can't claim to have thought of this back then.

I must have looked stricken as I tried to figure it all out, because my  48
mother put down her coffee cup and asked if I was O.K. She stopped just
short of feeling my forehead. I assured her I was fine, but something
within me had shifted, had given way to a heady doubt. When the wait-
ress came and slapped down our check—"Thank You," it read, "Dine out
more often"—I wondered if her lofty hairdo or the breasts on which her
nametag quaked were real. Wax carnations bloomed at every table.
Phony wood paneled the walls. Plastic food sat in a display case: fried
eggs, a hamburger sandwich, a sundae topped with a garish cherry.

## *CONSIDERATIONS*

1. In addition to the questions about gender that bothered the boy, what even
larger question seems to be forming as, at the end of the essay, he observes the wax carnations on every table, the phony wood paneling, the plastic food in a display case?

2. Thinking as a writer looking about for material to use in developing a thesis,
comment on the ways Cooper draws on childhood experiences to illustrate the points
he is making as an adult.

3. In addition to the shape of the restaurant's sign, "Burl's," what was there about
it that brought it to mind many years later? How is that relevant to how the eight-year-
old boy felt?

4. Would you say that Cooper grew up in a household where he felt free to ask his
parents about anything? Support your answer by quoting relevant passages in the essay.

5. Michelle Cliff's "If I Could Write This in Fire" (page 115) shows that she had
real doubts about *what* she was. Cooper expresses similar doubts. Do you think that
other children (some? many? most?) are troubled by such questions of identity? Use
your own experience or that of others to develop an essay on the subject.

6. "The continent of sex had drifted closer," Cooper writes at the end of paragraph 36. Is the writer's metaphor merely bizarre, or is it an effective use of his imagination? Consider all that is going on in the boy's mind. Can a writer be carried away by
his own figure of speech? See also the last sentence of paragraph 4 in Frank Conroy's "A
Yo-Yo Going Down" (page 136).

*John Daniel (b. 1948) was born in South Carolina and now lives
and teaches in Oregon. He won an Oregon Book Award for
Creative Non-Fiction, a genre at which he excels, writing essays
out of the natural world for* Audubon *and* Wilderness.

*We take this excerpt from his book* Looking After *(1996),
about his mother and her remarkable life, which ends in the
Alzheimer's that he describes in prose sometimes realistic and
symbolic at the same time. Take note of how Daniel uses the last
leaf of autumn, at the end of the essay.*

— **22**

# JOHN DANIEL
## *Looking After*

1    In my mother's last years she ate her breakfast and lunch at a small
oak table in our kitchen, by a window that looks out on the limbs and
leaves of a Pacific dogwood. The tree, with ferns below it, makes a small,
dapple-lighted garden of that side of the house, screening us from Tom
the neighbor's place next door. The pink blossoms gave my mother pleasure in the spring—though, like me, she preferred dogwoods that bloom
white—and she also enjoyed the sparrows and finches and chickadees
that came to the bird feeder with a mossy roof that hung from the dogwood's central limbs. My mother took a long time with her meals. She
looked out the window as she ate, and sometimes the food on her plate
seemed to surprise her when she looked down and saw it. She usually sat
at the table long after I had finished my meal and gone out back again to
write or off in the car on errands. My mother spent many hours with that
dogwood tree.

2    I can see her clearly as I write this, and I can smell her, too. It's a
fresh and musty smell of sandalwood and damp sweat, of skin cream and
urine, and it's as vivid in my memory as her stooped back and curling
white hair, as clear as her slow, flat-footed shuffle in bare feet or slippers,
her hands flying out sporadically to a wall or table edge to steady her on

her way. That smell of her old age is as sure in my mind as her quick scowl and sharp remarks, her laughter and childlike smile, her frowning concentration as she tried to listen with her bad ears, the look of her reddened eyes behind her glasses as she doggedly tracked lines of print across page after page of the books and papers and magazines she kept piled beside her on her bed.

Her eyesight, unlike her hearing, stayed sharp until the end. As we     3
drove in the car she would sometimes speak out loud the names she read on street signs and billboards, as if to fix our location in memory—or maybe simply for the exercise, for the pleasure of forming words, for the happiness of being out of the house and in motion through the streets of Portland. Her eyes saw clearly the birds that came to the kitchen feeder, but she often asked their names. Sometimes she asked about the same bird at breakfast and again at lunch, sometimes at the same meal.

"What *is* that one," she would say, intently, "with the bright red     4
. . ." She gestured at her throat with her long, purpled fingers.

"That's the finch," I'd tell her.     5

*"Finch,"* she'd say. "That's what I thought."     6

A black tomcat, not ours, once in a while would rocket from the     7
ferns and almost capture a finch or sparrow, upsetting the feeder in a spray of millet and sunflower seed. My usual response was to charge out the back door and throw a stick of firewood at the fleeing cat. My mother would watch through the window, looking at me and the wobbling feeder as if the scene had never occurred before and was as delightful as anything that had ever happened in the history of the world. And sometimes a particular image would come to her, a known shape of words, a recurrent visitation from the mists and shadows of the past.

"Do you remember," she would ask, in that way she had of giving     8
each syllable its full enunciation, "when the cat brought a poor bird to the door, and I scolded it? And you were there, all of six"—she'd be smiling now—"and you said, 'Mother, it's a cat's *nature* to hunt birds.'"

"I remember," I'd tell her, though in truth I didn't remember saying     9
it so much as I remembered hearing her tell the story about me. I remembered being remembered. But I cherished those moments, brief and infrequent as they were, when the two of us could pause together in the shared light of each other's recall. In those moments we were all at home—me, my mother, the family and friends we spoke of. I felt myself resting then, relaxing from some continuous effort I hadn't known I'd been engaged in and would shortly resume.

Sometimes when she brought up a glimpse of the past, I would try     10
to draw her out, try to enlarge the landscape of her recall. But memory for my mother was a thing of moments, as mutable as the lightplay in the dogwood tree. What I searched for with my questions usually wasn't there. She knew the names I spoke—my father's, my brother's, the places we had lived—but much of the time the names had come loose from their moorings, like boats adrift on the sea. If I told a family story she

would recognize it with pleasure, but my mother in herself had few stories left.

11      In the hot summer months the dogwood leaves curled on the tree,
and then as fall arrived and the light turned pale, the leaves took on a
tinge of red—a subtle red, nothing vivid—and began to drop and gather
on the ground. The gray Northwestern season that starts in mid October
and lasts through late spring was hard on my mother's spirits. In the
spring she could watch the dogwood twigs hopefully for evidence of
buds. In the fall she could only watch the tree unleaving itself. By late
November of her last autumn the branches shook in the wind with only
a smattering of leaves still clinging, and there came a morning when
only one was left, on a lower branch near the window at my mother's
end of the breakfast table. She pointed it out to me, and again the next
few mornings. "Still there," she said, smiling as if with a secret we
shared.

12      One morning as I heard her feet begin to shuffle from her bedroom,
I glanced at the window and saw that the leaf had fallen. I pointed as I
poured her coffee. "It's gone," I said.

13      She gazed blankly out the window.

14      "The leaf is gone," I told her. "The last leaf."

15      "Oh," she answered vaguely. "The leaf."

16      Because it was absent from her present sight she had only the
faintest memory of it. The leaf was profoundly gone for her, and soon
would be absolutely gone, but in my own mind it still hangs on. I can see
it now, I can't stop seeing it: a dark curled form infused with red, a beautiful ghost that by chance or willfulness still holds to its place in the
world. In memory I circle and circle that leaf. I watch it much more carefully than I watched it before. I want to know what makes it hold on in
the cold wind, how it somehow emerged out of sap and fiber and grew in
the sun and remains now only by habit, by a spell of nature, by nothing
at all. It's only memory that holds it now, and memory, at last, that lets
it go.

## CONSIDERATIONS

1. In his opening paragraph, Daniel details at some length the trees, flowers, and
birds that occupy his mother at her breakfast and lunch. What do you think is his purpose in beginning the essay this way?

2. Daniel's own description of his mother in paragraph 2 is devoid of sentimentality. Investigate the term "sentimentality" and explain how and why this writer avoids
it. One way to do this would be to write a paragraph of your own, deliberately senti-
mentalizing the memories of his mother, to substitute for Daniel's. Which of the two
paragraphs is the more useful in terms of Daniel's intent?

3. Impaired memory is a notable feature of Alzheimer's disease, yet moments of
shared memory with his mother gave Daniel the feeling that "we were all at home . . .

I felt myself resting then, relaxing from some continuous effort I hadn't known I'd been engaged in and would shortly resume." Re-read paragraphs 8, 9, and 10 and explain the connection between memory and the "continuous effort" Daniel does not define.

4. What is going on, literally and metaphorically, in paragraph 16?

5. Sooner or later everyone must acknowledge the fact of aging. When and how does that acknowledgment come about? Except among the elderly, the subject is generally avoided. Why? Look into some of the several studies of aging available and write an essay that deals with some of these questions.

*Joan Didion (b. 1934) worked as an editor in New York and then returned to her native California, where she supports herself by writing. She has collaborated on screenplays (often with her husband, John Gregory Dunne), including* A Star Is Born *(1976). Best known for her novels—*Play It As It Lays *appeared in 1971 and* Democracy *in 1984—she is also admired for her essays, collected in* Slouching towards Bethlehem *(1969),* The White Album *(1979), and* After Henry *(1992). "Last Words" appeared in the* New Yorker.

*Didion begins this essay with a passage from Ernest Hemingway and analyzes its construction with a meticulous eye, an analysis basic to her thesis. After speaking of the effect of Hemingway's style on a generation of writers, she recounts his often difficult life. Her subject is the degradation of the author after his death by the exploitative publication of unfinished work.*

— **23** —————————————————————————

# JOAN DIDION
## *Last Words*

———————————————————————————————

In the late summer of that year we lived in a house in a village that looked across the river and the plain to the mountains. In the bed of the river there were pebbles and boulders, dry and white in the sun, and the water was clear and swiftly moving and blue in the channels. Troops went by the house and down the road and the dust they raised powdered the leaves of the trees. The trunks of the trees too were dusty and the leaves fell early that year and we saw the troops marching along the road and the dust rising and leaves, stirred by the breeze, falling and the soldiers marching and afterward the road bare and white except for the leaves.

1    So goes the famous first paragraph of Ernest Hemingway's *A Farewell to Arms*, which I was moved to reread by the recent announcement that what was said to be Hemingway's last novel would be published posthumously next year. That paragraph, which was published in

1929, bears examination: four deceptively simple sentences, one hundred and twenty-six words, the arrangement of which remains as mysterious and thrilling to me now as it did when I first read them, at twelve or thirteen, and imagined that if I studied them closely enough and practiced hard enough I might one day arrange one hundred and twenty-six such words myself. Only one of the words has three syllables. Twenty-two have two. The other hundred and three have one. Twenty-four of the words are "the," fifteen are "and." There are four commas. The liturgical cadence of the paragraph derives in part from the placement of the commas (their presence in the second and fourth sentences, their absence in the first and third), but also from that repetition of "the" and of "and," creating a rhythm so pronounced that the omission of "the" before the word "leaves" in the fourth sentence ("and we saw the troops marching along the road and the dust rising and leaves, stirred by the breeze, falling") casts exactly what it was meant to cast, a chill, a premonition, a foreshadowing of the story to come, the awareness that the author has already shifted his attention from late summer to a darker season. The power of the paragraph, offering as it does the illusion but not the fact of specificity, derives precisely from this kind of deliberate omission, from the tension of withheld information. In the late summer of *what* year? *What* river, *what* mountains, *what* troops?

We all know the "life" of the man who wrote that paragraph. The rather reckless attractions of the domestic details became fixed in the national memory stream: *Ernest and Hadley have no money, so they ski at Cortina all winter. Pauline comes to stay. Ernest and Hadley are at odds with each other over Pauline, so they all take refuge at Juan-les-Pins. Pauline catches cold, and recuperates at the Waldorf-Astoria.* We have seen the snapshots: the celebrated author fencing with the bulls at Pamplona, fishing for marlin off Havana, boxing at Bimini, crossing the Ebro with the Spanish loyalists, kneeling beside "his" lion or "his" buffalo or "his" oryx on the Serengeti Plain. We have observed the celebrated author's survivors, read his letters, deplored or found lessons in his excesses, in his striking of attitudes, in the humiliations of his claim to personal machismo, in the degradations both derived from and revealed by his apparent tolerance for his own celebrity.

"This is to tell you about a young man named Ernest Hemingway, who lives in Paris (an American), writes for the *transatlantic review* and has a brilliant future," F. Scott Fitzgerald wrote to Maxwell Perkins in 1924. "I'd look him up right away. He's the real thing." By the time "the real thing" had seen his brilliant future both realized and ruined, he had entered the valley of extreme emotional fragility, of depressions so grave that by February of 1961, after the first of what would be two courses of shock treatment, he found himself unable to complete even the single sentence he had agreed to contribute to a ceremonial volume for President John F. Kennedy. Early on the Sunday morning of July 2, 1961, the celebrated author got out of his bed in Ketchum, Idaho, went downstairs, took a double-barreled Boss shotgun from a storage room in the cellar, and emptied both barrels into the center of his forehead. "I went downstairs," his fourth wife, Mary Welsh Hemingway, reported in her 1976 memoir, *How It Was*, "saw a crumpled heap of bathrobe and blood, the shotgun lying in the disintegrated flesh, in the front vestibule of the sitting room."

4       The didactic momentum of the biography was such that we sometimes forgot that this was a writer who had in his time made the English language new, changed the rhythms of the way both his own and the next few generations would speak and write and think. The very grammar of a Hemingway sentence dictated, or was dictated by, a certain way of looking at the world, a way of looking but not joining, a way of moving through but not attaching, a kind of romantic individualism distinctly adapted to its time and source. If we bought into those sentences, we would see the troops marching along the road, but we would not necessarily march with them. We would report, but not join. We would make, as Nick Adams made in the Nick Adams stories and as Frederic Henry made in *A Farewell to Arms*, a separate peace: "In the fall the war was always there, but we did not go to it any more."

5       So pervasive was the effect of this Hemingway diction that it became the voice not only of his admirers but even of those whose approach to the world was in no way grounded in romantic individualism. I recall being surprised, when I was teaching George Orwell in a class at Berkeley in 1975, by how much of Hemingway could be heard in his sentences. "The hills opposite us were grey and wrinkled like the skins of elephants," Orwell had written in *Homage to Catalonia* in 1938. "The hills across the valley of the Ebro were long and white," Hemingway had written in "Hills Like White Elephants" in 1927. "A mass of Latin words falls upon the facts like soft snow, blurring the outlines and covering up all the details," Orwell had written in *Politics and the English Language* in 1946. "I was always embarrassed by the words sacred, glorious, and sacrifice and the expression in vain," Hemingway had written in *A Farewell to Arms* in 1929. "There were many words that you could not stand to hear and finally only the names of places had dignity."

6       This was a man to whom words mattered. He worked at them, he understood them, he got inside them. When he was twenty-four years old and reading submissions to Ford Madox Ford's *transatlantic review* he would sometimes try rewriting them, just for practice. His wish to be survived by only the words he determined fit for publication would have seemed clear enough. "I remember Ford telling me that a man should always write a letter thinking of how it would read to posterity," he wrote to Arthur Mizener in 1950. "This made such a bad impression on me that I burned every letter in the flat including Ford's." In a letter dated May 20, 1958, addressed "To my Executors" and placed in his library safe at La Finca Vigia, he wrote, "It is my wish that none of the letters writ-

ten by me during my lifetime shall be published. Accordingly, I hereby request and direct you not to publish or consent to the publication by others of any such letters."

His widow and executor, Mary Welsh Hemingway, describing the 7 burden of this restriction as one that "caused me continuous trouble, and disappointment to others," eventually chose to violate it, publishing excerpts from certain letters in *How It Was* and granting permission to Carlos Baker to publish some six hundred others in his *Ernest Hemingway: Selected Letters, 1917–1961.* "There can be no question about the wisdom and rightness of the decision," Baker wrote, for the letters "will not only instruct and entertain the general reader but also provide serious students of literature with the documents necessary to the continuing investigation of the life and achievements of one of the giants of twentieth-century American fiction."

The peculiarity of being a writer is that the entire enterprise in- 8 volves the mortal humiliation of seeing one's own words in print. The risk of publication is the grave fact of the life, and, even among writers less inclined than Hemingway to construe words as the manifest expression of personal honor, the notion that words one has not risked publishing should be open to "continuing investigation" by "serious students of literature" could not be calculated to kindle enthusiasm. "Nobody likes to be tailed," Hemingway himself had in 1952 advised one such investigator, Charles A. Fenton of Yale, who on the evidence of the letters was tormenting Hemingway by sending him successive drafts of what would be *The Apprenticeship of Ernest Hemingway: The Early Years.* "You do not like to be tailed, investigated, queried about, by any amateur detective no matter how scholarly or how straight. You ought to be able to see that, Fenton." A month later Hemingway tried again. "I think you ought to drop the entire project," he wrote to Fenton, adding, "It is impossible to arrive at any truth without the co-operation of the person involved. That co-operation involves very nearly as much effort as for a man to write his autobiography." A few months later, he was still trying:

> In the first page or pages of your Mss. I found so many errors of fact that I could spend the rest of this winter re-writing and giving you the true gen and I would not be able to write anything of my own at all. . . . Another thing: You have located unsigned pieces by me through pay vouchers. But you do not know which pieces were changed or re-written by the copy desk and which were not. I know nothing worse for a writer than for his early writing which has been re-written and altered to be published without permission as his own.
>
> Actually I know few things worse than for another writer to collect a fellow writer's journalism which his fellow writer has elected not to preserve because it is worthless and publish it.
>
> Mr. Fenton I feel very strongly about this. I have written you so before and I write you now again. Writing that I do not wish to

publish, you have no right to publish. I would no more do a thing
like that to you than I would cheat a man at cards or rifle his desk or
wastebasket or read his personal letters.

9      It might seem safe to assume that a writer who commits suicide
has been less than entirely engaged by the work he leaves unfinished, yet
there appears to have been not much question about what would happen
to the unfinished Hemingway manuscripts. These included not only
"the Paris stuff" (as he called it), or *A Moveable Feast* (as Scribner's
called it), which Hemingway had in fact shown to Scribner's in 1959 and
then withdrawn for revision, but also the novels later published under
the titles *Islands in the Stream* and *The Garden of Eden*, several Nick
Adams stories, what Mrs. Hemingway called the "original treatment" of
the bullfighting pieces published by *Life* before Hemingway's death (this
became *The Dangerous Summer*), and what she described as "his semi-
fictional account of our African safari," three selections from which she
had published in *Sports Illustrated* in 1971 and 1972.

10     What followed was the systematic creation of a marketable product, a discrete body of work different in kind from, and in fact tending to
obscure, the body of work published by Hemingway in his lifetime. So
successful was the process of branding this product that in October, ac-
cording to the House & Home section of the *New York Times*,
Thomasville Furniture Industries introduced an "Ernest Hemingway
Collection" at the International Home Furnishings Market in High
Point, North Carolina, offering "96 pieces of living, dining and bedroom
furniture and accessories" in four themes, "Kenya," "Key West,"
"Havana," and "Ketchum." "We don't have many heroes today," Marla
A. Metzner, the president of Fashion Licensing of America, told the
*Times*. "We're going back to the great icons of the century, as heroic
brands." Ms. Metzner, according to the *Times*, not only "created the
Ernest Hemingway brand with Hemingway's three sons, Jack, Gregory
and Patrick," but "also represents F. Scott Fitzgerald's grandchildren,
who have asked for a Fitzgerald brand."

11     That this would be the logical outcome of posthumous marketing
cannot have been entirely clear to Mary Welsh Hemingway. During
Hemingway's lifetime, she appears to have remained cool to the marketing impulses of A. E. Hotchner, whose thirteen-year correspondence
with Hemingway gives the sense that he regarded the failing author not
as the overextended and desperate figure the letters suggest but as an infinite resource, a mine to be worked, an element to be packaged into his
various entertainment and publishing "projects." The widow tried to
stop the publication of Hotchner's *Papa Hemingway*, and, although the
correspondence makes clear that Hemingway himself had both trusted
and relied heavily on its author, presented him in her own memoir
mainly as a kind of personal assistant, a fetcher of manuscripts, an
arranger of apartments, a Zelig apparition in crowd scenes. "When the

*Ile de France* docked in the Hudson River at noon, March 27, we were elated to find Charlie Sweeny, my favorite general, awaiting us, together with Lillian Ross, Al Horowitz, Hotchner and some others."

In this memoir, which is memorable mainly for the revelation of its author's rather trying mixture of quite striking competence and strategic incompetence (she arrives in Paris on the day it is liberated and scores a room at the Ritz, but seems bewildered by the domestic problem of how to improve the lighting of the dining room at La Finca Vigia), Mary Welsh Hemingway shared her conviction, at which she appears to have arrived in the face of considerable contrary evidence, that her husband had "clearly" expected her to publish "some, if not all, of his work." The guidelines she set for herself in this task were instructive: "Except for punctuation and the obviously overlooked 'ands' and 'buts' we would present his prose and poetry to readers as he wrote it, letting the gaps lie where they were."

12

Well, there you are. You care about the punctuation or you don't, and Hemingway did. You care about the "ands" and the "buts" or you don't, and Hemingway did. You think something is in shape to be published or you don't, and Hemingway didn't. "This is it; there are no more books," Charles Scribner III told the *New York Times* by way of announcing the "Hemingway novel" to be published in July of 1999, to celebrate the centennial year of his birth. This piece of work, for which the title *True at First Light* was chosen from the text ("In Africa a thing is true at first light and a lie by noon and you have no more respect for it than for the lovely, perfect weed-fringed lake you see across the sunbaked salt plain"), is said to be the novel on which Hemingway was trying intermittently to work between 1954, when he and Mary Welsh Hemingway returned from the safari in Kenya which provides its narrative, and his suicide in 1961.

13

This "African novel" seems to have presented at first only the resistance that characterizes the early stage of any novel. In September of 1954, Hemingway wrote to Bernard Berenson from Cuba about the adverse effect of air conditioning on this thing he was doing: "You get the writing done but it's as false as though it were done in the reverse of a greenhouse. Probably I will throw it all away, but maybe when the mornings are alive again I can use the skeleton of what I have written and fill it in with the smells and the early noises of the birds and all the lovely things of this finca which are in the cold months very much like Africa." In September of 1955, he wrote again to Berenson, this time on a new typewriter, explaining that he could not use his old one "because it has page 594 of the [African] book in it, covered over with the dust cover, and it is unlucky to take the pages out." In November of 1955, he reported to Harvey Breit, of the *New York Times*, "Am on page 689 and wish me luck kid." In January of 1956, he wrote to his attorney, Alfred Rice, that he had reached page 810.

14

15      There then falls, in the *Selected Letters*, a certain silence on the matter of this African novel. Eight hundred and ten pages or no, there comes a point at which every writer knows when a book is not working, and every writer also knows when the reserves of will and energy and memory and concentration required to make the thing work simply may not be available. "You just have to *go on* when it is worst and most helpless—there is only one thing to do with a novel and that is go straight on through to the end of the damn thing," Hemingway had written to F. Scott Fitzgerald in 1929, when Fitzgerald was blocked on the novel that would be published in 1934 as *Tender Is the Night.*

16      In 1929, Hemingway was thirty. His concentration, or his ability to "*go on* when it is worst and most helpless," was still such that he had continued rewriting *A Farewell to Arms* while trying to deal, in the aftermath of his father's suicide in December of 1928, with the concerns of his mother, his sixteen-year-old sister, and his thirteen-year-old brother. "Realize of course that thing for me to do is not worry but get to work—finish my book properly so I can help them out with the proceeds," he had written to Maxwell Perkins within days of his father's funeral, and six weeks later he delivered the finished manuscript. He had seen one marriage destroyed, but not yet three. He was not yet living with the residue of the two 1954 plane crashes that had ruptured his liver, his spleen, and one of his kidneys, collapsed his lower intestine, crushed a vertebra, left first-degree burns on his face and head, and caused concussion and losses of vision and hearing. "Alfred this was a very rough year even before we smashed up in the air-craft," he wrote to Alfred Rice, who had apparently questioned his tax deductions for the African safari:

> But I have a diamond mine if people will let me alone and let me dig the stones out of the blue mud and then cut and polish them. If I can do it I will make more money for the Government than any Texas oilman that gets his depreciation. But I have been beat-up worse than you can be and still be around and I should be working steadily on getting better and then write and not think nor worry about anything else.

17      "The literal details of writing," Norman Mailer once told an interviewer, "involve one's own physiology or metabolism. You begin from a standing start and have to accelerate yourself to the point of cerebration where the words are coming—well, and in order. All writing is generated by a certain minimum of ego: you must assume a position of authority in saying that the way I'm writing it is the only way it happened. Writer's block, for example, is simply a failure of ego." In August of 1956, Hemingway advised Charles Scribner, Jr., that he had "found it impossible to resume work on the Africa book without some disciplinary writing," and so was writing short stories.

In November of 1958, he mentioned to one of his children that he    18
wanted to "finish book" during a winter stay in Ketchum, but the
"book" at issue was now "the Paris stuff." In April of 1960, he told
Scribner to scratch this still untitled Paris book from the fall list: "Plenty
of people will probably think that we have no book and that it is like all
the outlines that Scott had and borrowed money on that he never could
have finished but you know that if I did not want the chance to make it
even better it could be published exactly as you saw it with a few corrections of Mary's typing." Ten months later, and five months before his
death, in a letter written to his editor at Scribner's between the two
courses of shock treatment administered to him at the Mayo Clinic in
Rochester, Minnesota, the writer tried, alarmingly, to explain what he
was doing:

> Have material arranged as chapters—they come to 18—and am
> working on the last one—No *19*—also working on title. This is very
> difficult. (Have my usual long list—something wrong with all of them
> but am working toward it—Paris has been used so often it blights
> anything.) In pages typed they run 7, 14, 5, 6, 9½, 6, 11, 9, 8, 9, 4½,
> 3½, 8, 10½, 14½, 38½, 10, 3, 3: 177 pages + 5½ pages + 1¼ pages.

I recall listening, some years ago at a dinner party in Berkeley, to a    19
professor of English present *The Last Tycoon* as irrefutable proof that
F. Scott Fitzgerald was a bad writer. The assurance with which this judgment was offered so stunned me that I had let it slip into the *donnée* of
the evening before I managed to object. *The Last Tycoon*, I said, was an
unfinished book, one we had no way of judging because we had no way of
knowing how Fitzgerald might have finished it. But of course we did, another guest said, and others joined in: We had Fitzgerald's "notes," we
had Fitzgerald's "outline," the thing was "entirely laid out." Only one of
us at the table that evening, in other words, saw a substantive difference
between writing a book and making notes for it, or "outlining it," or
"laying it out."

The most chilling scene ever filmed must be, for a writer, that mo-    20
ment in *The Shining* when Shelley Duvall looks at the manuscript on
which her husband has been working and sees, typed over and over again
on each of the hundreds of pages, only the single line: "All work and no
play makes Jack a dull boy." The manuscript for what became *True at
First Light* was, as Hemingway left it, some eight hundred and fifty pages
long. The manuscript as edited for publication is half that. This editing
was done by Hemingway's son Patrick, who has said that he limited his
editing to condensing (which inevitably works to alter what the author
may have intended, as anyone who has been condensed knows), changing only some of the place names, which may or may not have seemed a
logical response to the work of the man who wrote "There were many

words that you could not stand to hear and finally only the names of places had dignity."

21      This question of what should be done with what a writer leaves unfinished goes back, and is conventionally answered by citing works we might have lost had the dying wishes of their authors been honored. Virgil's *Aeneid* is mentioned. Franz Kafka's *The Trial* and *The Castle* are mentioned. In 1951, clearly shadowed by mortality, Hemingway judged that certain parts of a long four-part novel on which he had been working for a number of years were sufficiently "finished" to be published after his death, and specified his terms, which did not include the intrusion of any editorial hand and specifically excluded the publication of the unfinished first section. "The last two parts need no cutting at all," he wrote to Charles Scribner in 1951. "The third part needs quite a lot but it is very careful scalpel work and would need no cutting if I were dead. . . . The reason that I wrote you that you could always publish the last three parts separately is because I know you can in case through accidental death or any sort of death I should not be able to get the first part in proper shape to publish."

22      Hemingway himself, the following year, published the fourth part of this manuscript separately, as *The Old Man and the Sea*. The "first part" of the manuscript, the part not yet "in proper shape to publish," was, after his death, nonetheless published, as part of *Islands in the Stream*. In the case of the "African novel," or *True at First Light*, eight hundred and fifty pages reduced by half by someone other than their author can go nowhere the author intended them to go, but they can provide the occasion for a chat-show hook, a faux controversy over whether the part of the manuscript in which the writer on safari takes a Wakamba bride does or does not reflect a "real" event. The increasing inability of many readers to construe fiction as anything other than roman à clef, or the raw material of biography, is both indulged and encouraged. The *New York Times*, in its announcement of the publication of the manuscript, quoted Patrick Hemingway to this spurious point: "'Did Ernest Hemingway have such an experience?' he said from his home in Bozeman, Mont. 'I can tell you from all I know—and I don't know everything—he did not.'"

23      This is a denial of the idea of fiction, just as the publication of unfinished work is a denial of the idea that the role of the writer in his or her work is to make it. Those excerpts from *True at First Light* already published can be read only as something not yet made, notes, scenes in the process of being set down, words set down but not yet written. There are arresting glimpses here and there, fragments shored against what the writer must have seen as his ruin, and a sympathetic reader might well believe it possible that had the writer lived (which is to say had the writer found the will and energy and memory and concentration) he might have shaped the material, written it into being, made it work as the story the glimpses suggest, that of a man returning to a place he

loved and finding himself at three in the morning confronting the knowledge that he is no longer the person who loved it and will never now be the person he had meant to be. But of course such a possibility would have been in the end closed to this particular writer, for he had already written that story, in 1936, and called it "The Snows of Kilimanjaro." "Now he would never write the things that he had saved to write until he knew enough to write them well," the writer in "The Snows of Kilimanjaro" thought as he lay dying of gangrene in Africa. And then, this afterthought, the saddest story: "Well, he would not have to fail at trying to write them either."

## CONSIDERATIONS

1. What is the point of Didion's meticulous analysis of the Hemingway paragraph? Would the same method produce comparable results if applied to any other author? Try it out on another fiction writer in your text—Raymond Carver, Louise Erdrich, Flannery O'Connor, Tillie Olsen, Eudora Welty. Report the results and your conclusions about them in a short essay.

2. "There are many words that you could not stand to hear and finally only the names of places had dignity," wrote Hemingway. What were some of the words he referred to? Bear in mind that he wrote those lines in the late 1920s when the horrors of World War I had not been forgotten. Write an essay explaining why you think Hemingway could not stand them. Feel free to mention words that you cannot stand and, of course, explain.

3. In paragraph 5, Didion refers to George Orwell's famous essay "Politics and the English Language" (page 484) when she discusses Hemingway's fiction. Read the Orwell essay with Didion's comments in mind, then read the Hemingway short story "Hills Like White Elephants" (page 292), and decide whether or not Didion, Hemingway, and Orwell are concerned about the same thing.

4. Asked in an interview how much rewriting of his work he did, Hemingway said, "I re-wrote the ending to *Farewell to Arms,* the last page of it, thirty-nine times before I was satisfied." In another interview, the American humorist S. J. Perelman, when asked how many drafts of a story he writes, answered: "Thirty-seven. I once tried doing thirty-three, but something was lacking." What do you think Perelman was up to? Look up the term "parody" before you answer.

5. What did Didion find significant when a furniture maker introduced an "Ernest Hemingway Collection," and how did she use that peculiar bit of merchandising in her essay?

6. In paragraph 14, Hemingway reveals in a letter an odd little superstition that explains why he couldn't use his old typewriter for the letter. Do you admit to any little superstitions of your own? What superstitions have you observed in others? Build an essay on the part—large or small—that superstitions play in decision-making.

*Frederick Douglass (1817–1895) was born a slave in Maryland and escaped to Massachusetts in 1838. Later, he lectured against slavery and wrote of his experience. "Plantation Life" comes from* A Narrative of the Life of Frederick Douglass, an American Slave, Written by Himself *(1845). During the Civil War, he organized two regiments of black troops in Massachusetts; in the Reconstruction period, he worked for the government.*

*With his detailed memory, in a calm and dignified language, Frederick Douglass calmly sketches the atrocities of slavery in the United States. He did not view the problem from a distance.*

— **24** —

# FREDERICK DOUGLASS
## *Plantation Life*

1    My master's family consisted of two sons, Andrew and Richard; one daughter, Lucretia, and her husband, Captain Thomas Auld. They lived in one house, upon the home plantation of Colonel Edward Lloyd. My master was Colonel Lloyd's clerk and superintendent. He was what might be called the overseer of the overseers. I spent two years of childhood on this plantation in my old master's family. . . . As I received my first impressions of slavery on this plantation, I will give some description of it, and of slavery as it there existed. The plantation is about twelve miles north of Easton, in Talbot county, and is situated on the border of Miles River. The principal products raised upon it were tobacco, corn, and wheat. These were raised in great abundance; so that, with the products of this and the other farms belonging to him, he was able to keep in almost constant employment a large sloop, in carrying them to market at Baltimore. This sloop was named *Sally Lloyd*, in honor of one of the colonel's daughters. My master's son-in-law, Captain Auld, was master of the vessel; she was otherwise manned by the colonel's own slaves. Their names were Peter, Isaac, Rich, and Jake. These were esteemed very highly by the other slaves, and looked upon as the privileged ones of the plantation; for it was no small affair, in the eyes of the slaves, to be allowed to see Baltimore.

2    Colonel Lloyd kept from three to four hundred slaves on his home plantation, and owned a large number more on the neighboring farms belonging to him. The names of the farms nearest to the home plantation

were Wye Town and New Design. "Wye Town" was under the overseer-ship of a man named Noah Willis. New Design was under the overseer-ship of a Mr. Townsend. The overseers of these, and all the rest of the farms, numbering over twenty, received advice and direction from the managers of the home plantation. This was the great business place. It was the seat of government for the whole twenty farms. All disputes among the overseers were settled here. If a slave was convicted of any high misdemeanor, became unmanageable, or evinced a determination to run away, he was brought immediately here, severely whipped, put on board the sloop, carried to Baltimore, and sold to Austin Woolfolk, or some other slave-trader, as a warning to the slaves remaining.

Here, too, the slaves of all the other farms received their monthly    3
allowance of food, and their yearly clothing. The men and women slaves received, as their monthly allowance of food, eight pounds of pork, or its equivalent in fish, and one bushel of corn meal. Their yearly clothing consisted of two coarse linen shirts, one pair of linen trousers, like the shirts, one jacket, one pair of trousers for winter, made of coarse negro cloth, one pair of stockings, and one pair of shoes; the whole of which could not have cost more than seven dollars. The allowance of the slave children was given to their mothers, or the old women having the care of them. The children unable to work in the field had neither shoes, stock-ings, jackets, nor trousers, given to them; their clothing consisted of two coarse linen shirts per year. When these failed them, they went naked until the next allowance-day. Children from seven to ten years old, of both sexes, almost naked, might be seen at all seasons of the year.

There were no beds given the slaves, unless one coarse blanket be    4
considered such, and none but the men and women had these. This, however, is not considered a very great privation. They find less diffi-culty from the want of beds, than from the want of time to sleep; for when their day's work in the field is done, the most of them having their washing, mending, and cooking to do, and having few or none of the or-dinary facilities for doing either of these, very many of their sleeping hours are consumed in preparing for the field the coming day; and when this is done, old and young, male and female, married and single, drop down side by side, on one common bed,—the cold, damp floor,—each covering himself or herself with their miserable blankets; and here they sleep till they are summoned to the field by the driver's horn. At the sound of this, all must rise, and be off to the field. There must be no halt-ing; every one must be at his or her post; and woe betides them who hear not this morning summons to the field; for if they are not awakened by the sense of hearing, they are by the sense of feeling: no age nor sex finds any favor. Mr. Severe, the overseer, used to stand by the door of the quar-ter, armed with a large hickory stick and heavy cowskin, ready to whip any one who was so unfortunate as not to hear, or, from any other cause, was prevented from being ready to start for the field at the sound of the horn.

5    Mr. Severe was rightly named: he was a cruel man. I have seen him whip a woman, causing the blood to run half an hour at the time; and this, too, in the midst of her crying children, pleading for their mother's release. He seemed to take pleasure in manifesting his fiendish barbarity. Added to his cruelty, he was a profane swearer. It was enough to chill the blood and stiffen the hair of an ordinary man to hear him talk. Scarce a sentence escaped him but that was commenced or concluded by some horrid oath. The field was the place to witness his cruelty and profanity. His presence made it both the field of blood and of blasphemy. From the rising till the going down of the sun, he was cursing, raving, cutting, and slashing among the slaves of the field, in the most frightful manner. His career was short. He died very soon after I went to Colonel Lloyd's; and he died as he lived, uttering, with his dying groans, bitter curses and horrid oaths. His death was regarded by the slaves as the result of a merciful providence.

6    Mr. Severe's place was filled by a Mr. Hopkins. He was a very different man. He was less cruel, less profane, and made less noise, than Mr. Severe. His course was characterized by no extraordinary demonstrations of cruelty. He whipped, but seemed to take no pleasure in it. He was called by the slaves a good overseer.

7    The home plantation of Colonel Lloyd wore the appearance of a country village. All the mechanical operations for all the farms were performed here. The shoemaking and mending, the blacksmithing, cartwrighting, coopering, weaving, and grain-grinding, were all performed by the slaves on the home plantation. The whole place wore a businesslike aspect very unlike the neighboring farms. The number of houses, too, conspired to give it advantage over the neighboring farms. It was called by the slaves the *Great House Farm*. Few privileges were esteemed higher, by the slaves of the out-farms, than that of being selected to do errands at the Great House Farm. It was associated in their minds with greatness. A representative could not be prouder of his election to a seat in the American Congress, than a slave on one of the out-farms would be of his election to do errands at the Great House Farm. They regarded it as evidence of great confidence reposed in them by their overseers; and it was on this account, as well as a constant desire to be out of the field from under the driver's lash, that they esteemed it a high privilege, one worth careful living for. He was called the smartest and most trusty fellow, who had this honor conferred upon him the most frequently. The competitors for this office sought as diligently to please their overseers, as the office-seekers in the political parties seek to please and deceive the people. The same traits of character might be seen in Colonel Lloyd's slaves, as are seen in the slaves of the political parties.

8    The slaves selected to go to the Great House Farm, for the monthly allowance for themselves and their fellow-slaves, were peculiarly enthusiastic. While on their way, they would make the dense old woods, for miles around, reverberate with their wild songs, revealing at once the

highest joy and the deepest sadness. They would compose and sing as they went along, consulting neither time nor tune. The thought that came up, came out—if not in the word, in the sound;—and as frequently in the one as in the other. They would sometimes sing the most pathetic sentiment in the most rapturous tone, and the most rapturous sentiment in the most pathetic tone. Into all of their songs they would manage to weave something of the Great House Farm. Especially would they do this, when leaving home. They would then sing most exultingly the following words:—

> I am going away to the Great House Farm!
> A, yea! O, Yea! O!

This they would sing, as a chorus, to words which to many would seem unmeaning jargon, but which, nevertheless, were full of meaning to themselves. I have sometimes thought that the mere hearing of those songs would do more to impress some minds with the horrible character of slavery, than the reading of whole volumes of philosophy on the subject could do.

I did not, when a slave, understand the deep meaning of those rude 9 and apparently incoherent songs. I was myself within the circle; so that I neither saw nor heard as those without might see and hear. They told a tale of woe which was then altogether beyond my feeble comprehension; they were tones loud, long, and deep; they breathed the prayer and complaint of souls boiling over with the bitterest anguish. Every tone was a testimony against slavery, and a prayer to God for deliverance from chains. The hearing of those wild notes always depressed my spirit, and filled me with ineffable sadness. I have frequently found myself in tears while hearing them. The mere recurrence of those songs, even now, afflicts me; and while I am writing these lines, an expression of feeling has already found its way down my cheek. To those songs I trace my first glimmering conception of the dehumanizing character of slavery. I can never get rid of that conception. Those songs still follow me, to deepen my hatred of slavery, and quicken my sympathies for my brethren in bonds. If any one wishes to be impressed with the soul-killing effects of slavery, let him go to Colonel Lloyd's plantation, and, on allowance-day, place himself in the deep pine woods, and there let him, in silence, analyze the sounds that shall pass through the chambers of his soul,—and if he is not thus impressed, it will only be because "there is no flesh in his obdurate heart."

I have often been utterly astonished, since I came to the north, to 10 find persons who could speak of the singing, among slaves, as evidence of their contentment and happiness. It is impossible to conceive of a greater mistake. Slaves sing most when they are most unhappy. The songs of the slave represent the sorrows of his heart; and he is relieved by them, only as an aching heart is relieved by its tears. At least, such is my experience.

I have often sung to drown my sorrow, but seldom to express my happiness. Crying for joy, and singing for joy, were alike uncommon to me while in the jaws of slavery. The singing of a man cast away upon a desolate island might be as appropriately considered as evidence of contentment and happiness, as the singing of a slave; the songs of the one and of the other are prompted by the same emotion.

## CONSIDERATIONS

1. Is there anything to suggest, at the end of paragraph 7, that Douglass had a talent for satire?

2. In paragraphs 2 and 7, Douglass sketches the operations of the home plantation and its relationship to the outlying farms owned by the same man. Does the arrangement sound feudal? How did the plantation system differ from feudalism?

3. "I was myself within the circle; so that I neither saw nor heard as those without might see and hear," writes Douglass in paragraph 9. Is a fish aware that its medium is water? Are you, as a student, always conscious of the knowledge you acquire?

4. What single phenomenon, according to Douglass, taught him the most moving and enduring lesson about the dehumanizing character of slavery? In what way did that lesson surprise those who had not had Douglass's experience?

5. Paragraph 5 offers a good example of Douglass's typical sentence structure: a linear series of independent clauses, with little or no subordination, producing a blunt, stop-and-go effect. Without losing any of the information provided, rewrite the paragraph, reducing the number of sentences from twelve to six. Do this by converting some of the sentences to phrases, modifying clauses, or, in some cases, single-word modifiers.

6. Read Brent Staples's "Just Walk On By" (page 535) and/or Shelby Steele's "I'm Black, You're White, Who's Innocent?" (page 539), and write an essay on the changes in race relations through the years between the account of Douglass and those of Staples and/or Steele.

*Gerald Early (b. 1952) is an essayist and a student of the genre. At Washington University, where he directs the African and Afro-American Studies Program and teaches English, he presents a course called "The Art of the Essay." He has edited essay collections and assembled his own in books like* Tuxedo Junction *(1990), from which we take this example. A year later, he published* The Culture of Bruising: Essays on Prizefighting, Literature, and Modern American Culture.

*"Life with Daughters: Watching the Miss America Pageant" builds itself on a series of oppositions: male and female, black and white, past and present. Watch how, with the appearance of ease or relaxation, Early explores complexities of our culture, writing out of experience and reflection—in the classic tradition of the essay.*

— 25 ——————————————————————

# GERALD EARLY
## *Life with Daughters: Watching the Miss America Pageant*

The theater is an expression of our dream life—of our unconscious aspirations.

> —David Mamet, "A Tradition of the Theater as Art,"
> *Writing in Restaurants*

Aunt Hester went out one night,—where or for what I do not know,—and happened to be absent when my master desired her presence.

> —Frederick Douglass,
> *Narrative of the Life of Frederick Douglass*

Adults, older girls, shops, magazines, newspapers, window signs—all the world had agreed that a blue-eyed, yellow-haired, pink-skinned doll was what every girl child treasured.

> —Toni Morrison, *The Bluest Eye*

"Life with Daughters" from *Tuxedo Junction* by Gerald Early. Reprinted by permission of Gerald Early.

1      It is now fast become a tradition—if one can use that word to describe a habit about which I still feel a certain amount of shamefacedness—for our household to watch the Miss America contest on television every year. The source of my embarrassment is that this program remains, despite its attempts in recent years to modernize its frightfully antique quality of "women on parade," a kind of maddeningly barbarous example of the persistent, hard, crass urge to sell: from the plugs for the sponsor that are made a part of the script (that being an antique of fifties and sixties television; the show does not remember its history so much as it seems bent on repeating it) to the constant references to the success of some of the previous contestants and the reminders that this is some sort of scholarship competition, the program has all the cheap earnestness of a social uplift project being played as a musical revue in Las Vegas. Paradoxically, it wishes to convince the public that it is a common entertainment while simultaneously wishing to convey that it is more than mere entertainment. The Miss America pageant is the worst sort of "Americanism," the soft smile of sex and the hard sell of toothpaste and hair dye ads wrapped in the dreamy ideological gauze of "making it through one's own effort." In a perverse way, I like the show; it is the only live television left other than sports, news broadcasts, performing arts award programs, and speeches by the president. I miss live TV. It was the closest thing to theater for the masses. And the Miss America contest is as it has been for some time, the most perfectly rendered theater in our culture, for it so perfectly captures what we yearn for: a low-class ritual, a polished restatement of vulgarity, that wants to open the door to high-class respectability by way of plain middle-class anxiety and ambition. Am I doing all right? the contestants seem to ask in a kind of reassuring, if numbed, way. The contest brings together all the American classes in a show-biz spectacle of classlessness and tastelessness.

2      My wife has been interested in the Miss America contest since childhood, and so I ascribe her uninterrupted engagement with America's cultural passage into fall (Miss America, like college and pro football, signifies for us as a nation the end of summer; the contest was invented, back in 1921, by Atlantic City merchants to prolong the summer season past Labor Day) as something mystically and uniquely female. She, as a black woman, had a long-standing quarrel with the contest until Vanessa Williams was chosen the first black Miss America in September 1983. Somehow she felt vindicated by Williams for all those years as a black girl in Dallas, watching white women win the crown and thumb their noses at her, at her blackness, at her straightened hair, her thick lips, her wide nose. She played with white Barbie dolls as a little girl and had, I suppose, a "natural," or at least an understandable and predictable, interest in seeing the National White Barbie Doll chosen every year because for such a long time, of course, the Miss America contest, with few exceptions, was a totemic preoccupation with and repre-

sentation of a particularly stilted form of patriarchal white supremacy. In short, it was a national white doll contest. And well we know that every black girl growing up in the fifties and early sixties had her peculiar love-hate affair with white dolls, with mythicized white femininity. I am reminded of this historical instance: everyone knows that in the *Brown versus Topeka Board of Education* case (the case that resulted in the Supreme Court decision to integrate public schools) part of the sociological evidence used by the plaintiffs to show the psychological damage suffered by blacks because of Jim Crow was an account by Kenneth Clarke of how, when offered a choice between a black doll and a white doll, little black girls invariably chose the white doll because they thought it "prettier."

On the front page of the January 6, 1962, *Pittsburgh Courier,* a black weekly, is a picture of a hospitalized black girl named Connie Smith holding a white doll sent to her by Attorney General Robert Kennedy. Something had occurred between 1954, when the Supreme Court made its decision, and 1962 that made it impossible for Kennedy to send the girl a black doll, and this impossibility was to signal, ironically, that the terms of segregation and the terms of racial integration, the very icon of them, were to be exactly the same. Kennedy could not send the girl a black doll, as it would have implied, in the age of integration, that he was, in effect, sending her a Jim Crow toy, a toy that would emphasize the girl's race. In the early sixties such a gesture would have been considered condescending. To give the black girl a white doll in the early sixties was to mainstream the black girl into the culture, to say that she was worthy of the same kind of doll that a white girl would have. But how can it be that conservatism and liberalism, segregation and integration, could produce, fantastically, the same results, the identical iconography: a black girl hugging a white doll because everyone thinks it is best for her to have it? How can it be that at one time the white doll is the sign of the black girl's rejection and inferiority and fewer than ten years later it is the sign of her acceptance and redemption? Those who are knowledgeable about certain aspects of the black mind or the collective black consciousness realize, of course, that the issues of segregation and integration, of conservatism and liberalism, of acceptance and rejection, of redemption and inferiority, are all restatements of the same immovable and relentless reality of the meaning of American blackness; that this is all a matter of the harrowing and compelling intensity that is called, quaintly, race pride. And in this context, the issue of white dolls, this fetishization of young white feminine beauty, and the complexity of black girlhood becomes an unresolved theme stated in a strident key. Blacks have preached for a long time about how to heal their daughters of whiteness: in the November 1908 issue of *The Colored American Magazine,* E. A. Johnson wrote an article entitled "Negro Dolls for Negro Babies," in which he said, "I am convinced that one of the best ways to teach Negro children to respect their own color would be to see to it that the children

3

be given colored dolls to play with. . . . To give a Negro child a white doll means to create in it a prejudice against its own color, which will cling to it through life." Lots of black people believed this and, for all I know, probably still do, as race pride, or the lack thereof, burns and crackles like a current through most African-American public and private discourse. Besides, it is no easy matter to wish white dolls away.

4      A few years ago I was thumbing through an album of old family photographs and saw one of me and my oldest sister taken when I was four and she was nine. It struck me, transfixed me really, as it was a color photo and most of the old family pictures taken when I was a boy were black-and-white because my mother could not afford to have color pictures developed. We, my sister and I, are sitting on an old stuffed blue chair and she is holding a white doll in her hand, displaying it for the picture. I remember the occasion very well, as my sister was to be confirmed in our small, all-black Episcopal church that day, and she was, naturally, proud of the moment and wanted to share it with her favorite toy. That, I remembered, was why these were color pictures. It was a special day for the family, a day my mother wanted to celebrate by taking special pictures. My mother is a very dark woman who has a great deal of race pride and often speaks about my sisters' having black dolls. I was surprised, in looking at the picture recently, that they ever owned a white one, that indeed a white one had been a favorite.

5      My wife grew up—enjoyed the primary years of black girlhood, so to speak—during the years 1954 through 1962; she was about five or six years younger than my oldest sister. She lived in a southern state, or a state that was a reasonable facsimile of a southern state. She remembers that signs for colored and white bathrooms and water fountains persisted well into the mid-sixties in Texas. She remembers also Phyllis George, the Miss America from Denton, Texas, who went on to become a television personality for several years. She has always been very interested in George's career, and she has always disliked her. "She sounds just like a white girl from Texas," my wife likes to say, always reminding me that while both blacks and whites in Texas have accents, they do not sound alike. George won the contest in 1971, my wife's freshman year at the University of Pennsylvania and around the time she began to wear an Afro, a popular hairstyle for young black women in the days of "our terrible blackness" or "our black terribleness." It was a year fraught with complex passages into black womanhood for her. To think that a white woman from Texas should win the Miss America title that year! For my wife, the years of watching the Miss America contest were nothing more, in some sense continue to be nothing more, than an expression of anger made all the worse by the very unconscious or semiconscious nature of it. But if the anger has been persistent, so has her enormous capacity to "take it"; for in all these years it has never occurred to her to refuse to watch because, like the black girl being offered the white doll, like all black folk being offered white gifts, she has absolutely no idea

how that is done, and she is not naïve enough to think that a simple refusal would be an act of empowerment. Empowerment comes only
through making demands of our bogeymen, not by trying to convince
ourselves we are not tormented. Yet, paradoxically, among blacks there
is the bitter hope that a simplistic race pride will save us, a creed that
masks its complex contradictions beneath lapping waves of bourgeois
optimism and bourgeois anguish; for race pride clings to the opposing notions that the great hope (but secret fear) of an African-American future
is, first, that blacks will always remain black and, second, that the great
fear (but secret hope) of an African-American future is that blacks will
not always remain black but evolve into something else. Race pride,
which at its most insistent argues that blackness is everything, becomes,
in its attempt to be the psychological quest for sanity, a form of dementia that exists as a response to that form of white dementia that says
blackness is nothing. Existing as it does as a reactive force battling
against a white preemptive presumption, race pride begins to take on the
vices of an unthinking dogma and the virtues of a disciplined religious
faith, all in the same instance. With so much at stake, race pride become
both the act of making a virtue of a necessity and making a necessity of a
virtue and, finally, making a profound and touching absurdity of both
virtue and necessity. In some ways my wife learned her lessons well in
her youth: she never buys our daughters white dolls.

My daughters, Linnet, age ten, and Rosalind, age seven, have be-   6
come staunch fans of beauty contests in the last three years. In that time
they have watched, in their entirety, several Miss America pageants, one
Miss Black America contest, and one Miss USA. At first, I ascribed this
to the same impulse that made my wife interested in such events when
she was little: something secretly female, just as an interest in professional sports might be ascribed to something peculiarly male. Probably it
is a sort of resentment that black girls harbor toward these contests. But
that could not really be the case with my daughters. After all, they have
seen several black entrants in these contests and have even seen black
winners. They also have black dolls.

Back in the fall of 1983 when Vanessa Williams became Miss   7
America, we, as a family, had our picture taken with her when she visited St. Louis. We went, my wife and I, to celebrate the grand moment
when white American popular culture decided to embrace black women
as something other than sexual subversives or fat, kindly maids cleaning
up and caring for white families. We had our own, well, royalty, and royal
origins means a great deal to people who have been denied their myths
and their right to human blood. White women reformers may be ready to
scrap the Miss America contest. (And the contest has certainly responded to the criticism it has been subjected to in recent years by mut-
ing some of the fleshier aspects of the program while, in its attempts to
be even more the anxiety-ridden middle-class dream-wish, emphasizing
more and more the magic of education and scholarly attainments.) It is

now the contest that signifies the quest for professionalism among bourgeois women, and the first achievement of the professional career is to win something in a competition. But if there is a movement afoot to bring down the curtain finally on Miss America, my wife wants no part of it: "Whites always want to reform and end things when black people start getting on the gravy train they've been enjoying for years. What harm does the Miss America contest do?" None, I suppose, especially since black women have been winning lately.

8      Linnet and Rosalind were too young when we met Vanessa Williams to recall anything about the pictures, but they are amazed to see themselves in a bright, color Polaroid picture with a famous person, being part of an event that does not strike a chord in their consciousness because they cannot remember being alive when it happened. I often wonder if they attach any significance to the pictures at all. They think Vanessa is very pretty, prettier than their mother, but they attach no significance to being pretty—that is to say, no real value; they would not admire someone simply because he or she was good-looking. They think Williams is beautiful, but they do not wish that she were their mother. And this issue of being beautiful is not to be taken lightly in the life of a black girl. About two years ago Linnet started coming home from school wishing aloud that her hair was long and blond so that she could fling it about, the way she saw many of her white classmates doing. As she attends a school that is more than 90 percent white, it seemed inevitable to my wife that one of our daughters would become sensitive about her appearance. At this time Linnet's hair was not straightened and she wore it in braids. Oddly, despite the fact that she wanted a different hairstyle that would permit her hair to "blow in the wind," so to speak, she vehemently opposed having it straightened, although my wife has straightened hair, after having worn an Afro for several years. I am not sure why Linnet did not want her hair straightened; perhaps, after seeing her teenaged cousin have her hair straightened on several occasions, the process of hair straightening seemed distasteful or disheartening or frightening. Actually, I do not think Linnet wanted to change her hair to be beautiful; she wanted to be like everyone else.[1] But perhaps this is simply wishful thinking here or playing with words because Linnet must have felt her difference as being a kind of ugliness. Yet she is not a girl who is subject to illusion. Once, about a year earlier, when she had had a particularly rough day in school, I told her, in a father's patronizing way with a daughter, that I thought she was the most beautiful girl in the world. She looked at me strangely when I said that and then replied matter-of-factly: "I don't think I'm beautiful at all. I think I'm just ordinary. There is nothing wrong with that, is there, Daddy? Just to be ordinary?" "Are you unhappy to be ordinary?" I asked. She thought for a moment, then said quietly and finally, "No. Are you?"

9      Hair straightening, therefore, was not an option and would not have been even if Linnet had wanted it, because my wife was opposed to having Linnet's hair straightened at her age. At first, Linnet began going to

school with her hair unbraided. Unfortunately, this turned out to be a disastrous hairdo, as her hair shrank during the course of a day to a tangled mess. Finally, my wife decided to have both Linnet and Rosalind get short Afro haircuts. Ostensibly, this was to ease the problem of taking swim lessons during the summer. In reality, it was to end Linnet's wishes for a white hairstyle by, in effect, foreclosing any possibility that she could remotely capture such a look. Rosalind's hair was cut so that Linnet would not feel that she was being singled out. (Alas, the trials of being both the second and the younger child!) At first, the haircuts caused many problems in school. Some of the children—both black and white—made fun of them. Brillo heads, they were called, and fungus and Afro heads. One group of black girls at school refused to play with Linnet. "You look so ugly with that short hair," they would say. "Why don't you wear your hair straight like your mom. Your mom's hair is so pretty." Then, for the first time, the girls were called niggers by a white child on their school bus, although I think neither the child nor my daughters completely understood the gravity of that obscenity. People in supermarkets would refer to them as boys unless they were wearing dresses. Both girls went through a period when they suffered most acutely from that particularly American disease, that particularly African-American disease, the conjunction of oppression and exhibitionistic desire: self-consciousness. They thought about their hair all the time. My wife called the parents of the children who teased them. The teasing stopped for the most part, although a few of the black girls remained so persistent that the white school counselor suggested that Linnet's and Rosalind's hair be straightened. "I'm white," he said, "and maybe I shouldn't get into this, but they might feel more comfortable if they wore a different hairstyle." My wife angrily rejected that bit of advice. She had them wear dresses more often to make them look unmistakably like girls, although she refused out of hand my suggestion of having their ears pierced. She is convinced that pierced ears are just a form of mutilation, primitive tattooing, or scarring passing itself off as something fashionable. Eventually, the girls became used to their hair. Now, after more than a year, they hardly think about it, and even if Linnet wears a sweat suit or jeans, no one thinks she is a boy because she is budding breasts. Poor Rosalind still suffers on occasion in supermarkets because she shows no outward signs of sexual maturity. Once, while watching Linnet look at her mother's very long and silken straight hair, the hair that the other black girls at school admire, always calling it pretty, I asked her if she would like to have hers straightened.

"Not now," she said. "Maybe when I'm older. It'll be something different."  10

"Do you think you will like it?" I asked.  11

"Maybe," she said.  12

And in that "maybe," so calmly and evenly uttered, rests the complex contradictions, the uneasy tentative negotiations of that which cannot be compromised yet can never be realized in this flawed world as an  13 ideal; there is, in that "maybe," the epistemology of race pride for black American women so paradoxically symbolized by their straightened hair. In the February 1939 issue of *The Atlantic Monthly*, a black woman named Kimbal Goffman (possibly a pseudonym) wrote an essay entitled "Black Pride" in which she accused blacks of being ashamed of their heritage and, even more damningly in some of her barbs obviously aimed at black women, of their looks:

> Why are so many manufacturers becoming rich through the manufacture of bleaching preparations? Why are hair-straightening combs found in nearly every Negro home? Why is the following remark made so often to a newborn baby, when grandma or auntie visits it for the first time? "Tell Mother she must pinch your nose every morning. If she doesn't, you're gonna have a sure 'nough darky nose."

14    According to Goffman, blacks do not exploit what society has given them; they are simply ashamed to have what they have, tainted as it is with being associated with a degraded people, and long to be white or to have possessions that would accrue a kind of white status. In the essay, blacks in general receive their share of criticism but only black women are criticized in a gender-specific way that their neurotic sense of inferiority concerning physical appearance is a particularly dangerous form of reactionism as it stigmatizes each new generation. According to Goffman, it is black women, because they are mothers, who perpetuate their sense of inferiority by passing it on to their children. In this largely Du Boisian argument, Goffman advises, "Originality is the backbone of all progress." And, in this sense, originality means understanding blackness as something uncontrolled or uninfluenced by what whites say it is. This is the idealism of race pride that demands both purity and parity. Exactly one year later, in the February 1940 issue of *The Brown American*, a black magazine published in Philadelphia, Lillian Franklin McCall wrote an article about the history of black women beauty shop owners and entrepreneurs entitled "Appointment at Seven." The opening paragraph is filled with dollar signs:

> The business of straightening milady's insistent curls tinkles cash registers in the country to the tune of two million and a half dollars a year. And that covers merely the semi-monthly session with the hairdresser for the estimated four million of Eve's sepia adult daughters by national census. Today there is a growing trend to top off the regular, "Shampoo and wave," with a facial; and, perhaps, a manicure. New oil treatments and rinses prove a lure, too, so milady finds her beauty budget stepped up from approximately $39 yearly for an average $1.25 or $1.50 "hair-do," to $52.00 per year if she adds a facial to the beauty rite, and $10 more, for the manicure.

In a Booker T. Washington tone, McCall goes on to describe how   15
the establishment of a black beauty culture serves as a source of empowerment for black women:

> Brown business it is, in all its magnitude for Miss Brown American
> receives her treatments from the hands of Negro beauticians and her
> hair preparations and skin dreams come, usually from Negro
> laboratories.

She then tells the reader that leading companies in this field were   16
founded by black women: Madame C. J. Walker, Mrs. Annie Turbo
Malone, Madame Sara Spencer Washington. And one is struck by the ab-
sences that this essay evokes, not only in comparison to Goffman's piece
but also to Elsie Johnson McDougald's major manifesto on black women,
"The Task of Negro Womanhood" that appeared in Alain Locke's seminal 1925 anthology of African-American thought, *The New Negro*. In
McDougald's piece, which outlines all the economic status and achievements of black women at the time, there is absolutely no mention of
black beauty culture, no mention of Madame C. J. Walker, although her
newspaper ads were among the biggest in black newspapers nationwide
during the twenties. (And why did McDougald not mention black
women's beauty workers and businesspeople along with the nurses, do-
mestics, clerks, and teachers she discusses at length? It can scarcely be
because she, as a trained and experienced writer on black sociological
matters, did not think of it.) It is not simply money or black woman's industry or endeavor that makes the black woman present or a presence; it
is beauty culture generally that finally brings her into being, and specifically, her presence is generated by her hair. What for one black woman
writer, Goffman, is an absence and thus a sign of degradation, is for another a presence and a sign of economic possibilities inherent in feminine aesthetics.

What did I see as a boy when I passed the large black beauty shop on   17
Broad and South streets in Philadelphia where the name of its owner,
Adele Reese, commanded such respect or provoked such jealousy? What
did I see there but a long row of black women dressed immaculately in
white tunics, washing and styling the hair of other black women? That
was a sign of what culture, of what set of politics? The sheen of those
straightened heads, the entire enterprise of the making of black feminine
beauty: Was it an enactment of a degradation inspirited by a bitter inferiority or was it a womanly laying on of hands where black women were,
in their way, helping themselves to live through and transcend their
degradation? As a boy, I used to watch and wonder as my mother
straightened my sisters' hair every Saturday night for church on Sunday
morning. Under a low flame on the stove, the hot comb would glow
dully; from an open jar of Apex bergamot hair oil or Dixie Peach, my
mother would extract blobs and place them on the back of one hand,

deftly applying the oil to strands of my sisters' hair with the other. And the strange talk about a "light press" or a "heavy press" or a "close press" to get the edges and the ends; the concern about the hair "going back" if caught in the rain. Going back where, I wondered. To Africa? To the bush? And the constant worry and vigil about burning, getting too close to the scalp. I can remember hearing my sisters' hair sizzle and crackle as the comb passed through with a kind of pungent smell of actually burning hair. And I, like an intentional moth, with lonely narrow arcs, hovered near this flame of femininity with a fascinated impertinence. Had I witnessed the debilitating nullity of absence or was it the affirmation of an inescapable presence? Had I witnessed a mutilation or a rite of devotion? Black women's hair is, I decided even as a boy, unintelligible. And now I wonder, is the acceptance of the reigns of black women as Miss America a sign that black beauty has become part of the mainstream culture? Is the black woman now truly a presence?

18      We, I and my wife and our daughters, sat together and watched the latest Miss America contest. We did what we usually do. We ate popcorn. We laughed at all the talent numbers, particularly the ones when the contestants were opera singers or dancers. We laughed when the girls tried to answer grand social questions—such as "How can we inspire children to achieve and stay in school?" or "How can we address the problem of mainstreaming physically disadvantaged people?"—in thirty seconds. In fact, as Rosalind told me after the show, the main reason my daughters watch the Miss America pageant is that "it's funny." My daughters laugh because they cannot understand why the women are doing what they are doing, why they are trying so hard to please, to be pleasing. This must certainly be a refreshing bit of sanity, as the only proper response for such a contest is simply to dismiss it as hilarious; this grandiose version of an elocution, charm school, dance and music recital, which is not a revelation of talent but a reaffirmation of bourgeois cultural conditioning. And this bit of sanity on my daughters' part may prove hopeful for our future, for our American future, for our African-American future, if black girls are, unlike my wife when she was young, no longer angry. When it was announced that Miss Missouri, Debbye Turner, the third black to be Miss America, was the winner, my children were indifferent. It hardly mattered to them who won, and a black woman's victory meant no more than if any other contestant had prevailed. "She's pretty," Linnet said. She won two dollars in a bet with my wife, who did not think it possible that another black Miss America would be chosen. "Vanessa screwed up for the whole race," she told me once. "It's the race burden, the sins of the one become the original sins of us all." Linnet said simply, "She'll win because she is the best." Meritocracy is still a valid concept with the young.

19      For me, it was almost to be expected that Miss Turner would win. First, she received more precontest publicity than any other contestant in

recent years, with the possible exception of the black woman who was chosen Miss Mississippi a few years ago. Second, after the reign of Vanessa Williams, one would think that the Miss America powers that be very much wanted to have another black win and have a successful reign so that the contest itself could both prove its good faith (to blacks) and forestall criticism from white feminists and liberals (who are always put in a difficult position when the object of their disapproval is a black woman). As with the selection of Williams, the contest gained a veneer of postmodernist social and political relevance not only by selecting a black again but by having an Asian, a kidney donor, and a hearing-impaired woman among the top ten finalists. This all smacks of Affirmative Action or the let's-play-fair-with-the-underrepresented doctrine, which, as Miss Virginia pointed out after the contest, smacks of politics. But the point she missed, of course, is the point that all people who oppose Affirmative Action miss. The selection process for the Miss America contest has always been political. Back in the days when only white college women, whose main interest in most instances was a degree in MRS, could win, the contest was indeed just as political as it is now, a clear ideological bow to both patriarchal ideals and racism. It is simply a matter of which politics you prefer, and while no politics are perfect, some are clearly better than others. But in America, it must be added, the doctrine of fair play shouldn't even be graced with such a sophisticated term as "political." It is more our small-town, bourgeois Christian, muscular myth of ethical rectitude, the tremendous need Americans feel to be decent. So Miss Turner is intended to be both the supercession of Vanessa Williams—a religious vet student whose ambitions are properly, well, postmodernist Victorianism, preach do-goodism, evoke the name of God whenever you speak of your ambitions, and live with smug humility—and the redemption of the image of black women in American popular culture, since the Miss America contest is one of the few vehicles of display and competition for women in popular culture.

And if my daughters have come to one profound penetration of this cultural rite, it is that the contest ought to be laughed at in some ways, as most of the manifestations of popular culture ought to be for being the shoddy illusions that they are. For one always ought to laugh at someone or a group of someones who are trying to convince you that nothing is something—and that is not really the same as someone trying to convince you that you can have something for nothing, because in the popular culture business, the price for nothing is the same as the price for something; this "nothing is something" is, in fact, in most cases what the merchandising of popular culture is all about. (But as my mother reminded me as a boy: Nothing is nothing and something is something. Accept no substitutes!) For my children, the contest can be laughed at because it is so completely meaningless to them; they know it is an illusion despite its veneer as a competition. And it is that magical word

20

"competition," which is used over and over again all night long by the hosts and hostesses of the Miss America show (a contest, like most others these days, from the SATs to professional sports, that is made up of a series of competitions within the framework of larger competitions in such a pyramid that the entire structure of the outside world, for the bourgeois mind, is a frightful maze, a strangulating skein of competitions), that is the touchstone of reality, the momentous signifier that the sponsors of the pageant hope will give this extravaganza new significance and new life. For everything that we feel is important now is a matter of competition, beating out someone else for a prize, for some cheap prestige, a moment of notice before descending to cipherhood again; competition ranging from high culture (literary prizes, which seem to be awarded every day in the week, and classical music competitions for every instrument in a symphony orchestra, because of course for high culture one can never have enough art) to mid-culture (the entire phenomenon of American education, from academic honors to entrance requirements for prestigious schools, because of course for the middle class one can never have enough education or enough professionalism) to low culture (playing the lottery and various forms of gambling, because of course for the lower class one can never hope enough for money). And the more stringent and compulsively expressed the competition is (and the Miss America contest has reached a new height of hysteria in both the stridency and compulsion of the competition), the more legitimate and noteworthy it is.

21      Everyone in our culture wants to win a prize. Perhaps that is the grand lesson we have taken with us from kindergarten in the age of the perversions of Dewey-style education: Everyone gets a ribbon, and praise becomes a meaningless narcotic to soothe egoistic distemper. And in our bourgeois coming-of-age, we simply crave more and more ribbons and praise, the attainment of which becomes all the more delightful and satisfying if they are gotten at someone else's expense. Competition, therefore, becomes in the end a kind of laissez-faire psychotherapy that structures and orders our impossible rages of ambition, our rages to be noticed. But competition does not produce better people (a myth we have swallowed whole); it does not even produce better candidates; it simply produces more desperately grasping competitors. The "quality" of the average Miss America contestant is not significantly better now than it was twenty-five years ago, although the desires of today's contestants may meet with our approval (who could possibly disapprove of a black woman who wishes to be a vet in this day of careerism as the expression of independence and political empowerment), but then the women of twenty-five years ago wanted what their audiences approved of as well. That is not necessarily an advance or progress; that is simply a recognition that we are all bound by the mood and temper of our time. So, in this vast competition, this fierce theatrical warfare where all the women

are supposed to love their neighbor while they wish to beat her brains out, this warfare so pointedly exposed before the nation, what we have chosen is not the Royal American Daughter (although the contest's preoccupation with the terminology of aristocracy mirrors the public's need for such a person as the American princess) but rather the Cosmopolitan Girl. As the magazine ad states:

> Can a girl be too busy? I'm taking seventeen units at Princeton, pushing on with my career during vacations and school breaks, study singing and dancing when I can, try never to lose track of my five closest chums, steal the time for Michael Jackson and Thomas Hardy, work for an anti-drug program for kids and, oh yes, I hang out with three horses, three cats, two birds and my dog Jack. My favorite magazine says "too busy" just means you don't want to miss anything. . . . I love that magazine. I guess you can say I'm That Cosmopolitan Girl.

When one reads about these women in the Miss America contest,    22
that is precisely what they sound like: the Cosmopolitan Girl who knows how to have serious fun, and she has virtually nothing with which to claim our attention except a moralistic bourgeois diligence. To use a twenties term: she sounds "swell." She is an amalgam of both lead characters portrayed by Patty Duke on her old TV show: the studious, serious kid and the "typical" wacky but good-hearted suburban teenager, or, to borrow Ann Douglas's concept, she is the Teen Angel: the bourgeois girl who can do everything, is completely self-absorbed with her leisure, and has a heart of gold. Once again, with the Miss America contest we have America's vehement preoccupation with innocence, with its inability to deal with the darkness of youth, the darkness of its own uselessly expressed ambition, the dark complexity of its own simplistic morality of sunshine and success, the darkness, righteous rage, and bitter depth of its own daughters. Once again, when the new Miss America, victorious and smiling, walks down the runway, we know that runway, that victory march, to be the American catwalk of supreme bourgeois self-consciousness and supreme illusion. We are still being told that nothing is something.

Nonetheless, the fact that Miss Turner won struck both my wife    23
and me as important, as something important for the race. We laughed during the contest, but we did not laugh when she was chosen. We wanted her to win very much; it is impossible to escape that need to see the race uplifted, to thumb your nose at whites in a competition. It is impossible for blacks not to want to see their black daughters elevated to the platforms where white women are. Perhaps this tainted desire, an echoing "Ballad of the Brown Girl" that resounds in the unconscious psyche of all black people, is the unity of feeling that is the only race

pride blacks have ever had since they became Americans; for race pride for the African American, finally, is something that can only be understood as existing on the edge of tragedy and history and is, finally, that which binds both together to make the African American the darkly and richly complicated person he or she is. In the end, both black women magazine writers quoted earlier were right: race pride is transcending your degradation while learning to live in it and with it. To paraphrase an idea of Dorothy Sayers, race pride must teach blacks that they are not to be saved *from* degradation but saved *in* it.

24    A few days after the contests I watched both my daughters playing Barbies, as they call it. They squat on the floor on their knees, moving their dolls around through an imaginary town and in imaginary houses. I decided to join them and squatted down too, asking them the rules of their game, which they patiently explained as though they did not mind having me, the strange adult, invade their children's world. I told them it was hard for me to squat and asked if I could simply sit down, but they said that one always plays Barbies while squatting. It was a rule that had to be obeyed. As they went along, explaining relationships among their myriad dolls and the several landscapes, as complicated a genealogy as anything Faulkner ever dreamed up, a theater as vast as the entire girlhood of the world, they told me that one particular black Ken doll and one particular black Barbie doll were married and that the dolls had a child. Then Rosalind held up a white doll that someone, probably a grandparent, had given them (my wife is fairly strict on the point of our daughters' not having white dolls, but I guess a few have slipped through), explaining that this doll was the daughter of the black Ken and Barbie.

25    "But," I said, "how could two black dolls have a white daughter?"

26    "Oh," said Rosalind, looking at me as if I were an object deserving of only her indulgent pity, "we're not racial. That's old-fashioned. Don't you think so, Daddy? Aren't you tired of all that racial stuff?"

27    Bowing to that wisdom which, it is said, is the only kind that will lead us to Christ and to ourselves, I decided to get up and leave them to their play. My knees had begun to hurt and I realized, painfully, that I was much too old, much too at peace with stiffness and inflexibility, for children's games.

## Note

1. Richard Wright tells a story in his 1956 account of the Bandung conference, entitled *The Color Curtain*, that emphasizes the absence of the black woman. He relates how a white woman journalist knocks on his hotel room door during the course of the conference and confides the strange behavior of her roommate— a black woman journalist from Boston. Her roommate walks

around in the middle of the night and the white woman often covertly spies her in "a dark corner of the room . . . bent over a tiny blue light, a very low and a very blue flame. . . . It seemed like she was combing her hair, but I wasn't sure. Her right arm was moving and now and then she would look over her shoulder toward my bed." The white woman thinks that the black woman is practicing voodoo. But Wright soon explains that the black woman is simply straightening her hair.

> "But why would she straighten her hair? Her hair seems all right" [the white woman journalist asks].
>     "Her hair is all right. But it's not straight. It's kinky. But she does not want you, a white woman, to see her when she straightens her hair. She would feel embarrassed"
>     "Why?"
>     "Because you were born with straight hair, and she wants to look as much like you as possible. . . ."
>     The woman stared at me, then clapped her hands to her eyes and exclaimed:
>     "Oh!"
>     I leaned back and thought: here in Asia, where everybody was dark, the poor American Negro woman was worried about the hair she was born with. Here, where practically nobody was white, her hair would have been acceptable; no one would have found her "inferior" because her hair was kinky; on the contrary, the Indonesians would perhaps have found her different and charming.

The conversation continues with an account of the black woman's secretive skin-lightening treatments. What is revealing in this dialogue, which takes on both political and psychoanalytic proportions, is the utter absence of the black woman's voice, her presence. She is simply the dark, neurotic ghost that flits in the other room while the black male and the white female, both in the same room, one with dispassionate curtness and the other with sentimentalized guilt, consider the illness that is enacted before them as a kind of bad theater. Once again, the psychopathology of the black American is symbolized by the black woman's straightened hair, by her beauty culture.

## CONSIDERATIONS

1. Early prefaces his essay with not one or two but three epigraphs. What purpose does an epigraph serve that a title does not? Is it possible that multiple epigraphs might be more of a confusion than an asset?

2. Compare Early's style with that of other writers in your text on the subjects of race and color: Julia Alvarez, Michelle Cliff, Zora Neal Hurston, Frederick Douglass, Brent Staples, Shelby Steele.

3. Beginning with paragraph 8, Early tells how his two young daughters worried about their appearance, especially their hair style. Thinking of your own experience growing up and those of others you know, write a personal essay on self-consciousness in which you make a strong connection with Linnet and Rosalind.

4. In what significant way could one say that Gerald Early, writing on the Miss America pageant, and Shirley Abbott, writing on the "Southern belle" (page 1), are writing on the same subject?

5. "The contest," writes Early, "brings together all the American classes in a show-biz spectacle of classlessness and tastelessness." Do you agree? Respond in terms of the particulars on which the author bases his generalization.

6. In paragraphs 20 and 21, the author writes disparagingly of a widely held American value—competition. Why does he devalue it, and where are you on the subject?

*Gretel Ehrlich (b. 1946) grew up in California, went east to study, and eventually settled in Wyoming, which she first visited in 1976 to film a documentary for PBS. From making films and writing poems—she has published two poetry collections—she has more recently turned to prose. "About Men" comes from an essay collection,* The Solace of Open Spaces, *which appeared in 1985. In 1988 she published a novel called* Heart Mountain *and in 1991 another essay collection,* Islands, the Universe, Home. *In 1995 she published* Life in the Saddle *and* Yellowstone: Land of Fire and Ice. *She married a Wyoming rancher and lives in the Big Horn Basin ten miles from a paved road.*

*Ehrlich sets forth a myth or a stereotype and contradicts it. Her prose is simple, clear, and direct. Notice how her passion of personal observation leads her into analysis of character.*

— 26 ——————————————————————————

# GRETEL EHRLICH
## *About Men*

———————————————————————————————

When I'm in New York but feeling lonely for Wyoming I look for 1
the Marlboro ads in the subway. What I'm aching to see is horseflesh, the glint of a spur, a line of distant mountains, brimming creeks, and a reminder of the ranchers and cowboys I've ridden with for the last eight years. But the men I see in those posters with their stern, humorless looks remind me of no one I know here. In our hellbent earnestness to romanticize the cowboy we've ironically disesteemed his true character. If he's "strong and silent" it's because there's probably no one to talk to. If he "rides away into the sunset" it's because he's been on horseback since four in the morning moving cattle and he's trying, fifteen hours later, to get home to his family. If he's "a rugged individualist" he's also part of a team: ranch work is teamwork and even the glorified open-range cowboys of the 1880s rode up and down the Chisholm Trail in the company of twenty or thirty other riders. Instead of the macho, trigger-happy man our culture has perversely wanted him to be, the cowboy is more apt to be convivial, quirky, and softhearted. To be "tough" on a ranch has

nothing to do with conquests and displays of power. More often than not, circumstances—like the colt he's riding or an unexpected blizzard—are overpowering him. It's not toughness but "toughing it out" that counts. In other words, this macho, cultural artifact the cowboy has become is simply a man who possesses resilience, patience, and an instinct for survival. "Cowboys are just like a pile of rocks—everything happens to them. They get climbed on, kicked, rained and snowed on, scuffed up by wind. Their job is 'just to take it,'" one old-timer told me.

2      A cowboy is someone who loves his work. Since the hours are long—ten to fifteen hours a day—and the pay is $30, he has to. What's required of him is an odd mixture of physical vigor and maternalism. His part of the beef-raising industry is to birth and nurture calves and take care of their mothers. For the most part his work is done on horseback and in a lifetime he sees and comes to know more animals than people. The iconic myth surrounding him is built on American notions of heroism: the index of a man's value as measured in physical courage. Such ideas have perverted manliness into a self-absorbed race for cheap thrills. In a rancher's world, courage has less to do with facing danger than with acting spontaneously—usually on behalf of an animal or another rider. If a cow is stuck in a boghole he throws a loop around her neck, takes his dally (a half hitch around the saddle horn), and pulls her out with horsepower. If a calf is born sick, he may take her home, warm her in front of the kitchen fire, and massage her legs until dawn. One friend, whose favorite horse was trying to swim a lake with hobbles on, dove under water and cut her legs loose with a knife, then swam her to shore, his arm around her neck lifeguard-style, and saved her from drowning. Because these incidents are usually linked to someone or something outside himself, the westerner's courage is selfless, a form of compassion.

3      The physical punishment that goes with cowboying is greatly underplayed. Once fear is dispensed with, the threshold of pain rises to meet the demands of the job. When Jane Fonda asked Robert Redford (in the film *Electric Horseman*) if he was sick as he struggled to his feet one morning, he replied, "No, just bent." For once the movies had it right. The cowboys I was sitting with laughed in agreement. Cowboys are rarely complainers; they show their stoicism by laughing at themselves.

4      If a rancher or cowboy has been thought of as a "man's man"—laconic, hard-drinking, inscrutable—there's almost no place in which the balancing act between male and female, manliness and femininity, can be more natural. If he's gruff, handsome, and physically fit on the outside, he's androgynous at the core. Ranchers are midwives, hunters, nurturers, providers, and conservationists all at once. What we've interpreted as toughness—weathered skin, calloused hands, a squint in the eye and a growl in the voice—only masks the tenderness inside. "Now don't go telling me these lambs are cute," one rancher warned me the first day I walked into the football-field-sized lambing sheds. The next thing I knew he was holding a black lamb. "Ain't this little rat good-lookin'?"

So many of the men who came to the West were Southerners—men 5
looking for work and a new life after the Civil War—that chivalrousness
and strict codes of honor were soon thought of as western traits. There
were very few women in Wyoming during territorial days, so when they
did arrive (some as mail-order brides from places like Philadelphia) there
was a standoffishness between the sexes and a formality that persists
now. Ranchers still tip their hats and say, "Howdy, ma'am" instead of
shaking hands with me.

Even young cowboys are often evasive with women. It's not that 6
they're Jekyll and Hyde creatures—gentle with animals and rough on
women—but rather, that they don't know how to bring their tenderness
into the house and lack the vocabulary to express the complexity of what
they feel. Dancing wildly all night becomes a metaphor for the explosive
emotions pent up inside, and when these are, on occasion, released,
they're so battery-charged and potent that one caress of the face or one "I
love you" will peal for a long while.

The geographical vastness and the social isolation here make emo- 7
tional evolution seem impossible. Those contradictions of the heart between respectability, logic, and convention on the one hand, and impulse,
passion, and intuition on the other, played out wordlessly against the par-
adisical beauty of the West, give cowboys a wide-eyed but drawn look.
Their lips pucker up, not with kisses but with immutability. They may
want to break out, staying up all night with a lover just to talk, but they
don't know how and can't imagine what the consequences will be. Those
rare occasions when they do bare themselves result in confusion. "I feel as
if I'd sprained my heart," one friend told me a month after such a meeting.

My friend Ted Hoagland wrote, "No one is as fragile as a woman
but no one is as fragile as a man." For all the women here who use "fra- 8
gileness" to avoid work or as a sexual ploy, there are men who try to hide
theirs, all the while clinging to an adolescent dependency on women to
cook their meals, wash their clothes, and keep the ranch house warm in
winter. But there is true vulnerability in evidence here. Because these
men work with animals, not machines or numbers, because they live
outside in landscapes of torrential beauty, because they are confined to a
place and a routine embellished with awesome variables, because calves
die in the arms that pulled others into life, because they go to the mountains as if on a pilgrimage to find out what makes a herd of elk tick, their
strength is also a softness, their toughness, a rare delicacy.

## CONSIDERATIONS ——————————————————————————

1. Although Ehrlich writes informally, her vocabulary may give some readers a
little trouble. Consider unfamiliar words such as "disesteemed," "artifact," "iconic,"
"stoicism," "laconic," "androgynous." Just looking them up in the dictionary may not be

enough. Examine the same words in their immediate context: "we've ironically *dises-teemed* his true character"; "this macho, cultural *artifact* the cowboy has become"; "the *iconic* myth surrounding him is built on American notions of heroism"; "cowboys are rarely complainers; they show their *stoicism* by laughing at themselves"; "a man's man—*laconic*, hard-drinking, inscrutable"; "he's *androgynous* at the core. Ranchers are midwives, hunters, nurturers, providers, and conservationists all at once." A third step, if you want to make these new words your own, would be to use them in your own writing.

2. The real nature of the cowboy, writes Ehrlich, is hidden beneath a set of myths and stereotypes implanted deeply in our consciousness by Hollywood movies and cheap fiction. Is this more true of the cowboy than of people in other walks of life—say, a policeman, a sailor, an artist, a shopkeeper, a student, a teacher? Build an essay on your responses to the question.

3. Ehrlich closes her essay with a set of contradictions. In what way do such contradictions make sense, and why would an author risk confusing the reader with them?

4. Ehrlich's "About Men," Joan Didion's "Last Words," and Margaret Atwood's "Alien Territory" are all concerned with habits of life conventionally thought of as masculine. Are these subjects distorted by the fact that the writers are women? Do their approaches differ from the way male writers might have written about the same topics?

5. Read the little dialog that opens Daniel Boorstin's essay "The Pseudo-Event." Then comment on Ehrlich's turning to Marlboro advertisements in her homesickness for the life she had known in Wyoming. How does she make the reader aware that she herself is conscious of the irony?

*Ralph Ellison (1914–1994), born in Oklahoma, won the National Book Award in 1953 for his novel* The Invisible Man. *His essays are collected in* Shadow and Act *(1964). For forty years and more, Ellison lectured and wrote on literature and race. A year after his death the University Press of Mississippi published* Conversations with Ralph Ellison.*

*Ralph Ellison writes of his struggles under circumstances many writers never need to face. This essay is personal narrative, like many essays, in the service of understanding a self as it derives from its society.*

— 27 —————————————————————

# RALPH ELLISON
## *On Becoming a Writer*

———————————————————————

In the beginning writing was far from a serious matter; it was a re- 1
flex of reading, an extension of a source of pleasure, escape, and instruction. In fact, I had become curious about writing by way of seeking to
understand the aesthetic nature of literary power, the devices through
which literature could command my mind and emotions. It was not,
then, the *process* of writing which initially claimed my attention, but
the finished creations, the artifacts, poems, plays, novels. The act of
learning writing technique was, therefore, an amusing investigation of
what seemed at best a secondary talent, an exploration, like dabbling in
sculpture, of one's potentialities as a "Renaissance Man." This, surely,
would seem a most unlikely and even comic concept to introduce here;
and yet, it is precisely because I come from where I do (the Oklahoma of
the years between World War I and the Great Depression) that I must introduce it, and with a straight face.

Anything and everything was to be found in the chaos of 2
Oklahoma; thus the concept of the Renaissance Man has lurked long
within the shadow of my past, and I shared it with at least a half dozen of
my Negro friends. How we actually acquired it I have never learned, and
since there is no true sociology of the dispersion of ideas within the
American democracy, I doubt if I ever shall. Perhaps we breathed it in

with the air of the Negro community of Oklahoma City, the capital of that state whose Negroes were often charged by exasperated white Texans with not knowing their "place." Perhaps we took it defiantly from one of them. Or perhaps I myself picked it up from some transplanted New Englander whose shoes I had shined on a Saturday afternoon. After all, the most meaningful tips do not always come in the form of money, nor are they intentionally extended. Most likely, however, my friends and I acquired the idea from some book or some idealistic Negro teacher, some dreamer seeking to function responsibly in an environment which at its more normal took on some of the mixed character of nightmare and of dream.

3    One thing is certain, ours was a chaotic community, still characterized by frontier attitudes and by that strange mixture of the naive and sophisticated, the benign and malignant, which makes the American past so puzzling and its present so confusing; that mixture which often affords the minds of the young who grow up in the far provinces such wide and unstructured latitude, and which encourages the individual's imagination—up to the moment "reality" closes in upon him—to range widely and, sometimes, even to soar.

4    We hear the effects of this in the Southwestern jazz of the 30's, that joint creation of artistically free and exuberantly creative adventurers, of artists who had stumbled upon the freedom lying within the restrictions of their musical tradition as within the limitations of their social background, and who in their own unconscious way have set an example for any Americans, Negro or white, who would find themselves in the arts. They accepted themselves and the complexity of life as they knew it, they loved their art and through it they celebrated American experience definitively in sound. Whatever others thought or felt, this was their own powerful statement, and only non-musical assaults upon their artistic integrity—mainly economically inspired changes of fashion—were able to compromise their vision.

5    Much of so-called Kansas City jazz was actually brought to perfection in Oklahoma by Oklahomans. It is an important circumstance for me as a writer to remember, because while these musicians and their fellows were busy creating out of tradition, imagination, and the sounds and emotions around them, a freer, more complex, and driving form of jazz, my friends and I were exploring an idea of human versatility and possibility which went against the barbs or over the palings of almost every fence which those who controlled social and political power had erected to restrict our roles in the life of the country. Looking back, one might say that the jazzmen, some of whom we idolized, were in their own way better examples for youth to follow than were most judges and ministers, legislators and governors (we were stuck with the notorious Alfalfa Bill Murray). For as we viewed these pillars of society from the confines of our segregated community we almost always saw crooks, clowns, or hypocrites. Even the best were revealed by their attitudes to-

ward us as lacking the respectable qualities to which they pretended and for which they were accepted outside by others, while despite the outlaw nature of their art, the jazzmen were less torn and damaged by the moral compromises and insincerities which have so sickened the life of our country.

Be that as it may, our youthful sense of life, like that of many Negro    6 children (though no one bothers to note it—especially the specialists and "friends of the Negro" who view our Negro-American life as essentially non-human) was very much like that of Huckleberry Finn, who is universally so praised and enjoyed for the clarity and courage of his moral vision. Like Huck, we observed, we judged, we imitated and evaded as we could the dullness, corruption, and blindness of "civilization." We were undoubtedly comic because, as the saying goes, we weren't supposed to know what it was all about. But to ourselves we were "boys," members of a wild, free, outlaw tribe which transcended the category of race. Rather we were Americans born into the forty-sixth state, and thus, into the context of Negro-American post–Civil War history, "frontiersmen." And isn't one of the implicit functions of the American frontier to encourage the individual to a kind of dreamy wakefulness, a state in which he makes—in all ignorance of the accepted limitations of the possible rash efforts, quixotic gestures, hopeful testings of the complexity of the known and the given?

Spurring us on in our controlled and benign madness was the vora-    7 cious reading of which most of us were guilty and the vicarious identification and empathetic adventuring which it encouraged. This was due, in part, perhaps to the fact that some of us were fatherless—my own father had died when I was three—but most likely it was because boys are natural romantics. We were seeking examples, patterns to live by, out of a freedom which for all its being ignored by the sociologists and subtle thinkers, was implicit in the Negro situation. Father and mother substitutes also have a role to play in aiding the child to help create himself. Thus we fabricated our own heroes and ideals catch-as-catch-can, and with an outrageous and irreverent sense of freedom. Yes, and in complete disregard of ideas of respectability or the surreal incongruity of some of our projections. Gamblers and scholars, jazz musicians and scientists, Negro cowboys and soldiers from the Spanish-American and First World Wars, movie stars and stunt men, figures from the Italian Renaissance and literature, both classical and popular, were combined with the special virtues of some local bootlegger, the eloquence of some Negro preacher, the strength and grace of some local athlete, the ruthlessness of some businessman-physician, the elegance in dress and manners of some head-waiter or hotel doorman.

Looking back through the shadows upon this absurd activity, I real-    8 ize now that we were projecting archetypes, recreating folk figures, legendary heroes, monsters even, most of which violated all ideas of social hierarchy and order and all accepted conceptions of the hero handed down by cultural, religious, and racist tradition. But we, remember, were under the intense spell of the early movies, the silents as well as the talkies; and in our community, life was not so tightly structured as it would have been in the traditional South—or even in deceptively *"free"* Harlem. And our imaginations processed reality and dream, natural man and traditional hero, literature and folklore, like maniacal editors turned loose in some frantic film-cutting room. Remember, too, that being boys, yet in the play-stage of our development, we were dream-serious in our efforts. But serious nevertheless, for *culturally* play is a preparation, and we felt that somehow the human ideal lay in the vague and constantly shifting figures—sometimes comic but always versatile, picaresque, and self-effacingly heroic—which evolved from our wildly improvisatory projections: figures neither white nor black, Christian nor Jewish, but representative of certain desirable essences, of skills and powers, physical, aesthetic, and moral.

9   The proper response to these figures was, we felt, to develop ourselves for the performance of many and diverse roles, and the fact that certain definite limitations had been imposed upon our freedom did not lessen our sense of obligation. Not only were we to prepare but we were to perform—not with mere competence but with an almost reckless verve; with, may we say (without evoking the quaint and questionable notion of *négritude*) Negro-American style? Behind each artist there stands a traditional sense of style, a sense of the felt tension indicative of expressive completeness, a mode of humanizing reality and of evoking a feeling of being at home in the world. It is something which the artist shares with the group, and part of our boyish activity expressed a yearning to make any and everything of quality *Negro-American*; to appropriate it, possess it, recreate it in our own group and individual images.

10   And we recognized and were proud of our group's own style wherever we discerned it, in jazzmen and prize-fighters, ballplayers, and tap dancers; in gesture, inflection, intonation, timbre, and phrasing. Indeed, in all those nuances of expression and attitude which reveal a culture. We did not fully understand the cost of that style, but we recognized within it an affirmation of life beyond all question of our difficulties as Negroes.

11   Contrary to the notion currently projected by certain specialists in the "Negro problem" which characterizes the Negro American as self-hating and defensive, we did not so regard ourselves. We felt, among ourselves at least, that we were supposed to be whoever we would and could be and do anything and everything which other boys did, and do it better. Not defensively, because we were ordered to do so; nor because it was held in the society at large that we were naturally, as Negroes, limited—but because we demanded it of ourselves. Because to measure up to our own standards was the only way of affirming our notion of manhood.

12   Hence it was no more incongruous, as seen from our own particular perspective in this land of incongruities, for young Negro Oklahomans to

project themselves as Renaissance men than for white Mississippians to see themselves as ancient Greeks or noblemen out of Sir Walter Scott. Surely our fantasies have caused far less damage to the nation's sense of reality, if for no other reason than that ours were expressive of a more democratic ideal. Remember, too, as William Faulkner made us so vividly aware, that the slaves often took the essence of the aristocratic ideal (as they took Christianity) with far more seriousness than their masters, and that we, thanks to the tight telescoping of American history, were but two generations from that previous condition. Renaissance men, indeed!

I managed, by keeping quiet about it, to cling to our boyish ideal   13 during three years in Alabama, and I brought it with me to New York, where it not only gave silent support to my explorations of what was then an unknown territory, but served to mock and caution me when I became interested in the Communist ideal. And when it was suggested that I try my hand at writing it was still with me.

The act of writing requires a constant plunging back into the   14 shadow of the past where time hovers ghostlike. When I began writing in earnest I was forced, thus, to relate myself consciously and imaginatively to my mixed background as American, as Negro-American, and as a Negro from what in its own belated way was a pioneer background. More important, and inseparable from this particular effort, was the necessity of determining my true relationship to that body of American literature to which I was most attracted and through which, aided by what I could learn from the literatures of Europe, I would find my own voice and to which I was challenged, by way of achieving myself, to make some small contribution, and to whose composite picture of reality I was obligated to offer some necessary modifications.

This was no matter of sudden insight but of slow and blundering   15 discovery, of a struggle to stare down the deadly and hypnotic temptation to interpret the world and all its devices in terms of race. To avoid this was very important to me, and in light of my background far from simple. Indeed, it was quite complex, involving as it did, a ceaseless questioning of all those formulas which historians, politicians, sociologists, and an older generation of Negro leaders and writers—those of the so-called "Negro Renaissance"—had evolved to describe my group's identity, its predicament, its fate, and its relation to the larger society and the culture which we share.

Here the questions of reality and personal identity merge. Yes, and   16 the question of the nature of the reality which underlies American fiction and thus the human truth which gives fiction viability. In this quest, for such it soon became, I learned that nothing could go unchallenged; especially that feverish industry dedicated to telling Negroes who and what they are, and which can usually be counted upon to deprive both humanity and culture of their complexity. I had undergone, not too many months before taking the path which led to writing, the humiliation of being taught in a class in sociology at a Negro college (from Park and Burgess, the leading textbook in the field) that Negroes represented the "lady of the races." This contention the Negro instructor passed blandly along to us without even bothering to wash his hands, much less his teeth. Well, I had no intention of being bound by any such humiliating definition of my relationship to American literature. Not even to those works which depicted Negroes negatively. Negro Americans have a highly developed ability to abstract desirable qualities from those around them, even from their enemies, and my sense of reality could reject bias while appreciating the truth revealed by achieved art. The pleasure which I derived from reading had long been a necessity, and in the *act* of reading, that marvelous collaboration between the writer's artful vision and the reader's sense of life, I had become acquainted with other possible selves; freer, more courageous and ingenuous and, during the course of the narrative at least, even wise.

17        At the time I was under the influence of Ernest Hemingway, and his description, in *Death in the Afternoon*, of his thinking when he first went to Spain became very important as translated in my own naïve fashion. He was trying to write, he tells us,

> and I found the greatest difficulty aside from knowing truly what
> you really felt, rather than what you were supposed to feel, and had
> been taught to feel, was to put down what really happened in action;
> what the actual things were which produced the emotion that you
> experienced. . . .

18        His statement of moral and aesthetic purpose which followed focused on my own search to relate myself to American life through literature. For I found the greatest difficulty for a Negro writer was the problem of revealing what he truly felt, rather than serving up what Negroes were supposed to feel, and were encouraged to feel. And linked to this was the difficulty, based upon our long habit of deception and evasion, of depicting what really happened within our areas of American life, and putting down with honesty and without bowing to ideological expediencies the attitudes and values which give Negro-American life its sense of wholeness and which render it bearable and human and, when measured by our own terms, desirable.

19        I was forced to this awareness through my struggles with the craft of fiction; yes, and by my attraction (soon rejected) to Marxist political theory, which was my response to the inferior status which society sought to impose upon me (I did not then, now, or ever *consider* myself inferior).

20        I did not know my true relationship to America—what citizen of the U.S. really does?—but I did know and accept how I felt inside. And I also knew, thanks to the old Renaissance Man, what I expected of myself in the matter of personal discipline and creative quality. Since by the

grace of the past and the examples of manhood picked willy-nilly from the continuing present of my background, I rejected all negative definitions imposed upon me by others, there was nothing to do but search for those relationships which were fundamental.

In this sense fiction became the agency of my efforts to answer the questions, Who am I, what am I, how did I come to be? What shall I make of the life around me, what celebrate, what reject, how confront the snarl of good and evil which is inevitable? What does American society *mean* when regarded out of my *own* eyes, when informed by my *own* sense of the past and viewed by my *own* complex sense of the present? How, in other words, should I think of myself and my pluralistic sense of the world, how express my vision of the human predicament, without reducing it to a point which would render it sterile before that necessary and tragic—though enhancing—reduction which must occur before the fictive vision can come alive? It is quite possible that much potential fiction by Negro Americans fails precisely at this point: through the writers' refusal (often through provincialism or lack of courage or through opportunism) to achieve a vision of life and resourcefulness of craft commensurate with the complexity of their actual situation. Too often they fear to leave the uneasy sanctuary of race to take their chances in the world of art.

21

## CONSIDERATIONS

1. Ellison's opening statement that writing was "a reflex of reading" points to the experience of many other students and writers (see Richard Wright's "The Library Card") and implies an important relationship between the two activities. Are reading and writing two sides of the same coin? (See also the editors' "Preface" to this volume.)

2. Look in a good dictionary for a definition of "Renaissance man" and explain why this concept is central to an understanding of Ellison's essay.

3. "I found the greatest difficulty for a Negro writer was the problem of revealing what he truly felt, rather than serving up what Negroes are supposed to feel," writes Ellison in paragraph 18. Could a writer who happened to be a woman, or a teenager, or a Mexican, or a Jew have a similar difficulty?

4. Read Maya Angelou's "Mr. Red Leg" (page 25), and comment on the idea that that character could have been used by Ellison to illustrate what he talks about in paragraph 8.

5. Does Ellison's remark that "boys are natural romantics," in paragraph 7, help explain his first sentence in paragraph 8? Do you think that sentence is limited to the boys of one race or class? Use your own experience to write an essay on the subject.

6. Which author would be most likely to agree with the first sentence of Ellison's paragraph 14: Alice Walker, William Stafford, Kyoko Mori, or Toni Morrison? Explain.

*Nora Ephron (b. 1941), daughter of two screenwriters, grew up in Hollywood wanting to move to New York and become a writer. She did. She began by working for* Newsweek *and soon was contributing articles to the* New Yorker *and a monthly column to* Esquire. *Most of her writing is about women and manages to be at once funny and serious, profound and irreverent—and on occasion outrageous. In 1983 she published a novel entitled* Heartburn *that, in 1986, was made into a film. Her essays are collected in* Wallflower at the Orgy *(1970); in* Crazy Salad *(1972), from which we take this essay on growing up flat-chested; and most recently in* Nora Ephron Collected *(1991).*

*"This is a true story. Everything in this story is a true story." We believe her partly because she talks of her old shame, partly because her self-deprecating humor takes the shame away. Imagine this essay if it lacked humor.*

— 28 ————————————————————————

# NORA EPHRON
## *A Few Words about Breasts: Shaping Up Absurd*

1    I have to begin with a few words about androgyny. In grammar school, in the fifth and sixth grades, we were all tyrannized by a rigid set of rules that supposedly determined whether we were boys or girls. The episode in *Huckleberry Finn* where Huck is disguised as a girl and gives himself away by the way he threads a needle and catches a ball—that kind of thing. We learned that the way you sat, crossed your legs, held a cigarette and looked at your nails, your wristwatch, the way you did these things instinctively was absolute proof of your sex. Now obviously most children did not take this literally, but I did. I thought that just one slip, just one incorrect cross of my legs or flick of an imaginary cigarette ash would turn me from whatever I was into the other thing; that would be all it took, really. Even though I was outwardly a girl and had many of

the trappings generally associated with the field of girldom—a girl's name, for example, and dresses, my own telephone, an autograph book—I spent the early years of my adolescence absolutely certain that I might at any point gum it up. I did not feel at all like a girl. I was boyish. I was athletic, ambitious, outspoken, competitive, noisy, rambunctious. I had scabs on my knees and my socks slid into my loafers and I could throw a football. I wanted desperately not to be that way, not to be a mixture of both things but instead just one, a girl, a definite indisputable girl. As soft and as pink as a nursery. And nothing would do that for me, I felt, but breasts.

I was about six months younger than everyone in my class, and so   2 for about six months after it began, for six months after my friends had begun to develop—that was the word we used, develop—I was not particularly worried. I would sit in the bathtub and look down at my breasts and know that any day now, any second now, they would start growing like everyone else's. They didn't. "I want to buy a bra," I said to my mother one night. "What for?" she said. My mother was really hateful about bras, and by the time my third sister had gotten to the point where she was ready to want one, my mother had worked the whole business into a comedy routine. "Why not use a Band-Aid instead?" she would say. It was a source of great pride to my mother that she had never even had to wear a brassiere until she had her fourth child, and then only because her gynecologist made her. It was incomprehensible to me that anyone would ever be proud of something like that. It was the 1950s, for God's sake. Jane Russell. Cashmere sweaters. Couldn't my mother see that? *I am too old to wear an undershirt.* Screaming. Weeping. Shouting. "Then don't wear an undershirt," said my mother. "But I want to buy a bra," "What for?"

I suppose that for most girls, breasts, brassieres, that entire thing,   3 has more trauma, more to do with the coming of adolescence, of becoming a woman, than anything else. Certainly more than getting your period, although that too was traumatic, symbolic. But you could *see* breasts; they were there; they were visible. Whereas a girl could claim to have her period for months before she actually got it and nobody would ever know the difference. Which is exactly what I did. All you had to do was make a great fuss over having enough nickels for the Kotex machine and walk around clutching your stomach and moaning for three to five days a month about The Curse and you could convince anybody. There is a school of thought somewhere in the women's lib/women's mag/gynecology establishment that claims that menstrual cramps are purely psychological, and I lean toward it. Not that I didn't have them finally. Agonizing cramps, heating-pad cramps, go-down-to-the-school-nurse-and-lie-on-the-cot cramps. But unlike any pain I have ever suffered, I adored the pain of cramps, welcomed it, wallowed in it, bragged about it. "I can't go. I have cramps." "I can't do that. I have cramps." And most of all, gigglingly, blushingly: "I can't swim. I have cramps." Nobody ever used the hard-core word. Menstruation. God, what an awful word. Never that. "I have cramps."

4      The morning I first got my period, I went into my mother's bedroom to tell her. And my mother, my utterly-hateful-about-bras mother, burst into tears. It was really a lovely moment, and I remember it so clearly not just because it was one of the two times I ever saw my mother cry on my account (the other was when I was caught being a six-year-old kleptomaniac), but also because the incident did not mean to me what it meant to her. Her little girl, her firstborn, had finally become a woman. That was what she was crying about. My reaction to the event, however, was that I might well be a woman in some scientific, textbook sense (and could at least stop faking every month and stop wasting all those nickels). But in another sense—in a visible sense—I was as androgynous and as liable to tip over into boyhood as ever.

5      I started with a 28AA bra. I don't think they made them any smaller in those days, although I gather that now you can buy bras for five year olds that don't have any cups whatsoever in them; trainer bras they are called. My first brassiere came from Robinson's Department Store in Beverly Hills. I went there alone, shaking, positive they would look me over and smile and tell me to come back next year. An actual fitter took me into the dressing room and stood over me while I took off my blouse and tried the first one on. The little puffs stood out on my chest. "Lean over," said the fitter (to this day I am not sure what fitters in bra departments do except to tell you to lean over). I leaned over, with the fleeting hope that my breasts would miraculously fall out of my body and into the puffs. Nothing.

6      "Don't worry about it," said my friend Libby some months later, when things had not improved. "You'll get them after you're married."

7      "What are you talking about?" I said.

8      "When you get married," Libby explained, "your husband will touch your breasts and rub them and kiss them and they'll grow."

9      That was the killer. Necking I could deal with. Intercourse I could deal with. But it had never crossed my mind that a man was going to touch my breasts, that breasts had something to do with all that, petting, my God they never mentioned petting in my little sex manual about fertilization of the ovum. I became dizzy. For I knew instantly—as naïve as I had been only a moment before—that only part of what she was saying was true: the touching, rubbing, kissing part, not the growing part. And I knew that no one would ever want to marry me. I had no breasts. I would never have breasts.

10      My best friend in school was Diana Raskob. She lived a block from me in a house full of wonders. English muffins, for instance. The Raskobs were the first people in Beverly Hills to have English muffins for breakfast. They also had an apricot tree in the back, and a badminton court, and a subscription to *Seventeen* magazine, and hundreds of games

like Sorry and Parcheesi and Treasure Hunt and Anagrams. Diana and I spent three or four afternoons a week in their den reading and playing and eating. Diana's mother's kitchen was full of the most colossal assortment of junk food I have ever been exposed to. My house was full of apples and peaches and milk and homemade chocolate-chip cookies—which were nice, and good for you, but-not-right-before-dinner-or-you'll-spoil-your-appetite. Diana's house had nothing in it that was good for you, and what's more, you could stuff it in right up until dinner and nobody cared. Bar-B-Q potato chips (they were the first in them, too), giant bottles of ginger ale, fresh popcorn with melted butter, hot fudge sauce on Baskin-Robbins jamoca ice cream, powdered-sugar doughnuts from Van de Kamps. Diana and I had been best friends since we were seven; we were about equally popular in school (which is to say, not particularly), we had about the same success with boys (extremely intermittent) and we looked much the same. Dark. Tall. Gangly.

It is September, just before school begins. I am eleven years old,   11 about to enter the seventh grade, and Diana and I have not seen each other all summer. I have been to camp and she has been somewhere like Banff with her parents. We are meeting, as we often do, on the street midway between our two houses and we will walk back to Diana's and eat junk and talk about what has happened to each of us that summer. I am walking down Walden Drive in my jeans and my father's shirt hanging out and my old red loafers with the socks falling into them and coming toward me is . . . I take a deep breath . . . a young woman. Diana. Her hair is curled and she has a waist and hips and a bust and she is wearing a straight skirt, an article of clothing I have been repeatedly told that I will be unable to wear until I have the hips to hold it up. My jaw drops, and suddenly I am crying, crying hysterically, can't catch my breath sobbing. My best friend has betrayed me. She has gone ahead without me and done it. She has shaped up.

Here are some things I did to help:   12
Bought a Mark Eden Bust Developer.   13
Slept on my back for four years.   14
Splashed cold water on them every night because some French ac-   15 tress said in *Life* magazine that that was what *she* did for her perfect bustline.

Ultimately, I resigned myself to a bad toss and began to wear   16 padded bras. I think about them now, think about all those years in high school I went around in them, my three padded bras, every single one of them with different sized breasts. Each time I changed bras I changed sizes: one week nice perky but not too obtrusive breasts, the next medium-sized slightly pointed ones, the next week knockers, true knockers; all the time, whatever size I was, carrying around this rubberized appendage on my chest that occasionally crashed into a wall and was poked inward and had to be poked outward—I think about all that and wonder how anyone kept a straight face through it. My parents, who normally had no restraints about needling me—why did they say nothing as they watched my chest go up and down? My friends, who would periodically inspect my breasts for signs of growth and reassure me—why didn't they at least counsel consistency?

17      And the bathing suits. I die when I think about the bathing suits. That was the era when you could lay an uninhabited bathing suit on the beach and someone would make a pass at it. I would put one on, an absurd swimsuit with its enormous bust built into it, the bones from the suit stabbing me in the rib cage and leaving little red welts on my body, and there I would be, my chest plunging straight downward absolutely vertically from my collarbone to the top of my suit and then suddenly, wham, out came all that padding and material and wiring absolutely horizontally.

18      Buster Klepper was the first boy who ever touched them. He was my boyfriend my senior year of high school. There is a picture of him in my high-school yearbook that makes him look quite attractive in a Jewish, horn-rimmed glasses sort of way, but the picture does not show the pimples, which were air-brushed out, or the dumbness. Well, that isn't really fair. He wasn't dumb. He just wasn't terribly bright. His mother refused to accept it, refused to accept the relentlessly average report cards, refused to deal with her son's inevitable destiny in some junior college or other. "He was tested," she would say to me, apropos of nothing, "and it came out 145. That's near-genius." Had the word under-achiever been coined, she probably would have lobbed that one at me, too. Anyway, Buster was really very sweet—which is, I know, damning with faint praise, but there it is. I was the editor of the front page of the high-school newspaper and he was editor of the back page; we had to work together, side by side, in the print shop, and that was how it started. On our first date, we went to see *April Love* starring Pat Boone. Then we started going together. Buster had a green coupe, a 1950 Ford with an engine he had handchromed until it shone, dazzled, reflected the image of anyone who looked into it, anyone usually being Buster polishing it or the gas-station attendants he constantly asked to check the oil in order for them to be overwhelmed by the sparkle on the valves. The car also had a boot stretched over the back seat for reasons I never understood; hanging from the rearview mirror, as was the custom, was a pair of angora dice. A previous girl friend named Solange who was famous throughout Beverly Hills High School for having no pigment in her right eyebrow had knitted them for him. Buster and I would ride around town, the two of us seated to the left of the steering wheel. I would shift gears. It was nice.

19      There was necking. Terrific necking. First in the car, overlooking Los Angeles from what is now the Trousdale Estates. Then on the bed of his parents' cabana at Ocean House. Incredibly wonderful, frustrating necking, I loved it, really, but no further than necking, please don't, please, because there I was absolutely terrified of the general implica-

tions of going-a-step-further with a near-dummy and also terrified of his finding out there was next to nothing there (which he knew, of course; he wasn't that dumb).

I broke up with him at one point. I think we were apart for about     20 two weeks. At the end of that time I drove down to see a friend at a boarding school in Palos Verdes Estates and a disc jockey played *April Love* on the radio four times during the trip. I took it as a sign. I drove straight back to Griffith Park to a golf tournament Buster was playing in (he was the sixth-seeded teen-age golf player in Southern California) and presented myself back to him on the green of the 18th hole. It was all very dramatic. That night we went to a drive-in and I let him get his hand under my protuberances and onto my breasts. He really didn't seem to mind at all.

*"Do you want to marry my son?" the woman asked me.*     21
*"Yes," I said.*     22
*I was nineteen years old, a virgin, going with this woman's son,*     23 *this big strange woman who was married to a Lutheran minister in New Hampshire and pretended she was Gentile and had this son, by her first husband, this total fool of a son who ran the hero-sandwich concession at Harvard Business School and whom for one moment one December in New Hampshire I said—as much out of politeness as anything else— that I wanted to marry.*

*"Fine," she said. "Now, here's what you do. Always make sure*     24 *you're on top of him so you won't seem so small. My bust is very large, you see, so I always lie on my back to make it look smaller, but you'll have to be on top most of the time."*

*I nodded. "Thank you," I said.*     25
*"I have a book for you to read," she went on. "Take it with you*     26 *when you leave. Keep it." She went to the bookshelf, found it, and gave it to me. It was a book on frigidity.*

*"Thank you," I said.*     27
This is a true story. Everything in this article is a true story, but I     28 feel I have to point out that that story in particular is true. It happened on December 30, 1960. I think about it often. When it first happened, I naturally assumed that the woman's son, my boyfriend, was responsible. I invented a scenario where he had had a little heart-to-heart with his mother and had confessed that his only objection to me was that my breasts were small; his mother then took it upon herself to help out. Now I think I was wrong about the incident. The mother was acting on her own, I think: that was her way of being cruel and competitive under the guise of being helpful and maternal. You have small breasts, she was saying; therefore you will never make him as happy as I have. Or you have small breasts; therefore you will doubtless have sexual problems. Or you have small breasts; therefore you are less woman than I am. She was, as it happens, only the first of what seems to me to be a never-

ending string of women who have made competitive remarks to me about breast size. "I would love to wear a dress like that," my friend Emily says to me, "but my bust is too big." Like that. Why do women say these things to me? Do I attract these remarks the way other women attract married men or alcoholics or homosexuals? This summer, for example. I am at a party in East Hampton and I am introduced to a woman from Washington. She is a minor celebrity, very pretty and Southern and blonde and outspoken and I am flattered because she has read something I have written. We are talking animatedly, we have been talking no more than five minutes, when a man comes up to join us. "Look at the two of us," the woman says to the man, indicating me and her. "The two of us together couldn't fill an A cup." Why does she say that? It isn't even true, dammit, so why? Is she even more addled than I am on this subject? Does she honestly believe there is something wrong with her size breasts, which, it seems to me, now that I look hard at them, are just right. Do I unconsciously bring out competitiveness in women? In that form? What did I do to deserve it?

29    As for men.

30    There were men who minded and let me know they minded. There were men who did not mind. In any case, I always minded.

31    And even now, now that I have been countlessly reassured that my figure is a good one, now that I am grown up enough to understand that most of my feelings have very little to do with the reality of my shape, I am nonetheless obsessed by breasts. I cannot help it. I grew up in the terrible Fifties—with rigid stereotypical sex roles, the insistence that men be men and dress like men and women be women and dress like women, the intolerance of androgyny—and I cannot shake it, cannot shake my feelings of inadequacy. Well, that time is gone, right? All those exaggerated examples of breast worship are gone, right? Those women were freaks, right? I know all that. And yet, here I am, stuck with the psychological remains of it all, stuck with my own peculiar version of breast worship. You probably think I am crazy to go on like this: here I have set out to write a confession that is meant to hit you with the shock of recognition and instead you are sitting there thinking I am thoroughly warped. Well, what can I tell you? If I had had them, I would have been a completely different person. I honestly believe that.

32    After I went into therapy, a process that made it possible for me to tell total strangers at cocktail parties that breasts were the hang-up of my life, I was often told that I was insane to have been bothered by my condition. I was also frequently told, by close friends, that I was extremely boring on the subject. And my girl friends, the ones with nice big breasts, would go on endlessly about how their lives had been far more miserable than mine. Their bra straps were snapped in class. They couldn't sleep on their stomachs. They were stared at whenever the word "mountain" cropped up in geography. And *Evangeline*, good God what they went through every time someone had to stand up and recite the Prologue to

Longfellow's *Evangeline*: "*. . . stand like druids of eld . . . / With beards that rest on their bosoms.*" It was much worse for them, they tell me. They had a terrible time of it, they assure me. I don't know how lucky I was, they say.

I have thought about their remarks, tried to put myself in their place, considered their point of view. I think they are full of shit.    33

## CONSIDERATIONS

1. Nora Ephron's account offends some readers and attracts others for the same reason—the frank and casual exploration of a subject that generations have believed unmentionable. This problem is worth investigating: Are there, in fact, subjects that should not be discussed in the popular press? Are there words a writer must not use? Why? And who should make the list of things not to be talked about?

2. Imagine an argument about Ephron's article between a feminist and an antifeminist. What ammunition could each find in the article? Write the dialog as you hear it.

3. Ephron reports that from a very early age she worried that she might not be "a girl, a definite indisputable girl." Is this anxiety as uncommon as she thought it was? Is worry about one's sex an exclusively female problem? See Bernard Cooper's "Burl" (page 143).

4. Are our ideas about masculinity and femininity changing? How are such ideas determined? How important are they in shaping personality and in channeling thoughts? See Margaret Atwood's "Alien Territory" (page 36).

5. Ephron's article is a good example of the very informal essay. What does she do that makes it so informal? Consider both diction and sentence structure.

6. How can one smile at others' problems—or at one's own disappointments, for that matter? How can Ephron see humor now in what she thought of as tragic then? Provide an example from your own experience.

7. What advantage does Ephron hope to gain when, in paragraph 11, she suddenly changes from past to present tense? Explain; then experiment with the same maneuver in one of your essays.

*Louise Erdrich (b. 1954) grew up in North Dakota. Her heritage is partly Turtle Mountain Chippewa (much of her fiction is drawn from Native American sources) and partly German American. Her Chippewa mother and her German-American father taught at a Bureau of Indian Affairs boarding school. She traveled east to attend Dartmouth College.*

*Although she has published volumes of poetry, she is best known for a tetralogy of novels out of Native American culture in its relationship to the white world:* Love Medicine *(1984 and 1993),* The Beet Queen *(1986),* Tracks *(1988), and* The Bingo Palace *(1994). She has written essays, children's stories, and short fiction also. She has four children and now lives in Minnesota.*

*"The Leap" is a remarkably plotted and written story of a picaresque life and a heroic act of mother love. See how she plants information or exposition at the beginning of her tale in order to make her conclusion both startling and believable.*

— **29** —

# LOUISE ERDRICH
## *The Leap*

1    My mother is the surviving half of a blindfold trapeze act, not a fact I think about much even now that she is sightless, the result of encroaching and stubborn cataracts. She walks slowly through her house here in New Hampshire, lightly touching her way along walls and running her hands over knickknacks, books, the drift of a grown child's belongings and castoffs. She has never upset an object or as much as brushed a magazine onto the floor. She has never lost her balance or bumped into a closet door left carelessly open.

2    It has occurred to me that the catlike precision of her movements in old age might be the result of her early training, but she shows so little of the drama or flair one might expect from a performer that I tend to forget the Flying Avalons. She has kept no sequined costume, no photographs, no fliers or posters from that part of her youth. I would, in fact, tend to think that all memory of double somersaults and heart-stopping

catches had left her arms and legs were it not for the fact that sometimes, as I sit sewing in the room of the rebuilt house in which I slept as a child, I hear the crackle, catch a whiff of smoke from the stove downstairs, and suddenly the room goes dark, the stitches burn beneath my fingers, and I am sewing with a needle of hot silver, a thread of fire.

I owe her my existence three times. The first was when she saved   3
herself. In the town square a replica tent pole, cracked and splintered, now stands cast in concrete. It commemorates the disaster that put our town smack on the front page of the Boston and New York tabloids. It is from those old newspapers, now historical records, that I get my information. Not from my mother, Anna of the Flying Avalons, nor from any of her in-laws, nor certainly from the other half of her particular act, Harold Avalon, her first husband. In one news account it says, "The day was mildly overcast, but nothing in the air or temperature gave any hint of the sudden force with which the deadly gale would strike."

I have lived in the West, where you can see the weather coming for   4
miles, and it is true that out here we are at something of a disadvantage. When extremes of temperature collide, a hot and cold front, winds generate instantaneously behind a hill and crash upon you without warning. That, I think, was the likely situation on that day in June. People probably commented on the pleasant air, grateful that no hot sun beat upon the striped tent that stretched over the entire center green. They bought their tickets and surrendered them in anticipation. They sat. They ate caramelized popcorn and roasted peanuts. There was time, before the storm, for three acts. The White Arabians of Ali-Khazar rose on their hind legs and waltzed. The Mysterious Bernie folded himself into a painted cracker tin, and the Lady of the Mists made herself appear and disappear in surprising places. As the clouds gathered outside, unnoticed, the ringmaster cracked his whip, shouted his introduction, and pointed to the ceiling of the tent, where the Flying Avalons were perched.

They loved to drop gracefully from nowhere, like two sparkling   5
birds, and blow kisses as they threw off their plumed helmets and high-collared capes. They laughed and flirted openly as they beat their way up again on the trapeze bars. In the final vignette of their act, they actually would kiss in midair, pausing, almost hovering as they swooped past one another. On the ground, between bows, Harry Avalon would skip quickly to the front rows and point out the smear of my mother's lipstick, just off the edge of his mouth. They made a romantic pair all right, especially in the blindfold sequence.

That afternoon, as the anticipation increased, as Mr. and Mrs.   6
Avalon tied sparkling strips of cloth onto each other's face and as they puckered their lips in mock kisses, lips destined "never again to meet," as one long breathless article put it, the wind rose, miles off, wrapped itself into a cone, and howled. There came a rumble of electrical energy, drowned out by the sudden roll of drums. One detail not mentioned by the press, perhaps unknown—Anna was pregnant at the time, seven

months and hardly showing, her stomach muscles were that strong. It seems incredible that she would work high above the ground when any fall could be so dangerous, but the explanation—I know from watching her go blind—is that my mother lives comfortably in extreme elements. She is one with the constant dark now, just as the air was her home, familiar to her, safe, before the storm that afternoon.

7    From opposite ends of the tent they waved, blind and smiling, to the crowd below. The ringmaster removed his hat and called for silence, so that the two above could concentrate. They rubbed their hands in chalky powder, then Harry launched himself and swung, once, twice, in huge calibrated beats across space. He hung from his knees and on the third swing stretched wide his arms, held his hands out to receive his pregnant wife as she dove from her shining bar.

8    It was while the two were in midair, their hands about to meet, that lightning struck the main pole and sizzled down the guy wires, filling the air with a blue radiance that Harry Avalon must certainly have seen through the cloth of his blindfold as the tent buckled and the edifice toppled him forward, the swing continuing and not returning in its sweep, and Harry going down, down into the crowd with his last thought, perhaps, just a prickle of surprise at his empty hands.

9    My mother once said that I'd be amazed at how many things a person can do within the act of falling. Perhaps, at the time, she was teaching me to dive off a board at the town pool, for I associate the idea with midair somersaults. But I also think she meant that even in that awful doomed second one could think, for she certainly did. When her hands did not meet her husband's, my mother tore her blindfold away. As he swept past her on the wrong side, she could have grasped his ankle, the toe-end of his tights, and gone down clutching him. Instead, she changed direction. Her body twisted toward a heavy wire and she managed to hang on to the braided metal, still hot from the lightning strike. Her palms were burned so terribly that once healed they bore no lines, only the blank scar tissue of a quieter future. She was lowered, gently, to the sawdust ring just underneath the dome of the canvas roof, which did not entirely settle but was held up on one end and jabbed through, torn, and still on fire in places from the giant spark, though rain and men's jackets soon put that out.

10    Three people died, but except for her hands my mother was not seriously harmed until an overeager rescuer broke her arm in extricating her and also, in the process, collapsed a portion of the tent bearing a huge buckle that knocked her unconscious. She was taken to the town hospital, and there she must have hemorrhaged, for they kept her, confined to her bed, a month and a half before her baby was born without life.

11    Harry Avalon had wanted to be buried in the circus cemetery next to the original Avalon, his uncle, so she sent him back with his brothers. The child, however, is buried around the corner, beyond this house and just down the highway. Sometimes I used to walk there just to sit. She

was a girl, but I rarely thought of her as a sister or even as a separate person really. I suppose you could call it the egocentrism of a child, of all young children, but I considered her a less finished version of myself.

When the snow falls, throwing shadows among the stones, I can   12
easily pick hers out from the road, for it is bigger than the others and in the shape of a lamb at rest, its legs curled beneath. The carved lamb looms larger as the years pass, though it is probably only my eyes, the vision shifting, as what is close to me blurs and distances sharpen. In odd moments, I think it is the edge drawing near, the edge of everything, the unseen horizon we do not really speak of in the eastern woods. And it also seems to me, although this is probably an idle fantasy, that the statue is growing more sharply etched, as if, instead of weathering itself into a porous mass, it is hardening on the hillside with each snowfall, perfecting itself.

It was during her confinement in the hospital that my mother met   13
my father. He was called in to look at the set of her arm, which was complicated. He stayed, sitting at her bedside, for he was something of an armchair traveler and had spent his war quietly, at an air force training grounds, where he became a specialist in arms and legs broken during parachute training exercises. Anna Avalon had been to many of the places he longed to visit—Venice, Rome, Mexico, all through France and Spain. She had no family of her own and was taken in by the Avalons, trained to perform from a very young age. They toured Europe before the war, then based themselves in New York. She was illiterate.

It was in the hospital that she finally learned to read and write, as a   14
way of overcoming the boredom and depression of those weeks, and it was my father who insisted on teaching her. In return for stories of her adventures, he graded her first exercises. He bought her her first book, and over her bold letters, which the pale guides of the penmanship pads could not contain, they fell in love.

I wonder if my father calculated the exchange he offered: one form   15
of flight for another. For after that, and for as long as I can remember, my mother has never been without a book. Until now, that is, and it remains the greatest difficulty of her blindness. Since my father's recent death, there is no one to read to her, which is why I returned, in fact, from my failed life where the land is flat. I came home to read to my mother, to read out loud, to read long into the dark if I must, to read all night.

Once my father and mother married, they moved onto the old farm   16
he had inherited but didn't care much for. Though he'd been thinking of moving to a larger city, he settled down and broadened his practice in this valley. It still seems odd to me, when they could have gone anywhere else, that they chose to stay in the town where the disaster had occurred, and which my father in the first place had found so constricting. It was my mother who insisted upon it, after her child did not survive. And then, too, she loved the sagging farmhouse with its scrap of

what was left of a vast acreage of woods and hidden hay fields that stretched to the game park.

17    I owe my existence, the second time then, to the two of them and the hospital that brought them together. That is the debt we take for granted since none of us asks for life. It is only once we have it that we hang on so dearly.

18    I was seven the year the house caught fire, probably from standing ash. It can rekindle, and my father, forgetful around the house and perpetually exhausted from night hours on call, often emptied what he thought were ashes from cold stoves into wooden or cardboard containers. The fire could have started from a flaming box, or perhaps a buildup of creosote inside the chimney was the culprit. It started right around the stove, and the heart of the house was gutted. The baby-sitter, fallen asleep in my father's den on the first floor, woke to find the stairway to my upstairs room cut off by flames. She used the phone, then ran outside to stand beneath my window.

19    When my parents arrived, the town volunteers had drawn water from the fire pond and were spraying the outside of the house, preparing to go inside after me, not knowing at the time that there was only one staircase and that it was lost. On the other side of the house, the superannuated extension ladder broke in half. Perhaps the clatter of it falling against the walls woke me, for I'd been asleep up to that point.

20    As soon as I awakened, in the small room that I now use for sewing, I smelled the smoke. I followed things by the letter then, was good at memorizing instructions, and so I did exactly what was taught in the second-grade home fire drill. I got up, I touched the back of my door before opening it. Finding it hot, I left it closed and stuffed my rolled-up rug beneath the crack. I did not hide under my bed or crawl into my closet. I put on my flannel robe, and then I sat down to wait.

21    Outside, my mother stood below my dark window and saw clearly that there was no rescue. Flames had pierced one side wall, and the glare of the fire lighted the massive limbs and trunk of the vigorous old elm that had probably been planted the year the house was built, a hundred years ago at least. No leaf touched the wall, and just one thin branch scraped the roof. From below, it looked as though even a squirrel would have had trouble jumping from the tree onto the house, for the breadth of that small branch was no bigger than my mother's wrist.

22    Standing there, beside Father, who was preparing to rush back around to the front of the house, my mother asked him to unzip her dress. When he wouldn't be bothered, she made him understand. He couldn't make his hands work, so she finally tore it off and stood there in her pearls and stockings. She directed one of the men to lean the broken half of the extension ladder up against the trunk of the tree. In surprise, he complied. She ascended. She vanished. Then she could be seen among the leafless branches of late November as she made her way up and,

along her stomach, inched the length of a bough that curved above the branch that brushed the roof.

Once there, swaying, she stood and balanced. There were plenty of people in the crowd and many who still remember, or think they do, my mother's leap through the ice-dark air toward that thinnest extension, and how she broke the branch falling so that it cracked in her hands, cracked louder than the flames as she vaulted with it toward the edge of the roof, and how it hurtled down end over end without her, and their eyes went up, again, to see where she had flown.

I didn't see her leap through air, only heard the sudden thump and looked out my window. She was hanging by the backs of her heels from the new gutter we had put in that year, and she was smiling. I was not surprised to see her, she was so matter-of-fact. She tapped on the window. I remember how she did it, too. It was the friendliest tap, a bit tentative, as if she was afraid she had arrived too early at a friend's house. Then she gestured at the latch, and when I opened the window she told me to raise it wider and prop it up with the stick so it wouldn't crush her fingers. She swung down, caught the ledge, and crawled through the opening. Once she was in my room, I realized she had on only under-clothing, a bra of the heavy stitched cotton women used to wear and step-in, lace-trimmed drawers. I remember feeling light-headed, of course, terribly relieved, and then embarrassed for her to be seen by the crowd undressed.

I was still embarrassed as we flew out the window, toward earth, me in her lap, her toes pointed as we skimmed toward the painted target of the fire fighter's net.

I know that she's right. I knew it even then. As you fall there is time to think. Curled as I was, against her stomach, I was not startled by the cries of the crowd or the looming faces. The wind roared and beat its hot breath at our back, the flames whistled. I slowly wondered what would happen if we missed the circle or bounced out of it. Then I wrapped my hands around my mother's hands. I felt the brush of her lips and heard the beat of her heart in my ears, loud as thunder, long as the roll of drums.

## CONSIDERATIONS

1. How does Erdrich build suspense for the final performance of the Flying Avalons? Consider how the same technique might work in a narrative essay of your own.

2. Find a couple of ironic incidents in the story, and explain why irony is such a useful tool for a writer.

3. What is there in our introduction to the speaker's mother that suggests she might laugh at the people described in the first paragraph of Donald Hall's "Keeping Things" (page 266)?

4. What would have been lost if Erdrich, instead of writing in paragraph 15, "I wonder if my father calculated the exchange he offered: one form of flight for another," had written out exactly what exchange her father might have had in mind?

5. In an otherwise realistically written story, "The Leap" contains one sentence that could only be called fantastic—or, possibly, surreal. Find that sentence and explain its significance.

6. How much time is covered by the story?

7. Sometimes writers cannot resist burying a story yet to be told in the one they're telling us at the moment. Does that occur in "The Leap"?

*Robert Finch (b. 1943) was born in New Jersey beside the Passaic River, which he has called "one of the ten dirtiest rivers in America." He settled on Cape Cod full-time in 1972, where he has been director of publications for the Cape Cod Museum of Natural History. He has written* Common Ground: A Naturalist's Cape Cod *(1981),* The Primal Place *(1983), and* Outlands *(1986). In 1990 he edited* The Norton Book of Nature Writing. *In 1993 the National Park Service issued Finch's official handbook,* Cape Cod: Its Natural and Cultural History. *In the same year, he edited a Cape Cod reader called* A Place Apart. *The essays in* Common Ground, *from which we take "Very Like a Whale," first appeared as weekly columns syndicated in four Cape Cod newspapers.*

*This column begins "One day last week . . ." with the relaxed intimacy that a columnist can use. This writing is personal, a man's own thoughts, and it is addressed to neighbors, some of whom have shared the writer's experience. His writing has a clearer sense of audience than most essays have; it can say "we" without seeming presumptuous. See how, starting from the premise of common experience, Finch can move to uncommon knowledge and speculation.*

— 30 ————————————————————————

# ROBERT FINCH
## *Very Like a Whale*

————————————————————————

One day last week at sunset I went back to Corporation Beach in 1
Dennis to see what traces, if any, might be left of the great, dead finback whale that had washed up there several weeks before. The beach was not as hospitable as it had been that sunny Saturday morning after Thanksgiving when thousands of us streamed over the sand to gaze and look. A few cars were parked in the lot, but these kept their inhabitants. Bundled up against a sharp wind, I set off along the twelve-foot swath of trampled beach grass, a raw highway made in a few hours by ten thousand feet that day.

2        I came to the spot where the whale had beached and marveled that such a magnitude of flesh could have been there one day and gone the next. But the carcass had been hauled off and the tide had smoothed and licked clean whatever vestiges had remained. The cold, salt wind had lifted from the sands the last trace of that pervasive stench of decay that clung to our clothes for days, and now blew clean and sharp into my nostrils.

3        The only sign that anything unusual had been there was that the beach was a little too clean, not quite so pebbly and littered as the surrounding areas, as the grass above a new grave is always fresher and greener. What had so manifestly occupied this space a short while ago was now utterly gone. And yet the whale still lay heavily on my mind; a question lingered, like a persistent odor in the air. And its dark shape, though now sunken somewhere beneath the waves, still loomed before me, beckoning, asking something.

4        What was it? What had we seen? Even the several thousand of us that managed to get down to the beach before it was closed off did not see much. Whales, dead or alive, are protected these days under the Federal Marine Mammals Act, and shortly after we arrived, local police kept anyone from actually touching the whale. I could hardly regret this, since in the past beached whales, still alive, have had cigarettes put out in their eyes and bits of flesh hacked off with pocket knives by souvenir seekers. And so, kept at a distance, we looked on while the specialists worked, white-coated, plastic-gloved autopsists from the New England Aquarium, hacking open the thick hide with carving knives and plumbing its depth for samples to be shipped to Canada for analysis and determination of causes of death. What was it they were pulling out? What fetid mystery would they pluck from that huge coffin of dead flesh? We would have to trust them for the answer.

5        But as the crowds continued to grow around the whale's body like flies around carrion, the question seemed to me, and still seems, not so much why did the whale die, but why had we come to see it? What made this dark bulk such a human magnet, spilling us over onto private lawns and fields? I watched electricians and oil truck drivers pulling their vehicles off the road and clambering down to the beach. Women in high heels and pearls, on their way to Filene's, stumbled through the loose sand to gaze at a corpse. The normal human pattern was broken and a carnival atmosphere was created, appropriate enough in the literal sense of "a farewell to the flesh." But there was also a sense of pilgrimage in those trekking across the beach, an obligation to view such a thing. But for what? Are we really such novices to death? Or so reverent toward it?

6        I could understand my own semiprofessional interest in the whale, but what had drawn these hordes? There are some obvious answers, of course: a break in the dull routine, "something different." An old human desire to associate ourselves with great and extraordinary events. We placed children and sweethearts in front of the corpse and clicked cameras. "Ruthie and the whale." "Having a whale of a time on Cape Cod."

Curiosity, the simplest answer, doesn't really answer anything.   7
What, after all, did we learn by being there? We were more like children
at a zoo, pointing and poking, or Indians on a pristine beach, gazing in innocent wonder at strange European ships come ashore. Yet, as the biologists looted it with vials and plastic bags and the press captured it on
film, the spectators also tried to *make* something of the whale. Circling
around it as though for some hold on its slippery bulk, we grappled it
with metaphors, lashed similes around its immense girth. It lay upside
down, overturned "like a trailer truck." Its black skin was cracked and
peeling, red underneath, "like a used tire." The distended, corrugated
lower jaw, "a giant accordion," was afloat with the gas of putrefaction
and, when pushed, oscillated slowly "like an enormous waterbed." Like
our primitive ancestors, we still tend to make images to try to comprehend the unknown.

But what were we looking at? Or more to the point, from what per-   8
spective were we looking at it? What did we see in it that might tell us
why we had come? A male finback whale—*Balaenoptera physalus*—a
baleen cetacean. The second largest creature ever to live on earth. An intelligent and complex mammal. A cause for conservationists. A remarkably adapted swimming and eating machine. Perfume, pet food,
engineering oil. A magnificent scientific specimen. A tourist attraction.
A media event, a "day to remember." A health menace, a "possible car-
rier of a communicable disease." A municipal headache and a naviga-
tional hazard. Material for an essay.

On the whale's own hide seemed to be written its life history,   9
which we could remark but not read. The right fluke was almost entirely
gone, lost in some distant accident or battle and now healed over with a
white scar. The red eye, unexpectedly small and mammalian, gazed out
at us with fiery blankness. Like the glacial scratches sometimes found on
our boulders, there were strange marks or grooves in the skin around the
anal area, perhaps caused by scraping the ocean bottom.

Yet we could not seem to scratch its surface. The whale—dead, im-   10
mobile, in full view—nonetheless shifted kaleidoscopically before our
eyes. The following morning it was gone, efficiently and sanitarily removed, like the week's garbage. What was it we saw? I have a theory,
though probably (as they say in New England) it hardly does.

There is a tendency these days to defend whales and other endan-   11
gered animals by pointing out their similarities to human beings.
Cetaceans, we are told, are very intelligent. They possess a highly complex language and have developed sophisticated communications systems that transmit over long distances. They form family groups,
develop social structures and personal relationships, and express loyalty
and affection toward one another. Much of their behavior seems to be
recreational: they sing, they play. And so on.

These are not sentimental claims. Whales apparently do these   12
things, at least as far as our sketchy information about their habits

warrants such interpretations. And for my money, any argument that helps to preserve these magnificent creatures can't be all bad.

13        I take exception to this approach not because it is wrong, but because it is wrongheaded and misleading. It is exclusive, anthropocentric, and does not recognize nature in its own right. It implies that whales and other creatures have value only insofar as they reflect man himself and conform to his ideas of beauty and achievement. This attitude is not really far removed from that of the whalers themselves. To consume whales solely for their nourishment of human values is only a step from consuming them for meat and corset staves. It is not only presumptuous and patronizing, but it is misleading and does both whales and men a grave disservice. Whales have an inalienable right to exist, not because they resemble man *or* because they are useful to him, but simply because they do exist, because they have a proven fitness to the exactitudes of being on a global scale matched by few other species. If they deserve our admiration and respect, it is because, as Henry Beston put it, "They are other nations, caught with ourselves in the net of life and time, fellow prisoners of the splendour and travail of life."

14        But that still doesn't explain the throngs who came pell-mell to stare and conjecture at the dead whale that washed up at Corporation Beach and dominated it for a day like some extravagant *memento mori*. Surely we were not flattering ourselves, consciously or unconsciously, with any human comparisons to that rotting hulk. Nor was there much, in its degenerate state, that it had to teach us. And yet we came—why?

15        The answer may be so obvious that we have ceased to recognize it. Man, I believe, has a crying need to confront otherness in the universe. Call it nature, wilderness, the "great outdoors," or what you will—we crave to look out and behold something other than our own human faces staring back at us, expectantly and increasingly frustrated. What the human spirit wants, as Robert Frost said, "Is not its own love back in copy-speech,/ But counter-love, original response."

16        This sense of otherness is, I feel, as necessary a requirement to our personalities as food and warmth are to our bodies. Just as an individual, cut off from human contact and stimulation, may atrophy and die of loneliness and neglect, so mankind is today in a similar, though more subtle, danger of cutting himself off from the natural world he shares with all creatures. If our physical survival depends upon our devising a proper use of earth's materials and produce, our growth as a species depends equally upon our establishing a vital and generative relationship with what surrounds us.

17        We need plants, animals, weather, unfettered shores and unbroken woodland, not merely for a stable and healthy environment, but as an antidote to introversion, a preventive against human inbreeding. Here in particular, in the splendor of natural life, we have an extraordinary reservoir of the Cape's untapped possibilities and modes of being, ways of experiencing life, of knowing wind and wave. After all, how many

neighborhoods have whales wash up in their backyards? To confine this world in zoos or in exclusive human terms does injustice not only to nature, but to ourselves as well.

Ever since his beginnings, when primitive man adopted totems and animal spirits to himself and assumed their shapes in ritual dance, *Homo sapiens* has been a superbly imitative animal. He has looked out across the fields and seen and learned. Somewhere along the line, though, he decided that nature was his enemy, not his ally, and needed to be confined and controlled. He abstracted nature and lost sight of it. Only now are we slowly realizing that nature can be confined only by narrowing our own concepts of it, which in turn narrows us. That is why we came to see the whale. 18

We substitute human myth for natural reality and wonder why we starve for nourishment. "Your Cape" becomes "your Mall," as the local radio jingle has it. Thoreau's "huge and real Cape Cod . . . a wild, rank place with no flattery in it," becomes the Chamber of Commerce's "Rural Seaside Charm"—until forty tons of dead flesh wash ashore and give the lie to such thin, flattering conceptions, flesh whose stench is still the stench of life that stirs us to reaction and response. That is why we came to see the whale. Its mute, immobile bulk represented that ultimate, unknowable otherness that we both seek and recoil from, and shouted at us louder than the policeman's bullhorn that the universe is fraught, not merely with response or indifference, but incarnate assertion. 19

Later that day the Dennis Board of Health declared the whale carcass to be a "health menace" and warned us off the beach. A health menace? More likely an intoxicating, if strong, medicine that might literally bring us to our senses. 20

But if those of us in the crowd failed to grasp the whale that day, others did not have much better luck. Even in death the whale escaped us: the tissue samples taken in the autopsy proved insufficient for analysis and the biologists concluded, "We will never know why the whale died." The carcass, being towed tail-first by a Coast Guard cutter for a final dumping beyond Provincetown, snapped a six-inch hawser. Eluding further attempts to reattach it, it finally sank from sight. Even our powers of disposal, it seemed, were questioned that day. 21

And so, while we are left on shore with the memory of a deflated and stinking carcass and of bullhorns that blared and scattered us like flies, somewhere out beyond the rolled waters and the shining winter sun, the whale sings its own death in matchless, sirenian strains. 22

## CONSIDERATIONS

1. A feature of Finch's style in "Very Like a Whale" is his skillful use of figurative language. In paragraph 3, for example, he compares the cleaned-up beach to "grass above a new grave," and his question to the whale that "still lay heavily on my mind."

Other examples are the question that "lingered, like a persistent odor," and the dark shape of the whale, long gone beneath the waves, that "still loomed" before him. Locate and underline a dozen more figures of speech in the essay. Decide whether they are merely decorative or significantly functional in the essay.

2. Does Finch's title sound familiar, but you just can't place it? Look up the phrase in *Familiar Quotations* by John Bartlett. Does it take on a new meaning when used as the title of this essay? How much thought do you give to the titles of your own essays?

3. Where does Finch first set forth the thesis of his essay? What responsibility does a thesis expressed as a question place on the writer? Does Finch meet that responsibility?

4. With the exception of the first three lines, what is the conspicuous grammatical form used in paragraph 8? Try changing each of the items in the series to a more conventional form. Can you now justify Finch's style in this paragraph?

5. Why does Finch object to a common approach by people concerned about preserving "nature"? See paragraph 13. Would he, for instance, find George Orwell's response to the death of an elephant (see "Shooting an Elephant") "sentimental," "exclusive," or "anthropocentric"? See also Henry David Thoreau's "Journal: November 30, 1858" (page 616).

6. What is the significance of the next to last word of Finch's essay?

*Janet Frame (b. 1924) comes from New Zealand. She has written poems as well as novels, and three volumes of reminiscence— memory out of particular circumstances, concluding in self-analysis.*

*Writers start as readers. They become collectors of words. They dwell on the sounds of words, even cherishing words they don't understand; thus, the plot of "Jewels" unfolds.*

*The painter Degas once told the poet Mallarme that he had an idea for a poem. Mallarme answered that poems were made not with ideas but with words.*

— 31 —

# JANET FRAME
## *Jewels*

Words, first words, are as traumatic as first love and first death. When we are young, presented with mature experienced words and lacking the mental imagery to receive them, we hospitably give them what we have in our minds only to find that we have invited them to live a falsehood which we believed to be truth. I am reminded of a word which caused much hope and suffering to me in my earliest years and which has accompanied me through my life, and because of its privileged metaphorical status, it will also attend my death. It is among the aristocracy of language because we have chosen to put it there. 1

The word is *jewel.* 2

I first heard the word "jewel" when I was very young, and its meaning was immediately clear, with the word becoming its meaning. Precious, a treasure, a glittering gem or stone in a choice of many colors and shapes and textures. 3

I knew that I would never own a jewel. I learned the names of jewels: ruby, sapphire, topaz, carnelian, fire opal, agate, moonstone, bloodstone, jasper, diamond. When my mother, in a poetic frame of mind, glanced out of the window in the early morning and observed that the lawn was covered with jewels, I learned not to take her remark literally; nor when she spoke of a relative or friend as being a "jewel," though I 4 found it hard to accept these falsehoods and I resented the confusion I felt over my inability to discern where to put a word when it was given to me, whether among the real or the unreal, especially when to me all was real. I could say that by the time I was seven I had almost an open mind about language; I was prepared for any shock, and as vigilant as a soldier on sentry duty in my encounters with words, yet I was caught unawares at school one day, in my eighth year, when I overheard a fellow pupil say to his friend,

5    "In Class Two they sit in *jewel* desks. Class Two is the only classroom with *jewel* desks."

6    You may imagine the effect of this news. From that moment I switched my hopes from dreams of Olympic glory (I was a fast runner) to those of acquiring a fortune in jewels. *Jewel desks.* In my saner moments I could not believe it was possible. My curiosity about the room with the jewel desks became intense, and as I was too shy to ask for details I had to live in a torture of wondering, with at least the consolation that when I was promoted to Class Two my curiosity would be satisfied. When I passed the door to Class Two it was always closed, and I could hear murmurs from within, which I interpreted as murmurs of wonder and pleasure as Class Two inspected the jewels in a special hour devoted to jewel inspection and appreciation.

7    It began to seem impossible that I could live through the remaining three months of the year until I became eligible to share the jewels. I had a growing fear that the supply might end, as no doubt the jewels were distributed to Class Two pupils, on loan or permanently; I noticed some bulky schoolbags being carried home in the afternoons. Also, I was worried about the evident secrecy. Except for that one day when I overheard the news, I heard no one speak of the jewel desks. Once, casually, making it half a question, half a statement, I said to another boy, "In Class Two you sit in a jewel desk."

8    "Yeah," he said. "A jewel desk."

9    He was uninterested, or he appeared to be; perhaps he had his own plans about the jewels and was confiding in no one.

10    One day when school was out and I was late going home, I walked along the corridor and I was about to pass the room when I noticed the door was open, and with an awful racing of my heart, I peeped in. I saw the desks, not single desks like ours, but long heavy desks with two lift-up seats to a desk. Not a jewel in sight. Obviously, they were removed each afternoon and locked in the class cupboard, and as if to confirm this, there was the teacher at that moment turning the key in the class cupboard. I had just missed seeing the jewels! It was almost as thrilling as having seen them.

11    Still, I might have gone crazy with wondering and planning had I not had an unexpected good fortune. One day, on the strength of being Excellent in Comprehension, Spelling and Arithmetic, and being able to recite unfalteringly in their correct order the ten longest rivers, highest

mountain peaks, deepest lakes in the world, I, and Gloria Bone, were promoted to Class Two.

"You can move your books after school," the teacher said. "And go  12
to Class Two tomorrow."

After school we took our books to Class Two where, as I expected,  13
the jewels were already locked away for the night.

"We'll be sitting in jewel desks," Gloria Bone said, so loudly that I  14
hushed her.

"What do you mean, Sh-sh-sh? Everyone knows you sit in jewel  15
desks in Class Two."

I was alarmed. I saw my fortune disappearing. I dug Gloria Bone  16
with my elbow which was effectively sharp. "Blabber," I said.

The teacher took our promotion cards to the class cupboard, opened  17
it, put the cards quickly inside, and relocked it, seeming, to my inflamed
imagination, to glance significantly at me as she turned the key in the
lock. Her glance promised, Distribution for new pupils of sapphires, diamonds, rubies, carnelian, bloodstone, immediately after the Lord's
Prayer and Hymn Singing tomorrow morning. What a stupendous
promise! Nothing, I thought, must be allowed to interfere with the distribution of the jewels. Perhaps there would be a special hymn for the occasion,

> When he cometh, when he cometh
> to make up his jewels,
> all his jewels, precious jewels,
> his loved and his own . . .

Or perhaps we would sing that hymn where the reckless (how reckless!) saints were "casting down their golden crowns around the glassy
sea."

There's a limit to patience. When I had been three days in Class Two  18
and there was still no sign of the promised jewels I decided to ask about
them. I said to my neighbor who sat with me in the new type of desk,

"I thought these were meant to be jewel desks."  19

His reply mystified me. "They *are* jewel desks. Can't you see?"  20

Here was a problem. It had not occurred to me that the jewels were  21
invisible, the kind you read about, which could become visible if you
were good, clever, self-sacrificing, courageous. Reluctant to admit that I
might be none of these, I tried a new approach.

"Are you ever allowed to take them home? You know—a handful—  22
to . . . to . . . (I was about to say to keep or to spend when I suspected
this might be classified as unself-sacrificing) you know, to give to your
mother so she can see again, or to your father so he can voyage round the
world in his spare time."

My classmate was matter-of-fact. He closed the lid of his desk  23
carefully.

24    "I didn't know that your mother was blind or that your father was wanting to voyage around the world," he said sarcastically.

25    "She isn't. He isn't."

26    "Then what the heck are you talking about? I think you must be touched. What do you mean? A handful of what?"

27    Why could he not understand?

28    "Listen," I said desperately. "I'm talking about the *jewels* from the *jewel* desks, the *jewel* desks we're sitting in now."

29    "Jewel desks? Jewel desks?"

30    Then he tittered down the scale, in sudden delight. "You mean *duel* desks." He spelled the word—d-u-e-l. "Duel desks. Duel meaning two, a fight with swords. Fighting a duel. A duel desk. Are some people dumb! You don't mean you really thought these were jewel desks with diamonds and rubies and precious stones?"

31    His disbelief was infectious; I began to wonder if I had believed it myself. Diamonds, rubies, sapphires, agate, moonstone, bloodstones?

32    "Not exactly," I said, a traitor to my dreams. "Not exactly."

33    It did not seem fair that one word could promise so much, could have held so much power to organize and disorganize my life. How could I have been so at the mercy of one word? My betrayal by the word "jewel" was a lasting blow dealt to me by the language I was encouraged to be at home in.

34    That night when I came home from school, I opened our dictionary and by chance found both the words *duel* and *dual.* I read, dual: pertaining to two, shared by two, twofold, double; duel: a combat between two persons fought with deadly weapons by agreement, in the presence of witnesses.

35    It's *dual* desks, I thought, realizing that even my classmate, unknowingly, was a victim of the treachery of the language. His interpretation of "duel" desks might cause him more suffering than mine had. Duel desks. Duel. A combat fought by two people with deadly weapons by agreement, in the presence of witnesses. He could be preparing a catastrophe for himself.

36    I prized the information given to me by the dictionary, and the generous way it offered up its words to anyone who turned its pages. I had never before prized information though I knew others did, and I was familiar with its power to grant victory in many battles both with other children and with adults. I realize now that I did receive the jewels I had been promised. I had opened the dictionary and I had been showered with the inescapable words which, if I worked, could become my allies instead of my enemies. The word "jewel" remained with me in a special place among the indelible impressions of my life and it was like meeting a first love or a first hate when years afterward, opening the English examination paper in the Public Service examination for accountants, I read, Paraphrase the following:

Dear beauteous death, the jewel of the just,
shining nowhere but in the dark.
What mysteries do lie beyond thy dust
could man outlook that mark!

There have been deaths in my life which touched the pressure     37
points of my experience, enriching it as if by fine jewels (the word serving me at last) which in their new setting revealed more clearly their
own brilliance, density, perfections and imperfections. The idea of death
as a jewel seems to me fair recompense for my painful association with
the word; it allows me to indulge in an exquisite annihilation of the to-
getherness in which it once disguised itself. Dual indeed! Or duel! A
combat fought by agreement with deadly weapons, in the presence of
witnesses.

It is good to see death returning to Class Two where, imagining we     38
sit together, we sit alone.

## CONSIDERATIONS

1. Janet Frame's childhood confusion grew out of a class of words called
homonyms—two or more words that have the same sound and often the same spelling
but that differ in meaning, as in dual/duel, base/base, horse/hoarse, told/tolled,
turn/tern, dew/due, bear/bare. The same definition applies to puns. Make a little collection—say, fifteen minutes' worth—of words with double or triple meanings; then write
a short essay on the problems (and the fun) caused by the presence of so many
homonyms in the English language.
2. Why is it unlikely that Janet Frame's problem with "jewel" would have arisen
had she grown up in Iowa instead of New Zealand?
3. "I found it hard to accept these falsehoods," writes Frame in paragraph 4
about her mother's figurative use of words like "jewel." She resented "the confusion I
felt over my inability to discern where to put a word . . . , whether among the real or
the unreal, especially when to me all was real." Find good examples of figurative language in any of the readings of this text, and use some of them in discussing your own
experience in learning to sort out the figurative and the literal.
4. In her closing line, the author writes, ". . . imagining we sit together, we sit
alone." Has that thought ever occurred to you while sitting in a classroom or a church
or a stadium full of people? Comment or explain.

*Joan Frank (b. 1949) was born in Arizona and went to college at
the University of California (Davis). She served in the Peace Corps
in West Africa, lived for several years in Hawaii, and has published
short stories as well as essays. She currently lives in Northern
California, and her book of collected short stories,* Boys Keep Being
Born, *was published in 2001 by the University of Missouri Press.*

*Here she remembers a disturbing moment from her freshman
year at college. She committed a small crime. Arrested, she was
aided by a public defender who became an angel of compassion.
See how she records, with an intimacy of detail, her mood of
desperation.*

— 32 ——————————————————————————

# JOAN FRANK
## *Petty Theft*

———————————————————————————————

1    When I was 18 and had just left home to begin college, I moved
through my life the way you drive through a fog. I crept along squinting,
blinded by the reflection of my own confused desires in the million little
mirroring droplets of other people's lives. Frightened by the fierceness of
others' purposes, unsure what in the world I actually wanted, I wandered
between classes in a haze.

2    Though groomed all my short life as an exceptional student, part of
me was still the spaced-out child who strolled in a dream to the corner
store for a cream soda, and who sometimes, with no particular thought
for it, also pocketed a candy bar or a bottle of cologne.

3    I don't know that I did it often, or that I ever stopped to consider
why. I know my friends stole things occasionally, but mainly as what is
called "a lark"—not making a career of it, though harder types boasted of
elaborate methods for spiriting off record albums and clothing.

4    No, I only remember doing it because it seemed easy, and for a kind
of low-grade thrill: I had not paid, yet here was the delicious prize toted
successfully out the door (heart beating fast) and now safely home with
me, real and usable and pleasure-giving—possibly slightly more so for
the illicit getting of it.

———————————————

"Petty Theft" by Joan Frank, *Chicago Tribune Magazine,* August 27, 1995.
Reprinted by permission of the author.

This occasional shoplifting habit simply rode along with me down the freeway in my dusty pea-green Volkswagen beetle, together with other small possessions and habits—the acoustic guitar, the battered jeans with fringes forming at the ripped knees, the Baez and Clapton albums, the old Royal portable typewriter my father had given me; the Salinger and Rilke books, the taste for bologna sandwiches and chocolate milk—habits that resumed themselves unthinkingly on arrival, in a little cabin I rented near the town's train station.

Thus it was just a reflexive afterthought, on visiting the local drugstore, to drop the extra items into my big floppy shoulder sack before purchasing other things at the checkout counter.

I can still see the quality of daylight beckoning through the glass exit door as I stood there. In my bag were a small bottle of bright-yellow daily multiple vitamins and a generic pair of nylon hose. Of course, like most working students, I was usually broke; but never literally starving, so I can only assume the vitamins and hose must have counted as slightly more exotic in my lexicon of spending.

I wish I could tell you that I suffered deep moral grapplings, or at least bouts of fancy rationalizing and equivocation, but it wasn't so. I had every expectation of walking calmly home, as I had always done. But this time a man quietly stopped me just outside the door, asking to examine the contents of my bag, and then the heedless dream became a surreal one.

I was led to an office in the store, questioned by people with reproachful faces. I remember realizing with dull but building anguish, as if forced awake from a drugged sleep, that somehow I had just done possibly the worst thing I could ever do—not because of great care then for its effect on my life, but because my father might be told.

Police must have been phoned, but I have no recollection of it, nor of being loaded into a squad car or being fingerprinted or booked. The next scene in my mental archives cuts directly to the office of a woman who was assigned me as counsel: the public defender.

I will never forget her, and if I had only found the wits to keep her name, I would surely be writing her today. She was large, earth-mother-shaped, not pretty, but comfortable. Straight ashen hair to shoulder-level, pinned back neatly on either side. She may have been 30—a spaced-out 18 does not judge ages well. She spoke to me softly but with seriousness; not coddling; but direct and businesslike. I'll call her Sandy.

In her book-lined office, Sandy asked me what had happened, and I must have summoned all my courage to answer her truthfully: that I had lifted the things with no clear sense of any compelling reason. I told her I was terrified that word of this would reach my father, a beloved professor in a college down the road, and I felt I would rather be destroyed than allow him to know such petty horribleness about me. It would not only hurt and dismay but deplete him, I knew, and he surely did not deserve a second's blame for it—which of course he would take on.

13    He had reared my sister and me from my mother's death, seven years earlier, and in my eyes he could do little wrong. I missed having a mother terribly, but took great solace in my pained, gentle father.

14    Sandy explained I was still considered a minor by the State, or at least quasi-minor—that is, in five years without mishap, the record of this incident could be sealed. Sealed! Meaning: It would not seep like black oil into the snowy-clean years before me; meaning, I could later apply for jobs and passports and Peace Corps and grad school (all of which I did), and never have to check the box that asks, "Have you ever been arrested or in serious violation of the law?"—a checkmark presumably removing the young seeker from her first choices or from ever being considered herself a first choice.

15    What Sandy did during prep time, and in the courtroom where she petitioned the judge to allow sealing the record—the simple, galvanizing thing she did—was to treat me, and the situation, with composure and dignity. She never scolded; never made cracks, never goaded or humiliated me, never exacted promises or pleas.

16    She could doubtless read in my face the impact of the experience, seeing it had been punishment enough—and to her eternal credit, allowed me what a wise friend calls the dignity of fact, without insisting on making doomsday inferences. It is a manner I still remember when I'm dealing with kids—relatives, friends, students. Each has his or her right to that dignity, of course—but for some, like me at 18, it is a kind of revelation to be shown it, a sly, and quite elegant, wake-up call. I hope I thanked her well.

## CONSIDERATIONS

1. There are several ways to tell others about a youthful misstep: some go about it shamefacedly, some brag about it, some attempt to minimize it. How would you describe the tone Joan Frank uses in her confession? What words or phrases are indicators of that tone?

2. "The needs of a society determine its ethics," writes Maya Angelou in "Mr. Red Leg" (page 25), as she tells of a successful swindle of a racist white man by two ingenious black men. Is there a similar expression of the notion of relative ethics in Frank's account? It might help to consider how her shoplifting might have been treated one hundred or two hundred years ago.

3. Frank's story is filled with very specific details. What do these contribute to the success of the piece?

4. Most of "Petty Theft" is told plainly and literally, but in paragraphs 1 and 14, the author uses rather striking metaphors, like sudden splashes of color in an otherwise black-and-white photograph. Is she simply yielding to a temptation to be "fancy," or are those figures of speech real assets in the essay? Explain.

5. Writing of the attorney who spoke for her in court, Frank says, "to her eternal credit, [she] allowed me what a wise friend calls the dignity of fact, without insisting on making doomsday inferences." Explain "the dignity of fact" and invent some "doomsday inferences" that might have been expressed about the girl.

Robert Frost (1874–1963) was born in California and became the great poet of New England. He published many books of poetry and won the Pulitzer Prize three times. A popular figure, Frost was admired as a gentle, affectionate, avuncular figure given to country sayings. The private Frost, however, was another man—guilty, jealous, bitter, sophisticated, occasionally triumphant, and always complicated. President Kennedy asked Robert Frost to read a poem at his inauguration in 1961. Because the sunlight dazzled his eyes, the old man could not read the poem that he had composed for the occasion, and instead he recited "The Gift Outright" from memory. With its emphasis on the nature of citizenship and its sense of history, the poem was wholly appropriate for the occasion. In the last line, thinking of the occasion, Frost changed "would" to "will." In 1995 the Library of America issued Robert Frost's work in one volume.

— 33 ——————————————————

# ROBERT FROST
## *The Gift Outright*

———————————————————

The land was ours before we were the land's.
She was our land more than a hundred years
Before we were her people. She was ours
In Massachusetts, in Virginia,
But we were England's, still colonials,                           5
Possessing what we still were unpossessed by,
Possessed by what we now no more possessed.
Something we were withholding made us weak
Until we found out that it was ourselves
We were withholding from our land of living,                     10
And forthwith found salvation in surrender.
Such as we were we gave ourselves outright
(The deed of gift was many deeds of war)
To the land vaguely realizing westward,
But still unstoried, artless, unenhanced,                        15
Such as she was, such as she would become.

———————————

*Martin Gansberg (b. 1920) edited and reported for the* New York
Times *for forty years. This story, written in 1964, has been widely
reprinted. Largely because of Gansberg's account, the murder of
Kitty Genovese has become an infamous example of citizen
apathy. When Gansberg returned to the neighborhood fifteen years
afterward, revisiting the place of the murder with a television
crew, the people had not changed: still, no one wanted to get
involved.*

*Gansberg's style, organization, and paragraphs are
appropriate to a reporter's news story, usually not a structural
model for an essay. He begins with the peak and point of his story.
The information that follows provides background to his initial
statement. Because newspaper columns are narrow and blocks of
print are hard to read without indentation, journalists make short
paragraphs. Notice how this staccato rhythm, in skilled hands,
adds emphasis and power to this shocking story.*

# — 34 —————

# MARTIN GANSBERG
## *38 Who Saw Murder Didn't Call the Police*

1    For more than half an hour 38 respectable, law-abiding citizens in
Queens watched a killer stalk and stab a woman in three separate attacks in Kew Gardens.

2    Twice their chatter and the sudden glow of their bedroom lights interrupted him and frightened him off. Each time he returned, sought her
out, and stabbed her again. Not one person telephoned the police during
the assault; one witness called after the woman was dead.

3    That was two weeks ago today.

4    Still shocked is Assistant Chief Inspector Frederick M. Lussen, in
charge of the borough's detectives and a veteran of 25 years of homicide
investigations. He can give a matter-of-fact recitation on many murders.

But the Kew Gardens slaying baffles him—not because it is a murder, but because the "good people" failed to call the police.

"As we have reconstructed the crime," he said, "the assailant had three chances to kill this woman during a 35-minute period. He returned twice to complete the job. If we had been called when he first attacked, the woman might not be dead now." 5

This is what the police say happened beginning at 3:20 A.M. in the staid, middle-class, tree-lined Austin Street area: 6

Twenty-eight-year-old Catherine Genovese, who was called Kitty by almost everyone in the neighborhood, was returning home from her job as manager of a bar in Hollis. She parked her red Fiat in a lot adjacent to the Kew Gardens Long Island Rail Road Station, facing Mowbray Place. Like many residents of the neighborhood, she had parked there day after day since her arrival from Connecticut a year ago, although the railroad frowns on the practice. 7

She turned off the lights of her car, locked the door, and started to walk the 100 feet to the entrance of her apartment at 82–70 Austin Street, which is in a Tudor building, with stores in the first floor and apartments on the second. 8

The entrance to the apartment is in the rear of the building because the front is rented to retail stores. At night the quiet neighborhood is shrouded in the slumbering darkness that marks most residential areas. 9

Miss Genovese noticed a man at the far end of the lot, near a seven-story apartment house at 82–40 Austin Street. She halted. Then nervously, she headed up Austin Street towards Lefferts Boulevard, where there is a call box to the 102nd Police Precinct in nearby Richmond Hill. 10

She got as far as a street light in front of a bookstore before the man grabbed her. She screamed. Lights went on in the 10-story apartment house at 82–67 Austin Street, which faces the bookstore. Windows slid open and voices punctuated the early-morning stillness. 11

Miss Genovese screamed: "Oh, my God, he stabbed me! Please help me! Please help me!" 12

From one of the upper windows in the apartment house, a man called down: "Let that girl alone!" 13

The assailant looked up at him, shrugged and walked down Austin Street toward a white sedan parked a short distance away. Miss Genovese struggled to her feet. 14

Lights went out. The killer returned to Miss Genovese, now trying to make her way around the side of the building by her parking lot to get to her apartment. The assailant stabbed her again. 15

"I'm dying!" she shrieked. "I'm dying!" 16

Windows were opened again, and lights went on in many apartments. The assailant got into his car and drove away. Miss Genovese staggered to her feet. A city bus, O–10, the Lefferts Boulevard line to Kennedy International Airport, passed. It was 3:35 A.M. 17

18    The assailant returned. By then, Miss Genovese had crawled to the back of the building where the freshly painted doors to the apartment house held out hope for safety. The killer tried the first door; she wasn't there. At the second door, 82–62 Austin Street, he saw her slumped on the floor at the foot of the stairs. He stabbed her a third time—fatally.

19    It was 3:50 by the time the police received their first call, from a man who was a neighbor of Miss Genovese. In two minutes they were at the scene. The neighbor, a 70-year-old woman, and another woman were the only persons on the street. Nobody else came forward.

20    The man explained that he had called the police after much deliberation. He had phoned a friend in Nassau County for advice and then he had crossed the roof of the building to the apartment of the elderly woman to get her to make the call.

21    "I didn't want to get involved," he sheepishly told the police.

22    Six days later, the police arrested Winston Moseley, a 29-year-old business-machine operator, and charged him with homicide. Moseley had no previous record. He is married, has two children and owns a home at 133–19 Sutter Avenue, South Ozone Park, Queens. On Wednesday, a court committed him to Kings County Hospital for psychiatric observation.

23    When questioned by the police, Moseley also said that he had slain Mrs. Annie May Johnson, 24, of 146–12 133rd Avenue, Jamaica, on Feb. 29 and Barbara Kralik, 15, of 174–17 140th Avenue, Springfield Gardens, last July. In the Kralik case, the police are holding Alvin L. Mitchell, who is said to have confessed that slaying.

24    The police stressed how simple it would have been to have gotten in touch with them. "A phone call," said one of the detectives, "would have done it." The police may be reached by dialing "O" for operator or SPring 7–3100.

25    Today witnesses from the neighborhood, which is made up of one-family homes in the $35,000 to $60,000 range with the exception of the two apartment houses near the railroad station, find it difficult to explain why they didn't call the police.

26    A housewife, knowingly if quite casually, said, "We thought it was a lover's quarrel." A husband and wife both said, "Frankly, we were afraid." They seemed aware of the fact that events might have been different. A distraught woman, wiping her hands on her apron, said, "I didn't want my husband to get involved."

27    One couple, now willing to talk about that night, said they heard the first screams. The husband looked thoughtfully at the bookstore where the killer first grabbed Miss Genovese.

28    "We went to the window to see what was happening," he said, "but the light from our bedroom made it difficult to see the street." The wife, still apprehensive, added: "I put out the light and we were able to see better."

29    Asked why they hadn't called the police, she shrugged and replied: "I don't know."

A man peeked out from a light opening in the doorway to his apart-   30
ment and rattled off an account of the killer's second attack. Why hadn't
he called the police at the time? "I was tired," he said without emotion.
"I went back to bed."

It was 4:25 A.M. when the ambulance arrived to take the body of   31
Miss Genovese. It drove off. "Then," a solemn police detective said, "the
people came out."

## CONSIDERATIONS

1. Obviously—though not overtly—Gansberg's newspaper account condemns
the failure of ordinary citizens to feel socially responsible. Explain how the writer
makes his purpose obvious without openly stating it. Compare his method with
Orwell's use of implication in "A Hanging" (page 479).

2. In paragraph 7, Gansberg tells us that Catherine Genovese was called Kitty and
that she drove a red Fiat. Are these essential details? If not, why does this writer use them?

3. Newspapers use short paragraphs for visual relief. If you were making this
story into a narrative essay, how might you change the paragraphing?

4. Is Gansberg's opening sentence a distortion of the facts? Read his account
carefully before you answer; then explain and support your answer with reference to
other parts of the story.

5. Gansberg's newspaper report was published nearly forty years ago. Are similar
incidents more common now? Were they more common in the 1960s than in the 1940s
or 1930s or 1920s? How about in the 1970s, 1980s, 1990s, and now the new century?
In what way does media coverage alter our impressions? What sources could you use to
find the facts?

*Rumer Godden (1907–1998) grew up in India. If she and her sisters played outdoors with their dolls, she remembered in later life, they risked losing them to monkeys. She was educated and spent most of her life in the United Kingdom. Her first well-known novel was* **Black Narcissus** *(1939). She wrote many books for children.*

*Rumer Godden's satirical imaginary correspondence ridicules the dumbing down of our culture. Publishers as well as television producers and newspaper owners condescend to the intelligence and knowledge of the public—which is us. Recently critics have pointed out revisions made between the English and the American editions of the Harry Potter series, in which American readers are presumed incapable of understanding English English.*

*This phenomenon is not new, but it is progressive. Godden's essay was published in 1963. See how its satirical point, as the reader follows the exchange of letters, derives from the stubborn obtuseness of an imagined correspondent.*

— 35 ————————————————————————

# RUMER GODDEN
## *An Imaginary Correspondence*

————————————————————————

*An imaginary correspondence between Mr V. Andal, editor of the De Base Publishing Company, Inc., and the ghost of Miss Beatrix Potter,[1] using the word* ghost *in the old meaning of soul or spirit. She would be shocked to its depth if she knew some of the things that are going on nowadays in the world of children's books.*

_____

"An Imaginary Correspondence" by Rumer Godden, copyright © 1963 by Rumer Godden. First appeared in *The Horn Book Magazine,* reprinted in *Only Connect* by Egoff, Stubbs and Ashley (Oxford University Press). Reprinted by permission of Curtis Brown Ltd.

[1]Some of Beatrix Potter's remarks are taken from her letters.

## Mr V. Andal to Miss B. Potter

January 18, 1963

Dear Miss Potter:

I am editing for the De Base Publishing Company, Inc., an unusual 1
series of books aimed at beginning readers. The general title is
'Masterpieces for Mini-Minds', and the series will consist of reissues, in
a modern production, of famous books that have become classics for
children, so that the first reading of the very young will also be an introduction to their own great authors. We are approaching, among others,
Hans Andersen, Edward Lear, Lewis Carroll, George MacDonald, Anna
Sewell, and Andrew Lang.

The works will be produced whole and entire, though with certain 2
modifications to the text to make them suitable for children of 1963:
with this in view we have decided on a limited vocabulary of 450 different words. I have had a list of words prepared by a trio of philologists and
I would be glad to send it to you if you are interested. Other words may
be added as long as they are within the grasp of a reader from 5 to 8.

Mr Al Loy, our president, has authorized me to pay an advance of 3
$3,000 against royalty upon receipt of an acceptable manuscript along
the lines indicated. In addition to the advance, there should be continuing payments, for the books will have, besides quality writing, the collaboration of the best illustrators and should enjoy a huge sale.

I hope you will be one of the contributors to this project. If you 4
would like to edit your own book, I will be delighted to send you the
word list, from which departures can, of course, be made (as long as they
come within this age range). If you would rather we edited, this will be
undertaken with the utmost care and the De Base Company will be
pleased to send you a check for $3,000 as soon as I forward your work.

Cordially,
V. ANDAL

I send you Hans Andersen's 'Ti-ny Thum-my' to see. (Originally is- 5
sued as 'Thumbelina', and I think now much improved.)

## Miss B. Potter to Mr V. Andal

26th January, 1963.

Dear Mr Andal,

Thank you for your letter. That a request for a fresh issue of my 6
books should reach me after so many years is heartening. The cheque
you offer is certainly generous; there are several acres round Sawrey that
could with advantage be purchased and given to our National Trust.
Publication with another firm would vex my old publishers very much,
and I don't like breaking with old friends, but possibly we might arrange

to have something published on the American market that would not interfere with my normal sales.

7       I presume you will want *Peter Rabbit.* I believe my attitude of mind towards my own successful publications has been comical. At one time I almost loathed Peter Rabbit, I was so sick of him. I still cannot understand his perennial success. I myself prefer *The Tailor of Gloucester,* and send you both books to see.

Yours sincerely,
BEATRIX POTTER

8       N.B. My books are illustrated by myself.
9       N.B. I do not understand your second paragraph. How can a work be 'whole and entire' if it is modified? How can a philologist, however gifted, know what words I need? Perhaps I have misunderstood you.

## Mr V. Andal to Miss Potter

February 4, 1963

Dear Miss Potter:
10       I hasten to thank you for 'Peter Rabbit', a most charming tale, and am sure that, when made larger (it must be enlarged—people like to get their money's worth) and given good illustrations, it will make a magnificent book for our series; we shall have our reader's report in a day or two when I shall write to you again. 'The Tailor of Gloucester' I have, for the moment, put aside. It has an old-fashioned air about it that might puzzle a child, but perhaps it might be reissued as a 'period piece'. The words would need a great deal of simplification: 'worn to a ravelling'—what could a child make of that?
11       I am sorry my letter was not clear. The modifications about such words are only those needed to make language more assimilatory to the children of today. In this connection, we believe the advice of our philologists is of value; they are often able to help an author to put his, or her, delightful thoughts into plain words—simple enough for a child to understand.

Yours very sincerely,
V. ANDAL

## Miss Potter to Mr V. Andal

10th February, 1963.

Dear Mr Andal,
12       Again I do not understand. What do you mean by 'reader's report'? When I sent the manuscript of *Peter Rabbit* to Mr Warne, my original

publisher, he read it, made up his mind he liked it, accepted it, and that was settled. Do you really need other people to do this for you? It seems to me a fuss over a very small matter.

I have too much common sense to think that *Peter Rabbit* could 13 ever be magnificent; he is an ordinary small brown rabbit. Nor do I like the idea of the book being enlarged. I have never heard that size was a guarantee of quality, and must point out that my books were made small to fit children's hands, not to impress the grownups.

As for the philologists: if an author needs help in putting thought 14 into plain and simple words he, or she, should not try to be an author. It would seem to me you are in danger of using 'simple' in the sense of mentally deficient. Are children nowadays so much less intelligent than their parents?

I have been told I write good prose. I think I write carefully because 15 I enjoy my writing and enjoy taking pains over it. I write to please myself; my usual way is to scribble and cut out and write it again and again. The shorter, the plainer—the better. And read the Bible (unrevised version and Old Testament) if I feel my style wants chastening.

> Yours sincerely,
> BEATRIX POTTER

N.B. My books, as I said, *are* illustrated. 16

## Mr Andal to Miss Potter

> February 19, 1963

My dear respected lady:

While disliking having to cross swords with someone as eminent as 17 yourself, I really must enlighten you to the fact that the Old Testament, as reading, is almost totally out of date, not only for children but adults. It has been replaced by the epic screen pictures which, sequestered as you are in your native Cumberland, you may not have seen. These movies are money-spinners, which is heartening as it endorses our belief that there is life in old tales yet—if properly presented. (One of our 'master-pieces' is Genesis, retold in uno- or duo-syllable words.)

Mr Warne could perhaps make his own decision to publish an im- 18 portant manuscript (which is what we want to make 'Peter Rabbit' in this new illustrated edition), but that was years ago. Publishing nowadays is such a costly business that we need expert advice. Properly handled, in attractive wrappers, perhaps packaged with one or two others, and well advertised, books for juveniles can become really big business, which is why I hope you will consider carefully our reader's report and let us guide you.

> Your well-wisher,
> V. ANDAL

## Miss Potter to Mr Andal

22nd February, 1963.

Dear Sir,

19   I am not 'eminent' as you call it but a plain person who believes in saying what she thinks.

20   Your publishing would not be so costly without all these 'experts' and elaborate notions; indeed, your last letter reads as if you were selling grocery, not books. In my day, philologists kept to what is their real work: to enrich a child's heritage of words—not diminish it.

Yours faithfully,
BEATRIX POTTER

21   N.B. The illustrations in my books are integral with the text. They may *not* be separated.

## Mr Andal to Miss Potter

March 7, 1963

Dear Miss Potter:

22   It is with pleasurable anticipation that I send you our detailed reader's report. It has taken a little time to get it—some work was necessary—but, as you will see, apart from some words in the text, some details of plot, new illustrations, fresh names and a larger size for the book, very little has had to be changed.

23   I very much hope you will co-operate in helping us to bring this classic little book within reach of our children.

Awaiting your favorable reactions,
Again yours cordially,
V. ANDAL

24   REPORT AND RECOMMENDATIONS FOR MODERNIZATION OF TEXT AND ILLUSTRATIONS OF 'PETER RABBIT' BY BEATRIX POTTER

'Mother' must read 'Momma' throughout.

| | | |
|---|---|---|
| p. 45 | '. . . some friendly sparrows . . . flew to him in great excitement, and implored him to exert himself.' | Not all children will be able to identify sparrows; suggest the more general 'birdies'; last five words especially difficult; suggest 'to try again' or 'try harder'. |
| p. 52 | 'Kertyschoo' for sneezing | Unfamiliar. 'Tishoo' is more usual. |
| p. 58 | 'Lippity lippity' | Not in the dictionary. |

| p. 69   'Scr-r-ritch' | Might confuse. Onomatopoeia, though allowable, should not distort a word. |
| Same page 'Scuttered' | Unfamiliar again. Suggest 'ran away and hid', which has the advantage that three out of four words have only three letters. |
| p. 80   'Camomile tea' | Not in use now. Suggest 'tranquilizer' or 'sedative'. |

As well as word limitation, the De Base Publishing Company has decided to use a certain 'thought limitation' so that parents may entrust their children's reading to us with complete confidence. In this connection:

p. 10   We do not think father should have been made into rabbit pie. Mr McGregor is altogether a too Jehovah-like figure. We want children to *like* people rather than have that out-of-date respect. They must not be left thinking that a little rabbit can be blamed for trespassing and stealing: it was, rather, that he was deprived of lettuce and radishes. Mr McGregor must be made a sympathetic figure.

ILLUSTRATIONS
We now have a report from our art panel, and though these illustrations have charm we believe fresh ones should be used. The rabbits' furniture and clothing are out of date; i.e., the red cloaks used by Flopsy, Mopsy and Cottontail; the length of Mrs Rabbit's skirts; the suspended pan and open cooking fire on p. 8. We therefore propose to commission a young Mexican who specializes in vivid outline drawing. (Less expensive to reproduce.)

NOMENCLATURE
Our bureau reports that while 'Peter' is familiar to most children, Flopsy, Mopsy and Cottontail must be retitled.

## Cable from Miss Potter to Mr Andal, 12 March 1963
### RETURN PETER RABBIT AT ONCE                                          25

## Mr Andal to Miss Potter

March 13, 1963

Dear Miss Potter:
We are sorry you have taken this attitude, which I confess seems to        26
us unrealistic and does not take into account public opinion (supported by our own careful poll statistics). We are having much the same

reaction from Mr Edward Lear. We saw a charming first version[2] of his poem, 'The Owl and the Pussy-Cat', which then had the lines:

> They sailed away
> For a year and a day
> To the land where the palm tree grows.

and:

> They dined on mince
> and slices of quince
> which they ate with a silver spoon.

lines quite innocuous and satisfactory; but now he has come up with 'bong tree' for the first lines, and 'runcible spoon' for the second, words not only unusual but not even in the dictionary.

27    As he insists on keeping these we have had to return his manuscript as, at your own request, we are returning yours. We can only tell you that it is our opinion, formed by expert advice, that in its present form, parents, teachers, and children will not buy, nor understand, nor like 'Peter Rabbit'.

Yours respectfully,
V. ANDAL

## Miss Potter to Mr V. Andal

24th March, 1963.

28    Seven million have. I rest in peace.

[1963]

---

### CONSIDERATIONS

1. Satirists can work savagely and shockingly or quietly (see Margaret Atwood's "Alien Territory," page 36) and good-humoredly, as Rumer Godden does in "An Imaginary Correspondence." However, satire, in whatever form it takes, is a species of attack with a definite target in its sights. What is Godden's target, and what are some of her weapons?

2. Have you had any experience with children's books or textbooks that have been scientifically simplified? If not, investigate one or two. Your college librarian can help you find them. Finally, write a short, argumentative essay taking sides with either Rumer Godden or Mr. V. Andal.

---

[2]The lines that follow are authentic and are in the first draft of 'The Owl and the Pussy-Cat'.

3. The reading level of a given book is usually determined by applying one of several available formulas, most of them using as criteria the average length of the sentences and the number of words not included in a predetermined vocabulary. As those numbers go up, so does the level of difficulty and hence the grade- or age-level of the book. Or so, at least, say the experts. Thinking back through your reading experience, what do you think? What other factors might affect the difficulty of reading a given book?

4. Do you think Mr. V. Andal's version of the lines from "The Owl and the Pussy-Cat" is an improvement over Mr. Edward Lear's? Why or why not?

*Stephen Jay Gould (b. 1941) is a paleontologist who teaches at*
*Harvard and writes scientific essays for the general reader. He*
*calls himself "an evolutionist," for Darwin and the theory of*
*evolution live at the center of his mind. Five of his books collect*
*periodical essays—*Ever Since Darwin *(1977),* The Panda's Thumb
*(1980),* Hen's Teeth and Horse's Toes *(1983),* Bully for Brontosaurus
*(1991), and* Eight Little Piggies *(1993).*

*This criticism of textbooks comes from* Bully for
Brontosaurus. *Gould's lively mind, eager to use scientific method*
*for public thinking, seeks out diverse subjects and often discovers*
*a political flavor in matters not usually perceived as political.*

## — 36

# STEPHEN JAY GOULD
## *The Case of the Creeping Fox*
## *Terrier Clone*

1      When Asta the fox terrier exhumed the body of the Thin Man, his
delightfully tipsy detective master, Nick Charles, exclaimed, "You're not
a terrier; you're a police dog" (*The Thin Man*, MGM 1934 original with
William Powell and Myrna Loy). May I now generalize for Asta's breed in
the case of the telltale textbook.

2      The wisdom of our culture abounds with mottoes that instruct us
to acknowledge the faults within ourselves before we criticize the failings of others. These words range from clichés about pots and kettles to
various sayings of Jesus: "And why beholdest thou the mote that is in thy
brother's eye, but perceivest not the beam that is in thine own eye?" (Luke
6:41); "He that is without sin among you, let him first cast a stone at her"
(John 8:7). I shall follow this wisdom by exposing my own profession in
trying to express what I find so desperately wrong about the basic tool of
American teaching, the textbook.

In March 1987, I spent several hours in the exhibit hall of the 3
National Science Teachers Association convention in Washington, D.C.
There I made an informal, but reasonably complete, survey of evolution
as treated (if at all) in major high-school science textbooks. I did find
some evidence of adulteration, pussyfooting, and other forms of capitulation to creationist pressure. One book, *Life Science*, by L. K. Bierer, K. F.
Liem, and E. P. Silberstein (Heath, 1987), in an accommodation that at
least makes you laugh while you weep for lost integrity in education,
qualifies every statement about the ages of fossils—usually in the most
barbarous of English constructions, the passive infinitive. We discover
that trilobites are "believed to have lived 500–600 million years ago,"
while frozen mammoths are "thought to have roamed the tundra 22,000
years ago." But of one poor bird, we learn with terrible finality, "There
are no more dodoes living today." Their extinction occurred within the
bounds of biblical literalism and need not be hedged.

But I was surprised and pleased to note that most books contained 4
material at reasonable length about evolution, and with no explicit signs
of tampering to appease creationists. Sins imposed by others were minimal. But I then found the beam in our own eye and became, if anything,
more distressed than by any capitulation to the yahoos. The problem
does not lie in what others are doing to us, but in what we are doing to
ourselves. In book after book, the evolution section is virtually cloned.
Almost all authors treat the same topics, usually in the same sequence,
and often with illustrations changed only enough to avoid suits for pla-
giarism. Obviously, authors of textbooks are copying material on a massive scale and passing along to students an ill-considered and virtually
Xeroxed version with a rationale lost in the mists of time.

Just two months after making this depressing observation, I read 5
Diane B. Paul's fascinating article "The Nine Lives of Discredited Data"
(*The Sciences*, May 1987). Paul analyzed the sections on heritability of
IQ from twenty-eight textbooks on introductory genetics published between 1978 and 1984. She paid particular attention to their treatment of
Sir Cyril Burt's data on identical twins raised separately. We now know
that these "studies" represent one of the most striking cases of fraud in
twentieth-century science—for Burt invented both data and coworkers.
His sad story had been well publicized, and all authors of texts published
since 1978 surely knew that Burt's data had been discredited and could
not be used. Several texts even included discussions of the Burt scandal
as a warning about caution and scrutiny in science.

But Paul then found that nearly half these books continued to cite 6
and use Burt's data, probably unconsciously. Of nineteen textbooks that
devoted more than a paragraph to the subject of genetics and IQ, eleven
based their conclusions about high heritability on a review article published in *Science* in 1963. This review featured a figure that ten of these
textbooks reproduced either directly or in slightly altered and simplified
form. This figure includes, as a prominent feature, the results of Sir Cyril

Burt (not yet suspect in 1963). We must conclude that the authors of these texts either had not read the 1963 article carefully or had not consulted it at all. Paul infers (correctly, I am sure) that this carelessness arises because authors of textbooks copy from other texts and often do not read original sources. How else to explain the several books that discussed the Burt scandal explicitly and then, unbeknownst to their authors, used the same discredited data in a figure?

7    Paul argues that the increasing commercialization of textbooks has engendered this virtual cloning of contents. Textbook publishing is a big business, replete with market surveys, fancy art programs, and subsidiary materials in the form of slide sets, teachers' guides, even test-making and grading services. The actual text of the book can become secondary and standardized; and departure from a conventional set of topics could derail an entire industry of supporting materials. Teachers are also locked into a largely set curriculum based on this flood of accoutrements. Paul concludes: "Today's textbooks are thicker, slicker, more elaborate, and more expensive than they used to be. They are also more alike. Indeed, many are virtual clones, both stylistic and substantive, of a market leader."

8    The marketplace rules. Most publishing houses are now owned by conglomerates—CBS, Raytheon, and Coca-Cola among them—with managers who never raise their eyes from the financial bottom line, know little or nothing about books, and view the publishing arm of their diversified empire as but one more item for the ultimate balance. I received a dramatic reminder of this trend last week when I looked at the back cover of my score for Mozart's *Coronation Mass*, now under rehearsal in my chorus. It read: "Kalmus Score. Belwin Mills Publishing Company, distributed by Columbia Pictures Publication, a unit of the Coca-Cola Company." I don't say that Bill Cosby or Michael Jackson or whoever advertises the stuff doesn't like Mozart; I merely suspect that Don Giovanni can't be high on the executive agenda when the big boys must worry about such really important issues as whether or not to market Cherry Coke (a resounding "yes" vote from this old New York soda fountain junkie).

9    Paul quotes a leading industry analyst from the 1984 *Book Publishing Annual*. Future textbooks, the analyst argues, will have "more elaborate designs and greater use of color. . . . The ancillary packages will become more comprehensive. . . . New, more aggressive marketing plans will be needed just to maintain a company's position. The quality of marketing will make the difference." Do note the conspicuous absence of any mention whatsoever about the quality of the text itself.

10    Paul is obviously correct in arguing that this tendency to cloning has accelerated remarkably as concerns of the market overwhelm scholarly criteria in the composition of textbooks. But I believe that the basic tendency has always been present and has a human as well as a corporate face. Independent thought has always been more difficult than borrow-

ing, and authors of textbooks have almost always taken the easier way out. Of course I have no objection to the similar recording of information by textbooks. No author can know all the byways of a profession, and all must therefore rely on written sources for areas not enlightened by personal expertise. I speak instead of the thoughtless, senseless, and often false copying of phrase, anecdote, style of argument, and sequence of topics that perpetuates itself by degraded repetition from text to text and thereby loses its anchor in nature.

I present an example that may seem tiny and peripheral in import. 　11
Nevertheless, and perhaps paradoxically, such cases provide our best evidence for thoughtless copying. When a truly important and well-known fact graces several texts in the same form, we cannot know whether it has been copied from previous sources or independently extracted from any expert's general knowledge. But when a quirky little senseless item attains the frequency of the proverbial bad penny, copying from text to text is the only reasonable interpretation. There is no other source. My method is no different from the standard technique of bibliographic scholars, who establish lineages of texts by tracing errors (particularly for documents spread by copyists before the invention of printing).

When textbooks choose to illustrate evolution with an example 　12
from the fossil record, they almost invariably trot out that greatest warhorse among case studies—the history of horses themselves. The standard story begins with an animal informally called *Eohippus* (the dawn horse), or more properly, *Hyracotherium*. Since evolutionary increase in size is a major component of the traditional tale, all texts report the diminutive stature of ancestral *Hyracotherium*. A few give actual estimates or measurements, but most rely upon a simile with some modern organism. For years, I have been much amused (and mildly bothered) that the great majority of texts report *Hyracotherium* as "like a fox-terrier" in size. I was jolted into action when I found myself writing the same line, and then stopped. "Wait a minute," said my inner voice, "beyond some vague memories of Asta last time I watched a Thin Man movie, I haven't the slightest idea what a fox terrier is. I can't believe that the community of textbook authors includes only dog fanciers—so if I don't know, I'll bet most of them don't either." Clearly, the classic line has been copied from text to text. Where did it begin? What has been its history? Is the statement even correct?

My immediate spur to action came from a most welcome and unex- 　13
pected source. I published a parenthetical remark about the fox terrier issue ending with a serious point: "I also wonder what the textbook tradition of endless and thoughtless copying has done to retard the spread of original ideas."

I have, over the years, maintained a correspondence about our fa- 　14
vorite common subject with Roger Angell of the *New Yorker*, who is, among other things, the greatest baseball writer ever. I assumed that his letter of early April would be a scouting report for the beginning of a new

season. But I found that Roger Angell is a man of even more dimensions than I had realized; he is also a fox terrier fancier. He had read my parenthetical comment and wrote, "I am filled with excitement and trepidation at the prospect of writing you a letter about science instead of baseball."

15        Angell went on to suggest a fascinating and plausible explanation for the origin of the fox terrier simile (no excuse, of course, for its later cloning). Fox terriers were bred "to dig out foxes from their burrows, when a fox had gone to earth during a traditional British hunt." Apparently, generations of fox-hunting gentlemen selected fox terriers not only for their functional role in the hunt but also under a breeder's artifice to make them look as much like horses as possible. Angell continues, "The dogs rode up on the saddle during the hunt, and it was a pretty conceit for the owner-horseman to appear to put down a little simulacrum of a horse when the pack of hounds and the pink-coated throng had arrived at an earth where the animal was to do his work." He also pointed out that fox terriers tend to develop varied patches of color on a basically white coat and that a "saddle" along the back is "considered desirable and handsome." Thus, Angell proposed his solution: "Wouldn't it seem possible that some early horse geologist, in casting about for the right size animal to fit his cliché-to-be, might have settled, quite unconsciously, on a breed of dog that fitted the specifications in looks as well as size?"

16        This interesting conjecture led me to devise the following, loosely controlled experiment. I asked David Backus, my research assistant, to record every simile for *Hyracotherium* that he could find in the secondary literature of texts and popular books during more than a century since O. C. Marsh first recognized this animal as a "dawn horse." We would then use these patterns in attempting to locate original sources for favored similes in the primary literature of vertebrate paleontology. We consulted the books in my personal library as a sample, and compiled a total of eighty-six descriptions. The story turns out to be much more ascertainable and revealing than I had imagined.

17        The tradition of simile begins at the very beginning. Richard Owen, the great British anatomist and paleontologist, described the genus *Hyracotherium* in 1841. He did not recognize its relationship with horses (he considered this animal, as his chosen name implies, to be a possible relative of hyraxes, a small group of Afro-Asian mammals, the "coneys" of the Bible). In this original article, Owen likened his fossil to a hare in one passage and to something between a hog and a hyrax in another. Owen's simile plays no role in later history because other traditions of comparison had been long established before scientists realized that Owen's older discovery represented the same animal that Marsh later named *Eohippus*. (Hence, under the rules of taxonomy, Owen's inappropriate and uneuphonious name takes unfortunate precedence over Marsh's lovely *Eohippus*.)

The modern story begins with Marsh's description of the earliest    18
horses in 1874. Marsh pressed "go" on the simile machine by writing,
"This species was about as large as a fox." He also described the larger
descendant *Miohippus* as sheeplike in size.

Throughout the nineteenth century all sources that we have found    19
(eight references, including such major figures as Joseph Le Conte,
Archibald Geikie, and even Marsh's bitter enemy E. D. Cope) copy
Marsh's favored simile—they all describe *Eohippus* as fox-sized. We are
confident that Marsh's original description is the source because most
references also repeat his statement that the *Miohippus* is the size of a
sheep. How, then, did fox terriers replace their prey?

The first decade of our century ushered in a mighty Darwinian    20
competition among three alternatives and led to the final triumph of fox
terriers. By 1910, three similes were battling for survival. Marsh's original fox suffered greatly from competition, but managed to retain a share
of the market at about 25 percent (five of twenty citations between 1900
and 1925 in our sample—a frequency that has been maintained ever
since (see accompanying figure)). Competition came from two stiff
sources, however—both from the American Museum of Natural History
in New York.

First, in 1903, W. D. Matthew, vertebrate paleontologist at the    21
Museum, published his famous pamphlet *The Evolution of the Horse* (it
remained in print for fifty years, and was still being sold at the Museum
shop when I was a child). Matthew wrote: "The earliest known ancestors
of the horse were small animals not larger than the domestic cat."
Several secondary sources picked up Matthew's simile during this quarter century (also five of twenty references between 1900 and 1925), but
felines have since faded (only one of fifteen references since 1975), and I
do not know why.

Second, the three-way carnivorous competition of vulpine, feline,    22
and canine began in earnest when man's best friend made his belated appearance in 1904 under the sponsorship of Matthew's boss, American
Museum president and eminent vertebrate paleontologist Henry
Fairfield Osborn. Remember that no nineteenth-century source (known
to us) had advocated a canine simile, so Osborn's late entry suffered a
temporal handicap. But Osborn was as commanding (and enigmatic) a
figure as American natural history has ever produced—a powerful patri-
cian in science and politics, imperious but kind, prolific and pompous,
crusader for natural history and for other causes of opposite merit
(Osborn wrote, for example, a glowing preface to the most influential
tract of American scientific racism, *The Passing of the Great Race*, by
his friend Madison Grant).

In the *Century Magazine* for November 1904, Osborn published a    23
popular article, "The Evolution of the Horse in America." (Given
Osborn's almost obsessively prolific spate of publications, we would not
be surprised if we have missed an earlier citation.) His first statement

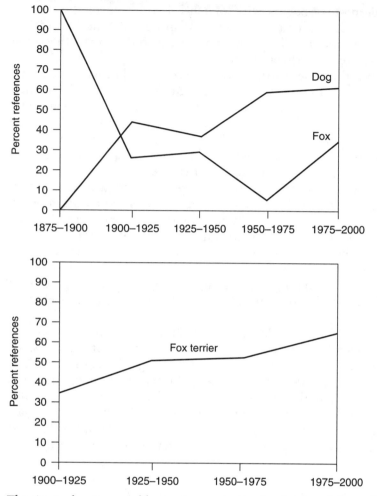

The rise to dominance of fox terriers as similes for the size of the earliest horses. Top graph: Increasing domination of dogs over foxes through time. Lower graph: Increase in percentage of fox terrier references among sources citing dogs as their simile. Graph by Iromie Weeramantry. Reprinted by permission of *Natural History* magazine.

about *Eohippus* introduces the comparison that would later win the competition:

> We may imagine the earliest herds of horses in the Lower Eocene (*Eohippus*, or "dawn horse" stage) as resembling a lot of small fox-terriers in size. . . . As in the terrier, the wrist (knee) was near the ground, the hand was still short, terminating in four hoofs, with a part of the fifth toe (thumb) dangling at the side.

Osborn provides no rationale for his choice of breeds. Perhaps he    24
simply carried Marsh's old fox comparison unconsciously in his head and
chose the dog most similar in name to the former standard. Perhaps
Roger Angell's conjecture is correct. Osborn certainly came from a social
set that knew about fox hunting. Moreover, as the quotation indicates,
Osborn extended the similarity of *Eohippus* and fox terrier beyond mere
size to other horselike attributes of this canine breed (although, in other
sources, Osborn treated the whippet as even more horselike, and even
mounted a whippet's skeleton for an explicit comparison with *Eohippus*).
Roger Angell described his fox terrier to me: "The back is long and
straight, the tail is held jauntily upward like a trotter's, the nose is elongated and equine, and the forelegs are strikingly thin and straight. In motion, the dog comes down on these forelegs in a rapid and distinctive,
stiff, flashy style, and the dog appears to walk on his tiptoes—on hooves,
that is."

In any case, we can trace the steady rise to domination of dog simi-    25
les in general, and fox terriers in particular, ever since. Dogs reached
nearly 50 percent of citations (nine of twenty) between 1900 and 1925,
but have now risen to 60 percent (nine of fifteen) since 1975. Meanwhile,
the percentage of fox terrier citations among dog similes had also
climbed steadily, from one-third (three of nine) between 1900 and 1925
to one-half (eight of sixteen) between 1925 and 1975, to two-thirds (six of
nine) since 1975. Osborn's simile has been victorious.

Copying is the only credible source for these shifts of popularity—    26
first from experts; then from other secondary sources. Shifts in fashion
cannot be recording independent insights based on observation of specimens. *Eohippus* could not, by itself, say "fox" to every nineteenth-
century observer and "dog" to most twentieth-century writers. Nor can I
believe that two-thirds of all dog-inclined modern writers would independently say, "Aha, fox terrier" when contemplating the dawn horse.
The breed is no longer so popular, and I suspect that most writers, like
me, have only the vaguest impression about fox terriers when they copy
the venerable simile.

In fact, we can trace the rise to dominance of fox terriers in our ref-    27
erences. The first post-Osborn citation that we can find (Ernest Ingersoll,
*The Life of Animals*, Macmillan, 1906) credits Osborn explicitly as author of the comparison with fox terriers. Thereafter, no one cites the
original, and I assume that the process of text copying text had begun.

Two processes combined to secure the domination of fox terriers.    28
First, experts began to line up behind Osborn's choice. The great vertebrate paleontologist W. B. Scott, for example, stood in loyal opposition in
1913, 1919, and 1929 when he cited both alternatives of fox and cat. But
by 1937, he had switched: "*Hyracotherium* was a little animal about the
size of a fox-terrier, but horse-like in all parts." Second, dogs became
firmly ensconced in major textbooks. Both leading American geology

textbooks of the early twentieth century (Chamberlin and Salisbury, 1909 edition, and Pirsson and Schuchert, 1924 edition) opt for canines, as does Hegner's zoology text (1912) and W. Maxwell Read's fine children's book (a mainstay of my youth) *The Earth for Sam* (1930 edition).

29    Fox terriers have only firmed up their position ever since. Experts cite this simile, as in A. S. Romer's leading text, *Vertebrate Paleontology* (3rd edition, 1966): "'*Eohippus*' was a small form, some specimens no larger than a fox terrier." They have also entered the two leading high-school texts: (1) Otto and Towle (descendant of Moon, Mann, and Otto, the dominant text for most of the past fifty years): "This horse is called *Eohippus*. It had four toes and was about the size of a fox-terrier" (1977 edition); (2) the *Biological Sciences Curriculum Study, Blue Edition* (1968): "The fossil of a small four-toed animal about the size of a fox-terrier was found preserved in layers of rock." College texts also comply. W. T. Keeton, in his *Biological Science*, the Hertz of the profession, writes (1980 edition): "It was a small animal, only about the size of a fox-terrier." Baker and Allen's *The Study of Biology*, a strong Avis, agrees (1982 edition): "This small animal *Eohippus* was not much bigger than a fox-terrier."

30    You may care little for dawn horses or fox terriers and might feel that I have made much of nothing in this essay. But I cite the case of the creeping fox terrier clone not for itself, but rather as a particularly clear example of a pervasive and serious disease—the debasement of our textbooks, the basic tool of written education, by endless, thoughtless copying.

31    My younger son started high school last month. For a biology text, he is using the 4th edition of *Biology: Living Systems*, by R. F. Oram, with consultants P. J. Hummer and R. C. Smoot (Charles E. Merrill, 1983, but listed on the title page, following our modern reality of conglomeration, as a Bell and Howell Company). I was sad and angered to find several disgraceful passages of capitulation to creationist pressure. Page one of the chapter on evolution proclaims in a blue sidebar: "The theory of evolution is the most widely accepted scientific explanation of the origin of life and changes in living things. You may wish to investigate other theories." Similar invitations are not issued for any other well-established theory. Students are not told that "most folks accept gravitation, but you might want to check out levitation" or that "most people view the earth as a sphere, but you might want to consider the possibility of a plane." When the text reaches human history, it doesn't even grant majority status to our evolutionary consensus: "Humans are indeed unique, but because they are also organisms, many scientists believe that humans have an evolutionary history."

32    Yet, as I argued at the outset, I find these compromises to outside pressure, disgraceful though they be, less serious than the internal disease of cloning from text to text. There is virtually only one chapter on evolution in all high-school biology texts, copied and degraded, then copied and degraded again. My son's book is no exception. This chapter begins with a discussion of Lamarck and the inheritance of acquired char-

acters. It then moves to Darwin and natural selection and follows this basic contrast with a picture of a giraffe and a disquisition of Lamarckian and Darwinian explanations for long necks. A bit later, we reach industrial melanism in moths and dawn horses of you-know-what size.

What is the point of all this? I could understand this development if   33
Lamarckism were a folk notion that must be dispelled before introducing Darwin, or if Lamarck were a household name. But I will lay 100 to 1 that few high-school students have ever heard of Lamarck. Why begin teaching evolution by explicating a false theory that is causing no confusion? False notions are often wonderful tools in pedagogy, but not when they are unknown, are provoking no trouble, and make the grasp of an accepted theory more difficult. I would not teach more sophisticated college students this way; I simply can't believe that this sequence works in high school. I can only conclude that someone once wrote the material this way for a reason lost in the mists of time, and that authors of textbooks have been dutifully copying "Lamarck . . . Darwin . . . giraffe necks" ever since.

(The giraffe necks, by the way, make even less sense. This venerable   34
example rests upon no data at all for the superiority of Darwinian explanation. Lamarck offered no evidence for his interpretation and only introduced the case in a few lines of speculation. We have no proof that the long neck evolved by natural selection for eating leaves at the tops of acacia trees. We only prefer this explanation because it matches current orthodoxy. Giraffes do munch the topmost leaves, and this habit obviously helps them to thrive, but who knows how or why their necks elongated? They may have lengthened for other reasons and then been fortuitously suited for acacia leaves.)

If textbook cloning represented the discovery of a true educational   35
optimum, and its further honing and propagation, then I would not object. But all evidence—from my little story of fox terriers to the larger issue of a senseless but nearly universal sequence of Lamarck, Darwin, and giraffe necks—indicates that cloning bears an opposite and discouraging message. It is the easy way out, a substitute for thinking and striving to improve. Somehow I must believe—for it is essential to my notion of scholarship—that good teaching requires fresh thought and genuine excitement, and that rote copying can only indicate boredom and slipshod practice. A carelessly cloned work will not excite students, however pretty the pictures. As an antidote, we need only the most basic virtue of integrity—not only the usual, figurative meaning of honorable practice but the less familiar, literal definition of wholeness. We will not have great texts if authors cannot shape content but must serve a commercial master as one cog in an ultimately powerless consortium with other packagers.

To end with a simpler point amid all this tendentiousness and gen-   36
erality: Thoughtlessly cloned "eternal verities" are often false. The latest estimate I have seen for the body size of *Hyracotherium* (MacFadden,

1986), challenging previous reconstructions congenial with the standard simile of much smaller fox-terriers, cites a weight of some twenty-five kilograms, or fifty-five pounds.

37        Lassie come home!

## CONSIDERATIONS

1. In paragraph 3, Gould refers to "the most barbarous of English constructions, the passive infinitive." Why is he so exercised over that construction?

2. Look briefly at a writer who prefers long paragraphs—Henry Thoreau, for instance, in his "Civil Disobedience" (page 595), Joan Didion (page 156), Gerald Early (page 171), or Frederick Douglass (page 166)—and then at a writer on the other end of the scale—such as Sven Birkerts (page 56) or Martin Gansberg (page 228). Where would Gould fall on such a scale? Is there such a thing as a standard paragraph length?

3. Does Gould have a distinct thesis statement? If so, where does it first appear?

4. In paragraph 4, Gould uses the term "yahoos." What does it mean, and what is its source?

5. Are all of Gould's statements to be taken seriously? Provide examples.

6. Gould does not get down to the main example of his thesis until paragraph 11. What is the point of all the material in those preceding paragraphs?

7. Discussing the conventional explanation of the length of the giraffe's neck, Gould says, "We only prefer this explanation because it matches current orthodoxy." How is that relevant to his whole essay? Might his comment apply as well to other fields of human activity—religion, say, or art, or politics, or business? Why are humans so fond of "current orthodoxy"? Try to answer these questions in a well-argued essay.

*Harvey Green (b. 1946) published* The Uncertainty of Everyday
Life, *from which we take "The Radio Age," in 1992. He is
professor of history at Northeastern University, and his earlier
books include* The Life of the Home: An Intimate View of Women
in Victorian America *and* Fit for America: Health, Fitness, Sport,
and American Society 1830–1940. *He lives in New Ipswich, New
Hampshire.*

*The historian writes a research paper, using with clarity of
purpose statistics gathered from many sources. Note how his
information is progressive as well as inclusive, moving from
numbers of listeners, to the advent of advertising, to the design of
radios themselves, to the content of programming. He eschews
making parallels to television—but the reader is bound to.*

— 37 —————————————————————

# HARVEY GREEN
## *The Radio Age 1915–1945*

————————————————————————

In the three decades preceding the end of World War II the amount    1
of time expended at ease and the variety of leisure activities had expanded for millions. Innovations in the industries of play were both enduring, such as radio and the talking cinema, and faddish and ephemeral,
such as mah-jongg. Americans of nearly all classes experienced in one
way or another what has been rightly termed the "golden age" of sport
and dancing. Prohibition may have cramped the style of some for a
while, but speakeasies and other "clubs" eased that difficulty. A drink
could be had with considerable speed in most cities if the thirsty knew
where to look and were stout of heart, since the quality of the hooch was
often frightening. Ultimately there were enough forms of entertainment
that were cheap enough that many of them became true mass media and
mass diversions, in spite of the Depression.

————————

## A Cultural Revolution

2       The most important leisure-time innovation of the era was the radio. For Secretary of Commerce Herbert Hoover in 1921, it was "an instrument of beauty and learning." But for others, such as Bruce Bliven, editor of *The New Republic*, radio programming was "outrageous rubbish, both verbal and musical." Undaunted by Bliven's condemnation and perhaps encouraged by Hoover's hyperbole, the popularity of radio grew rapidly. By 1924, 5 million homes nationwide had at least one set, and Americans had spent $350 million on radios and radio parts, or one-third of all the money spent on furniture. Within the first eight years of the industry's life it had become a $500 million industry with more than 500 local stations. For every 1,000 Americans in 1928, 50 radios were owned. A January 1, 1929, survey conducted for the National Broadcasting Company by Massachusetts Institute of Technology professor Daniel Starch found that one-third of all American homes owned a radio, and that 80 percent of all radio owners listened daily. In addition, he found that rural and urban listener programming preferences were virtually identical, which suggested to some optimists that radio programmers had discovered—or created—some of the unifying elements in American culture.

3       The severity of the Depression did not slow radio's phenomenal growth. By 1934, 60 percent of all American homes had radios, and radio listening had become Americans' favorite pastime, according to a survey conducted by the National Recreation Association, published as *The Leisure of 5,000 People*. Americans owned 43.2 percent of all the radios in the world. By 1939 the number of radios in American homes totaled 44 million, 86 percent of all households owned at least one set, and the average listener tuned in for four and one-half hours daily. There were, in addition, 6.5 million radios in automobiles. In 1940, the entire population spent 1 billion hours weekly listening to the radio, about seven times as much time as they passed at the movies.

4       Working-class Americans often saved money by building their own sets. After buying a germanium crystal for about $2 at a hardware or department store, the do-it-yourself radio builder only had to connect it to a wire wound in a coil, and attach the whole thing to a board. Then, after wiring a headset into the apparatus and twisting the coil until sound began to crackle, all that remained were adjustments until a comprehensible sound came through. Putting the headset in a hollow vessel created a loudspeaker of sorts.

## Early Programming

5       Radio in the 1920s was for the most part a local affair, and it reflected the interests and talents of either urban neighborhoods or farming areas. Much of the early urban programming was nonprofit, operated by ethnic,

religious, and labor groups. In 1925, 28 percent of the nation's 571 stations were owned by educational or religious groups. Many predominantly English-language stations broadcast "nationality hours" in the languages of the most powerful or most numerous ethnic groups of the cities they served. In the countryside commercial stations were at first more common, for the most part because businesses were about the only source of capital available to those who wanted to begin operating a station.

Commercial radio soon infiltrated all areas of the country, because broadcasting in areas in which people were highly concentrated could be very profitable. The commercial alleged to have been the first of the genre was aired on August 28, 1922. It was for real estate, and was broadcast over station WEAF in New York City. By the mid-1920s radio station managers discovered that manufacturers would pay for air time providing they could have some fraction of a fifteen-minute time slot to pitch their wares. Some advertisers at first declined to use the medium, fearing that the radio ad was too much of an intrusion into the intimacy of the parlor or bedroom. But by 1927, when the National Broadcasting Company established the first national network, the advertising business had shed its reservations. The radio was an immediate personal experience—as the cinema was not—and was for many advertisers a dream come true. One slick trick was to buy enough time to name the show after a product. The *Eveready Hour* debuted in 1926 on fourteen stations, and in the 1927–1928 season thirty-nine companies sponsored shows on NBC, while four did so on the newer Columbia Broadcasting System. The next year sixty-five sponsors bought time from the networks for a total of more than $25 million.

By the 1930s, tuning in the radio (which was at times a testing task requiring an attentive listener) brought Americans advertisements that were louder, more frequent, and more boisterous in their claims for products than the subdued descriptive ads of the late 1920s had been. Radio ads took up an increasing percentage of corporations' advertising budgets, and led to a corresponding drop in monies spent on advertising in other media. Between 1928 and 1934, radio ads grew 316 percent nationally, newspaper ads declined by 30 percent, and magazine ads dropped 45 percent; 246 daily newspapers ceased publication, in part a result of the Depression and in part because of their losses in advertising revenue.

Early commercially made radio sets were often crude, industrial-looking objects, conglomerations of dials, diodes, wires, resistors, capacitors, and speakers. At first, and until about 1927, the technology of the thing was miraculous, and the look of it was properly scientific and laboratorylike. But by the late twenties diodes were not enough of a statement: The miracle of sound was taken for granted, and a newer sign of the future and of technology was marketed. The workings, like those of the appliances of the era, were encased in new materials, such as Bakelite, or in basic box furniture forms designed to indicate "future" or "modern." Veneering the cases with different colored woods using the linear and streamlined decorative designs of the era's graphic arts gave a sense of movement to radios, and many floor consoles were designed to look like a piece of parlor furniture that was more tech-moderne than a sofa. The latter merely provided a comfortable place to sit or recline; the radio cabinet contained the wizardry of science and technology. Machine-age designs did not appeal to every radio owner, however. "Colonial" and other "historical" forms were also broadly popular, in spite of the incongruity of encasing a thoroughly modern communication system in furniture that represented the preindustrial world. Perhaps these forms of eras long gone were an unconscious comfort to those who wanted the benefits of the new technology and the illusion of "simpler" times before machines and industry had taken over American culture.

9      Music was the most common form of programming broadcast in the early 1920s. Sporting events and plays were distant second and third most common broadcast genres, and news reports occurred every hour on the hour. In cities classical music dominated early radio programming, consistent with the conviction that the medium had its greatest potential as an agent of uplift and that classical European music was the best form of "higher" culture. The first live symphony concert was broadcast in 1926, as Serge Koussevitzky led the Boston Symphony Orchestra in a concert heard by an estimated 1 million listeners. Music appreciation shows and weekly concerts were aired through the 1930s, and the Metropolitan Opera began broadcasts in 1931. In 1938 an estimated 12 million people heard the Met broadcasts regularly during the opera season. WQXR, New York, began a classical-only program in 1937, and the New York Yankees baseball team sponsored a program of classical music interspersed with major league scores.

10      Popular music gradually surpassed, but did not completely supplant, classical music on urban radio stations. In 1938 the Federal Communications Commission conducted a survey of the content of 62,000 radio hours, and found that one-third of the air time was devoted to commercials. Of the remaining 40,000 hours, one-half were devoted to music, and popular music dominated that segment; 9 percent of the time was for drama, 9 percent for variety programming, 8.5 percent for news and sports, 5.2 percent for religion, 2.2 percent for special events, and 13.7 percent for "miscellaneous," mostly talking, shows. Country music stations operated in nearly all the nation's rural areas, sometimes bringing the music of Nashville's Grand Old Opry (which began broadcasting the show under that name in 1927, after a few years as station WSM's "Barn Dance"), but usually carrying the performances of itinerant singers and bands that played at the station for a week or two and then moved on. West Virginia miner Aaron Barkham remembered when "the first radio come to Mingo County . . . in 1934. That was a boon. It was a little job, got more squeals and squeaks than anything else. Everybody

came from miles around to look at it. We didn't have any electricity. So we hooked up two car batteries. We got 'Grand Old Opry' on it."

The radio brought a new style of singing, termed "crooning," to    11
Americans, in addition to comic songs, ditties, and country music. The most famous of the crooners—Bing Crosby and Rudy Vallee were two of the best known—developed a slow and smooth delivery that featured sliding into notes as opposed to the clipped style of more formal singers. In 1935 another unique American form of music and song joined the airwaves when the "singing cowboy," Gene Autry, began his evening show and enormously lucrative career as movie star, singer, and entrepreneur. Radio play of recorded music did not actually cut into record or sheet music sales, but record sales became the measure of how often and for how long tunes were aired.

## Amos 'n' Andy; The "Soaps"

Perhaps as significant because of their national popularity, if not    12
their percentage of the air time, were two other types of programs—comedy and daytime drama. The great age of radio comedy began (on a national scale) in the summer of 1929. Just a couple of months before the crash, two Chicago radio actors went national with a show that had been a local success for a few years. Freeman Gosden and Charles J. Correll "blacked up" their voices as Sam 'n' Henry, two "indigent colored boys" known as "the Gumps" in Chicago.

After changing stations in Chicago, and their names to Amos 'n'    13
Andy, they linked up with NBC and shuffled into American homes with the help of Pepsodent toothpaste. The most popular radio show of the 1930s, it eventually dominated the listening lives of middle-class and working Americans, including some African-Americans, in spite of the show's demeaning racial stereotypes. First aired at eleven P.M. eastern time, the network switched to seven because parents complained that their children refused to go to sleep until the show was over. When people in the mountain and Pacific time zones complained that they were still at work when the show aired, the network broadcast it again at eleven-thirty P.M. eastern time. Restaurants broadcast the show, and movie houses scheduled showings around the fifteen-minute adventures of the two urban hustlers, sometimes actually stopping a film to bring in the broadcast. Telephone calls dropped off precipitously at seven and eleven-thirty, and only the president had air rights over them.

*Amos 'n' Andy* succeeded brilliantly among the white middle-class    14
audience that loved them because they epitomized coping with the Depression in a manner that posed no threat to the established order. The black protagonists—one a middle-class aspirant who never quite got it right in spite of his schemes (Amos), and the other a lazy, clownish,

but ultimately shrewd manipulator (Andy)—were obsessed with money and money-getting. The show's hokey moralism reinforced the idea that hard work and industriousness (and implicitly not labor organization or strikes) were the keys to success. Their struggles were those of the population as a whole, but they were depicted as if the scuffling of everyday life were appropriate for them, and not for the white folks. Three-quarters of a million blacks didn't think so: They signed a petition protesting the depiction of African-Americans on the show. Nothing much happened. *Amos 'n' Andy* became a television show after World War II, still steeped in stereotypes, but at least with black actors.

15    Other comedy shows brought vaudeville performers such as Eddie Cantor and George Burns and his allegedly dingbat wife, Gracie Allen, to the radio, and made-for-radio shows such as *Fibber McGee and Molly* made fun of everything about American married life, often with barely disguised slights of ethnic groups.

16    Daytime drama programs, originally sponsored by soap companies, seized a significant market share during the afternoons. Figuring that the bulk of the listeners at home during the day were women, and that they were the major purchasers of soap products, the companies put their money behind an array of extremely successful serial dramas that soon after their introduction were termed "soap operas." Three such shows were on the air in 1931. There were ten in 1934, nineteen in 1935, thirty-one in 1936 and 1937, and sixty-one in 1939.

17    Most offered plots revolving around personal struggle—with finance, with lovers and husbands, or between classes. Most had strong women as central characters, reflecting the gender, the problems, and the desires of their listeners. The shows' formulaic plots oversimplified the problems of personal interaction, and in keeping with the experience and identity of their working- and middle-class audiences, the characters were plain simple folk. Like "Old Ma Perkins," they embodied the mythic American culture that had been overwhelmed by the greedy and unprincipled economic onslaught that had caused the Depression.

18    Ma Perkins was a widow who had "spent all her life taking care of her home, washing and cooking and raising her family." When her husband died she took over the lumberyard that he had run. She was a fountain of down-home wisdom in Rushville Center, reaffirming the "basic" social values of accommodation, cooperation, and comfort with one's social and economic position. In these dramas men were largely irrelevant, or absent, with the exception of older, nonthreatening figures. What order there was in the turmoil of Rushville Center or in the class-conscious lives of Stella Dallas, Helen Trent, or Our Gal Sunday (other famous "soap" heroines) was the result of wise, struggling, and strong women. Maybe the promise of the machine and the modern was a hollow one after all, a slick urban sophisticated hoax on the basically sound values of town, farm, and village. The villains were the easily identifiable (and overdrawn) stereotypes of city life: rich men, hollow socialites,

painted women, shysters, crooks, hoods, and hustlers. Amos 'n' Andy were urban but safe: They were clownish, almost rural chicken-stealers in the city, nonthreatening because they were black, unsuccessful, and segregated. In the "soaps" the greedy high-rollers were white, successful, and everywhere.

Evening radio serial dramas often starred motion-picture cowboy 19 heroes such as Gene Autry or radio creations such as the Lone Ranger. The masked man was a typical Depression-era hero: a renegade Texas Ranger who rode with an outcast and sage Indian who had rescued him and nursed him back to health. The Lone Ranger, like Dashiell Hammett's Sam Spade and other detectives in the popular mystery novels of the era, was an outlaw, and a symbol of a society with little faith in its established institutions. The regular lawmen in this and other western series were usually good men at best buffaloed by crime, and at worst simply inept and occasionally crooked. The Ranger was a vigilante, and potentially a dangerous example of the man who took the law into his own hands, a Machiavellian do-gooder who rejected the limitations of law and law enforcement, even though his goals were justice. By the middle of 1939 the Ranger had ridden more than 1,000 times, on hundreds of stations, as often as three times in a week. For the Lone Ranger, Gene Autry, and other western heroes, as well as for Ma Perkins and the rest of the "soap" heroes, the key was to return, if not to "those thrilling days of yesteryear," as the Ranger and Tonto did, then to the values of those years, as Ma, Stella, and Helen did.

## News and Sports

News and sports shows were often spectacularly popular, gathering 20 as much as one-half the audience if the event was truly monumental. These were often one-shot affairs, such as the second Joe Louis–Max Schmeling heavyweight fight, which got a "Crosley" rating of 57.6 percent of the radios turned on and measured by the Crosley company. Politics entered the radio era in 1928, when an estimated 40 million listeners heard Al Smith and Herbert Hoover speak on election eve. The largest single line item (20 percent of the total) in the Republican party's campaign budget in 1928 was for radio ads. The Republicans bought 30 more hours of radio time in 1932 than they had in 1928, when they purchased 42.5 hours, to the Democrats' 51.5 hours (the same amount as in 1928). It backfired on Hoover, who came across as stodgy and distant in the face of a great human crisis. Roosevelt used radio to convey a personal and caring presence. Later, his "Fireside Chats" were also big scorers, garnering 30 to 40 percent of the listening audience. The World Series, the Kentucky Derby, and the Rose Bowl were similar big winners. Workers in the plant and on the farm regularly listened to baseball games all through the spring and summer if they could bring them in on the radio.

21      Listeners perhaps were comforted by the repetition of the hourly news that punctuated the day. News stories did not break with regularity or very often, but the news bulletin and its dramatic urgency (especially as World War II began to take shape in 1938 and 1939) kept many radios on, even if the listeners were only half attentive. In 1934 there were 4,670 interruptions of normal programming for news bulletins, nearly one-half of them relating to the "crime of the century," the kidnapping and death of the Lindbergh baby.

22      The war in Europe provided radio news with its greatest opportunity to establish the medium as the most reliable medium for the delivery of information. The crisis of the late 1930s also provided CBS with the opportunity to make up ground on NBC, the first and largest network. Pictures did not lie, but they were not instantaneous and they were not personal. Live reporting brought the crisis home and did it with immediacy and drama. A legendary group of reporters—among them H. V. Kaltenborn, Edward R. Murrow, and Robert Trout—brought interviews with political leaders, battlefield reports from Spain in 1936, and later from eastern Europe as Hitler began to overrun the region. Daily broadcasts from Berlin, Prague, Rome, London, and Munich began in 1938, and bulletins from two minutes to two hours in length during the Czechoslovakian crisis of September 1938 established news as more popular than entertainment and CBS as the top news network. Murrow's famous "This is London" opening brought the reality of the Blitz to Americans in a way that complemented and perhaps outdid the power of the photograph. In early 1938, the Columbia University Office of Radio Research reported that its surveys found that less than one-half of the public preferred radio to print journalism; after the Munich crisis, two-thirds preferred radio news to newspapers and magazines.

## CONSIDERATIONS ———————————————————————

1. In the 1930s questionnaires directed at householders asked if there was a radio in the home. Ten years later, they simply asked how many radios—as today the question is not whether you have a television set or a computer, but how many. Think about this rapid multiplication of the mass media in American life, and build an essay around your conclusions.

2. Why did advertisers at first decline to use the medium of radio? Can you imagine that happening today? Why would those early advertisers have been horrified by our telemarketing industry?

3. Why does Green use quotation marks around the words "simpler" in the last sentence of paragraph 8 and "higher" in paragraph 9?

4. Conduct a survey of your own among older men and women of your acquaintance as a way of testing Green's statements about the loyalty of listeners, especially women, to such long running shows as *Ma Perkins, Stella Dallas, Helen Trent,* or *Our Gal Sunday*. Sum up your findings in an essay that might be classified as social commentary.

5. In Green's discussion of the radio show *Amos 'n' Andy*, the two leading characters sound rather like the two black con-men described by Maya Angelou in "Mr. Red Leg" (page 25). Read her account and then reread the three paragraphs Green devotes to the show, paying particular attention to his explanation of why *Amos 'n' Andy* was so amazingly popular with the white middle-class. Write an essay on the mass media as a means of shaping our notions of race or class.

6. In paragraph 9, Green reports that an early conviction about radio was that it "had its greatest potential as an agent of uplift." Add to his history by describing—say, as a footnote to his essay—what has happened to classical music on radio since the 1940s.

*John Haines (b. 1924) homesteaded in Alaska from 1947 through 1969, at the address "Mile 68, Richardson Highway." He lives now in Montana and often visits American universities to teach. He is first of all a poet, who has published many books, including* At the End of This Summer: Poems 1948–54 *in 1997. He has collected two volumes of essays. "Death Is a Meadowlark" comes from* The Stars, the Snow, the Fire *(1989).*

*Everyone thinks about death. See how this poet embodies his feelings in images, using few abstractions. The essay moves from personal observation to self-realization by way of story and image. Here is man fearful of the death he observes, even when redeemed by the song of a meadowlark. And here is man the predator.*

— 38 ——————————————————————————————

# JOHN HAINES
## *Death Is a Meadowlark*

——————————————————————————————

1    Long before I went to live in the woods my awareness of death seemed to have a depth beyond any exact recall. It existed as a memory composed of discontinuous images: a snake crushed on the summer roadway, reeking in the sun—how dull and flattened it was compared to the live snake, supple and glistening, I had seen in the grass a week before. A drowned and bloated frog I had pulled from the bottom of a backyard pool and held in my hand: a wonder—why did it not breathe? A bird in whose decaying nostrils small white worms were coiling. These were the naked things of an uninstructed childhood in which there was little instinctive fear.

2    And had I not seen as a child the crushed body of a woman sprawled at the city curbing? She had jumped from a window ledge many stories above, and lay concealed by the brown heap of her clothing. Nothing else of her was visible from where I stood, clutched by my mother on a crowded downtown street. There had been the sound of a scream, a sudden rush of air, a glimpse of a spread shape flying down, and the thudding shock of her landing. I was hurried away, and I saw no more.

And there had been also my own near death by drowning late in the    3
first decade of my life. Death had taken the form of a watery green darkness into which I was sinking, slowed and numbed by the depth and cold,
while above me the strange, lost sight of sunlight faded from the surface.

It was not then, but a later time, when I was about thirteen. We lived    4
on the edge of uninhabited countryside at the end of a street in suburban
California. From our backyard a pathway led uphill into open fields.

One Sunday morning in spring, after the family had returned from    5
church and we had eaten a late breakfast, I went for a long walk alone
over the fields. I do not remember what was on my mind then, confused
by the unsorted emotions of youth or, as it may have been, delighting in
the open sky and the sun on the warm grasses.

The pathway soon merged with a narrow country road. The bare    6
soil in the wheeltracks was damp from the winter rains, and there was an
occasional shallow pool of water in a deeper rut. As I came over the crest
of the hill I saw something lying at the side of the road just ahead of me.
When I came up to it, I saw that it was a rabbit, and that it was dead. Its
brown and white fur was torn and its belly ripped open.

I came closer and stopped before it. Just for a moment I stood there    7
looking down at the torn, but still intact animal. The blue bulge of its
gut lay half-spilled from the body and shone brightly, glazed with blood,
in the morning sunlight. A few flies already buzzed around it.

A nameless panic gripped me. I heard the buzzing of the flies and    8
other insects, and somewhere close but out of sight a meadowlark was
singing. There was nothing else around, no other sign of man, of animal
or bird of prey. Beyond the hill crest not even a housetop showed above
the yellow grasses. I was alone under the sun in an open field with death,
unmistakable, physical death.

It was not just that still form lying at the edge of the road, nor the    9
blood that was dried upon its fur; I had seen things like it before. It was
something new—an awakening that fastened on the incredible shining
blueness of the inside turned outside, the innermost part ripped from its
place and spilled into the light where it did not belong. Gazing, fixed before it in the sunlight, I felt, perhaps for the first time, an absolute alone-
ness. And I who at that age loved solitude, knew that this was death, the
loneliest solitude of all.

In terror I began to walk, away from the scene, over the grassy slope    10
of the hill, but looking behind me all the while as if I expected that quiet,
mutilated form to rise from the damp ground and follow me. Perhaps I
feared that somewhere in that silent, sunny countryside, in the grass,
even in the voice of the meadowlark, death itself was waiting.

I do not know what sermon I had half-listened to that morning in    11
church; something that had deepened my mood and prompted my
walk—something about mortality, was it, of death and the hereafter, of
reward and damnation? I don't remember. Yet somehow I felt deeply that
I was guilty, but of what I did not know.

12 I walked a long way that morning, troubled and confused. I returned over the same path on my way home. As fearful as I had been, both re-pelled and attracted, I had to see that form of death again. I had to know.

13 But when I came again to the place in the road, on the rounded hill-top, there was nothing there. I looked around, thinking I had mistaken the location, and that the dead rabbit was somewhere close by. Its ab-sence now was even more alarming. Had I really seen it? But yes, for here in the brown soil at the edge of the grass was a small, darkened spot that appeared to be blood, and near it a little patch of rabbit fur.

14 I struggled with explanations. Something—hawk or fox—disturbed originally by my coming, had run off and left its victim in the road. And when I had gone, it returned to claim its food.

15 Still the feeling of dread remained as I walked on toward home. I think now that I told no one of what I had seen, but kept it as a secret, something shared between me, the grass, and the unseen meadowlark. The impression of that morning stayed with me for a long time, and for a while I avoided that part of the road on my walks. When later I crossed the hill at that spot, alone or with friends, I half-expected to see the rab-bit again, to have it rise before me from the grass without warning, and with that large, incredibly distended bulge of its stomach, veined with fat, gleaming so brightly blue and green in the sun. But a ghost-image was all I had; a latent emotion charged with mistrust, and a lingering fear.

16 Transitory in the field, under the sun, slowly disintegrating under blows of the summer rain, an image of the world's stupendous accident. An instant of inexplicable calm, as on the bright, cold winter day I found a redpoll frozen on a snowbank at the entrance to the homestead road. There was nothing to tell me how the bird came to die there. It may have been stunned by the wind gust from a passing car, or it may have fallen asleep while feeding on the blown seeds of the few weed stalks that showed above the snow, and momentarily warming itself in the cold sun. There was not a mark on its body, not a feather disturbed. Under the downy fluff the tiny feet were stiffened; the eyes were half-closed and crystalized; at either side of the nostrils lay a delicate whisker of frost. The rusty crown of its head was bright with color, and the flushed breast seemed almost warm to my touch. But it was absolutely still, the breast and the heart within it joined in a lump of ice. I held the bird for a moment before putting it to rest again in the snow. It seemed to weigh nothing at all.

17 In that tiny, quenched image of vitality, a bird like a leaf dropped by the wind in passing, I felt something of our common, friable substance—a shared vulnerability grasped once with insight and passion, and then too easily forgotten. Necessarily forgotten, perhaps, for to keep such a thing constantly before one might be intolerable; the identification would wound too deeply.

18 I see again the worn, chalk-white skull of a caribou left behind on the fall tundra many years ago. One half of an antler poked up from the

deep moss in which the skull was lying; the moss and the accumulation of old leaves and plant debris had nearly buried the rest of it from view.

When I tilted the skull slightly, I saw that a thin, green mold clung to    19
the bone below the soil line. There had been no trace there for a long time of meat, of marrow or gristle. All else was bleached, chalky and crumbling: the upper jaw with a few loose molars, the long thin nostril bone, the eye-sockets, and the mouldering hollows behind the ears. The remaining antler revealed the worn tooth-marks of rodents who in past years, when the skull was still fresh, had gnawed it for the calcium in the bone.

The small lichens and mosses that had taken root upon the skull    20
were breaking down whatever was left of its structure. It seemed to me as I walked away and turned to view it from a little distance, that the skull was like a small vessel, abandoned by captain and crew; rudderless and demasted, it was sinking into the moss and frozen sod. The wet, green sea-life of the tundra washed over the pale wreck in tiny waves year after year, and sooner or later sun, rain and frost would claim it completely. Farewell.

On a snowy day early in October I was sitting at breakfast alone in    21
the house at Richardson, gloomy with the knowledge that the moose season had closed and I had yet to get my meat for the winter. I had hunted for better than two weeks, all through the cool, dry days of late September, and had seen nothing but tracks. Winter was coming, there was snow on the ground, nearly eight inches of it already, and I knew that in order to find a moose now I would have to go far into the hills for it, and by the time I got it, late in the rut, the meat was sure to be lean and tough.

As I was cleaning up the breakfast pans and dishes, I thought I heard    22
a sound outside, rather like a low grunt, and one of the dogs chained in the yard gave a sharp "woof." I went to the door and looked out. To my astonishment I saw a large bull moose stalking slowly uphill through the snowy garden.

The moose, plainly in view against the white, cleared ground,    23
paused and looked down toward the house and yard. In those few moments of what seemed to be a kind of mutual recognition, it struck me that the moose was not in the best of condition, that perhaps it had been beaten in a fight, or was overtaken by weariness. But no matter—here was my meat, and right in the yard.

I had a rifle at my hand, but at that moment a car went by on the road    24
below the house, driving slowly because of the fresh snowfall. As keenly as I wanted that moose, I feared that it would be seen if I shot it there in plain view and out of season. I waited, and watched the moose climb the open hill and go out of sight over the crest toward the potato patch.

I decided immediately to follow it, to take another way up the hill    25
and head it off, since the moose seemed to be in no hurry. I dressed myself quickly in overshoes, cap, jacket and gloves, and with the rifle in hand I took off up the hill through the falling snow.

26    I climbed through the woods, following a trail I had cut the year before. I did not dare to stop for rest, but plowed on, hoping that the snowfall and the laden branches would dampen any sound I was making. In a short time I reached the top of a narrow ridge where the trail began to level off. And there I found the tracks of the moose who had just passed before me. He could not be far ahead. Panting, stumbling at times in the fresh snow, I followed those tracks, determined to catch up with that moose or fall in the snow from trying.

27    Within a quarter of a mile I came to a place where the trail straightened and I could see some distance ahead of me. Another twenty yards, and I caught up with the moose, now a large brown bulk blurred by the falling snow, standing in the birches. He was stopped in the trail, his head half-turned, looking back in my direction.

28    Trembling from the long climb, I raised the rifle, trying for some kind of shooting rest against the nearest tree. As I was doing this, the moose, alerted now, broke into a trot and began to move swiftly ahead. I had no time for a better shot; he would soon be out of sight, and I was too badly winded from the climb to pursue him any further. I aimed for a spot just below the tail stump and fired.

29    At the sound of the shot the moose jumped, ran forward at a faster pace, and stopped. As I approached him, he turned to one side of the trail and stepped slowly into the woods, as if he would think awhile on what had happened. In the one large, dark eye turned toward me I could see a kind of blunted panic and bewilderment. I was ready to shoot again, not knowing if I really had him, when he staggered, felt for better footing, and fell heavily on his right side with a soft, cushioned *swoosh*, sending a shower of dry snow into the air. Once he tried to raise his head, then let it fall. As I came near I saw his chest heave out a mighty sigh, and one leg stiffen slightly. And then the woods were silent in the falling snow.

30    The open eye of the moose gazed blank and dull into the treestroked whiteness. A few wet flakes fell on the eyelids, melted on the warm nostrils, and sank into the long, unmoving ears.

31    The great, dark bulk was still. I felt, as I always do at such times, a strange and painful combination of emotions, if what one feels then can be called emotion precisely—a mingling of awe, of regret, of elation and relief. There was a quiet space in which to breathe, to acknowledge that something urgent and needed had been accomplished, all anxiety and uncertainty for the moment done with.

32    I returned down the snowy trail to the house to get my knife, my axe and saw, and a length of rope. And once more up the trail, I was soon at work on the carcass. First, I cut off the head with its heavy antlers. Then I tied a foreleg to a tree, and pushed and balanced the heavy, inert bulk onto its back. As always, it was strenuous work for a single man. But now death was forgotten. A transformation had taken place, and what had been a vital and breathing creature, capable of perception and of movement, was now only meat and salvage—a hairy mound of bone and muscle.

When I cut through the hide and strained inner tissue of the     33
paunch, a cloud of red steam burst on the snowy air. And soon I could see
deep into the steaming red cavity divided from the upper torso by the
taut, muscular wall of the diaphragm. Working by feel alone in the hot
soupiness of the rib cage, I loosened the windpipe, then pulled the stomach and the intestines clear, tumbling the heavy, stretched bag and ropy
folds onto the snow. There was no fat on the veil nor around the kidneys,
but I had not expected to find any. The meat would be lean, but it was
better than no meat at all.

And now, with the entire inner part open to the light, I found that     34
my single bullet had traveled the length of the body cavity, just under the
spine, and had cut the blood vessels around the heart. Death had been
swift, and little meat was spoiled.

That afternoon I dragged the quarters downhill through the snow     35
and hung them on the rack behind the house. A week later a strong wind
blew from the south, much of the snow melted, and a springlike warmth
sailed through the woods. Where the killed moose had lain, the shaded
snow thawed, then froze again, forming a kind of sunken circle that was
stained pink and yellow, and matted with hair and leaves. It was soon to
be covered by a fresh snowfall, and in a far month to come, to melt and
be once more a part of the spring earth.

## CONSIDERATIONS

1. How and why does Haines avoid falling into sentimentality as he describes
the death of the moose?

2. Some readers might insist that Haines's focus on death is a morbid preoccupation. Take up that idea and either support it or contradict it by what you find in the essay.

3. How and when does the meadowlark show up in the essay? Explain why you
think it became such an important part of the title.

4. Haines is not only a keen observer, but also a lover of nature, yet he gives us a
detailed account of tracking, killing, and butchering a moose. Is there a contradiction
there, or does the whole of the essay remove that possibility?

5. Compare Haines on death with Jane Kenyon on "Season of Change and Loss"
(page 341) in a discussion of their different approaches to understanding and accepting
natural processes.

6. Staring at a dead rabbit, Haines discovered that death was "an absolute alone-
ness . . . the loneliest solitude of all." How old was he then? Compare and contrast his
experience with your own when you first confronted death.

*Donald Hall (b. 1928), co-editor of* A Writer's Reader, *was born in Connecticut and has spent the last twenty years writing on an ancestral farm in New Hampshire. Best known as a poet, he is author of* The One Day, *a book-length poem, which won the National Books Critics Circle Award and The Los Angeles Times Book Award in 1989. His most recent collection of poems is* Without *(1998). He has also published a book of short stories, books for children (including* Ox Cart Man, *which was awarded the Caldecott Medal in 1980), and many essays. We take "Keeping Things" from his collection* Here at Eagle Pond.*

*In 1975 Hall resigned from a professorship and moved with his wife Jane Kenyon (pages 339–345) to an old family farm in New Hampshire, where he still lives and writes. Notice how "Keeping Things" tells stories of his return, using detail to support the story, revealing emotion sometimes by extravagant language. "I would as soon sell my ancestors' bones for soup. . . ."*

— **39** ——————————————————————————————

# DONALD HALL
## *Keeping Things*

———————————————————————————————————

1      On the second floor of our house there is a long, unfinished room that my family has always called the back chamber. It is the place the broken chair ascends to when it is too weak for sitting on; the broken lamp finds its shelf there, the toolbox its roost after the carpenter's death. You do not throw things away: You cannot tell when they might come in handy. My great-grandfather was born in 1826 and died in 1914; some of his clothes remain in the back chamber, waiting to come in handy.

2      His name was Benjamin Keneston, and he had two sons and three daughters, the youngest my grandmother Kate, who died at ninety-seven in 1975. Most of Ben's children were long-lived; when they survived their spouses they would come home, bringing a houseful of furniture with them. They never called this place anything but home, or used the word for any other place, though they might have lived and worked elsewhere

for fifty years. Both Luther and Nannie returned to live in cottages near the farm, and Kate kept bedrooms at the house in their names—Luther's room, Nannie's room—for when they were sick. Their extra furniture went to the back chamber, or above the back chamber in a loft, or in the dark hole that extends under eaves in the old part of the house without windows or electric lights.

When we potter in the back chamber today, we find a dozen knocked-down double beds, one painted with gold designs and the slogan *Sleep Balmy Sleep* on dark veneer. We find something like thirty chairs: captain's chairs, rockers with a rocker missing, Morris chairs, green painted kitchen chairs, pressed-wood upright dining room chairs, uncomfortable stuffed parlor chairs; most of them lack a strut or a leg but live within distance of repair. We find a sewing machine that my grandmother sewed on for sixty years and a 1903 perambulator she wheeled my mother in. Two sisters came after my mother, and the back chamber is well furnished with dolls' furniture: tiny chests of drawers, small rockers and small captain's chairs, prams, cradles, and a miniature iron cookstove, like the big Glenwood range in the kitchen below, with an oven door that swings open, firebox, stove lids, and a tiny iron skillet that fits a stovetop opening. We find fat old wooden skis and sleds with bentwood runners. One ancient stove, with castiron floral reliefs, we cleaned up and use in Jane's study, which used to be Nannie's room. We find toolboxes, postcard collections, oil lamps, electric lamps, pretty cardboard boxes, books by Joe Lincoln and Zane Grey, cribs, carpetbags, loveseats, and a last for making shoes. We find three spinning wheels, two of them broken and a third intact, dispatched upstairs when Ward's replaced homespun; as the family remembers, Benjamin's wife Lucy Buck Keneston was a wonderful spinner. We find a dozen quilts too frail for cleaning, showing bright squares of the cut-up dresses of seamstresses born to the early Republic. We find six or seven chests full of dead people's clothing, Ben Keneston's among them. In a dark row stand four baby highchairs; one made from stout brown wood is more than seventy years old, first used by my mother's younger sister Nan, next by me, later by my children; two wicker highchairs are older, and a frail wooden one older still. I don't know which of them my grandmother sat in.

In the back chamber we keep the used and broken past. Of course it is also a dispensary. When my daughter moved from her University of New Hampshire dormitory to an apartment in Dover, she outfitted her flat from unbroken furniture out of the back chamber. With glue and dowels, the apartments of children and grandchildren could be filled for fifty years. In, and out again: the past hovering in the dusty present like motes, a future implicit in shadowy ranks of used things, usable again. We do not call these objects antiques; they were never removed from use as testimony to affluence. Twice a year, as I show somebody through the house, somebody decides that I am in need of counseling: "You've got a fortune here." I keep my temper. None of it would fetch a great price, but even if it would, I would as soon sell my ancestors' bones for soup as I would sell their top hats, chairs, tool chests, and pretty boxes. Someday when we are dead let them go to auction, if they are not repaired and dispersed.

5      Continually we discover new saved things, and my wonder is not for the things themselves but for the saving of them. Could Kate really have thought, when she put away a 1917 agricultural bulletin, that it might come in handy someday? The back chamber bespeaks attachment to the outlived world. On a long, narrow cardboard box an old hand has written, "Wool was from B. C. Keneston's sheep carded and ready for spinning at Otterville"—where there was a carding mill—"in 1848." When we open it, we find protected by mothballs a few pounds of one-hundred-and-forty-year-old sheep's wool, preserved for preservation's sake, so that we may touch our fingers to the wool our ancestor's fingers sheared. (Was 1848 his first crop from his first sheep? He was twenty-two that year.) This back chamber is like the parlor walls covered with family portraits, like the graveyard with its Vermont slate and New Hampshire granite; it keeps the dead.

6      When we moved into the old house after my grandmother's death, it needed work. (She was seventy-four when my grandfather died. He had kept the house up, and after his death she could not afford to hire help. My mother paid to keep the house painted and the roof dry.) Now as we painted and shingled, dug out the cesspool, planted daffodils, put in a leachfield, fertilized hayfields, jacked up the woodshed for a new sill, re-placed clapboards, and mulched old roses, our neighbors let us know that they were pleased. In this countryside, everyone over fifty had watched white wooden houses lose paint and tilt inward as their roofs sagged, and finally whole square-built houses collapse into their own cellarholes. Everyone here takes interest in preserving things, in landscape and build-ingscape, even if everyone knows that in a hundred years fire will con-sume all these houses.

7      One outbuilding was too far gone for us to bring it back. Built at the turn of this century just north of the house, the saphouse had been the site of prodigious syrup making. In 1913 my grandfather, with the help of his father-in-law and Freeman Morrison, made five hundred gallons to sell for a dollar each, and put the windfall into land. Because it takes about forty gallons of sap to make a gallon of syrup—the pale sap is wa-tery; it is hard to taste the sweetness—he hauled twenty thousand gal-lons of maple sap that year, in the two or three weeks of sugaring. First he tapped the huge old trees of the sugarbush on Ragged Mountain, set-ting one or more buckets at each tree to collect the dripping liquid; then he visited each tree each day, emptying the buckets into twenty-gallon pails he carried on a yoke across his shoulders; then he walked through the snowy woods to the ox sledge, where he poured the sap into milk cans; when the cans were full he eased his oxen to a funnel uphill from the saphouse and piped his crop down to the saphouse's holding tank.

When I was little and visited the farm in March, if I hit upon sugar-   8
ing time, I walked the sugarbush with him. The crop is best when days
are warm and nights freezing. To keep the sap boiling, somebody has to
tend the fire twenty-four hours a day; Freeman, who was a night owl,
stayed up all night and much of the day to feed the fire. He pushed whole
trees, foot by foot, over the snow through the saphouse's open doors into
the firebox. Freeman and my grandfather had built the saphouse under
the supervision of my grandfather's father-in-law, informally called
Uncle Ben. (Formally he was Benjamin Cilley Keneston, to distinguish
him from his father, who was plain Benjamin. When I was a child I liked
knowing that I was part Cilley.) BCK died in 1914, sixty-six years after he
sheared the sheep's wool in the back chamber. Although I never knew
him, I have been aware of his presence since I was a child, and living in
his house I feel him every day, not only in the photograph on the living
room wall or the top hat under the stairs. If we find a tar-brand for sheep
it is *K*. He was diminutive and powerful, and it must have been hard for
my grandfather Wesley Wells to marry his daughter, move into his
house, and take direction from him. Yet I never caught a shade of resentment in the stories my grandfather told me.

     We hated to pull the saphouse down. My grandfather used it last to   9
make a few gallons in March 1950. That autumn he had a heart attack,
sold the cows, and never used the saphouse again. He died in March
1953. When we moved into his house in 1975 we found an unopened
quart from his last crop of syrup on a shelf in the rootcellar. Maybe if I
had been truest to family practices I would have carried it up to the back
chamber unopened but labeled for future generations to wonder at.
However, we opened it, we ate it on pancakes, and when we had almost
finished it, we poured the last drops into a store-bought gallon—figuring
that for a few decades at least, if we continued emptying old gallons into
new ones, we could imagine molecular survival for my grandfather's final quart.

     The saphouse leaned over, a third out of the vertical. The shedlike   10
door gapped loose. I no longer entered it, because sometime the roof
would collapse and I would not let it collapse on me. Rot feathered the
timbers up from the ground, the tarpaper roof was swaybacked, and the
lead pipe sagged as it rose up-mountain from the rotten galvanized holding tank. Twenty years before, my grandmother Kate had sold the evapo-
rator—big tin tray over the firebox—to somebody building a new
saphouse; somebody else had bought the buckets. Every now and then, a
pickup braked in front of the house and a stranger offered to tear the saphouse down for us, in return for the old wood that he could salvage.
There's a market for old wood: beams for what is called restoration,
planks to be cut up for picture frames. I refused these offers, wanting to
keep the old wood, and probably because I inherited or acquired the desire to keep things. Also I remembered the sheepbarn. Two men tore it
down for my grandmother when it started to lean over; they promised,

as all the pickup people promised, to clean it up real good. But when these fellows had removed the solid wood they left a mess of rotten board and shingle that weeds grew to cover, a treacherous vegetal-archaeological heap you could break a leg in, where woodchucks bred for generations until we hired a dozer and a truck to haul the mess to the dump.

11      We tied a cable around the saphouse walls, hitched the cable to a four-wheel-drive pickup, and pulled it down. The frail boards stretched apart like a clasped bunch of straw when you unclench your fist. Sun touched bright unweathered boards that had seen no light since Wesley and Freeman lifted them from the sawmill's pile and hammered them in place. Store nails pulled from the corner four-by-fours. At the door we found long, irregular hammered iron pins, which Freeman had pounded out at his forge in the shop that stood not twenty yards away—the shop also gone now, all traces gone except the grindstone's base that leaned beside it.

12      We tossed rotten boards in the pickup's bed, stacked the good wood and hauled it for storage to the cowbarn with its kept-up roof. At day's end we drove the junk to the town dump. In a wheelbarrow we collected old bottles, one intact sap bucket, a float, an enamel funnel, and an elegantly shaped handmade shovel. Two huge tapered iron hinges bore a hammer's prints. We tucked the ironwork in a corner of the woodshed (where firewood covers it half the year) among ax heads, scythe blades, and the frail graceful trident of a pitchfork. Freeman forged some of this iron with his engineering-generalist's skill—who turned baseball bats on a lathe, tanned leather and made shoes, built ladders and hayricks and playhouses and wooden spoons and stone walls, repaired cutlery and milk pails, moved rocks and pulled stumps—but some of the work is finer than Freeman's; I fancy the hand of John Wells, Wesley's father, who fought at Vicksburg and returned to be blacksmith and farrier on a hill west of Danbury.

13      Soon grass and saplings would cover the debris we left behind, bricks and small pieces of wood, chowder of rusted metal, spread now in a drift of old leaves that blew into the saphouse autumns past, gray-brown and fragile. High in the center stood the one monument that remained like the saphouse's tombstone, the long brick hive of fire, firebox into which Freeman had pushed whole trees. Seventy-five-year-old mortar spilled at the edge of bricks pink as a baby's mouth. I remember hearing that BCK liked to butter bricks; he must have done this work. Maybe in a hundred years a hiker walking down Ragged Mountain will find this brickwork among new maples.

14      When we were done, birches cast late-day shadows across the little field between the house and the place where the saphouse used to be. Then we noticed an odd-shaped white stone where there had been a corner four-by-four. It was flat and looked carved. We lifted it up and saw

that beneath it there was another piece just like it, and when we turned
the top one over, we understood two things at once: The two pieces fitted where they had broken in the middle, and it was a tombstone.
Cleaning it off, I read the name and dates of my great-great-grandfather,
BCK's father, BENJAMIN KENISTON 1789–1863. Because I knew his grave in
the old Andover graveyard, because I remembered the sturdy, legible
stone above it, I understood that this was his *first* gravestone, that it had
broken, that his son BCK had replaced it—and brought it home and put it
to use.

The first month we moved here, going through an old desk, we     15
found a yellowed piece of stationery headed by an indistinct photograph
of Mount Kearsarge and the words *B. C. Keneston Eagle Pond Farm.* (It
was BCK who changed the spelling of the family name, to distance himself from some Keniston cousins.) The pond is west of the farm, thirty
acres of water—a lake anywhere else. No one alive remembered that
name for the place. Although it had not stuck, I decided to make use of
it, not for piety of reference but to ease the minds of urban and suburban
correspondents who find it hard to believe that a town's name can be address enough. So BCK solved a problem: All that first year, the dead
helped out.

Mostly they demanded attention. I could not decide whether     16
Freeman or BCK demanded more. (My grandparents, whom I knew so
well and loved so much, demanded little; I thought of them without being reminded.) BCK, whom I had never known, had picked this place out;
it was he who deserved credit for staking the claim to Kearsarge and to
Eagle Pond. It was he who bought the pew at the South Danbury church
he helped to found, where his daughter Kate played the organ Sundays
from the age of fourteen to ninety-two. (Is seventy-eight years at the
same organ a neo-Calvinist record?) It was fitting, then, that my one
glimpse of his ghost, looking suspiciously like my favorite photograph of
him, occurred in church one Sunday. He vanished as soon as I saw him. If
every Sunday I caught sight of my grandmother's black sequined hat,
bobbing next to the green glass lampshade above the organ, that vision
seemed natural enough.

Freeman insisted on his presence in a manner perfectly material.     17
He had stenciled his name all over the house. Cousin Freeman moved in
as a boy when his family was burned out; he preferred Uncle Ben and
Aunt Lucy to his parents and loved Kate like a little sister. His father
took him away and put him to work when he was sixteen, but for the
rest of his life he kept returning to this place that he loved. I remember
him old and sick, wrapped in a blanket, tucked into the rocker by the
kitchen range, attended by Kate grown old. He stenciled his name on the
underside of stairs leading to the back chamber, which we could see as
we walked down to the rootcellar. He stenciled his name on the bottom
of a drawer in the pantry, on the underside of the windowsill in his

room, and on shingles we found wedged under a box in the toolshed. When we turned something over or lifted something up, we half expected to see Freeman's name, as if his face with its playful eyes leapt up like a jack-in-the-box. He stenciled his name, as it were, on everybody who knew him.

18      My ghost stories are mostly unconscious memory. When we had lived here only a few weeks a stranger knocked on the front door; his trailer had broken down and he needed a large monkey wrench. I started to say that I had no big wrench, but before I could speak something took hold of me. Asking the man to wait I gave myself over to whatever possessed me and let it direct me out of the kitchen, into the toolshed toward the woodshed door; my right hand rose unbidden toward a flat shelf over that door where the big wrench resided, and had resided forever, covered now with thirty years of dust and spider webs. Something similar happened when I bought a sickle at Thornley's store to chop down weeds in the backyard. I cut Lexington plant until my back stopped me, then walked with my silvery crescent into the toolshed where I would find something to hang it on; I did not know why I headed for a particular place, but when I raised my hand toward the naily ceiling, I saw three frail rusted sickles hanging there already.

19      Not everything that happened was memory. Once my wife heard her name called repeatedly in the barn when no one was there to say it. Once after someone helping us cleaned a shed loft, and threw away old shoes and clothing we would not have thrown away, Jane felt in the loft some violence, anger, or even evil, as if something terrible had happened there; maybe it was only resentment over things lost. And there was something else soon after we moved in, although we did not hear about it for two years. It happened to a visitor—skeptical, secular, unsuperstitious, hesitant to speak of it, unable to understand what she saw. It was just a *seeing.* As she stood in our living room, she saw someone in the doorway of the kitchen, someone who was not there: a short man, bearded, wearing overalls and a hat. Both BCK and Freeman were short, bearded, wore overalls and a hat.

20      These experiences virtually stopped after that first year, but there was an exception. When we had lived here six years, we finally afforded a new bathroom. The old one was Sears 1937: cold, shabby, showerless. We tore it off the side of the house and put a new bathroom (with shower and laundry) into our old bedroom, extending a new bedroom onto the north lawn. For warmth in winter we extended the rootcellar under the new room, which obliged us to raise the north side of the house on jacks and bulldoze underneath it. We dug out rotten sills and replaced them; ripping a wall from the old bedroom we exposed 1803 carpentry; the wallpaper of the family Troy was nine layers deep; in one wall we found cardboard insulation from a box of breakfast cereal, Washington's Crisps, and a picture of the general with bright red lips.

It was the first major alteration of the house's shape since BCK ex-   21
panded it in 1865, when it became the extended farmhouse familiar in
New Hampshire—outbuildings not separated but linked one to one,
moving in slow file backward to the hill. To haul firewood in winter we
pass through a kitchen door into the toolshed, which is another repository almost like the back chamber: saws, levels, crowbars, old nails,
screws, bolts, shovels, rakes, hoes, sickles, awls, drills and their bits,
hammers, hammerheads, traps, stovepipe, lanterns, wrenches, screw-
drivers; and the practice organ Kate learned to play on, moved from the
parlor to the toolshed in 1927 when my mother and father displayed
wedding presents in the parlor—and at the southeast corner of the toolshed we go through another door into the woodshed. This door is made
from planks nailed to crossplanks, and it latches by a smooth oblong of
wood—touched ten million times like Saint Peter's toe to a soft and
shiny texture—which turns on a bolt and sticks at a thumb of wood below. Because we must carry wood many times a day, much of the year,
we have unfixed the latch to open this door thousands of times, walked
into the woodshed, loaded up with logs, and walked back out again,
latching the door behind us. But while we were tearing things up, something new happened, not once or twice but seven times: While we were
fetching logs, this woodshed door swung closed behind us, and the
wooden latch turned by itself and locked us inside the woodshed.

It never happened once in the years before; in the years since we   22
stopped sawing and hammering, it has not happened again. This locking
up was not malicious, because it is easy enough to get out of the woodshed by a door that leads outside. Not malicious, just an annoying prank.

The steadiest presence remains in the possessions, rooms, and arti-   23
facts of the dead. Living in their house, we take over their practices and
habits, which makes us feel close to them and to the years that they
knew. I always wanted to live in this house with the old people, and now
I do, even though they are dead. I don't live in their past; they inhabit my
present, where I live as I never lived before. I used to survive, like many
people, half in a daydream of future reward that is a confession of present
malaise: the vacation trip, the miraculous encounter. When I moved
here, at first I feared the fulfillment of desire, as if I would be punished
for possessing what I wanted so much; there was a brief time when I
drove ten miles under the speed limit and buckled up to move the car in
the driveway; but contentment was relentless and would not let me go
until I studied the rapture of the present tense. It turns out that the fulfillment of desire is to stop desiring, to live in the full moon and the
snow, in the direction the wind comes from, in the animal scent of the
alive second.

The dead were welcoming. I worried about usurping their place un-   24
til two dreams helped me. In one I discovered that my grandfather—who
was working the farm, now, in my dream—had disappeared and I

thought him dead, only to see him striding up the dirt road from Andover (a road paved before I was born), leading a file of zoo animals: ostrich, bear, elephant, lion, tiger. He had traded the cows and sheep for these exotic creatures, proving (as I take the dream) that I was permitted to raise poems on this farm instead of stock. The other dream was more to the point of disappearances; a large voice pronounced, "The blow of the ax resides in the acorn."

25      If there is no connected past, we lack the implication of persistence after our own death. The preserved or continuous past implies the possibility that oneself may continue, in place or object or even in spirit, a ring of time that revolves, revisits, and contains. As a child I heard about a bone ring. When John Wells fought at Vicksburg he stood next to a young man named George Henry Butler, who came from a farm on New Canada Road; people from the same neighborhoods fought together in that war. As they were shelled, Wells took cover behind a great tree, which allowed him to stand upright; Butler squatted in a hole beside him. When the cannonade continued Wells offered to switch places with Butler, to let him stretch for a bit, and when they had changed places, a cannonball crashed through the tree and took off the young man's head. My great-grandfather emptied Butler's pockets, and when he mustered out and walked home to Danbury turned over the dead soldier's possessions to his family.

26      John Wells's son Wesley married George Henry Butler's cousin Kate Keneston, and one object from those pockets came down to her. A few years ago it disappeared. No one could find it in the house, and we thought it was gone forever. We lamented the lost connection with a young man killed in the Civil War. Then we discovered it in a box of buttons in the back chamber: a finger ring carved out of bone, eight-sided, scratched with little decorations, small and yellowed—a bone ring I take as emblem of this place.

## *CONSIDERATIONS*

1. How does Hall avoid the vague meanderings so characteristic of such reminiscing?

2. In what ways, if any, does "Keeping Things" suggest that the author is primarily a poet? Are there things in the essay that surprise you when you think of the author as a poet? How do you go about distinguishing poetry from prose? Look at some of the poems in the text and discuss your findings.

3. What trait of Hall's great-grandfather is illustrated by the anecdote about an odd-shaped white stone found in the remnants of the leveled saphouse?

4. Examine some older houses in your town, paying particular attention to parts that were additions to the original structure and keeping in mind the changes Hall describes in paragraph 21. Report your findings by reconstructing—a little imagination

will help—the routines and ways of life, the changes in the family, and the economic ups and downs reflected in those changes of the house.

　　5. ". . . a bone ring I take as emblem of this place." Hall's concluding sentence. What does he mean by "emblem," and why does he think the bone ring a suitable one for his place?

　　6. Several other authors in your text—Patricia Hampl, Raymond Carver, Wallace Stegner, and E. B. White, for example—make important use of the past in their essays. Read one or more of these; then explain, with examples, how Hall's essay differs from the others.

*Patricia Hampl (b. 1946) was born in St. Paul, Minnesota, where she lives now. She received an MFA at the Iowa Writers Workshop and was a founding member of The Loft, a Twin Cities institution promoting literature and the arts. She has published stories, poems, and essays in the* New Yorker, Paris Review, *and* American Poetry Review. *In 1981 she received a Houghton Mifflin Literary Fellowship for her memoir,* A Romantic Education.

*To meditate on memory, Hampl uses photographs first— impersonal ones, personal ones—and moves on to intense memories of her own youth, which are entwined with recollections of her immigrant family, sources of the first photographs. Notice how the structure of her essay shapes a conclusion.*

— **40** —————————————————————————

# PATRICIA HAMPL
## *Holding Old Negatives Up to the Light*

1      I was five and was sitting on the floor of the vestibule hallway of my grandmother's house where the one bookcase had been pushed. The bookcase wasn't in the house itself—ours wasn't a reading family. I was holding in my lap a book of sepia photographs bound in a soft brown cover, stamped in flaking gold with the title *Zlatá Praha*, Golden Prague, views of the nineteenth century.

2      The album felt good, soft. First, the Hradčany Castle and its gardens, then a close-up of the astronomical clock, a view of the baroque jumble of Malá Strana. Then a whole series of photographs of the Vltava River, each showing a different bridge, photograph after pale photograph like a wild rose that opens petal by petal, exposing itself effortlessly, as if there were no such thing as regret. All the buildings in the pictures were hazy, making it seem that the air, not the stone, held the contour of the baroque villas intact.

3      I didn't know how to read yet, and the Czech captions under the pictures were no more comprehensible to me than English would have

been. I liked the soft, fleshlike pliancy of the book. I knew the pictures were of Europe, and that Europe was far away, unreachable. Still, it had something to do with me, with my family. I sat in the cold vestibule, turning the pages of the Prague album. I was flying; I was somewhere else. I was not in St. Paul, Minnesota, and I was happy.

My grandmother appeared at the doorway. Her hands were on her   4
stout hips, and she wanted me to come out of the unheated hallway. She wanted me to eat coffee cake in the kitchen with everybody else, and I had been hard to find. She said, "Come eat," as if this were the family motto.

As she turned to go, she noticed the album. In a second she was   5
down on the floor with me, taking the album carefully in her hands, turning the soft, felt pages. "Oh," she said, "Praha." She looked a long time at one picture, I don't remember which one, and then she took a white handkerchief out of her pinafore apron pocket, and dabbed at the tears under her glasses. She took off the wire-rim glasses and made a full swipe.

Her glasses had made deep hollows on either side of her nose, two   6
small caves. They looked as if, with a poke, the skin would give way like a ripe peach, and an entrance would be exposed into her head, into the skull, a passageway to the core of her brain. I didn't want her head to have such wounds. Yet I liked them, these unexpected dips in a familiar landscape.

"So beautiful," she was crying melodramatically over the album.   7
"So beautiful." I had never seen an adult cry before. I was relieved, in some odd way, that there was crying in adulthood, that crying would not be taken away.

My grandmother hunched down next to me in the hallway; she held   8
the album, reciting the gold-stamped captions as she turned the pages and dabbed at her eyes. She was having a good cry. I wanted to put my small finger into the two little caves of puckered skin, the eyeless sockets on either side of her large, drooping nose. Strange wounds, I wanted to touch them. I wanted to touch her, my father's mother. She was so *foreign*.

Looking repeatedly into the past, you do not necessarily become   9
fascinated with your own life, but rather with the phenomenon of memory. The act of remembering becomes less autobiographical; it begins to feel tentative, aloof. It becomes blessedly impersonal.

The self-absorption that seems to be the impetus and embarrass-   10
ment of autobiography turns into (or perhaps always was) a hunger for the world. Actually, it begins as hunger for *a* world, one gone or lost, effaced by time or a more sudden brutality. But in the act of remembering, the personal environment expands, resonates beyond itself, beyond its "subject," into the endless and tragic recollection that is history.

We look at old family photographs in which we stand next to black,   11
boxy Fords and are wearing period costumes, and we do not gaze fascinated because there we are young again, or there we are standing, as we

never will again in life, next to our mother. We stare and drift because there we are . . . historical. It is the dress, the black car that dazzle us now and draw us beyond our mother's bright arms which once caught us. We reach into the attractive impersonality of something more significant than ourselves.

12      We embrace the deathliness and yet we are not dead. We are impersonal and yet ourselves. The astonishing power and authority of memory derive from this paradox. Here, in memory, we live *and* die. We do "live again" in memory, but differently: in history as well as in biography. And when these two come together, forming a narrative, they approach fiction. The imprecision of memory causes us to create, to extend remembrance into narrative. It sometimes seems, therefore, that what we remember is not—could not be—true. And yet it is *accurate*. The imagination, triggered by memory, is satisfied that this is so.

13      We trust memory against all the evidence: it is selective, subjective, cannily defensive, unreliable as fact. But a single red detail remembered—a hat worn in 1952, the nail polish applied one summer day by an aunt to her toes, separated by balls of cotton, as we watched—has more real blood than the creatures around us on a bus as, for some reason, we think of that day, that hat, those bright feet. That world. This power of memory probably comes from its kinship with the imagination. In memory each of us is an artist: each of us creates. The Kingdom of God, the nuns used to tell us in school, is within you. We may not have made a religion of memory, but it is our passion, and along with (sometimes in opposition to) science, our authority. It is a kingdom of its own.

14      Psychology, which is somehow *our* science, the claustrophobic discipline of the century, has made us acknowledge the value of remembering—even at the peril of shame. But it is especially difficult to reach back into the merely insignificant, into a family life where, it seemed, nothing happened, where there wasn't the ghost of a pretension. That is a steelier resistance because to break through what is unimportant and as anonymous as dirt a greater sense of worthlessness must be overcome. At least shame is interesting; at least it is hidden, the sign of anything valuable. But for a past to be overlooked, discarded because it was not only useless but simply without interest—that is a harsher heritage. In fact, is it a heritage?

15      It seems as if I spent most of my twenties holding a lukewarm cup of coffee, hunched over a table, talking. Innumerable cups of coffee, countless tables: the booths of the Gopher Grill at the University of Minnesota where, probably around 1965, I first heard myself use the word *relationship*; a little later, the orange formica table of a federal prison where "the man I live with" (there still is no other term) was serving a sentence for draft resistance; and the second-hand tables of a dozen apartments, the wooden farmhouse table of a short-lived commune— table after table, friend after friend, rehashing our hardly ended (or not ended) childhoods. I may have the tables wrong; maybe the formica one

was in the farmhouse, the oak one in the prison, maybe the chairs in the prison were orange and the table gray. But they are fixtures, nailed down, not to be moved: memories.

This generation has written its memoirs early; we squeezed every   16 childhood lemon for all it was worth: my mother this, my father that. Our self-absorption was appalling. But I won't go back—not yet—on that decade. It was also the time when my generation, as "a generation," was most political, most involved. The people I sat with, picking at our individual pasts, wearing nightgowns till noon as we analyzed within a millimeter our dreams and their meanings (that is, how they proved this or that about our parents), finally put on our clothes, went outside and, in various ways that are too easily forgotten, tried to end a war which we were the first, as a group, to recognize was disastrous. In fact, our protest against the war is what made us a generation, even to ourselves.

Perhaps no American generation—certainly not our parents who   17 were young during the Depression—had a childhood as long as ours. The war kept us young. We stayed in school, endlessly, it seemed, and our protest kept us in the child's position: we alternately "rebelled" against and pestered the grownups for what we wanted—an end to the war. Those who fought the war had no such long, self-reflective youths. Childhood belonged to us, who stayed at home. And we became the "sixties generation."

Our certainty that the war was wrong became entangled with our   18 analysis of our families and our psyches not only because we were given to self-reflection and had a lot of time on our hands. We combed through our dreams and our childhoods with Jung's *Man and His Symbols* at the ready, and were looking for something, I now think, that was neither personal nor familial and perhaps not even psychological. We had lost the national connection and were heartsick in a cultural way. I don't think we knew that; I didn't, anyway. But at home I didn't talk psychology, I talked politics, arguing with a kind of angry misery whose depths confused me and made my family frightened for me, and probably of me. But there was no real argument—I did all the talking; my family, gathered for Sunday dinner, looked glumly at the gravy on their plates as if at liquid Rorschach blots that might suggest why I, the adored child, had come to this strange pass. They weren't "for the way," but the belligerent way I was against it dismayed them and caused them to fall silent, waiting for me to stop. I had opinions, I spoke of my "position" on things.

One night my uncle, trying to meet me halfway, said, "Well, when I   19 was in Italy during the War . . ."

"How do you defend that analogy?" I snapped at him, perhaps   20 partly because for them "the War" was still the Second World War. My family couldn't seem, for a long time, to *focus* on Vietnam. But my uncle retreated in the face of the big guns of my new English-major lingo.

On Thanksgiving one year I left the table to find *I. F. Stone's*   21 *Weekly* and read parts of it to the assembled family in a ringing,

triumphantly angry voice. "But," my father said when I finished, as if
I. F. Stone had been compiling evidence about me and not the Johnson administration, "you used to be so *happy*—the happiest person I ever met."

22        "What does that have to do with anything?" I said.

23        Yet he was right. My unhappiness (but I didn't think of myself as
unhappy) was a confusion of personal and public matters, and it was
made more intense by the fact that I had been happy ("the happiest person!") and now I couldn't remember what that happiness had been—just
childhood? But many childhoods are miserable. And I couldn't remember
exactly how the happiness stopped. I carry from that time the feeling
that private memory is not just private and not just memory. Yet the re-
sistances not against memory but against the significance of memory remain strong.

24        I come from people who have always been polite enough to feel that
nothing has ever happened to them. They have worked, raised families,
played cards, gone on fishing trips together, risen to grief and admirable
bitterness and, then, taken patiently the early death that robbed them of
a brother, a son. They have not dwelt on things. To dwell, that appropriate word, as if the past were a residence, faintly morbid and barbaric: the
dwellings of prehistoric men. Or, the language of the Bible: "The Word
was made flesh, and dwelt amongst us."

25        I have dwelt, though. To make a metaphor is to make a fuss, and I
am a poet, though it seems that is something one cannot claim for oneself; anyway, I write poetry. I am enough of them, my kind family, to be
repelled by the significance of things, to find poetry, with its tendency to
make connections and to break the barriers between past and present,
slightly embarrassing.

26        It would be impossible to look into the past, even a happy one (especially a happy one), were it not for the impersonality that dwells in the
most intimate fragments, the integuments that bind even obscure lives
to history and, eventually, history to fiction, to myth.

27        I will hold up negative after family negative to the light. I will
dwell. Dwell in the house of the dead and in the living house of my relatives. I'm after junk. I want to make something out of what my family
says is nothing. I suppose that is what I was up to when my grandmother
called me out of the vestibule, away from the bookcase and the views of
Prague, to eat my dinner with everybody else.

## CONSIDERATIONS

1. "Looking repeatedly into the past," writes Hampl, "you do not necessarily become fascinated with your own life, but rather with the phenomenon of memory." How
reliable do you find the individual or collective memory of your family? How do old
photos or other mementos verify or challenge your memories?

2. Why, according to Hampl, is psychology "our" science? And why does she put quotation marks around the word? Whose "our" is she talking about?

3. As a poet, Hampl makes expert use of images, both literal and figurative. Underline a few examples and discuss their value versus more abstract language, such as that of paragraph 14.

4. In paragraph 25, the author, speaking of poetry, mentions "its tendency to make connections and to break the barriers between past and present." Look for evidence of these two qualities in some of the poems in your text, and report your findings in a short essay.

5. The author's family meant one thing by "the War," and she another. What was the misunderstanding? Can you match that with a similar misunderstanding you and your family experienced? Describe it in a short narrative, perhaps including some dialog.

6. "Our self-absorption was appalling," says Hampl of her generation. Would you say the same thing about yours? Explain.

*Jean Hegland (b. 1956) did graduate work and taught composition at Eastern Washington University. Now she lives with her family in northern California, writing fiction and essays, and teaches creative writing at Santa Rosa Junior College. "The Fourth Month"—part of* The Life Within: Celebration of a Pregnancy *(1991)—appeared in* Spiritual Mothering *in 1989. In 1996, she published her first novel,* Into the Forest.

*Hegland's essay carries to the reader the feelings and sensations of a woman during pregnancy—by her adroit use of metaphor and image. See how her language communicates intimate feeling to a reader she presumes not to have experienced pregnancy.*

— **41**

# JEAN HEGLAND
## *The Fourth Month*

Woman is the artist of the imagination and the child in the womb is the canvas whereon she painteth her pictures.

—*Paracelsus (1493–1541)*

1    For several days I thought they were just the soft rumblings of my own guts, these dim twistings low in my belly. But then one morning as we lay in bed, the twister's father put his hand on my stomach and felt a nudge at the same time I felt a poke. After months of gyrating unobserved, this creature had finally made itself indisputably known, its delicate flutters like a message from a distant planet or a deserted island—there is life here, too! It tapped against its father's palm once more, and then was still, indifferent to our sudden joy, to the hot blaze of tears in its parents' eyes.

2    It feels like a kiss, this quickening, like another's tongue slipping and curling inside my mouth. The Eskimos said that the aurora borealis was the playing of unborn children. I have seen only the dim, southern version of those northern lights, but still, this sensation is like that, ghostly, lovely, a dance performed in the darkness of another world.

Now as I go about my days, I am aware of the baby brewing inside 3
me, and it surprises me that the pattern of my life is not completely
transformed by this quickening. At night, when I lie next to Douglas, I
feel the tumbling of the child we have set in motion, and I think I am a
priestess privy to the mysteries of the gods. But at other times this tick-
ling in my guts comes as no surprise. Like the passing of gas, or the beating of a heart, it is a familiar feeling, comfortable, homey, and often it
seems usual, normal, to have this movement inside me.

I feel newly fond of this old body, now that it is more than just the 4
vehicle of my own continuance. I have forgiven its many curves and soft-
nesses, and I am proud of the neat little bulge of my belly, pleased with
my swollen breasts and their thick brown nipples. No longer mine, more
than myself, I have become a catalyst, a resource, a riddle. I am a boat
which contains an ocean, a basket filling with a single egg. I am a cradle,
a crucible, a garden.

"Quicken" means to come to life, and it does seem as though this 5
baby had just begun, now that I can feel its presence. And now that I can
distinguish between us, I feel more connection to it than I did before.
With these first quiet nudges comes the nascence of love.

In Egypt, they say that the heart sees the baby before the eye. But 6
even a heart must be able to see before it can love. Our organs cannot
love themselves, and even a heart can only love what is outside of and
other than itself, because such a great part of loving is that longing to
bridge that distance. Now that it is tangibly separate from me, I find myself asking the lover's question of this finger-length child tucked beneath
my heart: dear Riddle, what is it like for you? They say that already your
face, with its newly finished lips, is like no one else's face. Already, the
lines that tell your fortune are etched into your pea-sized palms. Already,
the whorls have risen on the pads of your fingertips and in the flesh of
your feet. What is it like to have that face, those feet and hands?

I wish I could be a twin in your womb, to know what it is you 7
know. I wish I could hear the sounds and silences that your ears have just
begun to hear, could feel the currents of amniotic fluid on your raw skin,
and the elastic give of the walls that contain you. I wish I could learn exactly what this time is like for you. But as I ask those questions to which
I know I will never find answers, I learn something else. I learn that
imagination is the essence of love.

## CONSIDERATIONS

1. In what way does the author of "The Fourth Month" prepare us for the surprising conclusion: "I learn that imagination is the essence of love"?

2. Although "The Fourth Month" is a subjective expression of what the pregnant
woman experiences, the writer's research is skillfully put to work in this short essay.
Find examples of that research.

3. How does her awareness of her developing baby affect the mother's image of herself?

4. Each of the chapters of Hegland's book *The Life Within*, from which "The Fourth Month" was taken, begins with a quotation from a different source. What do you think of an author's use of such material? Can you imagine using one of Ambrose Bierce's "Devil's Definitions" at the head of an essay you might write?

5. How might Diane Ackerman have made use of Hegland's essay in "The Importance of Touch" (page 10)?

6. Hegland's intense focus on birth might be interesting to compare or contrast with John Haines's concentration on death—see "Death Is a Meadowlark (page 260)—particularly with reference to their respective writing styles.

*Lillian Hellman (1905–1984) was a playwright, born in New Orleans, who grew up in New Orleans and New York City. After graduating from New York University, she went to work in publishing.* The Children's Hour *(1934), her first great success on Broadway, was followed by her most famous play,* The Little Foxes *(1939), and* Watch on the Rhine *(1941). She also wrote the book for Leonard Bernstein's musical* Candide.

*Hellman's later works were autobiographical and include* Pentimento *(1973),* Scoundrel Time *(1977), and* An Unfinished Woman, *which won the National Book Award in 1970. These narratives were collected into one volume with new commentary by the author:* Three *(1979). In 1980 she published* Maybe: A Story.

*The anecdote below, which is from* An Unfinished Woman, *tells of a climactic episode in the transition from childhood to adolescence and shows the rebelliousness, strong feeling, and independence that become themes of the autobiography.*

— **42** ─────────────────────────────

# LILLIAN HELLMAN
## *Runaway*

───────────────────────────────────────

It was that night that I disappeared, and that night that Fizzy said I  1
was disgusting mean, and Mr. Stillman said I would forever pain my mother and father, and my father turned on both of them and said he would handle his family affairs himself without comments from strangers. But he said it too late. He had come home very angry with me: the jeweler, after my father's complaints about his unreliability, had found the lock of hair in the back of the watch. What started out to be a mild reproof on my father's part soon turned angry when I wouldn't explain about the hair. (My father was often angry when I was most like him.) He was so angry that he forgot that he was attacking me in front of the Stillmans, my old rival Fizzy, and the delighted Mrs. Dreyfus, a new, rich boarder who only that afternoon had complained about my bad

manners. My mother left the room when my father grew angry with me. Hannah, passing through, put up her hand as if to stop my father and then, frightened of the look he gave her, went out to the porch. I sat on the couch, astonished at the pain in my head. I tried to get up from the couch, but one ankle turned and I sat down again, knowing for the first time the rampage that could be caused in me by anger. The room began to have other forms, the people were no longer men and women, my head was not my own. I told myself that my head had gone somewhere and I have little memory of anything after my Aunt Jenny came into the room and said to my father, "Don't you remember?" I have never known what she meant, but I knew that soon after I was moving up the staircase, that I slipped and fell a few steps, that when I woke up hours later in my bed, I found a piece of angel cake—an old love, an old custom—left by my mother on my pillow. The headache was worse and I vomited out of the window. Then I dressed, took my red purse, and walked a long way down St. Charles Avenue. A St. Charles Avenue mansion had on its back lawn a famous doll's-house, an elaborate copy of the mansion itself, built years before for the small daughter of the house. As I passed this showpiece, I saw a policeman and moved swiftly back to the doll palace and crawled inside. If I had known about the fantasies of the frightened, that ridiculous small house would not have been so terrible for me. I was surrounded by ornate, carved reproductions of the mansion furniture, scaled for children, bisque figurines in miniature, a working toilet seat of gold leaf in suitable size, small draperies of damask with a sign that said "From the damask of Marie Antoinette," a miniature samovar with small bronze cups, and a tiny Madame Récamier couch on which I spent the night, my legs on the floor. I must have slept, because I woke from a nightmare and knocked over a bisque figurine. The noise frightened me, and since it was now almost light, in one of those lovely mist mornings of late spring when every flower in New Orleans seems to melt and mix with the air, I crawled out. Most of that day I spent walking, although I had a long session in the ladies' room of the railroad station. I had four dollars and two bits, but that wasn't much when you meant it to last forever and when you knew it would not be easy for a fourteen-year-old girl to find work in a city where too many people knew her. Three times I stood in line at the railroad ticket windows to ask where I could go for four dollars, but each time the question seemed too dangerous and I knew no other way of asking.

2      Toward evening, I moved to the French Quarter, feeling sad and envious as people went home to dinner. I bought a few Tootsie Rolls and a half loaf of bread and went to the St. Louis Cathedral in Jackson Square. (It was that night that I composed the prayer that was to become, in the next five years, an obsession, mumbled over and over through the days and nights: "God forgive me, Papa forgive me, Mama forgive me, Sophronia, Jenny, Hannah, and all others, through this time and that time, in life and in death." When I was nineteen, my father, who had

made several attempts through the years to find out what my lip movements meant as I repeated the prayer, said, "How much would you take
to stop that? Name it and you've got it." I suppose I was sick of the nonsense by that time because I said, "A leather coat and a feather fan," and
the next day he bought them for me.) After my loaf of bread, I went looking for a bottle of soda pop and discovered, for the first time, the whore-
house section around Bourbon Street. The women were ranged in the
doorways of the cribs, making the first early evening offers to sailors,
who were the only men in the streets. I wanted to stick around and see
how things like that worked, but the second or third time I circled the
block, one of the girls called out to me. I couldn't understand the words,
but the voice was angry enough to make me run toward the French
Market.

The Market was empty except for two old men. One of them called    3
to me as I went past, and I turned to see that he had opened his pants and
was shaking what my circle called "his thing." I flew across the street
into the coffee stand, forgetting that the owner had known me since I
was a small child when my Aunt Jenny would rest from her marketing
tour with a cup of fine, strong coffee.

He said, in the patois, *"Que faites, ma 'fant? Je suis fermó."*    4

I said, *"Rein. My tante attend"* —Could I have a doughnut?    5

He brought me two doughnuts, saying one was *lagniappe*, but I    6
took my doughnuts outside when he said, *"Mais où est vo' tante à
c'heure?"*

I fell asleep with my doughnuts behind a shrub in Jackson Square.    7
The night was damp and hot and through the sleep were many voices
and, much later, there was music from somewhere near the river. When
all sounds had ended, I woke, turned my head, and knew I was being
watched. Two rats were sitting a few feet from me. I urinated on my
dress, crawled backwards to stand up, screamed as I ran up the steps of
St. Louis Cathedral and pounded on the doors. I don't know when I
stopped screaming or how I got to the railroad station, but I stood against
the wall trying to tear off my dress and only knew I was doing it when
two women stopped to stare at me. I began to have cramps in my stomach of a kind I had never known before. I went to the ladies' room and sat
bent in a chair, whimpering with pain. After a while the cramps stopped,
but I had an intimation, when I looked into the mirror, of something
happening to me: my face was blotched, and there seemed to be circles
and twirls I had never seen before, the straight blonde hair was damp
with sweat, and a paste of green from the shrub had made lines on my
jaw. I had gotten older.

Sometime during that early morning I half washed my dress,    8
threw away my pants, put cold water on my hair. Later in the morning
a cleaning woman appeared, and after a while began to ask questions
that frightened me. When she put down her mop and went out of the
room, I ran out of the station. I walked, I guess, for many hours, but

when I saw a man on Canal Street who worked in Hannah's office, I realized that the sections of New Orleans that were known to me were dangerous for me.

9    Years before, when I was a small child, Sophronia and I would go to pick up, or try on, pretty embroidered dresses that were made for me by a colored dressmaker called Bibettera. A block up from Bibettera's there had been a large ruin of a house with a sign, ROOMS—CLEAN—CHEAP, and cheerful people seemed always to be moving in and out of the house. The door of the house was painted a bright pink. I liked that and would discuss with Sophronia why we didn't live in a house with a pink door.

10    Bibettera was long since dead, so I knew I was safe in this Negro neighborhood. I went up and down the block several times, praying that things would work and I could take my cramps to bed. I knocked on the pink door. It was answered immediately by a small young man.

11    I said, "Hello." He said nothing.

12    I said, "I would like to rent a room, please."

13    He closed the door but I waited, thinking he had gone to get the lady of the house. After a long time, a middle-aged woman put her head out of a second-floor window and said, "What you at?"

14    I said, "I would like to rent a room, please. My mama is a widow and has gone to work across the river. She gave me money and said to come here until she called for me."

15    "Who your mama?"

16    "Er. My mama."

17    "What you at? Speak out."

18    "I told you. I have money . . ." But as I tried to open my purse, the voice grew angry.

19    "This is a nigger house. Get you off. *Vite.*"

20    I said, in a whisper, "I know. I'm part nigger."

21    The small young man opened the front door. He was laughing. "You part mischief. Get the hell out of here."

22    I said, "Please"—and then, "I'm related to Sophronia Mason. She told me to come. Ask her."

23    Sophronia and her family were respected figures in New Orleans Negro circles, and because I had some vague memory of her stately bow to somebody as she passed this house, I believed they knew her. If they told her about me I would be in trouble, but phones were not usual then in poor neighborhoods, and I had no other place to go.

24    The woman opened the door. Slowly I went into the hall.

25    I said, "I won't stay long. I have four dollars and Sophronia will give more if . . ."

26    The woman pointed up the stairs. She opened the door of a small room. "Washbasin place down the hall. Toilet place behind the kitchen. Two-fifty and no fuss, no bother."

27    I said, "Yes, ma'am, yes ma'am," but as she started to close the door, the young man appeared.

"Where your bag?"                                                                            28

"Bag?"                                                                                       29

"Nobody put up here without no bag."                                                         30

"Oh. You mean the bag with my clothes? It's at the station. I'll go    31
and get it later . . ." I stopped because I knew I was about to say I'm sick,
I'm in pain, I'm frightened.

He said, "I say you lie. I say you trouble. I say you get out."          32

I said, "And I say you shut up."                                         33

Years later, I was to understand why the command worked, and to    34
be sorry that it did, but that day I was very happy when he turned and
closed the door. I was asleep within minutes.

Toward evening, I went down the stairs, saw nobody, walked a few    35
blocks and bought myself an oyster loaf. But the first bite made me feel
sick, so I took my loaf back to the house. This time, as I climbed the steps,
there were three women in the parlor, and they stopped talking when
they saw me. I went back to sleep immediately, dizzy and nauseated.

I woke to a high, hot sun and my father standing at the foot of the    36
bed staring at the oyster loaf.

He said, "Get up now and get dressed."                                  37

I was crying as I said, "Thank you, Papa, but I can't."                 38

From the hall, Sophronia said, "Get along up now. *Vite*. The morn-    39
ing is late."

My father left the room. I dressed and came into the hall carrying    40
my oyster loaf. Sophronia was standing at the head of the stairs. She
pointed out, meaning my father was on the street.

I said, "He humiliated me. He did. I won't . . ."                       41

She said, "Get you going or I will never see you whenever again."       42

I ran past her to the street. I stood with my father until Sophronia    43
joined us, and then we walked slowly, without speaking, to the streetcar
line. Sophronia bowed to us, but she refused my father's hand when he
attempted to help her into the car. I ran to the car meaning to ask her to
take me with her, but the car moved and she raised her hand as if to stop
me. My father and I walked again for a long time.

He pointed to a trash can sitting in front of a house. "Please put    44
that oyster loaf in the can."

At Vanalli's restaurant, he took my arm. "Hungry?"                      45

I said, "No, thank you, Papa."                                          46

But we went through the door. It was, in those days, a New Orleans    47
custom to have an early black coffee, go to the office, and after a few
hours have a large breakfast at a restaurant. Vanalli's was crowded, the
headwaiter was so sorry, but after my father took him aside, a very small
table was put up for us—too small for my large father, who was accom-
modating himself to it in a manner most unlike him.

He said, "Jack, my rumpled daughter would like cold crayfish, a    48
nice piece of pompano, separate bowl of Béarnaise sauce, don't ask me
why, French fried potatoes . . ."

49   I said, "Thank you, Papa, but I am not hungry. I don't want to be here."

50   My father waved the waiter away and we sat in silence until the crayfish came. My hand reached out instinctively and then drew back.

51   My father said, "Your mother and I have had an awful time."

52   I said, "I'm sorry about that. But I don't want to go home, Papa."

53   He said, angrily, "Yes, you do. But you want me to apologize first. I do apologize but you should not have made me say it."

54   After a while I mumbled, "God forgive me, Papa forgive me, Mama forgive me, Sophronia, Jenny, Hannah . . ."

55   "Eat your crayfish."

56   I ate everything he had ordered and then a small steak. I suppose I had been mumbling throughout my breakfast.

57   My father said, "You're talking to yourself. I can't hear you. What are you saying?"

58   "God forgive me, Papa forgive me, Mama forgive me, Sophronia, Jenny . . ."

59   My father said, "Where do we start your training as the first Jewish nun on Prytania Street?"

60   When I finished laughing, I liked him again. I said, "Papa, I'll tell you a secret. I've had very bad cramps and I am beginning to bleed. I'm changing life."

61   He stared at me for a while. Then he said, "Well, it's not the way it's usually described, but it's accurate, I guess. Let's go home now to your mother."

62   We were never, as long as my mother and father lived, to mention that time again. But it was of great importance to them and I've thought about it all my life. From that day on I knew my power over my parents. That was not to be too important: I was ashamed of it and did not abuse it too much. But I found out something more useful and more dangerous: if you are willing to take the punishment, you are halfway through the battle. That the issue may be trivial, the battle ugly, is another point.

## CONSIDERATIONS

1. Hellman's recollection of running away at fourteen is complicated by her interrupting the narrative with flashbacks and episodes of later years. How can an author justify such breaks in the chronology of a story?

2. In paragraphs 33 and 34, as she is trying to talk her way into the rooming house in the black district, Hellman tells a young man to shut up and then adds, "Years later, I was to understand why the command worked, and to be sorry that it did." What did she later understand?

3. What was the "power over my parents" that Hellman learned from her runaway experience? If you have ever recognized that power—even used it—in your own dealings with family, describe the incident(s) in a short narrative essay.

4. Accounts of childhood escapades often suffer as the author idealizes or glamorizes them. Does Hellman successfully resist the temptation? What is your evidence?

5. The bases the fourteen-year-old runaway touched in her flight were actually part of a familiar world: a doll's house, a cathedral, a market, a railroad station. How does Hellman give her flight more than a touch of horror?

6. In what specific ways did her first menstrual period heighten and distort some of the things that happened—or seemed to happen—to the fourteen-year-old runaway? Discuss the ways in which physiological and psychological conditions seem to feed on each other. Read Eudora Welty's short story "A Worn Path (page 653) for a rather different treatment of physiology and psychology affecting one's perception.

7. Hellman's first paragraph may well be the longest single paragraph in your text. Look it over again for places it might have been broken into two or more paragraphs. Discuss your findings, and justify any changes you would make.

*Ernest Hemingway (1899–1961) was an ambulance driver and a soldier in World War I, and made use of these experiences in his novel* A Farewell to Arms *(1929). One of the Lost Generation of expatriate American writers who lived in Paris in the twenties—a time described in his memoir,* A Moveable Feast *(1964)—he was a great prose stylist and innovator, and received a Nobel Prize for Literature in 1954. Other Hemingway novels include* The Sun Also Rises *(1926),* To Have and Have Not *(1937), and* For Whom the Bell Tolls *(1940).*

*Many critics prefer Hemingway's short stories to his novels, and his early stories—"Hills Like White Elephants" among them—to his later ones. This early prose is plain, simple, and clean. In this story, pages of dialog virtually without narrative—or description or subjective interpretation—give us two characters in the wholeness of themselves.*

— **43** ——————————————————

# ERNEST HEMINGWAY
## *Hills Like White Elephants*

———————————————————————————

1     The hills across the valley of the Ebro were long and white. On this side there was no shade and no trees and the station was between two lines of rails in the sun. Close against the side of the station there was the warm shadow of the building and a curtain, made of strings of bamboo beads, hung across the open door into the bar, to keep out flies. The American and the girl with him sat at a table in the shade, outside the building. It was very hot and the express from Barcelona would come in forty minutes. It stopped at this junction for two minutes and went on to Madrid.

2     "What should we drink?" the girl asked. She had taken off her hat and put it on the table.

3     "It's pretty hot," the man said.

4     "Let's drink beer."

5     "Dos cervezas," the man said into the curtain.

———————————

"Big ones?" a woman asked from the doorway.                                    6

"Yes. Two big ones."                                                           7

The woman brought two glasses of beer and two felt pads. She put        8
the felt pads and the beer glasses on the table and looked at the man and
the girl. The girl was looking off at the line of hills. They were white in
the sun and the country was brown and dry.

"They look like white elephants," she said.                                    9

"I've never seen one." The man drank his beer.                                10

"No, you wouldn't have."                                                       11

"I might have," the man said. "Just because you say I wouldn't have     12
doesn't prove anything."

The girl looked at the bead curtain. "They've painted something on      13
it," she said. "What does it say?"

"Anis del Toro. It's a drink."                                                14

"Could we try it?"                                                            15

The man called "Listen" through the curtain.                                  16

The woman came out from the bar.                                              17

"Four reales."                                                                18

"We want two Anis del Toros."                                                 19

"With water?"                                                                 20

"Do you want it with water?"                                                  21

"I don't know," the girl said. "Is it good with water?"                       22

"It's all right."                                                             23

"You want them with water?" asked the woman.                                  24

"Yes, with water."                                                            25

"It tastes like licorice," the girl said and put the glass down.              26

"That's the way with everything."                                            27

"Yes," said the girl. "Everything tastes of licorice. Especially all the  28
things you've waited so long for, like absinthe."

"Oh, cut it out."                                                            29

"You started it," the girl said. "I was being amused. I was having a    30
fine time."

"Well, let's try and have a fine time."                                      31

"All right. I was trying. I said the mountains looked like white ele-   32
phants. Wasn't that bright?"

"That was bright."                                                           33

"I wanted to try this new drink. That's all we do, isn't it—look at    34
things and try new drinks?"

"I guess so."                                                                35

The girl looked across at the hills.                                         36

"They're lovely hills," she said. "They don't really look like white   37
elephants. I just meant the colouring of their skin through the trees."

"Should we have another drink?"                                             38

"All right."                                                                 39

The warm wind blew the bead curtain against the table.                       40

"The beer's nice and cool," the man said.                                   41

42   "It's lovely," the girl said.

43   "It's really an awfully simple operation, Jig," the man said. "It's not really an operation at all."

44   The girl looked at the ground the table legs rested on.

45   "I know you wouldn't mind it, Jig. It's really not anything. It's just to let the air in."

46   The girl did not say anything.

47   "I'll go with you and I'll stay with you all the time. They just let the air in and then it's all perfectly natural."

48   "Then what will we do afterwards?"

49   "We'll be fine afterwards. Just like we were before."

50   "What makes you think so?"

51   "That's the only thing that bothers us. It's the only thing that's made us unhappy."

52   The girl looked at the bead curtain, put her hand out and took hold of two of the strings of beads.

53   "And you think then we'll be all right and be happy."

54   "I know we will. You don't have to be afraid. I've known lots of people that have done it."

55   "So have I," said the girl. "And afterward they were all so happy."

56   "Well," the man said, "if you don't want to you don't have to. I wouldn't have you do it if you didn't want to. But I know it's perfectly simple."

57   "And you really want to?"

58   "I think it's the best thing to do. But I don't want you to do it if you don't really want to."

59   "And if I do it you'll be happy and things will be like they were and you'll love me?"

60   "I love you now. You know I love you."

61   "I know. But if I do it, then it will be nice again if I say things are like white elephants, and you'll like it?"

62   "I'll love it. I love it now but I just can't think about it. You know how I get when I worry."

63   "If I do it you won't ever worry?"

64   "I won't worry about that because it's perfectly simple."

65   "Then I'll do it. Because I don't care about me."

66   "What do you mean?"

67   "I don't care about me."

68   "Well, I care about you."

69   "Oh, yes. But I don't care about me. And I'll do it and then everything will be fine."

70   "I don't want you to do it if you feel that way."

71   The girl stood up and walked to the end of the station. Across, on the other side, were fields of grain and trees along the banks of the Ebro. Far away, beyond the river, were mountains. The shadow of a cloud moved across the field of grain and she saw the river through the trees.

"And we could have all this," she said. "And we could have every-   72
thing and every day we make it more impossible."

"What did you say?"   73

"I said we could have everything."   74

"We can have everything."   75

"No, we can't."   76

"We can have the whole world."   77

"No, we can't."   78

"We can go everywhere."   79

"No, we can't. It isn't ours any more."   80

"It's ours."   81

"No, it isn't. And once they take it away, you never get it back."   82

"But they haven't taken it away."   83

"We'll wait and see."   84

"Come on back in the shade," he said. "You mustn't feel that way."   85

"I don't feel any way," the girl said. "I just know things."   86

"I don't want you to do anything that you don't want to do—"   87

"Nor that isn't good for me," she said. "I know. Could we have an-   88
other beer?"

"All right. But you've got to realize—"   89

"I realize," the girl said. "Can't we maybe stop talking?"   90

They sat down at the table and the girl looked across at the hills on   91
the dry side of the valley and the man looked at her and at the table.

"You've got to realize," he said, "that I don't want you to do it if   92
you don't want to. I'm perfectly willing to go through with it if it means
anything to you."

"Doesn't it mean anything to you? We could get along."   93

"Of course it does. But I don't want anybody but you. I don't want   94
anyone else. And I know it's perfectly simple."

"Yes, you know it's perfectly simple."   95

"It's all right for you to say that, but I do know it."   96

"Would you do something for me now?"   97

"I'd do anything for you."   98

"Would you please please please please please please please stop   99
talking?"

He did not say anything but looked at the bags against the wall of   100
the station. There were labels on them from all the hotels where they
had spent nights.

"But I don't want you to," he said, "I don't care anything about it."   101

"I'll scream," the girl said.   102

The woman came out through the curtains with two glasses of beer   103
and put them down on the damp felt pads. "The train comes in five minutes," she said.

"What did she say?" asked the girl.   104

"That the train is coming in five minutes."   105

The girl smiled brightly at the woman, to thank her.   106

107    "I'd better take the bags over to the other side of the station," the man said. She smiled at him.

108    "All right. Then come back and we'll finish the beer."

109    He picked up the two heavy bags and carried them around the station to the other tracks. He looked up the tracks but could not see the train. Coming back, he walked through the bar-room, where people waiting for the train were drinking. He drank an Anis at the bar and looked at the people. They were all waiting reasonably for the train. He went out through the bead curtain. She was sitting at the table and smiled at him.

110    "Do you feel better?" he asked.

111    "I feel fine," she said. "There's nothing wrong with me. I feel fine."

## *CONSIDERATIONS*

1. Nearly all of Hemingway's story is dialog, often without identifying phrases such as "he said" or "she said." Does that lack make it difficult to decide which character is speaking? What, if anything, does the writer do to make up for missing dialog tags? Compare his practice with the way other short story writers in your text handle dialog.

2. If you have ever questioned the common statement that writers must pay careful attention to *every* word they use, spend a little time examining the way Hemingway uses "it," beginning where the couple starts talking about the operation. Try to determine the various possible antecedents for that neutral pronoun in each context where it occurs. Such an effort may help you discover one reason why Hemingway's spare, almost skeletal style is so powerful.

3. Why is Hemingway *not* explicit about the kind of operation the two characters are discussing? Is he simply trying to mystify the reader? Is he afraid of a censor? Does this omission provide something important for the reader?

4. Does the place itself (as represented in brief descriptive passages) contribute to the point of the story? Explain.

5. Why does Hemingway refuse to describe the two characters? From what the story offers, what do you know about them?

6. How might a feminist writer make use of Hemingway's story?

7. What might a marriage counselor do with it?

*Edward Hoagland (b. 1932) was born in New York City and lives there much of the year, alternating between Manhattan and the countryside of northern Vermont. He has written novels but is best known for his essays, many like "The Urge for an End" published in* Harper's.

*Hoagland's meditation on suicide, and on the prospects of death, upset many readers when* Harper's *published it. People do not wish to confront or admit their own fantasies of self-murder. Many times in his essays, Hoagland dares or forces himself to the edges of human feeling, using personal anecdotes, statistics, and anecdotes of the experiences of others. Note that the essence of Hoagland's essay, like the essence of Montaigne, who invented the essay, is relentless self-examination.*

## — 44

# EDWARD HOAGLAND
## *The Urge for an End*

A friend of mine, a peaceable soul who has been riding the New York subways for thirty years, finds himself stepping back from the tracks once in a while and closing his eyes as the train rolls in. This, he says, is not only to suppress an urge to throw himself in front of it but because every couple of weeks an impulse rises in him to push a stranger onto the tracks, any stranger, thus ending his own life too. He blames this partly on apartment living—"pigeonholes without being able to fly." 1

It is profoundly startling not to trust oneself after decades of doing so. I don't dare keep ammunition in my country house for a small rifle I bought secondhand two decades ago. The gun sat in a cupboard in the back room with the original box of .22 bullets under the muzzle all that time, seldom fired except at a few apples hanging in a tree every fall to remind me of my army training near the end of the Korean War, when I'd been considered quite a marksman. When I bought the gun I didn't trust either my professional competence as a writer or my competence as a father as much as I came to do, but certainly believed I could keep myself alive. I bought it for protection, and the idea that someday I might be afraid of shooting myself with the gun would have seemed inconceivable—laughable. 2

"The Urge for an End" by Edward Hoagland. Reprinted by permission of the author.

3    One's fifties can be giddy years, as anybody fifty knows. Chest pains, back pains, cancer scares, menopausal or prostate complications are not the least of it, and the fidelities of a lifetime, both personal and professional, may be called into question. Was it a mistake to have stuck so long with one's marriage, and to have stayed with a lackluster well-paying job? (Or *not* to have stayed and stuck?) People not only lose faith in their talents and their dreams or values; some simply tire of them. Grow tired, too, of the smell of fried-chicken grease, once such a delight, and the cold glutinosity of ice cream, the boredom of beer, the stop-go of travel, the hiccups of laughter, and of two rush hours a day, then the languor of weekends, of athletes as well as accountants, and even the frantic birdsong of spring—red-eyed vireos that have been clocked singing 22,000 times in a day. Life is a matter of cultivating the five senses (the sixth too), and an equilibrium with nature and what I think of as its subdivision, human nature, trusting no one completely but almost everyone at least a little; but this is easier said than done.

4    More than 30,000 Americans took their own lives last year, men mostly, with the highest rate being among those older than sixty-five. When I asked a friend of mine why three times as many men kill themselves as members of her own sex, she replied with sudden anger, "I'm not going to go into the self-indulgence of men." Suicide is an exasperating act as often as it is pitiable. "Committing" suicide is in bad odor in our culture even among those who don't believe that to cash in your chips ahead of time and hand back to God his gifts to you is a blasphemous sin. We the living, in any case, are likely to feel accused by this person who "voted with his feet." It appears to cast a subversive judgment upon the social polity as a whole that what was supposed to work in life—religion, family, friendship, commerce, and industry—did not; and furthermore, it "frightens the horses in the street," as Virginia Woolf once defined wrongful behavior (before she killed herself).

5    Many suicides inflict outrageous trauma, burning permanent injuries into the minds of their children, though they may have joked beforehand only of "taking a dive." And sometimes the gesture has a peevish or cowardly aspect, or seems to have been senselessly short-sighted as far as an outside observer can tell. There are desperate suicides and crafty suicides, people who do it to cause others trouble and people who do it to save others trouble, deranged exhibitionists who yell from a building ledge and closedmouthed, secretive souls who swim out into the ocean's anonymity. Suicide may in fact be an attempt to escape death, shortcut the dreadful deteriorating processes, abort one's natural trajectory, elude "the ruffian on the stairs," in A. E. Housman's phrase for a cruelly painful and anarchic death—make it neat and not messy. The deed can be grandiose or self-abnegating, vindictive or drably mousy, rationally plotted or plainly insane. People sidle toward death, intent upon outwitting their own bodies' defenses, or they may dramatize the chance to make one last, unambiguous, irrevocable decision, like a cap-

tain scuttling his ship—death before dishonor—leaping toward oblivion through a curtain of pain, like a frog going down the throat of a snake. One man I knew hosted a quietly affectionate evening with several unknowing friends on the night before he swallowed too many pills. Another waved an apologetic good-bye to a bystander on a bridge; rarely considerate, he turned apologetic in the last moment of life. Never physically inclined, he made a great vault toward the ice on the Mississippi.

In the army, we wore dog tags with a notch at one end by which   6 these numbered pieces of metal could be jammed between our teeth, if we lay dead and nameless on a battlefield, for later sorting. As "servicemen" our job would be to kill people who were pointed out to us as enemies, or make "the supreme sacrifice" for a higher good than enjoying the rest of our lives. Life was very much a possession, in other words— not only God's, but the soldier's own to dispose of. Working in an army hospital, I frequently did handle dead bodies, but this never made me feel I would refuse to kill another man whose uniform was pointed out to me as being inimical, or value my life more tremulously and vigilantly. The notion of dying for my country didn't appeal to me as much as dying freelance for my ideas (in the unlikely event I *could* do that), but I was ready. People were taught during the 1940s and '50s that one should be ready to die for one's beliefs. Heroes were revered because they had deliberately chosen to give up their lives. Life would not be worth living under the tyranny of an invader, and Nathan Hale apparently hadn't paused to consider whether God might have other uses for him besides being hanged. Nor did the pilot Colin Kelly hesitate before crashing his plane into a Japanese battleship, becoming America's first well-publicized hero in World War II.

I've sometimes wondered why people who know that they are ter-   7 minally ill, or who are headed for suicide, so very seldom have paused to take a bad guy along with them. It is lawless to consider an act of assassination, yet hardly more lawless, really, than suicide is regarded in some quarters. Government bureaucracies, including our own, in their majesty and as the executors of laws, regularly weigh the pros and cons of murdering foreign antagonists. Of course the answer is that most individuals are fortunately more timid as well as humbler in their judgment than government officialdom; but beyond that, when dying or suicidal, people no longer care enough to devote their final energies to doing good works of any kind—Hitler himself in their gun sights they would have passed up. Some suicides become so crushed and despairing that they can't recognize the consequences of anything they do; and it's not primarily vindictiveness that wreaks such havoc upon their survivors but their derangement from ordinary life.

Courting the idea is different from the real impulse. "When he   8 begged for help, we took him and locked him up," another friend of mine says, speaking of her husband. "Not till then. Wishing to be out of the situation you are in—feeling helpless and unable to cope—is not the same as wishing to be dead. If I actually wished to be dead, even my children's welfare would have no meaning."

9      You might think the ready option of divorce available lately would have cut suicide rates, offering an escape to battered wives, lovelorn husbands, and other people in despair. But it doesn't work that way. When the number of choices people have is increased, an entire range of possibilities opens up. The suicide rate among teenagers has nearly quadrupled since 1950, although the standard of comfort that their families enjoy has gone up. Black Americans, less affluent than white Americans, have a suicide rate about half that of whites.

10     Still, if a fiftyish fellow with fine teeth and a foolproof pension plan, a cottage at the beach and the Fourth of July weekend coming up, kills himself, it seems truculent. We would look at him bafflingly if he told us he no longer likes the Sturm und Drang of banging fireworks.

11     *Then stay at your hideaway!* we'd argue with him.

12     "Big mouths eat little mouths. Nature isn't 'timeless.' Whole lives are squeezed into three months or three days."

13     *What about your marriage?*

14     "She's become more mannish than me. I loved women. I don't believe in marriage between men."

15     *Remarry, then!*

16     "I've gone impotent, and besides, when I see somebody young and pretty I guess I feel like dandling her on my knee."

17     *Marriage is friendship. You can find someone your own age.*

18     "I'm tired of it."

19     *But how about your company?—it's positioned itself on the cutting edge of the silicon frontier. That's interesting.*

20     "I know what wins. It's less and less appetizing."

21     *You're not scared of death anymore?*

22     "It interests me less than it did."

23     *What are you so sick of? The rest of us keep going.*

24     "I'm tired of weathermen and sportscasters on the screen. Of being patient and also of impatience. I'm tired of the President, whoever the President happens to be, and sleeping badly, with forty-eight half hours in the day—of breaking two eggs every morning and putting sugar on something. I'm tired of the drone of my voice, but also of us jabbering like parrots at each other—of all our stumpy ways of doing everything."

25     *You're bored with yourself?*

26     "I'm maybe the least interesting person I know."

27     *But to kill yourself?*

28     "You know, it's a tradition, too," he remarks quietly, not making so bold as to suggest that the tradition is an honorable one, though his tone of voice might be imagined to imply this. "I guess I've always been a latent maverick."

Except in circumstances which are themselves a matter of life and     29
death, I'm reluctant to agree with the idea that suicide is not the result of
mental illness. No matter how reasonably the person appears to have examined his options, it goes against the grain of nature for him to destroy
himself. And any illness that threatens his life changes a person. Suicidal
thinking, if serious, can be a kind of death scare, comparable to suffering
a heart attack or undergoing a cancer operation. One survives such a
phase both warier and chastened. When—two years ago—I emerged from
a bad dip into suicidal speculation, I felt utterly exhausted and yet quite
fearless of ordinary dangers, vastly afraid of myself but much less scared
of extraneous eventualities. The fact of death may not be tragic; many
people die with a bit of a smile that captures their mouths at the last instant, and some who are revived after a deadly accident are reluctant to
be brought to life, resisting resuscitation, and carrying back confusing,
beamish, or ecstatic memories. But the same impetuosity that made him
throw himself out of a window might have enabled that person to love
life all the more if he'd been calibrated somewhat differently at the time
of the emergency. Death's edge is so abrupt and near that many who expect a short, momentary dive may be astounded to find that it is bottomless and change their minds and start to scream when they are only
halfway down.

Although my fright at my mind's anarchy superseded my fear of     30
death in the conventional guise of heart seizures, airplane crashes, and so
on, nightmares are more primitive, and in my dreams I continued to be
scared of a death not sought after—dying from driving too fast and losing
control of the car, breaking through thin ice while skating and drowning
in the cold, or falling off a cliff. When I am tense and sleeping raggedly,
my worst nightmare isn't drawn from anxious prep-school memories or
the bad spells of my marriages or any of adulthood's vicissitudes.
Nothing else from the past half-century has the staying power in my
mind of the elevated train rides that my father and I used to take down
Third Avenue to the Battery in New York City on Sunday afternoons
when I was three or four or five, so I could see the fish at the aquarium.
We were probably pretty good companions in those years, but the
wooden platforms forty feet up shook terribly as trains from both directions pulled in and out. To me they seemed worse than rickety—ready to
topple. And the roar was fearful, and the railings left large gaps for a child
to fall through, after the steep climb up the slatsided, windy, shaking
stairway from street level. It's a rare dream, but several times a year I
still find myself on such a perch, without his company or anybody else's,
on a boyish or a grown-up's mission, when the elevated platform begins
to rattle desperately, seesaw, heel over, and finally come apart, disinte-
grate, while I cling to struts and trusses.

My father, as he lay dying at home of bowel cancer, used to enjoy     31
watching Tarzan reruns on the children's hour of television. Like a
strong green vine, they swung him far away from his deathbed to a world

of skinnydipping, friendly animals, and scenic beauty linked to the lost realities of his adolescence in Kansas City. Earlier, when he was still able to walk without much pain, he'd paced the house for several hours at night, contemplating suicide, I expect, along with other anguishing thoughts, regrets, remembrances, and yearnings. I don't know how much of that decision was for his wife and children, how much was because he didn't want to be a "quitter," as he sometimes put it, and how much was due to his believing that life belongs to God (which I'm not even sure he did). He was not a churchgoer after his thirties. He had belonged to J. P. Morgan's church, St. George's, on Stuyvesant Square—Morgan was a hero of his—but when things went a little wrong for him at the Wall Street law firm he worked for, and he changed jobs and moved out to the suburbs, he became a skeptic on religious matters, and gradually, in the absence of faith of that previous kind, he adhered to a determined allegiance to the social order. Dwight D. Eisenhower instead of J. P. Morgan became the sort of hero he admired, and suicide would have seemed an act of insurrection against the laws and conventions of the society, internationalist-Republican, that he believed in.

32      I was never particularly afraid that I might plan a suicide, swallowing a bunch of pills and keeping them down—only of what I think of as Anna Karenina's kind of death. This most plausible self-killing in all of literature is frightening because it was unwilled, regretted at midpoint, and came as a complete surprise to Anna herself. After rushing impulsively, in great misery, to the Moscow railway station to catch a train, she ended up underneath another one, dismayed, astonished, and trying to climb out from under the wheels even as they crushed her. Many people who briefly verge on suicide undergo a mental somersault for a terrifying interval during which they're upside down, their perspective topsy-turvy, skidding, churning; and this is why I got rid of the bullets for my .22.

33      Nobody expects to trust his body overmuch after the age of fifty. Incipient cataracts or arthritis, outlandish snores, tooth-grinding, ankles that threaten to turn are part of the game. But not to trust one's *mind*? That's a surprise. The single attribute that older people were sure to have (we thought as boys) was a stodgy dependability, a steady temperance and caution. Adults might be vain, unimaginative, pompous, and callous, but they did have their affairs tightly in hand. It was not till my thirties that I began to know friends who were in their fifties on equal terms, and I remember being amused, piqued, and bewildered to learn that some of them still felt as marginal or rebellious or in a quandary about what to do with themselves for the next dozen years as my contemporaries were likely to. Even that close to retirement, some of them harbored a deep-seated contempt for the organizations they had been working for, ready to walk away from almost everybody they had known and the efforts of whole decades with very little sentiment. Nor did twenty years of marriage necessarily mean more than two or three—they

might be just as ready to walk away from that also, and didn't really register it as twenty years at all. Rather, life could be about to begin all over again. "Bummish" was how one man described himself, with a raffish smile—"Lucky to have a roof over my head"—though he'd just put a child through Yale. He was quitting his job and claimed with exasperation that his wife still cried for her mother in her sleep, as if they'd never been married.

The great English traveler Richard Burton quoted an Arab proverb 34 that speaks for many middle-aged men of the old-fashioned variety: "Conceal thy Tenets, thy Treasure and thy Travelling." These are serious matters, in other words. People didn't conceal their tenets in order to betray them, but to fight for them more opportunely. And except for kings and princelings, concealing whatever treasure one had went without saying. As for travel, a man's travels were also a matter of gravity. Travel was knowledge, ambiguity, dalliances or misalliances, divided loyalty, forbidden thinking; and besides, someday he might need to make a run for it and go to ground someplace where he had made some secret friends. Friends of mine whose husbands or whose wives have died have been quite startled afterward to discover caches of money or traveler's checks concealed around the house, or a bundle of cash in a safe-deposit box.

Burton, like any other desert adage-spinner (and most individuals 35 over fifty), would have agreed to an addition so obvious that it wasn't included to begin with: "Conceal thy Illnesses." I can remember how urgently my father worried that word would get out, after a preliminary operation for his cancer. He didn't want to be written off, counted out of the running at the corporation he worked for and in other enclaves of competition. Men often compete with one another until the day they die; comradeship consists of rubbing shoulders jocularly with a competitor. As breadwinners, they must be considered fit and sound by friend as well as foe, and so there's lots of truth to the most common answer I heard when asking why three times as many men as women kill themselves: "They keep their troubles to themselves"; "They don't know how to ask for help."

I'm not entirely like that, and I discovered that when I confided 36 something of my perturbation to a woman friend, she was likely to keep telephoning me or mailing cheery postcards, whereas a man would usually listen with concern, communicate his sympathy, and maybe intimate that he had pondered the same drastic course of action himself a few years back and would end up respecting my decision either way. Open-mindedness seems an important attribute to a good many men who pride themselves on being objective, hearing all sides of an issue, on knowing that truth and honesty do not always coincide with social dicta, and who may even cherish a subterranean outlaw streak that, like being ready to violently defend one's family, reputation, and country, is by tradition male.

37        Men, having been so much freer than women in society, used to feel they had less of a stake in the maintenance of certain churchly conventions and enjoyed speaking irreverently about various social truisms, including even the principle that people ought to die on schedule, not cutting in ahead of their assigned place in line. Contemporary women, after their triumphant irreverence during the 1960s and 1970s, cannot be generalized about so easily. They turn as skeptical and saturnine as any man. In fact, women attempt suicide more frequently, but favor pills or other methods, whereas two-thirds of the men who kill themselves use a gun: in 1985, 85 percent of suicides by means of firearms were committed by men. An overdose of medication hasn't the same finality. It may be reversible if the person is discovered quickly, or be subject to benign miscalculation to start with. Even if it works, perhaps it can be fudged by a kindly doctor in the recordkeeping. Like an enigmatic drowning or a single-car accident that baffles the suspicions of the insurance company, a suicide by drugs can be a way to avoid making a loud statement, and merely illustrate the final modesty of a person who didn't wish to ask for too much of the world's attention.

38        Unconsummated attempts at suicide can strike the rest of us as self-pitying, self-aggrandizing, or as plaintive plea-bargaining—"childish," we say, though actually the helplessness that echoes through a child's suicide is ghastly beyond any stunt of self-mutilation an adult may indulge in. It would be hard to define chaos better than as a world where children decide that they don't want to live.

39        Love is the solution to all dilemmas, we sometimes hear; and in those moments when the spirit bathes itself in beneficence and manages to transcend the static of personalities rubbing fur off of each other, indeed it is. Without love nothing matters, Paul told the Corinthians, a mystery which, if true, has no ready Darwinian explanation. Love without a significant sexual component and for people who are unrelated to us serves little practical purpose. It doesn't help us feed our families, win struggles, thrive, and prosper. It distracts us from the ordinary business of sizing people up and making a living, and is not even conducive to intellectual observation, because instead of seeing them, we see right through them to the bewildered child and dreaming adolescent who inhabited their bodies earlier, the now tired idealist who fell in and out of love, got hired and quit, bought cars and wore them out, liked black-eyed susans, blueberry muffins, and roosters crowing—liked roosters crowing better than skyscrapers but now likes skyscrapers better than roosters crowing. As swift as thought, we select the details that we need to see in order to be able to love them.

40        Yet at other times we'll dispense with these same poignancies and choose only their grunginess to look at, their pinched mouths and shifty eyes, their thirst for gin at noon and indifference to their kids, their greed for the best tidbit on the buffet table, and their penchant for poking their penises up the excretory end of other human beings. I tend to gaze quite

closely at the faces of priests I meet on the street to see if a lifetime of love has marked them noticeably. Real serenity or asceticism I no longer expect, and I take for granted the beefy calm that often goes with Catholic celibacy, but I am watching for the marks of love and often see mere resignation or tenacity.

Many men are romantics, likely to plunge, go for broke, take action in a spirit of exigency rather than waiting for the problem to resolve itself. Then, still as romantics, they may drift into despairing passivity, stare at the TV all day long, and binge with a bottle. Women too may turn frenetic for a while and then throw up their hands; but though they may not seem as grandiosely fanciful and romantic at the outset, they are more frequently believers—at least they seem to me to believe in God or in humanity, the future, and so on. We have above us the inviting eternity of "the heavens," if we choose to look at it, lying on our backs in the summer grass under starlight, some of which had left its source before mankind became man. But because we live in our heads more than in nature nowadays, even the summer sky is a mine field for people whose memories are mined. With the sky no longer humbling, and sunshine only a sort of convenience, and no godhead located anywhere outside of our own heads, every problem may seem insolubly interlocked. When the telephone has become impossible to answer at home, sometimes it finally becomes impossible to stride down the gangplank of a cruise ship in Mombasa too, although no telephones will ring for you there.

But if escapist travel is ruled out in certain emergencies, surely you can *pray*? Pray, yes; but to whom? That requires a bit of preparation. Rarely do people obtain much relief from praying if they haven't stood in line awhile to get a visa. It's an appealing idea that you can just *go*, and in a previous era perhaps you could have. But it's not so simple now. What do you believe in? Whom are you praying to? What are you praying for? There's no crèche on the courthouse lawn; you're not supposed to adhere exactly even to what your parent believed. Like psychotherapy, praying takes time, even if you know which direction to face when you kneel.

Love is powerfully helpful when the roof falls in—loving other people with a high and hopeful heart and as a kind of prayer. That feat too, however, requires new and sudden insights or long practice. The beatitude of loving strangers as well as friends—loving them on sight with a leap of empathy and intuition—is a form of inspiration, edging, of course, in some cases toward madness, as other states of beatitude can do. But there's no question that a genuine love for the living will stymie suicidal depressions not chemical in origin. Love is an elixir, changing the life of the lover. And many of us have experienced this—a temporary lightening of our leery, prickly disapproval of much of the rest of the world, when at a wedding or a funeral of shared emotion, or when we have fallen in love.

Yet the zest for life of those unusual men and women who make a great zealous success of living is due more often in good part to the crafty

41

42

43

44

pertinacity with which they manage to overlook the misery of others. You can watch them watch life beat the stuffing out of the faces of their friends and acquaintances, yet they themselves seem to outwit the dense delays of social custom, the tedious tick-tock of bureaucratic obfuscation, accepting loss and age and change and disappointment without suffering punctures in their stomach lining. Breathlessness or strange dull pains from their nether organs don't nonplus them. They fret and doubt in moderation, and love a lobster roast, squeeze lemon juice on living clams on the half shell to prove that the clams are alive, laugh as a robin tussles a worm out of the ground or a kitten flees a dog. Like the problem drinkers, pork eaters, and chain smokers who nevertheless finish out their allotted years, succumbing to a stroke at a nice round biblical age when the best vitamin-eating vegetarian has long since died, their faces become veritable walnuts of fine character, with the same smile lines as the rarer individual whose grin has been affectionate all of his life.

45      We spend our lives getting to know ourselves, yet wonders never cease. During my adolescent years my states of mind, though undulant, seemed seamless; even when I was unhappy, no cracks or fissures made me wonder if I was a danger to myself. My confidence was such that I treaded the slippery lips of waterfalls, fought forest fires, drove ancient cars cross-country night and day, and scratched the necks of menagerie leopards in the course of various adventures which enhanced the joy of being alive. The chemistry of the mind, because unfathomable, is more frightening. In the city, I live on the waterfront and occasionally will notice an agitated-looking figure picking his way along the pilings and stringpieces of the timbered piers nearby, staring at the sliding whorls on the surface of the Hudson as if teetering over an abyss. Our building, across the street, seems imposing from the water and over the years has acted as a magnet for a number of suicides—people who have dreaded the clammy chill, the onerous smothering essential to their first plan. One woman climbed out after jumping in and took the elevator to our roof (my neighbors remember how wringing wet she was), and leapt off, banging window ledges on the way down, and hit with the whap of a sack of potatoes, as others have.

46      But what is more remarkable than that a tiny minority of souls reach a point where they entrust their bodies to the force of gravity is that so few of the rest of us splurge an hour of a summer day gazing at the trees and sky. How many summers do we *have*?

47      People with sunny natures do seem to live longer than people who are nervous wrecks; yet mankind didn't evolve out of the animal kingdom by being unduly sunny-minded. Life was fearful and phantasmagoric, supernatural and preternatural, as well as encompassing the kind of clockwork regularity of our well-governed day. It had numerous superstitious elements, such as we are likely to catch a whiff of only when we're peering at a dead body. And it was not just our optimism but

our pessimistic premonitions, our dark moments as a species, our irrational, frightful speculations, our strange mutations upon the simple theme of love, and our sleepless, obsessive inventiveness—our dread as well as our faith—that made us human beings. Staking one's life on the more general good came to include risking suicide also. Brilliant, fecund people sometimes kill themselves.

*Joy to the world! . . . Let heaven and nature sing, and heaven and*    48
*nature sing.* The famous Christmas carol invokes not only glee but unity: heaven with nature, not always a Christian combination. It's a rapturous hymn, and no one should refuse to surrender to such a pitch of revelation when it comes. But the flip side of rapture can be a riptide of panic, or hysterical gloom. Our faces are not molded as if joy were a preponderant experience. (Nor is a caribou's or a thrush's.) Our faces in repose look stoic or battered, and people of the sunniest temperament sometimes die utterly unstrung, doubting everything they have ever believed in.

*Let heaven and nature sing!* But *is* there such harmony? Are God    49
and Mother Nature really the same? And will we risk burning our wings if we mount high enough to try to see? I've noticed that woods soil in Italy smells the same as woods soil in New England when you pick up a handful of it and enjoy its aromas—but is God there the same? It can be precarious to wonder. I don't rule out suicide as being unthinkable for people who have tried to live full lives, and don't regard it as negating the work and faith and even ecstasy they may have known before. In killing himself a person acknowledges his failures during a time span when perhaps heaven and earth had caught him like a pair of scissors—but not his life span. Man is different from animals in that he speculates, a high-risk activity.

## CONSIDERATIONS ───────────────────

1. In paragraph 3, Hoagland includes the one reason for suicide with which it is probably most difficult to argue. Identify that reason and argue with it if you can.

2. What do you see as the unifying idea of paragraph 5, in which no main idea is overtly stated?

3. Do a little research in the press on arguments over euthanasia and assisted suicide. Then, making some significant use of Hoagland's essay, write an essay leading to your conclusions.

4. "The Urge for an End" is an informal, personal essay in that Hoagland writes in the first person, relies heavily on his personal experience, and adopts a casual, slangy, almost playful tone. With an eye (and an ear) open to Hoagland's tone, study the essay and collect examples of language that create and maintain the writer's attitude.

5. Our expectations of each other figure frequently in Hoagland's essay. In paragraph 33, what was he surprised to learn about his expectations of older people?

6. In paragraphs 34 and 35, Hoagland refers to the tendency among older people to conceal their illnesses. Use your own experience with older people and/or your reading to build an essay confirming or refuting Hoagland's idea.

7. In the last third of his essay, Hoagland presents what he calls the world's best definition of chaos. What has that to do with suicide? (Hint: In paragraph 9, he reports, "The suicide rate among teenagers has nearly quadrupled since 1950. . . .")

8. In paragraph 41, the author writes that "we live in our heads more than in nature nowadays," and in paragraph 46, he wonders that "so few of the rest of us splurge an hour of a summer day gazing at the trees and sky." Read Robert Finch's essay "Very Like a Whale," especially paragraphs 15, 16, 17, and 18, and/or the entry from Henry David Thoreau's journal of November 30, 1858 and/or Barbara Kingsolver's "The Forest in the Seed." Draw from those readings and your own life to develop into an essay Hoagland's implication that nature might have a preventive or curative effect on would-be suicides.

*Andrew Holleran (b. 1943) has written essays for* New York *magazine and* Christopher Street, *as well as two novels:* Dancer from the Dance *(1978) and* Nights in Aruba *(1984).* Ground Zero *(1988) collects his essays, including "Bedside Manners."*

*Holleran's essay is both an excursion into hospitals and desperate illness and an essay on AIDS and its consequences in terms of suffering, compassion, and grief. See how he separates general observations about the sick and the healthy, and analyzes the difficulties of healthy people confronting the diseases of others—and describes the particulars of one disease.*

— 45

# ANDREW HOLLERAN
## *Bedside Manners*

"There is no difference between men so profound," wrote Scott Fitzgerald, "as that between the sick and the well." 1

There are many thoughts that fill someone's head as he walks across town on a warm July afternoon to visit a friend confined to a hospital room—and that is one of them. Another occurs to you as you wait for the light to change and watch the handsome young basketball players playing on the public court behind a chicken wire fence: Health is everywhere. The world has a surreal quality to it when you are on your way to the hospital to visit someone you care for who is seriously ill: Everyone in it, walking down the sidewalk, driving by in cars, rushing about on a basketball court with sweat-stained chests, exhausted faces, and wide eyes, seems to you extremely peculiar. They are peculiar because they are free: walking under their own power, nicely dressed, sometimes beautiful. Beauty does not lose its allure under the spell of grief. The hospital visitor still notices the smooth chests of the athletes in their cotton shorts as they leap to recover the basketball after it bounces off the rim. But everything seems strangely quiet—speechless—as if you were watching a movie on television with the sound turned off, as if everyone else in the world but you is totally unaware of something: that the act of walking across York Avenue under one's own power is essentially miraculous. 2

3    Every time he enters a hospital, the visitor enters with two simultaneous thoughts: He hates hospitals, and only people working in them lead serious lives. Everything else is selfish. Entering a hospital he always thinks, *I should work for a year as a nurse, an aide, a volunteer helping people, coming to terms with disease and death.* This feeling will pass the moment he leaves the hospital. In reality the visitor hopes his fear and depression are not evident on his face as he walks down the gleaming, silent hall from the elevator to his friend's room. He is trying hard to stay calm.

4    The door of the room the receptionist downstairs has told the visitor his friend is in is closed—and on it are taped four signs that are not on any of the other doors and are headlined, WARNING. The visitor stops as much to read them as to allow his heartbeat to subside before going in. He knows—from the accounts of friends who have already visited—he must don a robe, gloves, mask, and even a plastic cap. He is not sure if the door is closed because his friend is asleep inside or because the door to this room is always kept closed. So he pushes it open a crack and peers in. His friend is turned on his side, a white mound of bed linen, apparently sleeping.

5    The visitor is immensely relieved. He goes down the hall and asks a nurse if he may leave the *Life* magazine he brought for his friend and writes a note to him saying he was here. Then he leaves the hospital and walks west through the summer twilight as if swimming through an enchanted lagoon. The next day—once more crossing town—he is in that surreal mood, under a blue sky decorated with a few photogenic, puffy white clouds, certain that no one else knows . . . knows he or she is absurdly, preposterously, incalculably fortunate to be walking on the street. He feels once again that either the sound has been turned off or some other element (his ego, perhaps with all its anger, ambition, jealousy) has been removed from the world. The basketball players are different youths today but just as much worth pausing to look at. He enters the hospital one block east more calmly this time and requests to see his friend—who is allowed only two visitors at a time, and visits lasting no more than ten minutes. He goes upstairs, peeks around the door, and sees his friend utterly awake. The visitor's heart races as he steps back and puts on the gloves, mask, cap, and robe he has been told his friends all look so comical in. He smiles because he hopes the photograph that made him bring the copy of *Life* to the hospital—Russian women leaning against a wall in Leningrad in bikinis and winter coats, taking the sun on a February day—has amused his friend as much as it tickled him.

6    "Richard?" the visitor says as he opens the door and peeks in. His friend blinks at him. Two plastic tubes are fixed in his nostrils bringing him oxygen. His face is emaciated and gaunt, his hair longer, softer in appearance, wisps rising above his head. But the one feature the visitor cannot get over are his friend's eyes. His eyes are black, huge, and furious. Perhaps because his face is gaunt or perhaps because they really are

larger than usual, they seem the only thing alive in his face; as if his whole being were distilled and concentrated, poured, drained, into his eyes. They are shining, alarmed, and—there is no other word—furious. He looks altogether like an angry baby—or an angry old man—or an angry bald eagle.

And just as the hospital visitor is absorbing the shock of these livid    7
eyes, the sick man says in a furious whisper, "Why did you bring that dreadful magazine? I hate *Life* magazine! With that stupid picture! I wasn't amused! I wasn't amused at all! You should never have brought that dreck into this room!"

The visitor is momentarily speechless: It is the first time in their    8
friendship of ten years that anything abusive or insulting has ever been said; it is as astonishing as the gaunt face in which two huge black eyes burn and shine. But he sits down and recovers his breath and apologizes. The visitor thinks, *He's angry because I haven't visited him till now. He's angry that he's here at all, that he's sick.* And they begin to talk. They talk of the hospital food (which he hates too), of the impending visit of his mother (whose arrival he dreads), of the drug he is taking (which is experimental), and of the other visitors he has had. The patient asks the visitor to pick up a towel at the base of the bed and give it to him. The visitor complies. The patient places it across his forehead—and the visitor, who, like most people, is unsure what to say in this situation, stifles the question he wants to ask, *Why do you have a towel on your forehead?* The patient finally says, "Don't you think I look like Mother Theresa?" And the visitor realizes his friend has made a joke—as he did years ago in their house on Fire Island: doing drag with bedspreads, pillow cases, towels, whatever was at hand. The visitor does not smile—he is so unprepared for a joke in these circumstances—but he realizes, with relief, he is forgiven. He realizes what people who visit the sick often learn: It is the patient who puts the visitor at ease. In a few moments his ten minutes are up. He rises and says, "I don't want to tire you." He goes to the door and once beyond it he turns and looks back. His friend says to him, "I'm proud of you for coming."

"Oh—!" the visitor says and shakes his head. "Proud of *me* for com-    9
ing!" he tells a friend later that evening, after he has stripped off his gown and mask and gone home, through the unreal city of people in perfect health. "Proud of me! Can you imagine! To say that to me, to make *me* feel good! When he's the one in bed!" The truth is he is proud of himself the next time he visits his friend, for he is one of those people who looks away when a nurse takes a blood test and finds respirators frightening. He is like almost everyone—everyone except these extraordinary people who work in hospitals, he thinks, as he walks into the building. The second visit is easier, partly because it is the second, and partly because the patient is better—the drug has worked.

But he cannot forget the sight of those dark, angry eyes and the    10
plastic tubes and emaciated visage—and as he goes home that evening,

he knows there is a place whose existence he was not aware of before: the foyer of death. It is a place many of us will see at least once in our lives. Because modern medicine fights for patients who a century ago would have died without its intervention, it has created an odd place between life and death. One no longer steps into Charon's boat to be ferried across the River Styx—ill people are now detained, with one foot in the boat and the other still on shore. It is a place where mercy looks exactly like cruelty to the average visitor. It is a place that one leaves, if one is only a visitor, with the conviction that ordinary life is utterly miraculous, so that, going home from the hospital on the subway, one is filled with things one cannot express to the crowd that walks up out of the station or throngs the street of the block where he lives. But if the people caught in the revolving door between health and death could speak, would they not say—as Patrick Cowley reportedly did as he watched the men dancing to his music while he was fatally ill, "Look at those stupid queens. Don't they *know*?" Guard your health. It is all you have. It is the thin line that stands between you and hell. It is your miraculous possession. Do nothing to threaten it. Treat each other with kindness. Comfort your suffering friends. Help one another. Revere life. Do not throw it away for the momentous pleasures of lust, or even the obliteration of loneliness.

11   Many homosexuals wonder how they will die: where, with whom. Auden went back to Oxford, Santayana to the Blue Nuns in Rome. We are not all so lucky. Some men afflicted with AIDS returned to die in their family's home. Others have died with friends. Some have died bitterly and repudiated the homosexual friends who came to see them; others have counted on these people. Volunteers from the Gay Men's Health Crisis have cooked, cleaned, shopped, visited, taken care of people they did not even know until they decided to help. One thing is sure—we are learning how to help one another. We are discovering the strength and goodness of people we knew only in discotheques or as faces on Fire Island. We are following a great moral precept by visiting the sick. We are once again learning the awful truth Robert Penn Warren wrote years ago: "Only through the suffering of the innocent is the brotherhood of man confirmed." The most profound difference between men may well be that between the sick and the well, but compassionate people try to reach across the chasm and bridge it. The hospital visitor who conquers his own fear of something facing us all takes the first step on a journey that others less fearful than he have already traveled much further on: They are combining eros and agape as they rally round their stricken friends. As for the courage and dignity and sense of humor of those who are sick, these are beyond praise, and one hesitates where words are so flimsy. As for a disease whose latency period is measured in years, not months, there is no telling which side of the line dividing the sick and the well each of us will be on before this affliction is conquered. We may disdain the hysteria of policemen and firemen who call for masks, and

people who ask if it is safe to ride the subway, and television crews who will not interview AIDS patients. For they are not at risk—those who are, are fearlessly helping their own. This is the greatest story of the plague.

## CONSIDERATIONS

1. In his long closing paragraph, Holleran uses the words "eros" and "agape" in the same clause. Both Greek words could be translated "love." What difference is the author after? Or is he careless and guilty of redundancy?

2. Locate in that same closing paragraph the theme Holleran borrows from the Scott Fitzgerald quotation that opens the essay. Note that the second half of the sentence, following that restatement, begins with a "but," as though to imply that what follows the "but" is more important than what precedes it. How does that "but" alter Holleran's thesis?

3. In paragraph 2, Holleran uses on four occasions a device of punctuation much less frequently employed than, say, the comma or period. Review what you know of that device; study Holleran's use of it to determine what function(s) it performs in this passage; then try using it yourself in one of your own essays.

4. Holleran does not mention the word "AIDS" until his closing paragraph. How soon do you suspect that this is the disease his friend suffers from? What clues does Holleran give you? Does Holleran gain anything by forcing you to identify the disease without direct help?

5. Among other discoveries Holleran makes in visiting his friend is what he calls "the foyer of death. . . . a place where mercy looks exactly like cruelty to the average visitor." Explain this apparent contradiction.

6. How does Holleran avoid thrusting himself unduly into the reader's attention in discussing a situation as obviously intimate and personal as Holleran's concern for his friend hospitalized with AIDS?

7. Would Holleran's essay be as moving if the friend were dying of cancer rather than AIDS? What elements of important interest to contemporary Americans would be missing? What elements would remain the same?

*James D. Houston (b. 1933) was born in San Francisco and attended San Jose State University as well as Stanford University. He has received a grant from the National Endowment for the Arts, a Wallace Stegner Fellowship, and a Joseph Henry Jackson Award for Fiction. In 1973 he wrote* Farewell to Manzanar *with his wife, Jeanne Wakatsuki Houston, about her family's experience during the internment of Japanese-Americans. A television show based on the book received a Humanitas Prize in 1976. Some of his novels are* Continental Drift *(1978),* Love Life *(1985),* The Last Paradise *(1998), and* Snow Mountain Passage *(2001). In 1982* Californians: Searching for the Golden State *won an American Book Award from The Before Columbus Foundation. We take this essay from* Californians.*

*Houston writes a reminiscence that leaps from Pearl Harbor Day (December 7, 1941) to a moment twenty-five years later as he stands by his father's hospital bedside. Every detail, simile, and metaphor illuminates memory and creates the character of a father, and a son's feelings for his father. Note the device of a tattoo to link one era with another.*

—— **46** ——————————————————————

# JAMES D. HOUSTON
## *Sand, Tattoo, and the Golden Gate*

——————————————————————————————————

1    One Sunday when I was eight, the entire city of San Francisco was reduced to the size of a billboard. This was the Sunday we received the news that Japanese aircraft had bombed Pearl Harbor and crippled America's Pacific Fleet. The billboard stood at the corner of 25th Avenue and Irving Street, half a block from the house my father had made his first payment on three years earlier. In what is now the classic scene of how Americans received the news that launched us into World War II, we all sat around the radio staring at the floor or at the speaker. When the somber announcement ended, my father switched off the radio. The

mood in the room was so heavy I went outside, wandered up to the corner and huddled down behind the billboard I had come to rely on in
times of stress and uncertainty.

It was a sandlot billboard with two surfaces to plaster ads across.   2
They made a right angle just inside the concrete, one side facing 25th,
the other facing Irving. I never knew what the ads said. My world was behind the signs, where all the struts, cross-pieces, and footings met and
overlapped. Back there, when I was eight, you felt secure. The western
wall broke the wind that usually poured down Irving from the ocean,
twenty-five blocks away. If you fell from one of the cross-beams, or
jumped, as we often did, like pirates abandoning ship or pilots leaving a
flaming cockpit, the sand was there to break your fall. This whole district was built on sand, miles and miles of what had once been dunes
were covered with houses. In those days there were still more miles
waiting to be covered, dunes dotted with spiny beach grass of the same
variety growing in this vacant corner lot. Wherever a parcel of houses
ended and the dunes began, a little skirmish was going on. Half a sidewalk would be disappearing under wind-blown sand, sometimes half an
avenue would be disappearing. People who lived in the final row of
houses could look out across a mile or so of dunes and wonder how long
before the next row would go in, so that *their* lawns and cars would no
longer have to bear the brunt.

As a kid, I always wanted the sand to win. I loved the sand, hot or   3
cold, dry or wet, day or night. In that district, the Sunset District of San
Francisco, which was the world of my boyhood, sand was the alternative
to civilization and its discontents, and so it is no wonder that on the day
World War II broke out I wandered up to the corner sandlot to think.

None of my buddies were there, and I was glad. I wanted solitude. I   4
was not in the mood that day for abandoning ship or leaping from the
cockpit. Real planes could be appearing in the sky at any moment. This
is what my parents were talking about. This is what I expected. Hawaii
was twenty-four hundred miles west, with nothing between here and
there but open water. My father had been to Hawaii. He had been stationed at Pearl Harbor for a couple of years during the 1920s, with a submarine crew.

"If they have a mind to keep on bombing," he said, "they'll have to   5
fly clear over here 'fore they've got anything else to hit."

"You think they'll do it?" my mother asked.   6

"No tellin," he said. "They might be able to git here. But I don't   7
know how they'd ever git back. And if you cain't git back, there ain't
much use in gittin' here."

A tall strip of lattice separated the two sides of the billboard, right   8
at the corner, splintery boards painted green and nailed diagonally so you
could squat back there, hidden from cars, and peer through the diamonds
down Irving Street. I sat for a long time peering at the cloud bank above
the distant ocean, expecting to see planes emerge, fighters, bombers. At

times it seemed that the clouds *were* bombers, ingeniously disguised as broken clouds and moving toward the city like an inexorable fog.

9     Never before had the sky taken on such a threatening look. As the clouds drew nearer, my childish fears ebbed and flowed, and the air grew damp and cold. By the time they had covered the sun, my fearful solitude lost its savor. The day's news had emptied the streets. There was nothing else to do but go home. I came over the back fence, by way of another vacant lot, and from the yard I heard strange noises. I heard voices up on our roof.

10     It wasn't easy to get onto the roof. Counting the street-level garage, our house was actually three stories high. To reach the roof you had to carry a ladder up the back stairs to the second landing, and from there hoist yourself over the gutter. I saw the ladder leaning up there, climbed the stairs, climbed the ladder, got my chin to the gutter level, and found my mother and grandmother standing on the roof gazing west. This had never happened before. No one went up onto the roof but my father, from time to time, when a skylight needed putty. Seeing the women on the roof added to the strangeness of this day. Their panicky conversation confirmed the half-shaped worry I was carrying around. They too were looking for Japanese bombers and trying to decide what to do.

11     My grandmother was doing most of the deciding. Her idea was that we should head back to west Texas where it was safe. They had all come out from Texas the year before I was born, from a little Panhandle town right at the edge of the Dust Bowl. Shading her eyes, like a pioneer woman trying to see through mirages on a desert horizon, she kept saying things like, "Look! Look out there! Isn't that something flying to'rd the city? Look! Can you see it now?" Not only could she see and hear bombers over the Cliff House, she was certain San Francisco Bay was filling with enemy subs and that hidden infantry divisions would soon be marching out of Chinatown.

12     By the next afternoon a plan had taken shape. Three of us would leave first, me, my five-year-old sister, and Grandma. That way, at least the children would be saved. We would travel by train to Texas, where she still owned a farmhouse and a quarter-section of land. Grandma called the Southern Pacific terminal and reserved seats on the overnight train to Los Angeles, where we would meet up tomorrow with the southwest special heading east toward Phoenix and El Paso. She drew all her savings out of the Bank of America, which amounted to $300 or $400, money she had earned as a seamstress, doing alterations and hemstitching in her apartment here on the second floor. My mother packed our bags, cleaned us up and dressed us, so that by the time my father came home from work we were too baffled to cry, protest, or even speak.

13     The plan was perfect in all details but one: my father had not been consulted. The plan had taken shape after he had driven off to work that morning. When his old Plymouth pulled up to the curb, we were standing on the stairs waiting for him to drive us downtown to the terminal—

me in my woolen suit, my sister in a pinafore Grandma had sewn and over the pinafore a red coat with simulated fur collar. My mother twisted at her sweater sleeve, caught between having to watch her children ride out of her life for who knew how many months or years, and her dread of the first air raid. Grandma stood over us, dressed in her city clothes, her long cloth coat, her round black pillbox hat garnished with cherries; but underneath these clothes she was the ranch-country matriarch, determined to protect her herd.

Dad climbed out of the car, still wearing his overalls. He was a   14
painting contractor, worked jobs in all parts of the city—homes, apartment houses, office buildings. He smelled like paint. His bill cap was spotted with it, his shirt and his shoes. His hands were covered with a chalky film made of thinner and enamel residue. He had rolled up the sleeves of his blue shirt, so you could see a line across his wrists.

My mother broke into tears. "Dudley, please hurry. Load up as fast   15
as you can!"

Grandma, looking mournful, waited until he had reached the stairs.   16
"It's got to be, Dudley, it's just got to be."

He looked the situation over and finally said, "What has got to be?"   17

While they explained, he listened in stoic silence. He was not a   18
talker. He took great pride in all forms of handiwork, but never put much stock in words. When they finished explaining, he stood there for a long time saying nothing. He squinted down at my sister and me and blinked and worked his jaws and fingered one of the brass buttons on his overalls, testing the callused tip of his forefinger.

The air was so charged, it was painful. I was looking around for any-   19
thing else to concentrate on, and that was when I noticed his tattoo. It was a purple anchor. A rope curled around the anchor's stem, a purple eagle perched upon the crosspiece. At age eight my eyes were just about even with his forearm. What a relief to see his tattoo inches away. I gave it my full attention. I had looked at it many times, but on this day it occurred to me that the tattoo had not always been a feature of my father's arm. Someone had put it there. For the first time I wondered why, and when? His forearm was thick and brown, the hairs fine around the squinting eagle and the navy anchor. I thought I saw the eagle move. Was it breathing? Or was Dad barely squeezing his fist?

My mother had reached her limit. She cried, "Well, Dudley! My   20
goodness! You going to stand here all day?"

He waited a while longer. I saw a trapped look come into his eyes,   21
the voiceless alarm of a trapped animal. Then he blinked and the look went away. His jaws clenched one final time and his mouth opened. "Maybe I will," he said. "Maybe I'll stand here all day."

Grandma was a twenty-year widow who had raised her two chil-   22
dren—my mother and my uncle—all by herself on that semi-fertile, semi-prairie quarter-section. It had put iron in her eyes. She fixed this iron glare on my father. "I *do* believe we ought to be gittin' along, Dudley."

23    The eagle stopped breathing. The anchor came to rest. He said, "I believe we ought to hold off a few days."

24    My mother was appalled: "HOLD OFF!"

25    Grandma was willing to bargain. "Now Dudley," she began, "if it's the money you're thinkin' about, you needn't . . ."

26    He passed between them, up the stairs, into the house.

27    For three weeks the bags stayed packed, while we waited on his approval of the plan. During those weeks the city braced itself for invasion by land or sea or air. The west sides of all the street lamps were painted chocolate brown. We draped our windows, taped up every place where light might leak, and sat through practice blackouts, staying off the streets, listening for bombers. They never came. The landing barges never landed. Grandma put her money back into the Bank of America. The sand continued to creep toward the last row of houses where the dunes began. My father never again mentioned the escape plan, nor did he ever acknowledge or even hint that such a plan had existed.

28    Twenty-five years later, I was again looking closely at his tattoo. We were at the University of California Medical Center on Parnassus Avenue, and a nurse was probing around on his arm with a transfusion needle.

29    "Your veins are very thin," she said.

30    He looked insulted, misjudged, but said nothing. She tried his left arm. "This one will do," she said. "The veins are stronger." And she slanted the needle through his white flesh.

31    He glanced at her with eyes full of suspicion, eyes that knew his right arm should be stronger, since that was the one he used most. With lips pursed she adjusted a valve on the thin, clear tube rising from his arm, watched the tube turn red. A scarlet bubble rose in the jar above his bed.

32    "This will take about four hours."

33    The trapped look came into his eyes. He wanted to ask her why so long. I knew he wouldn't ask. It was not his style. He rarely asked—for advice, for assistance, for answers. She noted something on her clipboard and padded out into the corridor, while I sat staring at the purple tattoo shielding his tender vein, watching that old eagle's slitted and arrogant eye.

34    After a while he said to me, "Why does it take so long?"

35    "Probably makes it easier for your system to adjust, assimilate the new blood."

36    A faint smile, while his body shifted restlessly under the sheet, impatient with the forced waiting. His jaws squeezed, the bunched muscles bulged, his lips began to part. He was framing another sentence, but he wouldn't speak it yet. His eyes roamed the room and gradually came to rest on the red bottle. It was always that way with him, the long slow pondering. I was never sure whether that reserve came from indecision or from caring too much, brooding too long over what was right and best.

37    "You'd think," he said at last, "that they could get somethin' like this done in less than four hours."

His eyes followed the infrequent climb of bubbles through the 38
blood drawn from my arm earlier that day. My eyes were fixed again on
his tattoo, wondering if this new blood had yet flowed under it. I
searched for a richer hue in the eagle's wing, along the rope curling down
behind the anchor's stem. He was grizzled by that time, coming through
his third bout with intestinal cancer, a chronic ailment I connected to
his lifetime habit of holding too much inside. His skin was pale and his
blood thin, but the tattoo had not changed, the ink had not faded much
at all. The eagle had not moved, the rope had not frayed, nor had the anchor rusted since I first took careful note of it in December 1941, or for
that matter since his young right arm was decorated by the Filipino master on Hotel Street in downtown Honolulu one night back in 1926.

He saw me staring at his arm. I looked away, out the window, to- 39
ward the vista to the north. The medical center stands high up the side of
a steep wooded hill under the eucalyptus groves of Sutro Forest. From his
room you could gaze out across several blocks of vintage flats and rooming houses pressed wall to wall in the San Francisco manner and cascad-
ing down the slope below. The houses end at Golden Gate Park. Beyond
the park, beyond the Richmond District, beyond the city, rose the orange
spires of the bridge, peeking over the forested hills around the Presidio.

That view was easier to watch, and it started me thinking about his 40
life and mine. The spires had not been there when he first sailed into San
Francisco Bay, on his way home from Hawaii, on his way home to Texas,
when his tattoo was new. In those days there was a legendary waterway
known around the world as the Golden Gate, but as yet no bridge had
come rising out of the water to span it. He didn't stay long in Texas. A
few years later he was back, with his bride. Something glittered for him
here. I'm still not sure what it was, maybe all those things the bridge has
come to symbolize, maybe something else entirely. I can only guess. We
never talked about it. I do know this: the bridge and I are of the same
generation. As it happens, construction began in the year I was born. I
was three when police motorcycles escorted the first cars across. I grew
up taking it for granted.

As I sat next to the bed of my father, I remembered the times I 41
played along beaches in full view of the bridge, explored the Fort Point
ruins in the shadow of its towers, bicycled out to stop in the middle, between spires, to watch the ruffling, endless Pacific, framed by the city on
one side, the moss-ridged Coast Range on the other. On a sunny day the
hills of white buildings still quiver with a brightness you only see in
cities next to water. I wonder where I would have cycled had Grandma's
plan carried through, and what other skylines might have beguiled me?
And I wonder still at my father's particular form of delay. Was it uncertainty, or caution, or wisdom, or stubbornness, or fear that kept us in San
Francisco till the war was past and the smoke had cleared?

Whatever anchored us, I know now that it shapes you to grow up in 42
a city whose gate is golden. You leave, you return through its golden

gate. Such a glitter can blind you to certain things. It can color all your expectations. Sooner or later you learn that from those railings people regularly plunge to their death, sometimes traveling thousands of miles to make the famous leap. But by the time you know that, the spires have already imprinted their gleaming image, and it takes more than suicides or heavy traffic to erase the El Dorados flickering there.

## *CONSIDERATIONS*

1. As many another child has done in moments of anxiety, the eight-year-old Houston sought security in a special place after he heard the frightening news of the Pearl Harbor attack. He describes that hide-out in paragraph 2. Write an essay about your own childhood secret place that you relied on in times of stress and uncertainty. Use your descriptive skills, as Houston has done, but develop your essay around an attempt to explain the phenomenon.

2. What role does sand play in this essay of reminiscence? Why, for example, does Houston mention sand in paragraph 27?

3. Houston devotes a good deal of space in both halves of this essay to his father's tattoo. Explain why.

4. What is notable, from a writer's point of view, in Houston's depiction of his father's reaction to Grandma's evacuation plan?

5. Several writers in your text discuss or touch significantly on the idea of sense of place: for example, Wallace Stegner's "The Town Dump" (page 552), Mary TallMountain's "Outflight" (page 566), Wendell Berry's "A Native Hill" (page 42), Cynthia Huntington's "The Spiral" (page 324), and John McPhee's "The Search for Marvin Gardens" (page 389). Select one of those authors and compare his or her efforts to express convincingly a sense of place with those of Houston.

6. Reflecting back on his childhood, Houston more or less identifies himself with the Golden Gate Bridge. If you have a similar identification with some notable new structure or development in your hometown, describe that relationship.

*Langston Hughes (1902–1967) was a poet, novelist, playwright, and essayist who wrote with wit and energy; he was a leader in the emergence of black American literature in the twentieth century. More than twenty of his books remain in print, including* Selected Poems *(1959) and his autobiography,* I Wonder as I Wander *(1956).*

*He argues as well as he sings the blues—and he knows how to tell a story.*

## — 47

# LANGSTON HUGHES
## *Salvation*

I was saved from sin when I was going on thirteen. But not really 1
saved. It happened like this. There was a big revival at my Auntie Reed's church. Every night for weeks there had been much preaching, singing, praying, and shouting, and some very hardened sinners had been brought to Christ, and the membership of the church had grown by leaps and bounds. Then just before the revival ended, they held a special meeting for children, "to bring the young lambs to the fold." My aunt spoke of it for days ahead. That night I was escorted to the front row and placed on the mourners' bench with all the other young sinners, who had not yet been brought to Jesus.

My aunt told me that when you were saved you saw a light, and 2
something happened to you inside! And Jesus came into your life! And God was with you from then on! She said you could see and hear and feel Jesus in your soul. I believed her. I had heard a great many old people say the same thing and it seemed to me they ought to know. So I sat there calmly in the hot, crowded church, waiting for Jesus to come to me.

The preacher preached a wonderful rhythmical sermon, all moans 3
and shouts and lonely cries and dire pictures of hell, and then he sang a song about the ninety and nine safe in the fold, but one little lamb was left out in the cold. Then he said: "Won't you come? Won't you come to Jesus? Young lambs, won't you come?" And he held out his arms to all us

young sinners there on the mourners' bench. All the little girls cried. And some of them jumped up and went to Jesus right away. But most of us just sat there.

4      A great many old people came and knelt around us and prayed, old women with jet-black faces and braided hair, old men with work-gnarled hands. And the church sang a song about the lower lights are burning, some poor sinners to be saved. And the whole building rocked with prayer and song.

5      Still I kept waiting to *see* Jesus.

6      Finally all the young people had gone to the altar and were saved, but one boy and me. He was a rounder's son named Westley. Westley and I were surrounded by sisters and deacons praying. It was very hot in the church, and getting late now. Finally Westley said to me in a whisper: "God damn! I'm tired o' sitting here. Let's get up and be saved." So he got up and was saved.

7      Then I was left all alone on the mourners' bench. My aunt came and knelt at my knees and cried, while prayers and songs swirled all around me in the little church. The whole congregation prayed for me alone, in a mighty wail of moans and voices. And I kept waiting serenely for Jesus, waiting, waiting—but he didn't come. I wanted to see him, but nothing happened to me. Nothing! I wanted something to happen to me, but nothing happened.

8      I heard the songs and the minister saying: "Why don't you come? My dear child, why don't you come to Jesus? Jesus is waiting for you. He wants you. Why don't you come? Sister Reed, what is this child's name?"

9      "Langston," my aunt sobbed.

10     "Langston, why don't you come? Why don't you come and be saved? Oh, Lamb of God! Why don't you come?"

11     Now it was really getting late. I began to be ashamed of myself, holding everything up so long. I began to wonder what God thought about Westley, who certainly hadn't seen Jesus either, but who was now sitting proudly on the platform, swinging his knickerbockered legs and grinning down at me, surrounded by deacons and old women on their knees praying. God had not struck Westley dead for taking his name in vain or for lying in the temple. So I decided that maybe to save further trouble, I'd better lie, too, and say that Jesus had come, and get up and be saved.

12     So I got up.

13     Suddenly the whole room broke into a sea of shouting, as they saw me rise. Waves of rejoicing swept the place. Women leaped in the air. My aunt threw her arms around me. The minister took me by the hand and led me to the platform.

14     When things quieted down, in a hushed silence, punctuated by a few ecstatic "Amens," all the new young lambs were blessed in the name of God. Then joyous singing filled the room.

That night, for the last time in my life but one—for I was a big boy   15
twelve years old—I cried. I cried, in my bed alone, and couldn't stop. I
buried my head under the quilts, but my aunt heard me. She woke up
and told my uncle I was crying because the Holy Ghost had come into
my life, and because I had seen Jesus. But I was really crying because I
couldn't bear to tell her that I had lied, that I had deceived everybody in
the church, and I hadn't seen Jesus, and that now I didn't believe there
was a Jesus any more, since he didn't come to help me.

## CONSIDERATIONS

1. Hughes tells this critical episode of his childhood in a simple, straightforward,
unelaborated fashion, almost as though he were still a child telling the story as it happened. Why is it necessary to say "*almost* as though he were still a child"? How would
you go about recounting a critical moment in your childhood? Where does simple
childhood memory stop and adult judgment take over?

2. Hughes's disillusionment is an example of what is called "an initiation story."
Compare it with Lillian Hellman's autobiographical essay, or Louise Bogan's girlhood
memories, or Bernard Cooper's retracing of a boyhood awakening. Discuss the degrees
of awareness noticeable among these varied characters.

3. Why is it so important to the congregation of Auntie Reed's church that everyone, children included, acknowledge their salvation?

4. Why did Westley and Langston finally proclaim that they have been saved?
Explain why that is critical to the conclusion of the account.

5. In his final paragraph, Hughes writes, "That night, for the last time in my life
but one . . . I cried." He does not tell us, in this account, what that other time was.
Read a little more about his life, or simply use your imagination, and write a brief account of the other time.

*Cynthia Huntington (b. 1951) grew up in Pennsylvania and attended Michigan State University. During a fellowship at the Provincetown Arts Center in 1978, she fell in love with the Cape Cod she describes. Since then, she has taught at the University of California at Irvine and, more recently, at Dartmouth College in New Hampshire, taking every opportunity to return to Cape Cod. She has published two books of poems and* The Salt House: A Summer on the Dunes of Cape Cod *(1999), from which we take "The Spiral."*

*Writers have noted that their best work derives from what they best love. For one writer, it may be baseball or labor unions; for many others, it is the best loved place. Cynthia Huntington's shack is Euphoria, and this pun tells the truth. In this opening chapter of* The Salt House, *we feel Huntington's elation in every word.*

— **48** ——————————————————————————

# CYNTHIA HUNTINGTON
## *The Spiral*

———————————————————————————————————

1    We live on the inside curve of a spiral, where the peninsula turns around on itself and curls backward. The tip of this peninsula is still building, extending in a thin line as waves wash sand along the outer shore, nudging it north and west. Moving inward, counterclockwise, the spiral winds backward, to set this place apart in its own self-willed dreaming.

2    Out here beyond the last bedrock, past the crust of the glacial deposit, we live on a foothold of sand that is constantly moving. Everything eroded and nudged along shore ends up here, broken. Whole coastlines, boulders, good earth perhaps: they all arrive at last as sand. Sand keeps its forms barely longer than water; only the most recent wave or the last footprint stays on its surface.

3    Sleeping, we wake to sounds of water. Day and night the ocean mutters like a restless dreamer. We live beside it and sleep falling into its voices. Repeating, obsessive, the waves' syllables might almost become

"The Spiral" from *The Salt House: A Summer on the Dunes of Cape Cod* by Cynthia Huntington. Reprinted by permission of University Press of New England.

words, but do not, just as the sand pushed back and forth at the tide line will not quite hold a form, though the ocean molds it again and again.

At night the oil lamps shine on the boards, and windows hold the flames in their black pools, yellow and welcoming if you were returning here after some journey. The only other lights glimmer down past the beach where boats sail into the night sky; the furthest ones blink like low stars on the horizon. Then one star may take flight, glowing yellow or red or green, and turn out to be a small plane patrolling this outpost, scanning the black water with its radar. The shack rocks gently in wind. Set up on wood pilings against the second dune, it lets the wind under it, gently lifting. We lie apart in narrow bunks like shipmates, breathing softly. Bert turns in his sleep, smacking the mattress with an outflung arm, and the whole bed shakes and resettles. In the high bunk, I feel the shack sway like a boat at anchor, and I know there is nothing fixed or steady, only these currents carrying us along in the dark. The windows are effacing themselves now, as the inner and outer darkness meet at the surface of the glass. I can still see a little bit of sky there; I lift my hand to touch the rough boards of the ceiling, pierced by the sharp points of shingle nails. The boards quiver slightly as night winds blow across them. Wobbling on its axis, the planet twirls off in space, spun in thrall to a star. Only the pull of that great fire, and our opposite thrust away from it, hold us on course.

We live on the outermost, outward-reaching shore of Cape Cod, at no fixed address. In the past three years we have lived in a series of rooms: summer houses in winter, apartments carved out of old hotels, a studio over a lumber yard, all borrowed nests. Of all the borrowed places, this one is best, a little board shack stuck up on posts in the sand, surrounded by beach roses, beach grass and miles of dunes, anchored in sand that flows straight down into the sea.

The shack has a name, Euphoria, which at first struck me as a little silly and high-flown. It means elation, and has to do with the wind. The name came with it, along with other bits of history. In its present incarnation it is the property of Hazel Hawthorne Werner, who holds a lifetime lease with the Cape Cod National Seashore, where it stands. Hazel bought Euphoria in the 1940s from a woman from Boston who had come out to join her lover, who had another shack a ways down the beach. He camped in that shack and she camped in Euphoria until the war came and he went off to fight. The woman from Boston bought it, years before that, from a Coast Guardsman who had built it to house his wife on summer visits. Story has it, she saw the place and promptly fled to town.

Hazel wrote a novel about her life in the dunes in a shack she called Salt House. I like that name, the way it distills the airy ecstasy of Euphoria to something more elemental, a flavor sharper than wind or spirit, preserving the body of the world in something hard and white. The taste of salt is always on my tongue here, held in the air and on every surface, beading my skin. The air has a flavor, a bite; even the sun has edges, reflected and magnified by sand and water. We see more clearly, taste and feel, here inside the salt house of our bodies.

8    A single room of unfinished boards, Euphoria measures about twelve by sixteen, with a narrow deck in front, facing east, a wall of windows looking north, and a weathervane on a knobby pole, that twirls like crazy in the constant winds. The shack is unpainted except for a little sky-blue trim on the screen door and along the eaves. The rest is the color of old wood—I should say colors, sometimes grey or silver, sometimes brown, depending how much damp is in the air and how the light falls. There are gaps between the boards, and around the doors and windows where sunlight and rain leak in equally; you can look down at the floor and see light glancing through. So it is a not-quite substantial shelter, the idea of a house, but with none of a real house's constriction.

9    Inside are three tables, one under each window, bunk beds, a gas stove for cooking, and a wood stove for heat. We are equipped with six oil lamps, an enormous kettle bestriding both burners of the range, a dry sink, and a propane refrigerator which invariably breaks down in the heat of August. The front wall faces north across the Atlantic with two big windows we open by tugging on a rope slung over a pulley. Along the south wall another window gazes at the back end of a dune which is slowly collapsing toward the rear of the shack, held back by roots of bay and poison ivy. Day blows straight through when these windows are open, ruffling newspapers and sending loose papers flying. In the most sheltered corner, by the cookstove at the foot of the bunks, a high, narrow window catches the last light of sunset glinting on upended pots and pans drying in the dishrack after supper.

10    From Monomoy to Race Point, surfmen once walked this beach, night and day in all weathers. Twelve Coast Guard stations were strung across a forty-mile stretch, with halfway houses spaced between, where the patrols would meet and turn back. Each night their lights moved north and south, beams of oil lanterns and electric torches, and often a red flare sent up to signal a wreck. Back then these dunes were considered wasteland, though people from Provincetown would sometimes tramp across to cook picnic suppers over a bonfire of wreckage. Townsfolk called this "the back side," the town facing otherwise toward the harbor, and only the Coast Guard walked the beach at night.

11    Every spring, when the town starts to fill up with people and our winter's lease runs out, we pack up our books and winter clothes to store in a friend's basement and begin assembling provisions for the summer. Out here, the pump handle is screwed together and coaxed into operation, the outhouse retrieved from bushes where it rested on its side, and set up at a discreet distance from the shack. When all is ready, we load our gear on to our friend Bill Fitts's four-wheel-drive truck and move out

to the dunes. I unpack what we've brought: rice and oil, and beans, and canned things, books, flashlights, radio, sweatshirts, and things for the beach. Everything fits, in a corner or on a shelf, stowed neat and tight as on a small boat, which is what Euphoria most nearly resembles. I fill the oil lamps while Bert fixes the propane tank to the stove and we're in business. It's a forty-minute walk to town, uphill and down in soft sand—far enough so the summer crowds won't reach us. From here on, we carry our supplies overland in knapsacks—and carry our garbage out—along the old Coast Guard supply route, Snail Road, now just a ghost trail in the sand.

On a still evening, when the wind picks up from the south, we may 12 hear the traffic from the highway pumping into town. From the back shore, it's only two or three miles at any point across to Provincetown Harbor, where the town hugs the bayside and keeps the dunes at its back, and where Route Six, the mid-Cape highway, ends in a parking lot on a public beach. In summer the town fills with tourists and the narrow streets throb with voices and engines. We aren't so far from any of it— the big blue water tower sits on one horizon with the lights of the town ranged beyond it, and Park Service rangers drive down the beach every morning in their green pickups. All summer Air Force pilots train against attack of this coast; their loops and turnings overhead remind us who owns this shore. Grey, sluglike tankers carrying oil from feudal kingdoms lurk on the horizon, and fishing boats trail oil and purple spumes of gasoline. The radar domes in Truro glow at night above the dune called Ararat, and Highland Light sends its white flare around and around, cutting through the clouds with its peremptory beam.

When we have returned from our winter rooms, at the end of an- 13 other year's wandering, we settle ourselves for a look around, fill the small blue cups with water, and watch as evening comes on. Then it is time to light the lamps, and, not so much later, to put them out.

## CONSIDERATIONS

1. Spend a few minutes looking at a map that shows the coastline of Massachusetts; then draw your own sketch of the unique form of Cape Cod, and write a brief description of it. Finally, comment on Huntington's opening paragraph.

2. Identify and comment on a few phrases or passages that suggest that the author had something in mind besides describing a beach shack.

3. The author's residence on Cape Cod is clearly temporary and seasonal. Aside from details of the preparations each year for moving there, how does she capitalize on the transitory nature of living there?

4. In paragraph 12, the author says of the Air Force planes overhead, "their loops and turnings overhead remind us who owns this shore." To what "owners" does she refer? In the same paragraph, what does she refer to when she describes the tankers "carrying oil from feudal kingdoms"?

5. In *Walden*, Henry David Thoreau describes how he built his house in the woods by Walden Pond, near Concord, Massachusetts. Like Huntington's "Euphoria," Thoreau's was a humble, one-room, handmade affair, but there are interesting differences. As opposed to celebrating the airy transiency of life as Huntington does, Thoreau built his house to stay. "I hewed the main timbers six inches square . . . each stick was carefully mortised or tenoned. . . . The boards were carefully feather-edged and lapped, so that it was perfectly impervious to rain." Compare and contrast the two writers on the basis of their respective relationships to their places.

6. Although both Huntington and Wendell Berry (in his "A Native Hill," page 42) are meticulous in showing how their respective places change, their relationships to those places are radically different. Read enough of Berry's essay to discover that difference; then explain it.

*Zora Neale Hurston (1902–1960) grew up in Florida and went to Howard University. In New York, she was associated with Langston Hughes in the Harlem Renaissance. Her knowledge of southern black culture showed itself in novels (*Their Eyes Were Watching God, *1937) and in nonfiction. Her excellent work has especially surfaced in the wake of attention to feminism and black studies.*

*Her confidence in herself, her lack of self-pity or complaint, shines through "How It Feels to Be Colored Me." Notice how, in a dry and objective manner, she exposes the absurdity of racism.*

— **49** —

# ZORA NEALE HURSTON
## *How It Feels to Be Colored Me*

I am colored but I offer nothing in the way of extenuating circum- 1
stances except the fact that I am the only Negro in the United States whose grandfather on the mother's side was *not* an Indian chief.

I remember the very day that I became colored. Up to my thirteenth 2
year I lived in the little Negro town of Eatonville, Florida. It is exclusively a colored town. The only white people I knew passed through the town going to or coming from Orlando. The native whites rode dusty horses, the Northern tourists chugged down the sandy village road in automobiles. The town knew the Southerners and never stopped cane chewing when they passed. But the Northerners were something else again. They were peered at cautiously from behind curtains by the timid. The more venturesome would come out on the porch to watch them go past and got just as much pleasure out of the tourists as the tourists got out of the village.

The front porch might seem a daring place for the rest of the town, 3
but it was a gallery seat for me. My favorite place was atop the gate-post. Proscenium box for a born first-nighter. Not only did I enjoy the show, but I didn't mind the actors knowing that I liked it. I usually spoke to them in passing. I'd wave at them and when they returned my salute, I would say something like this: "Howdy-do-well-I-thank-you-where-you-

"How It Feels to Be Colored Me" from *The World Tomorrow* by Zora Neale Hurston. Reprinted by permission of the Estate of Zora Neale Hurston.

goin'?" Usually automobile or the horse paused at this, and after a queer exchange of compliments, I would probably "go a piece of the way" with them, as we say in farthest Florida. If one of my family happened to come to the front in time to see me, of course negotiations would be rudely broken off. But even so, it is clear that I was the first "welcome-to-our-state" Floridian, and I hope the Miami Chamber of Commerce will please take notice.

4       During this period, white people differed from colored to me only in that they rode through town and never lived there. They liked to hear me "speak pieces" and sing and wanted to see me dance the parse-me-la, and gave me generously of their small silver for doing these things, which seemed strange to me for I wanted to do them so much that I needed bribing to stop. Only they didn't know it. The colored people gave no dimes. They deplored any joyful tendencies in me, but I was their Zora nevertheless. I belonged to them, to the nearby hotels, to the county—everybody's Zora.

5       But changes came in the family when I was thirteen, and I was sent to school in Jacksonville. I left Eatonville, the town of the oleanders, as Zora. When I disembarked from the river-boat at Jacksonville, she was no more. It seemed that I had suffered a sea change. I was not Zora of Orange County any more, I was now a little colored girl. I found it out in certain ways. In my heart as well as in the mirror, I became a fast brown—warranted not to rub nor run.

6       But I am not tragically colored. There is no great sorrow dammed up in my soul, nor lurking behind my eyes. I do not mind at all. I do not belong to the sobbing school of Negrohood who hold that nature some-how has given them a low-down dirty deal and whose feelings are all hurt about it. Even in the helter-skelter skirmish that is my life, I have seen that the world is to the strong regardless of a little pigmentation more or less. No, I do not weep at the world—I am too busy sharpening my oyster knife.

7       Someone is always at my elbow reminding me that I am the grand-daughter of slaves. It fails to register depression with me. Slavery is sixty years in the past. The operation was successful and the patient is doing well, thank you. The terrible struggle that made me an American out of a potential slave said "On the line!" The Reconstruction said "Get set!"; and the generation before said "Go!" I am off to a flying start and I must not halt in the stretch to look behind and weep. Slavery is the price I paid for civilization, and the choice was not with me. It is a bully adventure and worth all that I have paid through my ancestors for it. No one on earth ever had a greater chance for glory. The world to be won and noth-ing to be lost. It is thrilling to think—to know that for any act of mine, I shall get twice as much praise or twice as much blame. It is quite excit-ing to hold the center of the national stage, with the spectators not knowing whether to laugh or to weep.

The position of my white neighbor is much more difficult. No 8
brown specter pulls up a chair beside me when I sit down to eat. No dark
ghost thrusts its leg against mine in bed. The game of keeping what one
has is never so exciting as the game of getting.

I do not always feel colored. Even now I often achieve the uncon- 9
scious Zora of Eatonville before the Hegira. I feel most colored when I
am thrown against a sharp white background.

For instance at Barnard. "Beside the waters of the Hudson" I feel 10
my race. Among the thousand white persons, I am a dark rock surged
upon, and overswept, but through it all, I remain myself. When covered
by the waters, I am; and the ebb but reveals me again.

Sometimes it is the other way around. A white person is set down in 11
our midst, but the contrast is just as sharp for me. For instance, when I sit
in the drafty basement that is The New World Cabaret with a white person, my color comes. We enter chatting about any little nothing that we
have in common and are seated by the jazz waiters. In the abrupt way that
jazz orchestras have, this one plunges into a number. It loses no time in
circumlocutions, but gets right down to business. It constricts the thorax
and splits the heart with its tempo and narcotic harmonies. This orchestra grows rambunctious, rears on its hind legs and attacks the tonal veil
with primitive fury, rending it, clawing it until it breaks through to the
jungle beyond. I follow those heathen—follow them exultingly. I dance
wildly inside myself; I yell within, I whoop; I shake my assegai above my
head, I hurl it true to the mark *yeeeeooww!* I am in the jungle and living
in the jungle way. My face is painted red and yellow and my body is
painted blue. My pulse is throbbing like a war drum. I want to slaughter
something—give pain, give death to what, I do not know. But the piece
ends. The men of the orchestra wipe their lips and rest their fingers. I
creep back slowly to the veneer we call civilization with the last tone and
find the white friend sitting motionless in his seat, smoking calmly.

"Good music they have here," he remarks, drumming the table 12
with his fingertips.

Music. The great blobs of purple and red emotion have not touched 13
him. He has only heard what I felt. He is far away and I see him but
dimly across the ocean and the continent that have fallen between us.
He is so pale with his whiteness then and I am *so* colored.

At certain times I have no race, I am *me*. When I set my hat at a cer- 14
tain angle and saunter down Seventh Avenue, Harlem City, feeling as
snooty as the lions in front of the Forty-Second Street Library, for instance. So far as my feelings are concerned, Peggy Hopkins Joyce on the
Boule Mich with her gorgeous raiment, stately carriage, knees knocking
together in a most aristocratic manner, has nothing on me. The cosmic
Zora emerges. I belong to no race nor time. I am the eternal feminine
with its string of beads.

15       I have no separate feeling about being an American citizen and colored. I am merely a fragment of the Great Soul that surges within the
boundaries. My country, right or wrong.

16       Sometimes, I feel discriminated against, but it does not make me
angry. It merely astonishes me. How *can* any deny themselves the pleasure of my company? It's beyond me.

17       But in the main, I feel like a brown bag of miscellany propped
against a wall. Against a wall in company with other bags, white, red and
yellow. Pour out the contents, and there is discovered a jumble of small
things priceless and worthless. A first-water diamond, an empty spool,
bits of broken glass, lengths of string, a key to a door long since crumbled
away, a rusty knife-blade, old shoes saved for a road that never was and
never will be, a nail bent under the weight of things too heavy for any
nail, a dried flower or two still a little fragrant. In your hand is the brown
bag. On the ground before you is the jumble it held—so much like the
jumble in the bags, could they be emptied, that all might be dumped in a
single heap and the bags refilled without altering the content of any
greatly. A bit of colored glass more or less would not matter. Perhaps that
is how the Great Stuffer of Bags filled them in the first place—who
knows?

## CONSIDERATIONS

1. Hurston does something unexpected in her brief opening paragraph. What is
she up to? And why?

2. An old American Indian saying observes, "Fish do not know their atmosphere
is water." Explain how Hurston demonstrates this truth.

3. What evidence can you provide that Hurston was enjoying herself as she
wrote "How It Feels to Be Colored Me"? Do you find anything like that in Brent
Staples's "Just Walk on By" (page 535)? Explain.

4. Basing your opinion on this one short essay, do you think a militant civil rights
group would enlist Zora Neale Hurston? Explain your answer.

5. Read "Two Kinds" by Amy Tan (page 581)—another account of a young girl
changing (well, almost) identities—and pay particular attention to the tone of her story,
as opposed to Hurston's essay. Describe their respective attitudes as you see them expressed in their writing styles.

*Thomas Jefferson (1743–1826) was the third president of the United States, and perhaps more truly the Father of His Country than George Washington was; or maybe we would only like to think so, for such paternity flatters the offspring. Jefferson was a politician, philosopher, architect, inventor, and writer. With an energy equal to his curiosity, he acted to improve the world: he wrote the Declaration of Independence; he wrote a life of Jesus; and he founded the University of Virginia, whose original buildings he designed. An arch-Republican, fearful of Alexander Hamilton's monarchical reverence for authority, Jefferson withheld support from the Constitution until he saw the Bill of Rights added to it.*

*We take this text from Garry Wills's* Inventing America *(1978); by juxtaposition, Wills demonstrates the revision of a classic.*

*This document is a model of formal, straightforward, yet passionate prose. "We hold these truths to be self-evident . . ."*

— 50 ———————————

# THOMAS JEFFERSON
## *The Declarations of Jefferson and of the Congress*

I will state the form of the declaration as originally reported. The parts struck out by Congress shall be distinguished by a black line drawn under them; & those inserted by them shall be placed in the margin or in a concurrent column:

A Declaration by the representatives of the United States 1
of America, in [General] Congress assembled.

When in the course of human events it becomes neces- 2
sary for one people to dissolve the political bands which have
connected them with another, and to assume the powers of
the earth, the separate & equal station to which the laws of
nature and of nature's god entitle them, a decent respect to the

"The Declarations of Jefferson and the Congress" by Thomas Jefferson from *Inventing America* by Garry Wills, Random House, Inc.

opinions of mankind requires that they should declare the causes which impel them to the separation.

3     We hold these truths to be self evident: that all men are created equal; that they are endowed by their creator with ∧    certain [inherent and] inalienable rights; that among these are life, liberty & the pursuit of happiness: that to secure these rights, governments are instituted among men, deriving their just powers from the consent of the governed; that whenever any form of government becomes destructive of these ends, it is the right of the people to alter or to abolish it, & to institute new government, laying it's foundation on such principles, & organising it's powers in such form, as to them shall seem most likely to effect their safety & happiness. Prudence indeed will dictate that governments long established should not be changed for light & transient causes; and accordingly all experience hath shewn that mankind are more disposed to suffer while evils are sufferable than to right themselves by abolishing the forms to which they are accustomed. But when a long train of abuses & usurpations [begun at a distinguished period and] pursuing invariably the same object, evinces a design to reduce them under absolute despotism it is their right, it is their duty to throw off such government, & to provide new guards for their future security. Such has been the patient sufferance of these colonies; & such is now the necessity which constrains them to ∧ [expunge] their former systems of govern-    alter ment. The history of the present king of Great Britain is a history of ∧ [unremitting] injuries & usurpations, [among which    repeated appears no solitary fact to contradict the uniform tenor of the rest but all have] ∧ in direct object the establishment of an ab-    all having solute tyranny over these states. To prove this let facts be submitted to a candid world [for the truth of which we pledge a faith yet unsullied by falsehood].

4     He has refused his assent to laws the most wholesome & necessary for the public good.

5     He has forbidden his governors to pass laws of immediate & pressing importance, unless suspended in their operation till his assent should be obtained; & when so suspended, he has utterly neglected to attend to them.

6     He has refused to pass other laws for the accommodation of large districts of people, unless those people would relinquish the right of representation in the legislature, a right inestimable to them, & formidable to tyrants only.

7     He has called together legislative bodies at places unusual, uncomfortable, and distant from the depository of their public records, for the sole purpose of fatiguing them into compliance with his measures.

He has dissolved representative houses repeatedly [&   8
<u>continually</u>] for opposing with manly firmness his invasions
on the rights of the people.

He has refused for a long time after such dissolutions to   9
cause others to be elected, whereby the legislative powers, incapable of annihilation, have returned to the people at large for
their exercise, the state remaining in the mean time exposed
to all the dangers of invasion from without & convulsions
within.

He has endeavored to prevent the population of these   10
states; for that purpose obstructing the laws for naturalization
of foreigners, refusing to pass others to encourage their migrations hither, & raising the conditions of new appropriations of
lands

obstructed           He has ∧ [<u>suffered</u>] the administration of justice [<u>totally</u>   11
by           <u>to cease in some of these states</u>] ∧ refusing his assent to laws
for establishing judiciary powers.

He has made [<u>our</u>] judges dependant on his will alone, for   12
the tenure of their offices, & the amount & paiment of their
salaries.

He has erected a multitude of new offices [<u>by a self as-</u>   13
<u>sumed power</u>] and sent hither swarms of new officers to har-
rass our people and eat out their substance.

He has kept among us in times of peace standing armies   14
[<u>and ships of war</u>] without the consent of our legislatures.

He has affected to render the military independent of, &   15
superior to the civil power.

He has combined with others to subject us to jurisdic-   16
tion foreign to our constitutions & unacknowledged by our
laws, giving his assent to their acts of pretended legislation
for quartering large bodies of armed troops among us; for protecting them by a mock-trial from punishment for any murders which they should commit on the inhabitants of these
states; for cutting off our trade with all parts of the world; for
in many cases     imposing taxes on us without our consent; for depriving us ∧
of the benefits of trial by jury; for transporting us beyond seas
to be tried to pretended offences; for abolishing the free system of English laws in a neighboring province, establishing
therein an arbitrary government, and enlarging it's boundaries, so as to render it at once an example and fit instrument
colonies         for introducing the same absolute rule into these ∧ [<u>states</u>];
for taking away our charters, abolishing our most valuable
laws, and altering fundamentally the forms of our governments; for suspending our own legislatures, & declaring
themselves invested with power to legislate for us in all cases
whatsoever.

17      He has abdicated government here ∧ [<u>withdrawing his</u> <u>governors, and declaring us out of his allegiance & protection</u>].

by declaring us
out of his
protection &
waging war
against us

18      He has plundered our seas, ravaged our coasts, burnt our towns, & destroyed the lives of our people.

19      He is at this time transporting large armies of foreign mercenaries to compleat the works of death, desolation & tyranny already begun with circumstances of cruelty and perfidy ∧ unworthy the head of a civilized nation.

scarcely
paralleled in
the most bar-
barous ages, &
totally

20      He has constrained our fellow citizens taken captive on the high seas to bear arms against their country, to become the executioners of their friends & brethren, or to fall themselves by their hands.

21      He has ∧ endeavored to bring on the inhabitants of our frontiers the merciless Indian savages, whose known rule of warfare is an undistinguished destruction of all ages, sexes, & conditions [<u>of existence</u>].

excited domes-
tic insurrec-
tions amongst
us, & has

22      [<u>He has incited treasonable insurrections of our fellow-</u> <u>citizens, with the allurements of forfeiture & confiscation of</u> <u>our property.</u>

23      <u>He has waged cruel war against human nature itself, vio-</u> <u>lating it's most sacred rights of life and liberty in the persons</u> <u>of a distant people who never offended him, captivating & car-</u> <u>rying them into slavery in another hemisphere or to incur mis-</u> <u>erable death in their transportation thither. This piratical</u> <u>warfare, the opprobrium of *infidel* powers, is the warfare of the</u> <u>*Christian* king of Great Britain. Determined to keep open a</u> <u>market where *Men* should be bought & sold, he has prosti-</u> <u>tuted his negative for suppressing every legislative attempt to</u> <u>prohibit or to restrain this execrable commerce. And that this</u> <u>assemblage of horrors might want no fact of distinguished die,</u> <u>he is now exciting those very people to rise in arms among us,</u> <u>and to purchase that liberty of which he has deprived them, by</u> <u>murdering the people on whom he also obtruded them: thus</u> <u>paying off former crimes committed against the *Liberties* of</u> <u>one people, with crimes which he urges them to commit</u> <u>against the *lives* of another</u>].

24      In every stage of these oppressions we have petitioned for redress in the most humble terms: our repeated petitions have been answered only by repeated injuries. A prince whose character is thus marked by every act which may define a tyrant is unfit to be the ruler of a ∧ people [<u>who mean to be free. Future</u> <u>ages will scarcely believe that the hardiness of one man adven-</u> <u>tured, within the short compass of twelve years only, to lay a</u> <u>foundation so broad & so undisguised for tyranny over a peo-</u> <u>ple fostered & fixed in principles of freedom</u>].

free

Nor have we been wanting in attentions to our British    25
brethren. We have warned them from time to time of attempts
by their legislature to extend ∧ [a] jurisdiction over ∧ [these our
states]. We have reminded them of the circumstances of our
emigration & settlement here, [no one of which could warrant
so strange a pretension: that these were effected at the expence
of our own blood & treasure, unassisted by the wealth or the
strength of Great Britain: that in constituting indeed our several forms of government, we had adopted one common king,
thereby laying a foundation for perpetual league & amity with
them: but that submission to their parliament was no part of
our constitution, nor ever in idea, if history may be credited:
and,] we ∧ appealed to their native justice and magnanimity ∧
[as well as to] the ties of our common kindred to disavow
these usurpations which ∧ [were likely to] interrupt our connection and correspondence. They too have been deaf to the
voice of justice & of consanguinity, [and when occasions have
been given them, by the regular course of their laws, of removing from their councils the disturbers of our harmony, they
have, by their free election, reestablished them in power. At
this very time too they are permitting their chief magistrate to
send over not only souldiers of our common blood, but Scotch
& foreign mercenaries to invade & destroy us. These facts
have given the last stab to agonizing affection, and manly
spirit bids us to renounce for ever these unfeeling brethren. We
must endeavor to forget our former love for them, and to hold
them as we hold the rest of mankind enemies in war, in peace
friends. We might have been a free and a great people together;
but a communication of grandeur & of freedom it seems is below their dignity. Be it so, since they will have it. The road to
happiness & to glory is open to us too. We will tread it apart
from them, and] ∧ acquiesce in the necessity which denounces
our [eternal] separation ∧!

*Left margin notes:*
an unwarrant-
able
us

have
and we have
conjured
them by
would inevita-
bly

we must there-
fore
and hold them
as we hold
the rest of
mankind ene-
mies in war,
in peace friends

We therefore the repre-
sentatives of the United
States of America in General
Congress assembled do in the
name, & by the authority of
the good people of these
[states reject & renounce all
allegiance & subjection to the
kings of Great Britain & all
others who may hereafter
claim by, through or under

We therefore the repre-    26
sentatives of the United
States of America in General
Congress assembled, appealing to the supreme judge of
the world for the rectitude of
our intentions, do in the
name, & by the authority of
the good people of these
colonies, solemnly publish &
declare that these United

them: we utterly dissolve all political connection which may heretofore have subsisted between us & the people of parliament of Great Britain: & finally we do assert & declare these colonies to be free & independant states,] & that as free & independant states, they have full power to levy war, conclude peace, contract alliances, establish commerce, & to do all other acts & things which independant states may of right do. And for the support of this declaration we mutually pledge to each other our lives, our fortunes & our sacred honour.

colonies are & of right ought to be free & independant states; that they are absolved from all allegiance to the British crown, and that all political connection between them & the state of Great Britain is, & ought to be, totally dissolved; & that as free & independant states they have full power to levy war, conclude peace, contract alliances, establish commerce & to do all other acts & things which independant states may of right do. And for the support of this declaration, with a firm reliance on the protection of divine providence we mutually pledge to each other our lives, our fortunes & our sacred honour.

## CONSIDERATIONS

1. What part of the original Declaration deleted by Congress most surprises you? Why?

2. Make a careful study of the first eight or ten changes imposed by Congress on Jefferson's original Declaration. Why do you think each was made?

3. Garry Wills says in his book *Inventing America* that the Declaration is easy to misunderstand because it "is written in the lost language of the Enlightenment." What was the Enlightenment? How does the language of that period differ from that of today? Should the Declaration be rewritten in modern English?

4. If you conclude that the Declaration should be rewritten, try your hand at it. Try, for instance, rewriting the famous third paragraph: "We hold these truths. . . ." Can you be sure you're not writing a parody? For an example of parody, see paragraphs 9, 10, and 11 in George Orwell's "Politics and the English Language" (page 484).

5. How is the Declaration organized? Does it break down into distinct parts? If so, what is the function of those parts?

6. We frequently see complaints that the "jargon" of government, academia, large corporations, political parties, and the military obscures or actually hides the ideas that presumably are being expressed. To what extent, if any, would you say that jargon affects what Jefferson and the Congress were saying in the Declaration?

*Jane Kenyon (1947–1995) grew up in Ann Arbor, Michigan, where she won a Hopwood Award at the University of Michigan. After 1975 she lived on a farm in New Hampshire, writing essays and poems, and in 1992 she received a Guggenheim Fellowship. In her lifetime, she published four books of poems, starting with* From Room to Room *in 1978 and concluding with* Constance *in 1993. She died of leukemia in 1995, and in 1996 her publisher issued* Otherwise: New and Selected Poems.

*This poem grew out of Kenyon's 1991 visit to the battlefield in Pennsylvania, just as the Gulf War was ending.*

---

## — 51

# JANE KENYON
### *Gettysburg: July 1, 1863*

---

The young man, hardly more
than a boy, who fired the shot
had looked at him with an air
not of anger but of concentration,
as if he were surveying a road,    5
or feeding a length of wood into a saw:
it had to be done just so.

The bullet passed through
his upper chest, below the collarbone.
The pain was not what he might    10
have feared. Strangely exhilarated
he staggered out of the pasture
and into a grove of trees.

He pressed and pressed
the wound, trying to staunch    15
the blood, but he could only press
what he could reach, and he could

not reach his back, where the bullet
had exited.
20        He lay on the earth
smelling the leaves and mosses,
musty and damp and cool
after the blaze of open afternoon.
How good the earth smelled,
25    as it had when he was a boy
hiding from his father who was
intent on strapping him for doing
his chores late one time too many.

A cowbird razzed from a rail fence.
30    It isn't mockery, he thought,
no malice in it . . . just a noise.
Stray bullets nicked the oaks
overhead. Leaves and splinters fell.

Someone near him groaned.
35    But it was his own voice he heard.
His fingers and feet tingled,
the roof of his mouth,
and the bridge of his nose . . .

He became dry, dry, and thought
40    of Christ, who said, *I thirst*.
His man-smell—the smell of his hair
and skin, his sweat, the salt smell
of his cock and the little ferny hairs
that two women had known—

45    left him, and a sharp, almost sweet
smell began to rise from his open mouth
in the warm shade of the oaks.
A streak of sun climbed the rough
trunk of a tree, but he did not
50    see it with his open eye.

*In 1999 Jane Kenyon's publisher issued* A Hundred White Daffodils, *a miscellaneous collection of her translations from Russian poet Anna Akhmatova, prose essays, newspaper columns, notes, and interviews. "Season of Change and Loss" appeared in the* Concord Monitor *(New Hampshire) on 28 October 1989. Her columns, addressed to the neighbors, allowed her to begin to write prose. The reader will observe that the poet shines through the prose.*

## — 52

# JANE KENYON
## *Season of Change and Loss*

All Saints' and All Souls' have circled around again: All Saints', a 1 celebration of the lives of the Christian saints and martyrs, and All Souls', a remembrance of the souls of ordinary believers through all time.

Maybe your faith does not mark these days, or maybe you belong to 2 no religious persuasion, or your persuasion is to have no persuasion, but you recognize the season "When yellow leaves, or none, or few, do hang/Upon those boughs which shake against the cold,/Bare ruin'd choirs, where late the sweet birds sang."

You may already have left the hose to drain down some sloping 3 place in the yard, planted a few bulbs, raked a few leaves. Possibly you've pulled down the winter sashes on the storm windows and noticed the increasingly strident calling of crickets from the grass. The autumn sun can't dry the dew from the lawn, even on the brightest afternoon. The grass is lush, spendthrift, doomed.

A few small, unharvested green tomatoes dangle from blackened 4 plants, having frozen modestly in their pots on the porch. The smell of them is pungent, close to the smell of edible food but a little off. Rainwater in the ashtray on the garden table freezes by night and thaws again by day.

Acorns drop from the oaks with a sound like rain, acorns this year 5 small but plentiful. They've come down without their tops so that we miss the childish pleasure of whistling on their caps. Geese fly over in sweet disorder, controlled chaos, one leader pulling the string for a while, then another emerging to take the leader's place. The dog looks up to see where the commotion is coming from.

6      Good-bye to flesh. Turtlenecks and woolens come out of drawers and garment bags smelling of naphthalene, and the resumption of sober activities in public places, and love in a cold climate. Good-bye to getting the paper barefoot, or nipping out to the kitchen garden for a handful of basil or chervil. The basket on top of the fridge fills with odd hats and gloves, and our sandals withdraw discreetly to the back of the closet.

7      Little deaths. Somewhere in the psyche all these changes and losses register as death. What shall we do against it? One might bake a pie, as Joyce Maynard has been doing all summer against the big kind of death—the death of her mother. "Comfort me with apples . . ." Just now there are many kinds: Macouns, Spartans, Gravensteins, Empires, Paula Reds, Baldwins, Northern Spies. It is a fine thing to build a pie, a bulwark against autumnal entropy.

8      Another defense against reality is to confront it—to admit the pervasiveness of change and loss and replacement. We are in fact like the grass that flourishes and withers, just as the psalmist says. Gardening teaches this lesson over and over, but some of us are slow to learn. We can only acknowledge the mystery, and go on planting burgundy lilies.

9      Walking. Something else to do besides baking pies and planting bulbs. The bugs are gone, and the deer hunt hasn't started in earnest. We're free to notice the multitude of drying vines and grasses, mushrooms and puffballs, like the one that's growing faster than a shopping mall in the backyard. The dog's afraid of it.

10     Leaves come down around us, and the profile of the land emerges again, coming clear as a thought. Now we see ledges and stone walls that had been obscured by ferns and brush all summer. Now we see architecture; some of us see bones.

11     At twilight the sedges are purple, and, as if to compensate for the loss of day, the sunsets become more resplendent than ever. These are the skies through which, my Methodist grandmother used to tell me, Jesus will come a second time into the world, trailing clouds of glory, to judge the quick and the dead.

12     Certainly diminishing light contributes to our sense of loss. Not for nothing that Christmas and Chanukah—celebrations of light's triumph over darkness—come when the sky is indigo by 4:30. Even before the stores have finished touting Halloween—All Hallows' Eve is a variant name for All Saints'—I begin to string sets of small white lights on the larger houseplants in the parlor.

13     No more mowing after supper in the buttery light. We come inside, where the evenings are long and silent. Baseball is dead; even Commissioner Giamatti is dead. There are books, the consolations of philosophy. There's one last cricket in the window well, sounding half-

convinced, and a spider I brought in unintentionally with the geraniums, who lives in the general area of the sink.

My plan is to live like the bears: to turn the compost a few more times, 　14
prowl around a little longer and then go to sleep until the white-throated sparrow, with its coarse and cheerful song, calls me out of the dark.

## CONSIDERATIONS ─────────────────────────

1. Take a few minutes to consider the series of modifiers that make up half of the last sentence of paragraph 3. Then write a paragraph or two on how each of these words might draw from a reader more than the writer put on the page. Do they all do the same thing? How are they related to the whole essay?

2. Where would you turn for help in identifying the lines quoted by Kenyon in paragraphs 2 and 7? Try *Familiar Quotations,* compiled originally in 1855 by John Bartlett, a Boston bookseller. It is now in its sixteenth edition, edited by Justin Kaplan. *Bartlett's* by this time has become as much a household word as *Webster* and *Roget.* While you're in that useful reference book, look for a few other quotations you think might serve the same purpose as did Kenyon's choice.

3. In paragraphs 7 and 8, Kenyon offers two ways to defend oneself against the reality of change and death. In a short essay, explain those two ways and set forth your own ideas on the subject.

4. Among the other authors of your text, John Daniel (page 152), Wendell Berry (page 42), Edward Hoagland (page 297), and Andrew Holleran (page 309) write about change in the sense that Kenyon deals with it. Which of the four would find her brief essay the most useful?

5. What do you think of Kenyon's plan, as set out in paragraph 14? What's yours?

*For five years, Jane Kenyon worked with Vera Sandomirsky
Dunham, a scholar of Russian literature, to translate twenty
poems by Anna Akhmatova. These poems are mostly
Akhmatova's early lyrics, which Kenyon called "brief, perfectly
made verses of passion and feeling." Kenyon felt that by
translating Akhmatova, she learned more about writing her own
poems than she did from any other study or endeavor.*

## — 53

# JANE KENYON
## *Two Poems by Anna Akhmatova*

I know, I know the skis
will begin again their dry creaking.
In the dark blue sky the moon is red,
and the meadow slopes so sweetly.

5    The windows of the palace burn
remote and still.
No path, no lane,
only the iceholes are dark.

Willow, tree of nymphs,
10   don't get in my way.
Shelter the black grackles, black
grackles among your snowy branches.

*1913*

Like a white stone in a deep well                                    5
one memory lies inside me.
I cannot and will not fight against it:
it is joy and it is pain.

It seems to me that anyone who looks
into my eyes will notice it immediately,                             10
becoming sadder and more pensive
than someone listening to a melancholy tale.

I remember how the gods turned people
into things, not killing their consciousness.
And now, to keep these glorious sorrows alive,
you have turned into my memory of you.

*1916*
*Slepnevo*

*Jamaica Kincaid (b. 1949) grew up in Antigua and came to the
United States when she was sixteen. She arrived as an au pair girl
and remained to study and to write. She has written essays and
fiction and has worked as a member of the staff of the New
Yorker. She has taught at Harvard and now lives and writes in
Vermont.*

*Kincaid's first England was a map. Then it was book
knowledge, as she was taught that England was the measure of
everything. She catalogs and expands this mental England—and
then visits the England of rain and reality. See how her essay
develops by comparison and contrast.*

## — 54

# JAMAICA KINCAID
## *On Seeing England for the First Time*

1    When I saw England for the first time, I was a child in school sitting
at a desk. The England I was looking at was laid out on a map gently,
beautifully, delicately, a very special jewel; it lay on a bed of sky blue—
the background of the map—its yellow form mysterious, because though
it looked like a leg of mutton, it could not really look like anything so familiar as a leg of mutton because it was England—with shadings of pink
and green, unlike any shadings of pink and green I had seen before, squig-
gly veins of red running in every direction. England was a special jewel
all right, and only special people got to wear it. The people who got to
wear England were English people. They wore it well and they wore it
everywhere: in jungles, in deserts, on plains, on top of the highest mountains, on all the oceans, on all the seas, in places where they were not
welcome, in places they should not have been. When my teacher had
pinned this map up on the blackboard, she said, "This is England"—and
she said it with authority, seriousness, and adoration, and we all sat up. It
was as if she had said, "This is Jerusalem, the place you will go to when
you die but only if you have been good." We understood then—we were
meant to understand then—that England was to be our source of myth
and the source from which we got our sense of reality, our sense of what

was meaningful, our sense of what was meaningless—and much about our own lives and much about the very idea of us headed that last list.

At the time I was a child sitting at my desk seeing England for the first time, I was already very familiar with the greatness of it. Each morning before I left for school, I ate a breakfast of half a grapefruit, an egg, bread and butter and a slice of cheese, and a cup of cocoa; or half a grapefruit, a bowl of oat porridge, bread and butter and a slice of cheese, and a cup of cocoa. The can of cocoa was often left on the table in front of me. It had written on it the name of the company, the year the company was established, and the words "Made in England." Those words, "Made in England," were written on the box the oats came in too. They would also have been written on the box the shoes I was wearing came in; a bolt of gray linen cloth lying on the shelf of a store from which my mother had bought three yards to make the uniform that I was wearing had written along its edge those three words. The shoes I wore were made in England; so were my socks and cotton undergarments and the satin ribbons I wore tied at the end of two plaits of my hair. My father, who might have sat next to me at breakfast, was a carpenter and cabinet maker. The shoes he wore to work would have been made in England, as were his khaki shirt and trousers, his underpants and undershirt, his socks and brown felt hat. Felt was not the proper material from which a hat that was expected to provide shade from the hot sun should be made, but my father must have seen and admired a picture of an Englishman wearing such a hat in England, and this picture that he saw must have been so compelling that it caused him to wear the wrong hat for a hot climate most of his long life. And this hat—a brown felt hat—became so central to his character that it was the first thing he put on in the morning as he stepped out of bed and the last thing he took off before he stepped back into bed at night. As we sat at breakfast a car might go by. The car, a Hillman or a Zephyr, was made in England. The very idea of the meal itself, breakfast, and its substantial quality and quantity was an idea from England; we somehow knew that in England they began the day with this meal called breakfast and a proper breakfast was a big breakfast. No one I knew liked eating so much food so early in the day; it made us feel sleepy, tired. But this breakfast business was Made in England like almost everything else that surrounded us, the exceptions being the sea, the sky, and the air we breathed.

At the time I saw this map—seeing England for the first time—I did not say to myself, "Ah, so that's what it looks like," because there was no longing in me to put a shape to those three words that ran through every part of my life, no matter how small; for me to have had such a longing would have meant that I lived in a certain atmosphere, an atmosphere in which those three words were felt as a burden. But I did not live in such an atmosphere. My father's brown felt hat would develop a hole in its crown, the lining would separate from the hat itself, and six weeks before he thought that he could not be seen wearing it—he was a very vain man—he would order another hat from England. And my mother taught me to eat my food in the English way: the knife in the right hand, the fork in the left, my elbows held still close to my side, the food carefully balanced on my fork and then brought up to my mouth. When I had finally mastered it, I overheard her saying to a friend, "Did you see how nicely she can eat?" But I knew then that I enjoyed my food more when I ate it with my bare hands, and I continued to do so when she wasn't looking. And when my teacher showed us the map, she asked us to study it carefully, because no test we would ever take would be complete without this statement: "Draw a map of England."

4      I did not know then that the statement "Draw a map of England" was something far worse than a declaration of war, for in fact a flat-out declaration of war would have put me on alert, and again in fact, there was no need for war—I had long ago been conquered. I did not know then that this statement was part of a process that would result in my erasure, not my physical erasure, but my erasure all the same. I did not know then that this statement was meant to make me feel in awe and small whenever I heard the word "England": awe at its existence, small because I was not from it. I did not know very much of anything then—certainly not what a blessing it was that I was unable to draw a map of England correctly.

5      After that there were many times of seeing England for the first time. I saw England in history. I knew the names of all the kings of England. I knew the names of their children, their wives, their disappointments, their triumphs, the names of people who betrayed them; I knew the dates on which they were born and the dates they died. I knew their conquests and was made to feel glad if I figured in them; I knew their defeats. I knew the details of the year 1066 (the Battle of Hastings, the end of the reign of the Anglo-Saxon kings) before I knew the details of the year 1832 (the year slavery was abolished). It wasn't as bad as I make it sound now; it was worse. I did like so much hearing again and again how Alfred the Great, traveling in disguise, had been left to watch cakes, and because he wasn't used to this the cakes got burned, and Alfred burned his hands pulling them out of the fire, and the woman who had left him to watch the cakes screamed at him. I loved King Alfred. My grandfather was named after him; his son, my uncle, was named after King Alfred; my brother is named after King Alfred. And so there are three people in my family named after a man they have never met, a man who died over ten centuries ago. The first view I got of England then was not unlike the first view received by the person who named my grandfather.

6      This view, though—the naming of the kings, their deeds, their disappointments—was the vivid view, the forceful view. There were other views, subtler ones, softer, almost not there—but these were the ones that made the most lasting impression on me, these were the ones that made me really feel like nothing. "When morning touched the sky" was

one phrase, for no morning touched the sky where I lived. The mornings where I lived came on abruptly, with a shock of heat and loud noises. "Evening approaches" was another, but the evenings where I lived did not approach; in fact, I had no evening—I had night and I had day and they came and went in a mechanical way: on, off; on, off. And then there were gentle mountains and low blue skies and moors over which people took walks for nothing but pleasure, when where I lived a walk was an act of labor, a burden, something only death or the automobile could relieve. And there were things that a small turn of a head could convey— entire worlds, whole lives would depend on this thing, a certain turn of a head. Everyday life could be quite tiring, more tiring than anything I was told not to do. I was told not to gossip, but they did that all the time. And they ate so much food, violating another of those rules they taught me: do not indulge in gluttony. And the foods they ate actually: it only sometime I could eat cold cuts after theater, cold cuts of lamb and mint sauce, and Yorkshire pudding and scones, and clotted cream, and sausages that came from up-country (imagine, "up-country"). And having troubling thoughts at twilight, a good time to have troubling thoughts, apparently; and servants who stole and left in the middle of a crisis, who were born with a limp or some other kind of deformity, not nourished properly in their mother's womb (that last part I figured out for myself; the point was, oh to have an untrustworthy servant); and wonderful cobbled streets onto which solid front doors opened; and people whose eyes were blue and who had fair skins and who smelled only of lavender, or sometimes sweet pea or primrose. And those flowers with those names: delphiniums, foxgloves, tulips, daffodils, floribunda, peonies; in bloom, a striking display, being cut and placed in large glass bowls, crystal, decorating rooms so large twenty families the size of mine could fit in comfortably but used only for passing through. And the weather was so remarkable because the rain fell gently always, only occasionally in deep gusts, and it colored the air various shades of gray, each an appealing shade for a dress to be worn when a portrait was being painted; and when it rained at twilight, wonderful things happened: people bumped into each other unexpectedly and that would lead to all sorts of turns of events—a plot, the mere weather caused plots. I saw that people rushed: they rushed to catch trains, they rushed toward each other and away from each other; they rushed and rushed and rushed. That word: rushed! I did not know what it was to do that. It was too hot to do that, and so I came to envy people who would rush, even though it had no meaning to me to do such a thing. But there they are again. They loved their children; their children were sent to their own rooms as a punishment, rooms larger than my entire house. They were special, everything about them said so, even their clothes; their clothes rustled, swished, soothed. The world was theirs, not mine; everything told me so.

If now as I speak of all this I give the impression of someone on the outside looking in, nose pressed up against a glass window, that is wrong. 7

My nose was pressed up against a glass window all right, but there was an iron vise at the back of my neck forcing my head to stay in place. To avert my gaze was to fall back into something from which I had been rescued, a hole filled with nothing, and that was the word for everything about me, nothing. The reality of my life was conquests, subjugation, humiliation, enforced amnesia. I was forced to forget. Just for instance, this: I lived in a part of St. John's, Antigua, called Ovals. Ovals was made up of five streets, each of them named after a famous English seaman—to be quite frank, an officially sanctioned criminal: Rodney Street (after George Rodney), Nelson Street (after Horatio Nelson), Drake Street (after Francis Drake), Hood Street, and Hawkins Street (after John Hawkins). But John Hawkins was knighted after a trip he made to Africa, opening up a new trade, the slave trade. He was then entitled to wear as his crest a Negro bound with a cord. Every single person living on Hawkins Street was descended from a slave. John Hawkins's ship, the one in which he transported the people he had bought and kidnapped, was called *The Jesus.* He later became the treasurer of the Royal Navy and rear admiral.

8      Again, the reality of my life, the life I led at the time I was being shown these views of England for the first time, for the second time, for the one-hundred-millionth time, was this: the sun shone with what sometimes seemed to be a deliberate cruelty; we must have done something to deserve that. My dresses did not rustle in the evening air as I strolled to the theater (I had no evening, I had no theater; my dresses were made of a cheap cotton, the weave of which would give way after not too many washings). I got up in the morning, I did my chores (fetched water from the public pipe for my mother, swept the yard), I washed myself, I went to a woman to have my hair combed freshly every day (because before we were allowed into our classroom our teachers would inspect us, and children who had not bathed that day, or had dirt under their fingernails, or whose hair had not been combed anew that day, might not be allowed to attend class). I ate that breakfast. I walked to school. At school we gathered in an auditorium and sang a hymn, "All Things Bright and Beautiful," and looking down on us as we sang were portraits of the Queen of England and her husband; they wore jewels and medals and they smiled. I was a Brownie. At each meeting we would form a little group around a flagpole, and after raising the Union Jack, we would say, "I promise to do my best, to do my duty to God and the Queen, to help other people every day and obey the scouts' law."

9      Who were these people and why had I never seen them, I mean really seen them, in the place where they lived? I had never been to England. No one I knew had ever been to England, or I should say, no one I knew had ever been and returned to tell me about it. All the people I knew who had gone to England had stayed there. Sometimes they left behind them their small children, never to see them again. England! I had seen England's representatives. I had seen the governor general at the public grounds at a ceremony celebrating the Queen's birthday. I had

seen an old princess and I had seen a young princess. They had both been extremely not beautiful, but who of us would have told them that? I had never seen England, really seen it, I had only met a representative, seen a picture, read books, memorized its history. I had never set foot, my own foot, in it.

The space between the idea of something and its reality is always wide and deep and dark. The longer they are kept apart—idea of thing, reality of thing—the wider the width, the deeper the depth, the thicker and darker the darkness. This space starts out empty, there is nothing in it, but it rapidly becomes filled up with obsession or desire or hatred or love—sometimes all of these things, sometimes some of these things, sometimes only one of these things. The existence of the world as I came to know it was a result of this idea of thing over here, reality of thing way, way over there. There was Christopher Columbus, an unlikable man, an unpleasant man, a liar (and so, of course, a thief) surrounded by maps and schemes and plans, and there was the reality on the other side of that width, that depth, that darkness. He became obsessed, he became filled with desire, the hatred came later, love was never a part of it. Eventually, his idea met the longed-for reality. That the idea of something and its reality are often two completely different things is something no one ever remembers; and so when they meet and find that they are not compatible, the weaker of the two, idea or reality, dies. That idea Christopher Columbus had was more powerful than the reality he met, and so the reality he met died. 10

And so finally, when I was a grown-up woman, the mother of two children, the wife of someone, a person who resides in a powerful country that takes up more than its fair share of a continent, the owner of a house with many rooms in it and of two automobiles, with the desire and will (which I very much act upon) to take from the world more than I give back to it, more than I deserve, more than I need, finally then, I saw England, the real England, not a picture, not a painting, not through a story in a book, but England, for the first time. In me, the space between the idea of it and its reality had become filled with hatred, and so when at last I saw it I wanted to take it into my hands and tear it into little pieces and then crumble it up as if it were clay, child's clay. That was impossible, and so I could only indulge in not-favorable opinions. 11

There were monuments everywhere; they commemorated victories, battles fought between them and the people who lived across the sea from them, all vile people, fought over which of them would have dominion over the people who looked like me. The monuments were useless to them now, people sat on them and ate their lunch. They were like markers on an old useless trail, like a piece of old string tied to a finger to jog the memory, like old decoration in an old house, dirty, useless, in the way. Their skins were so pale, it made them look so fragile, so weak, so ugly. What if I had the power to simply banish them from their land, 12 send boat after boatload of them on a voyage that in fact had no destination, force them to live in a place where the sun's presence was a constant? This would rid them of their pale complexion and make them look more like me, make them look more like the people I love and treasure and hold dear, and more like the people who occupy the near and far reaches of my imagination, my history, my geography, and reduce them and everything they have ever known to figurines as evidence that I was in divine favor, what if all this was in my power? Could I resist it? No one ever has.

13      And they were rude, they were rude to each other. They didn't like each other very much. They didn't like each other in the way they didn't like me, and it occurred to me that their dislike for me was one of the few things they agreed on.

14      I was on a train in England with a friend, an English woman. Before we were in England she liked me very much. In England she didn't like me at all. She didn't like the claim I said I had on England, she didn't like the views I had of England. I didn't like England, she didn't like England, but she didn't like me not liking it too. She said, "I want to show you my England, I want to show you the England that I know and love." I had told her many times before that I knew England and I didn't want to love it anyway. She no longer lived in England; it was her own country, but it had not been kind to her, so she left. On the train, the conductor was rude to her; she asked something, and he responded in a rude way. She became ashamed. She was ashamed at the way he treated her; she was ashamed at the way he behaved. "This is the new England," she said. But I liked the conductor being rude; his behavior seemed quite appropriate. Earlier this had happened: we had gone to a store to buy a shirt for my husband; it was meant to be a special present, a special shirt to wear on special occasions. This was a store where the Prince of Wales has his shirts made, but the shirts sold in this store are beautiful all the same. I found a shirt I thought my husband would like and I wanted to buy him a tie to go with it. When I couldn't decide which one to choose, the salesman showed me a new set. He was very pleased with these, he said, because they bore the crest of the Prince of Wales, and the Prince of Wales had never allowed his crest to decorate an article of clothing before. There was something in the way he said it; his tone was slavish, reverential, awed. It made me feel angry; I wanted to hit him. I didn't do that. I said, my husband and I hate princes, my husband would never wear anything that had a prince's anything on it. My friend stiffened. The salesman stiffened. They both drew themselves in, away from me. My friend told me that the prince was a symbol of her Englishness, and I could see that I had caused offense. I looked at her. She was an English person, the sort of English person I used to know at home, the sort who was nobody in England but somebody when they came to live among the people like me. There were many people I could have seen England with; that I was

seeing it with this particular person, a person who reminded me of the people who showed me England long ago as I sat in church or at my desk, made me feel silent and afraid, for I wondered if, all these years of our friendship, I had had a friend or had been in the thrall of a racial memory.

I went to Bath—we, my friend and I, did this, but though we were     15
together, I was no longer with her. The landscape was almost as familiar as my own hand, but I had never been in this place before, so how could that be again? And the streets of Bath were familiar, too, but I had never walked on them before. It was all those years of reading, starting with Roman Britain. Why did I have to know about Roman Britain? It was of no real use to me, a person living on a hot, drought-ridden island, and it is of no use to me now, and yet my head is filled with this nonsense, Roman Britain. In Bath, I drank tea in a room I had read about in a novel written in the eighteenth century. In this very same room, young women wearing those dresses that rustled and so on danced and flirted and some-times disgraced themselves with young men, soldiers, sailors, who were on their way to Bristol or someplace like that, so many places like that where so many adventures, the outcome of which was not good for me, began. Bristol, England. A sentence that began "That night the ship sailed from Bristol, England" would end not so good for me. And then I was driving through the countryside in an English motorcar, on narrow winding roads, and they were so familiar, though I had never been on them before; and through little villages the names of which I somehow knew so well though I had never been there before. And the countryside did have all those hedges and hedges, fields hedged in. I was marveling at all the toil of it, the planting of the hedges to begin with and then the care of it, all that clipping, year after year of clipping, and I wondered at the lives of the people who would have to do this, because wherever I see and feel the hands that hold up the world, I see and feel myself and all the people who look like me. And I said, "Those hedges" and my friend said that someone, a woman named Mrs. Rothchild, worried that the hedges weren't being taken care of properly; the farmers couldn't afford or find the help to keep up the hedges, and often they replaced them with wire fencing. I might have said to that, well if Mrs. Rothchild doesn't like the wire fencing, why doesn't she take care of the hedges herself, but I didn't. And then in those fields that were now hemmed in by wire fenc-ing that a privileged woman didn't like was planted a vile yellow flower-ing bush that produced an oil, and my friend said that Mrs. Rothchild didn't like this either; it ruined the English countryside, it ruined the tra-ditional look of the English countryside.

It was not at that moment that I wished every sentence, everything     16
I knew, that began with England would end with "and then it all died; we don't know how, it just all died." At that moment, I was thinking, who are these people who forced me to think of them all the time, who forced me to think that the world I knew was incomplete, or without

substance, or did not measure up because it was not England; that I was incomplete, or without substance, and did not measure up because I was not English. Who were these people? The person sitting next to me couldn't give me a clue; no one person could. In any case, if I had said to her, I find England ugly, I hate England; the weather is like a jail sentence, the English are a very ugly people, the food in England is like a jail sentence, the hair of English people is so straight, so dead looking, the English have an unbearable smell so different from the smell of people I know, real people of course, she would have said that I was a person full of prejudice. Apart from the fact that it is I—that is, the people who look like me—who made her aware of the unpleasantness of such a thing, the idea of such a thing, prejudice, she would have been only partly right, sort of right: I may be capable of prejudice, but my prejudices have no weight to them, my prejudices have no force behind them, my prejudices remain opinions, my prejudices remain my personal opinion. And a great feeling of rage and disappointment came over me as I looked at England, my head full of personal opinions that could not have public, my public, approval. The people I come from are powerless to do evil on grand scale.

17    The moment I wished every sentence, everything I knew, that began with England would end with "and then it all died, we don't know how, it just all died" was when I saw the white cliffs of Dover. I had sung hymns and recited poems that were about a longing to see the white cliffs of Dover again. At the time I sang the hymns and recited the poems, I could not really long to see them again because I had never seen them at all, nor had anyone around me at the time. But there we were, groups of people longing for something we had never seen. And so there they were, the white cliffs, but they were not that pearly majestic thing I used to sing about, that thing that created such a feeling in these people that when they died in the place where I lived they had themselves buried facing a direction that would allow them to see the white cliffs of Dover when they were resurrected, as surely they would be. The white cliffs of Dover, when finally I saw them, were cliffs, but they were not white; you would only call them that if the word "white" meant something special to you; they were dirty and they were steep; they were so steep, the correct height from which all my views of England, starting with the map before me in my classroom and ending with the trip I had just taken, should jump and die and disappear forever.

## CONSIDERATIONS

1. Despite a conventional rule against such usage, a half dozen or more of the sentences of paragraph 6 begin with "And." Why does Kincaid insist on ignoring that rule? What do you think she accomplishes by doing so?

2. Reread Kincaid's essay as a lesson in indoctrination, and explain how and why the indoctrination was carried out. Who was being indoctrinated and who (or what) was doing the indoctrinating? What were the results?

3. "The space between the idea of something and its reality is always wide and deep and dark," writes Kincaid in paragraph 10. Read Langston Hughes's "Salvation" (page 321), and discuss what he learned about idea versus reality, comparing it with Kincaid's experience. If you have had a similar awakening to the "wide and deep and dark" differences, make use of that in your essay.

4. Paragraph 2 is largely a mass of tiny detail—half a grapefruit, an egg, bread and butter, for instance. Why should the reader care what that little girl had for breakfast? Why did she, as an adult, care about that menu?

5. What does Kincaid refer to when she writes "those three words that ran through every part of my life"? Why might they have served as a title for her essay?

6. How does Kincaid make use of that famous tourist attraction, the white cliffs of Dover, in her closing paragraph? What could serve as a comparable topographical landmark for your country?

*Barbara Kingsolver (b. 1955) grew up in rural Kentucky and did her undergraduate work in Indiana and her graduate study of ecology in Arizona. She began publishing as a science writer for magazines and newspapers, and married a chemist. While she was pregnant, she was troubled by insomnia and during sleepless nights began her first novel,* The Bean Trees *(1988).*

*"The Forest in the Seeds" comes from her essay collection* High Tide in Tucson *(1995), an example of her closely observed writing about the natural world, as well as her meditation on another great observer, Henry David Thoreau (see pages 595–618).*

— 55 —————————————————————

# BARBARA KINGSOLVER
## *The Forest in the Seeds*

1    In the springtime of my twenty-fifth year, and my first as a graduate student in ecology, I was seriously introduced to biological field research. The project to which I was assigned involved sitting in a mesquite thicket in the southern Arizona sun, watching a species of territorial lizard do, quite frankly, almost nothing. For hours and hours, day after day. It was stultifying. When I'd signed on as a rookie animal behaviorist, I suppose I was thinking of Konrad Lorenz's curiously malimprinted geese, who thought he was Mama Goose and followed him around; or of legendary Iwo, the genius macaque, who invented grain winnowing and introduced it to her tribe. Visions of sandhill cranes danced in my head. And here I had washed up instead in the land of torpid lizards. I could only be grateful that my subjects at least had *heartbeats*, and pity my botanically inclined colleagues who were counting pollen grains under a microscope, or literally watching the grass grow.

2    Nature does not move in mysterious ways, really. She just moves so slowly we're inclined to lose patience and stop watching before she gets around to the revelations. The natural historians of the nineteenth century knew this, or at any rate they had no reason to expect bells and whistles, and they had the luxury of writing for an audience with an at-

tention span. Charles Darwin charmingly suggests as much in his introduction to *On the Origin of Species:* "It occurred to me, in 1837, that something might perhaps be made out of this question [of the origin of species] by patiently accumulating and reflecting on all sorts of facts which could possibly have any bearing on it." Twenty-two years later he'd reflected on everything from slave-making ants to the Greenland whale and set it all down on paper, and for any reader willing to spend a portion of a lifetime with it, it remains a thorough masterpiece.

Henry David Thoreau, Darwin's contemporary, shared the penchant for accumulation and reflection, and while he did not shake the scientific paradigm so profoundly, he brought to his work an expansive poetic sensibility. Like other modern fans of his who had long since finished all the Thoreau in print, I rejoiced when Bradley P. Dean compiled from the massive notebooks of Thoreau's last two years a collection of previously unpublished writings, *Faith in a Seed.* The book contains fragmentary treatises on wild fruits, weeds and grasses, and the succession of forest trees. But the centerpiece is Thoreau's last important manuscript, *The Dispersion of Seeds,* in which he meticulously noted methods of seed ripening and dispersal, germination, and growth of a great many species: pines, willows, cherries, milkweeds, eight kinds of tick clover, and virtually every other plant known to the neighborhood of Concord, Massachusetts. With a categorical thoroughness akin to Darwin's, Thoreau intended to prove his conviction—which was still in dispute at the time—that new plants do not spontaneously generate but, rather, grow always and only from seeds.

It's hard to imagine grown men of science being uncertain of a thing that our first-graders now might snub as a science-fair project. ("A bean in a Dixie cup? That's *kid stuff,*" mine once hooted.) So the energy Thoreau brings to this argument may seem quaint for its obsolescence. But there is something wonderful to be gained from a two-hundred-page walk through the woods with a scientist from a century and a quarter ago. Thoreau had just read *On the Origin of Species,* and was clearly moving away from the travelogue format of his "excursion" writings, toward an articulation of unifying principles; he was attempting to see the forest among his trees. In his observations of plant communities he touched on succession, allelopathy, and other concepts that would not have names until the birth of the science of ecology in the next century.

His gifts as a writer, though, transcended his contributions to natural science. Thoreau dismissed the notion that poetry and science are incompatible, and captured for his readers the simple wonder we hastily leave behind in the age of reason. "How impatient, how rampant, how precocious these osiers," he wrote of the willows along his pond. "Some derive their Latin name *Salix* from *salire,* 'to leap,' they spring up so rapidly—they are so salient. They have hardly made two shoots from the sand in as many springs, when silvery catkins burst out along them, and anon golden blossoms and downy seeds, spreading their race with incredible rapidity."

6    He admired the trees for their ingenuity, and praised the wind that catches their seeds for its unfailing providence. He carefully watched the ways and means of the seed-scattering creatures: squirrels, foxes, birds (including, nostalgically, the now extinct ivory-billed woodpecker), a wading moose or cow, or "a wading pickerel fisher of the old school, who does not mind if his clothes be wet," and even little boys who blow the seeds off dandelion heads to find out whether their mothers want them. ("If they blow off all the seeds at one puff, which they rarely do, then they are not wanted.")

7    As I made my leisurely way through Thoreau's final book I found myself turning down the corner of nearly every other page to note an arresting moment of prose; eventually I realized I was admiring not specific bits of information but the man himself. As a Transcendentalist, Thoreau understood that the scientist and the science are inseparable, and he insinuated himself into his observations in a way that modern science writers, we virtuosos of the passive voice, have been trained carefully to forsake.

8    "I went forth on the afternoon of October 17th," one section begins, "expressly to ascertain how chestnuts are propagated." American chestnuts are now as dead as the ivory-billed woodpeckers, but still a reader can watch this bearded, wide-eyed man—who would within two years of that journal entry be dead himself—inhaling an autumn day and focusing his powers not only on the chestnuts but also on his own heart and the folkloric tenor of his village. "A squirrel goes a-chestnutting perhaps as far as the boys do, and when he gets there he does not have to shake or club the tree, or wait for frost to open the burrs, but he walks up to the burrs and cuts them off and strews the ground with them before they have opened. . . . The jays scream and the red squirrels scold while you are clubbing and shaking the chestnut trees, for they are there on the same errand, and two of a trade never agree."

9    Another passage exclaims, "Consider what a vast work these forest planters are doing! So far as our noblest hardwood forests are concerned, the animals, especially squirrels and jays, are our greatest and almost only benefactors.

10    "But what is the character of our gratitude to these squirrels? . . . Are they on our pension list? Have we in any way recognized their services? . . . We should be more civilized as well as humane if we recognized once a year by some symbolical ceremony the part which the squirrel plays in the economy of Nature."

11    *Faith in a Seed* is infused with Thoreau's delight, his meticulous curiosity and his inspiring patience. Across the silence of 125 years, during which an unforeseeable glut of hurry has descended, he exhorts us to slow down and take notice, to learn how to watch seeds become trees. This is the kind of book that should be forced on students, probably

against their will. When I recall my lizard-watching days I can sympathize with their restlessness, but I also long for all of us to rescue ourselves from the tyranny of impatience. Like cartoon characters, we seem to be running full tilt through the air beyond the edge of the cliff with our minds on something else. In *Earth in the Balance,* Al Gore poignantly discusses this detached relationship between humans and our earth. He reports that in a 1991 poll that asked the American people for their views about the role we should play in the world, an incredible 93 percent supported a proposal for "the U.S. using its position to get other countries to join together to take action against world environmental problems." And yet at the same time, he writes, "Almost every poll shows Americans decisively rejecting higher taxes on fossil fuels, even though that proposal is one of the logical first steps in changing our policies in a manner consistent with a more responsible approach to the environment." Is it possible we just couldn't sit still long enough to make the connection?

Recently, as I gave a lecture to a college class on writing and environmental activism, a student asked me, "Why can't we just teach people about this stuff in TV commercials?" The question was both naïve and astute. As a nation we will never defer to the endangered spotted owl (let alone declare a National Squirrel Holiday, as Thoreau suggested) until we are much more widely educated. But the things we will have to know—concepts of food chain, habitat, selection pressure and adaptation, and the ways all species depend on others—are complex ideas that just won't fit into a thirty-second spot. Evolution can't be explained in a sound bite.

Even well-intentioned educational endeavors like carefully edited nature films, and the easy access to exotic animals offered by zoos, are tailored to our impatience. They lead us to expect nature will be all storm and no lull. It's a dangerous habit. Natural-history writer Robert Michael Pyle asks: "If we can watch rhinos mating in our living rooms, who's going to notice the wren in the back yard?"

The real Wild Kingdom is as small and brown as a wren, as tedious as a squirrel turning back the scales of a pine cone to capture its seeds, as quiet as a milkweed seed on the wind—the long, slow stillness between takes. This, I think, is the message in the bottle from Thoreau, the man who noticed a clump of seeds caught in the end of a cow's whisking tail and wondered enviously what finds were presenting themselves to the laborers picking wool in nearby factories. "I do not see," he wrote, "but the seeds which are ripened in New England may plant themselves in Pennsylvania. At any rate, I am interested in the fate or success of every such venture which the autumn sends forth."

What a life it must have been, to seize time for this much wonder. If only we could recover faith in a seed—and in all the other complicated marvels that can't fit in a sound bite. Then we humans might truly know the glory of knowing our place.

## CONSIDERATIONS

1. Do you care about the dispersion of seeds? Explain your answer and connect it to Kingsolver's essay. What do you think of Thoreau's suggestion of an annual ceremony to recognize the part that the squirrel plays in the economy of nature?

2. According to Kingsolver, what advantage did nineteenth-century naturalists have over our contemporaries? Explain how this fits into an important idea she expresses about the nature of nature.

3. Find an example, in paragraph 4, of Kingsolver's ability to breathe new life into what most of us would call a cliché. Why are writers advised to avoid clichés? Have a contest with a friend: see who can compile the longest list of clichés in five minutes.

4. In more than one passage, Kingsolver points out Thoreau's refusal to separate poetry and science. What do you know of the so-called war between the sciences and the humanities, still being waged on many college campuses? How might Kingsolver's essay contribute to your understanding of that conflict?

5. "This is the kind of book that should be forced on students, probably against their will," writes Kingsolver of Thoreau's *Faith in a Seed*. Whether she is serious or not, her remark should provoke some sort of response from anyone who calls himself or herself a student. What kind of book do you think should be forced on a student? Any kind? Why or why not?

6. In paragraph 12, the author describes a student's question as "both naïve and astute." She explains why she calls the question naïve, but what was astute about it?

*Maxine Hong Kingston (b. 1940) was born in California to parents who had emigrated from China. Her father came to the United States in 1924, and her mother followed in 1939. She attended the University of California at Berkeley, married, had a son, and moved to Hawaii. Her first book,* Woman Warrior: Memoirs of a Girlhood among Ghosts, *appeared in 1976 and won the National Book Critics Circle Award.*

*Kingston writes with elegance about growing up in two languages. Notice how silence is a reality—and also a metaphor.*

— 56 ——————————————————————————

# MAXINE HONG KINGSTON
## *Silence*

——————————————————————————

When I went to kindergarten and had to speak English for the first 1
time, I became silent. A dumbness—a shame—still cracks my voice in two, even when I want to say "hello" casually, or ask an easy question in front of the check-out counter, or ask directions of a bus driver. I stand frozen, or I hold up the line with the complete, grammatical sentence that comes squeaking out at impossible length. "What did you say?" says the cab driver, or "Speak up," so I have to perform again, only weaker the second time. A telephone call makes my throat bleed and takes up that day's courage. It spoils my day with self-disgust when I hear my broken voice come skittering out into the open. It makes people wince to hear it. I'm getting better, though. Recently I asked the postman for special-issue stamps; I've waited since childhood for postmen to give me some of their own accord. I am making progress, a little every day.

My silence was thickest—total—during the three years that I cov- 2
ered my school paintings with black paint. I painted layers of black over houses and flowers and suns, and when I drew on the blackboard, I put a layer of chalk on top. I was making a stage curtain, and it was the moment before the curtain parted or rose. The teachers called my parents to school, and I saw they had been saving my pictures, curling and cracking,

all alike and black. The teachers pointed to the pictures and looked serious, talked seriously too, but my parents did not understand English. ("The parents and teachers of criminals were executed," said my father.) My parents took the pictures home. I spread them out (so black and full of possibilities) and pretended the curtains were swinging open, flying up, one after another, sunlight underneath, mighty operas.

3      During the first silent year I spoke to no one at school, did not ask before going to the lavatory, and flunked kindergarten. My sister also said nothing for three years, silent in the playground and silent at lunch. There were other quiet Chinese girls not of our family, but most of them got over it sooner than we did. I enjoyed the silence. At first it did not occur to me I was supposed to talk or to pass kindergarten. I talked at home and to one or two of the Chinese kids in class. I made motions and even made some jokes. I drank out of a toy saucer when the water spilled out of the cup, and everybody laughed, pointing at me, so I did it some more. I didn't know that Americans don't drink out of saucers.

4      I liked the Negro students (Black Ghosts) best because they laughed the loudest and talked to me as if I were a daring talker too. One of the Negro girls had her mother coil braids over her ears Shanghai-style like mine; we were Shanghai twins except that she was covered with black like my paintings. Two Negro kids enrolled in Chinese school, and the teachers gave them Chinese names. Some Negro kids walked me to school and home, protecting me from the Japanese kids, who hit me and chased me and stuck gum in my ears. The Japanese kids were noisy and tough. They appeared one day in kindergarten, released from concentration camp, which was a tic-tac-toe mark, like barbed wire, on the map.

5      It was when I found out I had to talk that school become a misery, that the silence became a misery. I did not speak and felt bad each time that I did not speak. I read aloud in first grade, though, and heard the barest whisper with little squeaks come out of my throat. "Louder," said the teacher, who scared the voice away again. The other Chinese girls did not talk either, so I knew the silence had to do with being a Chinese girl.

6      Reading out loud was easier than speaking because we did not have to make up what to say, but I stopped often, and the teacher would think I'd gone quiet again. I could not understand "I." The Chinese "I" has seven strokes, intricacies. How could the American "I," assuredly wearing a hat like the Chinese, have only three strokes, the middle so straight? Was it out of politeness that this writer left off the strokes the way a Chinese has to write her own name small and crooked? No, it was not politeness; "I" is a capital and "you" is lower-case. I stared at that middle line and waited so long for its black center to resolve into tight strokes and dots that I forgot to pronounce it. The other troublesome word was "here," no strong consonant to hang on to, and so flat, when "here" is two mountainous ideographs. The teacher, who had already told me every day how to read "I" and "here," put me in the low corner under the stairs again, where the noisy boys usually sat.

When my second grade class did a play, the whole class went to the     7
auditorium except the Chinese girls. The teacher, lovely and Hawaiian,
should have understood about us, but instead left us behind in the classroom. Our voices were too soft or nonexistent, and our parents never
signed the permission slips anyway. They never signed anything unnecessary. We opened the door a crack and peeked out, but closed it again
quickly. One of us (not me) won every spelling bee, though.

I remember telling the Hawaiian teacher, "We Chinese can't sing     8
'land where our fathers died.'" She argued with me about politics, while I
meant because of curses. But how can I have that memory when I couldn't
talk? My mother says that we, like the ghosts, have no memories.

After American school, we picked up our cigar boxes, in which we     9
had arranged books, brushes, and an inkbox neatly, and went to Chinese
school, from 5:00 to 7:30 P.M. There we chanted together, voices rising
and falling, loud and soft, some boys shouting, everybody reading together, reciting together and not alone with one voice. When we had a
memorization test, the teacher let each of us come to his desk and say
the lesson to him privately, while the rest of the class practiced copying
or tracing. Most of the teachers were men. The boys who were so well
behaved in the American school played tricks on them and talked back
to them. The girls were not mute. They screamed and yelled during recess, when there were no rules; they had fistfights. Nobody was afraid of
children hurting themselves or of children hurting school property. The
glass doors to the red and green balconies with the gold joy symbols were
left wide open so that we could run out and climb the fire escapes. We
played capture-the-flag in the auditorium, where Sun Yat-sen and Chiang
Kai-shek's pictures hung at the back of the stage, the Chinese flag on
their left and the American flag on their right. We climbed the teak ceremonial chairs and made flying leaps off the stage. One flag headquarters
was behind the glass door and the other on stage right. Our feet
drummed on the hollow stage. During recess the teachers locked themselves up in their office with the shelves of books, copybooks, inks from
China. They drank tea and warmed their hands at a stove. There was no
play supervision. At recess we had the school to ourselves, and also we
could roam as far as we could go—downtown, Chinatown stores, home—
as long as we returned before the bell rang.

At exactly 7:30 the teacher again picked up the brass bell that sat on     10
his desk and swung it over our heads, while we charged down the stairs,
our cheering magnified in the stairwell. Nobody had to line up.

Not all of the children who were silent at American school found     11
voice at Chinese school. One new teacher said each of us had to get up
and recite in front of the class, who was to listen. My sister and I had
memorized the lesson perfectly. We said it to each other at home, one
chanting, one listening. The teacher called on my sister to recite first. It
was the first time a teacher had called on the second-born to go first. My
sister was scared. She glanced at me and looked away; I looked down at

my desk. I hoped that she could do it because if she could, then I would have to. She opened her mouth and a voice came out that wasn't a whisper, but it wasn't a proper voice either. I hoped that she would not cry, fear breaking up her voice like twigs underfoot. She sounded as if she were trying to sing through weeping and strangling. She did not pause or stop to end the embarrassment. She kept going until she said the last word, and then she sat down. When it was my turn, the same voice came out, a crippled animal running on broken legs. You could hear splinters in my voice, bones rubbing jagged against one another. I was loud, though. I was glad I didn't whisper.

12 How strange that the emigrant villagers are shouters, hollering face to face. My father asks, "Why is it I can hear Chinese from blocks away? Is it that I understand the language? Or is it they talk loud?" They turn the radio up full blast to hear the operas, which do not seem to hurt their ears. And they yell over the singers that wail over the drums, everybody talking at once, big arm gestures, spit flying. You can see the disgust on American faces looking at women like that. It isn't just the loudness. It is the way Chinese sounds, ching-chong ugly, to American ears, not beautiful like Japanese sayonara words with the consonants and vowels as regular as Italian. We make guttural peasant noise and have Ton Duc Thang names you can't remember. And the Chinese can't hear Americans at all; the language is too soft and western music unhearable. I've watched a Chinese audience laugh, visit, talk-story, and holler during a piano recital, as if the musician could not hear them. A Chinese-American, somebody's son, was playing Chopin, which has no punctuation, no cymbals, no gongs. Chinese piano music is five black keys. Normal Chinese women's voices are strong and bossy. We American-Chinese girls had to whisper to make ourselves American-feminine. Apparently we whispered even more softly than the Americans. Once a year the teachers referred my sister and me to speech therapy, but our voices would straighten out, unpredictably normal, for the therapists. Some of us gave up, shook our heads, and said nothing, not one word. Some of us could not even shake our heads. At times shaking my head no is more self-assertion than I can manage. Most of us eventually found some voice, however faltering. We invented an American-feminine speaking personality.

## CONSIDERATIONS

1. If you didn't know when Maxine Hong Kingston was born, how could you tell when she had the experiences she reports in first grade?

2. Some of the young girl's problems were caused by grown-ups misinterpreting her actions. Find a couple of such instances, and use them in an essay about being misinterpreted yourself as a child.

3. Write a short essay comparing and contrasting the two schools the author attended as a child. Conclude your paper with a paragraph in which you explain why you would choose one over the other.

4. Kingston may have had her troubles with English as a child, but "Silence" demonstrates her mastery of the language as an adult. Look through the essay, noting, for example, how she makes the written language meet the difficult challenge of describing sounds, especially those of the human voice. Read these passages aloud; then try your own hand at writing the sound of some voice you know well.

5. Is Kingston's "Silence" the same thing that Kenneth Maue writes about in "Quiet Is Freedom" (page 419)? Explain.

*Yusef Komunyakaa (b. 1947) comes from Bogalusa, Louisiana, and teaches creative writing and Afro-American studies at Indiana University. In 1969 and 1970 he served with the Army in Vietnam. His* Neon Vernacular: New and Selected Poems 1977–1989 *(1994) won the Pulitzer Prize. He published a book of essays in 1999 and* Pleasure Dome: New and Selected Poems 1975–1999 *in 2001. He teaches at Princeton University.*

## — 57

# YUSEF KOMUNYAKAA
## *Facing It*

My black face fades,
hiding inside the black granite.
I said I wouldn't,
dammit: No tears.
5    I'm stone, I'm flesh.
My clouded reflection eyes me
like a bird of prey, the profile of night
slanted against morning. I turn
this way—the stone lets me go.
10   I turn that way—I'm inside
the Vietnam Veterans Memorial
again, depending on the light
to make a difference.
I go down the 58,022 names,
15   half-expecting to find
my own in letters like smoke.
I touch the name Andrew Johnson;
I see the booby trap's white flash.
Names shimmer on a woman's blouse
20   but when she walks away
the names stay on the wall.
Brushstrokes flash, a red bird's
wings cutting across my stare.

The sky. A plane in the sky.
A white vet's image floats 25
closer to me, then his pale eyes
look through mine. I'm a window.
He's lost his right arm
inside the stone. In the black mirror
a woman's trying to erase names: 30
No, she's brushing a boy's hair.

*Phillip Lopate (b. 1943) writes poems and nonfiction: this essay comes from* **Against Joie de Vivre** *(1989). He has received fellowships from the Guggenheim Foundation and the National Endowment for the Arts, and his work has appeared in* **Best American Essays.** *He teaches at the University of Houston and Columbia University. In 1994 he edited* **The Art of the Personal Essay.** *He also edited* **Writing New York** *for the Library of America.*

*This man who writes about the personal essay, furnishing us a brief example, constructs his anecdote with the care of a craftsman for whom every transition must be exact and invisible. Note how Lopate moves from paragraph to paragraph, without signaling how he moves.*

## — 58 —————————————————————

# PHILLIP LOPATE
## *On Shaving a Beard*

1    I have just made a change that feels as dramatic, for the moment, as switching from Democrat to Republican. I have shaved off my beard. Actually I clipped it away with scissors first, then I went in for the kill with a safety razor. The first snip is the most tentative: you can still allow yourself the fantasy that you are only shaping and trimming, perhaps a raffish Vandyke will emerge. Then comes the moment when you make a serious gash in the carpet. You rub the neighboring whiskers over the patch to see if it can still be covered, but the die is cast, and with a certain glee the energy turns demolitionary.

2    As I cut away the clumps of darkness, a moon rises out of my face. It lights up the old canyon line of the jawbone. I am getting my face back. I lather up again and again and shave away the bristles until the skin is smooth as a newborn's—the red irritation spots where the skin has reacted to the unaccustomed blade seem a sort of diaper rash. When I am done, I look in the glass and my face itself is like a mirror, so polished and empty are the cheeks. I feel a little sorry for the tender boy-man re-

flected before me, his helpless features open to assault. The unguarded vacancy of that face! Now I will have to come to terms again with the weak chin, the domineering nose, the thin, sarcastic-pleading lips.

I look down at the reddish-gray curls in the sink. The men in my    3
family have always been proud that our beards grew in red, though the tops of our heads were black. It seems an absurd triviality for Nature to waste a gene on, but it is one of the most tangible ways that my father has felt united to his sons and we to him. A momentary regret passes through me.

Never mind: I have taken an action. I grew the beard originally be-    4
cause I had been restless and dissatisfied with myself; I shaved it for the same reason. How few cut-rate stratagems there are to better our mood; you can take a trip, go shopping, change your hair, see every movie in town—and the list is exhausted. Now I will have to be contented for a while. It is summer, the wrong time to start growing a beard again.

Because of the hot weather, I also have a ready-made excuse for any-    5
one who might ask why I gave up my beard. I know that the real reasons are more murky—they go to the heart of my insecurities as a man and my envy of others of my sex. When I meet a man I admire and he is wearing a beard, I immediately think about emulating him. The tribe of bearded men have a patriarchal firmness, a rabbinical kindly wisdom in their faces. They strike me as good providers. They resemble trees (their beards are nests) or tree cutters. In any case, mentally I place them in the forest, with flannel shirt and axe.

So I join this fraternity, and start to collect the equivalent of approv-    6
ing winks from other beardies, fellow conspirators in the League of Hirsutes. It feels good to be taken for an ancestor or pioneer. Then the novelty begins to wear off, the beard starts to itch, and I realize that inside I am no more rooted or masculinely capable than before. I start to envy clean-shaven men—their frank, open, attractively "vulnerable" faces. Some women will trust you more if you are clean-shaven; they profess to see beards as Mephistophelian masks, hiding the emotions. Early in the relationship, this may be a good reason to keep a beard. At a later point shaving it off becomes tantamount to a giddy declaration of love.

Other women, on the other hand, will tell you that a kiss without fa-    7
cial hair is like a roast beef sandwich without mustard. *They* consider beards a mark of virility, trustworthiness, and bohemian sensitivity. Obviously, the image systems break down in the face of individual tastes. Nevertheless, it is still possible to say that beards connote freedom, telling the boss off, an attitude of "gone fishing"; men often grow them on vacations, or after being booted from the White House staff, like Ehrlichman. (Even Admiral Poindexter grew a mustache.) Clean-shavenness, on the other hand, implies a subscription to the rules of society.

A major division in the bearded kingdom exists between those who    8
revel in no longer having to bother with maintenance, letting Nature have its luxuriant bushy way, and those who continue to keep a razor

nearby, prudently pruning or shaving the cheeks every few days. A well-clipped beard on a kindly man looks as proper as a well-kept lawn on Sunday. On the other hand, there are beards with a glint of cruelty—beards trimmed to Caligulaesque exactitude. I had thought to be one of the pruners, but went too far, lacking the razor-sharp finesse.

9   Having shaved the beard off, I take my first cautious steps into society. I am dreading those who will ask why I did it, then settle back for a long soul-bearing explanation. What will I reply to those who are quick to say, "I liked you better the other way"? My impulse is to step on their toes, but we must not punish honesty. Once, when I was teaching in P.S. 90, I shaved off my beard, and the children, who were familiar with me as a hairy man, were so outraged that all through the first day of the new regime, they ran alongside and punched me. Children are good at expressing a sense of betrayal at change.

10   Those who are bearded for the long haul either tend to view the new me with something like a Mennonite's disapproval at backsliding, or are relieved that one who had appeared a member of the brotherhood was exposed in the nick of time as turncoat. A few friends, who pride themselves on their observational powers, make helpful comments like: You look fatter. You look thinner. You look younger. You look older. The majority say nothing. At first I think they are being polite, not meaning to broach a subject that might make me self-conscious. Then, out of frustration at their not having noticed, I finally call my naked face to their attention. They say: "I *thought* there was something different about you but I couldn't put my finger on it. Besides, you keep going back and forth, Lopate, who can keep up?"

## CONSIDERATIONS

1. In his first sentence, Lopate had to make a choice between "from Democrat to Republican" and "from Republican to Democrat." Did he make the right choice? Explain.

2. Why is Lopate unable to state decisively how a man's beard affects the opposite sex?

3. Lopate's smoothly written essay seems effortless, but a careful reader will find many unusually apt word choices, evidence that the writer did not toss off the piece casually. Note some of those choices and explain why they are real contributions to the essay.

4. In what sense, if any, does Lopate's essay explore deeper territory than the whiskers on his face?

5. There are a few capitalized words and phrases in the essay that you may not recognize: Vandyke, League of Hirsutes, Mephistophelian, Caligulaesque, P.S. 90, and so on. What do you lose if you do not bother to look them up?

6. How might Lopate have made use of Gretel Ehrlich's "About Men" (page 187) as he ponders beard or no beard?

*Barry Lopez (b. 1945) was born in New York State and attended Notre Dame. He has made his living as a writer since the age of twenty-five;* Desert Notes *appeared in 1976 and* Of Wolves and Men *in 1978. The latter book earned Lopez the John Burroughs Medal for distinguished writing about natural history and nomination for an American Book Award. His essays and short stories appear in the best American magazines, where he is a leading defender of the natural world.* Arctic Dreams *came out to critical acclaim in 1985 and* About This Life *in 1998.*

*In an article about Lopez in* Sierra, *"On Sacred Ground," Nicholas O'Connell begins, "Instead of becoming a Trappist monk, writer Barry Lopez made his work a form of prayer." For the spirituality that O'Connell speaks of, look at the meticulous telling of his search.*

## — 59 —

# BARRY LOPEZ
## *The Stone Horse*

I

The deserts of southern California, the high, relatively cooler and wetter Mojave and the hotter, dryer Sonoran to the south of it, carry the signatures of many cultures. Prehistoric rock drawings in the Mojave's Coso Range, probably the greatest concentration of petroglyphs in North America, are at least three thousand years old. Big-game-hunting cultures that flourished six or seven thousand years before that are known from broken spear tips, choppers, and burins left scattered along the shores of great Pleistocene lakes, long since evaporated. Weapons and tools discovered at China Lake may be thirty thousand years old; and worked stone from a quarry in the Calico Mountains is, some argue, evidence that human beings were here more than 200,000 years ago.

Because of the long-term stability of such arid environments, much of this prehistoric stone evidence still lies exposed on the ground, accessible to anyone who passes by—the studious, the acquisitive, the

1

2

———
"The Stone Horse" from *Anataeus,* copyright by Barry Holstun Lopez. Reprinted by permission of Sterling Lord Literistic, Inc.

indifferent, the merely curious. Archaeologists do not agree on the sequence of cultural history beyond about twelve thousand years ago, but it is clear that these broken bits of chalcedony, chert, and obsidian, like the animal drawings and geometric designs etched on walls of basalt throughout the desert, anchor the earliest threads of human history, the first record of human endeavor here.

3      Western man did not enter the California desert until the end of the eighteenth century, 250 years after Coronado brought his soldiers into the Zuni pueblos in a bewildered search for the cities of Cibola. The earliest appraisals of the land were cursory, hurried. People traveled *through* it, en route to Santa Fe or the California coastal settlements. Only miners tarried. In 1823 what had been Spain's became Mexico's, and in 1848 what had been Mexico's became America's; but the bare, jagged mountains and dry lake beds, the vast and uniform plains of creosote bush and yucca plants, remained as obscure as the northern Sudan until the end of the nineteenth century.

4      Before 1940 the tangible evidence of twentieth-century man's passage here consisted of very little—the hard tracery of travel corridors; the widely scattered, relatively insignificant evidence of mining operations; and the fair expanse of irrigated fields at the desert's periphery. In the space of a hundred years or so the wagon roads were paved, railroads were laid down, and canals and high-tension lines were built to bring water and electricity across the desert to Los Angeles from the Colorado River. The dark mouths of gold, talc, and tin mines yawned from the bony flanks of desert ranges. Dust-encrusted chemical plants stood at work on the lonely edges of dry lake beds. And crops of grapes, lettuce, dates, alfalfa, and cotton covered the Coachella and Imperial valleys, north and south of the Salton Sea, and the Palo Verde Valley along the Colorado.

5      These developments proceeded with little or no awareness of earlier human occupations by cultures that preceded those of the historic Indians—the Mohave, the Chemehuevi, the Quechan. (Extensive irrigation began actually to change the climate of the Sonoran Desert, and human settlements, the railroads, and farming introduced many new, successful plants into the region.)

6      During World War II, the American military moved into the desert in great force, to train troops and to test equipment. They found the clear weather conducive to year-round flying, the dry air and isolation very attractive. After the war, a complex of training grounds, storage facilities, and gunnery and test ranges was permanently settled on more than three million acres of military reservations. Few perceived the extent or significance of the destruction of the aboriginal sites that took place during tank maneuvers and bombing runs or in the laying out of highways, railroads, mining districts, and irrigated fields. The few who intuited that something like an American Dordogne Valley lay exposed here were (only) amateur archaeologists; even they reasoned that the desert was too vast for any of this to matter.

After World War II, people began moving out of the crowded Los   7
Angeles basin into homes in Lucerne, Apple, and Antelope valleys in
the western Mojave. They emigrated as well to a stretch of resort land
at the foot of the San Jacinto Mountains that included Palm Springs,
and farther out to old railroad and military towns like Twentynine
Palms and Barstow. People also began exploring the desert, at first in
military-surplus jeeps and then with a variety of all-terrain and off-road
vehicles that became available in the 1960s. By the mid-1970s, the
number of people using such vehicles for desert recreation had increased
exponentially. Most came and went in innocent curiosity; the few who
didn't wreaked a havoc all out of proportion to their numbers. The disturbance of previously isolated archaeological sites increased by an order of magnitude. Many sites were vandalized before archaeologists,
themselves late to the desert, had any firm grasp of the bounds of human history in the desert. It was as though in the same moment an
Aztec library had been discovered intact various lacunae had begun to
appear.

The vandalism was of three sorts: the general disturbance usually   8
caused by souvenir hunters and by the curious and the oblivious; the
wholesale stripping of a place by professional thieves for black market
sale and trade; and outright destruction, in which vehicles were actually
used to ram and trench an area. By 1980, the Bureau of Land Management estimated that probably 35 percent of the archaeological sites in
the desert had been vandalized. The destruction at some places by rifles
and shotguns, or by power winches mounted on vehicles, was, if one
cared for history, demoralizing to behold.

In spite of public education, land closures, and stricter law enforce-   9
ment in recent years, the BLM estimates that, annually, about 1 percent
of the archaeological record in the desert continues to be destroyed or
stolen.

## II

A BLM archaeologist told me, with understandable reluctance,   10
where to find the intaglio. I spread my Automobile Club of Southern
California map of Imperial County out on his desk, and he traced the
route with a pink felt-tip pen. The line crossed Interstate 8 and then
turned west along the Mexican border.

"You can't drive any farther than about here," he said, marking a   11
small X. "There's boulders in the wash. You walk up past them."

On a separate piece of paper he drew a route in a smaller scale that   12
would take me up the arroyo to a certain point where I was to cross back
east, to another arroyo. At its head, on higher ground just to the north, I
would find the horse.

"It's tough to spot unless you know it's there. Once you pick it up   13
. . ." He shook his head slowly, in a gesture of wonder at its existence.

14     I waited until I held his eye. I assured him I would not tell anyone else how to get there. He looked at me with stoical despair, like a man who had been robbed twice, whose belief in human beings was offered without conviction.

15     I did not go until the following day because I wanted to see it at dawn. I ate breakfast at four A.M. in El Centro and then drove south. The route was easy to follow, though the last section of road proved difficult, broken and drifted over with sand in some spots. I came to the barricade of boulders and parked. It was light enough by then to find my way over the ground with little trouble. The contours of the landscape were stark, without any masking vegetation. I worried only about rattlesnakes.

16     I traversed the stone plain as directed, but, in spite of the frankness of the land, I came on the horse unawares. In the first moment of recognition I was without feeling. I recalled later being startled, and that I held my breath. It was laid out on the ground with its head to the east, three times life size. As I took in its outline I felt a growing concentration of all my senses, as though my attentiveness to the pale rose color of the morning sky and other peripheral images had now ceased to be important. I was aware that I was straining for sound in the windless air, and I felt the uneven pressure of the earth hard against my feet. The horse, outlined in a standing profile on the dark ground, was as vivid before me as a bed of tulips.

17     I've come upon animals suddenly before, and felt a similar tension, a precipitate heightening of the senses. And I have felt the inexplicable but sharply boosted intensity of a wild moment in the bush, where it is not until some minutes later that you discover the source of electricity—the warm remains of a grizzly bear kill, or the still moist tracks of a wolverine.

18     But this was slightly different. I felt I had stepped into an unoccupied corridor. I had no familiar sense of history, the temporal structure in which to think: This horse was made by Quechan people three hundred years ago. I felt instead a headlong rush of images: people hunting wild horses with spears on the Pleistocene veld of southern California; Cortés riding across the causeway into Montezuma's Tenochtitlán; a short-legged Comanche, astride his horse like some sort of ferret, slashing through cavalry lines of young men who rode like farmers; a hoof exploding past my face one morning in a corral in Wyoming. These images had the weight and silence of stone.

19     When I released my breath, the images softened. My initial feeling, of facing a wild animal in a remote region, was replaced with a calm sense of antiquity. It was then that I became conscious, like an ordinary tourist, of what was before me, and thought: this horse was probably laid out by Quechan people. But when? I wondered. The first horses they saw, I knew, might have been those that came north from Mexico in 1692 with Father Eusebio Kino. But Cocopa people, I recalled, also came this far north on occasion, to fight with their neighbors, the Quechan. And

*they* could have seen horses with Melchior Díaz, at the mouth of the Colorado River in the fall of 1540. So, it could be four hundred years old. (No one in fact knows.)

I still had not moved. I took my eyes off the horse for a moment to look south over the desert plain into Mexico, to look east past its head at the brightening sunrise, to situate myself. Then, finally, I brought my trailing foot slowly forward and stood erect. Sunlight was running like a thin sheet of water over the stony ground and it threw the horse into relief. It looked as though no hand had ever disturbed the stones that gave it its form.

The horse had been brought to life on ground called desert pavement, a tight, flat matrix of small cobbles blasted smooth by sand-laden winds. The uniform, monochromatic blackness of the stones, a patina of iron and magnesium oxides called desert varnish, is caused by long-term exposure to the sun. To make this type of low-relief ground glyph, or intaglio, the artist either selectively turns individual stones over to their lighter side or removes areas of stone to expose the lighter soil underneath, creating a negative image. This horse, about eighteen feet from brow to rump and eight feet from withers to hoof, had been made in the latter way, and its outline was bermed at certain points with low ridges of stone a few inches high to enhance its three-dimensional qualities. (The left side of the horse was in full profile; each leg was extended at 90 degrees to the body and fully visible, as though seen in three-quarter profile.)

I was not eager to move. The moment I did I would be back in the flow of time, the horse no longer quivering in the same way before me. I did not want to feel again the sequence of quotidian events—to be drawn off into deliberation and analysis. A human being, a four-footed animal, the open land. That was all that was present—and a "thoughtless" understanding of the very old desires bearing on this particular animal: to hunt it, to render it, to fathom it, to subjugate it, to honor it, to take it as a companion.

What finally made me move was the light. The sun now filled the shallow basin of the horse's body. The weighted line of the stone berm created the illusion of a mane and the distinctive roundness of an equine belly. The change in definition impelled me. I moved to the left, circling past its rump, to see how the light might flesh the horse out from various points of view. I circled it completely before squatting on my haunches. Ten or fifteen minutes later I chose another view. The third time I moved, to a point near the rear hooves, I spotted a stone tool at my feet. I stared at it a long while, more in awe than disbelief, before reaching out to pick it up. I turned it over in my left palm and took it between my fingers to feel its cutting edge. It is always difficult, especially with something so portable, to rechannel the desire to steal.

I spent several hours with the horse. As I changed positions and as the angle of the light continued to change I noticed a number of things. The angle at which the pastern carried the hoof away from the ankle was

20

21

22

23

24

perfect. Also, stones had been placed within the image to suggest at precisely the right spot the left shoulder above the foreleg. The line that joined thigh and hock was similarly accurate. The muzzle alone seemed distorted—but perhaps these stones had been moved by a later hand. It was an admirably accurate representation, but not what a breeder would call perfect conformation. There was the suggestion of a bowed neck and an undershot jaw, and the tail, as full as a winter coyote's, did not appear to be precisely to scale.

25      The more I thought about it, the more I felt I was looking at an individual horse, a unique combination of generic and specific detail. It was easy to imagine one of Kino's horses as a model, or a horse that ran off from one of Coronado's columns. What kind of horses would these have been? I wondered. In the sixteenth century the most sought-after horses in Europe were Spanish, the offspring of Arabian stock and Barbary horses that the Moors brought to Iberia and bred to the older, eastern European strains brought in by the Romans. The model for this horse, I speculated, could easily have been a palomino, or a descendant of horses trained for lion hunting in North Africa.

26      A few generations ago, cowboys, cavalry quartermasters, and draymen would have taken this horse before me under consideration and not let up their scrutiny until they had its heritage fixed to their satisfaction. Today, the distinction between draft and harness horses is arcane knowledge, and no image may come to mind for a blue roan or a claybank horse. The loss of such refinement in everyday conversation leaves me unsettled. People praise the Eskimo's ability to distinguish among forty types of snow but forget the skill of others who routinely differentiate between overo and tobiano pintos. Such distinctions are made for the same reason. You have to do it to be able to talk clearly about the world.

27      For parts of two years I worked as a horse wrangler and packer in Wyoming. It is dim knowledge now; I would have to think to remember if a buckskin was a kind of dun horse. And I couldn't throw a double-diamond hitch over a set of panniers—the packer's basic tie-down—without guidance. As I squatted there in the desert, however, these more personal memories seemed tenuous in comparison with the sweep of this animal in human time. My memories had no depth. I thought of the Hittite cavalry riding against the Syrians 3,500 years ago. And the first of the Chinese emperors, Ch'in Shih Huang, buried in Shensi Province in 210 B.C. with thousands of life-size horses and soldiers, a terra-cotta guardian army. What could I know of what was in the mind of whoever made this horse? Was there some racial memory of it as an animal that had once fed the artist's ancestors and then disappeared from North America? And then returned in this strange alliance with another race of men?

28      Certainly, whoever it was, the artist had observed the animal very closely. Certainly the animal's speed had impressed him. Among the first things the Quechan would have learned from an encounter with Kino's

horses was that their own long-distance runners—men who could run down mule deer—were no match for this animal.

From where I squatted I could look far out over the Mexican plain. Juan Bautista de Anza passed this way in 1774, extending El Camino Real into Alta California from Sinaloa. He was followed by others, all of them astride the magical horse; *gente de razón*, the people of reason, coming into the country of *los primitivos*. The horse, like the stone animals of Egypt, urged these memories upon me. And as I drew them up from some forgotten corner of my mind—huge horses carved in the white chalk downs of southern England by an Iron Age people; Spanish horses rearing and wheeling in fear before alligators in Florida—the images seemed tethered before me. With this sense of proportion, a memory of my own—the morning I almost lost my face to a horse's hoof—now had somewhere to fit.    29

I rose up and began to walk slowly around the horse again. I had taken the first long measure of it and was now looking for a way to depart, a new angle of light, a fading of the image itself before the rising sun, that would break its hold on me. As I circled, feeling both heady and serene at the encounter, I realized again how strangely vivid it was. It had been created on a barren bajada between two arroyos, as nondescript a place as one could imagine. The only plant life here was a few wands of ocotillo cactus. The ground beneath my shoes was so hard it wouldn't take the print of a heavy animal even after a rain. The only sounds I heard here were the voices of quail.    30

The archaeologist had been correct. For all its forcefulness, the horse is inconspicuous. If you don't care to see it you can walk right past it. That pleases him, I think. Unmarked on the bleak shoulder of the plain, the site signals to no one; so he wants no protective fences here, no informative plaque, to act as beacons. He would rather take a chance that no motorcyclist, no aimless wanderer with a flair for violence and a depth of ignorance, will ever find his way here.    31

The archaeologist had given me something before I left his office that now seemed peculiar—an aerial photograph of the horse. It is widely believed that an aerial view of an intaglio provides a fair and accurate depiction. It does not. In the photograph the horse looks somewhat crudely constructed; from the ground it appears far more deftly rendered. The photograph is of a single moment, and in that split second the horse seems vaguely impotent. I watched light pool in the intaglio at dawn; I imagine you could watch it withdraw at dusk and sense the same animation I did. In those prolonged moments its shape and so, too, its general character changed—noticeably. The living quality of the image, its immediacy to the eye, was brought out by the light-in-time, not, at least here, in the camera's frozen instant.    32

Intaglios, I thought, were never meant to be seen by gods in the sky above. They were meant to be seen by people on the ground, over a long    33 period of shifting light. This could even be true of the huge figures on the Plain of Nazca in Peru, where people could walk for the length of a day beside them. It is our own impatience that leads us to think otherwise.

34 This process of abstraction, almost unintentional, drew me gradually away from the horse. I came to a position of attention at the edge of the sphere of its influence. With a slight bow I paid my respects to the horse, its maker, and the history of us all, and departed.

## III

35 A short distance away I stopped the car in the middle of the road to make a few notes. I could not write down what I was thinking when I was with the horse. It would have seemed disrespectful, and it would have required another kind of attention. So now I patiently drained my memory of the details it had fastened itself upon. The road I'd stopped on was adjacent to the All American Canal, the major source of water for the Imperial and Coachella valleys. The water flowed west placidly. A disjointed flock of coots, small, dark birds with white bills, was paddling against the current, foraging in the rushes.

36 I was peripherally aware of the birds as I wrote, the only movement in the desert, and of a series of sounds from a village a half-mile away. The first sounds from this collection of ramshackle houses in a grove of cottonwoods were the distracted dawn voices of dogs. I heard them intermingled with the cries of a rooster. Later, the high-pitched voices of children calling out to each other came disembodied through the dry desert air. Now, a little after seven, I could hear someone practicing on the trumpet, the same rough phrases played over and over. I suddenly remembered how as children we had tried to get the rhythm of a galloping horse with hands against our thighs, or by fluttering our tongues against the roofs of our mouths.

37 After the trumpet, the impatient calls of adults summoning children. Sunday morning. Wood smoke hung like a lens in the trees. The first car starts—a cold eight-cylinder engine, of Chrysler extraction perhaps, goosed to life, then throttled back to murmur through dual mufflers, the obbligato music of a shade-tree mechanic. The rote bark of mongrel dogs at dawn, the jagged outcries of men and women, an engine coming to life. Like a thousand villages from West Virginia to Guadalajara.

38 I finished my notes—where was I going to find a description of the horses that came north with the conquistadors? Did their manes come forward prominently over the brow, like this one's, like the forelocks of Blackfeet and Assiniboin men in nineteenth-century paintings? I set the notes on the seat beside me.

39 The road followed the canal for a while and then arced north, toward Interstate 8. It was slow driving and I fell to thinking how the desert had changed since Anza had come through. New plants and ani-

mals—the MacDougall cottonwood, the English house sparrow, the chukar from India—have about them now the air of the native born. Of the native species, some—no one knows how many—are extinct. The populations of many others, especially the animals, have been sharply reduced. The idea of a desert impoverished by agricultural poisons and varmint hunters, by off-road vehicles and military operations, did not seem as disturbing to me, however, as this other horror, now that I had been those hours with the horse. The vandals, the few who crowbar rock art off the desert's walls, who dig up graves, who punish the ground that holds intaglios, are people who devour history. Their self-centered scorn, their disrespect for ideas and images beyond their ken, create the awful atmosphere of loose ends in which totalitarianism thrives, in which the past is merely curious or wrong.

I thought about the horse sitting out there on the unprotected plain.   40
I enumerated its qualities in my mind until a sense of its vulnerability receded and it became an anchor for something else. I remembered that history, a history like this one, which ran deeper than Mexico, deeper than the Spanish, was a kind of medicine. It permitted the great breadth of human expression to reverberate, and it did not urge you to locate its apotheosis in the present.

Each of us, individuals and civilizations, has been held upside down   41
like Achilles in the River Styx. The artist mixing his colors in the dim light of Altamira; an Egyptian ruler lying still now, wrapped in his byssus, stored against time in a pyramid; the faded Dorset culture of the Arctic; the Hmong and Samburu and Walbiri of historic time; the modern nations. This great, imperfect stretch of human expression is the clarification and encouragement, the urging and the reminder, we call history. And it is inscribed everywhere in the face of the land, from the mountain passes of the Himalayas to a nameless bajada in the California desert.

Small birds rose up in the road ahead, startled, and flew off. I prayed   42
no infidel would ever find that horse.

## CONSIDERATIONS

1. In paragraph 6, Lopez touches briefly on the massive effect after World War II of the American military converting huge tracts of desert country into training grounds for tank maneuvers, artillery practice, and bombing runs. His immediate concern was over the destruction of archaeological sites. Pursue the subject by researching the environmental effects of the military's use of that area, and report your findings in an expository essay.

2. Lopez divides his essay into three parts. Study their differences and explain how they serve the writer's purposes.

3. If nothing else, "The Stone Horse" could teach you the difference between looking and seeing. Study especially paragraphs 20 through 24. Then spend a little time

observing some sizeable work of sculpture on your campus or in your community. Record not only what you see, but also how you go about seeing.

4. What is an intaglio? Does Lopez's description clarify the term?

5. The author's concern over the safety of the stone horse is not unlike that of other conservationists who want to preserve, say, an old building in the path of advancing changes. The obvious fate of the old building is often the subject of protests, demonstrations, and campaigns by those who would preserve it. Do you think there could be similar protests over threats to the stone horse? Those who are in favor of (or who would profit from) the change would call it "progress" or "opportunity" or "development." What would you call it? Explain in an argumentative essay in which you make use of some proposed change in your hometown.

6. Read David Quammen's "So What?" (page 511). Is his worry about destruction of the biosphere the same as Barry Lopez's worry about destruction of the archaeological record? Explain.

*Thomas Lynch (b. 1948) was born in Detroit and now lives in the
town of Milford, Michigan, where he has been a funeral director
since 1974. His first book of poems,* Skating with Heather Grace,
*was published by Knopf in 1988. "Burying" appeared in the*
Quarterly *and was renamed as the title essay of* The Undertaking:
Life Studies from the Dismal Trade *(1997). More poetry has
appeared in* Grimalkin *(1994) and* Still Life *(1998).*

*Lynch takes a straighforward or even brash approach to this
account of his work. Reminiscences and opinions flash out at us,
often in startling on-line paragraphs, until he concludes with a
story of one death, one undertaking. See how this structure, broad
to narrow, develops the tone of the essay.*

— **60** —————————————————————

# THOMAS LYNCH
## *Burying*

———————————————————————

Every year I bury one hundred and fifty of my townspeople. 1
Another dozen or two I take to the crematory to be burned. I sell caskets,
burial vaults, and urns for the ashes. I have a sideline in headstones and
monuments. I do flowers on commission.

Apart from the tangibles, I sell the use of my building, eleven thou- 2
sand square feet, furnished and fixtured with an abundance of pastel and
chair rail and crown moldings. The whole lash-up is mortgaged and re-
mortgaged well into the next century. My rolling stock includes a hearse,
a limo, two Fleetwoods, and a mini-van with darkened windows our price
list calls a service vehicle and everyone in town calls the Dead Wagon.

I used to use the "unit pricing method"—the old package deal. It 3
meant you had only one number to look at. It was a large number. Now
everything is itemized. It's the law. So now there is a long list of items
and numbers and italicized disclaimers, something like a menu or the
Sears, Roebuck wish book, and sometimes the federally mandated options begin to look like cruise control or rear-window defrost. I wear
black most of the time, to keep folks in mind of the fact we're not talking Buicks here. At the bottom of the list is still a large number.

———————

"Burying" by Thomas Lynch from the *Quarterly*. Reprinted by permission of the
author.

4    In a good year the gross is close to half a million, 5 percent of which we hope to call profit. I am the only undertaker in this town. I have a corner on the market.

5    The market, such as it is, is figured on what is called the "crude death rate"—the number of deaths every year out of every thousand of persons.

6    Here is how it works.

7    Imagine a large room into which you coax one thousand people. You slam the doors in January, leaving them plenty of food and drink, color TVs, magazines, condoms. Your sample should have an age distribution heavy on Baby Boomers and their children—1.2 children per boomer. For every four normal people, there is one Old-Timer, who, if he or she wasn't in this big room, would probably be in Florida or Arizona or a nursing home. You get the idea. The group will include fifteen lawyers, one faith healer, three dozen real-estate agents, a video technician, several licensed counselors, and an Amway distributor. The rest will be between jobs, middle managers, ne'er-do-wells, or retired.

8    Now the magic part—come late December, when you throw open the doors, only 991.3, give or take, will shuffle out upright. Two hundred and sixty will now be selling Amway. The other 8.7 have become the crude death rate.

9    Here's another stat.

10    Of the 8.7 corpses, two-thirds will have been Old-Timers, 5 percent will be children, and the rest (2.75) will be Boomers—realtors and attorneys—one of whom was, no doubt, elected to public office during the year. What's more, three will have died of cerebral vascular or coronary difficulties, two of cancer, one each of vehicular mayhem, diabetes, and domestic violence. The spare change will be by act of God or suicide—most likely the faith healer.

11    The figure most often and most conspicuously missing from the insurance charts and demographics is the one I call THE BIG ONE, which refers to the number of people out of every one hundred born who will die. Over the long haul, THE BIG ONE hovers right around . . . well—dead nuts on 100. If this were on the charts, they would call it "Death expectancy" and no one would buy futures of any kind. But it is a useful number and has its lessons. Maybe you will want to figure out what to do with your life. Maybe it will make you feel a certain kinship to the rest of us. Maybe it will make you hysterical. Whatever the implications of a one hundred death expectancy, calculate how big a town this is and why mine produces for me steady, if sometimes unpredictable, labor.

12    They die around the clock here, without apparent preference for a day of the week, month of the year; there is no clear favorite in the way of season. Nor does the alignment of the stars, fullness of moon, or liturgical calendar have very much to do with it. The whereabouts are neither here nor there. They go off upright or horizontally, in Chevrolets and nursing homes, in bathtubs, on the interstates, in ERs, ORs, BMWs. And while it

may be so that we assign more equipment or more importance to deaths that create themselves in places marked by initials—ICU being somehow better than Greenbrier Convalescent Home—it is also true that the dead don't care. In this way, the dead I bury and burn are like the dead before them, for whom time and space have become mortally unimportant. This loss of interest is, in fact, one of the first sure signs that something serious is about to happen. The next thing is they quit breathing. At this point, to be sure, a "gunshot wound to the chest" or "shock and trauma" will get more ink than a CVA or ASHD, but no condition of death is any less permanent than any other. All will do. The dead don't care.

Nor does *who* much matter, either. To say "I'm okay, you're okay, and by the way, he's dead!" is, for the living, a kind of comfort.   13

It is why we drag rivers and comb plane wrecks.   14

It is why MIA is more painful than DOA.   15

It is why we have open caskets and classified obits.   16

Knowing is better than not knowing, and knowing it is you is terrif-   17
ically better than knowing it is me. Once I'm the dead guy, whether you're okay or he's okay won't much interest me. You can both go bag your asses, because the dead don't care.

Of course, the living, bound by their adverbs and their actuarials,   18
still do. Now there's the difference and why I'm in business. The living are careful and oftentimes caring. The dead are careless, or maybe it's care-less. Either way, they don't care. These are unremarkable and verifiable truths.

My former mother-in-law, herself an unremarkable and verifiable   19
truth, was always fond of holding forth with Cagneyesque bravada—to wit, "When I'm dead, just put me in a box and throw me in a hole." But whenever I would remind her that we did substantially that with *every-one*, the woman would grow sullen and a little cranky.

Later, over meat loaf and green beans, she would invariably give out   20
with "When I'm dead, just cremate me and scatter the ashes."

My former mother-in-law was trying to make carelessness sound   21
like fearlessness. The kids would stop eating and look at each other. The kids' mother would whine, "Oh, Mom, don't talk like that." I'd take out my lighter and begin to play with it.

In the same way, the priest that married me to this woman's daugh-   22
ter—a man who loved gold and gold ciboria and vestments made of Irish linen; a man who drove a great black sedan with a wine-red interior and who always had his eye on the cardinal's job—this same fellow, leaving the cemetery one day, felt called upon to instruct me thus: "No bronze coffin for me. No Sir! No orchids or roses or limousines. The plain pine box is the one I want, a quiet Low Mass, and the pauper's grave. No pomp and circumstances."

He wanted, he explained, to be an example of simplicity, of pru-   23
dence, of piety and austerity—all priestly and, apparently, Christian

virtues. When I told him that he needn't wait, that he could begin his ministry of good example yet today, that he could quit the country club and do his hacking at the public links and trade his brougham for a used Chevette, that free of his Florsheims and cashmeres and prime ribs, free of his bingo nights and building funds, he could become, for Christ's sake, the very incarnation of Francis himself, or Anthony of Padua; when I said, in fact, that I would be willing to assist him in this, that I would gladly distribute his CDs and credit cards among the needy of the parish, and that I would, when the sad duty called, bury him for nothing in the manner he would have by then become accustomed to; when I told the priest who had married me these things, he said nothing at all, but turned his wild eye on me in the manner in which the cleric must have looked on Sweeney years ago, before he cursed him, irreversibly, into a bird.*

24    What I was trying to tell the fellow was, of course, that being a dead saint is no more worthwhile than being a dead philodendron or a dead angelfish. Living is the rub, and always has been. Living saints still feel the flames and stigmata, the ache of chastity and the pangs of conscience. Once dead, they let their relics do the legwork, because, as I was trying to tell this priest, the dead don't care.

25    Only the living care.

26    And I am sorry to be repeating myself, but this is the central fact of my business—that there is nothing, once you are dead, that can be done *to you* or *for you* or *with you* or *about you* that will do you any good or any harm; that any damage or decency we do accrues to the living, to whom your death happens if it really happens to anyone. The living have to live with it; you don't. Theirs is the grief or gladness your death brings. And there is the truth, abundantly self-evident, that seems, now that I think of it, the one most elusive to my old in-laws, to the parish priest, and to perfect strangers who are forever accosting me in barbershops and in cocktail bars and at parent-teacher conferences, hell-bent or duty-bound on telling me what it is they want done with them when they are dead.

27    Give it a rest is the thing I say.

28    Once you are dead, put your feet up, call it a day, and let the old man or the missus or the thankless kids decide whether you are to be buried or burned or blown out of a cannon or left to dry out in a ditch. It's not your day to watch it, because the dead don't care.

29    Another reason people are always rehearsing their obsequies with me has to do with the fear of death, which is something anyone in his right mind has. It is healthy. It keeps us from playing in the traffic. I say pass it on to the kids.

---

*Lynch alludes to a medieval Irish poem in which Sweeney attacks a priest, who puts a curse on Sweeney and changes him into a bird. The poem was recently translated from the Celtic by the Irish poet Seamus Heaney who called it, "Sweeney Astray."

There is a belief—widespread among the women I have dated, local 30
Rotarians, and friends of my children—that I, being the undertaker here,
have some irregular fascination with, special interest in, inside information about, even attachment to, *the dead*. They assume, these people,
some perhaps with good reason, that I want their bodies.

It is an interesting concept. 31

But here's the truth. 32

Being dead is one—the worst, the last—but only one in a series of 33
calamities that afflicts our own and several other species. The list may
include, but is not limited to, gingivitis, bowel obstruction, contested divorce, tax audit, spiritual vexation, money trouble, political mischief,
and on and on and on. There is no shortage of *misery*. And I am no more
attracted to the dead than the dentist is to your bad gums, the doctor to
your rotten innards, or the accountant to your sloppy expense records. I
have no more stomach for misery than the banker or the lawyer, the pastor or the politico—because misery is careless and is everywhere. Misery
is the bad check, the exwife, the mob in the street, and the IRS—who,
like the dead, feel nothing, and, like the dead, *don't care*.

Which is not to say that the dead do not matter. 34

They do. 35

Last Monday morning, Milo Hornsby died. Mrs. Hornsby called at 36
2:00 A.M. to say that Milo had "expired" and would I take care of it, as if
his condition were like any other that could be renewed or somehow improved upon. At 2:00 A.M., yanked from sleep, I am thinking, put a quarter in Milo and call me in the morning. But Milo is dead. In a moment, in
a twinkling, Milo has slipped irretrievably out of our reach, beyond Mrs.
Hornsby and the children, beyond the women at the laundromat he
owned, beyond his comrades at the Legion Hall, the Grand Master of the
Masonic Lodge, his pastor at First Baptist, beyond the mailman, zoning
board, town council, and Chamber of Commerce; beyond us all, and any
treachery or any kindness we had in mind for him.

Milo is dead. 37

X's on his eyes, lights out, curtains. 38

Helpless, harmless. 39

Milo's dead. 40

Which is why I do not haul to my senses, coffee and a quick shave, 41
Homburg and great coat, warm up the Dead Wagon, and make for the
freeway in the early o'clock for Milo's sake but for his missus's sake, for
she who has become, in the same moment and same twinkling, like water to ice, the widow Hornsby. I go for her—because she still can cry and
care and pray and pay my bill.

The hospital that Milo died in is state of the art. There are signs on 42
every door declaring a part or process or bodily function. I like to think
that, taken together, the words would add up to something like the
Human Condition, but they never do. What's left of Milo, the remains,
are in the basement, between SHIPPING & RECEIVING and LAUNDRY ROOM.

Milo would like that if he were still liking anything. Milo's room is called PATHOLOGY.

43    The medical-technical parlance of death emphasizes disorder. We are forever dying of failures, of anomalies, of insufficiencies, of dysfunctions, arrests, accidents. These are either chronic or acute. The language of death certificates—Milo's says "Cardiopulmonary Failure"—is like the language of weakness. Likewise, Mrs. Hornsby, in her grief, will be said to be breaking down or falling apart or going to pieces, as if there were something structurally awry with her. It is as if death and grief were not part of the Order of Things, as if Milo's failure and his widow's weeping were, or ought to be, sources of embarrassment. "Doing well" for Mrs. Hornsby would mean that she is bearing up, braving the storm, or being strong for the children. We have willing pharmacists to help her with this. Of course, for Milo, doing well would mean he was back upstairs, holding his own, keeping the meters and monitors bleeping.

44    But Milo is downstairs, between SHIPPING & RECEIVING and LAUNDRY ROOM, in a stainless-steel drawer, wrapped in white plastic top to toe, and—because of his small head, wide shoulders, ponderous belly, and skinny legs, and the trailing white binding cord from his ankles and toe tags—he looks, for all the world, like a larger than life-size sperm. *The beginning of life*

45    I sign for him and get him out of there. At some level, I am still thinking Milo gives a shit, which by now we all know he doesn't—because the dead don't care.

46    Back at my place of business, upstairs in the embalming room, behind a door marked PRIVATE, Milo Hornsby is floating on a porcelain table under fluorescent lights. Unwrapped, outstretched, Milo is beginning to look a little more like himself—eyes wide open, mouth agape, returning to our gravity. I shave him, close his eyes, his mouth. We call this "setting the features." These are the features—eyes and mouth—that, in death, will never look the way they would look in life, when they are always opening, closing, focusing, signaling, telling us something. In death, what they tell us is they will not be doing anything anymore. The last detail to be managed is Milo's hands—one folded over the other, over the umbilicus, in an attitude of ease, of repose, of retirement.

47    They will not be doing anything anymore, either.

48    I wash his hands before positioning them.

49    When my wife moved out some years ago, I kept the children and the dirty laundry. It was big news in a small town. There was the gossip and the goodwill that places like this are famous for. And while there was plenty of talk, no one knew exactly what to say to me. They felt hopeless, I suppose. So they brought casseroles and beef stews, took the kids out to the movies or canoeing, brought their younger sisters around to visit me. What Milo did was sent his laundry van by twice a week for two months, until I had found a housekeeper. Milo would pick up five loads in the morning and return them by lunchtime, fresh and folded. I

never asked him to do this. I hardly knew him. I had never been in his home or in his laundromat. His wife had never known my wife. His children were too old to play with my children.

After my housekeeper was installed, I went to thank Milo and to pay my bill. The invoices detailed the number of loads, the washers and the dryers, detergent, bleaches, fabric softeners. I think the total came to sixty dollars. When I asked Milo what the charges were for pickup and delivery, for stacking and folding, for saving my life and the lives of my children, for keeping us in clean clothes and towels and bed linens, "Never mind that," Milo said, "one hand washes the other."   50

I place Milo's right hand over his left hand, then try the other way. Then back again. Then I decide that it does not matter, that one hand washes the other either way.   51

The embalming takes me about two hours.   52

It is daylight by the time I am done.   53

Every Monday morning Paddy Fulton comes to my office. He was damaged in some profound way in Korea. The details of his damage are unknown to the locals. Paddy Fulton has no limp or anything missing— so everyone thinks it was something he saw in Korea that left him a little simple, occasionally perplexed, the type to draw rein abruptly in his daylong walks, to consider the meaning of litter, pausing over bottle caps and gum wrappers. Paddy Fulton has a nervous smile and a deadfish handshake. He wears a baseball cap and thick eyeglasses. Every Sunday night Paddy goes to the I.G.A. and buys up the tabloids at the checkout stands with headlines that usually involve Siamese twins or movie stars or UFOs. Paddy is a speed reader and a math whiz—but because of his damage, he has never held a job and never applied for one. Every Monday morning, Paddy brings me clippings of stories under headlines like: 601 LB. MAN FALLS THRU COFFIN—A GRAVE SITUATION or EMBALMER FOR THE STARS SAYS ELVIS IS FOREVER. The Monday morning Milo died, Paddy's clipping had to do with an urn full of ashes that made grunting and groaning noises, that whistled sometimes, and that was expected to begin talking. Certain scientists in England could make no sense of it. They had run several tests. The ashes' widow, however—left with nine children and no estate—is convinced that her dearly beloved and greatly reduced husband is trying to give her winning numbers for the lottery. "Jacky would never leave us without good prospects," she says. "He loved his family more than anything." There is a picture of the two of them—the widow and the urn, the living and the dead, flesh and bronze, the Victrola and the Victrola's dog. She has her ear cocked, waiting.   54

We are always waiting. Waiting for some good word or for the winning numbers. Waiting for a sign or wonder, some signal from our dear dead that the dead still care. We are gladdened when they do outstanding things, when they arise from their graves or appear to us in dreams or fall from their caskets. It pleases us no end, as if there were no end; as if the dead still cared, had agendas, were yet alive.   55

56    But the sad and well-known fact of the matter is that most of us will stay in our caskets and be dead a long time, and that our urns and graves will never make a sound. Our reason and requiems, our headstones and High Masses, will neither get us in nor keep us out of heaven. The meaning of our lives, and the memories of them, will belong only to the living, just as our funerals do.

57    We heat graves here for winter burials, as a kind of foreplay before digging in, to loosen the frost's hold on the ground before the sexton and his backhoe do the opening. We buried Milo in the ground last Wednesday. It was, by then, the only thing to do. The mercy is that what we buried there, in an oak casket, just under the frost line, had ceased to be Milo. It was something else. Milo had become the idea of himself, a permanent fixture of the third person and past tense, his widow's loss of appetite and trouble sleeping, the absence in places where we look for him, our habits of him breaking, our phantom limb, our one hand washing the other.

## CONSIDERATIONS ————————————————————————

1. Why is Thomas Lynch less than reverential toward the dead? Is he disrespectful toward them?

2. Are the following words synonymous: *ironic, satiric, sardonic, cynical, humorous, witty, sarcastic*? After comparing their definitions in a good dictionary, which one would you select as the most descriptive of Lynch's tone (attitude) in his essay? Be prepared to back up your choice by referring to illustrative words, phrases, or passages in "Burying." If you think none of these words is appropriate, make a case for any other word you think would be better.

3. In paragraph 43, Lynch tells us of something he discovers by looking at the "parlance of death." What is his criticism of that jargon? Find an example of Lynch making fun of his own parlance. What other evidence do you find that Lynch enjoys playing with language?

4. Several other writers in this text—Raymond Carver, John Daniel, John Haines, Edward Hoagland, Jane Kenyon, and Andrew Holleran among them—write seriously about death or dying. Write an essay comparing one or more of these writers' works with Thomas Lynch's "Burying." Pay attention not only to what they say, but also to how they say it.

5. Some readers feel that Lynch is coldly commercial about his work. What passages might give them that impression? What evidence do you find that Lynch is not without feelings about the dead and their survivors? Would you want Lynch to take care of your body when you die? Explain.

6. What do you make of Lynch's method of explaining the "crude death rate"?

7. Look at some of Lynch's one-sentence paragraphs. How do you suppose he might defend them as paragraphs?

8. What did Milo's remark "One hand washes the other" mean to Lynch? Why did he hesistate in arranging Milo's hands?

*John McPhee (b. 1931) was born in Princeton, New Jersey, where he graduated from college, and where he still lives. His writing, largely for the* New Yorker, *has taken him far afield, to Florida for a book about oranges, to Maine for a book about birchbark canoes, and all over the country for encounters with the American wilderness. His first book,* A Sense of Where You Are *(1965), described Senator Bill Bradley as he played basketball for Princeton University—before a Rhodes Scholarship, the NBA, the United States Senate, and a run for the presidency. In 1977 he published a report on Alaska called* Coming into the Country. *Some of his recent titles are* Assembling California *(1993) and* The Ransom of Russian Art *(1994).* Annals of the Former World *(1998) collected McPhee's observations about geology and won the Pulitzer Prize.*

*Here, his structure is his essay. It helps to know that the Atlantic City that he describes was a broken-down resort town before it was revived from its decadence to become a mecca for gamblers. His back-and-forth form, the reader can observe, finds unity in diversity, a unity of American culture.*

— 61

# JOHN MCPHEE
## *The Search for Marvin Gardens*

Go. I roll the dice—a six and a two. Through the air I move my to- 1
ken, the flatiron, to Vermont Avenue, where dog packs range.

The dogs are moving (some are limping) through ruins, rubble, fire 2
damage, open garbage. Doorways are gone. Lath is visible in the crumbling walls of the buildings. The street sparkles with shattered glass. I have never seen, anywhere, so many broken windows. A sign—"Slow, Children at Play"—has been bent backward by an automobile. At the lighthouse, the dogs turn up Pacific and disappear. George Meade, Army engineer, built the lighthouse—brick upon brick, six hundred thousand

**389**

bricks, to reach up high enough to throw a beam twenty miles over the sea. Meade, seven years later, saved the Union at Gettysburg.

3      I buy Vermont Avenue for $100. My opponent is a tall, shadowy figure, across from me, but I know him well, and I know his game like a favorite tune. If he can, he will always go for the quick kill. And when it is foolish to go for the quick kill he will be foolish. On the whole, though, he is a master assessor of percentages. It is a mistake to underestimate him. His eleven carries his top hat to St. Charles Place, which he buys for $140.

4      The sidewalks of St. Charles Place have been cracked to shards by through-growing weeds. There are no buildings. Mansions, hotels once stood here. A few street lamps now drop cones of light on broken glass and vacant space behind a chain-link fence that some great machine has in places bent to the ground. Five plane trees—in full summer leaf, flecking the light—are all that live on St. Charles Place.

5      Block upon block, gradually, we are cancelling each other out—in the blues, the lavenders, the oranges, the greens. My opponent follows a plan of his own devising. I use the Hornblower & Weeks opening and the Zuricher defense. The first game draws tight, will soon finish. In 1971, a group of people in Racine, Wisconsin, played for seven hundred and sixty-eight hours. A game begun a month later in Danville, California, lasted eight hundred and twenty hours. These are official records, and they stun us. We have been playing for eight minutes. It amazes us that Monopoly is thought of as a long game. It is possible to play to a complete, absolute, and final conclusion in less than fifteen minutes, all within the rules as written. My opponent and I have done so thousands of times. No wonder we are sitting across from each other now in this best-of-seven series for the international singles championship of the world.

6      On Illinois Avenue, three men lean out from second-story windows. A girl is coming down the street. She wears dungarees and a bright-red shirt, has ample breasts and a Hadendoan Afro, a black halo, two feet in diameter. Ice rattles in the glasses in the hands of the men.

7      "Hey, sister!"

8      "Come on up!"

9      She looks up, looks from one to another to the other, looks them flat in the eye.

10     "What for?" she says, and she walks on.

11     I buy Illinois for $240. It solidifies my chances, for I already own Kentucky and Indiana. My opponent pales. If he had landed first on Illinois, the game would have been over then and there, for he has houses

built on Boardwalk and Park Place, we share the railroads equally, and we have cancelled each other everywhere else. We never trade.

In 1852, R. B. Osborne, an immigrant Englishman, civil engineer, 12 surveyed the route of a railroad line that would run from Camden to Absecon Island, New Jersey, traversing the state from the Delaware River to the barrier beaches of the sea. He then sketched in the plan of a "bathing village" that would surround the eastern terminus of the line. His pen flew glibly, framing and naming spacious avenues parallel to the shore—Mediterranean, Baltic, Oriental, Ventnor—and narrower trans-secting avenues: North Carolina, Pennsylvania, Vermont, Connecticut, States, Virginia, Tennessee, New York, Kentucky, Indiana, Illinois. The place as a whole had no name, so when he had completed the plan Osborne wrote in large letters over the ocean, "Atlantic City." No one ever challenged the name, or the names of Osborne's streets. Monopoly was invented in the early nineteen-thirties by Charles B. Darrow, but Darrow was only transliterating what Osborne had created. The rail-roads, crucial to any player, were the making of Atlantic City. After the rails were down, houses and hotels burgeoned from Mediterranean and Baltic to New York and Kentucky. Properties—building lots—sold for as little as six dollars apiece and as much as a thousand dollars. The original investors in the railroads and the real estate called themselves the Camden & Atlantic Land Company. Reverently, I repeat their names: Dwight Bell, William Coffin, John DaCosta, Daniel Deal, William Fleming, Andrew Hay, Joseph Porter, Jonathan Pitney, Samuel Richards— founders, fathers, forerunners, archetypical masters of the quick kill.

My opponent and I are now in a deep situation of classical 13 Monopoly. The torsion is almost perfect—Boardwalk and Park Place ver-sus the brilliant reds. His cash position is weak, though, and if I escape him now he may fade. I land on Luxury Tax, contiguous to but in sanctu-ary from his power. I have four houses on Indiana. He lands there. He concedes.

Indiana Avenue was the address of the Brighton Hotel, gone now. 14 The Brighton was exclusive—a word that no longer has retail value in the city. If you arrived by automobile and tried to register at the Brighton, you were sent away. Brighton-class people came in private rail-road cars. Brighton-class people had other private railroad cars for their horses—dawn rides on the firm sand at water's edge, skirts flying. Colonel Anthony J. Drexel Biddle—the sort of name that would constrict throats in Philadelphia—lived, much of the year, in the Brighton.

Colonel Sanders' fried chicken is on Kentucky Avenue. So is 15 Clifton's Club Harlem, with the Sepia Revue and the Sepia Follies, fea-turing the Honey Bees, the Fashions, and the Lords.

16        My opponent and I, many years ago, played 2,428 games of
Monopoly in a single season. He was then a recent graduate of the
Harvard Law School, and he was working for a downtown firm, looking
up law. Two people we knew—one from Chase Manhattan, the other
from Morgan, Stanley—tried to get into the game, but after a few rounds
we found that they were not in the conversation and we sent them
home. Monopoly should always be *mano a mano* anyway. My opponent
won 1,199 games, and so did I. Thirty were ties. He was called into the
Army, and we stopped just there. Now, in Game 2 of the series, I go immediately to jail, and again to jail while my opponent seines property. He
is dumbfoundingly lucky. He wins in twelve minutes.

17        Visiting hours are daily, eleven to two; Sunday, eleven to one;
evenings, six to nine. "NO MINORS, NO FOOD, Immediate Family Only
Allowed in Jail." All this above a blue steel door in a blue cement wall in
the windowless interior of the basement of the city hall. The desk
sergeant sits opposite the door to the jail. In a cigar box in front of him
are pills in every color, a banquet of fruit salad an inch and a half deep—
leapers, co-pilots, footballs, truck drivers, peanuts, blue angels, yellow
jackets, redbirds, rainbows. Near the desk are two soldiers, waiting to go
through the blue door. They are about eighteen years old. One of them is
trying hard to light a cigarette. His wrists are in steel cuffs. A military
policeman waits, too. He is a year or so older than the soldiers, taller,
studious in appearance, gentle, fat. On a bench against a wall sits a good-
looking girl in slacks. The blue door rattles, swings heavily open. A
turnkey stands in the doorway. "Don't you guys kill yourselves back
there now," says the sergeant to the soldiers.

18        "One kid, he overdosed himself about ten and a half hours ago,"
says the M.P.

19        The M.P., the soldiers, the turnkey, and the girl on the bench are
white. The sergeant is black. "If you take off the handcuffs, take off the
belts," says the sergeant to the M.P. "I don't want them hanging themselves back there." The door shuts and its tumblers move. When it opens
again, five minutes later, a young white man in sandals and dungarees
and a blue polo shirt emerges. His hair is in a ponytail. He has no beard.
He grins at the good-looking girl. She rises, joins him. The sergeant
hands him a manila envelope. From it he removes his belt and a small
notebook. He borrows a pencil, makes an entry in the notebook. He is
out of jail, free. What did he do? He offended Atlantic City in some way.
He spent a night in the jail. In the nineteen-thirties, men visiting
Atlantic City went to jail, directly to jail, did not pass Go, for appearing
in topless bathing suits on the beach. A city statute requiring all men to
wear full-length bathing suits was not seriously challenged until 1937,
and the first year in which a man could legally go bare-chested on the
beach was 1940.

Game 3. After seventeen minutes, I am ready to begin construction    20
on overpriced and sluggish Pacific, North Carolina, and Pennsylvania.
Nothing else being open, opponent concedes.

The physical profile of streets perpendicular to the shore is some-    21
thing like a playground slide. It begins in the high skyline of Boardwalk
hotels, plummets into warrens of "side-avenue" motels, crosses Pacific,
slopes through church missions, convalescent homes, burlesque houses,
rooming houses, and liquor stores, crosses Atlantic, and runs level
through the bombed out ghetto as far—Baltic, Mediterranean—as the eye
can see. North Carolina Avenue, for example, is flanked at its beach end
by the Chalfonte and the Haddon Hall (908 rooms, air-conditioned),
where, according to one biographer, John Philip Sousa (1854–1932) first
played when he was twenty-two, insisting, even then, that everyone call
him by his entire name. Behind these big hotels, motels—Barbizon,
Catalina—crouch. Between Pacific and Atlantic is an occasional house
from 1910—wooden porch, wooden mullions, old yellow paint—and two
churches, a package store, a strip show, a dealer in fruits and vegetables.
Then, beyond Atlantic Avenue, North Carolina moves on into the vast
ghetto, the bulk of the city, and it looks like Metz in 1919, Cologne in
1944. Nothing has actually exploded. It is not bomb damage. It is deep
and complex decay. Roofs are off. Bricks are scattered in the street.
People sit on porches, six deep, at nine on a Monday morning. When
they go off to wait in unemployment lines, they wait sometimes two
hours. Between Mediterranean and Baltic runs a chain-link fence, enclos-
ing rubble. A patrol car sits idling by the curb. In the back seat is a
German shepherd. A sign on the fence says, "Beware of Bad Dogs."

Mediterranean and Baltic are the principal avenues of the ghetto.    22
Dogs are everywhere. A pack of seven passes me. Block after block, there
are three-story brick row houses. Whole segments of them are abandoned, a thousand broken windows. Some parts are intact, occupied. A
mattress lies in the street, soaking in a pool of water. Wet stuffing is
coming out of the mattress. A postman is having a rye and a beer in the
Plantation Bar at nine-fifteen in the morning. I ask him idly if he knows
where Marvin Gardens is. He does not. "HOOKED AND NEED HELP? CON-
TACT N.A.R.C.O." "REVIVAL NOW GOING ON, CONDUCTED BY REVEREND H. HEN-
DERSON OF TEXAS." These are signboards on Mediterranean and Baltic.
The second one is upside down and leans against a boarded-up window of
the Faith Temple Church of God in Christ. There is an old peeling poster
on a warehouse wall showing a figure in an electric chair. "The Black
Panther Manifesto" is the title of the poster, and its message is, or was,
that "the fascists have already decided in advance to murder Chairman
Bobby Seale in the electric chair." I pass an old woman who carries a
bucket. She wears blue sneakers, worn through. Her feet spill out. She
wears red socks, rolled at the knees. A white handkerchief, spread over

her head, is knotted at the corners. Does she know where Marvin Gardens is? "I sure don't know," she says, setting down the bucket. "I sure don't know. I've heard of it somewhere, but I just can't say where." I walk on, through a block of shattered glass. The glass crunches underfoot like coarse sand. I remember when I first came here—a long train ride from Trenton, long ago, games of poker in the train—to play basketball against Atlantic City. We were half black, they were all black. We scored forty points, they scored eighty, or something like it. What I remember most is that they had glass backboards—glittering, pendent, expensive glass backboards, a rarity then in high schools, even in colleges, the only ones we played on all year.

23      I turn on Pennsylvania, and start back toward the sea. The windows of the Hotel Astoria, on Pennsylvania near Baltic, are boarded up. A sheet of unpainted plywood is the door, and in it is a triangular peephole that now frames an eye. The plywood door opens. A man answers my question. Rooms there are six, seven, and ten dollars a week. I thank him for the information and move on, emerging from the ghetto at the Catholic Daughters of America Women's Guest House, between Atlantic and Pacific. Between Pacific and the Boardwalk are the blinking vacancy signs of the Aristocrat and Colton Manor motels. Pennsylvania terminates at the Sheraton-Seaside—thirty-two dollars a day, ocean corner. I take a walk on the Boardwalk and into the Holiday Inn (twenty-three stories). A guest is registering. "You reserved for Wednesday, and this is Monday," the clerk tells him. "But that's all right. We have *plenty* of rooms." The clerk is very young, female, and has soft brown hair that hangs below her waist. Her superior kicks her.

24      He is a middle-aged man with red spiderwebs in his face. He is jacketed and tied. He takes her aside. "Don't say 'plenty,'" he says. "Say 'You are fortunate, sir. We have rooms available.'"

25      The face of the young woman turns sour. "We have all the rooms you need," she says to the customer, and, to her superior, "How's that?"

26      Game 4. My opponent's luck has become abrasive. He has Boardwalk and Park Place, and has sealed the board.

27      Darrow was a plumber. He was, specifically, a radiator repairman who lived in Germantown, Pennsylvania. His first Monopoly board was a sheet of linoleum. On it he placed houses and hotels that he had carved from blocks of wood. The game he thus invented was brilliantly conceived, for it was an uncannily exact reflection of the business milieu at large. In its depth, range, and subtlety, in its luck-skill ratio, in its sense of infrastructure and socioeconomic parameters, in its philosophical characteristics, it reached to the profundity of the financial community. It was as scientific as the stock market. It suggested the manner and means through which an underdeveloped world had been developed. It was chess at Wall Street level. "Advance token to the nearest Railroad

and pay owner twice the rental to which he is otherwise entitled. If Railroad is unowned, you may buy it from the Bank. Get out of Jail, free. Advance token to nearest Utility. If unowned, you may buy it from Bank. If owned, throw dice and pay owner a total ten times the amount thrown. You are assessed for street repairs: $40 per house, $115 per hotel. Pay poor tax of $15. Go to Jail. Go directly to Jail. Do not pass Go. Do not collect $200.

The turnkey opens the blue door. The turnkey is known to the in-　28 mates as Sidney K. Above his desk are ten closed-circuit TV screens—assorted viewpoints of the jail. There are three cellblocks—men, women, juvenile boys. Six days is the average stay. Showers are twice a week. The stool doors and the equipment that operates them were made in San Antonio. The prisoners sleep on bunks of butcher block. There are no mattresses. There are three prisoners to a cell. In winter, it is cold in here. Prisoners burn newspapers to keep warm. Cell corners are black with smudge. The jail is three years old. The men's block echoes with chatter. The man in the cell nearest Sidney K. is pacing. His shirt is covered with broad stains of blood. The block for juvenile boys is, by contrast, utterly silent—empty corridor, empty cells. There is only one prisoner. He is small and black and appears to be thirteen. He says he is sixteen and that he has been alone in here for three days.

"Why are you here? What did you do?"　　29

"I hit a jitney driver."　　30

The series stands at three all. We have split the fifth and sixth　31 games. We are scrambling for property. Around the board we fairly fly. We move so fast because we do our own banking and search our own deeds. My opponent grows tense.

Ventnor Avenue, a street of delicatessens and doctors' offices, is　32 leafy with plane trees and hydrangeas, the city flower. Water Works is on the mainland. The water comes over in submarine pipes. Electric Company gets power from across the state, on the Delaware River, in Deepwater. States Avenue, now a wasteland like St. Charles, once had gardens running down the middle of the street, a horse-drawn trolley, private homes. States Avenue was as exclusive as the Brighton. Only an apartment house, a small motel, and the All Wars Memorial Building— monadnocks spaced widely apart—stand along States Avenue now. Pawnshops, convalescent homes, and the Paradise Soul Saving Station are on Virginia Avenue. The soul-saving station is pink, orange, and yellow. In the windows flanking the door of the Virginia Money Loan Office are Nikons, Polaroids, Yashicas, Sony TVs, Underwood typewriters, Singer sewing machines, and pictures of Christ. On the far side of town, beside a single track and locked up most of the time, is the new railroad station, a small hut made of glazed firebrick, all that is left of the lines that built the city. An authentic phrenologist works on New York Avenue close to Frank's Extra Dry Bar and a church where the sermon today is "Death in the Pot." The church is of pink brick, has blue and amber windows and two red doors. St. James Place, narrow and twisting, is lined with boarding houses that have wooden porches on each of three stories, suggesting a New Orleans made of salt-bleached pine. In a vacant lot on Tennessee is a white Ford station wagon stripped to the chassis. The windows are smashed. A plastic Clorox bottle sits on the driver's seat. The wind has pressed newspaper against the chain-link fence around the lot. Atlantic Avenue, the city's principal thoroughfare, could be seventeen American Main Streets placed end to end—discount vitamins and Vienna Corset shops, movie theatres, shoe stores, and funeral homes. The Boardwalk is made of yellow pine and Douglas fir, soaked in pentachlorophenol. Downbeach, it reaches far beyond the city. Signs everywhere—on windows, lampposts, trash baskets—proclaim "Bienvenue Canadiens!" The salt air is full of Canadian French. In the Claridge Hotel, on Park Place, I ask a clerk if she knows where Marvin Gardens is. She asks, "Is it a floral shop?" I ask a cabdriver, parked outside. He says, "Never heard of it." Park Place is one block long. Pacific to Boardwalk. On the roof of the Claridge is the Solarium, the highest point in town—panoramic view of the ocean, the bay, the salt-water ghetto. I look down at the rooftops of the side-avenue motels and into swimming pools. There are hundreds of people around the rooftop pools, sunbathing, reading—many more people than are on the beach. Walls, windows, and a block of sky are all that is visible from these pools—no sand, no sea. The pools are craters, and with the people around them they are countersunk into the motels.

33      The seventh, and final, game is ten minutes old and I have hotels on Oriental, Vermont, and Connecticut. I have Tennessee and St. James. I have North Carolina and Pacific. I have Boardwalk, Atlantic, Ventnor, Illinois, Indiana. My fingers are forming a "V." I have mortgaged most of these properties in order to pay for others, and I have mortgaged the others to pay for the hotels. I have seven dollars. I will pay off the mortgages and build my reserves with income from the three hotels. My cash position may be low, but I feel like a rocket in an underground silo. Meanwhile, if I could just go to jail for a time I could pause there, wait there, until my opponent, in his inescapable rounds, pays the rates of my hotels. Jail, at times, is the strategic place to be. I roll boxcars from the Reading and move the flatiron to Community Chest. "Go to Jail. Go directly to Jail."

34      The prisoners, of course, have no pens and no pencils. They take paper napkins, roll them tight as crayons, char the ends with matches, and write on the walls. The things they write are not entirely idiomatic; for example, "In God We Trust." All is in carbon. Time is required in the

writing. "Only humanity could know of such pain." "God So Loved the World." "There is no greater pain than life itself." In the women's block now, there are six blacks, giggling, and a white asleep in red shoes. She is drunk. The others are pushers, prostitutes, an auto thief, a burglar caught with pistol in purse. A sixteen-year-old accused of murder was in here last week. These words are written on the wall of a now empty cell: "Laying here I see two bunks about six inches thick, not counting the one I'm laying on, which is hard as brick. No cushion for my back. No pillow for my head. Just a couple scratchy blankets which is best to use it's said. I wake up in the morning so shivery and cold, waiting and waiting till I am told the food is coming. It's on its way. It's not worth waiting for, but I eat it anyway. I know one thing when they set me free I'm gonna be good if it kills me."

How many years must a game be played to produce an Anthony J. 35 Drexel Biddle and chestnut geldings on the beach? About half a century was the original answer, from the first railroad to Biddle at his peak. Biddle, at his peak, hit an Atlantic City streetcar conductor with his fist, laid him out with one punch. This increased Biddle's legend. He did not go to jail. While John Philip Sousa led his band along the Boardwalk playing "The Stars and Stripes Forever" and Jack Dempsey ran up and down in training for his fight with Gene Tunney, the city crossed the high curve of its parabola. Al Capone held conventions here—upstairs with his sleeves rolled, apportioning among his lieutenant governors the states of the Eastern seaboard. The natural history of an American resort proceeds from Indians to French Canadians via Biddles and Capones. French Canadians, whatever they may be at home, are Visigoths here. Bienvenue Visigoths!

My opponent plods along incredibly well. He has got his fourth rail- 36 road, and patiently, unbelievably, he has picked up my potential winners until he has blocked me everywhere but Marvin Gardens. He has avoided, in the fifty-dollar zoning, my increasingly petty hotels. His cash flow swells. His railroads are costing me two hundred dollars a minute. He is building hotels on States, Virginia, and St. Charles. He has temporarily reversed the current. With the yellow monopolies and my blue monopolies, I could probably defeat his lavenders and his railroads. I have Atlantic and Ventnor. I need Marvin Gardens. My only hope is Marvin Gardens.

There is a plaque at Boardwalk and Park Place, and on it in relief is 37 the leonine profile of a man who looks like an officer in a metropolitan bank—"Charles B. Darrow, 1889–1967, inventor of the game of Monopoly." "Darrow," I address him, aloud. "Where is Marvin Gardens?" There is, of course, no answer. Bronze, impassive, Darrow looks south down the Boardwalk. "Mr. Darrow, please, where is Marvin

Gardens?" Nothing. Not a sign. He just looks south down the Boardwalk.

38      My opponent accepts the trophy with his natural ease and I make, from notes, remarks that are even less graceful than his.

39      Marvin Gardens is the one color-block Monopoly property that is not in Atlantic City. It is a suburb within a suburb, secluded. It is a planned compound of seventy-two handsome houses set on curvilinear private streets under yews and cedars, poplars and willows. The compound was built around 1920, in Margate, New Jersey, and consists of solid buildings of stucco, brick, and wood, with slate roofs, tile roofs, multimullioned porches, Giraldic towers, and Spanish grilles. Marvin Gardens, the ultimate outwash of Monopoly, is a citadel and sanctuary of the middle class. "We're heavily patrolled by police here. We don't take no chances. Me? I'm living here nine years. I paid seventeen thousand dollars and I've been offered thirty. Number one, I don't want to move. Number two, I don't need the money. I have four bedrooms, two and a half baths, front den, back den. No basement. The Atlantic is down there. Six feet down and you float. A lot of people have a hard time finding this place. People that lived in Atlantic City all their life don't know how to find it. They don't know where the hell they're going. They just know it's south, down the Boardwalk."

## CONSIDERATIONS

1. What is the most obvious stylistic feature of McPhee's essay?

2. On first reading, you might complain that McPhee provides no transitional aids as he jumps from the world of the game to the world of Atlantic City. A second reading should make you aware of McPhee's skillful transitional devices. Point out some of them and adopt them in your writing.

3. In what sense might one call McPhee's final paragraph a postscript?

4. Why could not McPhee find Marvin Gardens in his walks around Atlantic City?

5. What evidence do you find that McPhee's research was not confined to walking about the streets of Atlantic City?

6. In playing off his description of Atlantic City's slums against a Monopoly game, does McPhee trivialize the inner-city problems, or does the irony of his unusual account heighten them? Build an argument to support your answer.

7. How much information about your own city or town could you find by walking a few of its streets? Try it. Take copious notes on your observations and impressions. Then devise a thesis that would help you organize your material into an interesting essay.

8. Read Peter Marin's essay "Helping and Hating the Homeless" (page 404). Imagine the two writers, John McPhee and Peter Marin, comparing notes. Could they have made any significant use of each other's material? Explain in an essay drawing on both authors.

*Nancy Mairs (b. 1943) began life in California, went east to attend
college in Massachusetts, and has worked as a technical writer
and editor as well as a teacher at the high school and college
levels. She has published a book of poems,* In All the Rooms of the
Yellow House *(1984), and a collection of essays,* Plain Text:
Deciphering a Woman's Life *(1986), as well as* Remembering the
Bone House: An Erotics of Place and Space *(1989).* Ordinary Time
*appeared in 1993 and in 1994* Voice Lessons: On Becoming a
(Woman) Writer. *Nancy Mairs has multiple sclerosis, uses a
wheelchair, and in 1997 wrote* Waist High in the World: A Life
among the Non-disabled.

*Notice the shapeliness of Mairs's essay, her ways of moving
among ideas, her ability to tie things together*

— 62

# NANCY MAIRS
## *The Unmaking of a Scientist*

My daughter is dissecting a chicken. Her first. Her father, whose job      1
this usually is, has been derelict in his duties, and my hands are now too
weak to dissect much more than a zucchini. If she wants dinner (and she
does), she will make this pale, flabby carcass into eight pieces I can fit
into the skillet. I act as coach. To encourage her, I tell her that her great-
great-grandfather was a butcher. This is true, not something I have made
up to con her into doing a nasty job.

Now that she's gotten going, she is having a wonderful time. She      2
has made the chicken crow and flap and dance all over the cutting board,
and now it lies quiet under her short, strong fingers as she slices the
length of its breastbone. She pries back the ribs and peers into the cavity.
"Oh, look at its mesenteries!" she cries. I tell her I thought mesentery
was something you got from drinking the water in Mexico. She pokes at
some filmy white webs. Mesenteries, she informs me, are the membranes that hold the chicken's organs in place. My organs too. She flips
the chicken over and begins to cut along its spine. As her fingers search
out joints and the knife severs wing from breast, leg from thigh, she gives

"The Unmaking of a Scientist" from *Plain Text: Deciphering a Woman's Life* by
Nancy Mairs. Reprinted by permission of the University of Arizona Press.

me a lesson in the comparative anatomy of this chicken and the frog she and her friend Emily have recently dissected at school.

3      I am charmed by her enthusiasm and self-assurance. Since she was quite small, she has talked of becoming a veterinarian, and now that she is approaching adulthood, her purpose is growing firmer. During this, her junior year in a special high school, she is taking a college-level introductory course in biology. I took much the same course when I was a freshman in college. But if I entered that course with Anne's self-confidence, and I may very well have done so, I certainly had none of it by the time I wrote the last word of my final examination in my blue book and turned it in the following spring. As the result of Miss White and the quadrat report, I am daunted to the point of dysfunction by the notion of thinking or writing "scientifically."

4      That woman—damn that woman!—turned me into a scientific cripple, and did so in the name of science at a prestigious women's college that promised to school me in the liberal arts that I might "have life and have it abundantly." And really, I have had it abundantly, so I suppose I oughtn't to complain if it's been a little short in *Paramecia* and *Amanita phalloides* and *Drosophila melanogaster*, whose eyes I have never seen.

5      Still, Miss White should not have been allowed to teach freshman biology because she had a fatal idiosyncrasy (fatal, that is, to the courage of students, not to herself, though I believe she is dead now of some unrelated cause): She could not bear a well-written report. One could be either a writer or a scientist but not both, she told me one November afternoon, the grey light from a tall window sinking into the grain of the dark woodwork in her cramped office in the old Science Building, her fingers flicking the sheets of my latest lab write-up. She was washing her hands of me, I could tell by the weariness of her tone. She didn't even try to make me a scientist. For that matter, she didn't even point to a spot where I'd gone wrong and show me what she wanted instead. She simply wrinkled her nose at the odor of my writing, handed me the sheets, and sent me away. We never had another conference. At the end of the semester, I wrote my quadrat report, and Miss White failed it. She allowed me to rewrite it. I wrote it again, and she failed it again. Neither of us went for a third try.

6      All the same, I liked my quadrat, which was a twenty-by-twenty plot in the College Woods behind the Library. Mine was drab compared to some others: Pam Weprin's, I remember, had a brook running through it, in which she discovered goldfish. It turned out that her magical discovery had a drab explanation: In a heavy rain the water from Peacock Pond backed up and spilled its resident carp into the brook. Even so, her quadrat briefly held an excitement mine never did. Mine was, in fact, as familiar as a living room, since I had spent large portions of my youth tramping another such woods sixty miles north. The lichen grew on the north side of the trees. In the rain the humus turned black and rank.

Afterwards, a fallen log across one corner would sprout ears of tough, pale fungus.

Each freshman biology student received a quadrat. There were enough of us that we had to double up, but I never met my quadrat-mate or even knew her name. It occurs to me that I ought to have found out, ought to have asked her what she got on her quadrat report, but I was new to failure and knew no ways to profit from it. I simply did as I was told—visited my quadrat to observe its progress through the seasons and wrote up my observations—and then discovered that I had somehow seen and spoken wrong. I wish now that I had kept the report. I wonder exactly what I said in it. Probably something about ears of fungus. Good God.

With a D+ for the first semester I continued, perversely, to like biology, but I also feared it more and more. Not the discipline itself. I pinned and opened a long earthworm, marvelling at the delicately tinted organs. I dissected a beef heart, carefully, so as not to spoil it for stuffing and roasting at the biology department's annual beef-heart feast. For weeks I explored the interior of my rat, which I had opened neatly, like the shutters over a window. He was a homely thing, stiff, his fur yellow and matted from formaldehyde, and because he was male, not very interesting. Several students got pregnant females, and I envied them the intricate organs, the chains of bluish-pink fetuses. At the end of each lab, I would reluctantly close the shutters, swaddle my rat in his plastic bag, and slip him back into the crock.

No, biology itself had more fascination and delight than fear. But with each report I grew more terrified of my own insidious poetic nature, which Miss White sniffed out in the simplest statement about planaria or left ventricles. Years later, when I became a technical editor and made my living translating the garbled outbursts of scientists, I learned that I had done nothing much wrong. My understanding was limited, to be sure, but Miss White would have forgiven me ignorance, even stupidity I think, if I had sufficiently muddled the language. As it was, I finished biology with a C−, and lucky I was to get it, since the next year the college raised the passing grade from C− to C. I have always thought, indeed, that the biology department awarded me a passing grade simply so that they wouldn't have to deal with me another year.

And they didn't. Nor did anyone else. I never took another science course, although I surprised myself long afterward by becoming, perforce and precipitously, a competent amateur herpetologist. My husband arrived home one afternoon with a shoebox containing a young bull snake, or gopher snake as this desert variety is called, which he had bought for a quarter from some of his students at a school for emotionally disturbed boys so that they wouldn't try to find out how long a snake keeps wriggling without its head. This was Ferdinand, who was followed by two more bull snakes, Squeeze and Beowulf, and by a checkered garter snake named Winslow J. Tweed, a black racer named Jesse Owens, a Yuma king snake named Hrothgar, and numerous nameless and short-lived blind

7

8

9

10

snakes, tiny and translucent, brought to us by our cats Freya, Burton Rustle, and Vanessa Bell. I grew so knowledgeable that when my baby boa constrictor, Crictor, contracted a respiratory ailment, I found that I was more capable of caring for him than were any of the veterinarians in the city. In fact, I learned, veterinarians do not do snakes; I could find only one to give Crictor the shot of a broad-spectrum antibiotic he needed.

11        So I do do snakes. I have read scientific treatises on them. I know that the Latin name for the timber rattlesnake is *Crotalus horridus horridus*. I know that Australia has more varieties of venomous snakes than any other continent, among them the lethal sea snakes and the willfully aggressive tiger snake. I know how long one is likely to live after being bitten by a mamba (not long). I read the treatises; but I don't, of course, write them. Although as a technical editor I grew proficient at unraveling snarls in the writing of scientists. I have never, since Miss White, attempted scientific experimentation or utterance.

12        Aside from my venture into herpetology, I remain a scientific booby. I mind my stupidity. I feel diminished by it. And I know now that it is unnecessary, the consequence of whatever quirk of fate brought me into Miss White's laboratory instead of Miss Chidsey's or Dr. McCoy's. Miss White, who once represented the whole of scientific endeavor to me, was merely a woman with a hobbyhorse. I see through her. Twenty years later, I am now cynical enough to write a quadrat report badly enough to pass her scrutiny, whereas when I had just turned seventeen I didn't even know that cynicism was an option—knowledge that comes, I suppose, from having life abundantly. I've learned, too, that Miss White's bias, though unusually strong, was not peculiar to herself but arose from a cultural rift between the humanities and the sciences resulting in the assumption that scientists will naturally write badly, that they are, in fact, rhetorical boobies. Today I teach technical writing. My students come to me terrified of the word-world from which they feel debarred, and I teach them to breach the boundaries in a few places, to step with bravado at least a little way inside. Linguistic courage is the gift I can give them.

13        In return, they give me gifts that I delight in—explanations of vortex centrifuges, evaluations of copper-smelting processes, plans for extracting gums from paloverde beans. These help me compensate for my deficiencies, as do the works of the popularizers of science. Carl Sagan. Loren Eiseley. Lewis Thomas and his reverential reflections subtitled *Notes of a Biology Watcher*. Stephen Jay Gould. James Burke and Jacob Bronowski. Pierre Teilhard de Chardin. John McPhee, who has made me love rocks. Isaac Asimov. Elaine Morgan. I watch television too. *Nova. Odyssey. The Undersea World of Jacques Cousteau. The Body in Question.* But always I am aware that I am having translated for me the concepts of worlds I will never now explore for myself. I stand with my toes on the boundaries, peering, listening.

Anne has done a valiant job with the chicken. She's had a little 14
trouble keeping its pajamas on, and one of the thighs has a peculiar trape-
zoidal shape, but she's reduced it to a workable condition. I brown it in
butter and olive oil. I press in several cloves of garlic and then splash in
some white wine. As I work, I think of the worlds Anne is going to explore. Some of them are listed in the college catalogues she's begun to
collect: "Genetics, Energetics, and Evolution"; "Histology of Animals";
"Vertebrate Endocrinology"; "Electron Microscopy"; "Organic Synthesis"; "Animal Morphogenesis."

Anne can write. No one has yet told her that she can be a scientist 15
or a writer but not both, and I trust that no one ever will. The complicated world can ill afford such lies to its children. As she plunges from
my view into the thickets of calculus, embryology, and chemical ther-
modynamics, I will wait here for her to send me back messages. I love
messages.

## CONSIDERATIONS

1. What, precisely, is a quadrat? (*Hint:* It is not a member of the family *Muridae*
or of the genus *Rattus*, one specimen of which Mairs dissected as a girl in biology class.
It does, however, figure importantly in Mairs's disillusionment with science education.)
What do you think of the quadrat as a teaching or learning device?

2. Mairs does some interesting things with tenses in her essay. Study the changes
carefully. How might you try them in your own writing?

3. "The complicated world can ill afford such lies to its children," Mairs writes in
her closing paragraph. What lies does she mean? Why is she particularly well qualified
to point them out?

4. Another aspect to the preceding question opens up if one thinks about the
"cultural rift" Mairs writes about in paragraph 12 "between the humanities and the sciences." What does she know about that?

5. Are any of the science writers so admired by Mairs in paragraph 13 immediately available to you? Read one of those in your text, and explain why Mairs might admire him or her.

6. Imagine Nancy Mairs having coffee with Walther Prausnitz (page 507). What
might they have in common to talk about with regard to teaching and learning? Would
they agree on everything?

*Peter Marin (b. 1936) teaches at the University of California at
Santa Barbara in the departments of sociology and of English—a
double profession that probably makes him unique among
American academics. He has taught at colleges all over the
country, has directed a free school, has worked for the
government, and has written in many genres: poems, a novel, and
many essays of social criticism.*

*He likes especially to investigate people and ideas that
appear excluded from the center of American society. For several
years, he has spent much of his time in shelters and on the streets
of American cities. In 1994 he collected* Freedom and Its
Discontents, *subtitled* Reflections on Four Decades of American
Moral Experience.

## — 63 —

# PETER MARIN
*Helping and Hating the Homeless*

1    When I was a child, I had a recurring vision of how I would end as
an old man: alone, in a sparsely furnished second-story room I could picture quite precisely, in a walk-up on Fourth Avenue in New York, where
the secondhand bookstores then were. It was not a picture which frightened me. I liked it. The idea of anonymity and solitude and marginality
must have seemed to me, back then, for reasons I do not care to remember, both inviting and inevitable. Later, out of college, I took to the road,
hitchhiking and traveling on freights, doing odd jobs here and there,
crisscrossing the country. I liked that too: the anonymity and the absence of constraint and the rough community I sometimes found. I felt at
home on the road, perhaps because I felt at home nowhere else, and periodically, for years, I would return to that world, always with a sense of
relief and release.

2    I have been thinking a lot about that these days, now that transience and homelessness have made their way into the national consciousness, and especially since the town I live in, Santa Barbara, has
become well known because of the recent successful campaign to do

---

**404**

away with the meanest aspects of its "sleeping ordinances"—a set of foolish laws making it illegal for the homeless to sleep at night in public places. During that campaign I got to know many of the homeless men and women in Santa Barbara, who tend to gather, night and day, in a small park at the lower end of town, not far from the tracks and the harbor, under the rooflike, overarching branches of a gigantic fig tree, said to be the oldest on the continent. There one enters much the same world I thought, as a child, I would die in, and the one in which I traveled as a young man: a "marginal" world inhabited by all those unable to find a place in "our" world. Sometimes, standing on the tracks close to the park, you can sense in the wind, or in the smell of tar and ties, the presence and age of that material world: the way it stretches backward and inevitably forward in time, parallel to our own world, always present, always close, and yet separated from us—at least in the mind  by a gulf few of us are interested in crossing.

Late last summer, at a city council meeting here in Santa Barbara, I    3
saw, close up, the consequences of that strange combination of proximity and distance. The council was meeting to vote on the repeal of the sleeping ordinances, though not out of any sudden sense of compassion or justice. Council members had been pressured into it by the threat of massive demonstrations—"The Selma of the Eighties" was the slogan one heard among the homeless. But this threat that frightened the council enraged the town's citizens. Hundreds of them turned out for the meeting. One by one they filed to the microphone to curse the council and castigate the homeless. Drinking, doping, loitering, panhandling, defecating, urinating, molesting, stealing—the litany went on and on, was repeated over and over, accompanied by fantasies of disaster: the barbarian hordes at the gates, civilization ended.

What astonished me about the meeting was not what was said; one    4
could have predicted that. It was the power and depth of the emotion revealed: the mindlessness of the fear, the vengefulness of the fury. Also, almost none of what was said had anything to do with the homeless people I know—not the ones I once traveled with, not the ones in town. They, the actual homeless men and women, might not have existed at all.

If I write about Santa Barbara, it is not because I think the attitudes    5
at work here are unique. They are not. You find them everywhere in America. In the last few months I have visited several cities around the country, and in each of them I have found the same thing: more and more people in the streets, more and more suffering. (There are at least 350,000 homeless people in the country, perhaps as many as 3 million.) And, in talking to the good citizens of these cities, I found, almost always, the same thing: confusion and ignorance, or simple indifference, but anger too, and fear.

What follows here is an attempt to explain at least some of that    6
anger and fear, to clear up some of the confusion, to chip away at the indifference. It is not meant to be definitive; how could it be? The point is

to try to illuminate some of the darker corners of homelessness, those we ordinarily ignore, and those in which the keys to much that is now going on may be hidden.

7    The trouble begins with the word "homeless." It has become such an abstraction, and is applied to so many different kinds of people, with so many different histories and problems, that it is almost meaningless.

8    Homelessness, in itself, is nothing more than a condition visited upon men and women (and, increasingly, children) as the final stage of a variety of problems about which the word "homelessness" tells us almost nothing. Or, to put it another way, it is a catch basin into which pour all of the people disenfranchised or marginalized or scared off by processes beyond their control, those which lie close to the heart of American life. Here are the groups packed into the single category of "the homeless":

- Veterans, mainly from the war in Vietnam. In many American cities, vets make up close to 50 percent of all homeless males.
- The mentally ill. In some parts of the country, roughly a quarter of the homeless would, a couple of decades ago, have been institutionalized.
- The physically disabled or chronically ill, who do not receive any benefits or whose benefits do not enable them to afford permanent shelter.
- The elderly on fixed incomes whose funds are no longer sufficient for their needs.
- Men, women, and whole families pauperized by the loss of a job.
- Single parents, usually women, without the resources or skills to establish new lives.
- Runaway children, many of whom have been abused.
- Alcoholics and those in trouble with drugs (whose troubles often begin with one of the other conditions listed here).
- Immigrants, both legal and illegal, who often are not counted among the homeless because they constitute a "problem" in their own right.
- Traditional tramps, hobos, and transients, who have taken to the road or the streets for a variety of reasons and who prefer to be there.

9    You can quickly learn two things about the homeless from this list. First, you can learn that many of the homeless, before they were homeless, were people more or less like ourselves: members of the working or middle class. And you can learn that the world of the homeless has its roots in various policies, events, and ways of life for which some of us are responsible and from which some of us actually prosper.

10    We decide, as a people, to go to war, we ask our children to kill and to die, and the result, years later, is grown men homeless on the street.

We change, with the best intentions, the laws pertaining to the    11
mentally ill, and then, without intention, neglect to provide them with
services; and the result, in our streets, drives some of us crazy with rage.

We cut taxes and prune budgets, we modernize industry and shift    12
the balance of trade, and the result of all these actions and errors can be
read, sleeping form by sleeping form, on our city streets.

The liberals cannot blame the conservatives. The conservatives    13
cannot blame the liberals. Homelessness is the *sum total* of our dreams,
policies, intentions, errors, omissions, cruelties, kindnesses, all of it
recorded, in flesh, in the life of the streets.

You can also learn from this list one of the most important things    14
there is to know about the homeless—that they can be roughly divided
into two groups: those who have had homelessness forced upon them and
want nothing more than to escape it; and those who have at least in part
*chosen* it for themselves, and now accept, or in some cases, embrace it.

I understand how dangerous it is to introduce the idea of choice    15
into a discussion of homelessness. It can all too easily be used to justify
indifference or brutality toward the homeless, or to argue that they are
only getting what they "deserve." And yet it seems to me that it is only
by taking choice into account, in all of the intracacies of its various
forms and expressions, that one can really understand certain kinds of
homelessness.

The fact is, many of the homeless are not only hapless victims but    16
voluntary exiles, "domestic refugees," people who have turned not
against life itself but against *us*, our life, American life. Look for a moment at the vets. The price of returning to America was to forget what
they had seen or learned in Vietnam, to "put it behind them." But some
could not do that, and the stress of trying showed up as alcoholism, broken marriages, drug addiction, crime. And it showed up too as life on the
street, which was for some vets a desperate choice made in the name of
life—the best they could manage. It was a way of avoiding what might
have occurred had they stayed where they were: suicide, or violence done
to others.

We must learn to accept that there may indeed be people, and not    17
only vets, who have seen so much of our world, or seen it so clearly, that
to live in it becomes impossible. Here, for example, is the story of Alice,
a homeless middle-aged woman in Los Angeles, where there are, perhaps, 50,000 homeless people. It was set down a few months ago by one
of my students at the University of California, Santa Barbara, where I
taught for a semester. I had encouraged them to go find the homeless and
listen to their stories. And so, one day, when this student saw Alice foraging in a dumpster outside a McDonald's, he stopped and talked to her:

> She told me she had led a pretty normal life as she grew up and
> eventually went to college. From there she went on to Chicago to
> teach school. She was single and lived in a small apartment.

One night, after she got off the train after school, a man began to follow her to her apartment building. When she got to her door she saw a knife and the man hovering behind her. She had no choice but to let him in. The man raped her.

After that, things got steadily worse. She had a nervous breakdown. She went to a mental institution for three months, and when she went back to her apartment she found her belongings gone. The landlord had sold them to cover the rent she hadn't paid.

She had no place to go and no job because the school had terminated her employment. She slipped into depression. She lived with friends until she could muster enough money for a ticket to Los Angeles. She said she no longer wanted to burden her friends, and that if she had to live outside, at least Los Angeles was warmer than Chicago.

It is as if she began back then to take on the mentality of a street person. She resolved herself to homelessness. She's been out West since 1980, without a home or job. She seems happy, with her best friend being her cat. But the scars of memories still haunt her, and she is running from them, or should I say *him*.

18     This is, in essence, the same story one hears over and over again on the street. You begin with an ordinary life; then an event occurs—traumatic, catastrophic; smaller events follow, each one deepening the original wound; finally, homelessness becomes inevitable, or begins to *seem* inevitable to the person involved—the only way out of an intolerable situation. You are struck continually, hearing these stories, by something seemingly unique in American life, the absolute isolation involved. In what other culture would there be such an absence or failure of support from familial, social, or institutional sources? Even more disturbing is the fact that it is often our supposed sources of support—family, friends, government organizations—that have caused the problem in the first place.

19     Everything that happened to Alice—the rape, the loss of job and apartment, the breakdown—was part and parcel of a world gone radically wrong, a world, for Alice, no longer to be counted on, no longer worth living in. Her homelessness can be seen as flight, as failure of will or nerve, even, perhaps, as *disease*. But it can also be seen as a mute, furious refusal, a self-imposed exile far less appealing to the rest of us than ordinary life, but *better*, in Alice's terms.

20     We like to think, in America, that everything is redeemable, that everything broken can be magically made whole again, and that what has been "dirtied" can be cleansed. Recently I saw on television that one of the soaps had introduced the character of a homeless old woman. A woman in her thirties discovers that her long-lost mother has appeared in town, on the streets. After much searching the mother is located and identified and embraced; and then she is scrubbed and dressed in style, restored in a matter of days to her former upper-class habits and role.

A triumph—but one more likely to occur on television than in real    21
life. Yes, many of these on the streets could be transformed, rehabili-
tated. But there are others whose lives have been irrevocably changed,
damaged beyond repair, and who no longer want help, who no longer recognize the need for help, and whose experience in our world has made
them want only to be left alone. How, for instance, would one restore
Alice's life, or reshape it in a way that would satisfy *our* notion of what a
life should be? What would it take to return her to the fold? How to erase
the four years of homelessness, which have become as familiar to her,
and as much a home, as her "normal" life once was? Whatever we think
of the way in which she has resolved her difficulties, it constitutes a sad
peace made with the world. Intruding ourselves upon it in the name of
redemption is by no means as simple a task—or as justifiable a task—as
one might think.

It is important to understand too that however disorderly and dirty    22
and unmanageable the world of homeless men and women like Alice appears to us, it is not without its significance, and its rules and rituals.
The homeless in our cities mark out for themselves particular neighborhoods, blocks, buildings, doorways. They impose on themselves often
obsessively strict routines. They reduce their world to a small area, and
thereby protect themselves from a world that otherwise would be too
much to bear.

Pavlov, the Russian psychologist, once theorized that the two most    23
fundamental reflexes in all animals, including humans, are those involving freedom and orientation. Grab any animal, he said, and it will immediately struggle to accomplish two things: to break free and to orient
itself. And this is what one sees in so many of the homeless. Having been
stripped of all other forms of connection, and of most kinds of social
identity, they are left only with this: the raw stuff of nature, something
encoded in the cells—the desire to be free, the need for familiar space.
Perhaps this is why so many of them struggle so vehemently against us
when we offer them aid. They are clinging to their freedom and their
space, and they do not believe that this is what we, with our programs
and our shelters, mean to allow them.

Years ago, when I first came to California, bumming my way west,    24
the marginal world, and the lives of those in it, were very different from
what they are now. In those days I spent much of my time in hobo jungles
or on the skid rows of various cities, and just as it was easier back then to
"get by" in the easygoing beach towns on the California coast, or in the
bohemian and artistic worlds in San Francisco or Los Angeles or New
York, it was also far easier than it is now to survive in the marginal world.

It is important to remember this—important to recognize the im-    25
mensity of the changes that have occurred in the marginal world in the
past twenty years. Whole sections of many cities—the Bowery in New
York, the Tenderloin in San Francisco—were once ceded to the transient.

In every skidrow area in America you could find what you needed to survive: hash houses, saloons offering free lunches, pawnshops, surplus-clothing stores, and, most important of all, cheap hotels and flophouses and two-bit employment agencies specializing in the kinds of labor (seasonal, shape-up) transients have always done.

26      It was by no means a wonderful world. But it *was* a world. Its rituals were spelled out in ways most of the participants understood. In hobo jungles up and down the tracks, whatever there was to eat went into a common pot and was divided equally. Late at night, in empties criss-crossing the country, men would speak with a certain anonymous openness, as if the shared condition of transience created among them a kind of civility.

27      What most people in that world wanted was simply to be left alone. Some of them had been on the road for years, itinerant workers. Others were recuperating from wounds they could never quite explain. There were young men and a few women with nothing better to do, and older men who had no families or had lost their jobs or wives, or for whom the rigor and pressure of life had proved too demanding. The marginal world offered them a respite from the other world, a world grown too much for them.

28      But things have changed. There began to pour into the marginal world—slowly in the sixties, a bit faster in the seventies, and then faster still in the eighties—more and more people who neither belonged nor knew how to survive there. The sixties brought the counterculture and drugs; the streets filled with young dropouts. Changes in the law loosed upon the streets mentally ill men and women. Inflation took its toll, then recession. Working-class and even middle-class men and women—entire families—began to fall into a world they did not understand.

29      At the same time the transient world was being inundated by new inhabitants, its landscape, its economy, was shrinking radically. Jobs became harder to find. Modernization had something to do with it; machines took the place of men and women. And the influx of workers from Mexico and points farther south created a class of semipermanent workers who took the place of casual transient labor. More important, perhaps, was the fact that the forgotten parts of many cities began to attract attention. Downtown areas were redeveloped, reclaimed. The skid-row sections of smaller cities were turned into "old townes." The old hotels that once catered to transients were upgraded or torn down or became warehouses for welfare families—an arrangement far more profitable to the owners. The price of housing increased; evictions increased. The mentally ill, who once could afford to house themselves in cheap rooms, the alcoholics, who once would drink themselves to sleep at night in their cheap hotels, were out on the street—exposed to the weather and to danger, and also in plain and public view: "problems" to be dealt with.

30      Nor was it only cheap shelter that disappeared. It was also those "open" spaces that had once been available to those without other shel-

ter. As property rose in value, the nooks and crannies in which the homeless had been able to hide became more visible. Doorways, alleys, abandoned buildings, vacant lots—these "holes" in the cityscape, these gaps in public consciousness, became *real estate*. The homeless, who had been there all the time, were overtaken by economic progress, and they became intruders.

You cannot help thinking, as you watch this process, of what hap-   31
pened in parts of Europe in the eighteenth and nineteenth centuries: the effects of the enclosure laws, which eliminated the "commons" in the countryside and drove the rural poor, now homeless, into the cities. The centuries-old tradition of common access and usage was swept away by the beginnings of industrialism; land became *privatized*, a commodity. At the same time something occurred in the cultural psyche. The world itself, space itself, was subtly altered. It was no longer merely to be lived in; it was now to be owned. What was enclosed was not only the land. It was also *the flesh itself*; it was cut off from, denied access to, the physical world.

And one thinks too, when thinking of the homeless, of the   32
American past, the settlement of the "new" world which occurred at precisely the same time that the commons disappeared. The dream of freedom and equality that brought men and women here had something to do with *space*, as if the wilderness itself conferred upon those arriving here a new beginning: the Eden that had been lost. Once God had sent Christ to redeem men; now he provided a new world. Men discovered, or believed, that this world, and perhaps time itself, had no edge, no limit. Space was a sign of God's magnanimity. It was a kind of grace.

Somehow, it is all this that is folded into the sad shapes of the   33
homeless. In their mute presence one can sense, however faintly, the dreams of a world gone aglimmering, and the presence of our failed hopes. A kind of claim is made, silently, an ethic is proferred, or, if you will, a whole cosmology, one older than our own ideas of privilege and property. It is as if flesh itself were seeking, this one last time, the home in the world it has been denied.

Daily the city eddies around the homeless. The crowds flowing past   34
leave a few feet, a gap. We do not touch the homeless world. Perhaps we cannot touch it. It remains separate even as the city surrounds it.

The homeless, simply because they are homeless, are strangers,   35
alien—and therefore a threat. Their presence, in itself, comes to constitute a kind of violence; it deprives us of our sense of safety. Let me use myself as an example. I know, and respect, many of those now homeless on the streets of Santa Barbara. Twenty years ago, some of them would have been my companions and friends. And yet, these days, if I walk through the park near my home and see strangers bedding down for the night, my first reaction, if not fear, is a sense of annoyance and intrusion, of worry and alarm. I think of my teenage daughter, who often walks

through the park, and then of my house, a hundred yards away, and I am tempted—only tempted, but tempted, still—to call the "proper" authorities to have the strangers moved on. Out of sight, out of mind.

36     Notice: I do not bring them food. I do not offer them shelter or a shower in the morning. I do not even stop to talk. Instead, I think: my daughter, my house, my privacy. What moves me is not the threat of *danger*—nothing as animal as that. Instead there pops up inside of me, neatly in a row, a set of anxieties, ones you might arrange in a dollhouse living room and label: Family of bourgeois fears. The point is this: our response to the homeless is fed by a complex set of cultural attitudes, habits of thought, and fantasies and fears so familiar to us, so common, that they have become a *second* nature and might as well be instinctive, for all the control we have over them. And it is by no means easy to untangle this snarl of responses. What does seem clear is that the homeless embody all that bourgeois culture has for centuries tried to eradicate and destroy.

37     If you look to the history of Europe you find that homelessness first appears (or is first acknowledged) at the very same moment that bourgeois culture begins to appear. The same processes produced them both: the breakup of feudalism, the rise of commerce and cities, the combined triumphs of capitalism, industrialism, and individualism. The historian Fernand Braudel, in *The Wheels of Commerce*, describes, for instance, the armies of impoverished men and women who began to haunt Europe as far back as the eleventh century. And the makeup of these masses? Essentially the same then as it is now: the unfortunates, the throwaways, the misfits, the deviants.

> In the eighteenth century, all sorts and conditions were to be found in this human dross . . . widows, orphans, cripples . . . journeymen who had broken their contracts, out-of-work labourers, homeless priests with no living, old men, fire victims . . . war victims, deserters, discharged soldiers, would-be vendors of useless articles, vagrant preachers with or without licenses, "pregnant servant-girls and unmarried mothers driven from home," children sent out "to find bread or to maraud."

38     Then, as now, distinctions were made between the "homeless" and the supposedly "deserving" poor, those who knew their place and willingly sustained, with their labors, the emergent bourgeois world.

> The good paupers were accepted, lined up and registered on the official list; they had a right to public charity and were sometimes allowed to solicit it outside churches in the prosperous districts, when the congregation came out, or in market places. . . .
>      When it comes to beggars and vagrants, it is a very different story, and different pictures meet the eye: crowds, mobs,

processions, sometimes mass emigrations, "along the country
highways or the streets of the Towns and Villages," by beggars
"whom hunger and nakedness has driven from home." . . . The
towns dreaded these alarming visitors and drove them out as soon as
they appeared on the horizon.

And just as the distinctions made about these masses were the　39
same then as they are now, so too was the way society saw them. They
seemed to bourgeois eyes (as they still do) the one segment of society
that remained resistant to progress, unassimilable and incorrigible, inimical to all order.

It is in the nineteenth century, in the Victorian era, that you can　40
find the beginnings of our modern strategies for dealing with the homeless: the notion that they should be controlled and perhaps eliminated
through "help." With the Victorians we begin to see the entangling
of self-protection with social obligation, the strategy of masking self-
interest and the urge to control as *moral duty*. Michel Foucault has
spelled this out in his books on madness and punishment: the zeal with
which the overseers of early bourgeois culture tried to purge, improve,
and purify all of urban civilization—whether through schools and prisons, or, quite literally, with public baths and massive new water and
sewage systems. Order, ordure—this is, in essence, the tension at the
heart of bourgeois culture, and it was the singular genius of the
Victorians to make it the main component of their medical, aesthetic,
*and* moral systems. It was not a sense of justice or even empathy which
called for charity or new attitudes toward the poor; it was *hygiene*. The
very same attitudes appear in nineteenth-century America. Charles
Loring Brace, in an essay on homeless and vagrant children written in
1876, described the treatment of delinquents in this way: "Many of their
vices drop from them like the old and verminous clothing they left behind. . . . The entire change of circumstances seems to cleanse them of
bad habits." Here you have it all: *vices, verminous clothing, cleansing
them of bad habits*—the triple association of poverty with vice with dirt,
an equation in which each term comes to stand for all of them.

These attitudes are with us still; that is the point. In our own cen-　41
tury the person who has written most revealingly about such things is
George Orwell, who tried to analyze his own middle-class attitudes toward the poor. In 1933, in *Down and Out in Paris and London*, he wrote
about tramps:

> In childhood we are taught that tramps are blackguards . . . a
> repulsive, rather dangerous creature, who would rather die than
> work or wash, and wants nothing but to beg, drink or rob henhouses.
> The tramp monster is no truer to life than the sinister Chinaman of
> the magazines, but he is very hard to get rid of. The very word
> "tramp" evokes his image.

42     All of this is still true in America, though now it is not the word "tramp" but the word "homeless" that evokes the images we fear. It is the homeless who smell. Here, for instance, is part of a paper a student of mine wrote about her first visit to a Rescue Mission on skid row.

> The sermon began. The room was stuffy and smelly. The mixture of body odors and cooking was nauseating. I remember thinking: how can these people share this facility? They must be repulsed by each other. They had strange habits and dispositions. They were a group of dirty, dishonored, weird people to me.
> When it was over I ran to my car, went home, and took a shower. I felt extremely dirty. Through the day I would get flashes of that disgusting smell.

43     To put it as bluntly as I can, for many of us the homeless are *shit*. And our policies toward them, our spontaneous sense of disgust and horror, our wish to be rid of them—all of this has hidden in it, close to its heart, our feelings about excrement. Even Marx, that most bourgeois of revolutionaries, described the deviant *lumpen* in *The Eighteenth Brumaire of Louis Bonaparte* as "scum, offal, refuse of all classes." These days, in puritanical Marxist nations, they are called "parasites"—a word, perhaps not incidentally, one also associates with human waste.

44     What I am getting at here is the *nature* of the desire to help the homeless—what is hidden behind it and why it so often does harm. Every government program, almost every private project, is geared as much to the needs of those giving help as it is to the needs of the homeless. Go to any government agency, or, for that matter, to most private charities, and you will find yourself enmeshed, at once, in a bureaucracy so tangled and oppressive, or confronted with so much moral arrogance and contempt, that you will be driven back out into the streets for relief.

45     Santa Barbara, where I live, is as good an example as any. There are three main shelters in the city—all of them private. Between them they provide fewer than a hundred beds a night for the homeless. Two of the three shelters are religious in nature: the Rescue Mission and the Salvation Army. In the mission, as in most places in the country, there are elaborate and stringent rules. Beds go first to those who have not been there for two months, and you can stay for only two nights in any two-month period. No shelter is given to those who are not sober. Even if you go to the mission only for a meal, you are required to listen to sermons and participate in prayer, and you are regularly proselytized— sometimes overtly, sometimes subtly. There are obligatory, regimented showers. You go to bed precisely at ten: lights out, no reading, no talking. After the lights go out you will find fifteen men in a room with double-decker bunks. As the night progresses the room grows stuffier and hotter. Men toss, turn, cough, and moan. In the morning you are awakened pre-

cisely at five forty-five. Then breakfast. At seven-thirty you are back on the street.

The town's newest shelter was opened almost a year ago by a con-   46
sortium of local churches. Families and those who are employed have first call on the beds—a policy which excludes the congenitally homeless. Alcohol is not simply forbidden *in* the shelter; those with a history of alcoholism must sign a "contract" pledging to remain sober and chemical-free. Finally, in a paroxysm of therapeutic bullying, the shelter has added a new wrinkle: if you stay more than two days you are required to fill out and then discuss with a social worker a complex form listing what you perceive as your personal failings, goals, and strategies—all of this for men and women who simply want a place to lie down out of the rain!

It is these attitudes, in various forms and permutations, that you   47
find repeated endlessly in America. We are moved either to "redeem" the homeless or to punish them. Perhaps there is nothing consciously hostile about it. Perhaps it is simply that as the machinery of bureaucracy cranks itself up to deal with these problems, attitudes assert themselves automatically. But whatever the case, the fact remains that almost every one of our strategies for helping the homeless is simply an attempt to rearrange the world *cosmetically*, in terms of how it looks and smells to us. Compassion is little more than the passion for control.

The central question emerging from all this is, What does a society   48
owe to its members in trouble, and *how* is that debt to be paid? It is a question which must be answered in two parts: first, in relation to the men and women who have been marginalized against their will, and then, in a slightly different way, in relation to those who have chosen (or accept or even prize) their marginality.

As for those who have been marginalized against their wills, I think   49
the general answer is obvious: A society owes its members whatever it takes for them to regain their places in the social order. And when it comes to specific remedies, one need only read backward the various processes which have created homelessness and then figure out where help is likely to do the most good. But the real point here is not the specific remedies required—affordable housing, say—but the basis upon which they must be offered, the necessary underlying ethical notion we seem in this nation unable to grasp: that those who are the inevitable casualties of modern industrial capitalism and the free-market system are entitled, *by right*, and by the simple virtue of their participation in that system, to whatever help they need. They are entitled to have to find and hold their places in the society whose social contract they have, in effect, signed and observed.

Look at that for just a moment: the notion of a contract. The majority   50
of homeless Americans have kept, insofar as they could, to the terms of that contract. In any shelter these days you can find men and women who have worked ten, twenty, forty years, and whose lives have nonetheless

come to nothing. These are people who cannot afford a place in the world they helped create. And in return? Is it life on the street they have earned? Or the cruel charity we so grudgingly grant them?

51 But those marginalized against their will are only half the problem. There remains, still, the question of whether we owe anything to those who are voluntarily marginal. What about them: the street people, the rebels, and the recalcitrants, those who have torn up their social contracts or returned them unsigned?

52 I was in Las Vegas last fall, and I went out to the Rescue Mission at the lower end of town, on the edge of the black ghetto, where I first stayed years ago on my way west. It was twilight, still hot; in the vacant lot next door to the mission 200 men were lining up for supper. A warm wind blew along the street lined with small houses and salvage yards, and in the distance I could see the desert's edge and the smudge of low hills in the fading light. There were elderly alcoholics in line, and derelicts, but mainly the men were the same sort I had seen here years ago: youngish, out of work, restless and talkative, the drifters and wanderers for whom the word "wanderlust" was invented.

53 At supper—long communal tables, thin gruel, stale sweet rolls, ice water—a huge black man in his twenties, fierce and muscular, sat across from me. "I'm from the Coast, man," he said. "Never been away from home before. Ain't sure I like it. Sure don't like *this* place. But I lost my job back home a couple of weeks ago and figured, why wait around for another. I thought I'd come out here, see me something of the world."

54 After supper, a squat Portuguese man in his mid-thirties, hunkered down against the mission wall, offered me a smoke and told me: "Been sleeping in my car, up the street, for a week. Had my own business back in Omaha. But I got bored, man. Sold everything, got a little dough, came out here. Thought I'd work construction. Let me tell you, this is one tough town."

55 In a world better than ours, I suppose, men (or women) like this might not exist. Conservatives seem to have no trouble imagining a society so well disciplined and moral that deviance of this kind would disappear. And leftists envision a world so just, so generous, that deviance would vanish along with inequity. But I suspect that there will always be something at work in some men and women to make them restless with the systems others devise for them, and to move them outward toward the edges of the world, where life is always riskier, less organized, and easier going.

56 Do we owe anything to these men and women, who reject our company and what we offer and yet nonetheless seem to demand *something* from us?

57 We owe them, I think, at least a place to exist, a way to exist. That may not be a *moral* obligation, in the sense that our obligation to the involuntarily marginal is clearly a moral one, but it is an obligation nevertheless, one you might call an existential obligation.

Of course, it may be that I think we owe these men something be-   58
cause I have liked men like them, and because I want their world to be
there always, as a place to hide or rest. But there is more to it than that. I
think we as a society need men like these. A society needs its margins as
much as it needs art and literature. It needs holes and gaps, *breathing
spaces*, let us say, into which men and women can escape and live, when
necessary, in ways otherwise denied them. Margins guarantee to society
a flexibility, an elasticity, and allow it to accommodate itself to the natures and needs of its members. When margins vanish, society becomes
too rigid, too oppressive by far, and therefore inimical to life.

It is for such reasons that, in cultures like our own, marginal men   59
and women take on a special significance. They are all we have left to remind us of the narrowness of the received truths we take for granted.
"Beyond the pale," they somehow redefine the pale, or remind us, at
least, that *something* is still out there, beyond the pale. They preserve,
perhaps unconsciously, a dream that would otherwise cease to exist, the
dream of having a place in the world, and of being *left alone*.

Quixotic? Infantile? Perhaps. But remember Pavlov and his reflexes   60
coded in the flesh: animal, and therefore as if given by God. What we are
talking about here is *freedom*, and with it, perhaps, an echo of the dream
men brought, long ago, to wilderness America. I use the word "freedom"
gingerly, in relation to lives like these: skewed, crippled, emptied of
everything we associate with a full, or realized, freedom. But perhaps this
is the condition into which freedom has fallen among us. Art has been
"appreciated" out of existence; literature has become an extension of the
university, replete with tenure and pensions; and as for politics, the ide-
ologies which ring us round seem too silly or shrill by far to speak for life.
What is left, then, is this mute and intransigent independence, this
"waste" of life which refuses even interpretation, and which cannot be
assimilated to any ideology, and which therefore can be put to no one's
use. In its crippled innocence and the perfection of its superfluity it
amounts, almost, to a rebellion against history, and that is no small thing.

Let me put it as simply as I can: what we see on the streets of our   61
cities are two dramas, both of which cut to the troubled heart of the culture and demand from us a response we may not be able to make. There
is the drama of those struggling to survive by regaining their place in the
social order. And there is the drama of those struggling to survive outside
of it.

The resolution of both struggles depends on a third drama occurring   62
at the heart of the culture: the tension and contention between the magnanimity we owe to life and the darker tendings of the human psyche:
our fear of strangeness, our hatred of deviance, our love of order and control. How we mediate by default or design between those contrary forces
will determine not only the destinies of the homeless but also something
crucial about the nation, and perhaps—let me say it—about our own
souls.

## CONSIDERATIONS ───────────────────────────────

1. What advantage does Marin gain by starting his essay with his own youthful experience on the road?

2. What causes a word like "homeless" to lose much of its meaning? What other words do you know that have suffered a similar fate?

3. Paragraphs 10, 11, and 12 form a sequence of short, one-sentence units of very similar construction: "We decide . . . ," "We change . . . ," "We cut. . . ." What, if anything, does the writer gain that is worth the risk of sounding monotonous?

4. In more than one place in his essay, Marin divides the homeless into the involuntary and the voluntary. Why, then, in paragraph 15, does he say that it is "dangerous . . . to introduce the idea of choice into a discussion of homelessness"? Do your own ideas about the homeless include or exclude the fact that some people voluntarily remain outside society? Explain.

5. Why, according to Marin, do some of the homeless react violently to any offer of aid? How, according to you, should society react to those reactions?

6. Marin's paragraph 29, in which he touches on what has happened to old neighborhoods, brings to mind a relatively new word that he does not use, but that has become common in discussions of change in our cities—"gentrification." Why might it have made a useful contribution to that paragraph?

7. In paragraph 43, Marin puts it as "bluntly" as he can. Do you find his bluntness offensive or justifiable in this context?

8. How might Marin have made use of Hellman's essay "Runaway" (page 285) or John McPhee's "The Search for Marvin Gardens" (page 389)?

*Born in 1947, Kenneth Maue now works at applying the organizing
principles of music to everyday life, life without sound or scale or
melody. He wrote* Water in the Lake: Real Events for the
Imagination *(1979) to demonstrate these ideas. He has worked in
holistic health and in woodworking, and edited a magazine that
collected "writings about the quiet beauty and inner worth of
daily life."*

*"Quiet Is Freedom" is a mini-essay, composed of brilliant
writing in the small.*

— 64 —————————————————————————————

# KENNETH MAUE
## *Quiet Is Freedom*

———————————————————————————————————

All things I love dwell in quiet. I don't mean total lack of sound,   1
which is rare, and never perfect anyhow since we hear our own heartbeat, breathing, and nerves when other noises fade, but the soft, sparse
body of sound we hear in nature, empty rooms, and the deep of night.
Quiet is now so uncommon that many people don't know what it is
(when the radio's turned low?), or shun it. True quiet isn't so much a lack
of something as the presence of the world's wholeness. Noise, like pain,
is local, forcing attention into isolated spots; quiet, like love, reaches
out, linking ever-further chambers of being. Hearing quiet is an art, like
thinking, or reading books. There is more to quiet than meets the ears.

## CONSIDERATIONS ————————————————————————

1. A mini-essay is something like a poem in that the writer hopes through compression to cover a topic that could be the subject of a long article or even a book.
What does the writer gain through compression? What is he or she in danger of losing?
2. "There is more to quiet than meets the ears." Study this aphorism and the
paradox Maue sets up in the sentence beginning "True quiet isn't so much a lack. . . ."
Think of them as ways a writer can achieve compression. Try to use both techniques in
a mini-essay of your own.

———————

"Quiet Is Freedom" by Kenneth Maue, *Rollmag Newsletter*, 1993. Reprinted by permission of the author.

3. Another writer describes the ever-present television set in the American home as rather like the family dog—something there in the corner, on all the time, so familiar it is largely ignored. Is this an example of "white noise"? Would Maue settle for that as quiet? Explain.

4. Do you remember ever "hearing" quiet? When and where, and what did it sound like?

5. There are noises and noises: some are irritating intrusions and some are welcome additions to our life. Select a pair of closely related noises—for example, classical versus popular music, or leaf-blowers versus bamboo lawn rakes, or door buzzers versus chimes. Try a mini-essay that contrasts the items of the pair you select.

*N. Scott Momaday (b. 1934) is a Kiowa Indian, born on a
reservation in Oklahoma where his parents were teachers. For
many years, he was a professor at the University of Arizona.*
House Made of Dawn *(1968), which was his first novel, won the
Pulitzer Prize. He has published collections of folklore, books of
poems, and memoir. This essay introduced* The Way to Rainy
Mountain *in 1969.*

*Momaday has the voice of a storyteller and creates his essay
from stories—memory and history and legend. Note his ability to
interweave these elements.*

— 65 ————————————————————————

# N. SCOTT MOMADAY
## *The Way to Rainy Mountain*

—————————————————————————

A single knoll rises out of the plain in Oklahoma, north and west of    1
the Wichita Range. For my people, the Kiowas, it is an old landmark, and
they gave it the name Rainy Mountain. The hardest weather in the world
is there. Winter brings blizzards, hot tornadic winds arise in the spring,
and in summer the prairie is an anvil's edge. The grass turns brittle and
brown, and it cracks beneath your feet. There are green belts along the
rivers and creeks, linear groves of hickory and pecan, willow and witch
hazel. At a distance in July or August the steaming foliage seems almost
to writhe in fire. Great green and yellow grasshoppers are everywhere in
the tall grass, popping up like corn to sting the flesh, and tortoises crawl
about on the red earth, going nowhere in the plenty of time. Loneliness is
an aspect of the land. All things in the plain are isolate; there is no confusion of objects in the eye, but *one* hill or *one* tree or *one* man. To look
upon that landscape in the early morning, with the sun at your back, is
to lose the sense of proportion. Your imagination comes to life, and this,
you think, is where Creation was begun.

I returned to Rainy Mountain in July. My grandmother had died in    2
the spring, and I wanted to be at her grave. She had lived to be very old

and at last infirm. Her only living daughter was with her when she died, and I was told that in death her face was that of a child.

3    I like to think of her as a child. When she was born, the Kiowas were living the last great moment of their history. For more than a hundred years they had controlled the open range from the Smoky Hill River to the Red, from the headwaters of the Canadian to the fork of the Arkansas and Cimarron. In alliance with the Comanches, they had ruled the whole of the southern Plains. War was their sacred business, and they were among the finest horsemen the world has ever known. But warfare for the Kiowas was preeminently a matter of disposition rather than of survival, and they never understood the grim, unrelenting advance of the U.S. Cavalry. When at last, divided and ill-provisioned, they were driven onto the Staked Plains in the cold rains of autumn, they fell into panic. In Palo Duro Canyon they abandoned their crucial stores to pillage and had nothing then but their lives. In order to save themselves, they surrendered to the soldiers at Fort Sill and were imprisoned in the old stone corral that now stands as a military museum. My grandmother was spared the humiliation of those high gray walls by eight or ten years, but she must have known from birth the affliction of defeat, the dark brooding of old warriors.

4    Her name was Aho, and she belonged to the last culture to evolve in North America. Her forebears came down from the high country in western Montana nearly three centuries ago. They were a mountain people, a mysterious tribe of hunters whose language has never been positively classified in any major group. In the late seventeenth century they began a long migration to the south and east. It was a journey toward the dawn, and it led to a golden age. Along the way the Kiowas were befriended by the Crows, who gave them the culture and religion of the Plains. They acquired horses, and their ancient nomadic spirit was suddenly free of the ground. They acquired Tai-me, the sacred Sun Dance doll, from that moment the object and symbol of their worship, and so shared in the divinity of the sun. Not least, they acquired the sense of destiny, therefore courage and pride. When they entered upon the southern Plains they had been transformed. No longer were they slaves to the simple necessity of survival; they were a lordly and dangerous society of fighters and thieves, hunters and priests of the sun. According to their origin myth, they entered the world through a hollow log. From one point of view, their migration was the fruit of an old prophecy, for indeed they emerged from a sunless world.

5    Although my grandmother lived out her long life in the shadow of Rainy Mountain, the immense landscape of the continental interior lay like memory in her blood. She could tell of the Crows, whom she had never seen, and of the Black Hills, where she had never been. I wanted to see in reality what she had seen more perfectly in the mind's eye, and traveled fifteen hundred miles to begin my pilgrimage.

Yellowstone, it seemed to me, was the top of the world, a region of   6
deep lakes and dark timber, canyons and waterfalls. But, beautiful as it
is, one might have the sense of confinement there. The skyline in all directions is close at hand, the high wall of the woods and deep cleavages
of shade. There is a perfect freedom in the mountains, but it belongs to
the eagle and the elk, the badger and the bear. The Kiowas reckoned their
stature by the distance they could see, and they were bent and blind in
the wilderness.

Descending eastward, the highland meadows are a stairway to the   7
plain. In July the inland slope of the Rockies is luxuriant with flax and
buckwheat, stonecrop and larkspur. The earth unfolds and the limit of
the land recedes. Clusters of trees, and animals grazing far in the distance, cause the vision to reach away and wonder to build upon the
mind. The sun follows a longer course in the day, and the sky is immense beyond all comparison. The great billowing clouds that sail upon
it are shadows that move upon the grain like water, dividing light.
Farther down, in the land of the Crows and Blackfeet, the plain is yellow.
Sweet clover takes hold of the hills and bends upon itself to cover and
seal the soil. There the Kiowas paused on their way; they had come to
the place where they must change their lives. The sun is at home on the
plains. Precisely there does it have the certain character of a god. When
the Kiowas came to the land of the Crows, they could see the dark lees of
the hills at dawn across the Bighorn River, the profusion of light on the
grain shelves, the oldest deity ranging after the solstices. Not yet would
they veer southward to the caldron of the land that lay below; they must
wean their blood from the northern winter and hold the mountains a
while longer in their view. They bore Tai-me in procession to the east.

A dark mist lay over the Black Hills, and the land was like iron. At   8
the top of a ridge I caught sight of Devil's Tower upthrust against the gray
sky as if in the birth of time the core of the earth had broken through its
crust and the motion of the world was begun. There are things in nature
that engender an awful quiet in the heart of man; Devil's Tower is one of
them. Two centuries ago, because they could not do otherwise, the
Kiowas made a legend at the base of the rock. My grandmother said:

> Eight children were there at play, seven sisters and their brother.
> Suddenly the boy was struck dumb; he trembled and began to run
> upon his hands and feet. His fingers became claws, and his body was
> covered with fur. Directly there was a bear where the boy had been.
> The sisters were terrified; they ran, and the bear after them. They
> came to the stump of a great tree, and the tree spoke to them. It bade
> them climb upon it, and as they did so it began to rise into the air.
> The bear came to kill them, but they were just beyond its reach. It
> reared against the tree and scored the bark all around with its claws.
> The seven sisters were borne into the sky, and they became the stars
> of the Big Dipper.

From that moment, and so long as the legend lives, the Kiowas have kinsmen in the night sky. Whatever they were in the mountains, they could be no more. However tenuous their well-being, however much they had suffered and would suffer again, they had found a way out of the wilderness.

9        My grandmother had a reverence for the sun, a holy regard that now is all but gone out of mankind. There was a wariness in her, and an ancient awe. She was a Christian in her later years, but she had come a long way about, and she never forgot her birthright. As a child she had been to the Sun Dances; she had taken part in those annual rites, and by them she had learned the restoration of her people in the presence of Tai-me. She was about seven when the last Kiowa Sun Dance was held in 1887 on the Washita River above Rainy Mountain Creek. The buffalo were gone. In order to consummate the ancient sacrifice—to impale the head of a buffalo bull upon the medicine tree—a delegation of old men journeyed into Texas, there to beg and barter for an animal from the Goodnight herd. She was ten when the Kiowas came together for the last time as a living Sun Dance culture. They could find no buffalo; they had to hang an old hide from the sacred tree. Before the dance could begin, a company of soldiers rode out from Fort Sill under orders to disperse the tribe. Forbidden without cause the essential act of their faith, having seen the wild herds slaughtered and left to rot upon the ground, the Kiowas backed away forever from the medicine tree. That was July 20, 1890, at the great bend of the Washita. My grandmother was there. Without bitterness, and for as long as she lived, she bore a vision of deicide.

10        Now that I can have her only in memory, I see my grandmother in the several postures that were peculiar to her: standing at the wood stove on a winter morning and turning meat in a great iron skillet; sitting at the south window, bent above her beadwork, and afterwards, when her vision failed, looking down for a long time into the fold of her hands; going out upon a cane, very slowly as she did when the weight of age came upon her; praying. I remember her most often at prayer. She made long, rambling prayers out of suffering and hope, having seen many things. I was never sure that I had the right to hear, so exclusive were they of all mere custom and company. The last time I saw her she prayed standing by the side of her bed at night, naked to the waist, the light of a kerosene lamp moving upon her dark skin. Her long, black hair, always drawn and braided in the day, lay upon her shoulders and against her breasts like a shawl. I do not speak Kiowa, and I never understood her prayers, but there was something inherently sad in the sound, some merest hesitation upon the syllables of sorrow. She began in a high and descending pitch, exhausting her breath to silence; then again and again—and always the same intensity of effort, of something that is, and is not, like urgency in the human voice. Transported so in the dancing light among the shadows of her room, she seemed beyond the reach of time. But that was illusion; I think I knew then that I should not see her again.

Houses are like sentinels in the plain, old keepers of the weather 11
watch. There, in a very little while, wood takes on the appearance of great
age. All colors wear soon away in the wind and rain, and then the wood is
burned gray and the grain appears and the nails turn red with rust. The
windowpanes are black and opaque; you imagine there is nothing within,
and indeed there are many ghosts, bones given up to the land. They stand
here and there against the sky, and you approach them for a longer time
than you expect. They belong in the distance; it is their domain.

Once there was a lot of sound in my grandmother's house, a lot of 12
coming and going, feasting and talk. The summers there were full of excitement and reunion. The Kiowas are a summer people; they abide the
cold and keep to themselves, but when the season turns and the land becomes warm and vital they cannot hold still; an old love of going returns
upon them. The aged visitors who came to my grandmother's house
when I was a child were made of lean and leather, and they bore themselves upright. They wore great black hats and bright ample shirts that
shook in the wind. They rubbed fat upon their hair and wound their
braids with strips of colored cloth. Some of them painted their faces and
carried the scars of old and cherished enmities. They were an old council
of warlords, come to remind and be reminded of who they were. Their
wives and daughters served them well. The women might indulge themselves; gossip was at once the mark and compensation of their servitude.
They made loud and elaborate talk among themselves, full of jest and
gesture, fright and false alarm. They went abroad in fringed and flowered
shawls, bright beadwork and German silver. They were at home in the
kitchen, and they prepared meals that were banquets.

There were frequent prayer meetings, and great nocturnal feasts. 13
When I was a child I played with my cousins outside, where the lamp-
light fell upon the ground and the singing of the old people rose up
around us and carried away into the darkness. There were a lot of good
things to eat, a lot of laughter and surprise. And afterwards, when the
quiet returned, I lay down with my grandmother and could hear the frogs
away by the river and feel the motion of the air.

Now there is a funeral silence in the rooms, the endless wake of 14
some final word. The walls have closed in upon my grandmother's
house. When I returned to it in mourning, I saw for the first time in my
life how small it was. It was late at night, and there was a white moon,
nearly full. I sat for a long time on the stone steps by the kitchen door.
From there I could see out across the land; I could see the long row of
trees by the creek, the low light upon the rolling plains, and the stars of
the Big Dipper. Once I looked at the moon and caught sight of a strange
thing. A cricket had perched upon the handrail, only a few inches away
from me. My line of vision was such that the creature filled the moon
like a fossil. It had gone there, I thought, to live and die, for there, of all
places, was its small definition made whole and eternal. A warm wind
rose up and purled like the longing within me.

15      The next morning I awoke at dawn and went out on the dirt road to Rainy Mountain. It was already hot, and the grasshoppers began to fill the air. Still, it was early in the morning, and the birds sang out of the shadows. The long yellow grass on the mountain shone in the bright light, and a scissortail hied above the land. There, where it ought to be, at the end of a long and legendary way, was my grandmother's grave. Here and there on the dark stones were ancestral names. Looking back once, I saw the mountain and came away.

## CONSIDERATIONS

1. Momaday attempts a large, general topic—the quest and migrations of a people, the Kiowas—yet he concentrates on one person, his grandmother. Why? A beginning writer may find an important guiding principle in this answer.

2. Momaday's essay is studded with names of native plants, such as hickory, pecan, willow, witch hazel, flax, buckwheat, stonecrop, larkspur. What do particulars do for an account like this?

3. Momaday writes that according to their origin myth, the Kiowas entered the world "through a hollow log." Why do people preserve such myths? Are you aware of any comparable myths in our culture of supermarkets, freeways, and television? Or do you believe, with some social historians, that twenty-first-century Americans are a mythless people?

4. The sense of place seems to be important to human consciousness and identity. Compare Momaday's treatment of place with Wendell Berry's in "A Native Hill" (page 42) or Cynthia Huntington's in "The Spiral" (page 324).

5. After reading Momaday, read Daniel Boorstin's "The Pseudo-Event" (page 65). Might Boorstin describe Momaday as a man trying to wander *back* into his history? In paragraphs 9 and 10, Momaday tells us of his grandmother's intense pre-Christian religious beliefs and how those beliefs affected her whole tribe. If you have a particular religious belief, can you find there anything comparable to Aho's? Explain your answer in a short essay.

6. Do you *see* the image that Momaday wants us to see when he describes the cricket against the moon in paragraph 14? Why does the image belong in that paragraph? Invent a similar image—some little object held up by one of the astronauts against the pale earth a quarter million miles away—and describe it and the view.

*Kyoko Mori (b. 1957) was born in Kobe, Japan, and came to the United States when she was twenty. She studied in Illinois and Wisconsin, where she has taught. She has written a book of poems, novels, and works for children. In 1998 she published* Polite Lies: On Being a Woman Caught between Cultures.

*By traveling among scenes of her past and present, and then arriving later at the destination of art, Kyoko Mori finds her home. Her discovery of a new language in books unfamiliar to her brings her home to the words of others as well.*

— **66** —————————————————————

# KYOKO MORI
## *Coming Home to Books*

———————————————————————————

I have a recurring dream of water. At least once every month in a 1
dream, I stand on a seashore looking at a blue stretch of salt water, knowing that I am home. The dream may start out in another part of my hometown: the busy downtown shopping district, my grade school up on the hill. Or it may begin some place far away. Perhaps I am driving across a bridge on a country road in Wisconsin—below me, there is an ice-covered river, and ahead, another expanse of bare, brown fields. I turn the next corner, and suddenly I am face-to-face with the salt water of my childhood.

The landscapes of childhood are imprinted on our memories. Many 2
of us, miles, oceans, and years away from our first homes, return to them in our dreams. A friend who grew up in a small town in northern Wisconsin keeps dreaming of the one busy intersection in town that had four-way stop signs. In a dream, he might be walking on Seventh Avenue in New York, but when he crosses the street, he finds himself standing at the old intersection with an A & W behind him, a Mobil station ahead, and a grain mill down the street to the right. All new places, perhaps, point us back home.

My childhood landscape is Kobe, Japan—a city built on a narrow 3
strip of land between the mountains and the sea. No matter where you are in Kobe, you can see the mountains to the north or the sea to the

———————————

"Coming Home to Books" by Kyoko Mori from *Hungry Mind Review*, No. 38, Summer 1996. Reprinted by permission of *Ruminator Review*.

south. When people in Kobe give directions, they don't say *kita* (north) and *minami* (south); they say *vamagawa* (mountain-side) and *umigawa* (sea-side) even if they are in the middle of town, a few miles from either the mountains or the sea. Last time I was in Kobe, I took a cab with three people from Tokyo. The cab driver asked us if the building we wanted to go to was on the sea-side of the train station. A woman from Tokyo said, "No, no. The building is only a block from the station. It's not near the sea." "He means south," I told her, as though she did not speak the language and I were her interpreter.

4      Landscape, I thought, is more potent than culture. Tokyo is built on a very flat plain. To people who grew up there, the mountains of Kobe must seem overwhelming. All three of them kept squinting as they looked north, as though they could not quite believe what they saw. They were surprised to meet old men and women walking up and down the steep hills that are everywhere in the city. Though I had not lived in Kobe for eighteen years, I felt completely at home.

5      But this familiarity with childhood landscapes is only one way to feel at home. Happy as I was to see the mountains and the sea, I began to feel restless after a few hours in my hometown. In the end, I don't feel at home in Kobe or in any of Japan. On my short visits there, I realize that the country of my birth is no longer my home.

6      I have never lived in Japan as a full-grown adult. I left Kobe at twenty to finish my college education at Rockford College in Illinois. I moved to Wisconsin to study creative writing in Milwaukee and then to teach at a college in Green Bay. At thirty-nine, I have lived half of my life in the American Midwest. I am an American citizen. My life is here: my work as a writer, my job at the college, my close friends. I no longer have immediate family in Japan: both my parents and all my grandparents have passed away; my brother spends most of his time in Ecuador. Though I still have relatives and friends, I visit seldom and don't stay for more than a week at a time.

7      We mean so many things by *home.* Kobe would still be my home if home simply meant the place where we grew up, a place that is special to us because of our memories. But home also means a place where we have made a life for ourselves, where we feel a sense of purpose. I have never worked, voted, or paid taxes in Kobe, never supported a political cause or donated money or volunteered my time to help other people there. I could never call a place home without doing some of these things—without feeling that I have a part to play in the community.

8      In fact, I left Kobe and Japan at twenty because I did not want to play a part there. The country of my childhood, I saw, was not a good home for the independent-minded woman I wanted to become. Very few Japanese women pursued any profession, career, or cause they were dedicated to. Nearly all such women were unmarried; they were treated with polite silence and exclusion, barely hidden disparagement and con-

descension. The negative feelings they were subjected to were quite different from the reactions I would later see in America. Most Americans, it seems to me, want their unmarried or divorced friends to "meet someone" and "get married" because they believe that everyone would be happier with a loving partner than alone. Perhaps it's misguided to wish the same happiness on everyone, but the intentions are benign. In Japan, happiness is not a factor. A lot of married women claim that they are only staying married because they love their children, and yet, people speak disparagingly of women who stay single, dedicate themselves to their careers, and are perfectly happy. Women who leave their unhappy marriages are considered selfish. Marriage, clearly, is considered a duty, not a means to personal happiness. I left at twenty because I did not want to make my home in a place where I only had one acceptable choice and that choice had nothing to do with my personal happiness.

I don't regret leaving, but as a result, I have two halves of the whole    9
when it comes to home—home as a special place of childhood, home as a place where I can live, work, be part of the community, and feel happy. The two halves don't quite make a smooth whole. Driving through the endlessly flat landscapes of the Midwest, I long for the mountains and the sea, the dramatic rise and fall of land and water around me. Like most people who grew up near any sea, I stare at midwesterners with polite disbelief when they tell me that the Great Lakes are like the ocean: nobody who grew up near salt water would ever make such a claim. I am always lonely for a home where I can have everything: the past, the present, the future.

Lately, however, I've realized that there is yet another way to come    10
home. A few years ago, on my first visit to Cleveland, I stood in front of the paintings by van Gogh, Monet, Renoir, Cézanne, and Bonnard in the Impressionist wing of the museum. I felt oddly at home: I had stood in front of some of these paintings at different times, in different cities—going back decades to the first traveling Impressionist exhibits I saw with my mother in Kyoto when I was eight. More than twenty-five years later, I was standing, again, in the same space: six inches away from the canvas, the space my mother and I had occupied for a few seconds on that cloudy day in Kyoto. I felt comforted by the familiar paintings, just as I felt comforted by the familiar landscapes of Kobe.

This sense of home has little to do with actual places. The Impres-    11
sionists painted places I have never seen in my life: the gardens of Giverny, the bridges over the Seine, the rail works and grey cobblestones of Paris. All the same, these were the images my mother had loved and taught me to love: Bonnard's white explosion of apple blossoms, Monet's blurred light and water in his studies of water lilies. Perhaps it seems odd that I grew up in Japan looking at the works of French Impressionists rather than at traditional Japanese art, which I seldom viewed as a child. But these are the facts of my life, and the juxtaposition is not as odd as it

12      seems. The Impressionists, after all, had been inspired and influenced by Japanese woodblock prints: the arched bridge of Monet's water lily garden has an unmistakably Japanese shape.

12      Art brings me home through the beauty my mother taught me to love. Literature has the same effect. Books, too, can bring me home.

13      I grew up reading an eclectic assortment of mostly British and American novels—some meant for children, others not specifically so. My favorite books between the ages of eight and twenty, to name a few, were: *Emily of New Moon, Little Women, The Secret Garden, The Catcher in the Rye, Jane Eyre, Pride and Prejudice, Tess of the D'Urbervilles*. Returning to these books and authors now, I feel a sense of homecoming. Last winter, in bed with the flu, I started Edith Wharton's *The Age of Innocence*. Immediately, I was struck by the ironic narrative voice, the leisurely setting-up of the scene, the slow unfolding of the story which I knew would gain momentum and become a page-turner. I was back in the world of my favorite nineteenth- and early twentieth-century authors: Austen, Elliot, Hardy, Trollope. I was home.

14      Looking back at my favorite books, I also notice that few of the characters in these stories have a home they can take for granted. Jane Eyre and Emily Starr are orphans who struggle to find a home where they can feel accepted, useful, and loved. At the beginning of *Pride and Prejudice*, the Bennett sisters know that the home they grew up in will belong to the odious Mr. Collins after their father's death; the two oldest girls must marry well and provide a home for their younger sisters. Though the girls in *Little Women* live at home with their loving mother, their father's absence gives the home an unsettled feeling; throughout the book, their favorite game is a re-enactment of *The Pilgrim's Progress*, a quest for a heavenly home. In *The Catcher in the Rye*, Holden Caulfield briefly comes home only to hide in the closet, worry about the ducks in Central Park, and give his sister the broken pieces of a record. And yet, Holden wants desperately to come home, if not to his parents' apartment, then to the rye field where he can catch the falling kids, even if his dream is based on lyrics he remembers imperfectly.

15      Holden's rye field is very much like my sense of home: an imagined place that brings together the comforting elements of childhood. For Holden, these elements are the remembered song from his childhood, the dreamlike images of other children, and an urge to love and protect them. My version of home brings together the paintings and books my mother taught me to love. Cézanne's pears and the robins and ivy of *The Secret Garden* connect my childhood home to the home I have made in Wisconsin, where I write, teach, and look for the return of the migratory birds and wildflowers. I keep coming home to books just as my dreams bring me back to the expanse of blue water.

## CONSIDERATIONS

1. In paragraphs 2, 3, and 4, Mori makes the point that the landscapes of our childhood are "more potent than culture." But in the latter part of her essay, she seems to contradict that idea by showing how "culture"—that is, paintings and books—gave her a satisfying sense of home that "has little to do with actual places." Can you—or does she—reconcile the two conflicting ideas?

2. What do you think the effect would be on a young man or woman brought up in the landscape John McPhee describes in "The Search for Marvin Gardens" as opposed to that described by Mori? Explain in an essay built on the contrast between McPhee and Mori.

3. Mori begins and ends her essay with a recurring dream, thus using the dream as a unifying device that ties the essay together. If you have experienced a recurring dream, explain how you could use it as Mori does hers.

4. In paragraph 3, the author shows how people in Kobe use the mountains and the sea as reference points instead of "north" and "south." Similarly in Hawaii, natives refer to the "windward" and the "leeward" sides of their island rather than "east" and "west." Invent a pair of comparable directional terms that might have been used where you grew up. Then explain why those inventions might or might not work.

5. In what sense is Mori's essay about liberation? Is it the same kind of liberation expressed by Jamaica Kincaid in her "On Seeing England for the First Time"? Explain.

*Toni Morrison (b. 1931) was a teacher before she became a chief editor at Random House. She first published a novel in 1970.* Song of Solomon *(1977) established her as a fiction writer, and President Carter appointed her to the National Council of the Arts. In 1987 she published her best-known novel,* Beloved, *which won a Pulitzer Prize. In 1993 she became the first African-American woman to receive the Nobel Prize for Literature.*

*What do you say, in Stockholm, when you are given the Nobel Prize? If you are Toni Morrison, you begin by telling a story and use it to examine the gift and power and responsibility of language. Note that the occasion demands profundity and that Morrison finds depth by starting with a tale from an oral tradition.*

— 67 ———————————————————————

# TONI MORRISON
## *Nobel Lecture*

---

1    "Once upon a time there was an old woman. Blind but wise." Or was it an old man? A guru, perhaps. Or a griot soothing restless children. I have heard this story, or one exactly like it, in the lore of several cultures.

2    "Once upon a time there was an old woman. Blind. Wise."

3    In the version I know the woman is the daughter of slaves, black, American, and lives alone in a small house outside of town. Her reputation for wisdom is without peer and without question. Among her people she is both the law and its transgression. The honor she is paid and the awe in which she is held reach beyond her neighborhood to places far away; to the city where the intelligence of rural prophets is the source of much amusement.

4    One day the woman is visited by some young people who seem to be bent on disproving her clairvoyance and showing her up for the fraud they believe she is. Their plan is simple: they enter her house and ask the one question the answer to which rides solely on her difference from them, a difference they regard as a profound disability: her blindness. They stand before her, and one of them says, "Old woman, I hold in my hand a bird. Tell me whether it is living or dead."

From *Nobel Lectures, Literature 1991–1995.*

She does not answer, and the question is repeated. "Is the bird I am   5
holding living or dead?"

Still she doesn't answer. She is blind and cannot see her visitors, let   6
alone what is in their hands. She does not know their color, gender or
homeland. She only knows their motive.

The old woman's silence is so long, the young people have trouble   7
holding their laughter.

Finally she speaks and her voice is soft but stern. "I don't know",   8
she says. "I don't know whether the bird you are holding is dead or alive,
but what I do know is that it is in your hands. It is in your hands."

Her answer can be taken to mean: if it is dead, you have either   9
found it that way or you have killed it. If it is alive, you can still kill it.
Whether it is to stay alive, it is your decision. Whatever the case, it is
your responsibility.

For parading their power and her helplessness, the young visitors   10
are reprimanded, told they are responsible not only for the act of mockery but also for the small bundle of life sacrificed to achieve its aims. The
blind woman shifts attention away from assertions of power to the instrument through which that power is exercised.

Speculation on what (other than its own frail body) that bird-in the-   11
hand might signify has always been attractive to me, but especially so
now thinking, as I have been, about the work I do that has brought me to
this company. So I choose to read the bird as language and the woman as
a practiced writer. She is worried about how the language she dreams in,
given to her at birth, is handled, put into service, even withheld from her
for certain nefarious purposes. Being a writer she thinks of language
partly as a system, partly as a living thing over which one has control,
but mostly as agency—as an act with consequences. So the question the
children put to her: "Is it living or dead?" is not unreal because she
thinks of language as susceptible to death, erasure; certainly imperiled
and salvageable only by an effort of the will. She believes that if the bird
in the hands of her visitors is dead the custodians are responsible for the
corpse. For her a dead language is not only one no longer spoken or written, it is unyielding language content to admire its own paralysis. Like
statist language, censored and censoring. Ruthless in its policing duties,
it has no desire or purpose other than maintaining the free range of its
own narcotic narcissism, its own exclusivity and dominance. However
moribund, it is not without effect for it actively thwarts the intellect,
stalls conscience, suppresses human potential. Unreceptive to interroga-
tion, it cannot form or tolerate new ideas, shape other thoughts, tell another story, fill baffling silences. Official language smitheryed to
sanction ignorance and preserve privilege is a suit of armor polished to
shocking glitter, a husk from which the knight departed long ago. Yet
there it is: dumb, predatory, sentimental. Exciting reverence in school-
children, providing shelter for despots, summoning false memories of
stability, harmony among the public.

12      She is convinced that when language dies, out of carelessness, disuse, indifference and absence of esteem, or killed by fiat, not only she herself, but all users and makers are accountable for its demise. In her country children have bitten their tongues off and use bullets instead to iterate the voice of speechlessness, of disabled and disabling language, of language adults have abandoned altogether as a device for grappling with meaning, providing guidance, or expressing love. But she knows tongue-suicide is not only the choice of children. It is common among the infantile heads of state and power merchants whose evacuated language leaves them with no access to what is left of their human instincts for they speak only to those who obey, or in order to force obedience.

13      The systematic looting of language can be recognized by the tendency of its users to forgo its nuanced, complex, mid-wifery properties for menace and subjugation. Oppressive language does more than represent violence; it is violence; does more than represent the limits of knowledge; it limits knowledge. Whether it is obscuring state language or the faux-language of mindless media; whether it is the proud but calcified language of the academy or the commodity driven language of science; whether it is the malign language of law-without-ethics, or language designed for the estrangement of minorities, hiding its racist plunder in its literary cheek—it must be rejected, altered and exposed. It is the language that drinks blood, laps vulnerabilities, tucks its fascist boots under crinolines of respectability and patriotism as it moves relentlessly toward the bottom line and the bottomed-out mind. Sexist language, racist language, theistic language—all are typical of the policing languages of mastery, and cannot, do not permit new knowledge or encourage the mutual exchange of ideas.

14      The old woman is keenly aware that no intellectual mercenary, nor insatiable dictator, no paid-for politician or demagogue; no counterfeit journalist would be persuaded by her thoughts. There is and will be rousing language to keep citizens armed and arming; slaughtered and slaughtering in the malls, courthouses, post offices, playgrounds, bedrooms and boulevards; stirring, memorializing language to mask the pity and waste of needless death. There will be more diplomatic language to countenance rape, torture, assassination. There is and will be more seductive, mutant language designed to throttle women, to pack their throats like paté-producing geese with their own unsayable, transgressive words; there will be more of the language of surveillance disguised as research; of politics and history calculated to render the suffering of millions mute; language glamorized to thrill the dissatisfied and bereft into assaulting their neighbors; arrogant pseudo-empirical language crafted to lock creative people into cages of inferiority and hopelessness.

15      Underneath the eloquence, the glamor, the scholarly associations, however stirring or seductive, the heart of such language is languishing, or perhaps not beating at all—if the bird is already dead.

She has thought about what could have been the intellectual his-    16
tory of any discipline if it had not insisted upon, or been forced into, the
waste of time and life that rationalizations for and representations of
dominance required—lethal discourses of exclusion blocking access to
cognition for both the excluder and the excluded.

The conventional wisdom of the Tower of Babel story is that the    17
collapse was a misfortune. That it was the distraction, or the weight of
many languages that precipitated the tower's failed architecture. That
one monolithic language would have expedited the building and heaven
would have been reached. Whose heaven, she wonders? And what kind?
Perhaps the achievement of Paradise was premature, a little hasty if no
one could take the time to understand other languages, other views,
other narratives period. Had they, the heaven they imagined might have
been found at their feet. Complicated, demanding, yes, but a view of
heaven as life; not heaven as post-life.

She would not want to leave her young visitors with the impression    18
that language should be forced to stay alive merely to be. The vitality of
language lies in its ability to limn the actual, imagined and possible lives
of its speakers, readers, writers. Although its poise is sometimes in dis-
placing experience it is not a substitute for it. It arcs toward the place
where meaning may lie. When a President of the United States thought
about the graveyard his country had become, and said, "The world will
little note nor long remember what we say here. But it will never forget
what they did here," his simple words are exhilarating in their life-
sustaining properties because they refused to encapsulate the reality of
600,000 dead men in a cataclysmic race war. Refusing to monumental-
ize, disdaining the "final word", the precise "summing up", acknowledging their "poor power to add or detract", his words signal deference to
the uncapturability of the life it mourns. It is the deference that moves
her, that recognition that language can never live up to life once and for
all. Nor should it. Language can never "pin down" slavery, genocide,
war. Nor should it yearn for the arrogance to be able to do so. Its force, its
felicity is in its reach toward the ineffable.

Be it grand or slender, burrowing, blasting, or refusing to sanctify;    19
whether it laughs out loud or is a cry without an alphabet, the choice
word, the chosen silence, unmolested language surges toward knowledge, not its destruction. But who does not know of literature banned because it is interrogative; discredited because it is critical; erased because
alternate? And how many are outraged by the thought of a self-ravaged
tongue?

Word-work is sublime, she thinks, because it is generative; it makes    20
meaning that secures our difference, our human difference—the way in
which we are like no other life.

We die. That may be the meaning of life. But we do language. That    21
may be the measure of our lives.

22      "Once upon a time, . . ." visitors ask an old woman a question. Who are they, these children? What did they make of that encounter? What did they hear in those final words: "The bird is in your hands"? A sentence that gestures towards possibility or one that drops a latch? Perhaps what the children heard was "It's not my problem. I am old, female, black, blind. What wisdom I have now is in knowing I cannot help you. The future of language is yours."

23      They stand there. Suppose nothing was in their hands? Suppose the visit was only a ruse, a trick to get to be spoken to, taken seriously as they have not been before? A chance to interrupt, to violate the adult world, its miasma of discourse about them, for them, but never to them? Urgent questions are at stake, including the one they have asked: "Is the bird we hold living or dead?" Perhaps the question meant: "Could someone tell us what is life? What is death?" No trick at all; no silliness. A straightforward question worthy of the attention of a wise one. An old one. And if the old and wise who have lived life and faced death cannot describe either, who can?

24      But she does not; she keeps her secret; her good opinion of herself; her gnomic pronouncements; her art without commitment. She keeps her distance, enforces it and retreats into the singularity of isolation, in sophisticated, privileged space.

25      Nothing, no word follows her declaration of transfer. That silence is deep, deeper than the meaning available in the words she has spoken. It shivers, this silence, and the children, annoyed, fill it with language invented on the spot.

26      "Is there no speech," they ask her, "no words you can give us that help us break through your dossier of failures? Through the education you have just given us that is no education at all because we are paying close attention to what you have done as well as to what you have said? To the barrier you have erected between generosity and wisdom?

27      "We have no bird in our hands, living or dead. We have only you and our important question. Is the nothing in our hands something you could not bear to contemplate, to even guess? Don't you remember being young when language was magic without meaning? When what you could say, could not mean? When the invisible was what imagination strove to see? When questions and demands for answers burned so brightly you trembled with fury at not knowing?

28      "Do we have to begin consciousness with a battle heroines and heroes like you have already fought and lost leaving us with nothing in our hands except what you have imagined is there? Your answer is artful, but its artfulness embarrasses us and ought to embarrass you. Your answer is indecent in its self-congratulation. A made-for-television script that makes no sense if there is nothing in our hands.

29      "Why didn't you reach out, touch us with your soft fingers, delay the sound bite, the lesson, until you knew who we were? Did you so despise our trick, our modus operandi you could not see that we were baf-

fled about how to get your attention? We are young. Unripe. We have heard all our short lives that we have to be responsible. What could that possibly mean in the catastrophe this world has become; where, as a poet said, "nothing needs to be exposed since it is already barefaced." Our inheritance is an affront. You want us to have your old, blank eyes and see only cruelty and mediocrity. Do you think we are stupid enough to perjure ourselves again and again with the fiction of nationhood? How dare you talk to us of duty when we stand waist deep in the toxin of your past?

"You trivialize us and trivialize the bird that is not in our hands. Is there no context for our lives? No song, no literature, no poem full of vitamins, no history connected to experience that you can pass along to help us start strong? You are an adult. The old one, the wise one. Stop thinking about saving your face. Think of our lives and tell us your particularized world. Make up a story. Narrative is radical, creating us at the very moment it is being created. We will not blame you if your reach exceeds your grasp; if love so ignites your words they go down in flames and nothing is left but their scald. Or if, with the reticence of a surgeon's hands, your words suture only the places where blood might flow. We know you can never do it properly—once and for all. Passion is never enough, neither is skill. But try. For our sake and yours forget your name in the street; tell us what the world has been to you in the dark places and in the light. Don't tell us what to believe, what to fear. Show us belief's wide skirt and the stitch that unravels fear's caul. You, old woman, blessed with blindness, can speak the language that tells us what only language can: how to see without pictures. Language alone protects us from the scariness of things with no names. Language alone is meditation.

"Tell us what it is to be a woman so that we may know what it is to be a man. What moves at the margin. What it is to have no home in this place. To be set adrift from the one you knew. What it is to live at the edge of towns that cannot bear your company.

"Tell us about ships turned away from shorelines at Easter, placenta in a field. Tell us about a wagonload of slaves, how they sang so softly their breath was indistinguishable from the falling snow. How they knew from the hunch of the nearest shoulder that the next stop would be their last. How, with hands prayered in their sex, they thought of heat, then sun. Lifting their faces as though it was there for the taking. Turning as though there for the taking. They stop at an inn. The driver and his mate go in with the lamp leaving them humming in the dark. The horse's void steams into the snow beneath its hooves and its hiss and melt are the envy of the freezing slaves.

"The inn door opens: a girl and a boy step away from its light. They climb into the wagon bed. The boy will have a gun in three years, but now he carries a lamp and a jug of warm cider. They pass it from mouth to mouth. The girl offers bread, pieces of meat and something more: a glance into the eyes of the one she serves. One helping for each man, two for each woman. And a look. They look back. The next stop will be their last. But not this one. This one is warmed."

34    It's quiet again when the children finish speaking, until the woman breaks into the silence.

35    "Finally", she says, "I trust you now. I trust you with the bird that is not in your hands because you have truly caught it. Look. How lovely it is, this thing we have done—together."

## CONSIDERATIONS

1. Morrison's dense paragraph 11 is her interpretation of the folk story about the blind but wise old woman. Without arguing with her interpretation, write a paragraph to clarify in your own mind what she means by a "dead language" and why she comes down so hard on it.

2. "Official language smitheryed to sanction ignorance. . . ." The unfamiliar word in that phrase is not to be found in contemporary dictionaries, but they do list "smithereens" (fragments or bits) and "smithery" (the art and trade of the smith or craftsman). You are therefore forced to derive the meaning of Morrison's word from the context. Explain what you decided and how you arrived at that conclusion.

3. Another writer in this text, Janet Frame, also devotes her essay to language. Read her "Jewels" (page 219), and comment on the difference between her focus and Morrison's.

4. Morrison refers to the Tower of Babel story in paragraph 17. Look up the story in the book of Genesis (11:1 through 9). What do you think of her reading of that famous story? Explain, making use of both the Morrison essay and the biblical account.

5. "Language can never 'pin down' slavery, genocide, war," writes Morrison in paragraph 18. Can language "pin down" freedom, equality, peace? What does she mean by "Its force, its felicity is in its reach toward the ineffable"? What is she trying to pin down with her language?

6. Morrison casts her Nobel lecture in the form of a parable. Similarly, writers of the scriptures of most of the world's religions present parables—the story of the Prodigal Son, for example. Where else have you run into parables? What is the defining feature of a parable that is of importance to any writer?

7. To what degree would Morrison agree with George Orwell in his "Politics and the English Language" (page 484)? Support your answer by referring to relevant passages in both writers' works.

*Flannery O'Connor (1925–1964) was born in Savannah and moved with her family to her mother's birthplace, Milledgeville, Georgia, at the age of twelve. When she was fifteen, her father died of the inherited degenerative disease lupus. She received her B.A. at Milledgeville's Georgia State College for Women (now Georgia College and State University) and then studied fiction writing at the University of Iowa. From 1947 until 1951 she spent time in New York and Connecticut. When she discovered that she was ill, she returned to live with her mother on the Milledgeville farm called Andalusia, surrounded by pet peacocks and peahens, writing her remarkable fiction and staying in touch with friends by letter. She died of lupus when she was thirty-eight.*

*In 1979 a selection of Flannery O'Connor's letters, edited by Sally Fitzgerald, appeared in* The Habit of Being. *The letters are affectionate, often funny, rich with literary and religious thought. The following excerpts begin with two letters about her story "A Good Man Is Hard to Find." The first is a passage from a letter addressed to novelist John Hawkes, a leading writer of O'Connor's generation. In the passage, O'Connor speaks of the theology of her story. The second letter, "To a Professor of English," is prefaced by Sally Fitzgerald's explanatory note. The letter that follows is another to John Hawkes. In it, O'Connor's Catholicism is clear and certain; Hawkes is of another mind. The last letter is addressed to Alfred Corn, who is now a well-known poet. In 1962 he was an undergraduate at Emory University in Atlanta, Georgia; after he heard Flannery O'Connor speak to an English class, he wrote her about a subject that troubled him.*

# — 68 —

# FLANNERY O'CONNOR
## *From Flannery O'Connor's Letters*

### To John Hawkes

14 April 60

Thanks for your letter of some time back. I have been busy keeping   1
my blood pressure down while reading various reviews of my book.

Some of the favorable ones are as bad as the unfavorable; most reviewers seem to have read the book in fifteen minutes and written the review in ten. . . . I hope that when yours comes out you'll fare better.

2      It's interesting to me that your students naturally work their way to the idea that the Grandmother in "A Good Man" is not pure evil and may be a medium for Grace. If they were Southern students I would say this was because they all had grandmothers like her at home. These old ladies exactly reflect the banalities of the society and the effect of the comical rather than the seriously evil. But Andrew [Lytle] insists that she is a witch, even down to the cat. These children, yr. students, know their grandmothers aren't witches.

3      Perhaps it is a difference in theology, or rather the difference that ingrained theology makes in the sensibility. Grace, to the Catholic way of thinking, can and does use as its medium the imperfect, purely human, and even hypocritical. Cutting yourself off from Grace is a very decided matter, requiring a real choice, act of will, and affecting the very ground of the soul. The Misfit is touched by the Grace that comes through the old lady when she recognizes him as her child, as she has been touched by the Grace that comes through him in his particular suffering. His shooting her is a recoil, a horror at her humanness, but after he has done it and cleansed his glasses, the Grace has worked in him and he pronounces his judgment: she would have been a good woman if *he* had been there every moment of her life. True enough. In the Protestant view, I think Grace and nature don't have much to do with each other. The old lady, because of her hypocrisy and humanness and banality couldn't be a medium for Grace. In the sense that I see things the other way, I'm a Catholic writer.

## To a Professor of English

*A professor of English had sent Flannery the following letter: "I am writing as spokesman for three members of our department and some ninety university students in three classes who for a week now have been discussing your story 'A Good Man Is Hard to Find.' We have debated at length several possible interpretations, none of which fully satisfies us. In general we believe that the appearance of the Misfit is not 'real' in the same sense that the incidents of the first half of the story are real. Bailey, we believe, imagines the appearance of the Misfit, whose activities have been called to his attention on the night before the trip and again during the stopover at the roadside restaurant. Bailey, we further believe, identifies himself with the Misfit and so plays two roles in the imaginary last half of the story. But we cannot, after great effort, determine the point at which reality fades into illusion or reverie. Does the accident literally occur, or is it a part of Bailey's dream? Please believe me when I say we are not seeking an easy way out of our difficulty. We admire your story and have examined it with great care, but we are con-*

*vinced that we are missing something important which you in-
tended for us to grasp. We will all be very grateful if you comment
on the interpretation which I have outlined above and if you will
give us further comments about your intention in writing 'A Good
Man Is Hard to Find.'"*

She replied:

28 March 61

The interpretation of your ninety students and three teachers is fan-   1
tastic and about as far from my intentions as it could get to be. If it were
a legitimate interpretation, the story would be little more than a trick
and its interest would be simply for abnormal psychology. I am not interested in abnormal psychology.

There is a change of tension from the first part of the story to the   2
second where the Misfit enters, but this is no lessening of reality. This
story is, of course, not meant to be realistic in the sense that it portrays
the everyday doings of people in Georgia. It is stylized and its conventions are comic even though its meaning is serious.

Bailey's only importance is as the Grandmother's boy and the driver   3
of the car. It is the Grandmother who first recognizes the Misfit and who
is most concerned with him throughout. The story is a duel of sorts between the Grandmother and her superficial beliefs and the Misfit's more
profoundly felt involvement with Christ's action which set the world off
balance for him.

The meaning of a story should go on expanding for the reader the   4
more he thinks about it, but meaning cannot be captured in an interpretation. If teachers are in the habit of approaching a story as if it were a research problem for which any answer is believable so long as it is not
obvious, then I think students will never learn to enjoy fiction. Too
much interpretation is certainly worse than too little, and where feeling
for a story is absent, theory will not supply it.

My tone is not meant to be obnoxious. I am in a state of shock.   5

## To John Hawkes

28 November 61

I have been fixing to write you ever since last summer when we saw   1
the goat man.* We went up to north Georgia to buy a bull and when we
were somewhere above Conyers we saw up ahead a pile of rubble some
eight feet high on the side of the road. When we got about fifty feet from
it, we could begin to make out that some of the rubble was distributed
around something like a cart and that some of it was alive. Then we

---

*The founder of the Free Thinking Christian Mission, a wandering witness who
traveled with a cart and a clutch of goats.

began to make out the goats. We stopped in front of it and looked back. About half the goats were asleep, venerable and exhausted, in a kind of heap. I didn't see Chess. Then my mother located an arm around the neck of one of the goats. We also saw a knee. The old man was lying on the road, asleep amongst them, but we never located his face.

2      That is wonderful about the new baby. I can't equal that but I do have some new additions to my ménage. For the last few years I have been hunting a pair of swans that I could afford. Swans cost $250 a pair and that was beyond me. My friend in Florida, the one I wrote you about once, took upon herself to comb Florida for cheap swans. What she sets out to do, she does. . . . So now I am the owner of a one-eyed swan and her consort. They are Polish, or immutable swans and very tractable and I radiate satisfaction every time I look at them.

3      I had brief notes from Andrew [Lytle]* a couple of times lately. In fact he has a story of mine but I haven't heard from him whether he's going to use it or not. He said he had asked you to write an article about my fiction and that if he used my story I might want to send it to you. If he does take it and you write an article and want to see the story ["The Lame Shall Enter First"], I'll send it. It's about one of Tarwater's terrible cousins, a lad named Rufus Johnson, and it will add fuel to your theory though not legitimately I think.

4      You haven't convinced me that I write with the Devil's will or belong in the romantic tradition and I'm prepared to argue some more with you on this if I can remember where we left off at. I think the reason we can't agree on this is because there is a difference in our two devils. My Devil has a name, a history and a definite plan. His name is Lucifer, he's a fallen angel, his sin is pride, and his aim is the destruction of the Divine plan. Now I judge that your Devil is co-equal to God, not his creature; that pride is his virtue, not his sin; and that his aim is not to destroy the Divine plan because there isn't any Divine plan to destroy. My Devil is objective and yours is subjective. You say one becomes "evil" when one leaves the herd. I say that depends entirely on what the herd is doing.

5      The herd has been known to be right, in which case the one who leaves it is doing evil. When the herd is wrong, the one who leaves it is not doing evil but the right thing. If I remember rightly, you put that word, evil, in quotation marks which means the standards you judge it by there are relative; in fact you would be looking at it there with the eyes of the herd.

6      I think I would admit to writing what Hawthorne called "romances," but I don't think that has anything to do with the romantic mentality. Hawthorne interests me considerably. I feel more of a kinship with him than with any other American, though some of what he wrote I can't make myself read through to the end.

---

*Novelist and editor of the *Sewanee Review*.

I didn't write the note to *Wise Blood*. I just let it go as is. I thought 7
here I am wasting my time saying what I've written when I've already
written it and I could be writing something else. I couldn't hope to convince anybody anyway. A friend of mine wrote me that he had read a review in one of the university magazines of *The Violent Bear etc.* that said
that since the seeds that had opened one at a time in Tarwater's blood
were put there in the first place by the great uncle that the book was
about homosexual incest. When you have a generation of students who
are being taught to think like that, there's nothing to do but wait for another generation to come along and hope it won't be worse. . . .

I've introduced *The Lime Twig* to several people and they're all en- 8
thusiastic. Somebody has gone off with my copy now. I hope you are at
another one.

## To Alfred Corn

30 May 62

I think that this experience you are having of losing your faith, or as 1
you think, of having lost it, is an experience that in the long run belongs
to faith; or at least it can belong to faith if faith is still valuable to you,
and it must be or you would not have written me about this.

I don't know how the kind of faith required of a Christian living in 2
the 20th century can be at all if it is not grounded on this experience that
you are having right now of unbelief. This may be the case always and
not just in the 20th century. Peter said, "Lord, I believe. Help my unbelief." It is the most natural and most human and most agonizing prayer
in the gospels, and I think it is the foundation prayer of faith.

As a freshman in college you are bombarded with new ideas, or 3
rather pieces of ideas, new frames of reference, an activation of the intellectual life which is only beginning, but which is already running ahead
of your lived experience. After a year of this, you think you cannot believe. You are just beginning to realize how difficult it is to have faith
and the measure of a commitment to it, but you are too young to decide
you don't have faith just because you feel you can't believe. About the
only way we know whether we believe or not is by what we do, and I
think from your letter that you will not take the path of least resistance
in this matter and simply decide that you have lost your faith and that
there is nothing you can do about it.

One result of the stimulation of your intellectual life that takes 4
place in college is usually a shrinking of the imaginative life. This
sounds like a paradox, but I have often found it to be true. Students get so
bound up with difficulties such as reconciling the clashing of so many
different faiths such as Buddhism, Mohammedanism, etc., that they
cease to look for God in other ways. Bridges once wrote Gerard Manley
Hopkins and asked him to tell him how he, Bridges, could believe. He
must have expected from Hopkins a long philosophical answer. Hopkins

wrote back, "Give alms." He was trying to say to Bridges that God is to be experienced in Charity (in the sense of love for the divine image in human beings). Don't get so entangled with intellectual difficulties that you fail to look for God in this way.

5        The intellectual difficulties have to be met, however, and you will be meeting them for the rest of your life. When you get a reasonable hold on one, another will come to take its place. At one time, the clash of the different world religions was a difficulty for me. Where you have absolute solutions, however, you have no need of faith. Faith is what you have in the absence of knowledge. The reason this clash doesn't bother me any longer is because I have got, over the years, a sense of the immense sweep of creation, of the evolutionary process in everything, of how incomprehensible God must necessarily be to be the God of heaven and earth. You can't fit the Almighty into your intellectual categories. I might suggest that you look into some of the works of Pierre Teilhard de Chardin (*The Phenomenon of Man* et al.). He was a paleontologist—helped to discover Peking man—and also a man of God. I don't suggest you go to him for answers but for different questions, for that stretching of the imagination that you need to make you a skeptic in the face of much that you are learning, much of which is new and shocking but which when boiled down becomes less so and takes its place in the general scheme of things. What kept me a skeptic in college was precisely my Christian faith. It always said: wait, don't bite on this, get a wider picture, continue to read.

6        If you want your faith, you have to work for it. It is a gift, but for very few it is a gift given without any demand for equal time devoted to its cultivation. For every book you read that is anti-Christian, make it your business to read one that presents the other side of the picture; if one isn't satisfactory read others. Don't think that you have to abandon reason to be a Christian. A book that might help you is *The Unity of Philosophical Experience* by Etienne Gilson. Another is Newman's *The Grammar of Assent*. To find out about faith, you have to go to the people who have it and you have to go to the most intelligent ones if you are going to stand up intellectually to agnostics and the general run of pagans that you are going to find in the majority of people around you. Much of the criticism of belief that you find today comes from people who are judging it from the standpoint of another and narrower discipline. The Biblical criticism of the 19th century, for instance, was the product of historical disciplines. It has been entirely revamped in the 20th century by applying broader criteria to it, and those people who lost their faith in the 19th century because of it, could better have hung on in blind trust.

7        Even in the life of a Christian, faith rises and falls like the tides of an invisible sea. It's there, even where he can't see it or feel it, if he wants it to be there. You realize, I think, that it is more valuable, more mysterious, altogether more immense than anything you can learn or decide upon in college. Learn what you can, but cultivate Christian scepticism.

It will keep you free—not free to do anything you please, but free to be formed by something larger than your own intellect or the intellects of those around you.

I don't know if this is the kind of answer that can help you, but any time you care to write me, I can try to do better.

## CONSIDERATIONS

### Letter to John Hawkes, 14 April 1960

1. What does O'Connor mean when she says that some of the favorable reviews of her book "are as bad as the unfavorable"? How do you go about judging the quality of a book review? As a writer, how do you judge your instructors' comments on your own papers?

2. In paragraph 2, O'Connor suggests that the grandmother in her story is like a lot of grandmothers in the South, but in her letter to the professor of English, she says her story is not realistic in the "everyday" sense. Can you reconcile this apparent contradiction?

3. What does O'Connor mean by the term "Grace" in paragraph 3? Pursue the word in a good dictionary where you will find at least a dozen different definitions of the word. Keep in mind that she is using the word according to her own view of Catholic theology.

4. O'Connor says at the end of paragraph 3 that she is a Catholic writer. Does she mean that Protestant readers are not welcome or that Protestants could not understand her work? Is it possible to disagree with—or even disapprove of—a writer's ideas and still appreciate that writer's work? Explain.

5. While she does not always agree with John Hawkes's interpretations of her stories, O'Connor's letters to him (see also that of 11/28/61) express a good deal more respect for his ideas than can be found in her letter to a professor of English. Read a little of the work of John Hawkes to see if you can discover qualities he shares with O'Connor.

### Letter to a Professor of English, 28 March 1961

1. O'Connor says her story is realistic not in an "everyday" but in a "stylized" sense. Compare a paragraph or two of her story with a passage in Eudora Welty's "A Worn Path" to see if you can determine what O'Connor means by "stylized." You might also get some help on that word by consulting a history of art.

2. Find passages in "A Good Man Is Hard to Find" that will illustrate what O'Connor means by the grandmother's "superficial beliefs" and The Misfit's "more profoundly felt involvement." Does such a close examination of the story push you closer to or further away from O'Connor's belief that the heart of the story is a "duel of sorts" between the grandmother and The Misfit?

3. In paragraph 4, O'Connor makes an interesting distinction between "meaning" and "interpretation" as she deplores the "habit of approaching a story as if it were a research problem for which any answer is believable so long as it is not obvious." Discuss some experience of your own in which insistence on a particular interpretation (yours or anyone else's) interfered with the expanded meaning O'Connor mentions.

4. O'Connor says in her last paragraph that her tone in the letter "is not meant to be obnoxious." If you were the professor to whom she had written, what particular lines or words in the letter might you think gave it an obnoxious tone? Can you find any other writers in this book whose tone is obnoxious? Explain.

5. In what sense, if any, do you think a short story (or poem or novel or play or essay for that matter) can be taught? What assistance do you expect or want from your own instructor and/or text in reading a story like O'Connor's?

## Letter to John Hawkes, 28 November 1961

1. O'Connor's remarkable versatility in the use of the English language is demonstrated in her letters as well as in her stories. This letter to John Hawkes, for example, shows her ability to shift from one voice to another at will. Find examples.

2. At the end of paragraph 4, O'Connor tells Hawkes, "You say one becomes 'evil' when one leaves the herd. I say that depends entirely on what the herd is doing." Write an essay on relative versus absolute morality.

3. O'Connor, speaking of her interest in Hawthorne, makes a distinction between writing "romances" and having a "romantic mentality." What did Hawthorne mean by "romances," and why does O'Connor "feel more of a kinship with him than with any other American"?

4. O'Connor's letters are filled with brief reports on local events and people, like the one on the goat man in the letter to John Hawkes. Eudora Welty, in discussing one of her own short stories—see her essay "The Point of the Story"—says that her story began when she observed an old woman in Mississippi. How might O'Connor's observations of her surroundings have contributed to "A Good Man Is Hard to Find"?

## Letter to Alfred Corn, 30 May 1962

1. "You can't fit the Almighty into your intellectual categories," says O'Connor. Does she advise her correspondent to ignore the intellectual challenges of college? Study her discussion of the clash between intellectual inquiry and faith, especially in paragraphs 5 and 6, and write an essay on her conclusions.

2. How, according to O'Connor, can we know whether we believe or not? See paragraph 3; then compose a series of examples of O'Connor's idea.

3. Look over Consideration 1 regarding O'Connor's 1961 letter to John Hawkes and think about voice. How would you describe the voice in this letter to Alfred Corn? Does O'Connor play with changes of voice in this letter? Why?

4. Read Langston Hughes's essay "Salvation"; how might O'Connor have consoled the disillusioned boy?

5. Looking at the first sentence of O'Connor's letter to Alfred Corn, some students complain that she is too slippery or too cagey or too flexible to be believed. Study the sentence by drawing a picture of it, a sketch, or a diagram—anything to help clarify the way her mind is working in it. Try simplifying the sentence. Comment on the results of your study.

*Flannery O'Connor's first novel,* Wise Blood, *appeared in 1952 and her second and last,* The Violent Bear It Away, *in 1960. Most critics prefer her stories to her novels. All of her fiction—stories and novels together—is gathered together in one volume of The Library of America. During her lifetime she published one collection of stories, bearing the title of the story that follows. This was the story she usually read aloud when asked to read.*

## — 69 —————————————————————

# FLANNERY O'CONNOR
## *A Good Man Is Hard to Find*

---

The grandmother didn't want to go to Florida. She wanted to visit 1 some of her connections in east Tennessee and she was seizing every chance to change Bailey's mind. Bailey was the son she lived with, her only boy. He was sitting on the edge of his chair at the table, bent over the orange sports section of the *Journal.* "Now look here, Bailey," she said, "see here, read this," and she stood with one hand on her thin hip and the other rattling the newspaper at his bald head. "Here this fellow that calls himself The Misfit is aloose from the Federal Pen and headed toward Florida and you read here what it says he did to these people. Just you read it. I wouldn't take my children in any direction with the criminal like that aloose in it. I couldn't answer to my conscience if I did."

Bailey didn't look up from his reading so she wheeled around then 2 and faced the children's mother, a young woman in slacks, whose face was as broad and innocent as a cabbage and was tied around with a green headkerchief that had two points on the top like rabbit's ears. She was sitting on the sofa, feeding the baby his apricots out of a jar. "The children have been to Florida before," the old lady said. "You all ought to take them somewhere else for a change so they would see different parts of the world and be broad. They never have been to east Tennessee."

The children's mother didn't seem to hear her, but the eight-year- 3 old boy, John Wesley, a stocky child with glasses, said, "If you don't want to go to Florida, why dontcha stay at home?" He and the little girl, June Star, were reading the funny papers on the floor.

4   "She wouldn't stay at home to be queen for a day," June Star said without raising her yellow head.

5   "Yes, and what would you do if this fellow, The Misfit, caught you?" the grandmother asked.

6   "I'd smack his face," John Wesley said.

7   "She wouldn't stay at home for a million bucks," June Star said. "Afraid she'd miss something. She has to go everywhere we go."

8   "All right, Miss," the grandmother said. "Just remember that the next time you want me to curl your hair."

9   June Star said her hair was naturally curly.

10   The next morning the grandmother was the first one in the car, ready to go. She had her big black valise that looked like the head of a hippopotamus in one corner, and underneath it she was hiding a basket with Pitty Sing, the cat, in it. She didn't intend for the cat to be left alone in the house for three days because he would miss her too much and she was afraid he might brush against one of the gas burners and accidentally asphyxiate himself. Her son, Bailey, didn't like to arrive at a motel with a cat.

11   She sat in the middle of the back seat with John Wesley and June Star on either side of her. Bailey and the children's mother and the baby sat in the front and they left Atlanta at eight forty-five with the mileage on the car at 55890. The grandmother wrote this down because she thought it would be interesting to say how many miles they had been when they got back. It took them twenty minutes to reach the outskirts of the city.

12   The old lady settled herself comfortably, removing her white cotton gloves and putting them up with her purse on the shelf in front of the back window. The children's mother still had on slacks and still had her head tied up in a green kerchief, but the grandmother had on a navy blue straw sailor hat with a bunch of white violets on the brim and a navy blue dress with a small white dot in the print. Her collar and cuffs were white organdy trimmed with lace and at her neckline she had pinned a purple spray of cloth violets containing a sachet. In case of an accident, anyone seeing her dead on the highway would know at once that she was a lady.

13   She said she thought it was going to be a good day for driving, neither too hot nor too cold, and she cautioned Bailey that the speed limit was fifty-five miles an hour and that the patrolmen hid themselves behind billboards and small clumps of trees and sped out after you before you had a chance to slow down. She pointed out interesting details of the scenery: Stone Mountain; the blue granite that in some places came up to both sides of the highway; the brilliant red clay banks slightly streaked with purple; and the various crops that made rows of green lacework on the ground. The trees were full of silver-white sunlights and the meanest of them sparkled. The children were reading comic magazines and their mother had gone back to sleep.

"Let's go through Georgia fast so we don't have to look at it much,"    14
John Wesley said.

"If I were a little boy," said the grandmother, "I wouldn't talk about    15
my native state that way. Tennessee has the mountains and Georgia has
the hills."

"Tennessee is just a hillbilly dumping ground," John Wesley said,    16
"and Georgia is a lousy state too."

"You said it," June Star said.    17

"In my time," said the grandmother, folding her thin veined fingers,    18
"children were more respectful of their native states and their parents
and everything else. People did right then. Oh look at the cute little pick-
aninny!" she said and pointed to a Negro child standing in the door of a
shack. "Wouldn't that make a picture now?" she asked and they all
turned and looked at the little Negro out of the back window. He waved.

"He didn't have any britches on," June Star said.    19

"He probably didn't have any," the grandmother explained. "Little    20
niggers in the country don't have things like we do. If I could paint, I'd
paint that picture," she said.

The children exchanged comic books.    21

The grandmother offered to hold the baby and the children's mother    22
passed him over the front seat to her. She set him on her knee and
bounced him and told him about the things they were passing. She rolled
her eyes and screwed up her mouth and stuck her leathery thin face into
his smooth bland one. Occasionally he gave her a faraway smile. They
passed a large cotton field with five or six graves fenced in the middle of
it, like a small island. "Look at the graveyard!" the grandmother said,
pointing it out. "That was the old family burying ground. That belonged
to the plantation."

"Where's the plantation?" John Wesley asked.    23

"Gone With the Wind," said the grandmother. "Ha. Ha."    24

When the children finished all the comic books they had brought,    25
they opened the lunch and ate it. The grandmother ate a peanut butter
sandwich and an olive and would not let the children throw the box and
the paper napkins out the window. When there was nothing else to do
they played a game by choosing a cloud and making the other two guess
what shape it suggested. John Wesley took one the shape of a cow and
June Star guessed a cow and John Wesley said, no, an automobile, and
June Star said he didn't play fair, and they began to slap each other over
the grandmother.

The grandmother said she would tell them a story if they would    26
keep quiet. When she told a story, she rolled her eyes and waved her head
and was very dramatic. She said once when she was a maiden lady she
had been courted by a Mr. Edgar Atkins Teagarden from Jasper, Georgia.
She said he was a very good-looking man and a gentleman and that he
brought her a watermelon every Saturday afternoon with his initials cut
in it, E.A.T. Well, one Saturday, she said, Mr. Teagarden brought the

watermelon and there was nobody at home and he left it on the front porch and returned in his buggy to Jasper, but she never got the watermelon, she said, because a nigger boy ate it when he saw the initials, E.A.T.! This story tickled John Wesley's funny bone and he giggled and giggled but June Star didn't think it was any good. She said she wouldn't marry a man that just brought her a watermelon on Saturday. The grandmother said she would have done well to marry Mr. Teagarden because he was a gentleman and had bought Coca-Cola stock when it first came out and that he had died only a few years ago, a very wealthy man.

27      They stopped at The Tower for barbecued sandwiches. The Tower was a part-stucco and part-wood filling station and dance hall set in a clearing outside of Timothy. A fat man named Red Sammy Butts ran it and there were signs stuck here and there on the building and for miles up and down the highway saying, TRY RED SAMMY'S FAMOUS BARBECUE. NONE LIKE FAMOUS RED SAMMY'S! RED SAM! THE FAT BOY WITH THE HAPPY LAUGH. A VETERAN! RED SAMMY'S YOUR MAN!

28      Red Sammy was lying on the bare ground outside The Tower with his head under a truck while a gray monkey about a foot high, chained to a small chinaberry tree, chattered nearby. The monkey sprang back into the tree and got on the highest limb as soon as he saw the children jump out of the car and run toward him.

29      Inside, The Tower was a long dark room with a counter at one end and tables at the other and dancing space in the middle. They all sat down at a broad table next to the nickelodeon and Red Sam's wife, a tall burnt-brown woman with hair and eyes lighter than her skin, came and took their order. The children's mother put a dime in the machine and played "The Tennessee Waltz," and the grandmother said that tune always made her want to dance. She asked Bailey if he would like to dance but he only glared at her. He didn't have a naturally sunny disposition like she did and trips made him nervous. The grandmother's brown eyes were very bright. She swayed her head from side to side and pretended she was dancing in her chair. June Star said play something she could tap to so the children's mother put in another dime and played a fast number and June Star stepped out onto the dance floor and did her tap routine.

30      "Ain't she cute?" Red Sam's wife said, leaning over the counter. "Would you like to come be my little girl?"

31      "No, I certainly wouldn't," June Star said. "I wouldn't live in a broken-down place like this for a million bucks!" and she ran back to the table.

32      "Ain't she cute?" the woman repeated, stretching her mouth politely.

33      "Aren't you ashamed?" hissed the grandmother.

34      Red Sam came in and told his wife to quit lounging on the counter and hurry up with these people's order. His khaki trousers reached just to his hip bones and his stomach hung over them like a sack of meal swaying under his shirt. He came over and sat down at a table nearby and let out a combination sigh and yodel. "You can't win," he said. "You can't

win," and he wiped his sweating red face off with a gray handkerchief. "These days you don't know who to trust," he said. "Ain't that the truth?"

"People are certainly not nice like they used to be," said the  35
grandmother.

"Two fellers come in here last week," Red Sammy said, "driving a  36
Chrysler. It was an old beat-up car but it was a good one and these boys looked all right to me. Said they worked at the mill and you know I let them fellers charge the gas they bought? Now why did I do that?"

"Because you're a good man!" the grandmother said at once.  37

"Yes'm, I suppose so," Red Sam said as if he were struck with this  38
answer.

His wife brought the orders, carrying the five plates all at once with-  39
out a tray, two in each hand and one balanced on her arm. "It isn't a soul in this green world of God's that you can trust," she said. "And I don't count nobody out of that, not nobody," she repeated, looking at Red Sammy.

"Did you read about that criminal, The Misfit, that's escaped?"  40
asked the grandmother.

"I wouldn't be a bit surprised if he didn't attack this place right  41
here," said the woman. "If he hears about it being here, I wouldn't be none surprised to see him. If he hears it's two cent in the cash register, I wouldn't be a tall surprised if he . . ."

"That'll do," Red Sam said. "Go bring these people their Co'-  42
Colas," and the woman went off to get the rest of the order.

"A good man is hard to find," Red Sammy said. "Everything is get-  43
ting terrible. I remember the day you could go off and leave your screen door unlatched. Not no more."

He and the grandmother discussed better times. The old lady said  44
that in her opinion Europe was entirely to blame for the way things were now. She said the way Europe acted you would think we were made of money and Red Sam said it was no use talking about it, she was exactly right. The children ran outside into the white sunlight and looked at the monkey in the lacy chinaberry tree. He was busy catching fleas on himself and biting each one carefully between his teeth as if it were a delicacy.

They drove off again into the hot afternoon. The grandmother took  45
cat naps and woke up every few minutes with her own snoring. Outside of Toombsboro she woke up and recalled an old plantation that she had visited in this neighborhood once when she was a young lady. She said the house had six white columns across the front and that there was an avenue of oaks leading up to it and two little wooden trellis arbors on either side in front where you sat down with your suitor after a stroll in the garden. She recalled exactly which road to turn off to get to it. She knew that Bailey would not be willing to lose any time looking at an old house, but the more she talked about it, the more she wanted to see it once again and find out if the little twin arbors were still standing.

"There was a secret panel in this house," she said craftily, not telling the truth but wishing that she were, "and the story went that all the family silver was hidden in it when Sherman came through but it was never found. . . ."

46      "Hey!" John Wesley said. "Let's go see it! We'll find it! We'll poke at the wood work and find it! Who lives there? Where do you turn off at? Hey Pop, can't we turn off there?"

47      "We never have seen a house with a secret panel!" June Star shrieked. "Let's go to the house with the secret panel! Hey, Pop, can't we go see the house with the secret panel?"

48      "It's not far from here, I know," the grandmother said. "It wouldn't take over twenty minutes."

49      Bailey was looking straight ahead. His jaw was as rigid as a horse-shoe. "No," he said.

50      The children began to yell and scream that they wanted to see the house with the secret panel. John Wesley kicked the back of the front seat and June Star hung over her mother's shoulder and whined desperately into her ear that they never had any fun even on their vacation, that they could never do what THEY wanted to do. The baby began to scream and John Wesley kicked the back of the seat so hard that his father could feel the blows in his kidney.

51      "All right!" he shouted and drew the car to a stop at the side of the road. "Will you all shut up? Will you all just shut up for one second? If you don't shut up, we won't go anywhere."

52      "It would be very educational for them," the grandmother murmured.

53      "All right," Bailey said, "but get this. This is the only time we're going to stop for anything like this. This is the one and only time."

54      "The dirt road that you have to turn down is about a mile back," the grandmother directed. "I marked it when we passed."

55      "A dirt road," Bailey groaned.

56      After they had turned around and were headed toward the dirt road, the grandmother recalled other points about the house, the beautiful glass over the front doorway and the candle lamp in the hall. John Wesley said that the secret panel was probably in the fireplace.

57      "You can't go inside the house," Bailey said. "You don't know who lives there."

58      "While you all talk to the people in front, I'll run around behind and get in a window," John Wesley suggested.

59      "We'll all stay in the car," his mother said.

60      They turned onto the dirt road and the car raced roughly along in a swirl of pink dust. The grandmother recalled the times when there were no paved roads and thirty miles was a day's journey. The dirt road was hilly and there were sudden washes in it and sharp curves on dangerous embankments. All at once they would be on a hill, looking down over the blue tops of trees for miles around, then the next minute, they

would be in a red depression with the dust-coated trees looking down on them.

"This place had better turn up in a minute," Bailey said, "or I'm go-   61
ing to turn around."

The road looked as if no one had traveled on it in months.   62

"It's not much further," the grandmother said and just as she said   63
it, a horrible thought came to her. The thought was so embarrassing that
she turned red in the face and her eyes dilated and her feet jumped up,
upsetting her valise in the corner. The instant the valise moved, the
newspaper top she had over the basket under it rose with a snarl and
Pitty Sing, the cat, sprang onto Bailey's shoulder.

The children were thrown to the floor and their mother, clutching   64
the baby, was thrown out the door onto the ground; the old lady was
thrown into the front seat. The car turned over once and landed right-
side-up in a gulch on the side of the road. Bailey remained in the driver's
seat with the cat—gray-striped with a broad white face and an orange
nose—clinging to his neck like a caterpillar.

As soon as the children saw they could move their arms and legs,   65
they scrambled out of the car shouting, "We've had an ACCIDENT!" The
grandmother was curled up under the dashboard, hoping she was injured
so that Bailey's wrath would not come down on her all at once. The horrible thought she had had before the accident was that the house she had
remembered so vividly was not in Georgia but in Tennessee.

Bailey removed the cat from his neck with both hands and flung it   66
out the window against the side of a pine tree. Then he got out of the car
and started looking for the children's mother. She was sitting against the
side of the red gutted ditch, holding the screaming baby, but she only had
a cut down her face and a broken shoulder. "We've had an ACCIDENT!" the
children screamed in a frenzy of delight.

"But nobody's killed," June Star said with disappointment as the   67
grandmother limped out of the car, her hat still pinned to her head but
the broken front brim standing up at a jaunty angle and the violet spray
hanging off the side. They all sat down in the ditch, except the children,
to recover from the shock. They were all shaking.

"Maybe a car will come along," said the children's mother hoarsely.   68

"I believe I have injured an organ," said the grandmother, pressing   69
her side, but no one answered her. Bailey's teeth were clattering. He had
on a yellow sport shirt with bright parrots designed in it and his face was
as yellow as the shirt. The grandmother decided that she would not mention that the house was in Tennessee.

The road was about ten feet above and they could see only the tops   70
of the trees on the other side of it. Behind the ditch they were sitting in
there were more woods, tall and dark and deep. In a few minutes they
saw a car some distance away on top of a hill, coming slowly as if the occupants were watching them. The grandmother stood up and waved both
arms dramatically to attract their attention. The car continued to come

on slowly, disappeared around a bend and appeared again, moving even slower, on top of the hill they had gone over. It was a big black battered hearselike automobile. There were three men in it.

71     It came to a stop just over them and for some minutes, the driver looked down with a steady expressionless gaze to where they were sitting, and didn't speak. Then he turned his head and muttered something to the other two and they got out. One was a fat boy in black trousers and a red sweat shirt with a silver stallion embossed on the front of it. He moved around on the right side of them and stood staring, his mouth partly open in a kind of loose grin. The other had on khaki pants and a blue striped coat and a gray hat pulled down very low, hiding most of his face. He came around slowly on the left side. Neither spoke.

72     The driver got out of the car and stood by the side of it, looking down at them. He was an older man than the other two. His hair was just beginning to gray and he wore silver-rimmed spectacles that gave him a scholarly look. He had a long creased face and didn't have on any shirt or undershirt. He had on blue jeans that were too tight for him and he was holding a black hat and a gun. The two boys also had guns.

73     "We've had an ACCIDENT!" the children screamed.

74     The grandmother had the peculiar feeling that the bespectacled man was someone she knew. His face was as familiar to her as if she had known him all her life but she could not recall who he was. He moved away from the car and began to come down the embankment, placing his feet carefully so that he wouldn't slip. He had on tan and white shoes and no socks, and his ankles were red and thin. "Good afternoon," he said, "I see you all had you a little spill."

75     "We turned over twice!" said the grandmother.

76     "Oncet," he corrected. "We see it happen. Try their car and see will it run, Hiram," he said quietly to the boy with the gray hat.

77     "What you got that gun for?" John Wesley asked. "Whatcha gonna do with that gun?"

78     "Lady," the man said to the children's mother, "would you mind calling them children to sit down by you? Children make me nervous. I want all you all to sit down right together there where you're at."

79     "What are you telling us what to do for?" June Star asked.

80     Behind them the line of woods gaped like a dark open mouth. "Come here," said their mother.

81     "Look here now," Bailey began suddenly, "we're in a predicament! We're in . . ."

82     The grandmother shrieked. She scrambled to her feet and stood staring.

83     "You're The Misfit!" she said. "I recognized you at once!"

84     "Yes'm," the man said, smiling slightly as if he were pleased in spite of himself to be known. "But it would have been better for all of you, lady, if you hadn't of reckernized me."

85     Bailey turned his head sharply and said something to his mother that shocked the children. The old lady began to cry and The Misfit reddened.

"Lady," he said, "don't you get upset. Sometimes a man says things    86
he don't mean. I don't reckon he meant to talk to you thataway."

"You wouldn't shoot a lady, would you?" the grandmother said and    87
removed a clean handkerchief from her cuff and began to slap at her eyes
with it.

The Misfit pointed the toe of his shoe into the ground and made a    88
little hole and then covered it up again. "I would hate to have to," he said.

"Listen," the grandmother almost screamed, "I know you're a good    89
man. You don't look a bit like you have common blood. I know you must
come from nice people!"

"Yes mam," he said, "finest people in the world." When he smiled    90
he showed a row of strong white teeth. "God never made a finer woman
than my mother and my daddy's heart was pure gold," he said. The boy
with the red sweat shirt had come around behind them and was standing
with his gun at his hip. The Misfit squatted down on the ground. "Watch
them children, Bobby Lee," he said. "You know they make me nervous."
He looked at the six of them huddled together in front of him and he
seemed to be embarrassed as if he couldn't think of anything to say.
"Ain't a cloud in the sky," he remarked, looking up at it. "Don't see no
sun but don't see no cloud neither."

"Yes, it's a beautiful day," said the grandmother. "Listen," she said,    91
"you shouldn't call yourself The Misfit because I know you're a good
man at heart. I can just look at you and tell."

"Hush!" Bailey yelled. "Hush! Everybody shut up and let me han-    92
dle this!" He was squatting in the position of a runner about to spring
forward but he didn't move.

"I pre-chate that, lady," The Misfit said and drew a little circle in    93
the ground with the butt of his gun.

"It'll take a half a hour to fix this here car," Hiram called, looking    94
over the raised hood of it.

"Well, first you and Bobby Lee get him and that little boy to step    95
over yonder with you," The Misfit said, pointing to Bailey and John
Wesley. "The boys want to ask you something," he said to Bailey.
"Would you mind stepping back in them woods there with them?"

"Listen," Bailey began, "we're in a terrible predicament! Nobody    96
realizes what this is," and his voice cracked. His eyes were as blue and
intense as the parrots in his shirt and he remained perfectly still.

The grandmother reached up to adjust her hat brim as if she were    97
going to the woods with him but it came off in her hand. She stood staring at it and after a second she let it fall on the ground. Hiram pulled
Bailey up by the arm as if he were assisting an old man. John Wesley
caught hold of his father's hand and Bobby Lee followed. They went off
toward the woods and just as they reached the dark edge, Bailey turned
and supporting himself against a gray naked pine trunk, he shouted, "I'll
be back in a minute, Mamma, wait on me!"

"Come back this instant!" his mother shrilled but they all disap-    98
peared into the woods.

99       "Bailey Boy!" the grandmother called in tragic voice but she found she was looking at The Misfit squatting on the ground in front of her. "I just know you're a good man," she said desperately. "You're not a bit common!"

100      "Nome, I ain't a good man," The Misfit said after a second as if he had considered her statement carefully, "but I ain't the worst in the world neither. My daddy said I was a different breed of dog from my brothers and sisters. 'You know,' Daddy said, 'it's some that can live their whole life out without asking about it and it's others has to know why it is, and this boy is one of the latters. He's going to be into everything!' " He put on his black hat and looked up suddenly and then away deep into the woods as if he were embarrassed again. "I'm sorry, I don't have on a shirt before you ladies," he said, hunching his shoulders slightly. "We buried our clothes that we had on when we escaped and we're just making do until we can get better. We borrowed these from some folks we met," he explained.

101      "That's perfectly all right," the grandmother said. "Maybe Bailey has an extra shirt in his suitcase."

102      "I'll look and see terrectly," The Misfit said.

103      "Where are they taking him?" the children's mother screamed.

104      "Daddy was a card himself," The Misfit said. "You couldn't put anything over on him. He never got in trouble with the Authorities though. Just had the knack of handling them."

105      "You could be honest too if you'd only try," said the grandmother. "Think how wonderful it would be to settle down and live a comfortable life and not have to think about somebody chasing you all the time."

106      The Misfit kept scratching in the ground with the butt of his gun as if he were thinking about it. "Yes'm, somebody is always after you," he murmured.

107      The grandmother noticed how thin his shoulder blades were just behind his hat because she was standing up looking down on him. "Do you ever pray?" she asked.

108      He shook his head. All she saw was the black hat wiggle between his shoulder blades. "Nome," he said.

109      There was a pistol shot from the woods, followed closely by another. Then silence. The old lady's head jerked around. She could hear the wind move through the tree tops like a long satisfied insuck of breath. "Bailey Boy!" she called.

110      "I was a gospel singer for a while," The Misfit said. "I been most everything. Been in the arm service, both land and sea, at home and abroad, been twict married, been an undertaker, been with the railroads, plowed Mother Earth, been in a tornado, seen a man burnt alive oncet," and he looked up at the children's mother and the little girl who were sitting close together, their faces white and their eyes glassy; "I even seen a woman flogged," he said.

111      "Pray, pray," the grandmother began, "pray, pray . . . "

"I never was a bad boy that I remember of," The Misfit said in an al- 112
most dreamy voice, "but somewheres along the line I done something
wrong and got sent to the penitentiary. I was buried alive," and he looked
up and held her attention to him by a steady stare.

"That's when you should have started to pray," she said. "What did 113
you do to get sent to the penitentiary that first time?"

"Turn to the right, it was a wall," The Misfit said, looking up again 114
at the cloudless sky. "Turn to the left, it was a wall. Look up it was a
ceiling, look down it was a floor. I forgot what I done, lady. I set there and
set there, trying to remember what it was I done and I ain't recalled it to
this day. Oncet in a while, I would think it was coming to me, but it
never come."

"Maybe they put you in by mistake," the old lady said vaguely. 115

"Nome," he said. "It wasn't no mistake. They had the papers on me." 116

"You must have stolen something," she said. 117

The Misfit sneered slightly. "Nobody had nothing I wanted," he 118
said. "It was a head-doctor at the penitentiary said what I had done was
kill my daddy but I known that for a lie. My daddy died in nineteen
ought nineteen of the epidemic flu and I never had a thing to do with it.
He was buried in the Mount Hopewell Baptist churchyard and you can
go there and see for yourself."

"If you would pray," the old lady said, "Jesus would help you." 119

"That's right," The Misfit said. 120

"Well then, why don't you pray?" she asked trembling with delight 121
suddenly.

"I don't want no hep," he said, "I'm doing all right by myself." 122

Bobby Lee and Hiram came ambling back from the woods. Bobby 123
Lee was dragging a yellow shirt with bright blue parrots in it.

"Throw me that shirt, Bobby Lee," The Misfit said. The shirt came 124
flying at him and landed on his shoulder and he put it on. The grandmother couldn't name what the shirt reminded her of. "No, lady," The
Misfit said while he was buttoning it up, "I found out the crime don't
matter. You can do one thing or you can do another, kill a man or take a
tire off his car, because sooner or later you're going to forget what it was
you done and just be punished for it."

The children's mother had begun to make heaving noises as if she 125
couldn't get her breath. "Lady," he asked, "would you and that little girl
like to step off yonder with Bobby Lee and Hiram and join your husband?"

"Yes, thank you," the mother said faintly. Her left arm dangled help- 126
lessly and she was holding the baby, who had gone to sleep, in the other.
"Hep that lady up, Hiram," The Misfit said as she struggled to climb out
of the ditch, "and Bobby Lee, you hold onto that little girl's hand."

"I don't want to hold hands with him," June Star said. "He reminds 127
me of a pig."

The fat boy blushed and laughed and caught her by the arm and 128
pulled her off into the woods after Hiram and her mother.

129        Alone with The Misfit, the grandmother found that she had lost her
voice. There was not a cloud in the sky nor any sun. There was nothing
around her but woods. She wanted to tell him that he must pray. She
opened and closed her mouth several times before anything came out.
Finally she found herself saying, "Jesus. Jesus," meaning, Jesus will help
you, but the way she was saying it, it sounded as if she might be cursing.

130        "Yes'm," The Misfit said as if he agreed. "Jesus thrown everything
off balance. It was the same case with Him as with me except He hadn't
committed any crime and they could prove I had committed one because
they had the papers on me. Of course," he said, "they never shown me
any papers. That's why I sign myself now, I said long ago, you get you a
signature and sign everything you do and keep a copy of it. Then you'll
know what you done and you can hold up the crime to the punishment
and see do they match and in the end you'll have something to prove you
ain't been treated right. I call myself The Misfit," he said, "because I can't
make what all I done wrong fit with all I gone through in punishment."

131        There was a piercing scream from the woods, followed closely by a
pistol report. "Does it seem right to you, lady, that one is punished a
heap and another ain't punished at all?"

132        "Jesus!" the old lady cried. "You've got blood! I know you wouldn't
shoot a lady! I know you come from nice people! Pray! Jesus, you ought
not to shoot a lady. I'll give you all the money I've got!"

133        "Lady," The Misfit said, looking beyond her far into the woods,
"there was never a body that give the undertaker a tip."

134        There were two more pistol reports and the grandmother raised her
head like a parched old turkey hen crying for water and called, "Bailey
Boy, Bailey Boy!" as if her heart would break.

135        "Jesus was the only One that ever raised the dead," The Misfit continued, "and He shouldn't have done it. He thrown everything off balance. If He did what He said, then it's nothing for you to do but throw
away everything and follow Him, and if He didn't then it's nothing for
you to do but enjoy the few minutes you got left the best way you can—
by killing somebody or burning down his house or doing some other
meanness to him. No pleasure but meanness," he said and his voice had
become almost a snarl.

136        "Maybe He didn't raise the dead," the old lady mumbled, not knowing what she was saying and feeling so dizzy that she sank down in the
ditch with her legs twisted under her.

137        "I wasn't there so I can't say He didn't," The Misfit said. "I wisht I
had of been there," he said, hitting the ground with his fist. "It ain't right
I wasn't there because if I had of been there I would of known. Listen
lady," he said in a high voice, "if I had of been there I would of known
and I wouldn't be like I am now." His voice seemed about to crack and
the grandmother's head cleared for an instant. She saw the man's face
twisted close to her own as if he were going to cry and she murmured,
"Why, you're one of my babies. You're one of my own children!" She

reached out and touched him on the shoulder. The Misfit sprang back as if a snake had bitten him and shot her three times through the chest. Then he put his gun down on the ground and took off his glasses and began to clean them.

Hiram and Bobby Lee returned from the woods and stood over the   138
ditch, looking down at the grandmother who half sat and half lay in a puddle of blood with her legs crossed under her like a child's and her face smiling up at the cloudless sky.

Without his glasses, The Misfit's eyes were red-rimmed and pale and   139
defenseless-looking. "Take her off and throw her where you thrown the others," he said, picking up the cat that was rubbing itself against his leg.

"She was a talker, wasn't she?" Bobby Lee said, sliding down the   140
ditch with a yodel.

"She would of been a good woman," The Misfit said, "if it had been   141
somebody there to shoot her every minute of her life."

"Some fun!" Bobby Lee said.   142

"Shut up, Bobby Lee," The Misfit said. "It's no real pleasure in life."   143

## CONSIDERATIONS

1. To keep the children quiet, the grandmother tells the ridiculous story of Mr. Edgar Atkins Teagarden, who cut his initials E.A.T. in a watermelon. How do you account for O'Connor's including such an anecdote in a story about a psychopathic murderer?

2. One respected scholar and critic describes O'Connor's story as a "satire on the half-and-half Christian faced with nihilism and death." In what sense would the grandmother qualify as a "half-and-half Christian"? Is there anything in O'Connor's letters to John Hawkes and Alfred Corn that might help you understand what O'Connor thought a real Christian was?

3. Does this story contain characteristics of satire, as seen in Margaret Atwood's "Alien Territory," Stephen Jay Gould's "The Case of the Creeping Fox Terrier Clone," Jonathan Swift's "A Modest Proposal," or Mark Twain's "Was the World Made for Man"? If so, does that make all these pieces somewhat alike?

4. O'Connor borrows a line from her own story to serve as a title. Find the line, study the context, and comment on it as a title. Compare it with the titles of other short stories in the text.

5. When The Misfit tells the grandmother that "it would have been better for all of you, lady, if you hadn't of reckernized me," what purpose does his warning serve in furthering the story?

6. Study the depiction of four elderly women: the grandmother in O'Connor's story, Phoenix Jackson in Eudora Welty's "A Worn Path" (page 653), Miss Cooper in Louise Bogan's "Miss Cooper and Me" (page 61), and the author's mother in John Daniel's "Looking After" (page 152). Are any of the four women stereotypes? If not, how do the authors avoid making them so? Report your findings in an essay that could include your own observations of elderly women.

*Flannery O'Connor also wrote essays, collected after her death in a volume called* Mystery and Manners: Occasional Prose *(1969). This essay, which originally appeared in the* Georgia Bulletin *in 1963, addressed local and immediate problems. In the American twenty-first century, its insights remain urgent, as our culture, in O'Connor's word, becomes increasingly "fractured."*

— 70 —————————————————————————

# FLANNERY O'CONNOR
## *The Total Effect and the Eighth Grade*

1    In two recent instances in Georgia, parents have objected to their eighth- and ninth-grade children's reading assignments in modern fiction. This seems to happen with some regularity in cases throughout the country. The unwitting parent picks up his child's book, glances through it, comes upon passages of erotic detail or profanity, and takes off at once to complain to the school board. Sometimes, as in one of the Georgia cases, the teacher is dismissed and hackles rise in liberal circles everywhere.

2    The two cases in Georgia, which involved Steinbeck's *East of Eden* and John Hersey's *A Bell for Adano*, provoked considerable newspaper comment. One columnist, in commending the enterprise of the teachers, announced that students do not like to read the fusty works of the nineteenth century, that their attention can best be held by novels dealing with the realities of our own time, and that the Bible, too, is full of racy stories.

3    Mr. Hersey himself addressed a letter to the State School Superintendent in behalf of the teacher who had been dismissed. He pointed out that his book is not scandalous, that it attempts to convey an earnest message about the nature of democracy, and that it falls well within the limits of the principle of "total effect," that principle followed in legal cases by which a book is judged not for isolated parts but by the final effect of the whole book upon the general reader.

4    I do not want to comment on the merits of these particular cases. What concerns me is what novels ought to be assigned in the eighth and

ninth grades as a matter of course, for if these cases indicate anything, they indicate the haphazard way in which fiction is approached in our high schools. Presumably there is a state reading list which contains "safe" books for teachers to assign; after that it is up to the teacher.

English teachers come in Good, Bad, and Indifferent, but too fre-  5
quently in high schools anyone who can speak English is allowed to teach it. Since several novels can't easily be gathered into one textbook, the fiction that students are assigned depends upon their teacher's knowledge, ability, and taste: variable factors at best. More often than not, the teacher assigns what he thinks will hold the attention and interest of the students. Modern fiction will certainly hold it.

Ours is the first age in history which has asked the child what he  6
would tolerate learning, but that is a part of the problem with which I am not equipped to deal. The devil of Educationism that possesses us is the kind that can be "cast out only by prayer and fasting." No one has yet come along strong enough to do it. In other ages the attention of children was held by Homer and Virgil, among others, but, by the reverse evolutionary process, that is no longer possible; our children are too stupid now to enter the past imaginatively. No one asks the student if algebra pleases him or if he finds it satisfactory that some French verbs are irregular, but if he prefers Hersey to Hawthorne, his taste must prevail.

I would like to put forward the proposition, repugnant to most  7
English teachers, that fiction, if it is going to be taught in the high schools, should be taught as a subject and as a subject with a history. The total effect of a novel depends not only on its innate impact, but upon the experience, literary and otherwise, with which it is approached. No child needs to be assigned Hersey or Steinbeck until he is familiar with a certain amount of the best work of Cooper, Hawthorne, Melville, the early James, and Crane, and he does not need to be assigned these until he has been introduced to some of the better English novelists of the eighteenth and nineteenth centuries.

The fact that these works do not present him with the realities of  8
his own time is all to the good. He is surrounded by the realities of his own time, and he has no perspective whatever from which to view them. Like the college student who wrote in her paper on Lincoln that he went to the movies and got shot, many students go to college unaware that the world was not made yesterday; their studies began with the present and dipped backward occasionally when it seemed necessary or unavoidable.

There is much to be enjoyed in the great British novels of the nine-  9
teenth century, much that a good teacher can open up in them for the young student. There is no reason why these novels should be either too simple or too difficult for the eighth grade. For the simple, they offer simple pleasures; for the more precocious, they can be made to yield subtler ones if the teacher is up to it. Let the student discover, after reading the nineteenth-century British novel, that the nineteenth-century American novel is quite different as to its literary characteristics, and he will

thereby learn something not only about these individual works but about the sea-change which a new historical situation can effect in a literary form. Let him come to modern fiction with this experience behind him, and he will be better able to see and to deal with the more complicated demands of the best twentieth-century fiction.

10      Modern fiction often looks simpler than the fiction that preceded it, but in reality is more complex. A natural evolution has taken place. The author has for the most part absented himself from direct participation in the work and has left the reader to make his own way amid experiences dramatically rendered and symbolically ordered. The modern novelist merges the reader in experience; he tends to raise the passions he touches upon. If he is a good novelist, he raises them to effect by their order and clarity a new experience—the total effect—which is not in itself sensuous or simply of the moment. Unless the child has had some literary experience before, he is not going to be able to resolve the immediate passions the book arouses into any true, total picture.

11      It is here the moral problem will arise. It is one thing for a child to read about adultery in the Bible or in *Anna Karenina*, and quite another for him to read about it in most modern fiction. This is not only because in both the former instances adultery is considered a sin, and in the latter, at most, an inconvenience, but because modern writing involves the reader in the action with a new degree of intensity, and literary mores now permit him to be involved in any action a human being can perform.

12      In our fractured culture, we cannot agree on morals; we cannot even agree that moral matters should come before literary ones when there is a conflict between them. All this is another reason why the high schools would do well to return to their proper business of preparing foundations. Whether in the senior year students should be assigned modern novelists should depend both on their parents' consent and on what they have already read and understood.

13      The high-school English teacher will be fulfilling his responsibility if he furnishes the student a guided opportunity, through the best writing of the past, to come, in time, to an understanding of the best writing of the present. He will teach literature, not social studies or little lessons in democracy or the customs of many lands.

14      And if the student finds that this is not to his taste? Well, that is regrettable. Most regrettable. His taste should not be consulted; it is being formed.

## CONSIDERATIONS

1. How far must you read in O'Connor's essay before you know her chief concern? Does it occupy her attention in her first three paragraphs? If not, how can you defend the organization of this essay?

2. O'Connor argues in paragraph 8 that it is "all to the good" that the so-called classics do not present the child "with the realities of his own time." How does her reference to the college student writing about Lincoln apply to her argument? How would she offset a reader's insistence that children's reading be relevant to their own time?

3. To what extent does O'Connor's paragraph 10 help explain the principle of "total effect" mentioned in paragraph 3? Do you consider that principle a reasonable means of sorting out acceptable from unacceptable reading matter?

4. How would Margaret Atwood (see "Pornography") respond to O'Connor's solution to the moral problem mentioned in paragraph 12?

5. Write a response to O'Connor's answer to her question at the beginning of paragraph 14. Take into account the rest of her essay as well as your own feelings.

6. What nineteenth-century British and American novels do you remember well enough to compare with modern novels? If your answer is "none," are you in any position to argue with O'Connor?

7. In paragraph 11, O'Connor writes: "modern writing involves the reader in the action with a new degree of intensity, and literary mores now permit him to be involved in any action a human being can perform." What, precisely, is she talking about? Rephrase these ideas in your own language, providing specifics and illustrations where needed. What do you think of her statement as a reason why children should not be reading people like Flannery O'Connor?

*Michael Francis O'Donovan (1903–1966) was a great Irish story-writer born in Cork. Under his pseudonym Frank O'Connor, he wrote novels, criticism (most notably* The Lonely Voice: A Study of the Short Story, *in 1962), and biography, but his short stories are his most celebrated work. We take "Christmas" from his volume of autobiography called* An Only Child *(1961).*

*O'Connor's skill at telling a story, which made him a great writer of short fiction, shows itself in this memoir of his own childhood. Notice how, from the first phrases to the end, O'Connor uses common notions of Christmas as a backdrop to his own recollection.*

— 71 —————————————————————

# FRANK O'CONNOR
## *Christmas*

———————————————————————

1   Christmas was always the worst time of the year for me, though it began well, weeks before Christmas itself, with the Christmas numbers. Normally I read only boys' weeklies, but at this time of year all papers, juvenile and adult, seemed equally desirable, as though the general magic of the season transcended the particular magic of any one paper. School stories, detective stories, and adventure stories all emerged into one great Christmas story.

2   Christmas numbers were, of course, double numbers; their pale-green and red covers suddenly bloomed into glossy colours, with borders of red-berried holly. Even their titles dripped with snow. As for the pictures within, they showed roads under snow, and old houses under snow, with diamond-paned windows that were brilliant in the darkness. I never knew what magic there was in snow for me because in Ireland we rarely saw it for more than two or three days in the year, and that was usually in the late spring. In real life it meant little to me except that Father—who was always trying to make a manly boy of me as he believed himself to have been at my age—made me wash my face and hands in it to avert chilblains. I think its magic in the Christmas numbers depended on the

———————————
"Christmas" from *An Only Child* by Frank O'Connor, published by Alfred A. Knopf, 1961. Reprinted by arrangement with the Joan Daves Agency on behalf of the estate of the author.

contrast between it and the Christmas candles, the holly branches with
the red berries, the log fires, and the gleaming windows. It was the contrast between light and dark, life and death; the cold and darkness that
reigned when life came into the world. Going about her work, Mother
would suddenly break into song:

> Natum videte
> Regem angelorum . . .*

and I would join in. It was the season of imagination. My trouble was
that I already had more than my share of imagination.

Then there were no more Christmas numbers, but I managed to      3
preserve the spirit of them, sitting at my table with pencil and paper, trying to draw Christmas scenes of my own—dark skies and walls, bright
snow and windows. When I was older and could trace figures, these
turned into the figures of the manger scene, cut out and mounted on
cardboard to make a proper crib.

Christmas Eve was the culmination of this season, the day when      4
the promise of the Christmas numbers should be fulfilled. The shops already had their green and red streamers, and in the morning Mother decorated the house with holly and ivy. Much as I longed for it, we never
had red berried holly, which cost more. The Christmas candle, two feet
high and a couple of inches thick, was set in a jam crock, wrapped in
coloured paper, and twined about with holly. Everything was ready for
the feast. For a lot of the day I leaned against the front door or wandered
slowly down the road to the corner, trying to appear careless and indifferent so that no one should know I was really waiting for the postman.
Most of the Christmas mail we got came on Christmas Eve, and though I
don't think I ever got a present through the post, that did not in the least
diminish my expectations of one. Whatever experience might have
taught me, the Christmas numbers taught differently.

Father had a half-day on Christmas Eve, and came home at noon      5
with his week's pay in his pocket—that is, when he got home at all.
Mother and I knew well how easily he was led astray by out-of-works
who waited at the street corners for men in regular jobs, knowing that on
Christmas Eve no one could refuse them a pint. But I never gave that aspect of it much thought. It wasn't for anything so commonplace as
Father's weekly pay that I was waiting. I even ignored the fact that when
he did come in, there was usually an argument and sometimes a quarrel.
At ordinary times when he did not give Mother enough to pay the bills,
she took it with resignation, and if there was a row it was he who provoked it by asking: 'Well, isn't that enough for you?' But at Christmas

---

*From the 17th-century Latin hymn "Adeste Fideles" ("O Come, All Ye Faithful").
("Behold the birth of the King of angels.") St. Stephen's Day is observed in Catholic communities. O'Connor explains the custom in paragraphs 12 and 13.

she would fight and fight desperately. One Christmas Eve he came home and handed her the housekeeping money with a complacent air, and she looked at the coins in her hand and went white. 'Lord God, what am I to do with that?' I heard her whisper despairingly, and I listened in terror because she never invoked the name of God. Father suddenly blew up into the fury he had been cooking up all the way home—a poor, hard-working man deprived of his little bit of pleasure at Christmas time because of an extravagant wife and child. 'Well, what do you want it for?' he snarled. 'What do I want it for?' she asked distractedly, and went through her shopping list, which, God knows, must have been modest enough. And then he said something that I did not understand, and I heard her whispering in reply and there was a frenzy in her voice that I would not have believed possible; 'Do you think I'll leave him without it on the one day of the year?'

6      Years later I suddenly remembered the phrase because of its beauty, and realized that it was I who was to be left without a toy, and on this one day of the year that seemed to her intolerable. And yet I did not allow it to disturb me; I had other expectations, and I was very happy when the pair of us went shopping together, down Blarney Lane, past the shop in the big old house islanded in Goulnaspurra, where they sold the coloured cardboard cribs I coveted, with shepherds and snow, manger and star, and across the bridge to Myles's Toy Shop on the North Main Street. There in the rainy dusk, jostled by prams and drunken women in shawls, and thrust on one side by barefooted children from the lanes, I stood in wonder, thinking which treasure Santa Claus would bring me from the ends of the earth to show his appreciation of the way I had behaved in the past twelve months. As he was a most superior man, and I a most superior child, I saw no limit to the possibilities of the period, and no reason why Mother should not join in my speculations.

7      It was usually dark when we tramped home together, up Wyse's Hill, from which we saw the whole city lit up beneath us and the trams reflected in the water under Patrick's Bridge; or later—when we lived in Barrackton, up Summerhill, Mother carrying the few scraps of meat and the plum pudding from Thompson's and me something from the Penny Bazaar. We had been out a long time, and I was full of expectations of what the postman might have brought in the meantime. Even when he hadn't brought anything, I didn't allow myself to be upset, for I knew that the poor postmen were dreadfully overworked at this time of year. And even if he didn't come later, there was always the final Christmas-morning delivery. I was an optimistic child, and the holly over the mirror in the kitchen and the red paper in the lighted window of the huxter shop across the street assured me that the Christmas numbers were right and anything might happen.

8      There were lesser pleasures to look forward to, like the lighting of the Christmas candle and the cutting of the Christmas cake. As the youngest of the household I had the job of lighting the candle and saying

solemnly: 'The light of Heaven to our souls on the last day,' and Mother's principal worry was that before the time came Father might slip out to the pub and spoil the ritual, for it was supposed to be carried out by the oldest and the youngest, and Father, by convention, was the oldest, though, in fact, as I later discovered, he was younger than Mother.

In those days the cake and candle were supposed to be presented by the small shopkeeper from whom we bought the tea, sugar, paraffin oil, and so on. We could not afford to shop in the big stores where everything was cheaper, because they did not give credit to poor people, and most of the time we lived on credit. But each year our 'presents' seemed to grow smaller, and Mother would comment impatiently on the meanness of Miss O' or Miss Mac in giving us a tiny candle or a stale cake. (When the 1914 War began they stopped giving us the cake.) Mother could never believe that people could be so mean, but, where we were concerned, they seemed to be capable of anything. The lighted candle still left me with two expectations. However late it grew I never ceased to expect the postman's knock, and even when that failed, there was the certainty that Christmas Morning would set everything right.

But when I woke on Christmas Morning, I felt the season of imagination slipping away from me and the world of reality breaking in. If all Santa Claus could bring me from the North Pole was something I could have bought in Myles's Toy Shop for a couple of pence, he seemed to me to be wasting his time. Then the postman came, on his final round before a holiday that already had begun to seem eternal, and either he brought nothing for us, or else he brought the dregs of the Christmas mail, like a Christmas card from somebody who had just got Mother's card and remembered her existence at the last moment. Often, even this would be in an unsealed envelope and it would upset her for hours. It was strange in a woman to whom a penny was money that an unsealed envelope seemed to her the worst of ill-breeding, equivalent to the small candle or the stale cake—not a simple measure of economy, but plain, unadulterated bad taste.

Comparing Christmas gifts with other kids didn't take long or give much satisfaction, and even then the day was overshadowed by the harsh rule that I was not supposed to call at other children's houses or they at mine. This, Mother said, was the family season, which was all very well for those who had families but death to an only child. It was the end of the season of imagination, and there was no reason to think it would ever come again. Nothing had happened as it happened in the Christmas numbers. There was no snow; no relative had returned from the States with presents for everyone; there was nothing but Christmas Mass and the choir thundering out *Natum videte regem angelorum* as though they believed it, when any fool could see that things were just going on in the same old way. Mother would sigh and say: 'I never believe it's really Christmas until I hear the *Adeste*,' but if that was all that Christmas meant to her she was welcome to it. Most Christmas days I could have screamed with misery. I argued with Mother that other kids were just as depressed as I was, and dying to see me, but I never remember that she allowed me to stray far from the front door.

12    But, bad as Christmas Day was, St. Stephen's Day was terrible. It needed no imagination, only as much as was required to believe that you really had a dead wren on the holly bush you carried from door to door, singing:

> I up with me stick and I gave him a fall,
> And I brought him here to visit ye all.

13    Father was very contemptuous, watching this, and took it as another sign of the disappearance of youthful manliness, for in his young days not only did they wash their faces in snow, but on Christmas Day they raised the countryside with big sticks, killing wrens—or droleens, as we called them. Everyone knew that it was the droleen's chirping that had alerted the Roman soldiers in the Garden of Gethsemane and pointed out to them where Christ was concealed, and in Father's young days they had carried it around with great pomp, all the mummers disguised. It seemed to him positively indecent to ask for money on the strength of a dead wren that you didn't have. It wasn't the absence of the wren that worried Mother, even if he was an informer, for she adored birds and supported a whole regiment of them through the winter, but the fear that I would be a nuisance to other women as poor as herself who didn't have a penny to give the wren boys.

14    In the afternoon she and I went to see the cribs in the chapels. (There were none in the parish churches.) She was never strong enough to visit the seven cribs you had to visit to get the special blessing, but we always went to the chapel of the Good Shepherd Convent in Sunday's Well where she had gone to school. She was very loyal to those she called 'the old nuns,' the nuns who had been kind to her when she was a child.

15    One Christmas Santa Claus brought me a toy engine. As it was the only present I had received, I took it with me to the convent, and played with it on the floor while Mother and 'the old nuns' discussed old times and how much nicer girls used to be then. But it was a young man who brought us in to see the crib. When I saw the Holy Child in the manger I was very distressed, because little as I had, he had nothing at all. For me it was fresh proof of the incompetence of Santa Claus—an elderly man who hadn't even remembered to give the Infant Jesus a toy and who should have been retired long ago. I asked the young nun politely if the Holy Child didn't like toys, and she replied composedly enough: 'Oh, he does, but his mother is too poor to afford them.' That settled it. My mother was poor too, but at Christmas she at least managed to buy me something, even if it was only a box of crayons. I distinctly remember getting into the crib and putting the engine between his outstretched arms. I probably showed him how to wind it as well, because a small

baby like that would not be clever enough to know. I remember too the tearful feeling of reckless generosity with which I left him there in the nightly darkness of the chapel, clutching my toy engine to his chest.

Because somehow I knew even then exactly how that child felt—    16 the utter despondency of realizing that he had been forgotten and that nobody had brought him anything; the longing for the dreary, dreadful holidays to pass till his father got the hell out of the house, and the postman returned again with the promise of better things.

## CONSIDERATIONS

1. The boy's bitter disappointment seems to culminate in paragraph 11, when he says, upon listening to the choir sing "Adeste Fideles," "any fool could see that things were just going on in the same old way." At what point does disappointment become disillusionment? Compare O'Connor's Christmas experience with the conclusion of Langston Hughes's "Salvation" (page 321) or with Jamaica Kincaid's "On Seeing England for the First Time" (page 346).

2. O'Connor's preoccupation with the "magic" of snow in paragraph 2 prompts a question: Why did snow and holly berries and the red and green covers of the Christmas magazines strike the adult writer as he tells of his boyhood?

3. O'Connor describes himself on Christmas Eve, loitering about, "trying to appear careless and indifferent," as he waited for the postman to bring the Christmas mail. What current slang word would perfectly fit the boy's behavior, and why didn't O'Connor use it?

4. Some students complain that O'Connor does not explain St. Stephen's Day clearly enough for a reader to understand what was going on and why the boy felt even worse then than he did on Christmas day. Write an expository paragraph about St. Stephen's Day, perhaps mentioning an irony involved in the customs of that day as practiced in Ireland. What sources would you turn to for information?

5. If the O'Donovans were so poor, how did they manage a Christmas cake and a Christmas candle? Finding the answer should help fill in some of the social context important to the story.

6. Years later, O'Connor writes, "I suddenly remembered the phrase because of its beauty." He refers to something he overheard his mother say in response to his father's surliness. If you remember a comparable phrase or sentence someone close to you once said in a dark moment, build a short narrative essay leading up to that remark.

— 72 ———————————————————————

# TILLIE OLSEN
## *I Stand Here Ironing*

1    I stand here ironing, and what you asked me moves tormented back and forth with the iron.

2    "I wish you would manage the time to come in and talk with  me about your daughter. I'm sure you can help me understand her. She's a youngster who needs help and whom I'm deeply interested in helping."

3    "Who needs help." Even if I came, what good would it do? You think because I am her mother I have a key, or that in some way you could use me as a key? She has lived for nineteen years. There is all that life that has happened outside of me, beyond me.

4    And when is there time to remember, to sift, to weigh, to estimate, to total? I will start and there will be an interruption and I will have to gather it all together again. Or I will become engulfed with all I did or did not do, with what should have been and what cannot be helped.

5    She was a beautiful baby. The first and only one of our five that was beautiful at birth. You do not guess how new and uneasy her tenancy in her now-loveliness. You did not know her all those years she was thought homely, or see her poring over her baby pictures, making me tell her over and over how beautiful she had been—and would be, I would

tell her—and was now, to the seeing eye. But the seeing eyes were few or nonexistent. Including mine.

I nursed her. They feel that's important nowadays. I nursed all the children, but with her, with all the fierce rigidity of first motherhood, I did like the books then said. Though her cries battered me to trembling and my breasts ached with swollenness, I waited till the clock decreed. 6

Why do I put that first? I do not even know if it matters, or if it explains anything. 7

She was a beautiful baby. She blew shining bubbles of sound. She loved motion, loved light, loved color and music and textures. She would lie on the floor in her blue overalls patting the surface so hard in ecstasy her hands and feet would blur. She was a miracle to me, but when she was eight months old I had to leave her daytimes with the woman downstairs to whom she was no miracle at all, for I worked or looked for work and for Emily's father, who "could no longer endure" (he wrote in his good-bye note) "sharing want with us." 8

I was nineteen. It was the pre-relief, pre-WPA world of the depression. I would start running as soon as I got off the streetcar, running up the stairs, the place smelling sour, and awake or asleep to startle awake, when she saw me she would break into a clogged weeping that could not be comforted, a weeping I can hear yet. 9

After a while I found a job hashing at night so I could be with her days, and it was better. But it came to where I had to bring her to his family and leave her. 10

It took a long time to raise the money for her fare back. Then she got chicken pox and I had to wait longer. When she finally came, I hardly knew her, walking quick and nervous like her father, looking like her father, thin, and dressed in a shoddy red that yellowed her skin and glared at the pockmarks. All the baby loveliness gone. 11

She was two. Old enough for nursery school they said, and I did not know then what I know now—the fatigue of the long day, and the lacerations of group life in nurseries that are only parking places for children. 12

Except that it would have made no difference if I had known. It was the only place there was. It was the only way we could be together, the only way I could hold a job. 13

And even without knowing, I knew. I knew the teacher that was evil because all these years it has curled into my memory, the little boy hunched in the corner, her rasp, "why aren't you outside, because Alvin hits you? that's no reason, go out, scaredy." I knew Emily hated it even if she did not clutch and implore "don't go Mommy" like the other children, mornings. 14

She always had a reason why we should stay home. Momma, you look sick, Momma. I feel sick. Momma, the teachers aren't there today, they're sick. Momma, we can't go, there was a fire there last night. Momma, it's a holiday today, no school, they told me. 15

16    But never a direct protest, never rebellion. I think of our others in their three-, four-year-oldness—the explosions, the tempers, the denunciations, the demands—and I feel suddenly ill. I put the iron down. What in me demanded that goodness in her? And what was the cost, the cost to her of such goodness?

17    The old man living in the back once said in his gentle way: "You should smile at Emily more when you look at her." What *was* in my face when I looked at her? I loved her. There were all the acts of love.

18    It was only with the others I remembered what he said, and it was the face of joy, and not of care or tightness or worry I turned to them— too late for Emily. She does not smile easily, let alone almost always as her brothers and sisters do. Her face is closed and sombre, but when she wants, how fluid. You must have seen it in her pantomimes, you spoke of her rare gift for comedy on the stage that rouses a laughter out of the audience so dear they applaud and applaud and do not want to let her go.

19    Where does it come from, that comedy? There was none of it in her when she came back to me that second time, after I had had to send her away again. She had a new daddy now to learn to love, and I think perhaps it was a better time.

20    Except when we left her alone nights, telling ourselves she was old enough.

21    "Can't you go some other time, Mommy, like tomorrow?" she would ask. "Will it be just a little while you'll be gone? Do you promise?"

22    The time we came back, the front door open, the clock on the floor in the hall. She rigid awake. "It wasn't just a little while. I didn't cry. Three times I called you, just three times, and then I ran downstairs to open the door so you could come faster. The clock talked loud. I threw it away, it scared me what it talked."

23    She said the clock talked loud again that night I went to the hospital to have Susan. She was delirious with the fever that comes before red measles, but she was fully conscious all the week I was gone and the week after we were home when she could not come near the new baby or me.

24    She did not get well. She stayed skeleton thin, not wanting to eat, and night after night she had nightmares. She would call for me, and I would rouse from exhaustion to sleepily call back: "You're all right, darling, go to sleep, it's just a dream," and if she still called, in a sterner voice, "now go to sleep, Emily, there's nothing to hurt you." Twice, only twice, when I had to get up for Susan anyhow, I went in to sit with her.

25    Now when it is too late (as if she would let me hold and comfort her like I do the others) I get up and go to her at once at her moan or restless stirring. "Are you awake, Emily? Can I get you something?" And the answer is always the same: "No, I'm all right, go back to sleep, Mother."

They persuaded me at the clinic to send her away to a convalescent    26
home in the country where "she can have the kind of food and care you
can't manage for her, and you'll be free to concentrate on the new baby."
They still send children to that place. I see pictures on the society page of
sleek young women planning affairs to raise money for it, or dancing at
the affairs, or decorating Easter eggs or filling Christmas stockings for
the children.

They never have a picture of the children so I do not know if the    27
girls still wear those gigantic red bows and the ravaged looks on the
every other Sunday when parents can come to visit "unless otherwise
notified"—as we were notified the first six weeks.

Oh it is a handsome place, green lawns and tall trees and fluted    28
flower beds. High up on the balconies of each cottage the children stand,
the girls in their red bows and white dresses, the boys in white suits and
giant red ties. The parents stand below shrieking up to be heard and the
children shriek down to be heard, and between them the invisible wall
"Not To Be Contaminated by Parental Germs or Physical Affection."

There was a tiny girl who always stood hand in hand with Emily.    29
Her parents never came. One visit she was gone. "They moved her to
Rose College," Emily shouted in explanation. "They don't like you to
love anybody here."

She wrote once a week, the labored writing of a seven-year-old. "I    30
am fine. How is the baby. If I write my leter nicly I will have a star.
Love." There never was a star. We wrote every other day, letters she
could never hold or keep but only hear read—once. "We simply do not
have room for children to keep any personal possessions," they patiently
explained when we pieced one Sunday's shrieking together to plead how
much it would mean to Emily, who loved so to keep things, to be allowed to keep her letters and cards.

Each visit she looked frailer. "She isn't eating," they told us.    31

(They had runny eggs for breakfast or mush with lumps, Emily said    32
later, I'd hold it in my mouth and not swallow. Nothing ever tasted good,
just when they had chicken.)

It took us eight months to get her released home, and only the fact    33
that she gained back so little of her seven lost pounds convinced the social worker.

I used to try to hold and love her after she came back, but her body    34
would stay stiff, and after a while she'd push away. She ate little. Food
sickened her, and I think much of life too. Oh she had physical lightness
and brightness, twinkling by on skates, bouncing like a ball up and down
up and down over the jump rope, skimming over the hill; but these were
momentary.

She fretted about her appearance, thin and dark and foreign-looking    35
at a time when every little girl was supposed to look or thought she
should look a chubby blonde replica of Shirley Temple. The doorbell

sometimes rang for her, but no one seemed to come and play in the house or be a best friend. Maybe because we moved so much.

36    There was a boy she loved painfully through two school semesters. Months later she told me how she had taken pennies from my purse to buy him candy. "Licorice was his favorite and I brought him some every day, but he still liked Jennifer better'n me. Why, Mommy?" The kind of question for which there is no answer.

37    School was a worry to her. She was not glib or quick in a world where glibness and quickness were easily confused with ability to learn. To her overworked and exasperated teachers she was an overconscientious "slow learner" who kept trying to catch up and was absent entirely too often.

38    I let her be absent, though sometimes the illness was imaginary. How different from my now-strictness about attendance with the others. I wasn't working. We had a new baby, I was home anyhow. Sometimes, after Susan grew old enough, I would keep her home from school, too, to have them all together.

39    Mostly Emily had asthma, and her breathing, harsh and labored, would fill the house with a curiously tranquil sound. I would bring the two old dresser mirrors and her boxes of collections to her bed. She would select beads and single earrings, bottle tops and shells, dried flowers and pebbles, old postcards and scraps, all sorts of oddments; then she and Susan would play Kingdom, setting up landscapes and furniture, peopling them with action.

40    Those were the only times of peaceful companionship between her and Susan. I have edged away from it, that poisonous feeling between them, that terrible balancing of hurts and needs I had to do between the two, and did so badly, those earlier years.

41    Oh there are conflicts between the others too, each one human, needing, demanding, hurting, taking—but only between Emily and Susan, no, Emily toward Susan that corroding resentment. It seems so obvious on the surface, yet it is not obvious. Susan, the second child, Susan, golden- and curly-haired and chubby, quick and articulate and assured, everything in appearance and manner Emily was not; Susan, not able to resist Emily's precious things, losing or sometimes clumsily breaking them; Susan telling jokes and riddles to company for applause while Emily sat silent (to say to me later: that was *my* riddle, Mother, I told it to Susan); Susan, who for all the five years' difference in age was just a year behind Emily in developing physically.

42    I am glad for that slow physical development that widened the difference between her and her contemporaries, though she suffered over it. She was too vulnerable for that terrible world of youthful competition, of preening and parading, of constant measuring of yourself against every other, of envy. "If I had that copper hair," "If I had that skin. . . ." She tormented herself enough about not looking like the others, there was enough of the unsureness, the having to be conscious of words before

you speak, the constant caring—what are they thinking of me? without having it all magnified by the merciless physical drives.

Ronnie is calling. He is wet and I change him. It is rare there is 43
such a cry now. That time of motherhood is almost behind me when the ear is not one's own but must always be racked and listening for the child cry, the child call. We sit for a while and I hold him, looking out over the city spread in charcoal with its soft aisles of light. *"Shoogily,"* he breathes and curls closer. I carry him back to bed, asleep. *Shoogily*. A funny word, a family word, inherited from Emily, invented by her to say: *comfort*.

In this and other ways she leaves her seal, I say aloud. And startle 44
at my saying it. What do I mean? What did I start to gather together, to try and make coherent? I was at the terrible, growing years. War years. I do not remember them well. I was working, there were four smaller ones now, there was not time for her. She had to help be a mother, and house-keeper, and shopper. She had to set her seal. Mornings of crisis and near hysteria trying to get lunches packed, hair combed, coats and shoes found, everyone to school or Child Care on time, the baby ready for transportation. And always the paper scribbled on by a smaller one, the book looked at by Susan then mislaid, the homework not done. Running out to that huge school where she was one, she was lost, she was a drop; suffering over the unpreparedness, stammering and unsure in her classes.

There was so little time left at night after the kids were bedded 45
down. She would struggle over books, always eating (it was in those years she developed her enormous appetite that is legendary in our fam-ily) and I would be ironing, or preparing food for the next day, or writing V-mail to Bill, or tending the baby. Sometimes, to make me laugh, or out of her despair, she would imitate happenings or types at school.

I think I said once: "Why don't you do something like this in the 46
school amateur show?" One morning she phoned me at work, hardly un-derstandable through the weeping: "Mother, I did it. I won, I won; they gave me first prize; they clapped and clapped and wouldn't let me go."

Now suddenly she was Somebody, and as imprisoned in her differ- 47
ence as she had been in anonymity.

She began to be asked to perform at other high schools, even in col- 48
leges, then at city and statewide affairs. The first one we went to, I only recognized her that first moment when thin, shy, she almost drowned herself into the curtains. Then: Was this Emily? The control, the com-mand, the convulsing and deadly clowning, the spell, then the roaring, stamping audience, unwilling to let this rare and precious laughter out of their lives.

Afterwards: You ought to do something about her with a gift like 49
that—but without money or knowing how, what does one do? We have left it all to her, and the gift has as often eddied inside, clogged and clot-ted, as been used and growing.

50    She is coming. She runs up the stairs two at a time with her light graceful step, and I know she is happy tonight. Whatever it was that occasioned your call did not happen today.

51    "Aren't you ever going to finish the ironing, Mother? Whistler painted his mother in a rocker. I'd have to paint mine standing over an ironing board." This is one of her communicative nights and she tells me everything and nothing as she fixes herself a plate of food out of the icebox.

52    She is so lovely. Why did you want me to come in at all? Why were you concerned? She will find her way.

53    She starts up the stairs to bed. "Don't get me up with the rest in the morning." "But I thought you were having midterms." "Oh, those," she comes back in, kisses me, and says quite lightly, "in a couple of years when we'll all be atom-dead they won't matter a bit."

54    She has said it before. She *believes* it. But because I have been dredging the past, and all that compounds a human being is so heavy and meaningful in me, I cannot endure it tonight.

55    I will never total it all. I will never come in to say: She was a child seldom smiled at. Her father left me before she was a year old. I had to work her first six years when there was work, or I sent her home and to his relatives. There were years she had care she hated. She was dark and thin and foreign-looking in a world where the prestige went to blondeness and curly hair and dimples, she was slow where glibness was prized. She was a child of anxious, not proud, love. We were poor and could not afford for her the soil of easy growth. I was a young mother, I was a distracted mother. There were the other children pushing up, demanding. Her younger sister seemed all that she was not. There were years she did not want me to touch her. She kept too much in herself, her life was such she had to keep too much in herself. My wisdom came too late. She has much to her and probably nothing will come of it. She is a child of her age, of depression, of war, of fear.

56    Let her be. So all that is in her will not bloom—but in how many does it? There is still enough left to live by. Only help her to know—help make it so there is cause for her to know—that she is more than this dress on the ironing board, helpless before the iron.

## CONSIDERATIONS

1. Identify the "I" and the "you" in the first line of the story. Neither one is given a name. Is the "I" Tillie Olsen or a character she created to tell the story? Comment on the first-person point of view and how the story would change if an omniscient observer told it.

2. In the concluding paragraphs of the story, what is so shocking to the mother that she says, "I cannot endure it tonight"?

3. What is there about the story that makes the title memorable? And vice versa? Is the last sentence of the story to be read literally? Explain.

4. Some readers find themselves arguing about which character the story is about—Emily or the nameless mother. Can you settle that dispute?

5. The mother worries that she and Emily had not had enough closeness and demonstrations of mutual affection—as in paragraph 34. Read Diane Ackerman's "The Importance of Touch" (page 10), especially paragraph 11, and discuss the relevance of her report to Tillie Olsen's story.

6. All we know about Emily's father is that he walked out on her and her mother because he "could no longer endure sharing want with us." Why doesn't the author tell us more about him, and to what important truth about writing does that fact point?

*George Orwell was the pen name of Eric Blair (1903–1950), who was born in India of English parents, attended Eton on a scholarship, and returned to the East as a member of the Imperial Police. He quit his position after five years because he wanted to write and because he came to feel that imperialism was "very largely a racket." For eight years, he wrote with small success and lived in considerable poverty. His first book,* Down and Out in Paris and London *(1933), described those years. Further memoirs and novels followed, including* Burmese Days *(1935) and* Keep the Aspidistra Flying *(1938). His last books were the political fable* Animal Farm *(1945) and his great anti-utopia* 1984, *which appeared in 1949, shortly before his death. He died of tuberculosis, his health first afflicted when he was a police officer in Burma, undermined by years of poverty, and further worsened by a wound he received during the civil war in Spain.*

*Best known for his fiction, Orwell was essentially an essayist; even his novels are essays. He made his living most of his adult life by writing reviews and articles for English weeklies. His collected essays, reviews, and letters form an impressive four volumes. Politics is at the center of his work—a personal politics. After his disaffection from imperialism, he became a leftist and fought on the Loyalist side against Franco in Spain. (*Homage to Catalonia *comes out of this time.) But his experience of Communist duplicity there, and his early understanding of the paranoid totalitarianism of Stalin, turned him anti-Communist. He could swear allegiance to no party. His anti-Communism made him in no way conservative; he considered himself a socialist until his death, but other socialists would have nothing to do with him. He found politics shabby and politicians dishonest. With an empirical, English turn of mind, he looked skeptically at all saviors and panaceas.*

*"A Hanging" comes from Orwell's firsthand experience with imperialism and uses slight and peripheral detail. Note how the condemned man, when he avoids the puddle, locates the ordinariness of outrage.*

## — 73

# GEORGE ORWELL
## *A Hanging*

It was in Burma, a sodden morning of the rains. A sickly light, like   1
yellow tinfoil, was slanting over the high walls into the jail yard. We
were waiting outside the condemned cells, a row of sheds fronted with
double bars, like small animal cages. Each cell measured about ten feet
by ten and was quite bare within except for a plank bed and a pot for
drinking water. In some of them brown, silent men were squatting at the
inner bars, with their blankets draped around them. These were the condemned men, due to be hanged within the next week or two.

One prisoner had been brought out of his cell. He was a Hindu, a   2
puny wisp of a man, with a shaven head and vague liquid eyes. He had a
thick, sprouting moustache, absurdly too big for his body, rather like the
moustache of a comic man on the films. Six tall Indian warders were
guarding him and getting him ready for the gallows. Two of them stood
by with rifles and fixed bayonets, while the others handcuffed him,
passed a chain through his handcuffs and fixed it to their belts, and
lashed his arms tight to his sides. They crowded very close about him,
with their hands always on him in a careful, caressing grip, as though all
the while feeling him to make sure he was there. It was like men handling a fish which is still alive and may jump back into the water. But he
stood quite unresisting, yielding his arms limply to the ropes, as though
he hardly noticed what was happening.

Eight o'clock struck and a bugle call, desolately thin in the wet air,   3
floated from the distant barracks. The superintendent of the jail, who
was standing apart from the rest of us, moodily prodding the gravel with
his stick, raised his head at the sound. He was an army doctor, with a
grey toothbrush moustache and a gruff voice. "For God's sake hurry up,
Francis," he said irritably. "The man ought to have been dead by this
time. Aren't you ready yet?"

Francis, the head jailer, a fat Dravidian in a white drill suit and gold   4
spectacles, waved his black hand. "Yes sir, yes sir," he bubbled. "All iss
satisfactorily prepared. The hangman iss waiting. We shall proceed."

5      "Well, quick march, then. The prisoners can't get their breakfast till this job's over."

6      We set out for the gallows. Two warders marched on either side of the prisoner, with their rifles at the slope; two others marched close against him, gripping him by arm and shoulder, as though at once pushing and supporting him. The rest of us, magistrates and the like, followed behind. Suddenly, when we had gone ten yards, the procession stopped short without any order or warning. A dreadful thing had happened—a dog, come goodness knows whence, had appeared in the yard. It came bounding among us with a loud volley of barks and leapt round us wagging its whole body, wild with glee at finding so many human beings together. It was a large woolly dog, half Airedale, half pariah. For a moment it pranced around us, and then, before anyone could stop it, it had made a dash for the prisoner, and jumping up tried to lick his face. Everybody stood aghast, too taken aback even to grab the dog.

7      "Who let that bloody brute in here?" said the superintendent angrily. "Catch it, someone!"

8      A warder detached from the escort, charged clumsily after the dog, but it danced and gambolled just out of his reach, taking everything as part of the game. A young Eurasian jailer picked up a handful of gravel and tried to stone the dog away, but it dodged the stones and came after us again. Its yaps echoed from the jail walls. The prisoner, in the grasp of the two warders, looked on incuriously, as though this was another formality of the hanging. It was several minutes before someone managed to catch the dog. Then we put my handkerchief through its collar and moved off once more, with the dog still straining and whimpering.

9      It was about forty yards to the gallows. I watched the bare brown back of the prisoner marching in front of me. He walked clumsily with his bound arms, but quite steadily, with that bobbing gait of the Indian who never straightens his knees. At each step his muscles slid neatly into place, the lock of hair on his scalp danced up and down, his feet printed themselves on the wet gravel. And once, in spite of the men who gripped him by each shoulder, he stepped lightly aside to avoid a puddle on the path.

10     It is curious; but till that moment I had never realized what it means to destroy a healthy, conscious man. When I saw the prisoner step aside to avoid the puddle I saw the mystery, the unspeakable wrongness, of cutting a life short when it is in full tide. This man was not dying, he was alive just as we are alive. All the organs of his body were working—bowels digesting food, skin renewing itself, nails growing, tissues forming—all toiling away in solemn foolery. His nails would still be growing when he stood on the drop, when he was falling through the air with a tenth-of-a-second to live. His eyes saw the yellow gravel and the grey walls, and his brain still remembered, foresaw, reasoned—

even about puddles. He and we were a party of men walking together, seeing, hearing, feeling, understanding the same world; and in two minutes, with a sudden snap, one of us would be gone—one mind less, one world less.

The gallows stood in a small yard, separate from the main grounds 11 of the prison, and overgrown with tall prickly weeds. It was a brick erection like three sides of a shed, with planking on top, and above that two beams and a crossbar with the rope dangling. The hangman, a greyhaired convict in the white uniform of the prison, was waiting beside his machine. He greeted us with a servile crouch as we entered. At a word from Francis the two wards, gripping the prisoner more closely than ever, half led, half pushed him to the gallows and helped him clumsily up the ladder. Then the hangman climbed up and fixed the rope round the prisoner's neck.

We stood waiting, five yards away. The warders had formed in a 12 rough circle round the gallows. And then, when the noose was fixed, the prisoner began crying out to his god. It was a high, reiterated cry of "Ram! Ram! Ram! Ram!" not urgent and fearful like a prayer or cry for help, but steady, rhythmical, almost like the tolling of a bell. The dog answered the sound with a whine. The hangman, still standing on the gallows, produced a small cotton bag like a flour bag and drew it down over the prisoner's face. But the sound, muffled by the cloth, still persisted, over and over again: "Ram! Ram! Ram! Ram! Ram!"

The hangman climbed down and stood ready, holding the lever. 13 Minutes seemed to pass. The steady, muffled crying from the prisoner went on and on, "Ram! Ram! Ram!" never faltering for an instant. The superintendent, his head on his chest, was slowly poking the ground with his stick; perhaps he was counting the cries, allowing the prisoner a fixed number—fifty, perhaps, or a hundred. Everyone had changed colour. The Indians had gone grey like bad coffee, and one or two of the bayonets were wavering. We looked at the lashed, hooded man on the drop, and listened to his cries—each cry another second of life; the same thought was in all our minds; oh, kill him quickly, get it over, stop that abominable noise!

Suddenly the superintendent made up his mind. Throwing up his 14 head he made a swift motion with his stick. "Chalo!" he shouted almost fiercely.

There was a clanking noise, and then dead silence. The prisoner 15 had vanished, and the rope was twisting on itself. I let go of the dog, and it galloped immediately to the back of the gallows; but when it got there it stopped short, barked, and then retreated into a corner of the yard, where it stood among the weeds, looking timorously out at us. We went round the gallows to inspect the prisoner's body. He was dangling with his toes pointed straight downwards, very slowly revolving, as dead as a stone.

16    The superintendent reached out with his stick and poked the bare brown body; it oscillated slightly. *"He's* all right," said the superintendent. He backed out from under the gallows, and blew out a deep breath. The moody look had gone out of his face quite suddenly. He glanced at his wrist-watch. "Eight minutes past eight. Well, that's all for this morning, thank God."

17    The warders unfixed bayonets and marched away. The dog, sobered and conscious of having misbehaved itself, slipped after them. We walked out of the gallows yard, past the condemned cells with their waiting prisoners, into the big central yard of the prison. The convicts, under the command of warders armed with lathis, were already receiving their breakfast. They squatted in long rows, each man holding a tin pannikin, while two warders with buckets marched round ladling out rice; it seemed quite a homely, jolly scene, after the hanging. An enormous relief had come upon us now that the job was done. One felt an impulse to sing, to break into a run, to snigger. All at once everyone began chatting gaily.

18    The Eurasian boy walking beside me nodded towards the way we had come, with a knowing smile: "Do you know, sir, our friend (he meant the dead man) when he heard his appeal had been dismissed, he pissed on the floor of his cell. From fright. Kindly take one of my cigarettes, sir. Do you not admire my new silver case, sir? From the boxwallah, two rupees eight annas. Classy European style."

19    Several people laughed—at what, nobody seemed certain.

20    Francis was walking by the superintendent, talking garrulously: "Well, sir, all has passed off with the utmost satisfactoriness. It was all finished—flick! Like that. It iss not always so—oah, no! I have known cases where the doctor wass obliged to go beneath the gallows and pull the prisoner's legs to ensure decease. Most disagreeable!"

21    "Wriggling about, eh? That's bad," said the superintendent.

22    "Ach, sir, it iss worse when they become refractory! One man, I recall, clung to the bars of hiss cage when we went to take him out. You will scarcely credit, sir, that it took six wards to dislodge him, three pulling at each leg. We reasoned with him, 'My dear fellow,' we said, 'think of all the pain and trouble you are causing to us!' But no, he would not listen! Ach, he wass very troublesome!"

23    I found that I was laughing quite loudly. Everyone was laughing. Even the superintendent grinned in a tolerant way. "You'd better all come out and have a drink," he said quite genially. "I've got a bottle of whisky in the car. We could do with it."

24    We went through the big double gates of the prison into the road. "Pulling at his legs!" exclaimed a Burmese magistrate suddenly, and burst into a loud chuckling. We all began laughing again. At that moment Francis' anecdote seemed extraordinarily funny. We all had a drink together, native and European alike, quite amicably. The dead man was a hundred yards away.

## CONSIDERATIONS

1. Many readers have described Orwell's "A Hanging" as a powerful condemnation of capital punishment. Study Orwell's technique in drawing from his readers the desired inference. Can you imagine using Orwell's techniques in a piece that by implication favors capital punishment? Try writing a paragraph or two of such a piece.

2. Point out examples of Orwell's skillful use of detail to establish the place and mood of "A Hanging." Adapt his technique to your purpose in your next essay.

3. What minor incident caused Orwell suddenly to see "the unspeakable wrongness . . . of cutting a life short"? Why?

4. What effect, in paragraph 6, does the boisterous dog have on the players of this scene? On you, the reader? Explain in terms of the whole essay.

5. "One mind, one world less" is the way Orwell sums up the demise of the Hindu prisoner. Obviously, Orwell's statement is highly compressed, jamming into its short length many ideas, hopes, and fears. Write a short essay, opening up his aphorism so that your readers get some idea of what can be packed into five short words. For additional examples of compressed expression, see Ambrose Bierce's "Some Devil's Definitions" and any of the poems in this book.

6. The warden and others present were increasingly disconcerted by the prisoner's continued cry, "Ram! Ram! Ram! Ram!" But note Orwell's description of that cry in paragraphs 12 and 13. Does that description give you a clue as to the nature of the man's cry? Why doesn't Orwell explain it?

*In this famous essay, Orwell attacks the rhetoric of politics. He largely attacks the left—because his audience was an English intellectual class that was largely leftist.*

*But his points apply to all prose, whatever its politics or lack of politics. This essay codifies many of the general principles of good modern prose and has had much influence. See how, by example and argument, Orwell proposes for prose style an ethic of clarity.*

## — 74 —

# GEORGE ORWELL
## *Politics and the English Language*

1    Most people who bother with the matter at all would admit that the English language is in a bad way, but it is generally assumed that we cannot by conscious action do anything about it. Our civilization is decadent and our language—so the argument runs—must inevitably share in the general collapse. It follows that any struggle against the abuse of language is a sentimental archaism, like preferring candles to electric light or hansom cabs to aeroplanes. Underneath this lies the half-conscious belief that language is a natural growth and not an instrument which we shape for our own purposes.

2    Now, it is clear that the decline of a language must ultimately have political and economic causes: it is not due simply to the bad influence of this or that individual writer. But an effect can become a cause, reinforcing the original cause and producing the same effect in an intensified form, and so indefinitely. A man may take to drink because he feels himself to be a failure, and then fail all the more completely because he drinks. It is rather the same thing that is happening to the English language. It becomes ugly and inaccurate because our thoughts are foolish, but the slovenliness of our language makes it easier for us to have foolish thoughts. The point is that the process is reversible. Modern English, especially written English, is full of bad habits which spread by imitation

and which can be avoided if one is willing to take the necessary trouble. If one gets rid of these habits one can think more clearly, and to think clearly is a necessary first step towards political regeneration: so that the fight against bad English is not frivolous and is not the exclusive concern of professional writers. I will come back to this presently, and I hope that by that time the meaning of what I have said here will have become clearer. Meanwhile, here are five specimens of the English language as it is now habitually written.

These five passages have not been picked out because they are especially bad—I could have quoted far worse if I had chosen—but because they illustrate various of the mental vices from which we now suffer. They are a little below the average, but are fairly representative samples. I number them so that I can refer back to them when necessary: 3

> (1) I am not, indeed, sure whether it is not true to say that the Milton who once seemed not unlike a seventeenth-century Shelley had not become, out of an experience ever more bitter in each year, more alien [*sic*] to the founder of that Jesuit sect which nothing could induce him to tolerate.
>
> > —Professor Harold Laski
> > [Essay in *Freedom of Expression*]

> (2) Above all, we cannot play ducks and drakes with a native battery of idioms which prescribes such egregious collocations of vocables as the Basic *put up with* for *tolerate* or *put at a loss* for *bewilder*.
> > —Professor Lancelot Hogben [*Interglossa*]

> (3) On the one side we have the free personality: by definition it is not neurotic, for it has neither conflict nor dream. Its desires, such as they are, are transparent, for they are just what institutional approval keeps in the forefront of consciousness; another institutional pattern would alter their number and intensity; there is little in them that is natural, irreducible, or culturally dangerous. But *on the other side,* the social bond itself is nothing but the mutual reflection of these self-secure integrities. Recall the definition of love. Is not this the very picture of a small academic? Where is there a place in this hall of mirrors for either personality or fraternity?
> > —Essay on psychology in *Politics* [New York]

> (4) All the "best people" from the gentlemen's clubs, and all the frantic fascist captains, united in common hatred of Socialism and bestial horror of the rising tide of the mass revolutionary movement, have turned to acts of provocation, to foul incendiarism, to medieval legends of poisoned wells, to legalize their own destruction of proletarian organizations, and rouse the agitated petty-bourgeoisie to chauvinistic fervor on behalf of the fight against the revolutionary way out of the crisis.
> > —Communist pamphlet

(5) If a new spirit is to be infused into this old country, there is one thorny and contentious reform which must be tackled, and that is the humanization and galvanization of the B.C.C. Timidity here will bespeak canker and atrophy of the soul. The heart of Britain may be sound and of strong beat, for instance, but the British lion's roar at present is like that of Bottom in Shakepeares's *Midsummer Night's Dream*—as gentle as any sucking dove. A virile new Britain cannot continue indefinitely to be traduced in the eyes, or rather ears, of the world by the effete languors of Langham Place brazenly masquerading as "standard English." When the Voice of Britain is heard at nine o'clock, better far and infinitely less ludicrous to hear aitches honestly dropped than the present priggish, inflated, inhibited, schoolma'amish arch braying of blameless bashful mewing maidens!

—Letter in *Tribune*

4    Each of these passages has faults of its own, but, quite apart from avoidable ugliness, two qualities are common to all of them. The first is staleness of imagery; the other is lack of precision. The writer either has a meaning and cannot express it, or he inadvertently says something else, or he is almost indifferent as to whether his words mean anything or not. This mixture of vagueness and sheer incompetence is the most marked characteristic of modern English prose, and especially of any kind of political writing. As soon as certain topics are raised, the concrete melts into the abstract and no one seems able to think of turns of speech that are not hackneyed: prose consists less and less of *words* chosen for the sake of their meaning, and more and more of *phrases* tacked together like the sections of a prefabricated hen-house. I list below, with notes and examples, various of the tricks by means of which the work of prose-construction is habitually dodged:

## Dying Metaphors

5    A newly invented metaphor assists thought by evoking a visual image, while on the other hand a metaphor which is technically "dead" (e.g. *iron resolution*) has in effect reverted to being an ordinary word and can generally be used without loss of vividness. But in between these two classes there is a huge dump of worn-out metaphors which have lost all evocative power and are merely used because they save people the trouble of inventing phrases for themselves. Examples are: *Ring the changes on, take up the cudgels for, toe the line, ride roughshod over, stand shoulder to shoulder with, play into the hands of, no axe to grind, grist to the mill, fishing in troubled waters, on the order of the day, Achilles' heel, swan song, hotbed.* Many of these are used without knowledge of their meaning (what is a "rift," for instance?), and incompatible metaphors are frequently mixed, a sure sign that the writer is not

interested in what he is saying. Some metaphors now current have been twisted out of their original meaning without those who use them even being aware of the fact. For example, *toe the line* is sometimes written *tow the line*. Another example is *the hammer and the anvil*, now always used with the implication that the anvil gets the worst of it. In real life it is always the anvil that breaks the hammer, never the other way about: a writer who stopped to think what he was saying would be aware of this, and would avoid perverting the original phrase.

## Operators or Verbal False Limbs

These save the trouble of picking out appropriate verbs and nouns, and at the same time pad each sentence with extra syllables which give it an appearance of symmetry. Characteristic phrases are *render inoperative, militate against, make contact with, be subjected to, give rise to, give grounds for, have the effect of, play a leading part (role) in, make itself felt, take effect, exhibit a tendency to, serve the purpose of,* etc., etc. The keynote is the elimination of simple verbs. Instead of being a single word, such as *break, stop, spoil, mean, kill* a verb becomes a *phrase,* made up of a noun or adjective tacked on to some general-purpose verb such as *prove, serve, form, play, render.* In addition, the passive voice is wherever possible used in preference to the active, and noun constructions are used instead of gerunds (*by examination of* instead of *by examining*). The range of verbs is further cut down by means of the *-ize* and *de-* formations, and the banal statements are given an appearance of profundity by means of the *not un-* formation. Simple conjunctions and prepositions are replaced by such phrases as *with respect to, having regard to, the fact that, by dint of, in view of, in the interests of, on the hypothesis that;* and the ends of sentences are saved from anticlimax by such resounding commonplaces as *greatly to be desired, cannot be left out of account, a development to be expected in the near future, deserving of serious consideration, brought to a satisfactory conclusion* and so on and so forth.

## Pretentious Diction

Words like *phenomenon, element, individual* (as noun), *objective, categorical, effective, virtual, basic, primary, promote, constitute, exhibit, exploit, utilize, eliminate, liquidate,* are used to dress up simple statements and give an air of scientific impartiality to biased judgments. Adjectives like *epoch-making, epic, historic, unforgettable, triumphant, age-old, inevitable, inexorable, veritable,* are used to dignify the sordid processes of international politics, while writing that aims at glorifying war usually takes on an archaic color, its characteristic words being: *realm, throne, chariot, mailed fist, trident, sword, shield, buckler, banner, jackboot, clarion.* Foreign words and expressions such as *cul de sac,* *ancien régime, deus ex machina, mutatis mutandis, status quo, gleich-schaltung, weltanschauung,* are used to give an air of culture and elegance. Except for the useful abbreviations *i.e., e.g.,* and *etc.,* there is no real need for any of the hundreds of foreign phrases now current in English. Bad writers, and especially scientific, political and sociological writers, are nearly always haunted by the notion that Latin or Greek words are grander than Saxon ones, and unnecessary words like *expedite, ameliorate, predict, extraneous, deracinated, clandestine, subaqueous* and hundreds of others constantly gain ground from their Anglo-Saxon opposite numbers.* The jargon peculiar to Marxist writing (*hyena, hangman, cannibal, petty bourgeois, these gentry, lacquey, flunkey, mad dog, White Guard,* etc.) consists largely of words and phrases translated from Russian, German or French; but the normal way of coining a new word is to use a Latin or Greek root with the appropriate affix and, where necessary, the *-ize* formation. It is often easier to make up words of this kind (*deregionalize, impermissible, extramarital, nonfragmentary* and so forth) than to think up the English words that will cover one's meaning. The result, in general, is an increase in slovenliness and vagueness.

### Meaningless Words

8        In certain kinds of writing, particularly in an art criticism and literary criticism, it is normal to come across long passages which are almost completely lacking in meaning.** Words like *romantic, plastic, values, human, dead, sentimental, natural, vitality,* as used in art criticism, are strictly meaningless, in the sense that they not only do not point to any discoverable object, but are hardly ever expected to do so by the reader. When one critic writes, "The outstanding feature of Mr. X's work is its living quality," while another writes, "The immediately striking thing about Mr. X's work is its peculiar deadness," the reader accepts this as a simple difference of opinion. If words like *black* and *white* were involved, instead of the jargon words *dead* and *living,* he would see at once that language was being used in an improper way. Many political words are similarly abused. The word *Fascism* has now no meaning in so far as it signifies "something not desirable." The words *democracy, socialism,*

---

*An interesting illustration of this is the way in which the English flower names which were in use till very recently are being ousted by Greek ones, *snapdragons* becoming *antirrhinum, forget-me-not* becoming *myosotis,* etc. It is hard to see any practical reason for this change of fashion: it is probably due to an instinctive turning-away from the more homely word and a vague feeling that the Greek is scientific.

**Example: "Comfort's catholicity of perception and image, strangely Whitmanesque in range, almost the exact opposite in aesthetic compulsion, continues to evoke that trembling atmosphere accumulative hinting at a cruel, an inexorably serene timelessness. . . . Wrey Gardiner scores by aiming at simple bull's-eyes with precision. Only they are not so simple, and through his contented sadness runs more than the surface bitter-sweet of resignation." (*Poetry Quarterly.*)

*freedom, patriotic, realistic, justice,* have each of them several different meanings which cannot be reconciled with one another. In the case of a word like *democracy,* not only is there no agreed definition, but the attempt to make one is resisted from all sides. It is almost universally felt that when we call a country democratic we are praising it: consequently the defenders of every kind of régime claim that it is a democracy, and fear that they might have to stop using the word if it were tied down to any one meaning. Words of this kind are often used in a consciously dishonest way. That is, the person who uses them has his own private definition, but allows his hearer to think he means something quite different. Statements like *Marshal Pétain was a true patriot, The Soviet Press is the freest in the world, The Catholic Church is opposed to persecution,* are almost always made with intent to deceive. Other words used in variable meanings, in most cases more or less dishonestly, are: *class, totalitarian, science, progressive, reactionary, bourgeois, equality.*

Now that I have made this catalogue of swindles and perversions,      9
let me give another example of the kind of writing that they lead to. This time it must of its nature be an imaginary one. I am going to translate a passage of good English into modern English of the worst sort. Here is a well-known verse from *Ecclesiastes:*

I returned and saw under the sun, that the race is not to the swift,
nor the battle to the strong, neither yet bread to the wise, nor yet
riches to men of understanding, nor yet favour to men of skill, but
time and chance happeneth to them all.

Here it is in modern English:      10

Objective consideration of contemporary phenomena compels the
conclusion that success or failure in competitive activities exhibits
no tendency to be commensurate with innate capacity, but that a
considerable element of the unpredictable must invariably be taken
into account.

This is a parody, but not a very gross one. Exhibit (3), above, for in-      11
stance, contains several patches of the same kind of English. It will be seen that I have not made a full translation. The beginning and ending of the sentence follow the original meaning fairly closely, but in the middle the concrete illustrations—race, battle, bread—dissolve into the vague phrase "success or failure in competitive activities." This had to be so, because no modern writer of the kind I am discussing—no one capable of using phrases like "objective consideration of contemporary phenomena"—would ever tabulate his thoughts in that precise and detailed way. The whole tendency of modern prose is away from concreteness. Now analyze these two sentences a little more closely. The first contains forty-nine words but only sixty syllables, and all its words are those of

everyday life. The second contains thirty-eight words of ninety syllables: eighteen of its words are from Latin roots, and one from Greek. The first sentence contains six vivid images, and only one phrase ("time and chance") that could be called vague. The second contains not a single fresh, arresting phrase, and in spite of its ninety syllables it gives only a shortened version of the meaning contained in the first. Yet without a doubt it is the second kind of sentence that is gaining ground in modern English. I do not want to exaggerate. This kind of writing is not yet universal, and outcrops of simplicity will occur here and there in the worst-written page. Still, if you or I were told to write a few lines on the uncertainty of human fortunes, we should probably come much nearer to my imaginary sentence than to the one from *Ecclesiastes*.

12    As I have tried to show, modern writing at its worst does not consist in picking out words for the sake of their meaning and inventing images in order to make the meaning clearer. It consists in gumming together long strips of words which have already been set in order by someone else, and making the results presentable by sheer humbug. The attraction of this way of writing is that it is easy. It is easier—even quicker, once you have the habit—to say *In my opinion it is not an unjustifiable assumption that* than to say *I think*. If you use ready-made phrases, you not only don't have to hunt about for words; you also don't have to bother with the rhythms of your sentences, since these phrases are generally so arranged as to be more or less euphonious. When you are composing in a hurry—when you are dictating to a stenographer, for instance, or making a public speech—it is natural to fall into a pretentious, Latinized style. Tags like *a consideration which we should do well to bear in mind* or *a conclusion to which all of us would readily assent* will save many a sentence from coming down with a bump. By using stale metaphors, similes and idioms, you save much mental effort, at the cost of leaving your meaning vague, not only for your reader but for yourself. This is the significance of mixed metaphors. The sole aim of a metaphor is to call up visual image. When these images clash—as in *The Fascist octopus has sung its swan song, the jackboot is thrown into the melting pot*—it can be taken as certain that the writer is not seeing a mental image of the objects he is naming; in other words he is not really thinking. Look again at the examples I gave at the beginning of this essay. Professor Laski (1) uses five negatives in fifty-three words. One of these is superfluous, making nonsense of the whole passage, and in addition there is a slip *alien* for *akin*, making further nonsense, and several avoidable pieces of clumsiness which increase the general vagueness. Professor Hogben (2) plays ducks and drakes with a battery which is able to write prescriptions, and, while disapproving of the everyday phrase *put up with*, is unwilling to look *egregious* up in the dictionary and see what it means; (3), if one takes an uncharitable attitude towards it, is simply meaningless: probably one could work out its intended meaning by reading the whole of the article in which it occurs. In (4), the writer

knows more or less what he wants to say, but an accumulation of stale phrases chokes him, like tea leaves blocking a sink. In (5), words and meaning have almost parted company. People who write in this manner usually have a general emotional meaning—they dislike one thing and want to express solidarity with another—but they are not interested in the detail of what they are saying. A scrupulous writer, in every sentence that he writes, will ask himself at least four questions, thus: What am I trying to say? What words will express it? What image or idiom will make it clearer? Is this image fresh enough to have an effect? And he will probably ask himself two more: Could I put it more shortly? Have I said anything that is avoidably ugly? But you are not obliged to go to all this trouble. You can shirk it by simply throwing your mind open and letting the ready-made phrases come crowding in. They will construct your sentences for you—even think your thoughts for you, to a certain extent—and at need they will perform the important service of partially concealing your meaning even from yourself. It is at this point that the special connection between politics and the debasement of language becomes clear.

In our time it is broadly true that political writing is bad writing. 13 Where it is not true, it will generally be found that the writer is some kind of rebel, expressing his private opinions and not a "party line." Orthodoxy, of whatever color, seems to demand a lifeless, imitative style. The political dialects to be found in pamphlets, leading articles, manifestos, White Papers and the speeches of undersecretaries do, of course, vary from party to party, but they are all alike in that one almost never finds in them a fresh, vivid, home-made turn of speech. When one watches some tired hack on the platform mechanically repeating the familiar phrases—*bestial atrocities, iron heel, blood-stained tyranny, free people of the world, stand shoulder to shoulder*—one often has a curious feeling that one is not watching a live human being but some kind of dummy: a feeling which suddenly becomes stronger at moments when the light catches the speaker's spectacles and turns them into blank discs which seem to have no eyes behind them. And this is not altogether fanciful. A speaker who uses that kind of phraseology has gone some distance towards turning himself into a machine. The appropriate noises are coming out of his larynx, but his brain is not involved as it would be if he were choosing his words for himself. If the speech he is making is one that he is accustomed to make over and over again, he may be almost unconscious of what he is saying, as one is when one utters the responses in church. And this reduced state of consciousness, if not indispensable, is at any rate favorable to political conformity.

In our time, political speech and writing are largely the defense of 14 the indefensible. Things like the continuance of British rule in India, the Russian purges and deportations, the dropping of the atom bombs on Japan, can indeed be defended, but only by arguments which are too brutal for most people to face, and which do not square with the professed aims of political parties. Thus political language has to consist largely of euphemism, question-begging and sheer cloudy vagueness. Defenseless villages are bombarded from the air, the inhabitants driven out into the countryside, the cattle machine-gunned, the huts set on fire with incendiary bullets: this is called *pacification*. Millions of peasants are robbed of their farms and sent trudging along the roads with no more than they can carry: this is called *transfer of population* or *rectification of frontiers*. People are imprisoned for years without trial, or shot in the back of the neck or sent to die of scurvy in Arctic lumber camps: this is called *elimination of unreliable elements*. Such phraseology is needed if one wants to name things without calling up mental pictures of them. Consider for instance some comfortable English professor defending Russian totalitarianism. He cannot say outright: "I believe in killing off your opponents when you can get good results by doing so." Probably, therefore, he will say something like this:

15      "While freely conceding that the Soviet régime exhibits certain features which the humanitarian may be inclined to deplore, we must, I think, agree that a certain curtailment of the right to political opposition is an unavoidable concomitant of transitional periods, and that the rigors which the Russian people have been called upon to undergo have been amply justified in the sphere of concrete achievement."

16      The inflated style is itself a kind of euphemism. A mass of Latin words falls upon the facts like soft snow, blurring the outlines and covering up all the details. The great enemy of clear language is insincerity. When there is a gap between one's real and one's declared aims, one turns as it were instinctively to long words and exhausted idioms, like a cuttlefish squirting out ink. In our age there is no such thing as "keeping out of politics." All issues are political issues, and politics itself is a mass of lies, evasions, folly, hatred and schizophrenia. When the general atmosphere is bad, language must suffer. I should expect to find—this is a guess which I have not sufficient knowledge to verify—that the German, Russian and Italian languages have all deteriorated in the last ten or fifteen years, as a result of dictatorship.

17      But if thought corrupts language, language can also corrupt thought. A bad usage can spread by tradition and imitation, even among people who should and do know better. The debased language that I have been discussing is in some ways very convenient. Phrases like *a not unjustifiable assumption, leaves much to be desired, would serve no good purpose, a consideration which we should do well to bear in mind*, are a continuous temptation, a packet of aspirins at one's elbow. Look back through this essay, and for certain you will find that I have again and again committed the very faults I am protesting against. By this morning's post I have received a pamphlet dealing with conditions in Germany. The author tells me that he "felt impelled" to write it. I open it at random, and here is almost the first sentence that I see: "[The Allies] have an opportunity not only of achieving a radical transforma-

tion of Germany's social and political structure in such a way as to avoid a nationalistic reaction in Germany itself, but at the same time of laying the foundations of a co-operative and unified Europe." You see, he "feels impelled" to write—feels, presumably, that he has something new to say—and yet his words, like cavalry horses answering the bugle, group themselves automatically into the familiar dreary pattern. This invasion of one's mind by ready-made phrases (*lay the foundations, achieve a radical transformation*) can only be prevented if one is constantly on guard against them, and every such phrase anaesthetizes a portion of one's brain.

I said earlier that the decadence of our language is probably curable. 18 Those who deny this would argue, if they produced an argument at all, that language merely reflects existing social conditions, and that we cannot influence its development by any direct tinkering with words and constructions. So far as the general tone or spirit of a language goes, this may be true, but it is not true in detail. Silly words and expressions have often disappeared, not through any evolutionary process but owing to the conscious action of a minority. Two recent examples were *explore every avenue* and *leave no stone unturned*, which were killed by the jeers of a few journalists. There is a long list of flyblown metaphors which could similarly be got rid of if enough people would interest themselves in the job; and it should also be possible to laugh the *not un-* formation out of existence,* to reduce the amount of Latin and Greek in the average sentence, to drive out foreign phrases and strayed scientific words, and, in general, to make pretentiousness unfashionable. But all these are minor points. The defence of the English language implies more than this, and perhaps it is best to start by saying what it does *not* imply.

To begin with it has nothing to do with archaism, with the sal- 19 vaging of obsolete words and turns of speech, or with the setting up of a "standard English" which must never be departed from. On the contrary, it is especially concerned with the scrapping of every word or idiom which has outworn its usefulness. It has nothing to do with correct grammar and syntax, which are of no importance so long as one makes one's meaning clear, or with the avoidance of Americanisms, or with having what is called a "good prose style." On the other hand it is not concerned with fake simplicity and the attempt to make written English colloquial. Nor does it even imply in every case preferring the Saxon word to the Latin one, though it does imply using the fewest and shortest words that will cover one's meaning. What is above all needed is to let the meaning choose the word, and not the other way about. In prose, the worst thing one can do with words is to surrender to them. When you think of a concrete object, you think wordlessly, and then, if you want to describe the thing you have been visualizing you probably hunt about till

---

*One can cure oneself of the *not un-* formation by memorizing this sentence: *A not unblack dog was chasing a not unsmall rabbit across a not ungreen field.*

you find the exact words that seem to fit it. When you think of something abstract you are more inclined to use words from the start, and unless you make a conscious effort to prevent it, the existing dialect will come rushing in and do the job for you, at the expense of blurring or even changing your meaning. Probably it is better to put off using words as long as possible and get one's meaning as clear as one can through pictures or sensations. Afterwards one can choose—not simply *accept*—the phrases that will best cover the meaning, and then switch round and decide what impression one's words are likely to make on another person. This last effort of the mind cuts out all stale or mixed images, all prefabricated phrases, needless repetitions, and humbug and vagueness generally. But one can often be in doubt about the effect of a word or a phrase, and one needs rules that one can rely on when instinct fails. I think the following rules will cover most cases:

(i)   Never use a metaphor, simile or other figure of speech which you are used to seeing in print.

(ii)  Never use a long word where a short one will do.

(iii) If it is possible to cut a word out, always cut it out.

(iv)  Never use the passive where you can use the active.

(v)   Never use a foreign phrase, a scientific word or a jargon word if you can think of an everyday English equivalent.

(vi)  Break any of these rules sooner than say anything outright barbarous.

These rules sound elementary, and so they are, but they demand a deep change of attitude in anyone who has grown used to writing in the style now fashionable. One could keep all of them and still write bad English, but one could not write the kind of stuff that I quoted in those five specimens at the beginning of this article.

20       I have not here been considering the literary use of language, but merely language as an instrument for expressing and not for concealing or preventing thought. Stuart Chase and others have come near to claiming that all abstract words are meaningless, and have used this as a pretext for advocating a kind of political quietism. Since you don't know what Fascism is, how can you struggle against Fascism? One need not swallow such absurdities as this, but one ought to recognize that the present political chaos is connected with the decay of language, and that one can probably bring about some improvement by starting at the verbal end. If you simplify your English, you are freed from the worst follies of orthodoxy. You cannot speak any of the necessary dialects, and when you make a stupid remark its stupidity will be obvious, even to yourself. Political language—and with variations this is true of all political par-

ties, from Conservatives to Anarchists—is designed to make lies sound truthful and murder respectable, and to give an appearance of solidity to pure wind. One cannot change this all in a moment, but one can at least change one's own habits, and from time to time one can even, if one jeers loudly enough, send some worn-out and useless phrase—some *jackboot, Achilles' heel, hotbed, melting pot, acid test, veritable inferno* or other lump of verbal refuse—into the dustbin where it belongs.

## CONSIDERATIONS

1. To what extent do Orwell's complaints about political language help you understand Toni Morrison in her "Nobel Lecture" (page 432), in which she condemns language used to control and manipulate others? Working back and forth between the two writers, write an essay developing your answer to the question.

2. Assuming that Orwell's statement in paragraph 2, "the fight against bad English is not frivolous and is not the exclusive concern of professional writers," is the conclusion of a syllogism, reconstruct the major and minor premises of that syllogism by studying the steps Orwell takes to reach his conclusion.

3. Orwell documents his argument by quoting five passages by writers who wrote in the forties. From comparable sources, assemble a gallery of current specimens to help confirm or refute his contention that "the English language is in a bad way."

4. Orwell concludes with six rules. From the rest of his essay, how do you think he would define "anything outright barbarous" (in rule vi)?

5. Has Orwell broken some of his own rules? Point out and explain any examples you find. Look over his "Shooting an Elephant" and "A Hanging" as well as "Politics and the English Language."

6. In paragraph 16, Orwell asserts, "The inflated style is itself a kind of euphemism." Look up the meaning of "euphemism" and compile examples from your local newspaper. Do you agree with Orwell that they are "swindles and perversions"? Note how Ambrose Bierce counts on our understanding of euphemisms in his *Devil's Dictionary.*

*Like "A Hanging," "Shooting an Elephant" derives from Orwell's experience as a colonial police officer. Many political thinkers develop an ideology from theory. Orwell's politics grew from living the life he did and from writing with the clarity codified in "Politics and the English Language." In this essay, notice how Orwell condemns colonialism by condemning himself.*

— 75 ——————————————————————————————

# GEORGE ORWELL
## *Shooting an Elephant*

---

1     In Moulmein, in Lower Burma, I was hated by large numbers of people—the only time in my life that I have been important enough for this to happen to me. I was a sub-divisional police officer of the town, and in an aimless, petty kind of way anti-European feeling was very bitter. No one had the guts to raise a riot, but if a European woman went through the bazaars alone somebody would probably spit betel juice over her dress. As a police officer I was an obvious target and was baited whenever it seemed safe to do so. When a nimble Burman tripped me on the football field and the referee (another Burman) looked the other way, the crowd yelled with hideous laughter. This happened more than once. In the end the sneering yellow faces of young men that met me everywhere, the insults hooted after me when I was at a safe distance, got badly on my nerves. The young Buddhist priests were the worst of all. There were several thousands of them in the town and none of them seemed to have anything to do except stand on street corners and jeer at Europeans.

2     All this was perplexing and upsetting. For at that time I had already made up my mind that imperialism was an evil thing and the sooner I chucked up my job and got out of it the better. Theoretically—and secretly, of course—I was all for the Burmese and all against their oppressors, the British. As for the job I was doing, I hated it more bitterly than I can perhaps make clear. In a job like that you see the dirty work of

Empire at close quarters. The wretched prisoners huddling in the stinking cages of the lock-ups, the grey, cowed faces of the long-term convicts, the scarred buttocks of the men who had been flogged with bamboos—all these oppressed me with an intolerable sense of guilt. But I could get nothing into perspective. I was young and ill-educated and I had had to think out my problems in the utter silence that is imposed on every Englishman in the East. I did not even know that the British Empire is dying, still less did I know that it is a great deal better than the younger empires that are going to supplant it. All I knew was that I was stuck between my hatred of the empire I served and my rage against the evil-spirited little beasts who tried to make my job impossible. With one part of my mind I thought of the British Raj as an unbreakable tyranny, as something clamped down, in *saecula saeculorum*, upon the will of prostrate peoples; with another part I thought that the greatest joy in the world would be to drive a bayonet into a Buddhist priest's guts. Feelings like these are the normal by-products of imperialism; ask any Anglo-Indian official, if you can catch him off duty.

One day something happened which in a roundabout way was    3
enlightening. It was a tiny incident in itself, but it gave me a better glimpse than I had had before of the real nature of imperialism—the real motives for which despotic governments act. Early one morning the sub-inspector at a police station the other end of town rang me up on the phone and said that an elephant was ravaging the bazaar. Would I please come and do something about it? I did not know what I could do, but I wanted to see what was happening and I got on to a pony and started out. I took my rifle, an old .44 Winchester and much too small to kill an elephant, but I thought the noise might be useful *in terrorem*. Various Burmans stopped me on the way and told me about the elephant's doings. It was not, of course, a wild elephant, but a tame one which had gone "must." It had been chained up, as tame elephants always are when their attack of "must" is due, but on the previous night it had broken its chain and escaped. Its mahout, the only person who could manage it when it was in that state, had set out in pursuit, but had taken the wrong direction and was now twelve hours' journey away, and in the morning the elephant had suddenly reappeared in the town. The Burmese population had no weapons and were quite helpless against it. It had already destroyed somebody's bamboo hut, killed a cow and raided some fruit-stalls and devoured the stock; also it had met the municipal rubbish van and, when the driver jumped out and took to his heels, had turned the van over and inflicted violences upon it.

The Burmese sub-inspector and some Indian constables were wait-    4
ing for me in the quarter where the elephant had been seen. It was a very poor quarter, a labyrinth of squalid bamboo huts, thatched with palm-leaf, winding all over a steep hillside. I remember that it was a cloudy, stuffy morning at the beginning of the rains. We began questioning the people as to where the elephant had gone and, as usual, failed to get any

definite information. That is invariably the case in the East; a story always sounds clear enough at a distance, but the nearer you get to the scene of events the vaguer it becomes. Some of the people said that the elephant had gone in one direction, some said that he had gone in another, some professed not even to have heard of any elephant. I had almost made up my mind that the whole story was a pack of lies, when we heard yells a little distance away. There was a loud, scandalized cry of "Go away, child! Go away this instant!" and an old woman with a switch in her hand came round the corner of hut, violently shooing away a crowd of naked children. Some more women followed, clicking their tongues and exclaiming; evidently there was something that the children ought not to have seen. I rounded the hut and saw a man's dead body sprawling in the mud. He was an Indian, a black Dravidian coolie, almost naked, and he could not have been dead many minutes. The people said that the elephant had come suddenly upon him round the corner of the hut, caught him with its trunk, put its foot on his back and ground him into the earth. This was the rainy season and the ground was soft, and his face had scored a trench a foot deep and a couple of yards long. He was lying on his belly with arms crucified and head sharply twisted to one side. His face was coated with mud, the eyes wide open, the teeth bared and grinning with an expression of unendurable agony. (Never tell me, by the way, that the dead look peaceful. Most of the corpses I have seen looked devilish.) The friction of the great beast's foot had stripped the skin from his back as neatly as one skins a rabbit. As soon as I saw the dead man I sent an orderly to a friend's house nearby to borrow an elephant rifle. I had already sent back the pony, not wanting it to go mad with fright and throw me if it smelt the elephant.

5      The orderly came back in a few minutes with a rifle and five cartridges, and meanwhile some Burmans had arrived and told us that the elephant was in the paddy fields below, only a few hundred yards away. As I started forward practically the whole population of the quarter flocked out of the houses and followed me. They had seen the rifle and were all shouting excitedly that I was going to shoot the elephant. They had not shown much interest in the elephant when he was merely ravaging their homes, but it was different now that he was going to be shot. It was a bit of fun to them, as it would be to an English crowd; besides they wanted the meat. It made me vaguely uneasy. I had no intention of shooting the elephant—I had merely sent for the rifle to defend myself if necessary—and it is always unnerving to have a crowd following you. I marched down the hill, looking and feeling a fool, with the rifle over my shoulder and an ever-growing army of people jostling at my heels. At the bottom, when you got away from the huts, there was a metalled road and beyond that a miry waste of paddy fields a thousand yards across, not yet ploughed but soggy from the first rains and dotted with coarse grass. The elephant was standing eight yards from the road, his left side towards us.

He took not the slightest notice of the crowd's approach. He was tearing up bunches of grass, beating them against his knees to clean them and stuffing them into his mouth.

I had halted on the road. As soon as I saw the elephant I knew with 6 perfect certainty that I ought not to shoot him. It is a serious matter to shoot a working elephant—it is comparable to destroying a huge and costly piece of machinery—and obviously one ought not to do it if it can possibly be avoided. And at that distance, peacefully eating, the elephant looked no more dangerous than a cow. I thought then and I think now that his attack of "must" was already passing off; in which case he would merely wander harmlessly about until the mahout came back and caught him. Moreover, I did not in the least want to shoot him. I decided that I would watch him for a little while to make sure that he did not turn savage again, and then go home.

But at that moment, I glanced round at the crowd that had followed 7 me. It was an immense crowd, two thousand at the least and growing every minute. It blocked the road for a long distance on either side. I looked at the sea of yellow faces above the garish clothes—faces all happy and excited over this bit of fun, all certain that the elephant was going to be shot. They were watching me as they would watch a conjuror about to perform a trick. They did not like me, but with the magical rifle in my hands I was momentarily worth watching. And suddenly I realized that I should have to shoot the elephant after all. The people expected it of me and I had got to do it; I could feel their two thousand wills pressing me forward, irresistibly. And it was at this moment, as I stood there with the rifle in my hands, that I first grasped the hollowness, the futility of the white man's dominion in the East. Here was I, the white man with his gun, standing in front of the unarmed native crowd—seemingly the leading actor of the piece; but in reality I was only an absurd puppet pushed to and fro by the will of those yellow faces behind. I perceived in this moment that when the white man turns tyrant it is his own freedom that he destroys. He becomes a sort of hollow, posing dummy, the conventionalized figure of a sahib. For it is the condition of his rule that he shall spend his life in trying to impress the "natives," and so in every crisis he has got to do what the "natives" expect of him. He wears a mask, and his face grows to fit it. I had got to shoot the elephant. I had committed myself to doing it when I sent for the rifle. A sahib has got to act like a sahib; he has got to appear resolute, to know his own mind and do definite things. To come all that way, rifle in hand, with two thousand people marching at my heels, and then to trail feebly away, having done nothing—no, that was impossible. The crowd would laugh at me. And my whole life, every white man's life in the East, was one long struggle not to be laughed at.

But I did not want to shoot the elephant. I watched him beating his 8 bunch of grass against his knees, with that preoccupied grandmotherly air that elephants have. It seemed to me that it would be murder to shoot him. At that age I was not squeamish about killing animals, but I had never shot an elephant and never wanted to. (Somehow it always seems worse to kill a *large* animal.) Besides, there was the beast's owner to be considered. Alive, the elephant was worth at least a hundred pounds; dead, he would only be worth the value of his tusks, five pounds, possibly. But I had got to act quickly. I turned to some experienced-looking Burmans who had been there when we arrived, and asked them how the elephant had been behaving. They all said the same things: he took no notice of you if you left him alone, but he might charge if you went too close to him.

9      It was perfectly clear to me what I ought to do. I ought to walk up to within, say, twenty-five yards of the elephant and test his behavior. If he charged, I could shoot; if he took no notice of me, it would be safe to leave him until the mahout came back. But also I knew that I was going to do no such thing. I was a poor shot with a rifle and the ground was soft mud into which one would sink at every step. If the elephant charged and I missed him, I should have about as much chance as a toad under a steam-roller. But even then I was not thinking particularly of my own skin, only of the watchful yellow faces behind. For at that moment, with the crowd watching me, I was not afraid in the ordinary sense, as I would have been if I had been alone. A white man mustn't be frightened in front of "natives"; and so, in general, he isn't frightened. The sole thought in my mind was that if anything went wrong those two thousand Burmans would see me pursued, caught, trampled on and reduced to a grinning corpse like that Indian up the hill. And if that happened it was quite probable that some of them would laugh. That would never do. There was only one alternative. I shoved the cartridges into the magazine and lay down on the road to get a better aim.

10     The crowd grew very still, and a deep, low, happy sigh, as of people who see the theatre curtain go up at last, breathed from innumerable throats. They were going to have their bit of fun after all. The rifle was a beautiful German thing with cross-hair sights. I did not then know that in shooting an elephant one would shoot to cut an imaginary bar running from ear-hole to ear-hole. I ought, therefore, as the elephant was sideways on, to have aimed straight at his ear-hole; actually I aimed several inches in front of this, thinking the brain would be further forward.

11     When I pulled the trigger I did not hear the bang or feel the kick— one never does when a shot goes home—but I heard the devilish roar of glee that went up from the crowd. In that instant, in too short a time, one would have thought, even for the bullet to get there, a mysterious, terrible change had come over the elephant. He neither stirred nor fell, but every line of his body had altered. He looked suddenly stricken, shrunken, immensely old, as though the frightful impact of the bullet had paralysed him without knocking him down. At last, after what

seemed a long time—it might have been five seconds, I dare say—he sagged flabbily to his knees. His mouth slobbered. An enormous senility seemed to have settled upon him. One could have imagined him thousands of years old. I fired again into the same spot. At the second shot he did not collapse but climbed with desperate slowness to his feet and stood weakly upright, with legs sagging and head drooping. I fired a third time. That was the shot that did for him. You could see the agony of it jolt his whole body and knock the last remnant of strength from his legs. But in falling he seemed for a moment to rise, for as his hind legs collapsed beneath him he seemed to tower upward like a huge rock toppling, his trunk reaching skywards like a tree. He trumpeted, for the first and only time. And then down he came, his belly towards me, with a crash that seemed to shake the ground even where I lay.

I got up. The Burmans were already racing past me across the mud. 12 It was obvious that the elephant would never rise again, but he was not dead. He was breathing very rhythmically with long rattling gasps, his great mound of a side painfully rising and falling. His mouth was wide open. I could see far down into caverns of pale pink throat. I waited a long time for him to die, but his breathing did not weaken. Finally I fired my two remaining shots into the spot where I thought his heart must be. The thick blood welled out of him like red velvet, but still he did not die. His body did not even jerk when the shots hit him, the tortured breathing continued without pause. He was dying, very slowly and in great agony, but in some world remote from me where not even a bullet could damage him further. I felt I had got to put an end to that dreadful noise. It seemed dreadful to see the great beast lying there, powerless to move and yet powerless to die, and not even to be able to finish him. I sent back for my small rifle and poured shot after shot into his head and down his throat. They seemed to make no impression. The tortured gasps continued as steadily as the ticking of a clock.

In the end I could not stand it any longer and went away. I heard 13 later that it took him half an hour to die. Burmans were bringing dahs and baskets even before I left, and I was told they had stripped his body almost to the bones by the afternoon.

Afterwards, of course, there were endless discussions about the 14 shooting of the elephant. The owner was furious, but he was only an Indian and could do nothing. Besides, legally I had done the right thing, for a mad elephant has to be killed, like a mad dog, if its owner fails to control it. Among the Europeans opinion was divided. The older men said I was right, the younger men said it was a damn shame to shoot an elephant for killing a coolie, because the elephant was worth more than any damn Coringhee coolie. And afterwards I was very glad that the coolie had been killed; it put me legally in the right and it gave me sufficient pretext for shooting the elephant. I often wondered whether any of the others grasped that I had done it solely to avoid looking a fool.

## *CONSIDERATIONS* ————————————————————

1. Some of Orwell's remarks about the Burmese make him sound like a racist. Collect a few of them on a separate sheet of paper; then look for lines or phrases that counter the first samples. Discuss your findings, bearing in mind the purpose of Orwell's essay.

2. "In a job like that you see the dirty work of Empire at close quarters." If you ponder Orwell's capitalizing "Empire" (paragraph 2) and then substitute other abstract terms for "Empire"—say, Government, Poverty, War, Hatred—you may discover one of the most important principles of effective writing, a principle beautifully demonstrated by Orwell's whole account.

3. In paragraph 4, Orwell says, "the nearer you get to the scene of events the vaguer it becomes." Have you had an experience that would help you understand his remark? Would it hold true for the soldier caught in battle, a couple suffering a divorce, a football player caught in a pile-up on the line of scrimmage?

4. Some years after his experience in Burma, Orwell became a well-known opponent of fascism. How might shooting the elephant have taught him to detest totalitarianism?

5. "Somehow it always seems worse to kill a *large* animal," Orwell writes in paragraph 8. Why? Are some lives more valuable than others? See also "Very Like a Whale" by Robert Finch, page 213, or "Death Is a Meadowlark" by John Haines, page 260.

6. After two substantial paragraphs of agonizing detail, Orwell's elephant is still dying. Why does the writer draw it out so long? Write your own version of what Orwell covers in those passages, deliberately boiling it down to one brief paragraph. Then compare your version with Orwell's, and answer the question asked.

*Camille Paglia (b. 1947) grew up in New York State,
granddaughter of immigrants, daughter of a professor. She earned
a Ph.D. at Yale University and has taught at Bennington College
in Vermont and the University of the Arts in Philadelphia. In 1990
she published the book from which we take this passage about
cats.* Sexual Personae: Art and Decadence from Nefertiti to Emily
Dickinson *caused an uproar when it appeared. Paglia considers
herself a feminist but has been routinely denounced by feminists.
Her writing specializes in turning upside down all common
knowledge and common opinion.*

*"Cats" rushes headlong, typical of Paglia's prose, hurtling
through information and assertion. See how tightly her prose is
packed; it has no time for small talk.*

— 76 ——————————————————————————

# CAMILLE PAGLIA
## *Cats*

———————————————————————————————

One of the most misunderstood features of Egyptian life was the   1
veneration of cats, whose mummified bodies have been found by the
thousands. My theory is that the cat was the model for Egypt's unique
synthesis of principles. The modern cat, the last animal domesticated by
man, descends from *Felis lybica*, a North African wildcat. Cats are
prowlers, uncanny creatures of the night. Cruelty and play are one for
them. They live by and for fear, practicing being scared or spooking humans by sudden rushings and ambushes. Cats dwell in the occult, that
is, the "hidden." In the Middle Ages, they were hunted and killed for
their association with witches. Unfair? But the cat really *is* in league
with chthonian nature, Christianity's mortal enemy. The black cat of
Halloween is the lingering shadow of archaic night. Sleeping up to
twenty of every twenty-four hours, cats reconstruct and inhabit the
primitive night-world. The cat is telepathic—or at least thinks that it is.
Many people are unnerved by its cool stare. Compared to dogs, slavishly
eager to please, cats are autocrats of naked self-interest. They are both

amoral and immoral, consciously breaking rules. Their "evil" look at such times is no human projection: the cat may be the only animal who savors the perverse or reflects upon it.

2       Thus the cat is an adept of chthonian mysteries. But it has a hieratic duality. It is *eye-intense*. The cat fuses the Gorgon eye of appetite to the detached Apollonian eye of contemplation. The cat values invisibility, comically imagining itself undetectable as it slouches across a lawn. But it also fashionably loves to see and be seen; it is a spectator of life's drama, amused, condescending. It is a narcissist, always adjusting its appearance. When it is disheveled, its spirits fall. Cats have a sense of *pictorial composition:* they station themselves symmetrically on chairs, rugs, even a sheet of paper on the floor. Cats adhere to an Apollonian metric of mathematical space. Haughty, solitary, precise, they are arbiters of elegance—that principle I find natively Egyptian.

3       Cats are poseurs. They have a sense of *persona*—and become visibly embarrassed when reality punctures their dignity. Apes are more human but less beautiful: they posture but never pose. Hunkering, chattering, chest-beating, buttock-baring, apes are bumptious vulgarians lurching up the evolutionary road. The cat's sophisticated personae are masks of an advanced theatricality. Priest and god of its own cult, the cat follows a code of ritual purity, cleaning itself religiously. It makes pagan sacrifices to itself and may share its ceremonies with the elect. The day of a cat-owner often begins with the discovery of a neat pile of mole guts or mashed mouse limbs on the porch—Darwinian mementos. The cat is the least Christian inhabitant of the average home.

4       In Egypt the cat; in Greece the horse. The Greeks did not care for cats. They admired the horse and used it constantly in art and metaphor. The horse is an athlete, proud but serviceable. It accepts citizenship in a public system. The cat is a law unto itself. It has never lost its despotic air of Oriental luxury and indolence. It was too feminine for the male-loving Greeks. I spoke of Egypt's invention of femininity, an aesthetic of social practice removed from nature's brutal female machinery. Aristocratic Egyptian women's costume, an exquisite tunic of transparent pleated linen, must be called *slinky*, a word we still use for formfitting evening gowns. Slinkiness is the nocturnal stealth of cats. The Egyptians admired sleekness, in greyhounds, jackals, and hawks. Sleekness is smooth Apollonian contour. But slinkiness is the sinuous craft of daemonic darkness, which the cat carries into day.

5       Cats have secret thoughts, a divided consciousness. No other animal is capable of *ambivalence*, those ambiguous cross-currents of feeling, as when a purring cat simultaneously buries its teeth warningly in one's arm. The inner drama of a lounging cat is telegraphed by its ears, which swerve round toward a distant rustle as its eyes rest with false adoration on ours, and secondly by its tail, which flicks menacingly even while the cat dozes. Sometimes the cat pretends to have no relation to its

own tail, which it schizophrenically attacks. The twitching, thumping tail is the chthonian barometer of the cat's Apollonian world. It is the serpent in the garden, bumping and grinding with malice aforethought. The cat's ambivalent duality is dramatized in erratic mood-swings, abrupt leaps from torpor to mania, by which it checks our presumption: "Come no closer. I can never be known."

Thus the Egyptian veneration of cats was neither silly nor childish.   6 Through the cat, Egypt defined and refined its complex aesthetic. The cat was the symbol of that fusion of chthonian and Apollonian which no other culture achieved. The West's eye-intense pagan line begins in Egypt, as does the hard persona of art and politics. Cats are exemplars of both. The crocodile, also honored in Egypt, resembles the cat in its daily passage between two realms: hefting itself between water and earth, the spiky crocodile is the West's armoured ego, sinister, hostile, and ever-watchful. The cat is a time-traveller from ancient Egypt. It returns whenever sorcery or style is in vogue. In the Decadent aestheticism of Poe and Baudelaire, the cat regains its sphinxlike prestige and magnitude. With its taste for ritual and bloody spectacle, conspiracy and exhibitionism, the cat is pure pagan pomp. Uniting nocturnal primitivism to Apollonian elegance of line, it became the living paradigm of Egyptian sensibility. The cat, fixing its swift predatory energy in poses of Apollonian stasis, was the first to enact the frozen moment of perceptual stillness that is high art.

## CONSIDERATIONS

1. Language, like cats, cannot be understood by ignoring it. Paglia's essay provides a good opportunity for experimenting with ways to expand your vocabulary. Her essay includes at least a dozen words that might need your attention, including Apollonian, chthonian, Gorgon, narcissist, personae, schizophrenically, paradigm, hieratic, and ambivalence.

2. Understanding a sophisticated writer like Paglia depends on more than looking up a series of words. It helps greatly to think about the larger context in which the words appear. Bear in mind, for example, that "Cats" is part of a larger discussion of Egyptian art, not a selection from *The Care and Feeding of Household Pets*. The practical value of such a reminder would be clearly seen if you read a paragraph or two in a biologist's book about cats or the first paragraph of an encyclopedia article on cats.

3. Are Paglia's factual statements about the cat provable, or is she, in some instances, echoing highly subjective notions that have been handed down through generations of cat lovers and cat haters? Discuss specific examples and mix in whatever is relevant from your experience with cats.

4. "The cat is the least Christian inhabitant of the average home," writes Paglia in paragraph 3. On the face of it, the statement is rather silly, but how does Paglia go about giving it some substance?

5. Think of the ways Paglia used cats to show us something about ancient Egyptian culture: "Through the cat, Egypt defined and refined its complex aesthetic." Then select another animal that in our culture has come to represent or be identified with something larger than itself, for example, the Russian bear, the English bulldog, the American eagle, the French poodle, the African lion . . . or a bear market versus a bull market . . . or the Republicans' elephant versus the Democrats' donkey. Finally, write an essay like Paglia's in which the ostensible subject is really a means of understanding the larger entity or concept.

*Walther G. Prausnitz (b. 1924) was born in Germany and emigrated to the United States when the Nazis took power. He earned his Ph.D. at the University of Chicago and taught at Concordia College in Moorhead, Minnesota—Professor of English, Dean of Liberal Arts—from 1952 until his retirement in 1998.*

*A Christmas letter is not a genre usually represented in books like* A Writer's Reader, *but it is, after all, a common form of essay. Here, the retired teacher speaks of beginning his education again, a "frosh" or freshman at seventy-five. His thoughts on education and on reading speak to the beginning student from a student approaching the end of life. This similarity, this contrast, rides through his Christmas letter: "[T]here still remained an overwhelming and over-riding similarity."*

## — 77

# WALTHER G. PRAUSNITZ
## *Christmas Letter*

Dear good friends,

All my warmest wishes to each of you, for a blessed Christmas and 1
for much happiness in the new year, complete with good health and with peace and contentment. Last year I wrote to you with the uncertainties of a first year as professor emeritus before me; this year I can assure you that although I'm still far from being an expert, I am at least a survivor.

I devoted all of my scheduled work time to rereading and summa- 2
rizing; the notes I had taken on literally thousands of class assessments during the past twenty-five years, the research on student learning, and ways of translating what I had into something that was legally usable and—incidentally—worth reading. But the strangest development took place, not in my office but at home during many hours of leisurely evenings. And thereby hangs a tale:

I have spent many of my evening hours reading what I want to read. 3
Being a bookaholic who buys more books than he finds time for, I now had the leisure to look at what had accumulated, leisure for some

"Christmas Letter" from a self-published newsletter by Walther G. Prausnitz, Professor of English, emeritus, Concordia College, Moorhead, Minnesota. Reprinted by permission of the author.

systematic reading in fields in which I had been interested but to which I could bring only superficial knowledge. There seemed at first no pattern to my excursions, nor need there have been. After all, I'd followed self-imposed rigid patterns in my professional learning for close to fifty years, and now I felt entitled to relax. And so I read: books on cosmology, on world history, the Nazis, art history, the sources for the Old Testament, the development of medicine, the growth of life on earth—I had a marvelous time following many different interests.

4       Eventually, after about six or seven months of this information orgy I began to sober up; I became more selective. While still wanting to read more, and more intensively, in certain fields, I dropped others with no regret. I had started my search with an excitement and naivete comparable to that of many of the frosh I'd observed in college: I was ready to be taught, to become involved. But sometimes I became bored and frustrated, even angry. It was almost as if I had asked myself to start a college education again. I had a major which I had developed for half a century. But now it was time to fill in the "distribution requirements." And I found, just as college students do, some intriguing personalities, some hopeless pedants, some challenging thinkers, some of those experts who are able to speak only "for the edification of other experts": I found some good teachers and some poor ones.

5       But there was another development, also shared by college students. My excitement, thus my involvement, came when I found scholars who were systematic and orderly, who knew so much that they could keep in mind readers who knew how to think but who lacked information, scholars who not only knew their fields but who respected their readers. Similarly, I had little patience with persons who did not know how to involve their audience, who discouraged with their arbitrariness and their lack of vision. I "dropped their classes."

6       I had advantages which college students don't share; when I dropped a course I simply put the book on my shelf. And I could choose when to go to class. I gave some of my explorations a daily workout, and let others rest up for a while. (Students who do that get to talk with a dean.) And I had another (temporary) advantage over the college frosh; I am a more experienced reader than they, someone who is used to organizing new territories.

7       But there still remained an over-riding similarity, and the more I thought about it the more disturbing it became. In some fifty years of teaching in college, I have only very rarely encountered a frosh who wasn't awed and excited *at the start*. Dissatisfaction, boredom, frustration—those develop later.

8       And so, like the college student, I came to respect and admire those author/teachers who took me seriously, who could help me understand what their fields were about, *and* why those fields should be important to me. I have continued in some of those fields, even to working toward getting "a minor," learning to read aggressively rather than passively,

critically rather than helplessly. And I dropped the "courses" taught by writers who talked at instead of with me; who seemed so aloof they became arbitrary; who couldn't see the trees in their forests; who were condescending (even grudging) about what their readers might be able to grasp; who were boring because they could not explain themselves.

And it was then that I thought of something else. My main research ("my major") continues to focus on how students learn, and on how we teachers can strengthen that learning. My outside reading was to have been for fun. Well, I did have a lot of fun, but also I found myself thinking back to "the major." What do we teachers do to sustain the excitement which frosh bring to college, and what do we do to weaken, even destroy it? How do we help students to become involved, to consider a subject as something in which they have a personal stake? And what is it we do to make some fields no more than "distribution requirements to get out of the way"? I wonder if my dropping not only books but whole fields from my interest is similar to what happens to college students, except that what happens to them is part of a potentially developing or frustrated future; what happened to me just made for one exciting or boring evening. 9

And so I came back to where I had started: the obligation for teachers to involve students, to help them get a glimpse of the passion and responsibility of discovery. And that's enough to see me into the next millenium. Warmest greetings for you, and best wishes, a blessed Christmas, happiness and health in the new year, with much love from this particular "frosh" who has no plans to retire from continuing to learn how to learn. Please stay in touch. 10

Sincerely,

Walther G. Prausnitz

## CONSIDERATIONS

1. Reread the English professor's Christmas letter/essay. Trace his enjoyment in paralleling what he has done in his first year of retirement with what a college student does in his or her first year on campus. Then write a commentary on the value of such a parallel to a writer about education.

2. What does Prausnitz mean by "distribution requirements" in paragraphs 4 and 9. Why did they irritate him? Write a short essay on your own experience with such required courses based on your ideas about their value or lack of same.

3. Thinking of what Prausnitz called his "major," write a personal experience essay about a teacher who either did or did not "sustain the excitement which frosh bring to college."

4. Compare and contrast Prausnitz's Christmas letter with the customary photocopied letter detailing a family's high and low moments of the past year.

5. The facts that Prausnitz was a cellist with the local symphony and that his retirement reading ranged widely through many fields suggest that his interests and energies were not confined to his professional "major." In what sense do you see this variety as important to a teacher—or to anyone?

6. Although Prausnitz's letter is not a formal essay, he is careful to assist the reader by providing transitional words and phrases to connect a new paragraph with that which preceded it. Examine the beginnings and endings of his paragraphs, and jot down the transitional words and phrases he uses. Then examine one of your own essays to see if you might have improved it by following Prausnitz's model. Why are such transitional aids important?

7. Read Billy Collins's poem "Marginalia" (page 134). Are the readers Collins talks about the kind Prausnitz would call "aggresive and critical" or "passive and helpless"? How would you describe yourself as a reader? Explain.

David Quammen (b. 1948) writes a column for Outside called
"Natural Acts" and collected his witty and eccentric essays on
science in a volume under that title. He has written two novels,
and his essays have appeared in the New York Times Book
Review, Audubon, Esquire, and Rolling Stone. He graduated from
Yale University in 1970 and attended Oxford University on a
Rhodes Scholarship, where he earned a B. Litt. in 1973.

   After studying literature at both Oxford and Yale, Quammen
pursued graduate studies in zoology at the University of Montana.
His interests have always varied, ranging from the novels of
William Faulkner to the history of nuclear weapons. He once
worked as a trout-fishing guide but quit when he discovered that
he "sympathized too much with the fish."

   The Song of the Dodo (1996), from which we excerpt this
essay, is a blend of personal experiences in the Malay archipelago
and an exposition of the concepts and principles of biogeography.
Notice how, in his zeal for the preservation of the species,
Quammen collects and organizes facts in the service of passionate
argument. Facts become arguments.

— 78 ——————————————————————————————

# DAVID QUAMMEN
## So What?

————————————————————————————————————————

There's a voice that says: *So what?*

   It's not my voice, it's probably not yours, but it makes itself heard
in the arenas of public opinion, querulous and smug and fortified by just
a little knowledge, which as always is a dangerous thing. *So what if a
bunch of species go extinct? it says. Extinction is a natural process.
Darwin himself said so, didn't he? Extinction is the complement of evolution, making room for new species to evolve. There have always been
extinctions. So why worry about these extinctions currently being
caused by humanity?* And there has always been a pilot light burning in
your furnace. So why worry when your house is on fire?

1

2

3        Biologists and paleontologists speak of a background level of extinctions throughout the history of life. That background level is the routine average rate at which species disappear. It's generally offset by the rate of speciation, the rate at which new species evolve. These two together, extinction and speciation, constitute still another form of turnover—in this case, on the global scale. Rates of extinction in the remote past can't be calculated precisely, because gaps in the fossil record prevent us from knowing what has been lost. But a cautious paleontologist named David Jablonski has made an informed guess, placing the background level at "perhaps a few species per million years for most kinds of organisms." A few mammal species, a few bird species, a few fish species lost to extinction every million years—with that rate, evolution can keep up, adding a few species to each group by speciation. Such losses, counterbalanced by gains, yield no net loss of biological diversity. Extinction at that level, the background level, is an ordinary and sustainable process.

4        Against that background, a small number of big events have emerged to the foreground. These cataclysms, anything but ordinary, are the mass extinctions that scientists now recognize as major punctuation marks in the history of life. Some of them are famous: the Cretaceous extinction, the Permian extinction. In such a mass extinction, compressed within a relatively brief span of years, the extinction rate far exceeds the rate of speciation, and the richness of the biosphere plummets. Niches fall vacant. Intricate networks of ecological relationships are thrown into disarray. Entire ecosystems are left raw and ragged. Millions of years pass, then, before speciation fills the gaps and brings the overall diversity back up to previous levels.

5        No one knows just what caused the mass extinctions of the distant past. The competing hypotheses range from gradual climate change (reflected in habitat changes that proved intolerable for many species) to a so-far-undetected Death Star that orbits mutually with our sun, exerting cosmic gravitational drag and pulling a shitstorm of killer asteroids through the vicinity of Earth every twenty-six million years. The debate over the competing hypotheses is a fascinating story but not one I'm going to pursue here. It's enough to note that mass extinctions of the first magnitude occurred at just five points in distant geological time, and that each was caused by some indeterminate set of natural factors among which humanity (not yet on the scene then) can't be implicated. The Cretaceous extinction, 65 million years ago, claimed the last of the dinosaurs; the Permian extinction, 250 million years ago, eliminated more than half the extant families of invertebrate marine creatures. Other mass extinctions struck at the end of the Ordovician period (440 million years ago), in the late Devonian period (370 million years ago), and at the end of the Triassic period (215 million years ago, give or take a few million). Additionally, a sizable roster of large-bodied animals disappeared during the later millennia of the Pleistocene epoch, only tens of thousands of years ago, and in this case humanity *may* have been partly re-

sponsible; those Pleistocene extinctions occurred about the time that humans began hunting in armed and cooperative packs. Compared to the five big events, though, the Pleistocene spasm was minor, mostly confined to mammals.

And there have been still others, lesser episodes during which the extinction rate only modestly exceeded the background level. One way of defining a mass extinction as distinct from a lesser episode, according to Jablonski, is that it entails an extinction rate double the background level among many different plant and animal groups.     6

By this rigorous standard, we're experiencing one now.     7

It started a few thousand years ago, when humans from Neolithic cultures along the fringes of the continents began venturing across the open sea in primitive boats. Colonizing remote islands such as Madagascar, New Zealand, New Caledonia, and the Hawaiian archipelago, the human invaders promptly killed off some endemic bird species. Many of these extinct birds were giant forms, flightless and ecologically naïve. You've read enough by now to imagine how it went, island after island around the world. The Neolithic wave of human invasion had accomplished its damage centuries before the first Portuguese ship landed at Mauritius. But the results were similar, and the European-inflicted insular extinctions were actually just a second phase of the larger process. The case of the dodo was only one of hundreds.     8

From the time of the Neolithic voyages until the present, twenty percent of the world's bird species have gone extinct. During recent centuries, the rate of extinction has increased further and the range of jeopardy has widened—from birds to animals and plants of all kinds, and from islands to continents—as humanity's impact has grown in direct correlation with the growth of human population, technological efficaciousness, and hubris. Nowadays it's not just a question of dodos and elephant birds and moas. Nowadays we're losing a little of everything.     9

Within a few decades, if present trends continue, we'll be losing a *lot* of everything. As we extinguish a large portion of the planet's biological diversity, we will lose also a large portion of our world's beauty, complexity, intellectual interest, spiritual depth, and ecological health. You've heard this doom song before, so I won't chant all the dreary, important verses about how sterilizing our own biosphere represents a form of suicide. But I offer you, from some familiar authorities, a bit of numerical perspective on the scope of the damage being done. Paul Ehrlich, one of the grandfathers of conservation biology, who was a respected ecologist before he gained fame as a population-crisis maven, estimates that the current extinction rate, just among birds and mammals, is roughly a hundred times the background level. Ed Wilson, based on surveys of the diversity of invertebrates within tropical forests, estimates that the current loss of rainforest species is at least a thousand times above normal. Dan Simberloff, who is nobody's idea of a careless alarmist, has published a skeptical review of the evidence, titled "Are We on the Verge of a     10

Mass Extinction in Tropical Rain Forests?" Is the situation really so dire as the arm-wavers would have us believe? asks Simberloff. After thirteen pages of cool argument and conscientiously crunched numbers, he concludes that it is. Yes, Simberloff predicts, the current cataclysm of extinctions is indeed likely to stand among the worst half-dozen such events in the history of life on Earth.

11      This time around, *we're* the Death Star.

12      But with a difference. Our own devastating impact on the biosphere will probably be a singular event, not part of a recurrent pattern. Why? Because we probably won't survive long enough, as a species, to do it again. The richness of Earth's ecosystems might recover to previous levels within, oh, ten or twenty million years, assuming that *Homo sapiens* itself has meanwhile gone extinct too. When we ourselves do go, the sparrows and the cockroaches and the rats and the dandelions that survive us should eventually give rise to a full new inflorescence of diversity. I'll leave it to you to decide whether that represents a gloomy scenario or a cheery one.

13      Eons in the future, paleontologists from the planet Tralfamadore will look at the evidence and wonder what happened on Earth to cause such vast losses so suddenly at six points in time: at the end of the Ordovician, in the late Devonian, at the end of the Permian, at the end of the Triassic, at the end of the Cretaceous, and again about sixty-five million years later, in the late Quaternary, right around the time of the invention of the dugout canoe, the stone ax, the iron plow, the three-masted sailing ship, the automobile, the hamburger, the television, the bulldozer, the chain saw, and the antibiotic.

## CONSIDERATIONS

1. Why would Quammen's essay not be called a strictly scientific account? Back up your answer with specifics.

2. Quammen offers no solution to the ongoing processes of extinction. Why? Can you? How do you like being part of the "Death Star"?

3. In brief, Quammen says of our survival chances, do the numbers. Beginning with paragraph 6, trace the march of numbers to his conclusion. Then comment on the way he begins his essay.

4. Quammen is not writing a term paper, so he does not interrupt his argument with footnotes. What efforts does he make to show that he is not simply inventing the numbers to fit his argument?

5. Much of Quammen's essay is written in the present tense. What might a writer hope to gain by that?

6. Read Wendell Berry's essay "A Native Hill" (page 42). Then imagine Berry and Quammen talking with each other. Write a short dialog showing how they would or would not agree with each other's ideas about conservation.

*Ishmael Reed (b. 1938) was born in Tennessee. He has published eight novels, five books of poetry, and two essay collections. He has received awards from the National Institute of Arts and Letters, the American Civil Liberties Union, the National Endowment for the Arts, and the Guggenheim Foundation.* New and Selected Poems *appeared in 1989. His most recent fiction is* Airing Dirty Laundry *(1994). "America: The Multinational Society" started its life in* San Francisco Focus.

*"America: The Multinational Society" is an essay in its length, a booklong argument in the range and number of its historical summaries and ideas. Notice how they derive, as so often in the essay, from personal recollection and reflection.*

— **79** ——————————————————————————

# ISHMAEL REED
## *America: The Multinational Society*

---

At the annual Lower East Side Jewish Festival yesterday, a Chinese woman ate a pizza slice in front of Ty Thuan Duc's Vietnamese grocery store. Beside her a Spanish-speaking family patronized a cart with two signs: "Italian Ices" and "Kosher by Rabbi Alper." And after the pastrami ran out, everybody ate knishes.
—*New York Times*, 23 June 1983

On the day before Memorial Day, 1983, a poet called me to describe a city he had just visited. He said that one section included mosques, built by the Islamic people who dwelled there. Attending his reading, he said, were large numbers of Hispanic people, forty thousand of whom lived in the same city. He was not talking about a fabled city located in some mysterious region of the world. The city he'd visited was Detroit.

A few months before, as I was leaving Houston, Texas, I heard it announced on the radio that Texas's largest minority was Mexican-American, and though a foundation recently issued a report critical of bilingual education, the taped voice used to guide the passengers on the air trams connecting terminals in Dallas Airport is in both Spanish and English. If the trend continues, a day will come when it will be difficult to travel through some sections of the country without hearing commands in both English and Spanish; after all, for some western states, Spanish was the first written language and the Spanish style lives on in the western way of life.

3    Shortly after my Texas trip, I saw in an auditorium located on the campus of the University of Wisconsin at Milwaukee a Yale professor— whose original work on the influence of African cultures upon those of the Americas has led to his ostracism from some monocultural intellectual circles—walked up and down the aisle, like an old-time southern evangelist, dancing and drumming the top of the lectern, illustrating his points before some serious Afro-American intellectuals and artists who cheered and applauded his performance and his mastery of information. The professor was "white." After his lecture, he joined a group of Milwaukeeans in a conversation. All of the participants spoke Yoruban, though only the professor had ever traveled to Africa.

4    One of the artists told me that his paintings, which included African and Afro-American mythological symbols and imagery, were hanging in the local McDonald's restaurant. The next day I went to McDonald's and snapped pictures of smiling youngsters eating hamburgers below paintings that could grace the walls of any of the country's leading museums. The manager of the local McDonald's said, "I don't know what you boys are doing, but I like it," as he commissioned the local painters to exhibit in his restaurant.

5    Such blurring of cultural styles occurs in everyday life in the United States to a greater extent than anyone can imagine and is probably more prevalent than the sensational conflict between people of different backgrounds that is played up and often encouraged by the media. The result is what the Yale professor, Robert Thompson, referred to as a cultural bouillabaisse, yet members of the nation's present educational and cultural Elect still cling to the notion that the United States belongs to some vaguely defined entity they refer to as "Western civilization," by which they mean, presumably, a civilization created by the people of Europe, as if Europe can be viewed in monolithic terms. Is Beethoven's Ninth Symphony, which includes Turkish marches, a part of Western civilization, or the late nineteenth- and twentieth-century French paintings, whose creators were influenced by Japanese art? And what of the cubists, through whom the influence of African art changed modern painting, or the surrealists, who were so impressed with the art of the Pacific Northwest Indians that, in their map of North America, Alaska dwarfs the lower forty-eight in size?

6    Are the Russians, who are often criticized for their adoption of "Western" ways by Tsarist dissidents in exile, members of Western civilization? And what of the millions of Europeans who have black African and Asian ancestry, black Africans having occupied several countries for

hundreds of years? Are these "Europeans" members of Western civilization, or the Hungarians, who originated across the Urals in a place called Greater Hungary, or the Irish, who came from the Iberian Peninsula?

Even the notion that North America is part of Western civilization    7
because our "system of government" is derived from Europe is being challenged by Native American historians who say that the founding fathers, Benjamin Franklin especially, were actually influenced by the system of government that had been adopted by the Iroquois hundreds of years prior to the arrival of large numbers of Europeans.

Western civilization, then, becomes another confusing category    8
like Third World, or Judeo-Christian culture, as man attempts to impose his small-screen view of political and cultural reality upon a complex world. Our most publicized novelist recently said that Western civilization was the greatest achievement of mankind, an attitude that flourishes on the street level as scribbles in public restrooms: "White Power," "Niggers and Spics Suck," or "Hitler was a prophet," the latter being the most telling, for wasn't Adolph Hitler the archetypal monoculturalist who, in his pigheaded arrogance, believed that one way and one blood was so pure that it had to be protected from alien strains at all costs? Where did such an attitude, which has caused so much misery and depression in our national life, which has tainted even our noblest achievements, begin? An attitude that caused the incarceration of Japanese-American citizens during World War II, the persecution of Chicanos and Chinese-Americans, the near-extermination of the Indians, and the murder and lynchings of thousands of Afro-Americans.

Virtuous, hardworking, pious, even though they occasionally would    9
wander off after some fancy clothes, or rendezvous in the woods with the town prostitute, the Puritans are idealized in our schoolbooks as "a hardy band" of no-nonsense patriarchs whose discipline razed the forest and brought order to the New World (a term that annoys Native American historians). Industrious, responsible, it was their "Yankee ingenuity" and practicality that created the work ethic. They were simple folk who produced a number of good poets, and they set the tone for the American writing style, of lean and spare lines, long before Hemingway. They worshiped in churches whose colors blended in with the New England snow, churches with simple structures and ornate lecterns.

The Puritans were a daring lot, but they had a mean streak. They    10
hated the theater and banned Christmas. They punished people in a cruel and inhuman manner. They killed children who disobeyed their parents. When they came in contact with those whom they considered heathens or aliens, they behaved in such a bizarre and irrational manner that this chapter in the American history comes down to us as a late-movie horror film. They exterminated the Indians, who taught them how to survive in a world unknown to them, and their encounter with the calypso culture of Barbados resulted in what the tourist guide in Salem's Witches' House refers to as the Witchcraft Hysteria.

11      The Puritan legacy of hard work and meticulous accounting led to the establishment of a great industrial society; it is no wonder that the American industrial revolution began in Lowell, Massachusetts, but there was the other side, the strange and paranoid attitudes toward those different from the Elect.

12      The cultural attitudes of that early Elect continue to be voiced in everyday life in the United States: the president of a distinguished university, writing a letter to the *Times*, belittling the study of African civilizations; the television network that promoted its show on the Vatican art with the boast that this art represented "the finest achievements of the human spirit." A modern up-tempo state of complex rhythms that depends upon contacts with an international community can no longer behave as if it dwelled in a "Zion Wilderness" surrounded by beasts and pagans.

13      When I heard a schoolteacher warn the other night about the invasion of the American educational system by foreign curriculums, I wanted to yell at the television set, "Lady, they're already here." It has already begun because the world is here. The world has been arriving at these shores for at least ten thousand years from Europe, Africa, and Asia. In the late nineteenth and early twentieth centuries, large numbers of Europeans arrived, adding their cultures to those of the European, African, and Asian settlers who were already here, and recently millions have been entering the country from South America and the Caribbean, making Yale Professor Bob Thompson's bouillabaisse richer and thicker.

14      One of our most visionary politicians said that he envisioned a time when the United States could become the brain of the world, by which he meant the repository of all of the latest advanced information systems. I thought of that remark when an enterprising poet friend of mine called to say that he had just sold a poem to a computer magazine and that the editors were delighted to get it because they didn't carry fiction or poetry. Is that the kind of world we desire? A humdrum homogeneous world of all brains and no heart, no fiction, no poetry; a world of robots with human attendants bereft of imagination, of culture? Or does North America deserve a more exciting destiny? To become a place where the cultures of the world crisscross. This is possible because the United States is unique in the world: The world is here.

## CONSIDERATIONS

1. Reed's concluding sentence, "The world is here," runs, in one variation or another, through his essay as a sort of refrain. What, precisely, does he mean? Why does he deplore public speakers who take pride in being part of what they call the culture of the Western world?

2. What word does Reed use in describing Adolph Hitler that might be seen as the antonym of Reed's term "multinational"?

3. "America: The Multinational Society," in some ways, illustrates the difficulty of presenting broad, sweeping ideas in such a short essay. What is that difficulty, and how does Reed attempt to avoid it?

4. Is it fair, as some have done, to stigmatize Reed as a rabble-rousing demagogue seeking to subvert the American way of life? Explain.

5. What is "bouillabaisse," and why is it such a useful metaphor in Reed's argument?

6. Look over a few other essays in this text that bear on Reed's argument: for example, those of Michelle Cliff (page 115), Judith Ortiz Cofer (page 128), Bernard Cooper (page 143), Zora Neale Hurston (page 329), Maxine Hong Kingston (page 361), and N. Scott Momaday (page 421). Then write an essay on whether or not Reed's essay is a good summary of such accounts of diversity in American life and culture.

7. In what sense is a lynching a "multicultural" event?

*Charles Simic (b. 1938) left Yugoslavia when he was fifteen to become a leading American poet. He has written four collections of essays and many volumes of poetry, of which* A Wedding in Hell *(1994) is the most recent. In 1984 he was named a MacArthur Fellow, and he won the Pulitzer Prize for Poetry in 1990. He teaches at the University of New Hampshire. He wrote this essay for an issue of the literary magazine* Antaeus *devoted to the subject of food. Books of his essays are* Wonderful Words, Silent Truth *(1990) and* The Unemployed Fortune-Teller *(1994). His latest poems appear in* Jackstraws *(1999).*

*Someone asked Charles Simic, in an interview, "If you had not been a poet, what would you have done?" He answered, "I would have liked to own a small restaurant and do my own cooking." See how an essay can develop from light zeal, pleasing us by its enthusiasm.*

---

— **80** ——————————————————————————

# CHARLES SIMIC
## *On Food and Happiness*

---

1      Sadness and good food are incompatible. The old sages knew that wine lets the tongue loose, but one can grow melancholy with even the best bottle, especially as one grows older. The appearance of food, however, brings instant happiness. A *paella*, a *choucroute garnie*, a pot of *tripes à la mode de Caen*, and so many other dishes of peasant origin guarantee merriment. The best talk is around that table. Poetry and wisdom are its company. The true Muses are cooks. Cats and dogs don't stray far from the busy kitchen. Heaven is a pot of chili simmering on the stove. If I were to write about the happiest days of my life, many of them would have to do with food and wine and a table full of friends.

> Homer never wrote on any empty stomach.
> —Rabelais

2      One could compose an autobiography mentioning every memorable meal in one's life and it would probably make better reading than what

---

one ordinarily gets. Honestly, what would you rather have? The description of a first kiss, or of stuffed cabbage done to perfection?

I have to admit, I remember better what I ate than what I thought. 3 My memory is especially vivid about those far-off days from 1944 to 1949 in Yugoslavia when we were mostly starving. The black market flourished. Women exchanged their wedding rings and silk underwear for hams. Occasionally someone invited us to an illicit feast on a day everyone else was hungry.

I'll begin with the day I realized that there was more to food than 4 just stuffing yourself. I was nine years old. I ate Dobrosav Cvetkovic's *burek*, and I can still see it and taste it when I close my eyes.

*Burek* is a kind of pie made with fillo dough and stuffed with either 5 ground meat, cheese, or spinach. It is eaten everywhere in the Near East and Balkans. Like pizza today, it's usually good no matter where you get it, but it can also be a work of art. My father said that when Dobrosav retired from his bakery in Skopje, the mayor and his cronies, after realizing that he was gone, sent a police warrant after him. The cops brought him back in handcuffs! "Dobrosav," they said visiting him in jail, "how can you do a thing like that to us? At least make us one last *burek*, and then you can go wherever your heart desires."

I ate that famous *burek* forty-four years ago on a cold winter morn- 6 ing with snow falling. Dobrosav made it illegally in his kitchen and sold it to select customers who used to knock on his door and enter looking like foreign agents making a pickup. The day I was his guest—for the sake of my poor exiled father who was so good to Dobrosav—the *burek* came with meat. I ate every greasy crumb that fell out of my mouth on the table while old Dobrosav studied me the way a cat studies a bird in a cage. He wanted my opinion. I understood this was no fluke. Dobrosav knew something other *burek* makers did not. I believe I told him so. This was my first passionate outburst to a cook.

Then there was my aunt, Ivanka Bajalović. Every time I wiped my 7 plate clean she shook her head sadly. "One day," she'd say to me, "I'll make so much food you won't be able to finish it." With my appetite in those days that seemed impossible, but she did it! She found a huge pot ordinarily used to make soap and filled it with beans to "feed an army," as the neighbors said.

All Serbians, of whatever gender or age, have their own opinion as 8 to how this dish ought to be made. Some folk like it thicker, others soupier. Between the two extremes there are many nuances. Almost everybody adds bacon, pork ribs, sausage, paprika, and hot peppers. It's a class thing. The upper classes make it lean, the lower fatty. My aunt, who was educated in London and speaks English with a British accent to this day, made it like a ditchdigger's wife. The beans were spicy hot.

My uncle was one of those wonders of nature everybody envies, a 9 skinny guy who could eat all day long and never gain any weight. I'm sad to admit that I've no idea how much we actually ate that day. Anywhere between three and five platefuls is a good guess. These were European soup plates, nice and roomy, that could take loads of beans. It was summer afternoon. We were eating on a big terrace watched by nosy neighbors who kept score. At some point, I remember, I just slid off my chair onto the floor.

10       I'm dying, it occurred to me. My uncle was still wielding the spoon with his face deep in the plate. There was a kind of hush. In the beginning, everybody talked and kidded around, but now my aunt was exhausted and had gone in to lie down. There were still plenty of beans, but I was through. I couldn't move. Finally, even my uncle staggered off to bed, and I was left alone, sitting under the table, the heat intolerable, the sun setting, my mind blurry, thinking this is how a pig must feel.

11       On May 9, 1950, I asked all my relatives to give me money instead of presents for my birthday. When they did, I spent the entire day going with a friend from one pastry shop to another. We ate huge quantities of cream puffs, custard rolls, *dobos torta*, rum balls, pishingers, strudels with poppy seed, and other Viennese and Hungarian pastries. At dusk we had no money left. We were dragging ourselves in the general vicinity of the Belgrade railroad station when a man, out of breath and carrying a large suitcase, overtook us. He wondered if we could carry it for him to the station and we said we could. The suitcase was very heavy and it made a noise like it was full of silverware or burglar's tools, but we managed somehow to get it to his train. There, he surprised us by paying us handsomely for our good deed. Without a moment's thought we returned to our favorite pastry shop, which was closing at that hour and where the help eyed us with alarm as we ordered more ice cream and cake.

12       In 1951, I lived an entire summer in a village on the Adriatic coast. Actually, the house my mother, brother, and I roomed at was a considerable distance from the village on a stretch of sandy beach. Our landlady, a war widow, was a fabulous cook. In her home I ate squid for the first time and began my lifelong long affair with olives. All her fish was grilled with a little olive oil, garlic, and parsley. I still prefer it that way.

13       My favorite dish was a plate of tiny surf fish called *girice*, which were fried in corn flour. We'd eat them with our fingers, head and all. Since it's no good to swim after lunch, all the guests would take a long siesta. I remember our deliciously cool room, the clean sheets, the soothing sound of the sea, the aftertaste and smell of the fish, and the long naps full of erotic dreams.

14       There were two females who obsessed me in that place. One was a theater actress from Zagreb in the room next to ours who used to sunbathe with her bikini top removed when our beach was deserted and I was hiding in the bushes. The other was our landlady's sixteen-year-old daughter. I sort of tagged along after her. She must have been bored out of

her wits to allow a thirteen-year-old boy to keep her company. We used to swim out to a rock in the bay where there were wild grapes. We'd lie sunbathing and popping the little blue grapes in our mouths. And in the evening, once or twice, there was even a kiss, and then an exquisite risotto with mussels.

> He that with his soup will drink,
> When he's dead won't sleep a wink.
> —Old French Song

In Paris I went to what can only be described as a school for losers.    15
These were youngsters who were not destined for further glories of French education, but were en route to being petty bureaucrats and tradespeople. We ate lunch in school, and the food was mostly tolerable. We even drank red wine. The vegetable soup served on Tuesdays, however, was out of this world. One of the fat ladies I saw milling in the kitchen must have been a southerner, because the soup had a touch of Provence. For some reason, the other kids didn't care for it. Since the school rule was that you had to *manger* everything in your plate, and since I loved the soup so much, my neighbors at the table would let me have theirs. I'd end up by eating three or four servings of that thick concoction with tomatoes, green and yellow beans, potatoes, carrots, white beans, noodles, and herbs. After that kind of eating, I usually fell asleep in class after lunch only to be rudely awakened by one of my teachers and ordered to a blackboard already covered with numbers. I'd stand there bewildered and feeling sleepy while time changed into eternity, and nobody budged or said anything, and my only solace was the lingering taste in my mouth of that divine soup.

Some years back I found myself in Genoa at an elegant reception in    16
Palazzo Doria talking with the Communist mayor. "I love American food," he blurted out to me after I mentioned enjoying the local cuisine. I asked him what he had in mind. "I love potato chips," he told me. I had to agree, potato chips were pretty good.

When we came to the United States in 1954, it now seems like    17
that's all my brother and I ate. We sat in front of the TV eating potato chips out of huge bags. Our parents approved. We were learning English and being American. It's a wonder we have any teeth left today. We visited the neighborhood supermarket twice a day to sightsee the junk food. There were so many things to taste, and we were interested in them all. There was deviled ham, marshmallows, Spam, Hawaiian Punch, Fig Newtons, V-8 Juice, Mounds, Planter's Peanuts, and so much else, all good. Everything was good in America except for Wonder Bread, which we found disgusting.

It took me a few years to come to my sense. One day I met    18
Salvatore. He told me I ate like a dumb shit, and took me home to his

mother. Sal and his three brothers were all well-employed, unmarried, living at home, and giving their paychecks to Mom. The father was dead, so there were just these four boys to feed. She did not stop cooking. Every meal was like a peasant wedding feast. Of course, her sons didn't appreciate it as far as she was concerned. "Are you crazy, Mom?" they'd shout in a chorus each time she brought in another steaming dish. The old lady didn't flinch. The day I came she was happy to have someone else at the table who was more appreciative, and I did not spare the compliments.

19    She cooked southern Italian dishes. Lots of olive oil and garlic. I recollect with a sense of heightened consciousness her linguine with anchovies. We drank red Sicilian wine with it. She'd put several open bottles on the table before the start of the meal. I never saw anything like it. She'd lie to us and say there was nothing more to eat so we'd have at least two helpings, and then she'd bring some sausage and peppers, and some kind of roast after that.

20    After the meal we'd remain at the table, drinking and listening to old records of Beniamino Gigli and Feruccio Tagliavini. The old lady would still be around, urging on us a little more cheese, a little more cake. And then, just when we thought she had given up and gone to bed, she'd surprise us by bringing out a dish of fresh figs.

21    My late father, who never in his life refused another helping at the table, had a peculiarity common among gastronomes. The more he ate the more he talked about food. My mother was always amazed. We'd be done with a huge turkey roasted over sauerkraut and my father would begin reminiscing about a little breakfast-like sausage he had in some village on the Rumanian border in 1929, or a fish soup a blind woman made for him in Marseilles in 1945. Well, she wasn't completely blind, and besides she was pretty to look at—in any case, after three or four stories like that we'd be hungry again. My father had a theory that if you were still hungry, say for a hot dog, after a meal at Lutece, that meant that you were extraordinarily healthy. If a casual visitor to your house was not eating and drinking three minutes after his arrival, you had no manners. For people who had no interest in food, he absolutely had no comprehension. He'd ask them questions like an anthropologist, and go away seriously puzzled and worried. He told me toward the end of his life that the greatest mistake he ever made was accepting his doctor's advice to eat and drink less after he passed seventy-five. He felt terrible until he went back to his old ways.

22    One day we are walking up Second Avenue and talking. We get into an elaborate philosophical argument, as we often did. I feel like I've understood everything! I'm inspired! I'm quoting Kant, Descartes, Wittgenstein, when I notice he's no longer with me. I look around and locate him a block back staring into a shop window. I'm kind of pissed, especially since I have to walk to where he's standing, for he doesn't move or answer to my shouts. Finally, I tap him on the shoulder and he looks

at me, dazed. "Can you believe that?" he says and points to a window full of Hungarian smoked sausages, salamis, and pork rinds.

My friend, Mike De Porte, whose grandfather was a famous St. 23 Petersburg lawyer and who in his arguments combines a Dostoevskian probity and his grandfather's jurisprudence, claims that such obsession with food is the best proof that we have of the existence of the soul. Ergo, long after the body is satisfied, the soul is not. "Does that mean," I asked him, "that the soul is never satisfied?" He has not given me his answer yet. My own notion is that it is a supreme sign of happiness. When our souls are happy, they talk about food.

## CONSIDERATIONS

1. "I have to admit," writes Simic in paragraph 3, "I remember better what I ate than what I thought." Discuss in an essay how remembered tastes, smells, textures, colors, or shapes sometimes become powerful influences on our feelings, understandings, or behavior.

2. Does Simic's essay provide sufficient support for his thesis statement?

3. Why does Simic italicize words like *paella, choucroute garnie, tripes à la mode de Caen, burek, dobos torta,* and so on? How do you show italics in a typed manuscript?

4. In what ways do eating customs become keys—or, at least, introductions—to different cultures?

5. How do you think Simic would respond to the old question, "Do we eat to live or live to eat?" And how do you respond to the same question?

*Gary Soto (b. 1952) was born in Fresno and taught at the University of California in Berkeley. He has published many books of poems—including* The Elements of San Joaquin *(1977)* and Black Hair *(1985)—and more recently has written essays and reminiscence out of the Chicano experience, as well as fiction for children. This memoir comes from* A Summer Life *(1990). In 1995 he published* New and Selected Poems, *and in 1999 he received the Literature Award from the Hispanic Heritage Foundation.*

*In this affectionate reminiscence, observe how Soto uses images from memory, and memory of speech, to embody the relationship of the immigrant grandfather and the young Hispanic American.*

## — 81

# GARY SOTO
## *The Grandfather*

1    Grandfather believed a well-rooted tree was the color of money. His money he kept hidden behind portraits of sons and daughters or taped behind the calendar of an Aztec warrior. He tucked it into the sofa, his shoes and slippers, and into the tight-lipped pockets of his suits. He kept it in his soft brown wallet that was machine tooled with "MEXICO" and a campesino and donkey climbing a hill. He had climbed, too, out of Mexico, settled in Fresno and worked thirty years at Sun Maid Raisin, first as a packer and later, when he was old, as a watchman with a large clock on his belt.

2    After work, he sat in the backyard under the arbor, watching the water gurgle in the rose bushes that ran along the fence. A lemon tree hovered over the clothesline. Two orange trees stood near the alley. His favorite tree, the avocado, which had started in a jam jar from a seed and three toothpicks lanced in its sides, rarely bore fruit. He said it was the wind's fault, and the mayor's, who allowed office buildings so high that the haze of pollen from the countryside could never find its way into the city. He sulked about this. He said that in Mexico buildings only grew so tall. You could see the moon at night, and the stars were clear points all

---

the way to the horizon. And wind reached all the way from the sea, which was blue and clean, unlike the oily water sloshing against a San Francisco pier.

During its early years, I could leap over that tree, kick my bicycling legs over the top branch and scream my fool head off because I thought for sure I was flying. I ate fruit to keep my strength up, fuzzy peaches and branch-scuffed plums cooled in the refrigerator. From the kitchen chair he brought out in the evening, Grandpa would scold, "Hijo, what's the matta with you? You gonna break it." 3

By the third year, the tree was as tall as I, its branches casting a meager shadow on the ground. I sat beneath the shade, scratching words in the hard dirt with a stick. I had learned "Nile" in summer school and a dirty word from my brother who wore granny sunglasses. The red ants tumbled into my letters, and I buried them, knowing that they would dig themselves back into fresh air. 4

A tree was money. If a lemon cost seven cents at Hanoian's Market, then Grandfather saved fistfuls of change and more because in winter the branches of his lemon tree hung heavy yellow fruit. And winter brought oranges, juicy and large as softballs. Apricots he got by the bagfuls from a son, who himself was wise for planting young. Peaches he got from a neighbor, who worked the night shift at Sun Maid Raisin. The chile plants, which also saved him from giving up his hot, sweaty quarters, were propped up with sticks to support an abundance of red fruit. 5

But his favorite tree was the avocado because it offered hope and the promise of more years. After work, Grandpa sat in the back yard, shirtless, tired of flagging trucks loaded with crates of raisins, and sipped glasses of ice water. His yard was neat: five trees, seven rose bushes, whose fruit were the red and white flowers he floated in bowls, and a statue of St. Francis that stood in a circle of crushed rocks, arms spread out to welcome hungry sparrows. 6

After ten years, the first avocado hung on a branch, but the meat was flecked with black, an omen, Grandfather thought, a warning to keep an eye on the living. Five years later, another avocado hung on a branch, larger than the first and edible when crushed with a fork into a heated tortilla. Grandfather sprinkled it with salt and laced it with a river of chile. 7

"It's good," he said, and let me taste. 8

I took a big bite, waved a hand over my tongue, and ran for the garden hose gurgling in the rose bushes. I drank long and deep, and later ate the smile from an ice cold watermelon. 9

Birds nested in the tree, quarreling jays with liquid eyes and cool, pulsating throats. Wasps wove a horn-shaped hive one year, but we smoked them away with swords of rolled up newspapers lit with matches. By then, the tree was tall enough for me to climb to look into the neighbor's yard. But by then I was too old for that kind of thing and went about with my brother, hair slicked back and our shades dark as oil. 10

11        After twenty years, the tree began to bear. Although Grandfather complained about how much he lost because pollen never reached the poor part of town, because at the market he had to haggle over the price of avocados, he loved that tree. It grew, as did his family, and when he died, all his sons standing on each other's shoulders, oldest to youngest, could not reach the highest branches. The wind could move the branches, but the trunk, thicker than any waist, hugged the ground.

## CONSIDERATIONS

1. In what sense could one say that Soto's essay is a tribute to his grandfather? What else might be called a thematic thread running through it?

2. Select for study a few examples of Soto's use of figurative language. Then create some of your own in a short essay on a member of your family.

3. Read another account of a man recalling his boyhood, such as "Sand, Tattoo, and the Golden Gate" by James D. Houston, page 314, or "The Town Dump" by Wallace Stegner, page 552. Compare and contrast the respective techniques of that author and Soto.

4. What was there about the tree's first avocado that made the grandfather think neither old men nor growing boys were angels? He called it an omen. Was it some kind of sign or symbol? Take a little time to discriminate between "sign" and "symbol," and then explain the difference in the paragraph.

*William Stafford (1914–1993) was a poet who grew up in Kansas and taught for many years at Lewis and Clark College in Oregon. His* Traveling through the Dark *won the National Book Award in 1963, and in 1977 Stafford collected his poems into one volume called* Stories That Could Be True. *His essays appear in* Writing the Australian Crawl *(1978) and* You Must Revise Your Life *(1986). Robert Bly edited a selection of Stafford's poems in* The Darkness around Us Is Deep *(1993). Posthumous collections have followed. Stafford was the Consultant in Poetry at the Library of Congress in 1977, a position that has since been renamed and is now that of the Poet Laureate.*

*Stafford's poetry, and his personal account of writing poetry, looks simple at first glance, but the apparent simplicity reveals its depth as we reread. A French thinker said, "The style is the man." Reading about Stafford's way of writing, we sense the style as the man.*

— 82 —

# WILLIAM STAFFORD
## *A Way of Writing*

A writer is not so much someone who has something to say as he is someone who has found a process that will bring about new things he would not have thought of if he had not started to say them. That is, he does not draw on a reservoir; instead, he engages in an activity that brings to him a whole succession of unforeseen stories, poems, essays, plays, laws, philosophies, religions, or—but wait!

Back in school, from the first when I began to try to write things, I felt this richness. One thing would lead to another; the world would give and give. Now, after twenty years or so of trying, I live by that certain richness, an idea hard to pin, difficult to say, and perhaps offensive to some. For there are strange implications in it.

One implication is the importance of just plain receptivity. When I write, I like to have an interval before me when I am not likely to be interrupted. For me, this means usually the early morning, before others

1

2

3

"A Way of Writing" by William Stafford from *Field: Contemporary Poetry and Poetics*, #2 Spring 1970. Reprinted by permission of *Field*. Oberlin College, Oberlin, Ohio.

**529**

are awake. I get pen and paper, take a glance out the window (often it is dark out there), and wait. It is like fishing. But I do not wait very long, for there is always a nibble—and this is where receptivity comes in. To get started I will accept anything that occurs to me. Something always occurs, of course, to any of us. We can't keep from thinking. Maybe I have to settle for an immediate impression: it's cold, or hot, or dark, or bright, or in between! Or—well, the possibilities are endless. If I put down something, that thing will help the next thing come, and I'm off. If I let the process go on, things will occur to me that were not at all in my mind when I started. These things, odd or trivial as they may be, are somehow connected. And if I let them string out, surprising things will happen.

4    If I let them string out. . . . Along with initial receptivity, then, there is another readiness: I must be willing to fail. If I am to keep on writing, I cannot bother to insist on high standards. I must get into action and not let anything stop me, or even slow me much. By "standards" I do not mean "correctness"—spelling, punctuation, and so on. These details become mechanical for anyone who writes for awhile. I am thinking about what many people would consider "important" standards, such matters as social significance, positive values, consistency, etc. I resolutely disregard these. Something better, greater, is happening! I am following a process that leads so wildly and originally into new territory that no judgment can at the moment be made about values, significance, and so on. I am making something new, something that has not been judged before. Later others—and maybe I myself—will make judgments. Now, I am headlong to discover. Any distraction may harm the creating.

5    So, receptive, careless of failure, I spin out things on the page. And a wonderful freedom comes. If something occurs to me, it is all right to accept it. It has one justification: it occurs to me. No one else can guide me. I must follow my own weak, wandering, diffident impulses.

6    A strange bonus happens. At times, without my insisting on it, my writings become coherent; the successive elements that occur to me are clearly related. They lead by themselves to new connections. Sometimes the language, even the syllables that happen along, may start a trend. Sometimes the materials alert me to something waiting in my mind, ready for sustained attention. At such times, I allow myself to be eloquent, or intentional, or for great swoops (treacherous! not to be trusted!) reasonable. But I do not insist on any of that; for I know that back of my activity there will be the coherence of my self, and that indulgence of my impulses will bring recurrent patterns and meanings again.

7    This attitude toward the process of writing creatively suggests a problem for me, in terms of what others say. They talk about "skills" in writing. Without denying that I do have experience, wide reading, automatic orthodoxies and maneuvers of various kinds, I still must insist that I am often baffled about what "skill" has to do with the precious little area of confusion when I do not know what I am going to say and then

I find out what I am going to say. That precious interval I am unable to bridge by skill. What can I witness about it? It remains mysterious, just as all of us must feel puzzled about how we are so inventive as to be able to talk along through complexities with our friends, not needing to plan what we are going to say, but never stalled for long in our confident forward progress. Skill? If so, it is the skill we all have, something we must have learned before the age of three or four.

A writer is one who has become accustomed to trusting that grace, 8 or luck, or—skill.

Yet another attitude I find necessary: most of what I write, like 9 most of what I say in casual conversation, will not amount to much. Even I will realize, and even at the time, that it is not negotiable. It will be like practice. In conversation I allow myself random remarks—in fact, as I recall, that is the way I learned to talk—, so in writing I launch many expendable efforts. A result of this free way of writing is that I am not writing for others, mostly; they will not see the product at all unless the activity eventuates in something that later appears to be worthy. My guide is the self, and its adventuring in the language brings about communications.

This process-rather-than-substance view of writing invites a final, 10 dual reflection:

1. Writers may not be special—sensitive or talented in any usual sense. They are simply engaged in sustained use of a language skill we all have. Their "creations" come about through confident reliance on stray impulses that will, with trust, find occasional patterns that are satisfying.
2. But writing itself is one of the great, free human activities. There is scope for individuality, and elation, and discovery, in writing. For the person who follows with trust and forgiveness what occurs to him, the world remains always ready and deep, an inexhaustible environment, with the combined vividness of an actuality and flexibility of a dream. Working back and forth between experience and thought, writers have more than space and time can offer. They have the whole unexplored realm of human vision.

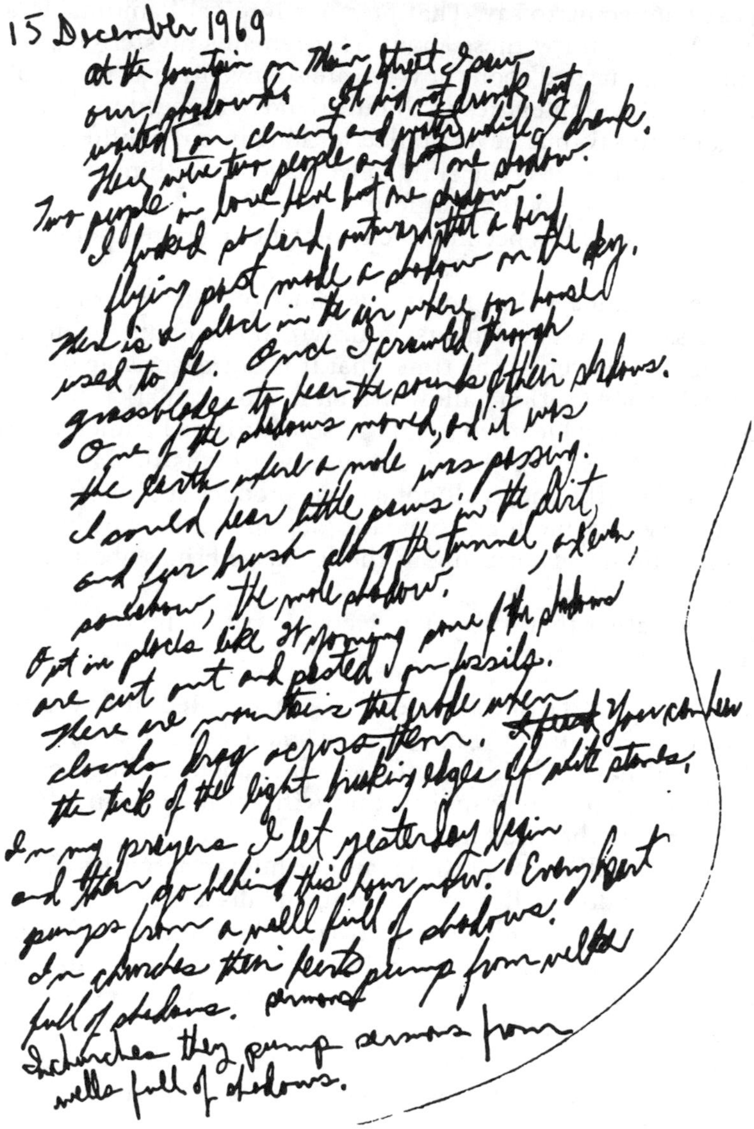

15 December 1969
At the fountain on Main Street I saw
our shadows. He did not drink but
waited on cement and water while I drank.
There were two people and but one shadow.
Two people in love have but one shadow.
I looked at [illegible], [illegible] a bird
flying past made a shadow on the sky.
There is a place in the air where our house
used to be. Once I crawled through
grassblades to hear the sounds of their shadows.
One of the shadows moved, and it was
the earth where a mole was passing.
I could hear little paws in the dirt,
and fur brush along the tunnel, and even,
somehow, the mole shadow.
Out in places like [illegible] some of the shadows
are cut out and pasted on fossils.
There are mountains that wobble when
clouds drag across them. ~~Streak~~ You can hear
the tick of the light breaking edges of white stones.
In my prayers I let yesterday begin
and then go behind this hour now. Every heart
pumps from a well full of shadows.
In churches their hearts pump from wells
full of shadows. sermons
In churches they pump sermons from
wells full of shadows.

A sample daily-writing sheet and the poem as revised.

Shadows

I

Out in places like Wyoming some of the shadows

are cut out and pasted on fossils.

There are mountains that erode when
clouds drag across them.  You can hear *the tick*

~~the tick~~ of the light breaking edges off white stones.

*a*
At ~~the~~ fountain on Main Street I saw

our shadow.  It did not drink but

waited on cement and water while I drank.

There were two people and but one shadow.

I looked up so hard outward that a bird

flying past made a shadow on the sky. ✗

There is a place in the air where ⌐our house

⌐used to be.

Once I crawled through grassblades to hear

the sounds of their shadows. One of the shadows

moved, and it was the earth where a mole

was passing.  I could hear little

paws in the dirt, and fur brush along

the tunnel, and even, somehow, the mole shadow.

*where*
In churches ~~their~~ hearts pump sermons

from wells full of shadows.

In my prayers I let yesterday begin

and then go behind this hour now.

## Shadows

Out in places like Wyoming some of the shadows
are cut out and pasted on fossils.
There are mountains that erode when
clouds drag across them. You hear the tick
of sunlight breaking edges off white stones.

5

At a fountain on Main Street I saw
our shadow. It did not drink but
waited on cement and water while I drank.
There were two people and but one shadow.
10      I looked up so hard outward that a bird
flying past made a shadow on the sky.
There is a place in the air where
our old house used to be.

Once I crawled through grassblades to hear
15      the sounds of their shadows. One shadow
moved, and it was the earth where a mole
was passing. I could hear little
paws in the dirt, and fur brush along
the tunnel, and even, somehow, the mole shadow.

20      In my prayers I let yesterday begin
and then go behind this hour now,
in churches where hearts pump sermons
from wells full of shadows.

## CONSIDERATIONS

1. Stafford is clearly and openly talking about himself—how *he* writes, what writing means to *him*—and yet most readers agree that he successfully avoids the egotism or self-consciousness that sours many first-person essays. Compare his style with three or four other first-person pieces in this book to see how he does it.

2. In his first paragraph, Stafford tells of an idea that might be called writing as discovery. Thinking back through your own writing, can you recall this experience—when, after struggling to write an essay or letter that you *had* to write, you discovered something you *wanted* to write? What did you do about it? More important, what might you do next time it happens?

3. What, according to Stafford, is more important to a writer than "social significance, or positive values, or consistency"?

4. Stafford is talking about writing a poem. How do his discoveries and conclusions bear on *your* problems in writing an essay? Be specific.

5. Do the opening and closing paragraphs differ in style? If so, what is the difference, and why does Stafford allow it?

6. Study the three versions of Stafford's poem "Shadows." Do you find anything that belies the easygoing impression his essay gives of Stafford at work? Explain.

7. Compare Stafford's advice with the suggestions of other authors in the text who talk about writing: Sven Birkerts, Joan Didion, Ralph Ellison, Alice Walker, Amy Tan, Eudora Welty, and James Thurber. What advice is most relevant to your current writing tasks?

*Brent Staples (b. 1951) is Assistant Metropolitan Editor at the* New
York Times. *He grew up in Chester, Pennsylvania, and received his
Ph.D. in psychology at the University of Chicago. He taught
briefly and then worked for several magazines and newspapers,
including the* Chicago Sun-Times, *before moving to New York.
"Just Walk On By" appeared in* Ms. *magazine in 1986. He
published* Parallel Time: Growing Up in Black and White *in 1994.*

— 83 ——————————————————————————

# BRENT STAPLES
## *Just Walk On By*

My first victim was a woman—white, well-dressed, probably in her    1
early twenties. I came upon her late one evening on a deserted street in
Hyde Park, a relatively affluent neighborhood in an otherwise mean, impoverished section of Chicago. As I swung onto the avenue behind her,
there seemed to be a discreet, uninflammatory distance between us. Not
so. She cast back a worried glance. To her, the youngish black man—a
broad six feet two inches with a beard and billowing hair, both hands
shoved into the pockets of a bulky military jacket—seemed menacingly
close. After a few more quick glimpses, she picked up her pace and was
soon running in earnest. Within seconds she disappeared into a cross
street.

That was more than a decade ago. I was 22 years old, a graduate stu-    2
dent newly arrived at the University of Chicago. It was in the echo of
that terrified woman's footfalls that I first began to know the unwieldy
inheritance I'd come into—the ability to alter public space in ugly ways.
It was clear that she thought herself the quarry of a mugger, a rapist, or
worse. Suffering a bout of insomnia, however, I was stalking sleep, not
defenseless wayfarers. As a softy who is scarcely able to take a knife to a
raw chicken—let alone hold it to a person's throat—I was surprised, embarrassed, and dismayed all at once. Her flight made me feel like an accomplice in tyranny. It also made it clear that I was indistinguishable
from the muggers who occasionally seeped into the area from the surrounding ghetto. That first encounter, and those that followed, signified

that a vast, unnerving gulf lay between nighttime pedestrians—particularly women—and me. And I soon gathered that being perceived as dangerous is a hazard in itself. I only needed to turn a corner into a dicey situation, or crowd some frightened, armed person in a foyer somewhere, or make an errant move after being pulled over by a policeman. Where fear and weapons meet—and they often do in urban America—there is always the possibility of death.

3    In that first year, my first away from my hometown, I was to become thoroughly familiar with the language of fear. At dark, shadowy intersections in Chicago, I could cross in front of a car stopped at a traffic light and elicit the *thunk, thunk, thunk, thunk* of the driver—black, white, male, or female—hammering down the door locks. On less traveled streets after dark, I grew accustomed to but never comfortable with people who crossed to the other side of the street rather than pass me. Then there were the standard unpleasantries with police, doormen, bouncers, cab drivers, and others whose business it is to screen out troublesome individuals *before* there is any nastiness.

4    I moved to New York nearly two years ago and I have remained an avid night walker. In central Manhattan, the near-constant crowd cover minimizes tense one-on-one street encounters. Elsewhere—visiting friends in SoHo, where sidewalks are narrow and tightly spaced buildings shut out the sky—things can get very taut indeed.

5    Black men have a firm place in New York mugging literature. Norman Podhoretz in his famed (or infamous) 1963 essay, "My Negro Problem—And Ours," recalls growing up in terror of black males; they "were tougher than we were, more ruthless," he writes—and as an adult on the Upper West Side of Manhattan, he continues, he cannot constrain his nervousness when he meets black men on certain streets. Similarly, a decade later, the essayist and novelist Edward Hoagland extols a New York where once "Negro bitterness bore down mainly on other Negroes." Where some see mere panhandlers, Hoagland sees "a mugger who is clearly screwing up his nerve to do more than just *ask* for money." But Hoagland has "the New Yorker's quick-hunch posture for broken-field maneuvering," and the bad guy swerves away.

6    I often witness that "hunch posture," from women after dark on the warrenlike streets of Brooklyn where I live. They seem to set their faces on neutral and, with their purse straps strung across their chests bandolier style, they forge ahead as though bracing themselves against being tackled. I understand, of course, that the danger they perceive is not a hallucination. Women are particularly vulnerable to street violence, and young black males are drastically overrepresented among the perpetrators of that violence. Yet these truths are no solace against the kind of alienation that comes of being ever the suspect, against being set apart, a fearsome entity with whom pedestrians avoid making eye contact.

7    It is not altogether clear to me how I reached the ripe old age of 22 without being conscious of the lethality nighttime pedestrians attributed

to me. Perhaps it was because in Chester, Pennsylvania, the small, angry industrial town where I came of age in the 1960s, I was scarcely noticeable against a backdrop of gang warfare, street knifings, and murders. I grew up one of the good boys, had perhaps a half-dozen fist fights. In retrospect, my shyness of combat has clear sources.

Many things go into the making of a young thug. One of those    8 things is the consummation of the male romance with the power to intimidate. An infant discovers that random flailings send the baby bottle flying out of the crib and crashing to the floor. Delighted, the joyful babe repeats those motions again and again, seeking to duplicate the feat. Just so, I recall the points at which some of my boyhood friends were finally seduced by the perception of themselves as tough guys. When a mark cowered and surrendered his money without resistance, myth and reality merged—and paid off. It is, after all, only manly to embrace the power to frighten and intimidate. We, as men, are not supposed to give an inch of our lane on the highway; we are to seize the fighter's edge in work and in play and even in love; we are to be valiant in the face of hostile forces.

Unfortunately, poor and powerless young men seem to take all this    9 nonsense literally. As a boy, I saw countless tough guys locked away; I have since buried several, too. They were babies, really a teenage cousin, a brother of 22, a childhood friend in his mid-twenties—all gone down in episodes of bravado played out in the streets. I came to doubt the virtues of intimidation early on. I chose, perhaps even unconsciously, to remain a shadow—timid, but a survivor.

The fearsomeness mistakenly attributed to me in public places of-    10 ten has a perilous flavor. The most frightening of these confusions occurred in the late 1970s and early 1980s when I worked as a journalist in Chicago. One day, rushing into the office of a magazine I was writing for with a deadline story in hand, I was mistaken for a burglar. The office manager called security and, with an *ad hoc* posse, pursued me through the labyrinthine halls, nearly to my editor's door. I had no way of proving who I was. I could only move briskly toward the company of someone who knew me.

Another time I was on assignment for a local paper and killing time    11 before an interview. I entered a jewelry store on the city's affluent Near North Side. The proprietor excused herself and returned with an enormous red Doberman pinscher straining at the end of a leash. She stood, the dog extended toward me, silent to my questions, her eyes bulging nearly out of her head. I took a cursory look around, nodded, and bade her good night. Relatively speaking, however, I never fared as badly as another black male journalist. He went to nearby Waukegan, Illinois, a couple of summers ago to work on a story about a murderer who was born there. Mistaking the reporter for the killer, police hauled him from his car at gunpoint and but for his press credentials would probably have tried to book him. Such episodes are not uncommon. Black men trade tales like this all the time.

12    In "My Negro Problem—And Ours," Podhoretz writes that the hatred he feels for blacks makes itself known to him through a variety of avenues—one being his discomfort with that "special brand of paranoid touchiness" to which he says blacks are prone. No doubt he is speaking here of black men. In time, I learned to smother the rage I felt at so often being taken for a criminal. Not to do so would surely have led to madness—via that special "paranoid touchiness" that so annoyed Podhoretz at the time he wrote the essay.

13    I began to take precautions to make myself less threatening. I move about with care, particularly late in the evening. I give a wide berth to nervous people on subway platforms during the wee hours, particularly when I have exchanged business clothes for jeans. If I happen to be entering a building behind some people who appear skittish, I may walk by, letting them clear the lobby before I return, so as not to seem to be following them. I have been calm and extremely congenial on those rare occasions when I've been pulled over by the police.

14    And on late-evening constitutionals along streets less traveled by, I employ what has proved to be an excellent tension-reducing measure. I whistle melodies from Beethoven and Vivaldi and the more popular classical composers. Even steely New Yorkers hunching toward nighttime destinations seem to relax, and occasionally they even join in the tune. Virtually everybody seems to sense that a mugger wouldn't be warbling bright, sunny selections from Vivaldi's *Four Seasons*. It is my equivalent of the cowbell that hikers wear when they know they are in bear country.

## CONSIDERATIONS

1. "Her flight made me feel like an accomplice in tyranny," writes Staples, in paragraph 2, of the young white woman who was frightened by his mere appearance. What "tyranny" is Staples talking about? Explain how he develops that idea (or its reversal) elsewhere in the essay.

2. Staples's technique for defusing potentially unpleasant or dangerous situations might be summed up in the title of his essay. Read one of the following authors in your text: Zora Neale Hurston (page 329), Ishmael Reed (page 515), Toni Morrison (page 432), or Richard Wright (page 679). Describe how you think that writer might respond to situations Staples mentions.

3. What do hikers wearing cowbells in bear country have to do with Staples's techniques for easing tension on his evening walks?

4. Is there any connection between the fear Staples encounters when he meets lone white men or women on the street at night and the fear of the homeless that many middle-class people feel? See Peter Marin's essay "Helping and Hating the Homeless."

5. Why was the word "hunching" a good choice in the second sentence of paragraph 14?

*Shelby Steele (b. 1946) is a Senior Fellow at the Hoover Institute at Stanford University in California, on leave from his professorship at San Jose State University. He has published essays in* Commentary, *the* New York Times Magazine, *and the* American Scholar, *as well as* Harper's, *which printed "I'm Black, You're White, Who's Innocent?" in 1988. His "On Being Black and Middle Class" appeared in* The Best American Essays of 1989. *His* The Content of Our Character: A New Vision of Race in America *won the National Book Critics Circle Award in 1991.*

*There's the highway crime known as DWB (Driving While Black), which derives from the racial profiling practiced by some police departments. In New York, an innocent black man was killed in a fusillade of police bullets when he reached for his wallet to prove his identity. Shelby Steele writes as a man whose appearance causes fear.*

*The large African-American middle class faces unique problems—in its integration with the white middle class and in its separation from the African-American mass. In exploring the problem, notice how Steele thinks, argues, and uses examples from his own experience.*

— **84** ———————————————————

# SHELBY STEELE
## *I'm Black, You're White, Who's Innocent?*

———————————————————

It is a warm, windless California evening, and the dying light that covers the redbrick patio is tinted pale orange by the day's smog. Eight of us, not close friends, sit in lawn chairs sipping chardonnay. A black engineer and I (we had never met before) integrate the group. A psychologist is also among us, and her presence encourages a surprising openness. But not until well after the lovely twilight dinner had been served, when the sky has turned to deep black and the drinks have long since changed to scotch, does the subject of race spring awkwardly upon us. Out of nowhere the engineer announces, with a coloring of accusation in his voice, that it bothers him to send his daughter to a school where she is

1

one of only three black children. "I didn't realize my ambition to get ahead would pull me into a world where my daughter would lose touch with her blackness," he says.

2    Over the course of the evening we have talked about money, infidelity, past and present addictions, child abuse, even politics. Intimacies have been revealed, fears named. But this subject, race, sinks us into one of those shaming silences where eye contact terrorizes. Our host looks for something in the bottom of his glass. Two women stare into the black sky as if to locate the Big Dipper and point it out to us. Finally, the psychologist seems to gather herself for a challenge, but it is too late. "Oh, I'm sure she'll be just fine," says our hostess, rising from her chair. When she excuses herself to get the coffee, the two sky gazers offer to help.

3    With three of us now gone, I am surprised to see the engineer still silently holding his ground. There is a willfulness in his eyes, an inner pride. He knows he has said something awkward, but he is determined not to give a damn. His unwavering eyes intimidate me. At last the host's head snaps erect. He has an idea. "The hell with coffee," he says. "How about some of the smoothest brandy you ever tasted?" An idea made exciting by the escape it offers. Gratefully we follow him back into the house, quickly drink his brandy, and say our good-byes.

4    An autopsy of this party might read: death induced by an abrupt and lethal injection of the American race issue. An accurate if superficial assessment. Since it has been my fate to live a rather integrated life, I have often witnessed sudden deaths like this. The threat of them, if not the reality, is a part of the texture of integration. In the late 1960s, when I was just out of college, I took a delinquent's delight in playing the engineer's role, and actually developed a small reputation for playing it well. Those were the days of flagellatory white guilt; it was such great fun to pinion some professor or housewife or, best of all, a large group of remorseful whites, with the knowledge of both their racism and their denial of it. The adolescent impulse to sneer at convention, to startle the middle-aged with doubt, could be indulged under the guise of racial indignation. And how could I lose? My victims—earnest liberals for the most part—could no more crawl out from under my accusations than Joseph K. in Kafka's *Trial* could escape the amorphous charges brought against him. At this odd moment in history the world was aligned to facilitate my immaturity.

5    About a year of this was enough: the guilt that follows most cheap thrills caught up to me, and I put myself in check. But the impulse to do it faded more slowly. It was one of those petty talents that is tied to vanity, and when there were ebbs in my self-esteem the impulse to use it would come alive again. In integrated situations I can still feel the faint itch. But then there are many youthful impulses that still itch, and now, just inside the door of mid-life, this one is least precious to me.

6    In the literature classes I teach, I often see how the presence of whites all but seduces some black students into provocation. When we come to a novel by a black writer, say Toni Morrison, the white students

can easily discuss the human motivations of the black characters. But, inevitably, a black student, as if by reflex, will begin to set in relief the various racial problems that are the background of these characters' lives. The student's tone will carry a reprimand: the class is afraid to confront the reality of racism. Classes cannot be allowed to die like dinner parties, however. My latest strategy is to thank that student for his or her moral vigilance, and then appoint the young man or woman as the class's official racism monitor. But even if I get a laugh—I usually do, but sometimes the student is particularly indignant, and it gets uncomfortable— the strategy never quite works. Our racial division is suddenly drawn in neon. Overcaution spreads like spilled paint. And, in fact, the black student who started it all does become a kind of monitor. The very presence of this student imposes a new accountability on the class.

I think those who provoke this sort of awkwardness are operating out of a black identity that obliges them to badger white people about race almost on principle. Content hardly matters. (For example, it made no sense for the engineer to expect white people to sympathize with his anguish over sending his daughter to school with *white* children.) Race indeed remains a source of white shame; the goal of these provocations is to put whites, no matter how indirectly, in touch with this collective guilt. In other words, these provocations I speak of are *power* moves, little shows of power that try to freeze the "enemy" in self-consciousness. They gratify and inflate the provocateur. They are the underdog's bite. And whites, far more secure in their power, respond with a self-contained and tolerant silence that is, itself, a show of power. What greater power than that of non-response, the power to let a small enemy sizzle in his own juices, to even feel a little sad at his frustration just as one is also complimented by it. Black anger always, in a way, flatters white power. In America, to know that one is not black is to feel an extra grace, a little boost of impunity.

I think the real trouble between the races in America is that the races are not just races but competing power groups—a fact that is easily minimized perhaps because it is so obvious. What is not so obvious is that this is true quite apart from the issue of class. Even the well-situated middle-class (or wealthy) black is never completely immune to that peculiar contest of power that his skin color subjects him to. Race is a separate reality in American society, an entity that carries its own potential for power, a mark of fate that class can soften considerably but not eradicate.

The distinction of race has always been used in American life to sanction each race's pursuit of power in relation to the other. The allure of race as a human delineation is the very shallowness of the delineation it makes. Onto this shallowness—mere skin and hair—men can project a false depth, a system of dismal attributions, a series of malevolent or ignoble stereotypes that skin and hair lack the substance to contradict. These dark projections then rationalize the pursuit of power. Your difference from me makes you bad, and your badness justifies, even demands, my pursuit of power over you—the oldest formula for aggression known to man. Whenever much importance is given to race, power is the primary motive.

10          But the human animal almost never pursues power without first convincing himself that he is *entitled* to it. And this feeling of entitlement has its own precondition: to be entitled one must first believe in one's innocence, at least in the area where one wishes to be entitled. By innocence I mean a feeling of essential goodness in relation to others and, therefore, superiority to others. Our innocence always inflates us and deflates those we seek power over. Once inflated we are entitled; we are in fact licensed to go after the power our innocence tells us we deserve. In this sense, *innocence is power.* Of course, innocence need not be genuine or real in any objective sense, as the Nazis demonstrated not long ago. Its only test is whether or not we can convince ourselves of it.

11          I think the racial struggle in America has always been primarily a struggle for innocence. White racism from the beginning has been a claim of white innocence and, therefore, of white entitlement to subjugate blacks. And in the '60s, as went innocence so went power. Blacks used the innocence that grew out of their long subjugation to seize more power, while whites lost some of their innocence and so lost a degree of power over blacks. Both races instinctively understand that to lose innocence is to lose power (in relation to each other). Now to be innocent someone else must be guilty, a natural law that leads the races to forge their innocence on each other's backs. The inferiority of the black always makes the white man superior; the evil might of whites makes blacks good. This pattern means that both races have a hidden investment in racism and racial disharmony, despite their good intentions to the contrary. Power defines their relations, and power requires innocence, which, in turn, requires racism and racial division.

12          I believe it was this hidden investment that the engineer was protecting when he made his remark—the white "evil" he saw in a white school "depriving" his daughter of her black heritage confirmed his innocence. Only the logic of power explained this—he bent reality to show that he was once again a victim of the white world and, as a victim, innocent. His determined eyes insisted on this. And the whites, in their silence, no doubt protected their innocence by seeing him as an ungracious troublemaker—his bad behavior underscoring their goodness. I can only guess how he was talked about after the party. But it isn't hard to imagine that his blunder gave everyone a lift. What none of us saw was the underlying game of power and innocence we were trapped in, or how much we needed a racial impasse to play that game.

13          When I was a boy of about twelve, a white friend of mine told me one day that his uncle, who would be arriving the next day for a visit, was a racist. Excited by the prospect of seeing such a man, I spent the following afternoon hanging around the alley behind my friend's house, watching from a distance as this uncle worked on the engine of his

Buick. Yes, here was evil and I was compelled to look upon it. And I saw evil in the tight angle of his elbow as he pumped his wrench to tighten nuts, I saw it in the blade-sharp crease of his chinos, in the pack of Lucky Strikes that threatened to slip from his shirt pocket as he bent, and in the way his concentration seemed to shut out the human world. He worked neatly and efficiently, wiping his hands constantly, and I decided that evil worked like this.

I felt a compulsion to have this man look upon me so that I could    14
see evil—so that I could see the face of it. But when he noticed me standing beside his toolbox, he said only, "If you're looking for Bobby, I think he went up to the school to play baseball." He smiled nicely and went back to work. I was stunned for a moment, but then I realized that evil could be sly as well, could smile when it wanted to trick you.

Need, especially hidden need, puts a strong pressure on perception,    15
and my need to have this man embody white evil was stronger than any contravening evidence. As a black person you always hear about racists but never meet any. And I needed to incarnate this odious category of humanity, those people who hated Martin Luther King Jr. and thought blacks should "go slow" or not at all. So, in my mental dictionary, behind the term "white racist," I inserted this man's likeness. I would think of him and say to myself, "There is no reason for him to hate black people. Only evil explains unmotivated hatred." And this thought soothed me; I felt innocent. If I hated white people, which I did not, at least I had a reason. His evil commanded me to assert in the world the goodness he made me confident of in myself.

In looking at this man I was *seeing for innocence*—a form of seeing    16
that has more to do with one's hidden need for innocence (and power) than with the person or group one is looking at. It is quite possible, for example, that the man I saw that day was not a racist. He did absolutely nothing in my presence to indicate that he was. I invested an entire afternoon in seeing not the man but in seeing my innocence through the man. *Seeing for innocence* is, in this way, the essence of racism—the use of others as a means to our own goodness and superiority.

The loss of innocence has always to do with guilt, Kierkegaard tells    17
us, and it has never been easy for whites to avoid guilt where blacks are concerned. For whites, *seeing for innocence* means seeing themselves and blacks in ways that minimize white guilt. Often this amounts to a kind of white revisionism, as when President Reagan declares himself "colorblind" in matters of race. The President, like many of us, may aspire to racial color blindness, but few would grant that he has yet reached this sublimely guiltless state. The statement clearly revises reality, moves it forward into some heretofore unknown America where all racial determinism will have vanished. I do not think that Ronald Reagan is a racist, as that term is commonly used, but neither do I think that he is capable of seeing color without making attributions, some of which may be negative—nor am I, or anyone else I've ever met.

18      So why make such a statement? I think Reagan's claim of color blindness with regard to race is really a claim of racial innocence and guiltlessness—the preconditions for entitlement and power. This was the claim that grounded Reagan's campaign against special entitlement programs—affirmative action, racial quotas, and so on—that black power had won in the '60s. Color blindness was a strategic assumption of innocence that licensed Reagan's use of government power against black power.

19      I do not object to Reagan's goals in this so much as the presumption of innocence by which he rationalized them. I, too, am strained to defend racial quotas and any affirmative action that supersedes merit. And I believe there is much that Reagan has to offer blacks. His emphasis on traditional American values—individual initiative, self-sufficiency, strong families—offers what I think is the most enduring solution to the demoralization and poverty that continue to widen the gap between blacks and whites in America. Even his de-emphasis of race is reasonable in a society where race only divides. But Reagan's posture of innocence undermines any beneficial interaction he might have with blacks. For blacks instinctively sense that a claim of racial innocence always precedes a power move against them. Reagan's pretense of innocence makes him an adversary, and makes his quite reasonable message seem vindictive. You cannot be innocent of a man's problem and expect him to listen.

20      I'm convinced that the secret of Reagan's "teflon" coating, his personal popularity apart from his policies and actions, has been his ability to offer mainstream America a vision of itself as innocent and entitled (unlike Jimmy Carter, who seemed to offer only guilt and obligation). Probably his most far-reaching accomplishment has been to reverse somewhat the pattern by which innocence came to be distributed in the '60s, when outsiders were innocent and insiders were guilty. Corporations, the middle class, entrepreneurs, the military—all villains in the '60s—either took on a new innocence in Reagan's vision or were designated as protectors of innocence. But again, for one man to be innocent another man must be bad or guilty. Innocence imposes, *demands*, division and conflict, a right/wrong view of the world. And this, I feel, has led to the underside of Reagan's achievement. His posture of innocence draws him into a partisanship that undermines the universality of his values. He can't sell these values to blacks and others because he has made blacks into the bad guys and outsiders who justify his power. It is humiliating for a black person to like Reagan because Reagan's power is so clearly derived from a distribution of innocence that leaves a black with less of it, and the white man with more.

21      Black Americans have always had to find a way to handle white society's presumption of racial innocence whenever they have sought to enter the American mainstream. Louis Armstrong's exaggerated smile honored the presumed innocence of white society—I will not bring you

your racial guilt if you will let me play my music. Ralph Ellison calls this "masking"; I call it bargaining. But whatever it's called, it points to the power of white society to enforce its innocence. I believe this power is greatly diminished today. Society has reformed and transformed—Miles Davis never smiles. Nevertheless, this power has not faded altogether; blacks must still contend with it.

Historically, blacks have handled white society's presumption of in-    22 nocence in two ways: they have bargained with it, granting white society its innocence in exchange for entry into the mainstream; or they have challenged it, holding that innocence hostage until their demand for entry (or other concessions) was met. A bargainer says, *I already believe you are innocent (good, fair-minded) and have faith that you will prove it.* A challenger says, *If you are innocent, then prove it.* Bargainers *give* in hope of receiving; challengers *withhold* until they receive. Of course, there is risk in both approaches, but in each case the black is negotiating his own self-interest against the presumed racial innocence of the larger society.

Clearly the most visible black bargainer on the American scene to-    23 day is Bill Cosby. His television show is a perfect formula for black bargaining in the '80s. The remarkable Huxtable family—with its doctor/lawyer parent combination, its drug-free, college-bound children, and its wise yet youthful grandparents—is a blackface version of the American dream. Cosby is a subscriber to the American identity, and his subscription confirms his belief in its fair-mindedness. His vast audience knows this, knows that Cosby will never assault their innocence with racial guilt. Racial controversy is all but banished from the show. The Huxtable family never discusses affirmative action.

The bargain Cosby offers his white viewers—I will confirm your    24 racial innocence if you accept me—is a good deal for all concerned. Not only does it allow whites to enjoy Cosby's humor with no loss of innocence, but it actually enhances their innocence by implying that race is not the serious problem for blacks that it once was. If anything, the success of this handsome, affluent black family points to the fair-mindedness of whites who, out of their essential goodness, changed society so that black families like the Huxtables could succeed. Whites can watch *The Cosby Show* and feel complimented on a job well done.

The power that black bargainers wield is the power of absolution.    25 On Thursday nights, Cosby, like a priest, absolves his white viewers, forgives and forgets the sins of the past. (Interestingly, Cosby was one of the first blacks last winter to publicly absolve Jimmy the Greek for his well-publicized faux pas about black athletes.) And for this he is rewarded with an almost sacrosanct status. Cosby benefits from what might be called a gratitude factor. His continued number-one rating may have something to do with the (white) public's gratitude at being offered a commodity so rare in our time; he tells his white viewers each week that they are okay, and that this black man is not going to challenge them.

26    When a black bargains, he may invoke the gratitude factor and find himself cherished beyond the measure of his achievement; when he challenges, he may draw the dark projections of whites and become a source of irritation to them. If he moves back and forth between these two options, as I think many blacks do today, he will likely baffle whites. It is difficult for whites to either accept or reject such blacks. It seems to me that Jesse Jackson is such a figure—many whites see Jackson as a challenger by instinct and a bargainer by political ambition. They are uneasy with him, more than a little suspicious. His powerful speech at the 1984 Democratic convention was a masterpiece of bargaining. In it he offered a Kinglike vision of what America could be, a vision that presupposed Americans had the fair-mindedness to achieve full equality—an offer in hope of a return. A few days after this speech, looking for rest and privacy at a lodge in Big Sur, he and his wife were greeted with standing ovations three times a day when they entered the dining room for meals. So much about Jackson is deeply American—his underdog striving, his irrepressible faith in himself, the daring of his ambition, and even his stubbornness. These qualities point to his underlying faith that Americans can respond to him despite his race, and this faith is a compliment to Americans, an offer of innocence.

27    But Jackson does not always stick to the terms of his bargain—he is not like Cosby on TV. When he hugs Arafat, smokes cigars with Castro, refuses to repudiate Farrakhan, threatens a boycott of major league baseball, or, more recently, talks of "corporate barracudas," "pension-fund socialism," and "economic violence," he looks like a challenger in bargainer's clothing, and his positions on the issues look like familiar protests dressed in white-paper formality. At these times he appears to be revoking the innocence so much else about him seems to offer. The old activist seems to come out of hiding once again to take white innocence hostage until whites prove they deserve to have it. In his candidacy there is a suggestion of protest, a fierce insistence on his *right* to run, that sends whites a message that he may secretly see them as a good bit less than innocent. His dilemma is to appear the bargainer while his campaign itself seems to be a challenge.

28    There are, of course, other problems that hamper Jackson's bid for the Democratic presidential nomination. He has held no elective office, he is thought too flamboyant and opportunistic by many, there are rather loud whispers of "character" problems. As an individual he may not be the best test of a black man's chances for winning so high an office. Still, I believe it is the aura of challenge surrounding him that hurts him most. Whether it is right or wrong, fair or unfair, I think no black candidate will have a serious chance at his party's nomination, much less the presidency, until he can convince white Americans that he can be trusted to preserve *their* sense of racial innocence. Such a candidate will have to use his power of absolution; he will have to flatly forgive and forget. He

will have to bargain with white innocence out of a genuine belief that it really exists. There can be no faking it. He will have to offer a vision that is passionately raceless, a vision that strongly condemns any form of racial politics. This will require the most courageous kind of leadership, leadership that asks all the people to meet a new standard.

Now the other side of American's racial impasse: How do blacks lay 29 claim to their racial innocence?

The most obvious and unarguable source of black innocence is the 30 victimization that blacks endured for centuries at the hands of a race that insisted on black inferiority as a means to its own innocence and power. Like all victims, what blacks lost in power they gained in innocence—innocence that, in turn, entitled them to pursue power. This was the innocence that fueled the civil rights movement of the '60s, and that gave blacks their first real power in American life—victimization metamorphosed into power via innocence. But this formula carries a drawback that I believe is virtually as devastating to blacks today as victimization once was. It is a formula that binds the victim to his victimization by linking his power to his status as a victim. And this, I'm convinced, is the tragedy of black power in America today. It is primarily a victim's power, grounded too deeply in the entitlement derived from past injustice and in the innocence that Western/Christian tradition has always associated with poverty.

Whatever gains this power brings in the short run through political 31 action, it undermines in the long run. Social victims may be collectively entitled, but they are all too often individually demoralized. Since the social victim has been oppressed by society, he comes to feel that his individual life will be improved more by changes *in* society than by his own initiative. Without realizing it, he makes society rather than himself the agent of change. The power he finds in his victimization may lead him to collective action against society, but it also encourages passivity within the sphere of his personal life.

This past summer I saw a television documentary that examined 32 life in Detroit's inner city on the twentieth anniversary of the riots there in which forty-three people were killed. A comparison of the inner city then and now showed a decline in the quality of life. Residents feel less safe than they did twenty years ago, drug trafficking is far worse, crimes by blacks against blacks are more frequent, housing remains substandard, and the teenage pregnancy rate has skyrocketed. Twenty years of decline and demoralization, even as opportunities for blacks to better themselves have increased. This paradox is not peculiar to Detroit. By many measures, the majority of blacks—those not yet in the middle class—are further behind whites today than before the victories of the civil rights movement. But there is a reluctance among blacks to examine this paradox, I think, because it suggests that racial victimization is not our real problem. If conditions have worsened for most of us as racism has receded, then much of the problem must be of our own making. But to fully admit this would cause us to lose the innocence we derive from our victimization. And we would jeopardize the entitlement we've always had to challenge society. We are in the odd and self-defeating position where taking responsibility for bettering ourselves feels like a surrender to white power.

33      So we have a hidden investment in victimization and poverty. These distressing conditions have been the source of our only real power, and there is an unconscious sort of gravitation toward them, a complaining celebration of them. One sees evidence of this in the near happiness with which certain black leaders recount the horror of Howard Beach and other recent (and I think over-celebrated) instances of racial tension. As one is saddened by these tragic events, one is also repelled at the way some black leaders—agitated to near hysteria by the scent of victim-power inherent in them—leap forward to exploit them as evidence of black innocence and white guilt. It is as though they sense the decline of black victimization as a loss of standing and dive into the middle of these incidents as if they were reservoirs of pure black innocence swollen with potential power.

34      *Seeing for innocence* pressures blacks to focus on racism and to neglect the individual initiative that would deliver them from poverty—the only thing that finally delivers anyone from poverty. With our eyes on innocence we see racism everywhere and miss opportunity even as we stumble over it. About 70 percent of black students at my university drop out before graduating—a flight from opportunity that racism cannot explain. It is an injustice that whites can *see for innocence* with more impunity than blacks can. The price whites pay is a certain blindness to themselves. Moreover, for white *seeing for innocence* continues to engender the bad faith of a long-disgruntled minority. But the price blacks pay is an ever-escalating poverty that threatens to make the worst off of them a permanent underclass. Not fair, but real.

35      Challenging works best for the collective, while bargaining is more the individual's suit. From this point on, the race's advancement will come from the efforts of its individuals. True, some challenging will be necessary for a long time to come. But bargaining is now—today—a way for the black individual to *join* the larger society, to make a place for himself or herself.

36      "Innocence is ignorance," Kierkegaard says, and if this is so, the claim of innocence amounts to an insistence on ignorance, a refusal to know. In their assertions of innocence both races carve out very functional areas of ignorance for themselves—territories of blindness that license a misguided pursuit of power. Whites gain superiority by *not* knowing blacks; blacks gain entitlement by *not* seeing their own responsibility for bettering themselves. The power each race seeks in relation to the other is grounded in a double-edged ignorance, ignorance of the self as well as the other.

The original sin that brought us to an impasse at the dinner party I   37
mentioned at the outset occurred centuries ago, when it was first decided
to exploit racial difference as a means to power. It was the determinism
that flowed karmically from this sin that dropped over us like a net that
night. What bothered me most was our helplessness. Even the engineer
did not know how to go forward. His challenge hadn't worked, and he'd
lost the option to bargain. The marriage of race and power depersonalized
us, changed us from eight people to six whites and two blacks. The easi-
est thing was to let silence blanket our situation, our impasse.

I think the civil rights movement in its early and middle years of-   38
fered the best way out of America's racial impasse: in this society, race
must not be a source of advantage or disadvantage for anyone. This is
fundamentally a *moral* position, one that seeks to breach the corrupt
union of race and power with principles of fairness and human equality:
if all men are created equal, then racial difference cannot sanction power.
The civil rights movement was conceived for no other reason than to redress that corrupt union, and its guiding insight was that only a moral
power based on enduring principles of justice, equality, and freedom
could offset the lower impulse in man to exploit race as a means to
power. Three hundred years of suffering had driven the point home, and
in Montgomery, Little Rock, and Selma, racial power was the enemy and
moral power the weapon.

An important difference between genuine and presumed innocence,   39
I believe, is that the former must be earned through sacrifice, while the
latter is unearned and only veils the quest for privilege. And there was
much sacrifice in the early civil rights movement. The Gandhian principle of non-violent resistance that gave the movement a spiritual center
as well as a method of protest demanded sacrifice, a passive offering of
the self in the name of justice. A price was paid in terror and lost life, and
from this sacrifice came a hard-earned innocence and a credible moral
power.

Non-violent passive resistance is a bargainer's strategy. It assumes   40
the power that is the object of the protest has the genuine innocence to
morally respond, and puts the protesters at the mercy of that innocence.
I think this movement won so many concessions precisely because of its
belief in the capacity of whites to be moral. It did not so much demand
that whites change as offer them relentlessly the opportunity to live by
their own morality—to attain a true innocence based on the sacrifice of
their racial privilege, rather than a false innocence based on presumed
racial superiority. Blacks always bargain with or challenge the larger society; but I believe that in the early civil rights years, these forms of negotiation achieved a degree of integrity and genuineness never seen
before or since.

In the mid-'60s all this changed. Suddenly a sharp *racial* conscious-   41
ness emerged to compete with the moral consciousness that had defined
the movement to that point. Whites were no longer welcome in the

movement, and a vocal "black power" minority gained dramatic visibility. Increasingly, the movement began to seek racial as well as moral power, and thus it fell into a fundamental contradiction that plagues it to this day. Moral power precludes racial power by denouncing race as a means to power. Now suddenly the movement itself was using race as a means to power, and thereby affirming the very union of race and power it was born to redress. In the end, black power can claim no higher moral standing than white power.

42    It makes no sense to say this shouldn't have happened. The sacrifices that moral power demands are difficult to sustain, and it was inevitable that blacks would tire of these sacrifices and seek a more earthly power. Nevertheless, a loss of genuine innocence and moral power followed. The movement, splintered by a burst of racial militancy in the late '60s, lost its hold on the American conscience and descended more and more to the level of secular, interest-group politics. Bargaining and challenging once again became racial rather than moral negotiations.

43    You hear it asked, why are there no Martin Luther Kings around today? I think one reason is that there are no black leaders willing to resist the seductions of racial power, or to make the sacrifices moral power requires. King understood that racial power subverts moral power, and he pushed the principles of fairness and equality rather than black power because he believed those principles would bring blacks their most complete liberation. He sacrificed race for morality, and his innocence was made genuine by that sacrifice. What made King the most powerful and extraordinary black leader of this century was not his race but his morality.

44    Black power is a challenge. It grants whites no innocence; it denies their moral capacity and then demands that they be moral. No power can long insist on itself without evoking an opposing power. Doesn't an insistence on black power call up white power? (And could this have something to do with what many are now calling a resurgence of white racism?) I believe that what divided the races at the dinner party I attended, and what divides them in the nation, can only be bridged by an adherence to those moral principles that disallow race as a source of power, privilege, status, or entitlement of any kind. In our age, principles like fairness and equality are ill-defined and all but drowned in relativity. But this is the fault of people, not principles. We keep them muddled because they are the greatest threat to our presumed innocence and our selective ignorance. Moral principles, even when somewhat ambiguous, have the power to assign responsibility and therefore to provide us with knowledge. At the dinner party we were afraid of so severe an accountability.

45    What both black and white Americans fear are the sacrifices and risks that true racial harmony demands. This fear is the measure of our racial chasm. And though fear always seeks a thousand justifications, none is ever good enough, and the problems we run from only remain to haunt us. It would be right to suggest courage as an antidote to fear, but the glory of the word might only intimidate us into more fear. I prefer the

word effort—relentless effort, moral effort. What I like most about this word are its connotations of everydayness, earnestness, and practical sacrifice. No matter how badly it might have gone for us that warm summer night, we should have talked. We should have made the effort.

## CONSIDERATIONS

1. "It was one of those petty talents that is tied to vanity, and when there were ebbs in my self-esteem the impulse to use it would come alive again," writes Steele in paragraph 5. What petty talent is he talking about, and what other similar "talents" can you think of?

2. In paragraph 17, Steele writes, "I do not think that Ronald Reagan is a racist, as that term is commonly used, but neither do I think that he is capable of seeing color without making attributions, some of which may be negative—nor am I, or anyone else I've ever met." Read Brent Staples's short report of his experiences in "Just Walk On By," and decide whether or not he would agree with Steele.

3. In his lengthy discussion of the racial struggle for innocence, beginning with the first sentence of paragraph 11, how does Steele make use of two well-known but different black figures?

4. Essential to the later development of his analysis are Steele's ideas that "innocence is power" and that "seeing for innocence is the essence of racism." Put into your own words, perhaps in outline form, the steps by which he arrives at those ideas from paragraph 8 through paragraph 16.

5. How does Steele explain his belief that black power is "the enemy," but moral power is "the weapon" in the blacks' fight for equality?

6. To what extent does Steele employ comparison and contrast in organizing his materials?

7. How could Steele justify devoting his first three paragraphs to a dinner party?

*Wallace Stegner (1909–1993) was a novelist of the western United States and an essayist devoted to the natural world. He won the Pulitzer Prize for* Angle of Repose *(1971) and the National Book Award for* The Spectator Bird *(1976). In 1990 he published his* Collected Stories *and in 1992* Where the Blackbird Sings to the Lemonade Springs. *He lived in California, where he taught for many years at Stanford University.*

*Memoir may often find its source not in a life's most memorable events but in a life's commonplaces made memorable. See how Stegner can move from the mundane to the sublime. "The dump was our poetry and our history."*

— 85 —————————————————————————————————————

# WALLACE STEGNER
## *The Town Dump*

1    The town dump of Whitemud, Saskatchewan, could only have been a few years old when I knew it, for the village was born in 1913 and I left there in 1919. But I remember the dump better than I remember most things in that town, better than I remember most of the people. I spent more time with it, for one thing; it has more poetry and excitement in it than people did.

2    It lay in the southeast corner of town, in a section that was always full of adventure for me. Just there the Whitemud River left the hills, bent a little south, and started its long traverse across the prairie and international boundary to join the Milk. For all I knew, it might have been on its way to join the Alph: simply, before my eyes, it disappeared into strangeness and wonder.

3    Also, where it passed below the dumpground, it ran through willowed bottoms that were a favorite campsite for passing teamsters, gypsies, sometimes Indians. The very straw scattered around those camps, the ashes of those strangers' campfires, the manure of their teams and saddle horses, were hot with adventurous possibilities.

———————————

It was as an extension, a living suburb, as it were, of the dump-   4
ground that we most valued those camps. We scoured them for artifacts
of their migrant tenants as if they had been archaeological sites full of
the secrets of ancient civilizations. I remember toting around for weeks
the broken cheek strap of a bridle. Somehow or other its buckle looked as
if it had been fashioned in a far place, a place where they were accustomed to flatten the tongues of buckles for reasons that could only be exciting, and where they made a habit of plating the metal with some
valuable alloy, probably silver. In places where the silver was worn away
the buckle underneath shone dull yellow: probably gold.

It seemed that excitement liked that end of town better than our   5
end. Once old Mrs. Gustafson, deeply religious and a little raddled in the
head, went over there with a buckboard full of trash, and as she was driving home along the river she looked and saw a spent catfish, washed in
from Cypress Lake or some other part of the watershed, floating on the
yellow water. He was two feet long, his whiskers hung down, his fins
and tail were limp. He was a kind of fish that no one had seen in the
Whitemud in the three or four years of the town's life, and a kind that
none of us children had ever seen anywhere. Mrs. Gustafson had never
seen one like him either; she perceived at once that he was the devil, and
she whipped up the team and reported him at Hoffman's elevator.

We could hear her screeching as we legged it for the river to see for   6
ourselves. Sure enough, there he was. He looked very tired, and he made
no great effort to get away as we pushed out a half-sunken rowboat from
below the flume, submerged it under him, and brought him ashore.
When he died three days later we experimentally fed him to two half-
wild cats, but they seemed to suffer no ill effects.

At that same end of town the irrigation flume crossed the river. It   7
always seemed to me giddily high when I hung my chin over its plank
edge and looked down, but it probably walked no more than twenty feet
above the water on its spidery legs. Ordinarily in summer it carried
about six or eight inches of smooth water, and under the glassy hurrying
of the little boxed stream the planks were coated with deep sun-warmed
moss as slick as frogs' eggs. A boy could sit in the flume with the water
walling up against his back, and grab a cross brace above him, and pull,
shooting himself sledlike ahead until he could reach the next brace for
another pull and another slide, and so on across the river in four scoots.

After ten minutes in the flume he would come out wearing a dozen   8
or more limber black leeches, and could sit in the green shade where
darning needles flashed blue, and dragonflies hummed and darted and
stopped, and skaters dimpled slack and eddy with their delicate transitory footprints, and there stretch the leeches out one by one while their
sucking ends clung and clung, until at last, stretched far out, they let go
with a tiny wet *puk* and snapped together like rubber bands. The smell of
the river and the flume and the clay cutbanks and the bars of that part of
the river was the smell of wolf willow.

9    But nothing in that end of town was as good as the dumpground that scattered along a little runoff coulee dipping down toward the river from the south bench. Through a historical process that went back, probably, to the roots of community sanitation and distaste for eyesores, but that in law dated from the Unincorporated Towns Ordinance of the territorial government, passed in 1888, the dump was one of the very first community enterprises, almost our town's first institution.

10    More than that, it contained relics of every individual who had ever lived there, and of every phase of the town's history.

11    The bedsprings on which the town's first child was begotten might be there; the skeleton of a boy's pet colt; two or three volumes of Shakespeare bought in haste and error from a peddler, later loaned in carelessness, soaked with water and chemicals in a house fire, and finally thrown out to flap their stained eloquence in the prairie wind.

12    Broken dishes, rusty tinware, spoons that had been used to mix paint; once a box of percussion caps, sign and symbol of the carelessness that most of those people felt about all matters of personal or public safety. We put them on the railroad tracks and were anonymously denounced in the *Enterprise.* There were also old iron, old brass, for which we hunted assiduously, by night conning junkmen's catalogues and the pages of the *Enterprise* to find how much wartime value there might be in the geared insides of clocks or in a pound of tea lead[1] carefully wrapped in a ball whose weight astonished and delighted us. Sometimes the unimaginable outside world reached in and laid a finger on us. I recall that, aged no more than seven, I wrote a St. Louis junk house asking if they preferred their tea lead and tinfoil wrapped in balls, or whether they would rather have it pressed flat in sheets, and I got back a typewritten letter in a window envelope instructing me that they would be happy to have it in any way that was convenient for me. They added that they valued my business and were mine very truly. Dazed, I carried that windowed grandeur around in my pocket until I wore it out, and for months I saved the letter as a souvenir of the wondering time when something strange and distinguished had singled me out.

13    We hunted old bottles in the dump, bottles caked with dirt and filth, half buried, full of cobwebs, and we washed them out at the horse trough by the elevator, putting in a handful of shot along with the water to knock the dirt loose; and when we had shaken them until our arms were tired, we hauled them off in somebody's coaster wagon and turned them in at Bill Anderson's pool hall, where the smell of lemon pop was so sweet on the dark pool-hall air that I am sometimes awakened by it in the night, even yet.

14    Smashed wheels of wagons and buggies, tangles of rusty barbed wire, the collapsed perambulator that the French wife of one of the town's doctors had once pushed proudly up the planked sidewalks and

---

[1]A protective leadfoil used to line shipping boxes of tea.

along the ditchbank paths. A welter of foul-smelling feathers and coyote-scattered carrion which was all that remained of somebody's dream of a chicken ranch. The chickens had all got some mysterious pip at the same time, and died as one, and the dream lay out there with the rest of the town's history to rustle to the empty sky on the border of the hills.

There was melted glass in curious forms, and the half-melted office    15
safe left from the burning of Bill Day's Hotel. On very lucky days we might find a piece of the lead casing that had enclosed the wires of the town's first telephone system. The casing was just the right size for rings, and so soft that it could be whittled with a jackknife. It was a material that might have made artists of us. If we had been Indians of fifty years before, that bright soft metal would have enlisted our maximum patience and craft and come out as ring and metal and amulet inscribed with the symbols of our observed world. Perhaps there were too many ready-made alternatives in the local drug, hardware, and general stores; perhaps our feeble artistic response was a measure of the insufficiency of the challenge we felt. In any case I do not remember that we did any more with the metal than to shape it into crude seal rings with our initials or pierced hearts carved in them; and these, though they served a purpose in juvenile courtship, stopped something short of art.

The dump held very little wood, for in that country anything burn-    16
able got burned. But it had plenty of old iron, furniture, papers, mattresses that were the delight of field mice, and jugs and demijohns[2] that were sometimes their bane, for they crawled into the necks and drowned in the rain water or redeye[3] that was inside.

If the history of our town was not exactly written, it was at least    17
hinted, in the dump. I think I had a pretty sound notion even at eight or nine of how significant was that first institution of our forming Canadian civilization. For rummaging through its foul purlieus I had several times been surprised and shocked to find relics of my own life tossed out there to rot or blow away.

The volumes of Shakespeare belonged to a set that my father had    18
bought before I was born. It had been carried through successive moves from town to town in the Dakotas, and from Dakota to Seattle, and from Seattle to Bellingham, and Bellingham to Redmond, and from Redmond back to Iowa, and from there to Saskatchewan. Then, stained in a stranger's house fire, these volumes had suffered from a house-cleaning impulse and been thrown away for me to stumble upon in the dump. One of the Cratchet girls had borrowed them, a hatchet-faced, thin, eager, transplanted Cockney girl with a frenzy, almost a hysteria, for reading. And yet somehow, through her hands, they found the dump, to become a symbol of how much was lost, how much thrown aside, how much carelessly or of necessity given up, in the making of a new country.

---

[2]A large bottle with a short, narrow neck, usually encased in wicker-work.
[3]Strong, cheap whiskey.

We had so few books that I was familiar with them all, had handled them, looked at their pictures, perhaps even read them. They were the lares and penates,[4] part of the skimpy impedimenta of household gods we had brought with us into Latium. Finding those three thrown away was a little like finding my own name on a gravestone.

19     And yet not the blow that something else was, something that impressed me even more with the dump's close reflection of the town's intimate life. The colt whose picked skeleton lay out there was mine. He had been incurably crippled when dogs chased our mare, Daisy, the morning after she foaled. I had labored for months to make him well; had fed him by hand, curried him, exercised him, adjusted the iron braces that I had talked my father into having made. And I had not known that he would have to be destroyed. One weekend I turned him over to the foreman of one of the ranches, presumably so that he could be cared for. A few days later I found his skinned body, with the braces still on his crippled front legs, lying on the dump.

20     Not even that, I think, cured me of going there, though our parents all forbade us on pain of cholera or worse to do so. The place fascinated us, as it should have. For this was the kitchen midden of all of the civilization we knew; it gave us the most tantalizing glimpses into our lives as well as into those of the neighbors. It gave us an aesthetic distance from which to know ourselves.

21     The dump was our poetry and our history. We took it home with us by the wagonload, bringing back into town the things the town had used and thrown away. Some little part of what we gathered, mainly bottles, we managed to bring back to usefulness, but most of our gleanings we left lying around barn or attic or cellar until in some renewed fury of spring cleanup our families carted them off to the dump again, to be rescued and briefly treasured by some other boy with schemes for making them useful. Occasionally something we really valued with a passion was snatched from us in horror and returned at once. That happened to the mounted head of a white mountain goat, somebody's trophy from old times and the far Rocky Mountains, that I brought home one day in transports of delight. My mother took one look and discovered that his beard was full of moths.

22     I remember that goat; I regret him yet. Poetry is seldom useful, but always memorable. I think I learned more from the town dump than I learned from school: more about people, more about how life is lived, not elsewhere but here, not in other times but now. If I were a sociologist anxious to study in detail the life of any community, I would go very early to its refuse piles. For a community may be as well judged by what it throws away—what it has to throw away and what it chooses to—as by any other evidence. For whole civilizations we have sometimes no more of the poetry and little more of the history than this.

---

[4]The benevolent spirits and gods of a Roman household. After the Greek victory in the Trojan war, the Trojans settled in the Latium region of Italy.

## CONSIDERATIONS

1. In paragraph 1, Stegner says that the dump "has more poetry and excitement in it than people did." In the next paragraph, he refers to the river Alph, an imaginary, mysterious river that Samuel Taylor Coleridge invented for his poem "Kubla Khan":

> Where Alph, the sacred river ran
> To caverns measureless to man
> Down to a sunless sea.

If Stegner does not mean this kind of poetry, what kind does he mean? Do you think the people of Whitemud thought there was poetry and excitement and history in what they threw on the town dump?

2. Stegner makes the muddy Canadian prairie town and its dump colorful through his choice of words: "whipped up the team," "as we legged it," "I hung my chin over its plank edge," "with the water walling up against his back." Find other examples of Stegner's live diction. Try substituting words or phrases of your own choosing for Stegner's examples—one way to discover the many possibilities once one slows down enough actually to think about the words.

3. In your memories of your own hometown, was there a particular place—perhaps a school, church, park, or attic—that seemed to be a repository of the record of your childhood or family or town? Write a descriptive essay with what you find.

4. Notice the pivotal word "But" at the beginning of paragraph 9. What is pivotal about it? Look over an essay of your own to see if you have used the word that way and, if not, why not.

5. Stegner makes his point about the dump as the town's history by bringing to our eyes, ears, noses, and fingers, and even our taste, very concrete, physical things that turn out to be, in his terms, historical—the piece of lead casing, for example, in paragraph 15. Make a careful list of everything Stegner uses to appeal to our senses. Then give some thought to why those sensory appeals seem to be so important to so many first-rate writers.

6. Writing somewhat enviously in the *New York Times* about Stegner's town dump, Ann Farrar Scott, after describing her childhood in a modern housing tract, concludes: "There is not much poetry or history, it seems to me, in what we throw away these days." Make a quick survey of what is actually thrown away in your neighborhood, and then respond to Scott's remark in an essay as studded with particulars as Stegner's.

*Jonathan Swift (1667–1745), the author of* Gulliver's Travels, *was a priest, a poet, and a master of English prose. Some of his strongest satire took the form of reasonable defense of the unthinkable, like his argument in favor of abolishing Christianity in the British Isles. Born in Dublin, he was angry all his life at England's misuse and mistreatment of the subject Irish people. In 1729 he made this modest proposal for solving the Irish problem.*

## — 86 —

# JONATHAN SWIFT
## *A Modest Proposal*

### For Preventing the Children of Poor People in Ireland from Being a Burden to Their Parents or Country, and for Making Them Beneficial to the Public

1    It is a melancholy object to those who walk through this great town or travel in the country, when they see the streets, the roads, and cabin doors, crowded with beggars of the female sex, followed by three, four, or six children, all in rags and importuning every passenger for an alms. These mothers, instead of being able to work for their honest livelihood, are forced to employ all their time in strolling to beg sustenance for their helpless infants, who, as they grow up, either turn thieves for want of work, or leave their dear native country to fight for the Pretender in Spain, or sell themselves to the Barbadoes.

2    I think it is agreed by all parties that this prodigious number of children in the arms, or on the backs, or at the heels of their mothers and frequently of their fathers, is in the present deplorable state of the kingdom a very great additional grievance; and therefore whoever could find out a fair, cheap, and easy method of making these children sound useful members of the commonwealth would deserve so well of the public as to have his statue set up for a preserver of the nation.

3    But my intention is very far from being confined to provide only for the children of professed beggars; it is of a much greater extent, and shall take in the whole number of infants at a certain age who are born of parents in effect as little able to support them as those who demand our charity in the streets.

As to my own part, having turned my thoughts for many years upon this important subject, and maturely weighed the several schemes of other projectors, I have always found them grossly mistaken in their computation. It is true, a child just dropped from its dam may be supported by her milk for a solar year, with little other nourishment; at most not above the value of two shillings, which the mother may certainly get, or the value in scraps, by her lawful occupation of begging; and it is exactly at one year old that I propose to provide for them in such a manner as instead of being a charge upon their parents or the parish, or wanting food and raiment for the rest of their lives, they shall on the contrary contribute to the feeding, and partly to the clothing, of many thousands.

There is likewise another great advantage in my scheme, that it will prevent those voluntary abortions, and that horrid practice of women murdering their bastard children, alas, too frequent among us, sacrificing the poor innocent babes, I doubt, more to avoid the expense than the shame, which would move tears and pity in the most savage and inhuman breast.

The number of souls in this kingdom being usually reckoned one million and a half, of these I calculate there may be about two hundred thousand couples whose wives are breeders; from which number I subtract thirty thousand couples who are able to maintain their own children, although I apprehend there cannot be so many under the present distress of the kingdom; but this being granted, there will remain an hundred and seventy thousand breeders. I again subtract fifty thousand for those women who miscarry, or whose children die by accident or disease within the year. There only remain an hundred and twenty thousand children of poor parents actually born. The question therefore is, how this number shall be reared and provided for, which, as I have already said, under the present situation of affairs, is utterly impossible by all the methods hitherto proposed. For we can neither employ them in handicraft or agriculture; we neither build houses (I mean in the country) nor cultivate land. They can very seldom pick up a livelihood by stealing till they arrive at six years old, except where they are of towardly parts; although I confess they learn the rudiments much earlier, during which time they can however be looked upon only as probationers, as I have been informed by a principal gentleman in the country of Cavan, who protested to me that he never knew above one or two instances under the age of six, even in a part of the kingdom so renowned for the quickest proficiency in that art.

I am assured by our merchants that a boy or a girl before twelve years old is no salable commodity; and even when they come to this age they will not yield above three pounds, or three pounds and half a crown at most on the Exchange; which cannot turn to account either to the parents or the kingdom, the charge of nutriment and rags having been at least four times that value.

8    I shall now therefore humbly propose my own thoughts, which I hope will not be liable to the least objection.

9    I have been assured by a very knowing American of my acquaintance in London, that a young healthy child well nursed is at a year old a most delicious, nourishing, and wholesome food, whether stewed, roasted, baked, or boiled; and I make no doubt that it will equally serve in a fricassee or a ragout.

10    I do therefore humbly offer it to public consideration that of the hundred and twenty thousand children, already computed, twenty thousand may be reserved for breed, whereof only one fourth part to be males, which is more than we allow to sheep, black cattle, or swine; and my reason is that these children are seldom the fruits of marriage, a circumstance not much regarded by our savages, therefore one male will be sufficient to serve four females. That the remaining hundred thousand may at a year old be offered in sale to the persons of quality and fortune through the kingdom, always advising the mother to let them suck plentifully in the last month, so as to render them plump and fat for a good table. A child will make two dishes at an entertainment for friends; and when the family dines alone, the fore or hind quarter will make a reasonable dish, and seasoned with a little pepper or salt will be very good boiled on the fourth day, especially in the winter.

11    I have reckoned upon a medium that a child just born will weigh twelve pounds, and in a solar year if tolerably nursed increaseth to twenty-eight pounds.

12    I grant this food will be somewhat dear, and therefore very proper for landlords, who, as they have already devoured most of the parents, seem to have the best title to the children.

13    Infant's flesh will be in season throughout the year, but more plentiful in March, and a little before and after. For we are told by a grave author, an eminent French physician, that fish being a prolific diet, there are more children born in Roman Catholic countries about nine months after Lent than at any other season; therefore, reckoning a year after Lent, the markets will be more glutted than usual, because the number of popish infants is at least three to one in this kingdom; and therefore it will have one other collateral advantage, by lessening the number of Papists among us.

14    I have already computed the charge of nursing a beggar's child (in which list I reckon all cottagers, laborers, and four fifths of the farmers) to be about two shillings per annum, rags included; and I believe no gentleman would repine to give ten shillings for the carcass of a good fat child, which, as I have said, will make four dishes of excellent nutritive meat, when he hath only some particular friend or his own family to dine with him. Thus the squire will learn to be a good landlord, and grow popular among the tenants; the mother will have eight shillings net profit, and be fit for work till she produces another child.

Those who are more thrifty (as I must confess the times require)    15
may flay the carcass; the skin of which artificially dressed will make admirable gloves for ladies, and summer boots for fine gentlemen.

As to our city of Dublin, shambles may be appointed for this pur-    16
pose in the most convenient parts of it, and butchers we may be assured
will not be wanting; although I rather recommend buying the children
alive, and dressing them hot from the knife as we do roasting pigs.

A very worthy person, a true lover of his country, and whose virtues    17
I highly esteem, was lately pleased in discoursing on this matter to offer
a refinement upon my scheme. He said that many gentlemen of his kingdom, having of late destroyed their deer, he conceived that the want of
venison might be well supplied by the bodies of young lads and maidens,
not exceeding fourteen years of age nor under twelve, so great a number
of both sexes in every country being now ready to starve for want of
work and service; and these to be disposed of by their parents, if alive, or
otherwise by their nearest relations. But with due deference to so excellent a friend and so deserving a patriot, I cannot be altogether in his sentiments, for as to the males, my American acquaintance assured me from
frequent experience that their flesh was generally tough and lean, like
that of our schoolboys, by continual exercise, and their taste disagreeable; and to fatten them would not answer the charge. Then as to the females, it would, I think with humble submission, be a loss to the public,
because they soon would become breeders themselves: and besides, it is
not improbable that some scrupulous people might be apt to censure
such a practice (although indeed very unjustly) as a little bordering upon
cruelty; which, I confess, hath always been with me the strongest objection against any project, how well soever intended.

But in order to justify my friend, he confessed that this expedient    18
was put into his head by the famous Psalmanazar, a native of the island
Formosa, who came from thence to London above twenty years ago, and
in conversation told my friend that in his country when any young person happened to be put to death, the executioner sold the carcass to persons of quality as a prime dainty; and that in his time the body of a
plump girl of fifteen, who was crucified for an attempt to poison the emperor, was sold to his Imperial Majesty's prime minister of state, and
other great mandarins of the court, in joints from the gibbet, at four hundred crowns. Neither indeed can I deny that if the same use were made of
several plump young girls in this town, who without one single groat to
their fortunes cannot stir abroad without a chair, and appear at the play-
house and assemblies in foreign fineries which they never will pay for,
the kingdom would not be the worse.

Some persons of a desponding spirit are in great concern about that    19
vast number of poor people who are aged, diseased, or maimed, and I
have been desired to employ my thoughts what course may be taken to
ease the nation of so grievous an encumbrance. But I am not in the least

pain upon that matter, because it is very well known that they are every day dying and rotting by cold and famine, and filth and vermin, as fast as can be reasonably expected. And as to the younger laborers, they are now in almost as hopeful a condition. They cannot get work, and consequently pine away for want of nourishment to a degree that if at any time they are accidentally hired to common labor, they have not strength to perform it; and thus the country and themselves are happily delivered from the evils to come.

20    I have too long digressed, and therefore shall return to my subject. I think the advantages by the proposal which I have made are obvious and many, as well as of the highest importance.

21    For first, as I have already observed, it would greatly lessen the number of Papists, with whom we are yearly overrun, being the principal breeders of the nation as well as our most dangerous enemies; and who stay at home on purpose to deliver the kingdom to the Pretender, hoping to take their advantage by the absence of so many good Protestants, who have chosen rather to leave their country than to stay at home and pay tithes against their conscience to an Episcopal curate.

22    Secondly, the poorer tenants will have something valuable of their own, which by law may be made liable to distress, and help to pay their landlord's rent, their corn and cattle being already seized and money a thing unknown.

23    Thirdly, whereas the maintenance of an hundred thousand children, from two years old and upwards, cannot be computed at less than ten shillings a piece per annum, the nation's stock will be thereby increased fifty thousand pounds per annum, besides the profit of a new dish introduced to the tables of all gentlemen of fortune in the kingdom who have any refinement in taste. And the money will circulate among ourselves, the goods being entirely of our own growth and manufacture.

24    Fourthly, the constant breeders, besides the gain of eight shillings sterling per annum by the sale of their children, will be rid of the charge of maintaining them after the first year.

25    Fifthly, this food would likewise bring great custom to taverns, where the vintners will certainly be so prudent as to procure the best recipes for dressing it to perfection, and consequently have their houses frequented by all the fine gentlemen, who justly value themselves upon their knowledge in good eating; and a skillful cook, who understands how to oblige his guests, will contrive to make it as expensive as they please.

26    Sixthly, this would be a great inducement to marriage, which all wise nations have either encouraged by rewards or enforced by laws and penalties. It would increase the care and tenderness of mothers toward their children, when they were sure of a settlement for life to the poor babes, provided in some sort by the public, to their annual profit instead of expense. We should see an honest emulation among the married women, which of them could bring the fattest child to the market. Men

would become as fond of their wives during the time of their pregnancy as they are now of their mares in foal, their cows in calf, or sows when they are ready to farrow; nor offer to beat or kick them (as is too frequent a practice) for fear of a miscarriage.

Many other advantages might be enumerated. For instance, the addition of some thousand carcasses in our exportation of barreled beef, the propagation of swine's flesh, and improvements in the art of making good bacon, so much wanted among us by the great destruction of pigs, too frequent at our tables, which are no way comparable in taste or magnificence to a well-grown, fat, yearling child, which roasted whole will make a considerable figure at a lord mayor's feast or any other public entertainment. But this and many others I omit, being studious of brevity.

Supposing that one thousand families in this city would be constant customers for infants' flesh, besides others who might have it at merry meetings, particularly weddings and christenings, I compute that Dublin would take off annually about twenty thousand carcasses, and the rest of the kingdom (where probably they will be sold somewhat cheaper) the remaining eighty thousand.

I can think of no one objection that will possibly be raised against this proposal, unless it should be urged that the number of people will be thereby much lessened in the kingdom. This I freely own, and it was indeed one principal design in offering it to the world. I desire the reader will observe, that I calculate my remedy for this one individual kingdom of Ireland and for no other that ever was, is, or I think ever can be upon earth. Therefore let no man talk to me of other expedients: of taxing our absentees at five shillings a pound; of using neither clothes nor household furniture except what is of our own growth and manufacture; of utterly rejecting the materials and instruments that promote foreign luxury; of curing the expensiveness of pride, vanity, idleness, and gaming in our women; of introducing a vein of parsimony, prudence, and temperance; of learning to love our country, in the want of which we differ even from Laplanders and the inhabitants of Topinamboo; of quitting our animosities and factions, nor acting any longer like the Jews, who were murdering one another at the very moment their city was taken; of being a little cautious not to sell our country and conscience for nothing; of teaching landlords to have at least one degree of mercy toward their tenants; lastly, of putting a spirit of honesty, industry, and skill into our shopkeepers; who, if a resolution could now be taken to buy only our native goods, would immediately unite to cheat and exact upon us in the price, the measure, and the goodness, nor could ever yet be brought to make one fair proposal of just dealing, though often and earnestly invited to it.

Therefore, I repeat, let no man talk to me of these and the like expedients, till he hath at least some glimpse of hope that there will ever be some hearty and sincere attempt to put them in practice.

31      But as to myself, having been wearied out for many years with offering vain, idle, visionary thoughts, and at length utterly despairing of success, I fortunately fell upon this proposal, which, as it is wholly new, so it hath something solid and real, of no expense and little trouble, full in our own power, and whereby we can incur no danger in disobliging England. For this kind of commodity will not bear exportation, the flesh being of too tender a consistence to admit a long continuance in salt, although perhaps I could name a country which would be glad to eat up our whole nation without it.

32      After all, I am not so violently bent upon my own opinions as to reject any offer proposed by wise men, which shall be found equally innocent, cheap, easy, and effectual. But before something of that kind shall be advanced in contradiction to my scheme, and offering a better, I desire the author or authors will be pleased maturely to consider two points. First, as things now stand, how they will be able to find food and raiment for an hundred thousand useless mouths and backs. And secondly, there being a round million of creatures in human figure throughout this kingdom, whose sole subsistence put into a common stock would leave them in debt two millions of pounds sterling, adding those who are beggars by profession to the bulk of farmers, cottagers, and laborers, with their wives and children who are beggars in effect; I desire those politicians who dislike my overture, and may perhaps be so bold to attempt an answer, that they will first ask the parents of these mortals whether they would not at this day think it a great happiness to have been sold for food at a year old in this manner I prescribe, and thereby have avoided such a perpetual scene of misfortunes as they have since gone through by the oppression of landlords, the impossibility of paying rent without money or trade, the want of common sustenance, with neither house nor clothes to cover them from the inclemencies of the weather, and the most inevitable prospect of entailing the like or greater miseries upon their breed forever.

33      I profess, in the sincerity of my heart, that I have not the least personal interest in endeavoring to promote this necessary work, having no other motive than the public good of my country, by advancing our trade, providing for infants, relieving the poor, and giving some pleasure to the rich. I have no children by which I can propose to get a single penny; the youngest being nine years old, and my wife past childbearing.

## CONSIDERATIONS

1. The biggest risk a satirist runs is that the reader will be too literal-minded to understand that a work is meant as satire. Can you imagine a reader missing the satiric nature of Swift's "A Modest Proposal"? It has happened many times. What might such a

reader think of the author? Consider the same problem with regard to Ambrose Bierce, Nora Ephron, Mark Twain, Margaret Atwood, Rumer Godden, or James Thurber. Write a paragraph on satire as a double-edged sword.

2.  One way to understand the making of satire is to see it as an exercise in tone, that is, attitude. Swift's diction suggests the utter seriousness and earnestness of his proposal. The more thorough he is in this, the more horrified the reader will be. Make a list of several examples of that particular diction, for instance, in paragraph 6, calling the wives "breeders" rather than "mothers."

3.  Swift does not announce his proposal until paragraph 9. What is his strategy in waiting so long?

4.  At one point, Swift's technique changes in that he derides a list of measures that, in all seriousness, he actually proposes. Study how he does this, and try your hand at it in a short satire of your own.

5.  How, if at all, is Swift's satire relevant today? Explain, using specifics from his essay and from what you know about the world around you. Peter Marin's "Helping and Hating the Homeless" (page 404) might be of some help in this.

6.  How does Swift anticipate and attempt to avoid charges of conflict of interest? How does that serve his satirical purposes?

*Mary TallMountain (1918–1994) was born beside the Yukon River in Alaska, which she had to leave for the United States during the terminal illness of her mother. She was active in the discovery and publication of Native American literature. She lived for many years in San Francisco and visited her own Alaskan culture more in memory than in person. Later, she was able to return, even to teach poetry in her late years to children in Alaskan villages.*

*The Native American experience often requires journeys between two worlds, revisiting a lost world. Observe how Mary TallMountain uses the device of flashback, by means of a dream, to make distinct her sensations of return.*

## — 87 —

# MARY TALLMOUNTAIN
## *Outflight, An Essay*

1    Galena Air Service's little Red Baron bounces and dawdles along, the pilot intent on where to thrust through a fluff of cirrus clouds. Why don't we fly around the enormous cloud bank? No, we skim through the towering top. Drafts jerk us up, down, and around. Here in the body of the cloud, the arctic chill says we're in Alaska. The other four passengers, and I, and the pilot, shiver in our down jackets but it's not long before the bushplane is buzzing out into the blue.

2    Jagged peaks needle up like shards of brown glass. Beyond, we crane at endless fragments of another cloud as we float before Denali, that breathtaking mountain renamed McKinley a long time ago. Today her snow cap lies under veils; her sorrel-colored attendants, Brooks, Hunter, Foraker, Russell, a grandeur arrayed below her. Beneath their snow lines countless blackish-green spruce trees stream down the slopes. Scientists call these four mountains massifs, and they *are* massive. They compose most of the Alaska Range. We will cross the less formidable Kuskokwim Mountains and the yet smaller Kaiyuh Mountains, before we arrive at our destination, the subarctic bush.

I'm busy reliving another autumn day in 1978, when I had flown    3
this route over the inconceivably vast Interior on my way to my birthplace. That was the day I had returned for the first time to my roots in
the Yukon village of Nulato, after an absence of fifty years. We had found
fewer clouds than these, and a more intense clarity of the air. The mountains had lain breathing the light, and the valley had stretched to the
horizons; the autumn gold and bronze of its surface formed a rough pit-
ted pumpkin pie magnified to the nth power.

This afternoon in Anchorage I had boarded a six-passenger Nomad    4
out to the River. In the seat ahead, a tall slim half-blood Native woman
was reading. She called to her daughter, Minnie, a chubby child about
five, who was tossing and catching a pair of purple beaded earrings while
chattering indiscriminately to the pilot, her mother, her puppy, and two
snoring young Indian men. She wore scrubbed cord coveralls and a sunflower yellow sweatshirt. Her hair was a sooty horsetail, eyes gleaming
blackberries. Crawling across my lap to look out the narrow windows of
the plane, she was the epitome of knees and elbows and energy. She was
delightfully huggable, I learned during one of her lap-crossings.

The two young Indians had no problems sleeping, but Minnie's    5
puppy couldn't even doze. She set up a tiny dirge. Bushplanes aren't always well insulated, winds bellow and engines roar; and sometimes the
plane does a jig in sudden, unexpected drafts. Minnie made faces and
clapped her palms over her ears, but it didn't help, so she consoled the
puppy with a wrestling match. This pup wasn't your real Alaska male-
mute, but she was the most cunning pup I'd ever met. She was the color
of a birch leaf in fall. A pale champagne-colored X lay across her shoulders, long flirty eyelashes the same color batted back and forth, and her
ears drooped like empty silk gloves. Minnie called her Sheba. When I
told Minnie how pretty Sheba was, my admiration encouraged Minnie's
mother to introduce herself as Vernita. She had come in on Alaska Air
from a visit to Seattle; our bush pilot was Garth; and the two snoozing
young Indians had been on R&R in Anchorage. I learned further that the
salmon runs were about over; it had been a real good year for dog salmon
and not so good for king. Blueberries, Vernita said, were falling off the
bushes; she had put three gallons in the freezer. Her husband had told her
on the phone he had shot his first moose of the season, and Vernita
sighed with a certain pride, saying her hands would be full for a week
skinning out, cutting up, and freezing that big moose. She thought it
would be an early winter this year. Something had told her, in the way
the balsam leaves were turning.

Garth remarked, "We're a hundred miles south of the Arctic    6
Circle," undoubtedly wanting to enlighten me, the newcomer the
Natives called *Cheechacko*.* We crossed the pale violet Kaiyuh Moun-
tains, site of our people's hunting grounds, I was informed, long kept a

---

*Cheechacko: Newcomer

deep religious secret from other bands of Indians along the River. The Yukon was visible now, a silver corkscrew lying in the folds of the enormous marsh country. Already the air was darkened by flocks of geese, flurrying and rising to take the southbound Pacific flyway, high above us and to the east. I felt the plane merely inched along in the immensity of space as we crossed the last lap of the central plain, but Garth remarked that the light played tricks. Ahead, the Yukon unfurled in a coil of river and creeks like ribbons of fallen sky. Garth showed me some islands the River had created by dropped silt in a huge flood a few years back. He pointed down to the curve of a marsh. "See the moose?" he asked.

7    I said, "I can't see it at all, it's just a dot!"

8    Vernita chuckled, but Garth got me off the hook, "He's just a dot from here. Down there, he's bigger than a piano."

9    Then I had rested back in my seat. It had been my first bushplane trip, and after four hours I was tired. Minnie and Sheba had curled up in her seat and were asleep. Looking at them, I thought I had been only as small as Minnie when I had left Alaska. How little I had known then, how little I had learned since, about this wild sweeping country of my birth. For a moment I regretted the years lost, but lulled by the vast river and sky, I felt safe and slept.

10    Now, an air pocket jolts into my half-dream. This isn't the Nomad! But what plane is it? Where are Minnie and Sheba? Why, of course, I realize, I've been dreaming about my first flight to the Yukon, seven years ago. This is 1985, and I'm in the Red Baron, and it's hovering. We're getting ready to set down at Nulato; I can see the shining galvanized iron roofs of the village. The pilot is apparently new to this run; with minute care he is studying wind drafts, always tricky here around the great up-jutting bulk of Cemetery Hill. There! He's got it. He swings the Baron sharply out over the River and back in a grand wheel, and we dip slow over the hill. It is capped with clusters of white-painted picket fences, sheltering the graves of one of the famous Alaskan cemeteries. The pickets gleam like white baubles in the afternoon sun, slanting above the silty red-grey River. We hiccup to a stop on the gravelly tarmac.

11    There's Cousin Andrew, outside. I see he has children with him. Maybe they are some of the young Koyukon Athabascans I've come to read my poetry for. Now I feel that I'm really home. The pilot jumps out, and for an instant we passengers crowd together in the narrow aisle, hearing the babble of welcoming voices. Then we step down into the sudden quiet of the gold aspens bending like sentinels toward us.

## CONSIDERATIONS

1. More than one famous writer—Thomas Wolfe comes to mind—has said, "You can't go home again." In what sense is Mary TallMountain trying to do this? Two other

writers in your text also look back thoughtfully—Patricia Hampl, "Holding Old Negatives Up to the Light" (page 276) and E. B. White, "Once More to the Lake" (page 668). If you have made—or even thought of making—such a backward journey in time, what were some of the difficulties and some of the pleasures? Is going home again merely a matter of finding the old address?

2. What purpose—or purposes—do you think the author had in mind in devoting so much space to the other passengers of the little plane?

3. "The Yukon was visible now, a silver corkscrew. . . . Ahead, the Yukon unfurled in a coil of river and creek like ribbons of fallen sky." Look for other examples of TallMountain's expert use of figures of speech. Compare them with some of the phrases in John Haines's "Death Is a Meadowlark" (page 260). Study how they are made; then experiment with some of your own invention in a short description of some prominent feature of your home landscape.

4. What *doesn't* TallMountain do that you might expect her to do in this account of her flight home? What does she gain by avoiding the expected?

*Amy Tan (b. 1952) was born in California, attended high school in Switzerland, and went to college in Oregon. While she worked writing computer manuals, she was inspired by the interlocking stories of Louise Erdrich (see page 206) to write her first novel,* The Joy Luck Club *(1989).*

*"Mother Tongue" concerns multiple heritages—the condition of so many Americans now—by examination of language. Amy Tan is bilingual within the same language. Maybe all of us learn to speak or write different languages, to different degrees and for different reasons.*

— 88 —

# AMY TAN
## *Mother Tongue*

1    I am not a scholar of English or literature. I cannot give you much more than personal opinions on the English language and its variations in this country or others.

2    I am a writer. And by that definition, I am someone who has always loved language. I am fascinated by language in daily life. I spend a great deal of my time thinking about the power of language—the way it can evoke an emotion, a visual image, a complex idea, or a simple truth. Language is the tool of my trade. And I use them all—all the Englishes I grew up with.

3    Recently, I was made keenly aware of the different Englishes I do use. I was giving a talk to a large group of people, the same talk I had already given to half a dozen other groups. The nature of the talk was about my writing, my life, and my book, *The Joy Luck Club.* The talk was going along well enough, until I remembered one major difference that made the whole talk sound wrong. My mother was in the room. And it was perhaps the first time she had heard me give a lengthy speech, using the kind of English I have never used with her. I was saying things like "The intersection of memory upon imagination" and "There is an aspect of my fiction that relates to thus-and-thus"—a speech filled with

carefully wrought grammatical phrases, burdened, it suddenly seemed to me, with nominalized forms, past perfect tenses, conditional phrases, all the forms of standard English that I had learned in school and through books, the forms of English I did not use at home with my mother.

Just last week, I was walking down the street with my mother, and     4
I again found myself conscious of the English I was using, the English I do use with her. We were talking about the price of new and used furniture and I heard myself saying this: "Not waste money that way." My husband was with us as well, and he didn't notice any switch in my English. And then I realized why. It's because over the twenty years we've been together I've often used that same kind of English with him, and sometimes he even uses it with me. It has become our language of intimacy, a different sort of English that relates to family talk, the language I grew up with.

So you'll have some idea of what this family talk I heard sounds     5
like, I'll quote what my mother said during a recent conversation which I videotaped and then transcribed. During this conversation, my mother was talking about a political gangster in Shanghai who had the same last name as her family's, Du, and how the gangster in his early years wanted to be adopted by her family, which was rich by comparison. Later, the gangster became more powerful, far richer than my mother's family, and one day showed up at my mother's wedding to pay his respects. Here's what she said in part:

"Du Yusong having business like fruit stand. Like off the street     6
kind. He is Du like Du Zong—but not Tsung-ming Island people. The local people call putong, the river east side, he belong to that side local people. That man want to ask Du Zong father take him in like become own family. Du Zong father wasn't look down on him, but didn't take seriously, until that man big like become a mafia. Now important person, very hard to inviting him. Chinese way, came only to show respect, don't stay for dinner. Respect for making big celebration, he shows up. Mean gives lots of respect. Chinese custom. Chinese social life that way. If too important won't have to stay too long. He come to my wedding. I didn't see, I heard it. I gone to boy's side, they have YMCA dinner. Chinese age I was nineteen."

You should know that my mother's expressive command of English     7
belies how much she actually understands. She reads the *Forbes* report, listens to *Wall Street Week*, converses daily with her stockbroker, reads all of Shirley MacLaine's books with ease—all kinds of things I can't begin to understand. Yet some of my friends tell me they understand 50 percent of what my mother says. Some say they understand 80 to 90 percent. Some say they understand none of it, as if she were speaking pure Chinese. But to me, my mother's English is perfectly clear, perfectly natural. It's my mother tongue. Her language, as I hear it, is vivid, direct, full of observation and imagery. That was the language that helped shape the way I saw things, expressed things, made sense of the world.

8        Lately, I've been giving more thought to the kind of English my mother speaks. Like others, I have described it to people as "broken" or "fractured" English. But I wince when I say that. It has always bothered me that I can think of no other way to describe it other than "broken," as if it were damaged and needed to be fixed, as if it lacked a certain wholeness and soundness. I've heard other terms used, "limited English," for example. But they seem just as bad, as if everything is limited, including people's perceptions of the limited English speaker.

9        I know this for a fact, because when I was growing up, my mother's "limited" English limited *my* perception of her. I was ashamed of her English. I believed that her English reflected the quality of what she had to say. That is, because she expressed them imperfectly her thoughts were imperfect. And I had plenty of empirical evidence to support me: the fact that people in department stores, at banks, and at restaurants did not take her seriously, did not give her good service, pretended not to understand her, or even acted as if they did not hear her.

10       My mother has long realized the limitations of her English as well. When I was fifteen, she used to have me call people on the phone to pretend I was she. In this guise, I was forced to ask for information or even to complain and yell at people who had been rude to her. One time it was a call to her stockbroker in New York. She had cashed out her small portfolio and it just so happened we were going to go to New York the next week, our very first trip outside California. I had to get on the phone and say in an adolescent voice that was not very convincing, "This is Mrs. Tan."

11       And my mother was standing in the back whispering loudly, "Why he don't send me check, already two weeks late. So mad he lie to me, losing me money."

12       And then I said in perfect English, "Yes, I'm getting rather concerned. You had agreed to send the check two weeks ago, but it hasn't arrived."

13       Then she began to talk more loudly. "What he want, I come to New York tell him front of his boss, you cheating me?" And I was trying to calm her down, make her be quiet, while telling the stockbroker, "I can't tolerate any more excuses. If I don't receive the check immediately, I am going to have to speak to your manager when I'm in New York next week." And sure enough, the following week there we were in front of this astonished stockbroker, and I was sitting there red-faced and quiet, and my mother, the real Mrs. Tan, was shouting at his boss in her impeccable broken English.

14       We used a similar routine just five days ago, for a situation that was far less humorous. My mother had gone to the hospital for an appointment, to find out about a benign brain tumor a CAT scan had revealed a month ago. She said she had spoken very good English, her best English, no mistakes. Still, she said, the hospital did not apologize when they said they had lost the CAT scan and she had come for nothing. She said they did not seem to have any sympathy when she told them she was anxious to know the exact diagnosis, since her husband and son had both died of

brain tumors. She said they would not give her any more information until the next time and she would have to make another appointment for that. So she said she would not leave until the doctor called her daughter. She wouldn't budge. And when the doctor finally called her daughter, me, who spoke in perfect English—lo and behold—we had assurances the CAT scan would be found, promises that a conference call on Monday would be held, and apologies for any suffering my mother had gone through for a most regrettable mistake.

I think my mother's English almost had an effect on limiting my possibilities in life as well. Sociologists and linguists probably will tell you that a person's developing language skills are more influenced by peers. But I do think that the language spoken in the family, especially in immigrant families which are more insular, plays a large role in shaping the language of the child. And I believe that it affected my results on achievement tests, IQ tests, and the SAT. While my English skills were never judged as poor, compared to math, English could not be considered my strong suit. In grade school I did moderately well, getting perhaps B's, sometimes B-pluses, in English and scoring perhaps in the sixtieth or seventieth percentile on achievement tests. But those scores were not good enough to override the opinion that my true abilities lay in math and science, because in those areas I achieved A's and scored in the ninetieth percentile or higher.   15

This was understandable. Math is precise; there is only one correct answer. Whereas, for me at least, the answers on English tests were always a judgment call, a matter of opinion and personal experience. Those tests were constructed around items like fill-in-the-blank sentence completion, such as "Even though Tom was ___, Mary thought he was ___." And the correct answer always seemed to be the most bland combinations of thoughts, for example, "Even though Tom was shy, Mary thought he was charming," with the grammatical structure "even though" limiting the correct answer to some sort of semantic opposites, so you wouldn't get answers like, "Even though Tom was foolish, Mary thought he was ridiculous." Well, according to my mother, there were very few limitations as to what Tom could have been and what Mary might have thought of him. So I never did well on tests like that.   16

The same was true with word analogies, pairs of words in which you were supposed to find some sort of logical, semantic relationship—for example, "*Sunset* is to *nightfall* as ___ is to ___." And here you would be presented with a list of four possible pairs, one of which showed the same kind of relationship: *red* is to *stoplight, bus* is to *arrival, chills* is to *fever, yawn* is to *boring*. Well, I could never think that way. I knew what the tests were asking, but I could not block out of my mind the images already created by the first pair, "*sunset* is to *nightfall*"—and I would see a burst of colors against a darkening sky, the moon rising, the lowering of a curtain of stars. And all the other pairs of words—red, bus, stoplight, boring—just threw up a mass of confusing   17 images, making it impossible for me to sort out something as logical as saying: "A sunset precedes nightfall" is the same as "a chill precedes a fever." The only way I would have gotten that answer right would have been to imagine an associative situation, for example, my being disobedient and staying out past sunset, catching a chill at night, which turns into feverish pneumonia as punishment, which indeed did happen to me.

18       I have been thinking about all this lately, about my mother's English, about achievement tests. Because lately I've been asked, as a writer, why there are not more Asian Americans represented in American literature. Why are there few Asian Americans enrolled in creative writing programs? Why do so many Chinese students go into engineering? Well, these are broad sociological questions I can't begin to answer. But I have noticed in surveys—in fact, just last week—that Asian students, as a whole, always do significantly better on math achievement tests than in English. And this makes me think that there are other Asian-American students whose English spoken in the home might also be described as "broken" or "limited." And perhaps they also have teachers who are steering them away from writing and into math and science, which is what happened to me.

19       Fortunately, I happen to be rebellious in nature and enjoy the challenge of disproving assumptions made about me. I became an English major my first year in college, after being enrolled as pre-med. I started writing nonfiction as a freelancer the week after I was told by my former boss that writing was my worst skill and I should hone my talents toward account management.

20       But it wasn't until 1985 that I finally began to write fiction. And at first I wrote using what I thought to be wittily crafted sentences, sentences that would finally prove I had mastery over the English language. Here's an example from the first draft of a story that later made its way into *The Joy Luck Club,* but without this line: "That was my mental quandary in its nascent state." A terrible line, which I can barely pronounce.

21       Fortunately, for reasons I won't get into today, I later decided I should envision a reader for the stories I would write. And the reader I decided upon was my mother, because these were stories about mothers. So with this reader in mind—and in fact she did read my early drafts—I began to write stories using all the Englishes I grew up with: the English I spoke to my mother, which for lack of a better term might be described as "simple"; the English she used with me, which for lack of a better term might be described as "broken"; my translation of her Chinese, which could certainly be described as "watered down"; and what I imagined to be her translation of her Chinese if she could speak in perfect English, her internal language, and for that I sought to preserve the essence, but neither an English nor a Chinese structure. I wanted to capture what language ability tests can never reveal: her intent, her passion, her imagery, the rhythms of her speech, and the nature of her thoughts.

Apart from what any critic had to say about my writing, I knew I 22 had succeeded where it counted when my mother finished reading my book and gave me her verdict: "So easy to read."

## CONSIDERATIONS

1. Amy Tan begins her essay on language by telling of "all the Englishes I grew up with" and then demonstrates two of them in paragraphs 3 and 6. How many Englishes do you know? Where and how and why do you shift from one to another? Is one "better" than another? If so, what are your criteria?

2. In paragraphs 10 through 14, Tan gives us additional demonstrations of her "mother tongue." What is her purpose in this, and how might you benefit from that as a writer?

3. Conventionally, in Great Britain it was (and to some extent still is) the spoken language that instantly categorized a person as "lower class" (undesirable) or "upper class" (desirable). Are you aware of, or guilty of, or have you been the victim of anything like that in your society? Explain in a short essay.

4. "I wanted to capture what language ability tests can never reveal . . . her intent . . . her passion . . . her imagery . . . her rhythms . . . and the nature of her thoughts," writes Tan toward the end of her essay. Are all those elements as difficult to capture or measure as she says? Why are some of them impossible?

5. Have you ever been ashamed of your own use of English or of another's? Why or why not? If you have, how did you get over it? Or did you?

*Poet Elizabeth Bishop, perfectly feminist, refused to be printed in anthologies of women's poetry, wanting to be regarded as a poet, not as a subdivision of poet. Someone has suggested that all adjectives are diminutives. Who wants to be known as a painter of southwestern Arkansas when one might be known as a painter? But in the essays of* A Writer's Reader, *subjects* do not *matter, as long as the essays remain excellent. We do a cluster of Amy Tan's essays not only because she writes so well but also because she writes out of our increasing American multiculturalism. This essay exemplifies the reasons for its inclusion.*

## —— 89 ——

# AMY TAN
## *In the Canon, For All the Wrong Reasons*

1      Several years ago I learned that I had passed a new literary milestone. I had made it to the Halls of Education under the rubric of "Multicultural Literature," also known in many schools as "Required Reading."

2      Thanks to this development, I now meet students who proudly tell me they're doing their essays, term papers, or master's theses on me. By that they mean that they are analyzing not just my books but me—my grade-school achievements, youthful indiscretions, marital status, as well as the movies I watched as a child, the slings and arrows I suffered as a minority, and so forth—all of which, with the hindsight of classroom literary investigation, prove to contain many Chinese omens that made it inevitable that I would become a writer.

3      Once I read a master's thesis on feminist writings, which included examples from *The Joy Luck Club.* The student noted that I had often used the number four, something on the order of thirty-two or thirty-six times—in any case, a number divisible by four. She pointed out that there were four mothers, four daughters, four sections of the book, four stories per section. Furthermore, there were four sides to a mah jong table, four directions of the wind, four players. More important, she pos-

tulated, my use of the number four was a symbol for the four stages of psychological development, which corresponded in uncanny ways to the four stages of some type of Buddhist philosophy I had never heard of before. The student recalled that the story contained a character called Fourth Wife, symbolizing death, and a four-year-old girl with a feisty spirit, symbolizing regeneration.

In short, her literary sleuthing went on to reveal a mystical and   4
rather Byzantine puzzle, which, once explained, proved to be completely brilliant and precisely logical. She wrote me a letter and asked if her analysis had been correct. How I longed to say "absolutely."

The truth is, if there are symbols in my work they exist largely by   5
accident or through someone else's interpretive design. If I wrote of "an orange moon rising on a dark night," I would more likely ask myself later if the image was a cliché, not whether it was a symbol for the feminine force rising in anger, as one master's thesis postulated. To plant symbols like that, you need a plan, good organizational skills, and a prescient understanding of the story you are about to write. Sadly, I lack those traits.

All this is by way of saying that I don't claim my use of the number   6
four to be a brilliant symbolic device. In fact, now that it's been pointed out to me in rather astonishing ways, I consider my overuse of the number to be a flaw.

Reviewers and students have enlightened me about not only how I   7
write but why I write. Apparently, I am driven to capture the immigrant experience, to demystify Chinese culture, to point out the differences between Chinese and American culture, even to pave the way for other Asian American writers.

If only I were that noble. Contrary to what is assumed by some stu-   8
dents, reporters, and community organizations wishing to bestow honors on me, I am not an expert on China, Chinese culture, mah jong, the psychology of mothers and daughters, generation gaps, immigration, illegal aliens, assimilation, acculturation, racial tension, Tiananmen Square, the Most Favored Nation trade agreements, human rights, Pacific Rim economics, the purported one million missing baby girls of China, the future of Hong Kong after 1997, or, I am sorry to say, Chinese cooking. Certainly I have personal opinions on many of these topics, but by no means do my sentiments and my world of make-believe make me an expert.

So I am alarmed when reviewers and educators assume that my   9
very personal, specific, and fictional stories are meant to be representative down to the nth detail not just of Chinese Americans but, sometimes, of all Asian culture. Is Jane Smiley's *A Thousand Acres* supposed to be taken as representative of all of American culture? If so, in what ways? Are all American fathers tyrannical? Do all American sisters betray one another? Are all American conscientious objectors flaky in love relationships?

10    Over the years my editor has received hundreds of permissions requests from publishers of college textbooks and multicultural anthologies, all of them wishing to reprint my work for "educational purposes."
One publisher wanted to include an excerpt from *The Joy Luck Club,* a
scene in which a Chinese woman invites her non-Chinese boyfriend to
her parents' house for dinner. The boyfriend brings a bottle of wine as a
gift and commits a number of social gaffes at the dinner table. Students
were supposed to read this excerpt, then answer the following question:
"If you are invited to a Chinese family's house for dinner, should you
bring a bottle of wine?"

11    In many respects, I am proud to be on the reading lists for courses
such as Ethnic Studies, Asian American Studies, Asian American
Literature, Asian American History, Women's Literature, Feminist
Studies, Feminist Writers of Color, and so forth. What writer wouldn't
want her work to be read? I also take a certain perverse glee in imagining
countless students, sleepless at three in the morning, trying to read *The
Joy Luck Club* for the next day's midterm. Yet I'm also not altogether
comfortable about my book's status as required reading.

12    Let me relate a conversation I had with a professor at a school in
southern California. He told me he uses my books in his literature class
but he makes it a point to lambast those passages that depict China as
backward or unattractive. He objects to any descriptions that have to do
with spitting, filth, poverty, or superstitions. I asked him if China in the
1930s and 1940s was free of these elements. He said, No, such descriptions are true; but he still believes it is "the obligation of the writer of
ethnic literature to create positive, progressive images."

13    I secretly shuddered and thought, Oh well, that's southern
California for you. But then, a short time later, I met a student from UC
Berkeley, a school that I myself attended. The student was standing in
line at a book signing. When his turn came, he swaggered up to me, then
took two steps back and said in a loud voice, "Don't you think you have
a responsibility to write about Chinese men as positive role models?"

14    In the past, I've tried to ignore the potshots. A *Washington Post* reporter once asked me what I thought of another Asian American writer
calling me something on the order of "a running dog whore sucking on
the tit of the imperialist white pigs."

15    "Well," I said, "you can't please everyone, can you?" I pointed out
that readers are free to interpret a book as they please, and that they are
free to appreciate or not appreciate the result. Besides, reacting to your
critics makes a writer look defensive, petulant, and like an all-around
bad sport.

16    But lately I've started thinking it's wrong to take such a laissez-faire
attitude. Lately I've come to think that I must say something, not so
much to defend myself and my work but to express my hopes for

American literature, for what it has the potential to become in the twenty-first century—that is, a truly American literature, democratic in the way it includes many colorful voices.

Until recently, I didn't think it was important for writers to express their private intentions in order for their work to be appreciated; I believed that any analysis of my intentions belonged behind the closed doors of literature classes. But I've come to realize that the study of literature does have its effect on how books are being read, and thus on what might be read, published, and written in the future. For that reason, I do believe writers today must talk about their intentions—if for no other reason than to serve as an antidote to what others say our intentions should be.

For the record, I don't write to dig a hole and fill it with symbols. I don't write stories as ethnic themes. I don't write to represent life in general. And I certainly don't write because I have answers. If I knew everything there is to know about mothers and daughters, Chinese and Americans, I wouldn't have any stories left to imagine. If I had to write about only positive role models, I wouldn't have enough imagination left to finish the first story. If I knew what to do about immigration, I would be a sociologist or a politician and not a long-winded storyteller.

So why do I write?

Because my childhood disturbed me, pained me, made me ask foolish questions. And the questions still echo. Why does my mother always talk about killing herself? Why did my father and brother have to die? If I die, can I be reborn into a happy family? Those early obsessions led to a belief that writing could be my salvation, providing me with the sort of freedom and danger, satisfaction and discomfort, truth and contradiction I can't find in anything else in life.

I write to discover the past for myself. I don't write to change the future for others. And if others are moved by my work—if they love their mothers more, scold their daughters less, or divorce their husbands who were not positive role models—I'm often surprised, usually grateful to hear from kind readers. But I don't take either credit or blame for changing their lives for better or for worse.

Writing, for me, is an act of faith, a hope that I will discover what I mean by "truth." I also think of reading as an act of faith, a hope that I will discover something remarkable about ordinary life, about myself. And if the writer and the reader discover the same thing, if they have that connection, the act of faith has resulted in an act of magic. To me, that's the mystery and the wonder of both life and fiction—the connection between two individuals who discover in the end that they are more the same than they are different.

And if that doesn't happen, it's nobody's fault. There are still plenty of other books on the shelf. Choose what you like.

## CONSIDERATIONS

1. What is the difference in the tone of Amy Tan's writing between the opening paragraphs and the rest of her essay? What does she do that results in a particular tone?

2. Study the second sentence of paragraph 8, which occupies all but the first and last lines of the paragraph. How would you describe Tan's reasons for such an uncommonly long series? Read it aloud before you answer the question.

3. Tan's comment on the way she writes—"I don't write to dig a hole and fill it with symbols"—is reminiscent of a story told by another talented writer, Mary McCarthy, about a student who reported that she had finished her story except for putting in the symbols. Read a little in a literary handbook about the nature of symbols to help you understand why symbols are not some decorative thing just dropped into a story or poem, but are part and parcel of the story and grow out of it. Read Ernest Hemingway's short story "Hills Like White Elephants" (page 292), and write about your decision that the landscape does or does not develop symbolic weight in that story.

4. In paragraph 20, Tan says she came to believe that writing provided her with a sort of freedom. Is that the same kind of freedom William Stafford talks about in the last paragraph of "A Way of Writing" (page 529)? Discuss in a short expository essay.

5. How do you think Amy Tan would respond to the idea that writers describing minority characters should avoid any negative aspect of those characters? Shelby Steele, in "I'm Black, You're White, Who's Innocent?" (page 539), has something to say on this subject. And what is your opinion?

*This story comes from* The Joy Luck Club *(1989). Notice how it reveals the sources of the author's thinking, and development, by a narrative in which the speaker alters without announcing alteration.*

# — 90

# AMY TAN
## *Two Kinds*

My mother believed you could be anything you wanted to be in 1 America. You could open a restaurant. You could work for the government and get good retirement. You could buy a house with almost no money down. You could become rich. You could become instantly famous.

"Of course you can be prodigy, too," my mother told me when I was 2 nine. "You can be best anything. What does Auntie Lindo know? Her daughter, she is only best tricky."

America was where all my mother's hopes lay. She had come here in 3 1949 after losing everything in China: her mother and father, her family home, her first husband, and two daughters, twin baby girls. But she never looked back with regret. There were so many ways for things to get better.

We didn't immediately pick the right kind of prodigy. At first my 4 mother thought I could be a Chinese Shirley Temple. We'd watch Shirley's old movies on TV as though they were training films. My mother would poke my arm and say, *"Ni kan"*—You watch. And I would see Shirley tapping her feet, or singing a sailor song, or pursing her lips in a very round O while saying, "Oh my goodness."

*"Ni kan,"* said my mother as Shirley's eyes flooded with tears. "You 5 already know how. Don't need talent for crying!"

Soon after my mother got this idea about Shirley Temple, she took me 6 to a beauty training school in the Mission district and put me in the hands of a student who could barely hold the scissors without shaking. Instead of getting big fat curls, I emerged with an uneven mass of crinkly black fuzz. My mother dragged me off to the bathroom and tried to wet down my hair.

7    "You look like Negro Chinese," she lamented, as if I had done this on purpose.

8    The instructor of the beauty training school had to lop off these soggy clumps to make my hair even again. "Peter Pan is very popular these days," the instructor assured my mother. I now had hair the length of a boy's, with straight-across bangs that hung at a slant two inches above my eyebrows. I liked the haircut and it made me actually look forward to my future fame.

9    If fact, in the beginning, I was just as excited as my mother, maybe even more so. I pictured this prodigy part of me as many different images, trying each one on for size. I was a dainty ballerina girl standing by the curtains, waiting to hear the right music that would send me floating on my tiptoes. I was like the Christ child lifted out of the straw manger, crying with holy indignity. I was Cinderella stepping from her pumpkin carriage with sparkly cartoon music filling the air.

10    In all of my imaginings, I was filled with a sense that I would soon become *perfect.* My mother and father would adore me. I would be beyond reproach. I would never feel the need to sulk for anything.

11    But sometimes the prodigy in me became impatient. "If you don't hurry up and get me out of here, I'm disappearing for good," it warned. "And then you'll always be nothing."

12    Every night after dinner, my mother and I would sit at the Formica kitchen table. She would present new tests, taking her examples from stories of amazing children she had read in *Ripley's Believe It or Not,* or *Good Housekeeping, Reader's Digest,* and a dozen other magazines she kept in a pile in our bathroom. My mother got these magazines from people whose houses she cleaned. And since she cleaned many houses each week, we had a great assortment. She would look through them all, searching for stories about remarkable children.

13    The first night she brought out a story about a three-year-old boy who knew the capitals of all the states and even most of the European countries. A teacher was quoted as saying the little boy could also pronounce the names of the foreign cities correctly.

14    "What's the capital of Finland?" my mother asked me, looking at the magazine story.

15    All I knew was the capital of California, because Sacramento was the name of the street we lived on in Chinatown. "Nairobi!" I guessed, saying the most foreign word I could think of. She checked to see if that was possibly one way to pronounce "Helsinki" before showing me the answer.

16    The tests got harder—multiplying numbers in my head, finding the queen of hearts in a deck of cards, trying to stand on my head without using my hands, predicting the daily temperatures in Los Angeles, New York, and London.

One night I had to look at a page from the Bible for three minutes     17
and then report everything I could remember. "Now Jehoshaphat had
riches and honor in abundance and . . . that's all I remember, Ma," I said.

And after seeing my mother's disappointed face once again, some-     18
thing inside of me began to die. I hated the tests, the raised hopes and
failed expectations. Before going to bed that night, I looked in the mirror
above the bathroom sink and when I saw only my face staring back—and
that it would always be this ordinary face—I began to cry. Such a sad,
ugly girl! I made high-pitched noises like a crazed animal, trying to
scratch out the face in the mirror.

And then I saw what seemed to be the prodigy side of me—because     19
I had never seen that face before. I looked at my reflection, blinking so I
could see more clearly. The girl staring back at me was angry, powerful.
This girl and I were the same. I had new thoughts, willful thoughts, or
rather thoughts filled with lots of won'ts. I won't let her change me, I
promised myself. I won't be what I'm not.

So now on nights when my mother presented her tests, I performed     20
listlessly, my head propped on one arm. I pretended to be bored. And I
was. I got so bored I started counting the bellows of the foghorns out on
the bay while my mother drilled me in other areas. The sound was comforting and reminded me of the cow jumping over the moon. And the
next day, I played a game with myself, seeing if my mother would give
up on me before eight bellows. After a while I usually counted only
one, maybe two bellows at most. At last she was beginning to give up
hope.

Two or three months had gone by without any mention of my be-     21
ing a prodigy again. And then one day my mother was watching *The Ed
Sullivan Show* on TV. The TV was old and the sound kept shorting out.
Every time my mother got halfway up from the sofa to adjust the set,
the sound would go back on and Ed would be there talking. As soon as
she sat down, Ed would go silent again. She got up, the TV broke into
loud piano music. She sat down. Silence. Up and down, back and forth,
quiet and loud. It was like a stiff embraceless dance between her and
the TV set. Finally she stood by the set with her hand on the sound
dial.

She seemed to be entranced by the music, a little frenzied piano     22
piece with this mesmerizing quality, sort of quick passages and then
teasing lilting ones before it returned to the quick playful parts.

"*Ni kan,*" my mother said, calling me over with hurried hand ges-     23
tures, "Look here."

I could see why my mother was fascinated by the music. It was be-     24
ing pounded out by a little Chinese girl, about nine years old, with a
Peter Pan haircut. The girl had the sauciness of a Shirley Temple. She
was proudly modest like a proper Chinese child. And she also did this

fancy sweep of a curtsy, so that the fluffy skirt of her white dress cascaded slowly to the floor like the petals of a large carnation.

25    In spite of these warning signs, I wasn't worried. Our family had no piano and we couldn't afford to buy one, let alone reams of sheet music and piano lessons. So I could be generous in my comments when my mother bad-mouthed the little girl on TV.

26    "Play note right, but doesn't sound good! No singing sound," complained my mother.

27    "What are you picking on her for?" I said carelessly. "She's pretty good. Maybe she's not the best, but she's trying hard." I knew almost immediately I would be sorry I said that.

28    "Just like you," she said. "Not the best. Because you not trying." She gave a little huff as she let go of the sound dial and sat down on the sofa.

29    The little Chinese girl sat down also to play an encore of "Anitra's Dance" by Grieg. I remember the song, because later on I had to learn how to play it.

30    Three days after watching *The Ed Sullivan Show*, my mother told me what my schedule would be for piano lessons and piano practice. She had talked to Mr. Chong, who lived on the first floor of our apartment building. Mr. Chong was a retired piano teacher and my mother traded house-cleaning services for weekly lessons and a piano for me to practice on every day, two hours a day, from four until six.

31    When my mother told me this, I felt as though I had been sent to hell. I whined and then kicked my foot a little when I couldn't stand it anymore.

32    "Why don't you like me the way I am? I'm *not* a genius! I can't play the piano. And even if I could, I wouldn't go on TV if you paid me a million dollars!" I cried.

33    My mother slapped me. "Who ask you to be genius?" she shouted. "Only ask you to be your best. For your sake. You think I want you to be genius? Hnnh! What for! Who ask you!"

34    "So ungrateful," I heard her mutter in Chinese. "If she had as much talent as she has temper, she would be famous now."

35    Mr. Chong, whom I secretly nicknamed Old Chong, was very strange, always tapping his fingers to the silent music of an invisible orchestra. He looked ancient in my eyes. He had lost most of the hair on top of his head and he wore thick glasses and had eyes that always looked tired and sleepy. But he must have been younger than I thought, since he lived with his mother and was not yet married.

36    I met old lady Chong once and that was enough. She had this peculiar smell like a baby that had done something in its pants. And her fingers felt like a dead person's, like an old peach I once found in the back of the refrigerator, the skin just slid off the meat when I picked it up.

I soon found out why Old Chong had retired from teaching piano. 37
He was deaf. "Like Beethoven!" he shouted to me. "We're both listening
only in our head!" And he would start to conduct his frantic silent
sonatas.

Our lessons went like this. He would open the book and point to 38
different things, explaining their purpose: "Key! Treble! Bass! No sharps
or flats! So this is C major! Listen now and play after me!"

And then he would play the C scale a few times, a simple chord, 39
and then, as if inspired by an old, unreachable itch, he gradually added
more notes and running trills and a pounding bass until the music was
really something quite grand.

I would play after him, the simple scale, the simple chord, and then 40
I just played some nonsense that sounded like a cat running up and down
on top of garbage cans. Old Chong smiled and applauded and then said,
"Very good! But now you must learn to keep time!"

So that's how I discovered that Old Chong's eyes were too slow to 41
keep up with the wrong notes I was playing. He went through the motions in half-time. To help me keep rhythm, he stood behind me, pushing
down on my right shoulder for every beat. He balanced pennies on top of
my wrists so I would keep them still as I slowly played scales and arpeg-
gios. He had me curve my hand around an apple and keep that shape
when playing chords. He marched stiffly to show me how to make each
finger dance up and down, staccato like an obedient little soldier.

He taught me all these things, and that was how I also learned I 42
could be lazy and get away with mistakes, lots of mistakes. If I hit the
wrong notes because I hadn't practiced enough, I never corrected myself.
I just kept playing in rhythm. And Old Chong kept conducting his own
private reverie.

So maybe I never really gave myself a fair chance. I did pick up the 43
basics pretty quickly, and I might have become a good pianist at that
young age. But I was so determined not to try, not to be anybody different
that I learned to play only the most ear-splitting preludes, the most dis-
cordant hymns.

Over the next year, I practiced like this, dutifully in my own way. 44
And then one day I heard my mother and her friend Lindo Jong both talking in a loud bragging tone of voice so others could hear. It was after
church, and I was leaning against the brick wall wearing a dress with stiff
white petticoats. Auntie Lindo's daughter, Waverly, who was about my
age, was standing farther down the wall about five feet away. We had
grown up together and shared all the closeness of two sisters squabbling
over crayons and dolls. In other words, for the most part, we hated each
other. I thought she was snotty. Waverly Jong had gained a certain
amount of fame as "Chinatown's Littlest Chinese Chess Champion."

"She bring home too many trophy," lamented Auntie Lindo that 45
Sunday. "All day she play chess. All day I have no time do nothing but

dust off her winnings." She threw a scolding look at Waverly, who pretended not to see her.

46      "You lucky you don't have this problem," said Auntie Lindo with a sigh to my mother.

47      And my mother squared her shoulders and bragged: "Our problem worser than yours. If we ask Jing-mei wash dish, she hear nothing but music. It's like you can't stop this natural talent."

48      And right then, I was determined to put a stop to her foolish pride.

49      A few weeks later, Old Chong and my mother conspired to have me play in a talent show which would be held in the church hall. By then, my parents had saved up enough to buy me a secondhand piano, a black Wurlitzer spinet with a scarred bench. It was the showpiece of our living room.

50      For the talent show, I was to play a piece called "Pleading Child" from Schumann's *Scenes from Childhood*. It was a simple, moody piece that sounded more difficult than it was. I was supposed to memorize the whole thing, playing the repeat parts twice to make the piece sound longer. But I dawdled over it, playing a few bars and then cheating, looking up to see what notes followed. I never really listened to what I was playing. I daydreamed about being somewhere else, about being someone else.

51      The part I liked to practice best was the fancy curtsy: right foot out, touch the rose on the carpet with a pointed foot, sweep to the side, left leg bends, look up and smile.

52      My parents invited all the couples from the Joy Luck Club to witness my debut. Auntie Lindo and Uncle Tin were there. Waverly and her two older brothers had also come. The first two rows were filled with children both younger and older than I was. The littlest ones got to go first. They recited simple nursery rhymes, squawked out tunes on miniature violins, twirled Hula Hoops, pranced in pink ballet tutus, and when they bowed or curtsied, the audience would sigh in unison, "Awww," and then clap enthusiastically.

53      When my turn came, I was very confident. I remember my childish excitement. It was as if I knew, without a doubt, that the prodigy side of me really did exist. I had no fear whatsoever, no nervousness. I remember thinking to myself, This is it! This is it! I looked out over the audience, at my mother's blank face, my father's yawn, Auntie Lindo's stiff-lipped smile, Waverly's sulky expression. I had on a white dress layered with sheets of lace, and a pink bow in my Peter Pan haircut. As I sat down I envisioned people jumping to their feet and Ed Sullivan rushing up to introduce me to everyone on TV.

54      And I started to play. It was so beautiful. I was so caught up in how lovely I looked that at first I didn't worry how I would sound. So it was a surprise to me when I hit the first wrong note and I realized something didn't sound quite right. And then I hit another and another followed that. A chill started at the top of my head and began to trickle down. Yet

I couldn't stop playing, as though my hands were bewitched. I kept thinking my fingers would adjust themselves back, like a train switching to the right track. I played this strange jumble through two repeats, the sour notes staying with me all the way to the end.

When I stood up, I discovered my legs were shaking. Maybe I had    55
just been nervous and the audience, like Old Chong, had seen me go through the right motions and had not heard anything wrong at all. I swept my right foot out, went down on my knee, looked up and smiled. The room was quiet, except for Old Chong, who was beaming and shouting "Bravo! Bravo! Well done!" But then I saw my mother's face, her stricken face. The audience clapped weakly, and as I walked back to my chair, with my whole face quivering as I tried not to cry, I heard a little boy whisper loudly to his mother, "That was awful," and the mother whispered back, "Well, she certainly tried."

And now I realized how many people were in the audience, the    56
whole world it seemed. I was aware of eyes burning into my back. I felt the shame of my mother and father as they sat stiffly throughout the rest of the show.

We could have escaped during the intermission. Pride and some    57
strange sense of honor must have anchored my parents to their chairs. And so we watched it all: the eighteen-year-old boy with a fake mustache who did a magic show and juggled flaming hoops while riding a unicycle. The breasted girl with white makeup who sang from *Madama Butterfly* and got honorable mention. And the eleven-year-old boy who won first prize playing a tricky violin song that sounded like a busy bee.

After the show, the Hsus, the Jongs, and the St. Clairs from the Joy    58
Luck Club came up to my mother and father.

"Lots of talented kids," Auntie Lindo said vaguely, smiling broadly.    59

"That was somethin' else," said my father, and I wondered if he was    60
referring to me in a humorous way, or whether he even remembered what I had done.

Waverly looked at me and shrugged her shoulders. "You aren't a ge-    61
nius like me," she said matter-of-factly. And if I hadn't felt so bad, I would have pulled her braids and punched her stomach.

But my mother's expression was what devastated me: a quiet, blank    62
look that said she had lost everything. I felt the same way, and it seemed as if everybody were now coming up, like gawkers at the scene of an accident, to see what parts were actually missing. When we got on the bus to go home, my father was humming the busy-bee tune and my mother was silent. I kept thinking she wanted to wait until we got home before shouting at me. But when my father unlocked the door to our apartment, my mother walked in and then went to the back, into the bedroom. No accusations. No blame. And in a way, I felt disappointed. I had been waiting for her to start shouting, so I could shout back and cry and blame her for all my misery.

63   I assumed my talent-show fiasco meant I never had to play the piano again. But two days later, after school, my mother came out of the kitchen and saw me watching TV.

64   "Four clock," she reminded me as if it were any other day. I was stunned, as though she were asking me to go through the talent-show torture again. I wedged myself more tightly in front of the TV.

65   "Turn off TV," she called from the kitchen five minutes later.

66   I didn't budge. And then I decided. I didn't have to do what my mother said anymore. I wasn't her slave. This wasn't China. I had listened to her before and look what happened. She was the stupid one.

67   She came out from the kitchen and stood in the arched entryway of the living room. "Four clock," she said once again, louder.

68   "I'm not going to play anymore," I said nonchalantly. "Why should I? I'm not a genius."

69   She walked over and stood in front of the TV. I saw her chest was heaving up and down in an angry way.

70   "No!" I said, and I now felt stronger, as if my true self had finally emerged. So this was what had been inside me all along.

71   "No! I won't!" I screamed.

72   She yanked me by the arm, pulled me off the floor, snapped off the TV. She was frighteningly strong, half pulling, half carrying me toward the piano as I kicked the throw rugs under my feet. She lifted me up and onto the hard bench. I was sobbing by now, looking at her bitterly. Her chest was heaving even more and her mouth was open, smiling crazily as if she were pleased I was crying.

73   "You want me to be someone that I'm not!" I sobbed. "I'll never be the kind of daughter you want me to be!"

74   "Only two kinds of daughters," she shouted in Chinese. "Those who are obedient and those who follow their own mind! Only one kind of daughter can live in this house! Obedient daughter!"

75   "Then I wish I wasn't your daughter. I wish you weren't my mother," I shouted. As I said these things I got scared. It felt like worms and toads and slimy things crawling out of my chest, but it also felt good, as if this awful side of me had surfaced, at last.

76   "Too late change this," said my mother shrilly.

77   And I could sense her anger rising to its breaking point. I wanted to see it spill over. And that's when I remembered the babies she had lost in China, the ones we never talked about. "Then I wish I'd never been born!" I shouted. "I wish I were dead! Like them."

78   It was as if I had said the magic words. Alakazam!—and her face went blank, her mouth closed, her arms went slack, and she backed out of the room, stunned, as if she were blowing away like a small brown leaf, thin, brittle, lifeless.

79   It was not the only disappointment my mother felt in me. In the years that followed, I failed her so many times, each time asserting my

own will, my right to fall short of expectations. I didn't get straight As. I didn't become class president. I didn't get into Stanford. I dropped out of college.

For unlike my mother, I did not believe I could be anything I 80 wanted to be. I could only be me.

And for all those years, we never talked about the disaster at the 81 recital or my terrible accusations afterward at the piano bench. All that remained unchecked, like a betrayal that was now unspeakable. So I never found a way to ask her why she had hoped for something so large that failure was inevitable.

And even worse, I never asked her what frightened me the most: 82 Why had she given up hope?

For after our struggle at the piano, she never mentioned my playing 83 again. The lessons stopped. The lid to the piano was closed, shutting out the dust, my misery, and her dreams.

So she surprised me. A few years ago, she offered to give me the pi- 84 ano, for my thirtieth birthday. I had not played in all those years. I saw the offer as a sign of forgiveness, a tremendous burden removed.

"Are you sure?" I asked shyly. "I mean, won't you and Dad miss it?" 85

"No, this your piano," she said firmly. "Always your piano. You 86 only one can play."

"Well, I probably can't play anymore," I said. "It's been years." 87

"You pick up fast," said my mother, as if she knew this was certain. 88 "You have natural talent. You could been genius if you want to."

"No I couldn't." 89

"You just not trying," said my mother. And she was neither angry 90 nor sad. She said it as if to announce a fact that could never be disproved. "Take it," she said.

But I didn't at first. It was enough that she had offered it to me. And 91 after that, every time I saw it in my parents' living room, standing in front of the bay windows, it made me feel proud, as if it were a shiny trophy I had won back.

Last week I sent a tuner over to my parents' apartment and had the 92 piano reconditioned, for purely sentimental reasons. My mother had died a few months before and I had been getting things in order for my father, a little bit at a time. I put the jewelry in special silk pouches. The sweaters she had knitted in yellow, pink, bright orange—all the colors I hated—I put those in moth-proof boxes. I found some old Chinese silk dresses, the kind with the little slits up the sides. I rubbed the old silk against my skin, then wrapped them in tissue and decided to take them home with me.

After I had the piano tuned, I opened the lid and touched the keys. It 93 sounded even richer than I imagined. Really, it was a very good piano. Inside the bench were the same exercise notes with handwritten scales, the same secondhand books with their covers held together with yellow tape.

94     I opened up the Schumann book to the dark little piece I had played at the recital. It was on the left-hand side of the page, "Pleading Child." It looked more difficult than I remembered. I played a few bars, surprised at how easily the notes came back to me.

95     And for the first time, or so it seemed, I noticed the piece on the right-hand side. It was called "Perfectly Contented." I tried to play this one as well. It had a lighter melody but the same flowing rhythm and turned out to be quite easy. "Pleading Child" was shorter but slower; "Perfectly Contented" was longer, but faster. And after I played them both a few times, I realized they were two halves of the same song.

## CONSIDERATIONS

1. After reading Amy Tan's story of two kinds of daughters, read Lillian Hellman's "Runaway" (page 285), about another girl who decided to be herself, and Langston Hughes's "Salvation" (page 321), about a boy who could not resist the pressure to be like everyone else. Then, by drawing on all three accounts and your own experience, write an argumentative essay on children and conformity.

2. With the exception of a few similes, Tan writes in a very literal style in this story. What effect does that plainness have on your response to what she is saying? Compare Tan's style with that of a writer like Jean Hegland, whose "The Fourth Month" (page 282) is rich with figures of speech. Make a few notes on how both pieces affect you; then write a short essay on your response to the two styles.

3. In "Two Kinds," the mother and daughter move both away from and toward each other in what might be called a kind of dance. Using the dance motif, describe a similarly variable relationship you have observed or experienced.

4. In Amy Tan's accompanying essay, "In the Canon, For All the Wrong Reasons," she talks chiefly about writing fiction. Is "Two Kinds" a work of fiction or nonfiction? How can you tell—or can you? What criteria might you use to make such a distinction? Are those criteria foolproof?

*Lewis Thomas (1913–1993) was a medical doctor, teacher, and writer, born in New York, where he became president of Memorial Sloan-Kettering Cancer Center. Earlier, he taught medicine at the University of Minnesota, was department chairman and dean at New York University-Bellevue, and was a dean at Yale Medical School.* The Lives of a Cell *won a National Book Award in 1975, and he wrote many subsequent books, including* The Fragile Species *(1992).* The New England Journal of Medicine *originally printed the articles collected in that volume, articles that at the same time make contributions to medicine and literature.*

*His scientific mind, like the best minds in whatever field, extended itself by language to investigate everything human, and to speculate beyond the human. This essay comes from* The Lives of a Cell.

— 91 —————————————————————————————

# LEWIS THOMAS
## *Ceti*

—————————————————————————————————

Tau Ceti is a relatively nearby star that sufficiently resembles our 1 sun to make its solar system a plausible candidate for the existence of life. We are, it appears, ready to begin getting in touch with Ceti, and with any other interested celestial body in more remote places, out to the edge. CETI is also, by intention, the acronym of the First International Conference on Communication with Extraterrestrial Intelligence, held in 1972 in Soviet Armenia under the joint sponsorship of the National Academy of Sciences of the United States and the Soviet Academy, which involved eminent physicists and astronomers from various countries, most of whom are convinced that the odds for the existence of life elsewhere are very high, with a reasonable probability that there are civilizations, one place or another, with technologic mastery matching or exceeding ours.

On this assumption, the conferees thought it likely that radio- 2 astronomy would be the generally accepted mode of interstellar communication, on grounds of speed and economy. They made a formal recommendation that we organize an international cooperative program, with new and immense radio telescopes, to probe the reaches of deep space for electromagnetic signals making sense. Eventually, we would plan to send out messages on our own and receive answers, but at the outset it seems more practical to begin by catching snatches of conversation between others.

3      So, the highest of all our complex technologies in the hardest of our sciences will soon be engaged, full scale, in what is essentially biologic research—and with some aspects of social science, at that.

4      The earth has become, just in the last decade, too small a place. We have the feeling of being confined—shut in; it is something like outgrowing a small town in a small county. The views of the dark, pocked surface of Mars, still lifeless to judge from the latest photographs, do not seem to have extended our reach; instead, they bring closer, too close, another unsatisfactory feature of our local environment. The blue noonday sky, cloudless, has lost its old look of immensity. The word is out that the sky is not limitless; it is finite. It is, in truth, only a kind of local roof, a membrane under which we live, luminous but confusingly refractile when suffused with sunlight; we can sense its concave surface a few miles over our heads. We know that it is tough and thick enough so that when hard objects strike it from the outside they burst into flames. The color photographs of the earth are more amazing than anything outside: we live inside a blue chamber, a bubble of air blown by ourselves. The other sky beyond, absolutely black and appalling, is wide-open country, irresistible for exploration.

5      Here we go, then. An extraterrestrial embryologist, having a close look at us from time to time, would probably conclude that the morphogenesis of the earth is coming along well, with the beginnings of a nervous system and fair-sized ganglions in the form of cities, and now with specialized, dish-shaped sensory organs, miles across, ready to receive stimuli. He may well wonder, however, how we will go about responding. We are evolving into the situation of a Skinner pigeon in a Skinner box, peering about in all directions, trying to make connections, probing.

6      When the first word comes in from outer space, finally, we will probably be used to the idea. We can already provide a quite good explanation for the origin of life, here or elsewhere. Given a moist planet with methane, formaldehyde, ammonia, and some usable minerals, all of which abound, exposed to lightning or ultraviolet irradiation at the right temperature, life might start off almost anywhere. The tricky, unsolved thing is how to get the polymers to arrange in membranes and invent replication. The rest is clear going. If they follow our protocol, it will be anaerobic life at first, then photosynthesis and the first exhalation of oxygen, then respiring life and the great burst of variation, then speciation, and, finally, some kind of consciousness. It is easy, in the telling.

I suspect that when we have recovered from the first easy acceptance of signs of life from elsewhere, and finished nodding at each other, and finished smiling, we will be in shock. We have had it our way, relatively speaking, being unique all these years, and it will be hard to deal with the thought that the whole, infinitely huge, spinning, clocklike apparatus around us is itself animate, and can sprout life whenever the conditions are right. We will respond, beyond doubt, by making connections after the fashion of established life, floating out our filaments, extending pili, but we will end up feeling smaller than ever, as small as a single cell, with a quite new sense of continuity. It will take some getting used to.

The immediate problem, however, is a much more practical, down-to-earth matter, and must be giving insomnia to the CETI participants. Let us assume that there is, indeed, sentient life in one or another part of remote space, and that we will be successful in getting in touch with it. What on earth are we going to talk about? If, as seems likely, it is a hundred or more light years away, there are going to be some very long pauses. The barest amenities, on which we rely for opening conversations—Hello, are you there?, from us, followed by Yes, hello, from them—will take two hundred years at least. By the time we have our party we may have forgotten what we had in mind.

We could begin by gambling on the rightness of our technology and just send out news of ourselves, like a mimeographed Christmas letter, but we would have to choose our items carefully, with durability of meaning in mind. Whatever information we provide must still make sense to us two centuries later, and must still seem important, or the conversation will be an embarrassment to all concerned. In two hundred years it is, as we have found, easy to lose the thread.

Perhaps the safest thing to do at the outset, if technology permits, is to send music. This language may be the best we have for explaining what we are like to others in space, with least ambiguity. I would vote for Bach, all of Bach, streamed out into space, over and over again. We would be bragging, of course, but it is surely excusable for us to put the best possible face on at the beginning of such an acquaintance. We can tell the harder truths later. And, to do ourselves justice, music would give a fairer picture of what we are really like than some of the other things we might be sending, like *Time*, say, or a history of the U.N. or Presidential speeches. We could send out our science, of course, but just think of the wincing at this end when the polite comments arrive two hundred years from now. Whatever we offer as today's items of liveliest interest are bound to be out of date and irrelevant, maybe even ridiculous. I think we should stick to music.

Perhaps, if the technology can be adapted to it, we should send some paintings. Nothing would better describe what this place is like, to an outsider, than the Cézanne demonstrations that an apple is really part fruit, part earth.

12    What kinds of questions should we ask? The choices will be hard, and everyone will want his special question first. What are your smallest particles? Did you think yourselves unique? Do you have colds? Have you anything quicker than light? Do you always tell the truth? Do you cry? There is no end to the list.

13    Perhaps we should wait a while, until we are sure we know what we want to know, before we get down to detailed questions. After all, the main question will be the opener: Hello, are you there? If the reply should turn out to be Yes, hello, we might want to stop there and think about that, for quite a long time.

## CONSIDERATIONS

1. If you were to decide on our first communication with life in outer space, what message would you send? Why?

2. Why must people working on interplanetary communication keep time in mind?

3. Thomas skillfully uses figurative language to help us see what he is talking about. Consider, for example, his description of our sky in paragraph 4. Try, in writing your own paragraph of description of the sky, by day or by night, to make it memorable.

4. Point out some stylistic features in Thomas's essay that account for the highly informal, even jaunty tone.

5. Thomas touches on the shock we will feel when we have proof that mankind is not, after all, unique. What does he mean by saying "we will end up feeling smaller than ever, as small as a single cell, with quite a new sense of continuity"?

6. How might conservationists like David Quammen, "So What?" (page 511), or Wendell Berry, "A Native Hill" (page 42), respond to Thomas's prediction in paragraph 7 that we will be in shock because "we have had it our way . . . being unique all these years"? Is that at all related to our conventional insistence on placing humankind at the peak of evolutionary development?

7. Discuss the role played by assumptions in an attempted communication. You might use as a starting point one of the following innocent-sounding questions:

Will you be home tonight?
How much is that doggy in the window?
Did you ever see such a gorgeous day?
Why did you vote for Senator Blowhard?
Was this paper turned in late?

*Henry David Thoreau (1817–1862) is one of the greatest American writers, and* Walden *one of the great American books. Thoreau attended Concord Academy, in the Massachusetts town where he was born and lived. Then he went to Harvard and completed his formal education, which was extensive in mathematics, literature, Greek, Latin, and French—and included smatterings of Spanish and Italian and some of the literature of India and China. He and his brother founded a school that lasted four years, and then he was a private tutor to a family. He also worked for his father, manufacturing pencils. But mostly Thoreau walked, meditated, observed nature, and wrote.*

*A friend of Ralph Waldo Emerson's, Thoreau was influenced by the older man, and by Transcendentalism—a doctrine that recognized the unity of man and nature. For Thoreau, an idea required testing by life itself; it never remained merely mental. In his daily work on his journals, and in the books he carved from them—*A Week on the Concord and Merrimack Rivers *(1849) as well as* Walden *(1854)—he observed the detail of daily life, human and natural, and he speculated on the universal laws he could derive from this observation.*

*"To know it by experience, and be able to give a true account of it"—these words could be carved on Thoreau's gravestone. "To give a true account" he became a great writer, a master of observation.*

*"Civil Disobedience" began as a lecture; it has become one of the most influential essays ever written, promulgating ideas of nonviolent resistance to injustice. Leo Tolstoy and Mahatma Ghandi cited Thoreau as a mentor. Thoreau went to prison when he refused to pay a poll tax because of his opposition to the Mexican War.*

— **92** —

# HENRY DAVID THOREAU
## *Civil Disobedience*

I heartily accept the motto, "That government is best which governs least"; and I should like to see it acted up to more rapidly and systematically. Carried out, it finally amounts to this, which also I

1

believe—"That government is best which governs not at all"; and when men are prepared for it, that will be the kind of government which they will have. Government is at best but an expedient; but most governments are usually, and all governments are sometimes, inexpedient. The objections which have been brought against a standing army, and they are many and weighty, and deserve to prevail, may also at last be brought against a standing government. The standing army is only an arm of the standing government. The government itself, which is only the mode which the people have chosen to execute their will, is equally liable to be abused and perverted before the people can act through it. Witness the present Mexican war, the work of comparatively a few individuals using the standing government as their tool; for, in the outset, the people would not have consented to this measure.

2      This American government—what is it but a tradition, though a recent one, endeavoring to transmit itself unimpaired to posterity, but each instant losing some of its integrity? It has not the vitality and force of a single living man; for a single man can bend it to his will. It is a sort of wooden gun to the people themselves. But it is not the less necessary for this; for the people must have some complicated machinery or other, and hear its din, to satisfy that idea of government which they have. Governments show thus how successfully men can be imposed on, even impose on themselves, for their own advantage. It is excellent, we must all allow. Yet this government never of itself furthered any enterprise, but by the alacrity with which it got out of its way. *It* does not keep the country free. *It* does not settle the West. *It* does not educate. The character inherent in the American people has done all that has been accomplished; and it would have done somewhat more, if the government had not sometimes got in its way. For government is an expedient by which men would fain succeed in letting one another alone; and, as has been said, when it is most expedient, the governed are most let alone by it. Trade and commerce, if they were not made of india-rubber, would never manage to bounce over the obstacles which legislators are continually putting in their way; and, if one were to judge these men wholly by the effects of their actions and not partly by their intentions, they would deserve to be classed and punished with those mischievous persons who put obstructions on the railroads.

3      But, to speak practically and as a citizen, unlike those who call themselves no-government men, I ask for, not at once no government, but *at once* a better government. Let every man make known what kind of government would command his respect, and that will be one step toward obtaining it.

4      After all, the practical reason why, when the power is once in the hands of the people, a majority are permitted, and for a long period continue, to rule is not because they are most likely to be in the right, nor because this seems fairest to the minority, but because they are physically the strongest. But a government in which the majority rule in all

cases cannot be based on justice, even as far as men understand it. Can there not be a government in which majorities do not virtually decide right and wrong, but conscience?—in which majorities decide only those questions to which the rule of expediency is applicable? Must the citizen ever for a moment, or in the least degree, resign his conscience to the legislator? Why has every man a conscience, then? I think that we should be men first, and subjects afterward. It is not desirable to cultivate a respect for the law, so much as for the right. The only obligation which I have a right to assume is to do at any time what I think right. It is truly enough said that a corporation has no conscience; but a corporation of conscientious men is a corporation *with* a conscience. Law never made men a whit more just; and, by means of their respect for it, even the well-disposed are daily made the agents of injustice. A common and natural result of an undue respect for law is, that you may see a file of soldiers, colonel, captain, corporal, privates, powder-monkeys, and all, marching in admirable order over hill and dale to the wars, against their wills, ay, against their common sense and consciences, which makes it very steep marching indeed, and produces a palpitation of the heart. They have no doubt that it is a damnable business in which they are all concerned; they are all peaceably inclined. Now, what are they? Men at all? or small movable forts and magazines, at the service of some unscrupulous man in power? Visit the Navy Yard, and behold a marine, such a man as an American government can make, or such as it can make a man with its black arts—a mere shadow and reminiscence of humanity, a man laid out alive and standing, and already, as one may say, buried, under arms with funeral accompaniments, though it may be,

> Not a drum was heard, not a funeral note,
>     As his corse to the rampart we hurried;
> Not a soldier discharged his farewell shot
>     O'er the grave where our hero we buried.*

The mass of men serve the state thus, not as men mainly, but as 5 machines, with their bodies. They are the standing army, and the militia, jailers, constables, *posse comitatus*, etc. In most cases there is no free exercise whatever of the judgment or of the moral sense; but they put themselves on a level with wood and earth and stones; and wooden men can perhaps be manufactured that will serve the purpose as well. Such command no more respect than men of straw or a lump of dirt. They have the same sort of worth only as horses and dogs. Yet such as these even are commonly esteemed good citizens. Others—as most legislators, politicians, lawyers, ministers, and office-holders—serve the state chiefly with their heads; and, as they rarely make any moral distinctions,

---

*"Not . . . buried": the opening lines of "Burial of Sir John Moore at Corunna," by the Irish clergyman-poet Charles Wolfe (1791–1823).

they are as likely to serve the devil, without *intending* it, as God. A very few—as heroes, patriots, martyrs, reformers in the great sense, and *men*—serve the state with their consciences also, and so necessarily resist it for the most part; and they are commonly treated as enemies by it. A wise man will only be useful as a man, and will not submit to be "clay," and "stop a hole to keep the wind away,"* but leave that office to his dust at least:

> I am too high-born to be propertied,
> To be a secondary at control,
> Or useful serving-man and instrument
> To any sovereign state throughout the world.[†]

6    He who gives himself entirely to his fellow men appears to them useless and selfish; but he who gives himself partially to them is pronounced a benefactor and philanthropist.

7    How does it become a man to behave toward this American government today? I answer, that he cannot without disgrace be associated with it. I cannot for an instant recognize that political organization as *my* government which is the *slave's* government also.

8    All men recognize the right of revolution; that is, the right to refuse allegiance to, and to resist, the government, when its tyranny or its inefficiency are great and unendurable. But almost all say that such is not the case now. But such was the case, they think, in the Revolution of '75. If one were to tell me that this was a bad government because it taxed certain foreign commodities brought to its ports, it is most probable that I should not make an ado about it, for I can do without them. All machines have their friction; and possibly this does enough good to counterbalance the evil. At any rate, it is a great evil to make a stir about it. But when the friction comes to have its machine, and oppression and robbery are organized, I say, let us not have such a machine any longer. In other words, when a sixth of the population of a nation which has undertaken to be the refuge of liberty are slaves, and a whole country is unjustly overrun and conquered by a foreign army, and subjected to military law, I think that it is not too soon for honest men to rebel and revolutionize. What makes this duty the more urgent is the fact that the country so overrun is not our own, but ours is the invading army.

9    Paley,[‡] a common authority with many on moral questions, in his chapter on the "Duty of Submission to Civil Government," resolves all civil obligation into expediency; and he proceeds to say that "so long as the interest of the whole society requires it, that is, so long as the estab-

---

*A . . . away: Cf. Shakespeare, *Hamlet*, V.i.236–37.

[†]"I . . . world": Cf. Shakespeare, *King John*, V.ii.79–82.

[‡]Paley: William Paley (1743–1805), British philosopher, whose moral utilitarianism is exemplified by this quotation from his *Principles of Moral and Political Philosophy* (1785).

lished government cannot be resisted or changed without public inconveniency, it is the will of God . . . that the established government be obeyed—and no longer. This principle being admitted, the justice of every particular case of resistance is reduced to a computation of the quantity of the danger and grievance on the one side, and of the probability and expense of redressing it on the other." Of this, he says, every man shall judge for himself. But Paley appears never to have contemplated those cases to which the rule of expediency does not apply, in which a people as well as an individual, must do justice, cost what it may. If I have unjustly wrested a plank from a drowning man, I must restore it to him though I drown myself. This, according to Paley, would be inconvenient. But he that would save his life, in such a case, shall lose it. This people must cease to hold slaves, and to make war on Mexico, though it cost them their existence as a people.

In their practice, nations agree with Paley; but does anyone think 　　10
that Massachusetts does exactly what is right at the present crisis?

> A drab of state, a cloth-o'-silver slut,
> To have her train borne up, and her soul train in the dirt.

Practically speaking, the opponents to a reform in Massachusetts are not a hundred thousand politicians at the South, but a hundred thousand merchants and farmers here, who are more interested in commerce and agriculture than they are in humanity, and are not prepared to do justice to the slave and to Mexico, *cost what it may*. I quarrel not with far-off foes, but with those who, near at home, co-operate with, and do the bidding of, those far away, and without whom the latter would be harmless. We are accustomed to say, that the mass of men are unprepared; but improvement is slow, because the few are not materially wiser or better than the many. It is not so important that many should be as good as you, as that there be some absolute goodness somewhere; for that will leaven the whole lump. There are thousands who are *in opinion* opposed to slavery and to the war, who yet in effect do nothing to put an end to them; who, esteeming themselves children of Washington and Franklin, sit down with their hands in their pockets, and say that they know not what to do, and do nothing; who even postpone the question of freedom to the question of free trade, and quietly read the prices-current along with the latest advices from Mexico, after dinner, and, it may be, fall asleep over them both. What is the price-current of an honest man and patriot today? They hesitate, and they regret, and sometimes they petition; but they do nothing in earnest and with effect. They will wait, well disposed, for others to remedy the evil, that they may no longer have it to regret. At most, they give only a cheap vote, and a feeble countenance and Godspeed, to the right, as it goes by them. There are nine hundred and ninety-nine patrons of virtue to one virtuous man. But it is easier to deal with the real possessor of a thing than with the temporary guardian of it.

11      All voting is a sort of gaming, like checkers or backgammon, with a slight moral tinge to it, a playing with right and wrong, with moral questions; and betting naturally accompanies it. The character of the voters is not staked. I cast my vote, perchance, as I think right; but I am not vitally concerned that that right should prevail. I am willing to leave it to the majority. Its obligation, therefore, never exceeds that of expediency. Even voting *for the right* is *doing* nothing for it. It is only expressing to men feebly your desire that it should prevail. A wise man will not leave the right to the mercy of chance, nor wish it to prevail through the power of the majority. There is but little virtue in the action of masses of men. When the majority shall at length vote for the abolition of slavery, it will be because they are indifferent to slavery, or because there is but little slavery left to be abolished by their vote. *They* will then be the only slaves. Only *his* voice can hasten the abolition of slavery who asserts his own freedom by his vote.

12      I hear of a convention to be held at Baltimore, or elsewhere, for the selection of a candidate for the Presidency, made up chiefly of editors, and men who are politicians by profession; but I think, what is it to any independent, intelligent, and respectable man what decision they may come to? Shall we not have the advantage of his wisdom and honesty, nevertheless? Can we not count upon some independent votes? Are there not many individuals in the country who do not attend conventions? But no: I find that the respectable man, so called, has immediately drifted from his position, and despairs of his country, when his country has more reason to despair of him. He forthwith adopts one of the candidates thus selected as the only *available* one, thus proving that he is himself *available* for any purposes of the demagogue. His vote is of no more worth than that of any unprincipled foreigner or hireling native, who may have been bought. O for a man who is a *man*, and, as my neighbor says, has a bone in his back which you cannot pass your hand through! Our statistics are at fault: the population has been returned too large. How many *men* are there to a square thousand miles in this country? Hardly one. Does not America offer any inducement for men to settle here? The American has dwindled into an Odd Fellow—one who may be known by the development of his organ of gregariousness, and a manifest lack of intellect and cheerful self-reliance; whose first and chief concern, on coming into the world, is to see that the almshouses are in good repair; and, before yet he has lawfully donned the virile garb, to collect a fund for the support of the widows and orphans that may be; who, in short, ventures to live only by the aid of the Mutual Insurance company, which has promised to bury him decently.

13      It is not a man's duty, as a matter of course, to devote himself to the eradication of any, even the most enormous, wrong; he may still properly have other concerns to engage him; but it is his duty, at least, to wash his hands of it, and, if he gives it no thought longer, not to give it practically his support. If I devote myself to other pursuits and contemplations, I

must first see, at least, that I do not pursue them sitting upon another man's shoulders. I must get off him first, that he may pursue his contemplations too. See what gross inconsistency is tolerated. I have heard some of my townsmen say, "I should like to have them order me out to help put down an insurrection of the slaves, or to march to Mexico—see if I would go"; and yet these very men have each, directly by their allegiance, and so indirectly, at least, by their money, furnished a substitute. The soldier is applauded who refuses to serve in an unjust war by those who do not refuse to sustain the unjust government which makes the war; is applauded by those whose own act and authority he disregards and sets at naught; as if the state were penitent to that degree that it hired one to scourge it while it sinned, but not to that degree that it left off sinning for a moment. Thus, under the name of Order and Civil Government, we are all made at last to pay homage to and support our own meanness. After the first blush of sin comes its indifference; and from immoral it becomes, as it were, *unmoral*, and not quite unnecessary to that life which we have made.

The broadest and most prevalent error requires the most disinterested virtue to sustain it. The slight reproach to which the virtue of patriotism is commonly liable, the noble are most likely to incur. Those who, while they disapprove of the character and measures of a government, yield to it their allegiance and support are undoubtedly its most conscientious supporters, and so frequently the most serious obstacles to reform. Some are petitioning the State to dissolve the Union, to disregard the requisitions of the President. Why do they not dissolve it to themselves—the union between themselves and the State—and refuse to pay their quota into its treasury? Do not they stand in the same relation to the State that the State does to the Union? And have not the same reasons prevented the State from resisting the Union which have prevented them from resisting the State?    14

How can a man be satisfied to entertain an opinion merely, and enjoy *it*? Is there any enjoyment in it, if his opinion is that he is aggrieved? If you are cheated out of a single dollar by your neighbor, you do not rest satisfied with knowing that you are cheated, or with saying that you are cheated, or even with petitioning him to pay you your due; but you take effectual steps at once to obtain the full amount, and see that you are never cheated again. Action from principle, the perception and the performance of right, changes things and relations; it is essentially revolutionary, and does not consist wholly with anything which was. It not only divides States and churches, it divides families; ay, it divides the *individual*, separating the diabolical in him from the divine.    15

Unjust laws exist: shall we be content to obey them, or shall we endeavor to amend them, and obey them until we have succeeded, or shall we transgress them at once? Men generally, under such a government as this, think that they ought to wait until they have persuaded the majority to alter them. They think that, if they should resist, the remedy    16 would be worse than the evil. But it is the fault of the government itself that the remedy *is* worse than the evil. *It* makes it worse. Why is it not more apt to anticipate and provide for reform? Why does it not cherish its wise minority? Why does it cry and resist before it is hurt? Why does it not encourage its citizens to be on the alert to point out its faults, and *do* better than it would have them? Why does it always crucify Christ, and excommunicate Copernicus and Luther, and pronounce Washington and Franklin rebels?

17     One would think, that a deliberate and practical denial of its authority was the only offence never contemplated by government: else, why has it not assigned its definite, its suitable and proportionate, penalty? If a man who has no property refuses but once to earn nine shillings for the State, he is put in prison for a period unlimited by any law that I know, and determined only by the discretion of those who placed him there; but if he should steal ninety times nine shillings from the State, he is soon permitted to go at large again.

18     If the injustice is part of the necessary friction of the machine of government, let it go, let it go: perchance it will wear smooth—certainly the machine will wear out. If the injustice has a spring, or a pulley, or a rope, or a crank, exclusively for itself, then perhaps you may consider whether the remedy will not be worse than the evil; but if it is of such a nature that it requires you to be the agent of injustice to another, then, I say, break the law. Let your life be a counter-friction to stop the machine. What I have to do is to see, at any rate, that I do not lend myself to the wrong which I condemn.

19     As for adopting the ways which the State has provided for remedying the evil, I know not of such ways. They take too much time, and a man's life will be gone. I have other affairs to attend to. I came into this world, not chiefly to make this a good place to live in, but to live in it, be it good or bad. A man has not everything to do, but something; and because he cannot do *everything*, it is not necessary that he should do *something* wrong. It is not my business to be petitioning the Governor or the Legislature any more than it is theirs to petition me; and if they should not hear my petition, what should I do then? But in this case the State has provided no way: its very Constitution is the evil. This may seem to be harsh and stubborn and unconciliatory; but it is to treat with the utmost kindness and consideration the only spirit that can appreciate or deserves it. So is all change for the better, like birth and death, which convulse the body.

20     I do not hesitate to say, that those who call themselves Abolitionists should at once effectually withdraw their support, both in person and property, from the government of Massachusetts, and not wait till they constitute a majority of one, before they suffer the right to prevail through them. I think that it is enough if they have God on their side, without waiting for that other one. Moreover, any man more right than his neighbors constitutes a majority of one already.

I meet this American government, or its representative, the State    21
government, directly, and face to face, once a year—no more—in the person of its tax-gatherer; this is the only mode in which a man situated as I
am necessarily meets it; and it then says distinctly, Recognize me; and
the simplest, the most effectual, and, in the present posture of affairs, the
indispensablest mode of treating with it on this head, of expressing your
little satisfaction with and love for it, is to deny it then. My civil neighbor, the tax-gatherer, is the very man I have to deal with—for it is, after
all, with men and not with parchment that I quarrel—and he has voluntarily chosen to be an agent of the government. How shall he ever know
well what he is and does as an officer of the government, or as a man, until he is obliged to consider whether he shall treat me, his neighbor, for
whom he has respect, as a neighbor and well-disposed man, or as a ma-
niac and disturber of the peace, and see if he can get over this obstruction
to his neighborliness without a ruder and more impetuous thought or
speech corresponding with his action. I know this well, that if one thousand, if one hundred, if ten men whom I could name—if ten *honest* men
only—ay, if *one* HONEST man, in this State of Massachusetts, *ceasing to
hold slaves,* were actually to withdraw from this copartnership, and be
locked up in the county jail therefor, it would be the abolition of slavery
in America. For it matters not how small the beginning may seem to be:
what is once well done is done forever. But we love better to talk about
it: that we say is our mission. Reform keeps many scores of newspapers
in its service, but not one man. If my esteemed neighbor, the State's ambassador,* who will devote his days to the settlement of the question of
human rights in the Council Chamber, instead of being threatened with
the prisons of Carolina, were to sit down the prisoner of Massachusetts,
that State which is so anxious to foist the sin of slavery upon her sister—
though at present she can discover only an act of inhospitality to be the
ground of a quarrel with her—the Legislature would not wholly waive
the subject the following winter.

Under a government which imprisons any unjustly, the true place    22
for a just man is also a prison. The proper place today, the only place
which Massachusetts has provided for her freer and less desponding spirits, is in her prisons, to be put out and locked out of the State by her own
act, as they have already put themselves out by their principles. It is
there that the fugitive slave, and the Mexican prisoner on parole, and the
Indian come to plead the wrongs of his race should find them; on that
separate, but more free and honorable, ground, where the State places
those who are not *with* her, but *against* her—the only house in a slave
State in which a free man can abide with honor. If any think that their
influence would be lost there, and their voices no longer afflict the ear of

---

*The State's ambassador: Samuel Hoar (1778–1856), Concord lawyer and congress-
man, was sent to Charleston, S.C., to represent black seamen from Massachusetts threatened with arrest and enslavement. Hoar was forcibly expelled from the port.

the State, that they would not be as an enemy within its walls, they do not know by how much truth is stronger than error, nor how much more eloquently and effectively he can combat injustice who has experienced a little in his own person. Cast your whole vote, not a strip of paper merely, but your whole influence. A minority is powerless while it conforms to the majority; it is not even a minority then; but it is irresistible when it clogs by its whole weight. If the alternative is to keep all just men in prison, or give up war and slavery, the State will not hesitate which to choose. If a thousand men were not to pay their tax-bills this year, that would not be a violent and bloody measure, as it would be to pay them, and enable the State to commit violence and shed innocent blood. This is, in fact, the definition of a peaceable revolution, if any such is possible. If the tax-gatherer, or any other public officer, asks me, as one has done, "But what shall I do?" my answer is, "If you really wish to do anything, resign your office." When the subject has refused allegiance, and the officer has resigned his office, then the revolution is accomplished. But even suppose blood should flow. Is there not a sort of blood shed when the conscience is wounded? Through this wound a man's real manhood and immortality flow out, and he bleeds to an everlasting death. I see this blood flowing now.

23      I have contemplated the imprisonment of the offender, rather than the seizure of his goods—though both will serve the same purpose—because they who assert the purest right, and consequently are most dangerous to a corrupt State, commonly have not spent much time in accumulating property. To such the State renders comparatively small service, and a slight tax is wont to appear exorbitant, particularly if they are obliged to earn it by special labor with their hands. If there were one who lived wholly without the use of money, the State itself would hesitate to demand it of him. But the rich man—not to make any invidious comparison—is always sold to the institution which makes him rich. Absolutely speaking, the more money, the less virtue; for money comes between a man and his objects, and obtains them for him; and it was certainly no great virtue to obtain it. It puts to rest many questions which he would otherwise be taxed to answer; while the only new question which it puts is the hard but superfluous one, how to spend it. Thus his moral ground is taken from under his feet. The opportunities of living are diminished in proportion as what are called the "means" are increased. The best thing a man can do for his culture when he is rich is to endeavor to carry out those schemes which he entertained when he was poor. Christ answered the Herodians according to their condition. "Show me the tribute-money," said he—and one took a penny out of his pocket—if you use money which has the image of Caesar on it, and which he has made current and valuable, that is, *if you are men of the State*, and gladly enjoy the advantages of Caesar's government, then pay him back some of his own when he demands it. "Render therefore to Caesar that which is Caesar's, and to God those things which are

God's"*—leaving them not wiser than before as to which was which; for they did not wish to know.

When I converse with the freest of my neighbors, I perceive that, 24 whatever they may say about the magnitude and seriousness of the question, and their regard for the public tranquility, the long and the short of the matter is, that they cannot spare the protection of the existing government, and they dread the consequences to their property and families of disobedience to it. For my own part, I should not like to think that I ever rely on the protection of the State. But, if I deny the authority of the State when it presents its tax bill, it will soon take and waste all my property, and so harass me and my children without end. This is hard. This makes it impossible for a man to live honestly, and at the same time comfortably, in outward respects. It will not be worth the while to accumulate property; that would be sure to go again. You must hire or squat somewhere, and raise but a small crop, and eat that soon. You must live within yourself, and depend upon yourself always tucked up and ready for a start, and not have many affairs. A man may grow rich in Turkey even, if he will be in all respects a good subject of the Turkish government. Confucius said: "If a state is governed by the principles of reason, poverty and misery are subjects of shame; if a state is not governed by the principles of reason, riches and honors are the subjects of shame." No: until I want the protection of Massachusetts to be extended to me in some distant Southern port, where my liberty is endangered, or until I am bent solely on building up an estate at home by peaceful enterprise, I can afford to refuse allegiance to Massachusetts, and her right to my property and life. It costs me less in every sense to incur the penalty of disobedience to the State than it would to obey. I should feel as if I were worth less in that case.

Some years ago, the State met me in behalf of the Church, and com- 25 manded me to pay a certain sum toward the support of a clergyman whose preaching my father attended, but never I myself. "Pay," it said, "or be locked up in the jail." I declined to pay.† But, unfortunately, another man saw fit to pay it. I did not see why the schoolmaster should be taxed to support the priest, and not the priest the schoolmaster; for I was not the State's schoolmaster, but I supported myself by voluntary subscription. I did not see why the lyceum should not present its tax bill, and have the State to back its demand, as well as the Church. However, at the request of the selectmen, I condescended to make some such statement as this in writing: "Know all men by these presents, that I, Henry Thoreau, do not wish to be regarded as a member of any incorporated society which I have not joined." This I gave to the town clerk; and he has it. The State, having thus learned that I did not wish to be regarded as a member of that church, has never made a like demand on me since;

---

*Matthew 22:21.

†"I . . . pay": Thoreau signed off from church taxes in 1838 and went to jail in July 1846, for refusing to pay his poll tax.

though it said that it must adhere to its original presumption that time. If I had known how to name them, I should then have signed off in detail from all the societies which I never signed on to; but I did not know where to find a complete list.

26        I have paid no poll-tax for six years. I was put into a jail once on this account, for one night; and, as I stood considering the walls of solid stone, two or three feet thick, the door of wood and iron, a foot thick, and the iron grating which strained the light, I could not help being struck with the foolishness of that institution which treated me as if I were mere flesh and blood and bones, to be locked up. I wondered that it should have concluded at length that this was the best use it could put me to, and had never thought to avail itself of my services in some way. I saw that, if there was a wall of stone between me and my townsmen, there was a still more difficult one to climb or break through before they could get to be as free as I was. I did not for a moment feel confined, and the walls seemed a great waste of stone and mortar. I felt as if I alone of all my townsmen had paid my tax. They plainly did not know how to treat me, but behaved like persons who are underbred. In every threat and in every compliment there was a blunder; for they thought that my chief desire was to stand the other side of that stone wall. I could not but smile to see how industriously they locked the door on my meditations, which followed them out again without let or hindrance, and *they* were really all that was dangerous. As they could not reach me, they had resolved to punish my body; just as boys, if they cannot come at some person against whom they have a spite, will abuse his dog. I saw that the State was half-witted, that it was timid as a lone woman with her silver spoons, and that it did not know its friends from its foes, and I lost all my remaining respect for it, and pitied it.

27        Thus the State never intentionally confronts a man's sense, intellectual or moral, but only his body, his senses. It is not armed with superior wit or honesty, but with superior physical strength. I was not born to be forced. I will breathe after my own fashion. Let us see who is the strongest. What force has a multitude? They only can force me who obey a higher law than I. They force me to become like themselves. I do not hear of *men* being *forced* to live this way or that by masses of men. What sort of life were that to live? When I meet a government which says to me, "Your money or your life," why should I be in haste to give it my money? It may be in a great strait, and not know what to do: I cannot help that. It must help itself; do as I do. It is not worth the while to snivel about it. I am not responsible for the successful working of the machinery of society. I am not the son of the engineer. I perceive that, when an acorn and a chestnut fall side by side, the one does not remain inert to make way for the other, but both obey their own laws, and spring and grow and flourish as best they can, till one, perchance, overshadows and destroys the other. If a plant cannot live according to its nature, it dies; and so a man.

The night in prison was novel and interesting enough. The prisoners   28
in their shirtsleeves were enjoying a chat and the evening air in the doorway, when I entered. But the jailer said, "Come, boys, it is time to lock
up"; and so they dispersed, and I heard the sound of their steps returning
into the hollow apartments. My room-mate was introduced to me by the
jailer as "a first-rate fellow and a clever man." When the door was locked,
he showed me where to hang my hat, and how he managed matters there.
The rooms were white-washed once a month; and this one, at least, was
the whitest, most simply furnished, and probably the neatest apartment
in the town. He naturally wanted to know where I came from, and what
brought me there; and, when I had told him, I asked him in my turn how
he came there, presuming him to be an honest man, of course; and, as the
world goes, I believe he was. "Why," said he, "they accuse me of burning
a barn; but I never did it." As near as I could discover, he had probably
gone to bed in a barn when drunk, and smoked his pipe there; and so a
barn was burnt. He had the reputation of being a clever man, had been
there some three months waiting for his trial to come on, and would have
to wait as much longer; but he was quite domesticated and contented,
since he got his board for nothing, and thought that he was well treated.

He occupied one window, and I the other; and I saw that if one   29
stayed there long, his principal business would be to look out the window. I had soon read all the tracts that were left there, and examined
where former prisoners had broken out, and where a grate had been
sawed off, and heard the history of the various occupants of that room;
for I found that even here there was a history and a gossip which never
circulated beyond the walls of the jail. Probably this is the only house in
the town where verses are composed, which are afterward printed in a
circular form, but not published. I was shown quite a long list of verses
which were composed by some young men who had been detected in an
attempt to escape, who avenged themselves by singing them.

I pumped my fellow-prisoner as dry as I could, for fear I should   30
never see him again; but at length he showed me which was my bed, and
left me to blow out the lamp.

It was like traveling into a far country, such as I had never expected   31
to behold, to lie there for one night. It seemed to me that I never had
heard the town clock strike before, nor the evening sounds of the village;
for we slept with the windows open, which were inside the grating. It
was to see my native village in the light of the Middle Ages, and our
Concord was turned into a Rhine stream, and visions of knights and castles passed before me. They were the voices of old burghers that I heard
in the streets. I was an involuntary spectator and auditor of whatever
was done and said in the kitchen of the adjacent village inn—a wholly
new and rare experience to me. It was a closer view of my native town. I
was fairly inside of it. I never had seen its institutions before. This is one
of its peculiar institutions; for it is a shire town. I began to comprehend
what its inhabitants were about.

32    In the morning, our breakfasts were put through the hole in the door, in small oblong-square tin pans, made to fit, and holding a pint of chocolate, with brown bread, and an iron spoon. When they called for the vessels again, I was green enough to return what bread I had left; but my comrade seized it, and said that I should lay that up for lunch or dinner. Soon after he was let out to work at haying in a neighboring field, whither he went every day, and would not be back till noon; so he bade me good-day, saying that he doubted if he should see me again.

33    When I came out of prison—for some one interfered, and paid that tax—I did not perceive that great changes had taken place on the common, such as he observed who went in a youth and emerged a tottering and gray-headed man; and yet a change had to my eyes come over the scene—the town, and State, and country—greater than any that mere time could effect. I saw yet more distinctly the State in which I lived. I saw to what extent the people among whom I lived could be trusted as good neighbors and friends; that their friendship was for summer weather only; that they did not greatly propose to do right; that they were a distinct race from me by their prejudices and superstitions, as the Chinamen and Malays are; that in their sacrifices to humanity they ran no risks, not even to their property; that after all they were not so noble but they treated the thief as he had treated them, and hoped, by a certain outward observance and a few prayers, and by walking in a particular straight though useless path from time to time, to save their souls. This may be to judge my neighbors harshly; for I believe that many of them are not aware that they have such an institution as the jail in their village.

34    It was formerly the custom in our village, when a poor debtor came out of jail, for his acquaintances to salute him, looking through their fingers, which were crossed to represent the grating of a jail window, "How do ye do?" My neighbors did not thus salute me, but first looked at me, and then at one another, as if I had returned from a long journey. I was put into jail as I was going to the shoemaker's to get a shoe which was mended. When I was let out the next morning, I proceeded to finish my errand, and, having put on my mended shoe, joined a huckleberry party, who were impatient to put themselves under my conduct; and in half an hour—for the horse was soon tackled—was in the midst of a huckleberry field, on one of our highest hills, two miles off, and then the State was nowhere to be seen.

35    This is the whole history of "My Prisons."*

36    I have never declined paying the highway tax, because I am as desirous of being a good neighbor as I am of being a bad subject; and as for supporting schools, I am doing my part to educate my fellow-countrymen now. It is for no particular item in the tax bill that I refuse to pay it. I simply wish to refuse allegiance to the State, to withdraw and stand aloof

---

*"My Prisons": English translation of the title *Le Mie Prigioni*, a record of his Austrian incarceration by the Italian patriot and poet Silvio Pellico (1789–1854).

from it effectually. I do not care to trace the course of my dollar, if I could, till it buys a man or a musket to shoot one with—the dollar is innocent— but I am concerned to trace the effects of my allegiance. In fact, I quietly declare war with the State, after my fashion, though I will still make what use and get what advantage of her I can, as is usual in such cases.

If others pay the tax which is demanded of me, from a sympathy     37 with the State, they do but what they have already done in their own case, or rather they abet injustice to a greater extent than the State re- quires. If they pay the tax from a mistaken interest in the individual taxed, to save his property, or prevent his going to jail, it is because they have not considered wisely how far they let their private feelings inter- fere with the public good.

This, then, is my position at present. But one cannot be too much     38 on his guard in such a case, lest his action be biased by obstinacy or an undue regard for the opinions of men. Let him see that he does only what belongs to himself and to the hour.

I think sometimes, Why, this people mean well, they are only igno-     39 rant; they would do better if they knew how: why give your neighbors his pain to treat you as they are not inclined to? But I think again, This is no reason why I should do as they do, or permit others to suffer much greater pain of a different kind. Again, I sometimes say to myself, When many millions of men, without heat, without ill will, without personal feeling of any kind, demand of you a few shillings only, without the pos- sibility, such is their constitution, of retracting or altering their present demand, and without the possibility, on your side, of appeal to any other millions, why expose yourself to this overwhelming brute force? You do not resist cold and hunger, the winds and the waves, thus obstinately; you quietly submit to a thousand similar necessities. You do not put your head into the fire. But just in proportion as I regard this as not wholly a brute force, but partly a human force, and consider that I have relations to those millions as to so many millions of men, and not of mere brute or inanimate things, I see that appeal is possible, first and instantaneously, from them to the Maker of them, and, secondly, from them to them- selves. But if I put my head deliberately into the fire, there is no appeal to fire or to the Maker of fire, and I have only myself to blame. If I could convince myself that I have any right to be satisfied with men as they are, and to treat them accordingly, and not according, in some respects, to my requisitions and expectations of what they and I ought to be, then, like a good Mussulman and fatalist, I should endeavor to be satisfied with things as they are, and say it is the will of God. And, above all, there is this difference between resisting this and a purely brute or natural force, that I can resist this with some effect; but I cannot expect, like Orpheus, to change the nature of the rocks and trees and beasts.

I do not wish to quarrel with any man or nation. I do not wish to     40 split hairs, to make fine distinctions, or set myself up as better than my neighbors. I seek rather, I may say, even an excuse for conforming to the laws of the land. I am but too ready to conform to them. Indeed, I have reason to suspect myself on this head; and each year, as the tax-gatherer comes round, I find myself disposed to review the acts and position of the general and State governments, and the spirit of the people, to discover a pretext for conformity.

> We must affect our country as our parents,
> And if at any time we alienate
> Our love or industry from doing it honor,
> We must respect effects and teach the soul
> Matter of conscience and religion,
> And not desire of rule or benefit.

I believe that the State will soon be able to take all my work of this sort out of my hands, and then I shall be no better a patriot than my fellow-countrymen. Seen from a lower point of view, the Constitution, with all its faults, is very good; the law and the courts are very respectable; even this State and this American government are, in many respects, very admirable, and rare things, to be thankful for, such as a great many have described them; but seen from a point of view a little higher, they are what I have described them; seen from a higher still, and the highest, who shall say what they are, or that they are worth looking at or thinking of at all?

41      However, the government does not concern me much, and I shall bestow the fewest possible thoughts on it. It is not many moments that I live under a government, even in this world. If a man is thought-free, fancy-free, imagination-free, that which *is not* never for a long time appearing *to be* to him, unwise rulers or reformers cannot fatally interrupt him.

42      I know that most men think differently from myself; but those whose lives are by profession devoted to the study of these or kindred subjects content me as little as any. Statesmen and legislators, standing so completely within the institution, never distinctly and nakedly behold it. They speak of moving society, but have no resting-place without it. They may be men of a certain experience and discrimination, and have no doubt invented ingenious and even useful systems, for which we sincerely thank them; but all their wit and usefulness lie within certain not very wide limits. They are wont to forget that the world is not governed by policy and expediency. Webster never goes behind government, and so cannot speak with authority about it. His words are wisdom to those legislators who contemplate no essential reform in the existing government; but for thinkers, and those who legislate for all time, he never once glances at the subject. I know of those whose serene and wise speculations on this theme would soon reveal the limits of his mind's range and hospitality. Yet, compared with the cheap professions of most reformers, and the still cheaper wisdom and eloquence of politicians in

general, his are almost the only sensible and valuable words, and we thank Heaven for him. Comparatively, he is always strong, original, and above all, practical. Still, his quality is not wisdom, but prudence. The lawyer's truth is not Truth, but consistency or a consistent expediency. Truth is always in harmony with herself, and is not concerned chiefly to reveal the justice that may consist with wrong-doing. He well deserves to be called, as he has been called, the Defender of the Constitution. There are really no blows to be given by him but defensive ones. He is not a leader, but a follower. His leaders are the men of '87. "I have never made an effort," he says, "and never propose to make an effort; I have never countenanced an effort, and never mean to countenance an effort, to disturb the arrangement as originally made, by which the various States came into the Union." Still thinking of the sanction which the Constitution gives to slavery, he says, "Because it was a part of the original compact—let it stand." Notwithstanding his special acuteness and ability, he is unable to take a fact out of its merely political relations, and behold it as it lies absolutely to be disposed of by the intellect—what, for instance, it behooves a man to do here in America today with regard to slavery—but ventures, or is driven, to make some such desperate answer as the following, while professing to speak absolutely, and as a private man—from which what new and singular code of social duties might be inferred? "The manner," says he, "in which the governments of those states where slavery exists are to regulate it is for their own consideration, under their responsibility to their constituents, to the general laws of propriety, humanity, and justice, and to God. Associations formed elsewhere, springing from a feeling of humanity, or any other cause, have nothing whatever to do with it. They have never received any encouragement from me, and they never will."

They who know of no purer sources of truth, who have traced up its 43 stream no higher, stand, and wisely stand, by the Bible and the Constitution, and drink at it there with reverence and humility; but they who behold where it comes trickling into his lake or that pool, gird up their loins once more, and continue their pilgrimage toward its fountainhead.

No man with a genius for legislation has appeared in America. They 44 are rare in the history of the world. There are orators, politicians, and eloquent men, by the thousand; but the speaker has not yet opened his mouth to speak who is capable of settling the much-vexed questions of the day. We love eloquence for its own sake, and not for any truth which it may utter, or any heroism it may inspire. Our legislators have not yet learned the comparative value of free trade and of freedom, of union, and of rectitude, to a nation. They have no genius or talent for comparatively humble questions of taxation and finance, commerce and manufactures and agriculture. If we were left solely to the wordy wit of legislators in Congress for our guidance, uncorrected by the seasonable experience and the effectual complaints of the people, America would not long retain her rank among the nations. For eighteen hundred years, though perchance I have no right to say it, the New Testament has been written; yet where is the legislator who has wisdom and practical talent enough to avail himself of the light which it sheds on the science of legislation?

45    The authority of government, even such as I am willing to submit to—for I will cheerfully obey those who know and can do better than I, and in many things even those who neither know nor can do so well—is still an impure one: to be strictly just, it must have the sanction and consent of the governed. It can have no pure right over my person and property but what I concede to it. The progress from an absolute to a limited monarchy, from a limited monarchy to a democracy, is a progress toward a true respect for the individual. Even the Chinese philosopher was wise enough to regard the individual as the basis of the empire. Is a democracy, such as we know it, the last improvement possible in government? Is it not possible to take a step further towards recognizing and organizing the rights of man? There will never be a really free and enlightened State until the State comes to recognize the individual as a higher and independent power, from which all its own power and authority are derived, and treats him accordingly. I please myself with imagining a State at last which can afford to be just to all men, and to treat the individual with respect as a neighbor; which even would not think it inconsistent with its own repose if a few were to live aloof from it, not meddling with it, nor embraced by it, who fulfilled all the duties of neighbors and fellow men. A State which bore this kind of fruit, and suffered it to drop off as fast as it ripened, would prepare the way for a still more perfect and glorious State, which also I have imagined, but not yet anywhere seen.

## CONSIDERATIONS

1. "But to be *liked,* you must never disagree. And if you never disagree, it's like breathing in and never breathing out!" This is a line from *The Night Thoreau Spent in Jail,* a widely produced play by Jerome Lawrence and Robert E. Lee (1971). Can you find lines in "Civil Disobedience" that sound a little like this Thoreau character in the play?

2. Thoreau, sometimes depicted as a grimly serious man, had his own dry sense of humor, as seen in paragraph 25, especially the last few sentences. What are the strengths and risks of using humor in a serious essay like "Civil Disobedience"?

3. Specifically, what paradoxical discovery did Thoreau make during his night in jail that made him lose all his remaining respect for the state? Might the same discovery have been made by Nelson Mandela? Explain.

4. Explain how Thoreau's radical statement, "I cannot for an instant recognize that political organization as *my* government which is the *slave's* government also," is tempered by the reader's awareness of the historical context. How might a similar awareness shape one's understanding of other memorable statements, such as "Our country, right or wrong!" made by American naval commander Stephen Decatur after subduing the Algerian pirates in 1815?

5. Is Thoreau a liberal or a conservative? Find evidence for your opinion in "Civil Disobedience."

6. Thoreau makes emphatic use of the word "expedient." Study his uses of the word and consider some alternatives. Compare it with our use of "appropriate" today, as in "Your behavior is not appropriate," instead of "Your behavior is not right."

7. Why does Thoreau say voting is more like a game than anything else? Do you agree? Would Toni Morrison, "Nobel Lecture" (page 432), agree?

8. Thoreau's famous statement, "Any man more right than his neighbors constitutes a majority of one already," has been applauded by many and deplored by many. Explain why this forthright statement has been so variously received, perhaps beginning with your own judgment of it.

*Thoreau was disgusted with fellow Northerners who accepted enforcement of the Fugitive Slave Act. Two entries from his journal, on two successive days, respond to one dreadful occasion involving the case of Anthony Burns. When a mob tried to free the fugitive slave, the government called out the militia to ensure that the trial was held. Burns was returned to the South, although his identity as an escaped slave was doubtful. Never again was the Fugitive Slave Act enforced in Massachusetts. Here is the first of those two entries.*

*Often Thoreau used his journals, especially his observations of the natural world, as mines from which he could extract the gold of his finished essays. But see how these notes served also to exercise his outrage.*

— **93** —

# HENRY DAVID THOREAU
## From *The Journals: June 16, 1854,* and *November 30, 1858*

### June 16, 1854

1    The effect of a good government is to make life more valuable,—of a bad government, to make it less valuable. We can afford that railroad and all merely material stock should depreciate, for that only compels us to live more simply and economically; but suppose the value of life itself should be depreciated. Every man in New England capable of the sentiment of patriotism must have lived the last three weeks with the sense of having suffered a vast, indefinite loss. I had never respected this government, but I had foolishly thought that I might manage to live here, attending to my private affairs, and forget it. For my part, my old and worthiest pursuits have lost I cannot say how much of their attraction, and I feel that my investment in life here is worth many per cent less since Massachusetts last deliberately and forcibly restored an innocent man, Anthony Burns, to slavery. I dwelt before in the illusion that my life passed somewhere only between heaven and hell, but now I cannot persuade myself that I do not dwell wholly within hell. The sight of that political organization called Massachusetts is to me morally covered with scoriæ and volcanic cinders, such as Milton imagined. If there is any hell more unprincipled than our rulers and our people, I feel curious

to visit it. Life itself being worthless, all things with it, that feed it, are worthless. Suppose you have a small library, with pictures to adorn the walls,—a garden laid out around—and contemplate scientific and literary pursuits, etc., etc., and discover suddenly that your villa, with all its contents, is located in hell, and that the justice of the peace is one of the devil's angels, has a cloven foot and forked tail,—do not these things suddenly lose their value in your eyes? Are you not disposed to sell at a great sacrifice?

I feel that, to some extent, the State has fatally interfered with my just and proper business. It has not merely interrupted me in my passage through Court Street on errands of trade, but it has, to some extent, interrupted me and every man on his onward and upward path, on which he had trusted soon to leave Court Street far behind. I have found that hollow which I had relied on for solid. 2

I am surprised to see men going about their business as if nothing had happened, and say to myself, "Unfortunates! they have not heard the news"; that the man whom I just met on horseback should be so earnest to overtake his newly bought cows running away,—since all property is insecure, and if they do not run away again, they may be taken away from him when he gets them. Fool! does he not know that his seed-corn is worth less this year,—that all beneficent harvests fail as he approaches the empire of hell? No prudent man will build a stone house under these circumstances, or engage in any peaceful enterprise which it requires a long time to accomplish. Art is as long as ever, but life is more interrupted and less available for a man's proper pursuits. It is time we had done referring to our ancestors. We have used up all our inherited freedom, like the young bird the albumen in the egg. It is not an era of repose. If we would save our lives, we must fight for them. 3

The discovery is what matter of men your countrymen are. They steadily worship mammon—and on the seventh day curse God with a tintamarre from one end of the *Union* to the other. I heard the other day of a meek and sleek devil of a Bishop Somebody, who commended the law and order with which Burns was given up. I would like before I sit down to a table to inquire if there is one in the company who styles himself or is styled Bishop, and he or I should go out of it. I would have such a man wear his bishop's hat and his clerical bib and tucker, that we may know him. 4

Why will men be such fools as [to] trust to lawyers for a *moral* reform? I do not believe that there is a judge in this country prepared to decide by the principle that a law is immoral and therefore of no force. They put themselves, or rather are by character, exactly on a level with the marine who discharges his musket in any direction in which he is ordered. They are just as much tools, and as little men. 5

*These passages come from his journal, the disciplined daily writing from which Thoreau shaped his finished books. Here he writes about*

*the bream—a small, silvery, flattish freshwater fish—not so much by*
*describing it as by recounting his reaction to it and by ruminating*
*on the relationship between people and the natural world.*

## November 30, 1858

1      I cannot but see still in my mind's eye those little striped breams
poised in Walden's glaucous water. They balance all the rest of the world in
my estimation at present, for this is the bream that I have just found, and
for the time I neglect all its brethren and am ready to kill the fatted calf on
its account. For more than two centuries have men fished here and have
not distinguished this permanent settler of the township. It is not like a
new bird, a transient visitor that may not be seen again for years, but there
it dwells and has dwelt permanently, who can tell how long? When my
eyes first rested on Walden the striped bream was poised on it, though I did
not see it, and when Tahatawan paddled his canoe there. How wild it
makes the pond and the township to find a new fish in it! America renews
her youth here. But in my account of this bream I cannot go a hair's breadth
beyond the mere statement that it exists,—the miracle of its existence, my
contemporary and neighbor, yet so different from me! I can only poise my
thought there by its side and try to think like a bream for a moment. I can
only think of precious jewels, of music, poetry, beauty, and the mystery of
life. I only see the bream in its orbit, as I see a star, but I care not to measure
its distance or weight. The bream, appreciated, floats in the pond as the
centre of the system, another image of God. Its life no man can explain
more than he can his own. I want you to perceive the mystery of the bream.
I have a contemporary in Walden. It has fins where I have legs and arms. I
have a friend among the fishes, at least a new acquaintance. Its character
will interest me, I trust, not its clothes and anatomy. I do not want it to eat.
Acquaintance with it is to make my life more rich and eventful. It is as if a
poet or an anchorite had moved into the town, whom I can see from time
to time and think of yet oftener. Perhaps there are a thousand of these
striped bream which no one had thought of in that pond—not their mere
impressions in stone, but in the full tide of the bream life.

2      Though science may sometimes compare herself to a child picking
up pebbles on the seashore, that is a rare mood with her; ordinarily her
practical belief is that it is only a few pebbles which are *not* known,
weighed and measured. A new species of fish signifies hardly more than
a new name. See what is contributed in the scientific reports. One
counts the fin-rays, another measures the intestines, a third daguerreo-
types a scale, etc., etc.; otherwise there's nothing to be said. As if all but
this were done, and these were very rich and generous contributions to
science. Her votaries may be seen wandering along the shore of the ocean
of truth, with their backs to that ocean, ready to seize on the shells
which are cast up. You would say that the scientific bodies were terribly
put to it for objects and subjects. A dead specimen of an animal, if it is

only preserved in alcohol, is just as good for science as a living one pre-served in its native element.

What is the amount of my discovery to me? It is not that I have got    3
one in a bottle, that it has got a name in a book, but that I have a little
fishy friend in the pond. How was it when the youth first discovered
fishes? Was it the number of their fin-rays or their arrangement, or the
place of the fish in some system that made the boy dream of them? Is it
these things that interest mankind in the fish, the inhabitant of the water? No, but a faint recognition of a living contemporary, a provoking
mystery. One boy thinks of fishes and goes a-fishing from the same motive that his brother searches the poets for rare lines. It is the poetry of
fishes which is their chief use; their flesh is their lowest use. The beauty
of the fish, that is what it is best worth the while to measure. Its place in
our systems is of comparatively little importance. Generally the boy
loses some of his perception and his interest in the fish; he degenerates
into a fisherman or an ichthyologist.

## CONSIDERATIONS

### June 16, 1854

1. In expressing disgust over the Fugitive Slave Act at work in his own state of
Massachusetts, Thoreau distinguishes between a high material standard of living and a
high valuing of life itself. Thus, he would be willing to dispense with railroads and other
creature comforts if the value of life could be preserved. Do you hold similar feelings?
Are you willing to trade civil liberties for comforts and conveniences? Is such a trade
necessary?

2. To show how the court decisions about Anthony Burns have changed his life,
Thoreau makes use of allusion—a literary device—when he refers to Milton's description of hell. If that allusion does not elicit the dramatic effect Thoreau intends, turn to
"Book 1" of Milton's *Paradise Lost.* In your next essay, try to employ an allusion—not
necessarily to Milton—to strengthen a point.

3. How does Thoreau use his knowledge of natural history to make credible his
statement that "We have used up all our inherited freedom"?

4. Can you connect Thoreau's thinking with any of the arguments over present
unrest in our cities?

5. Thoreau's journal is not a collection of hasty jottings but a sequence of
carefully composed mini-essays. Examine this, and describe what suggests to you
that, far from being mere memoranda, they are the finished work of a thoughtful
writer.

### November 30, 1858

1. Thoreau's excitement in describing the bream was generated by his discovery
of a species living unnoticed in Walden Pond. But why, according to him, can he do no
more than say that it exists? Why is that statement sufficient?

2. What kind of truth—scientific, philosophic, economic, aesthetic—can you find in Thoreau's statement that the bream "is the center of the system, another image of God"? Look carefully at his sentence in paragraph 1. Why pay particular attention to the word "appreciated," which is set off by commas?

3. What does Thoreau's excitement over discovering the bream have in common with Wendell Berry's "A Native Hill," Robert Finch's "Very Like a Whale," E. B. White's "Once More to the Lake," or John Haines's "Death Is a Meadowlark"?

4. Why, in his closing statement, does Thoreau consider both the fisherman and the ichthyologist pitiable?

5. "Mystery" is an important word in Thoreau's essay. What is there about the way scientists work that limits their appreciation of the mystery of creation? Perhaps Nancy Mairs's "The Unmaking of a Scientist" (page 399) would be of help on this question.

*James Thurber (1894–1961) was born in Columbus, Ohio, the
scene of many of his funniest stories. He graduated from Ohio
State University and, after a period as a newspaperman in Paris,
began to work for the* New Yorker. *For years, his comic writing
and his cartoons—drawings of sausage-shaped dogs and of men
and women forever at battle—were fixtures of that magazine. His
collections of essays, short stories, and cartoons include* The Owl
in the Attic and Other Perplexities *(1931),* The Seal in the Bedroom
and Other Predicaments *(1932),* My Life and Hard Times *(1933),*
Men, Women, and Dogs *(1943), and* Alarms and Diversions *(1957).
He also wrote an account of life on the* New Yorker *staff,* The
Years with Ross *(1959).* Selected Letters of James Thurber *appeared
in 1981.*

*An elegant stylist, Thurber was always fussy about language.
"Which" is an example not only of his fascination with
language—which became obsessive at times—but also of his
humor.*

---

## — 94

# JAMES THURBER
## *Which*

---

The relative pronoun "which" can cause more trouble than any
other word, if recklessly used. Foolhardy persons sometimes get lost in
which-clauses and are never heard of again. My distinguished contemporary, Fowler, cites several tragic cases, of which the following is one: "It
was rumoured that Beaconsfield intended opening the Conference with a
speech in French, his pronunciation of which language leaving everything
to be desired . . ." That's as much as Mr. Fowler quotes because, at his
age, he was afraid to go any farther.* The young man who originally got
into that sentence was never found. His fate, however, was not as terrible
as that of another adventurer who became involved in a remarkable

1

---

*Thurber refers to the Englishman H. W. Fowler (1858–1933), whose *A Dictionary
of Modern English Usage* has been a source of amusement and useful information since its
first edition in 1926.

which-mire. Fowler has followed his devious course as far as he safely could on foot: "Surely what applies to games should also apply to racing, the leaders of which being the very people from whom an example might well be looked for . . ." Not even Henry James could have successfully emerged from a sentence with "which," "whom," and "being" in it. The safest way to avoid such things is to follow in the path of the American author, Ernest Hemingway. In his youth he was trapped in a which-clause one time and barely escaped with his mind. He was going along on solid ground until he got into this: "It was the one thing of which, being very much afraid—for whom has not been warned to fear such things—he . . ." Being a young and powerfully built man, Hemingway was able to fight his way back to where he had started, and begin again. This time he skirted the treacherous morass in this way: "He was afraid of one thing. This was the one thing. He had been warned to fear such things. Everybody has been warned to fear such things." Today Hemingway is alive and well, and many happy writers are following along the trail he blazed.

2      What most people don't realize is that one "which" leads to another. Trying to cross a paragraph by leaping from "which" to "which" is like Eliza crossing the ice. The danger is in missing a "which" and falling in. A case in point is this: "He went up to a pew which was in the gallery, which brought him under a colored window which he loved and always quieted his spirit." The writer, worn out, missed the last "which"—the one that should come just before "always" in that sentence. But supposing he had got it in! We would have: "He went up to a pew which was in the gallery, which brought him under a colored window which he loved and which always quieted his spirit." Your inveterate whicher in this way gives the effect of tweeting like a bird or walking with a crutch, and is not welcome in the best company.

3      It is well to remember that one "which" leads to two and that two "whiches" multiply like rabbits. You should never start out with the idea that you can get by with one "which." Suddenly they are all around you. Take a sentence like this: "It imposes a problem which we either solve, or perish." On a hot night, or after a hard day's work, a man often lets himself get by with a monstrosity like that, but suppose he dictates that sentence bright and early in the morning. It comes to him typed out by his stenographer and he instantly senses that something is the matter with it. He tries to reconstruct the sentence, still clinging to the "which," and gets something like this: "It imposes a problem which we either solve, or which, failing to solve, we must perish on account of." He goes to the water-cooler, gets a drink, sharpens his pencil, and grimly tries again. "It imposes a problem which we either solve or which we don't solve . . ." He begins once more: "It imposes a problem which we either solve, or which we do not solve, and from which . . ." The more times he does it the more "whiches" he gets. The way out is simple. "We must either solve this problem, or perish." Never monkey with "which." Nothing except getting tangled up in a typewriter ribbon is worse.

## CONSIDERATIONS

1. James Thurber concentrates on one word from an important class of function words. These relative pronouns often complicate life for the writer wishing to write clear sentences more complex than "I see Spot. Spot is a dog. Spot sees me." What other words belong to this class? Do you find any of them tripping you up in your sentences?

2. A grammar lesson may seem a peculiar place to find humor, but humor is Thurber's habit, whatever his subject. How does he make his treatment of the relative pronoun "which" entertaining?

3. Compare Fowler's book with an American version such as Wilson Follett's *Modern American Usage*. Think about usage as the ultimate authority in establishing conventions of grammar, spelling, definition, and punctuation.

4. "One 'which' leads to another" is a play on the old saying "One drink leads to another." Consider how changing one word can revive a thought that otherwise would be hackneyed phrase. See how it is done by substituting a key word in several familiar sayings.

5. The two writers Thurber mentions, Henry James and Ernest Hemingway, are not idly chosen. Why not?

6. In addition to many books of humorous and satirical stories and essays, Thurber wrote several fairy tales for children, including *The Wonderful O* (1957), an account of what would happen if the letter "O" were banned from the language. Said one character: "We shall have mantels but no clocks, shelves without crocks, keys without locks, walls without doors, rugs without floors." Select some peculiarity of the language that tickles your imagination and try your hand, Thurber style, at developing it into a mock report.

*Barbara Tuchman (1912–1989) was born in New York, graduated from Radcliffe, and began her career as an editor and writer for* the Nation. *But her interests led her away from the politics of the moment to the politics of the past, which is to say, history.* The Guns of August, *which won the Pulitzer Prize in 1963, recounted the first weeks of the great war of 1914–1918.* Stilwell and the American Experience in China *won the Pulitzer Prize in 1972. Her major work,* A Distant Mirror: The Calamitous 14th Century *(1973), from which the following essay was adapted, brought her into the forefront of American historians. Although she appeared to have deserted modern history for medieval, she did no such thing. This "six-hundred-year-old mirror" reflects ourselves. Her last book was* The First Salute *(1988), an unusual approach to the story of the American Revolution.*

*Barbara Tuchman wrote clean exposition, laying out for us clearly what she meant us to understand, supplying detail adequate to her argument and fascinating in itself. She loved the feel and shape of an odd and illuminating detail; she collected it with gusto, and she used it with skill.*

— 95 ————————————————————————

# BARBARA TUCHMAN
## *History as Mirror*

———————————————————————————————

1     At a time when everyone's mind is on the explosions of the moment, it might seem obtuse of me to discuss the fourteenth century. But I think a backward look at that disordered, violent, bewildered, disintegrating, and calamity-prone age can be consoling and possibly instructive in a time of similar disarray. Reflected in a six-hundred-year-old mirror, a more revealing image of ourselves and our species might be seen than is visible in the clutter of circumstances under our noses. The value of historical comparison was made keenly apparent to the French medievalist, Edouard Perroy, when he was writing his book on the Hundred Years' War while dodging the Gestapo in World War II. "Certain ways of behav-

ing," he wrote, "certain reactions against fate, throw mutual light upon each other."

Besides, if one suspects that the twentieth century's record of inhu-    2
manity and folly represents a phase of mankind at its worst, and that our last decade of collapsing assumptions has been one of unprecedented discomfort, it is reassuring to discover that the human race has been in this box before—and emerged. The historian has the comfort of knowing that man (meaning, here and hereafter, the species, not the sex) is always capable of his worst; has indulged in it, painfully struggled up from it, slid back, and gone on again.

In what follows, the parallels are not always in physical events but    3
rather in the effect on society, and sometimes in both.

The afflictions of the fourteenth century were the classic riders of    4
the Apocalypse—famine, plague, war, and death, this time on a black horse. These combined to produce an epidemic of violence, depopulation, bad government, oppressive taxes, an accelerated breakdown of feudal bonds, working class insurrection, monetary crisis, decline of morals and rise in crime, decay of chivalry, the governing idea of the governing class, and above all, corruption of society's central institution, the Church, whose loss of authority and prestige deprived man of his accustomed guide in a darkening world.

Yet amidst the disintegration were sprouting, invisible to contem-    5
poraries, the green shoots of the Renaissance to come. In human affairs as in nature, decay is compost for new growth.

Some medievalists reject the title of decline for the fourteenth cen-    6
tury, asserting instead that it was the dawn of a new age. Since the processes obviously overlap, I am not sure that the question is worth arguing, but it becomes poignantly interesting when applied to ourselves. Do *we* walk amidst trends of a new world without knowing it? How far ahead is the dividing line? Or are we on it? What designation will our age earn from historians six hundred years hence? One wishes one could make a pact with the devil like Enoch Soames, the neglected poet in Max Beerbohm's story, allowing us to return and look ourselves up in the library catalogue. In that future history book, shall we find the chapter title for the twentieth century reading Decline and Fall, or Eve of Revival?

The fourteenth century opened with a series of famines brought on    7
when population growth outstripped the techniques of food production. The precarious balance was tipped by a series of heavy rains and floods and by a chilling of the climate in what has been called the Little Ice Age. Upon a people thus weakened fell the century's central disaster, the Black Death, an eruption of bubonic plague which swept the known world in the years 1347–1349 and carried off an estimated one-third of the population in two and a half years. This makes it the most lethal episode known to history, which is of some interest to an age equipped with the tools of overkill.

8    The plague raged at terrifying speed, increasing the impression of horror. In a given locality it accomplished its kill within four to six months, except in the larger cities, where it struck again in spring after lying dormant in winter. The death rate in Avignon was said to have claimed half the population, of whom ten thousand were buried in the first six weeks in a single mass grave. The mortality was in fact erratic. Some communities whose last survivors fled in despair were simply wiped out and disappeared from the map forever, leaving only a grassed-over hump as their mortal trace.

9    Whole families died, leaving empty houses and property a prey to looters. Wolves came down from the mountains to attack plague-stricken villages, crops went unharvested, dikes crumbled, salt water reinvaded and soured the lowlands, the forest crept back, and second growth, with the awful energy of nature unchecked, reconverted cleared land to waste. For lack of hands to cultivate, it was thought impossible that the world could ever regain its former prosperity.

10    Once the dark bubonic swellings appeared in armpit and groin, death followed rapidly within one to three days, often overnight. For lack of gravediggers, corpses piled up in the streets or were buried so hastily that dogs dug them up and ate them. Doctors were helpless, and priests lacking to administer that final sacrament so that people died believing they must go to hell. No bells tolled, the dead were buried without prayers or funeral rites or tears; families did not weep for the loss of loved ones, for everyone expected death. Matteo Villani, taking up the chronicle of Florence from the hands of his dead brother, believed he was recording the "extermination of mankind."

11    People reacted variously, as they always do: some prayed, some robbed, some tried to help, most fled if they could, others abandoned themselves to debauchery on the theory that there would be no tomorrow. On balance, the dominant reaction was fear and a desire to save one's own skin regardless of the closest ties. "A father did not visit his son, nor the son his father; charity was dead," wrote one physician, and that was not an isolated observation. Boccaccio in his famous account reports that "kinsfolk held aloof, brother was forsaken by brother . . . often times husband by wife; nay what is more, and scarcely to be believed, fathers and mothers were found to abandon their own children to their fate, untended, unvisited as if they had been strangers."

12    "Men grew bold," wrote another chronicler, "in their indulgence in pleasure. . . . No fear of God or law of man deterred a criminal. Seeing that all perished alike, they reflected that offenses against human or Divine law would bring no punishment for no one would live long enough to be held to account." This is an accurate summary, but it was written by Thucydides about the Plague of Athens in the fifth century B.C.—which indicates a certain permanence of human behavior.

13    The nightmare of the plague was compounded for the fourteenth century by the awful mystery of its cause. The idea of disease carried by in-

sect bite was undreamed of. Fleas and rats, which were in fact the carriers, are not mentioned in the plague writings. Contagion could be observed but not explained and thus seemed doubly sinister. The medical faculty of the University of Paris favored a theory of poisonous air spread by a conjunction of the planets, but the general and fundamental belief, made official by a papal bull, was that the pestilence was divine punishment for man's sins. Such horror could only be caused by the wrath of God. "In the year of our Lord, 1348," sadly wrote a professor of law at the University of Pisa, "the hostility of God was greater than the hostility of men."

That belief enhanced the sense of guilt, or rather the consciousness    14
of sin (guilt, I suspect, is modern; sin is medieval), which was always so close to the surface throughout the Middle Ages. Out of the effort to appease divine wrath came the flagellants, a morbid frenzy of self-punishment that almost at once found a better object in the Jews.

A storm of pogroms followed in the track of the Black Death,    15
widely stimulated by the flagellants, who often rushed straight for the Jewish quarter, even in towns which had not yet suffered the plague. As outsiders within the unity of Christendom the Jews were natural persons to suspect of evil design on the Christian world. They were accused of poisoning the wells. Although the Pope condemned the attacks as inspired by "that liar the devil," pointing out that Jews died of plague like everyone else, the populace wanted victims, and fell upon them in three hundred communities throughout Europe. Slaughtered and burned alive, the entire colonies of Frankfurt, Cologne, Manz, and other towns of Germany and the Lowlands were exterminated, despite the restraining efforts of town authorities. Elsewhere the Jews were expelled by judicial process after confession of well-poisoning was extracted by torture. In every case their goods and property, whether looted or confiscated, ended in the hands of the persecutors. The process was lucrative, as it was to be again in our time under the Nazis, although the fourteenth century had no gold teeth to rob from the corpses. Where survivors slowly returned and the communities revived, it was on worse terms than before and in walled isolation. This was the beginning of the ghetto.

Men of the fourteenth century were particularly vulnerable because    16
of the loss of credibility by the Church, which alone could absolve sin and offer salvation from hell. When the papal schism dating from 1378 divided the Church under two popes, it brought the highest authority in society into disrepute, a situation with which we are familiar. The schism was the second great calamity of the time, displaying before all the world the unedifying spectacle of twin vicars of God, each trying to bump the other off the chair of St. Peter, each appointing his own college of cardinals, each collecting tithes and revenues and excommunicating the partisans of his rival. No conflict of ideology was involved; the split arose from a simple squabble for the office of the papacy and remained no more than that for the fifty years the schism lasted. Plunged in this scandal, the Church lost moral authority, the more so as its two halves

scrambled in the political arena for support. Kingdoms, principalities, even towns, took sides, finding new cause for the endless wars that scourged the times.

17        The Church's corruption by worldliness long antedated the schism. By the fourteenth century the papal court at Avignon was called Babylon and rivaled temporal courts in luxury and magnificence. Its bureaucracy was enormous and its upkeep mired in a commercial traffic in spiritual things. Pardons, indulgences, prayers, every benefice and bishopric, everything the Church had or was, from cardinal's hat to pilgrim's relic, everything that represented man's relation to God, was for sale. Today it is the processes of government that are for sale, especially the electoral process, which is as vital to our political security as salvation was to the emotional security of the fourteenth century.

18        Men still craved God and spun off from the Church in sects and heresies, seeking to purify the realm of the spirit. They too yearned for a greening of the system. The yearning, and disgust with the Establishment, produced freak orders of mystics who lived in coeducational communes, rejected marriage, and glorified sexual indulgence. Passionate reformers ranged from St. Catherine of Siena, who scolded everyone in the hierarchy from the popes down, to John Wycliffe, who plowed the soil of Protestant revolt. Both strove to renew the Church, which for so long had been the only institution to give order and meaning to the untidy business of living on earth. When in the last quarter of the century the schism brought the Church into scorn and ridicule and fratricidal war, serious men took alarm. The University of Paris made strenuous and ceaseless efforts to find a remedy, finally demanding submission of the conflict to a supreme Council of the Church whose object should be not only reunification but reform.

19        Without reform, said the University's theologians in their letter to the popes, the damaging effect of the current scandal could be irreversible. In words that could have been addressed to our own secular potentate although he is—happily—not double, they wrote, "The Church will suffer for your overconfidence if you repent too late of having neglected reform. If you postpone it longer the harm will be incurable. Do you think people will suffer forever from your bad government? Who do you think can endure, amid so many other abuses . . . your elevation of men without literacy or virtue to the most eminent positions?" The echo sounds over the gulf of six hundred years with a timeliness almost supernatural.

20        When the twin popes failed to respond, pressure at last brought about a series of Church councils which endeavored to limit and constitutionalize the powers of the papacy. After a thirty-year struggle, the councils succeeded in ending the schism but the papacy resisted reform. The decades of debate only served to prove that the institution could not be reformed from within. Eighty years of mounting protest were to pass before pressure produced Luther and the great crack.

Despite the parallel with the present struggle between Congress    21
and the presidency, there is no historical law that says the outcome must
necessarily be the same. The American presidency at age two hundred is
not a massive rock of ages embedded in a thousand years of acceptance as
was the medieval Church, and should be easier to reform. One can wish
for Congress a better result than the councils had in the effort to curb the
executive—or at least one can hope.

The more important parallel lies in the decay of public confidence    22
in our governing institutions, as the fourteenth-century public lost confidence in the Church. Who believes today in the integrity of government?—or of business, or of law or justice or labor unions or the military
or the police? Even physicians, the last of the admired, are now in disfa-
vor. I have a theory that the credibility vacuum owes something to our
nurture in that conspiracy of fables called advertising, which we daily absorb without believing. Since public affairs and ideas and candidates are
now presented to us as a form of advertising, we automatically suspend
belief or suspect fraud as soon as we recognize the familiar slickness. I realize, of course, that the roots of disbelief go down to deeper ground.
Meanwhile the effect is a loss of trust in all authority which leaves us
guideless and dismayed and cynical—even as in the fourteenth century.

Over that whole century hung the smoke of war—dominated by the    23
Anglo-French conflict known to us, though fortunately not to them, as the
Hundred Years' War. (With the clock still ticking in Indochina, one won-
ders how many years there are still to go in that conflict.) Fought on
French soil and extending into Flanders and Spain, the Hundred Years' War
actually lasted for more than a century, from 1337 to 1453. In addition, the
English fought the Scots; the French fought incessant civil wars against
Gascons, Bretons, Normans, and Navarrese; the Italian republics fought
each other—Florence against Pisa, Venice against Genoa, Milan against
everybody; the kingdom of Naples and Sicily was fought over by claimants
from Hungary to Aragon; the papacy fought a war that included unbridled
massacre to reconquer the Papal States; the Savoyards fought the
Lombards; the Swiss fought the Austrians; the tangled wars of Bohemia,
Poland, and the German Empire defy listing; crusades were launched
against the Saracens, and to fill up any pauses the Teutonic Knights conducted annual campaigns against pagan Lithuania which other knights
could join for extra practice. Fighting was the function of the Second
Estate, that is, of the landed nobles and knights. A knight without a war or
tournament to go to felt as restless as a man who cannot go to the office.

Every one of these conflicts threw off Free Companies of mercenar-    24
ies, organized for brigandage under a professional captain, which became
an evil of the period as malignant as the plague. In the money economy
of the fourteenth century, armed forces were no longer feudal levies serving under a vassal's obligation who went home after forty days, but were
recruited bodies who served for pay. Since this was at great cost to the
sovereign, he cut off the payroll as soon as he safely could during halts of

truce or negotiation. Thrown on their own resources and having acquired a taste for plunder, the men-at-arms banded together in the Free Companies, whose savage success swelled their ranks with landless knights and squires and roving adventurers.

25    The companies contracted their services to whatever ruler was in need of troops, and between contracts held up towns for huge ransom, ravaged the countryside, and burned, pillaged, raped, and slaughtered their way back and forth across Europe. No one was safe, no town or village knew when it might be attacked. The leaders, prototypes of the *condottieri* in Italy, became powers and made fortunes and even became respectable like Sir John Hawkwood, commander of the famous White Company. Smaller bands, called in France the *tards-venus* (late-comers), scavenged like jackals, living off the land, plundering, killing, carrying off women, torturing peasants for their small horde of grain or townsmen for their hidden goods, and burning, always burning. They set fire to whatever they left behind, farmhouses, vineyards, abbeys, in a kind of madness to destroy the very sources off which they lived, or would live tomorrow. Destruction and cruelty became self-engendering, not merely for loot but almost one might say for sport. The phenomenon is not peculiar to any one time or people, as we know from the experience of our own century, but in the fourteenth century it seems to have reached a degree and an extent beyond explanation.

26    It must be added that in practice and often personnel the Free Companies were hardly distinguishable from the troops of organized official wars. About 80 percent of the activity of a declared war consisted of raids of plunder and burning through enemy territory. That paragon of chivalry, the Black Prince, could well have earned his name from the blackened ruins he left across France. His baggage train and men-at-arms were often so heavily laden with loot that they moved as slowly as a woman's litter.

27    The saddest aspect of the Hundred Years' War was the persistent but vain efforts of the belligerents themselves to stop it. As in our case, it spread political damage at home, and the cost was appalling. Moreover it harmed the relations of all the powers at a time when they were anxious to unite to repel the infidel at the gates. For Christendom was now on the defensive against the encroaching Turks. For that reason the Church, too, tried to end the war that was keeping Europe at odds. On the very morning of the fatal battle of Poitiers, two cardinals hurried with offers and counter-offers between the two armed camps, trying in vain to prevent the clash. During periods of truce the parties held long parleys lasting months and sometimes years in the effort to negotiate a definitive peace. It always eluded them, failing over questions of prestige, or put off by the feeling of whichever side held a slight advantage that one more push would bring the desired gains.

28    All this took place under a code of chivalry whose creed was honor, loyalty, and courtesy and whose purpose, like that of every social code

evolved by man in his long search for order, was to civilize and supply a pattern of rules. A knight's task under the code was to uphold the Church, defend his land and vassals, maintain the peace of his province, protect the weak and guard the poor from injustice, shed his blood for his comrade, and lay down his life if needs must. For the land-owning warrior class, chivalry was their ideology, their politics, their system—what democracy is to us or Marxism to the Communists.

Originating out of feudal needs, it was already slipping into  29
anachronism by the fourteenth century because the development of monarchy and a royal bureaucracy was taking away the knight's functions, economic facts were forcing him to commute labor dues for money, and a rival element was appearing in the urban magnates. Even his military prowess was being nullified by trained bodies of English longbowmen and Swiss pikemen, nonmembers of the warrior class who in feudal theory had no business in battle at all.

Yet in decadence chivalry threw its brightest light; never were its  30
ceremonies more brilliant, its jousts and tournaments so brave, its apparel so splendid, its manners so gay and amorous, its entertainments so festive, its self-glorification more eloquent. The gentry elaborated the forms of chivalry just *because* institutions around them were crumbling. They clung to what gave their status meaning in a desperate embrace of the past. This is the time when the Order of the Garter was founded by the King of England, the Order of the Star by the King of France, the Golden Fleece by the Duke of Burgundy—in deliberate imitation of King Arthur's Knights of the Round Table.

The rules still worked well enough among themselves, with occa-  31
sional notorious exceptions such as Charles of Navarre, a bad man appropriately known as Charles the Bad. Whenever necessity required him to swear loyal reconciliation and fealty to the King of France, his mortal enemy, he promptly engaged in treacherous intrigues with the King of England, leaving his knightly oaths to become, in the White House word, inoperative. On the whole, however, the nobility laid great stress on high standards of honor. It was vis-à-vis the Third Estate that chivalry fell so far short of the theory. Yet it remained an ideal of human relations, as Christianity remained an ideal of faith, that kept men reaching for the unattainable. The effort of society is always toward order, away from anarchy. Sometimes it moves forward, sometimes it slips back. Which is the direction of one's own time may be obscure.

The fourteenth century was further afflicted by a series of convul-  32
sions and upheavals in the working class, both urban and rural. Causes were various: the cost of constant war was thrown upon the people in hearth taxes, salt taxes, sales taxes, and debasement of coinage. In France the failure of the knights to protect the populace from incessant ravaging was a factor. It exacerbated the peasants' misery, giving it the energy of anger which erupted in the ferocious mid-century rising called the

*Jacquerie.* Shortage of labor caused by the plague had temporarily brought higher wages and rising expectations. When these were met, especially in England, by statutes clamping wages at pre-plague levels, the result was the historic Peasants' Revolt of 1381. In the towns, capitalism was widening the gap between masters and artisans, producing the sustained weavers' revolts in the cloth towns of Flanders and major outbreaks in Florence and Paris. In Paris, too, the merchant class rose against the royal councillors, whom they despised as both corrupt and incompetent. To frighten the regent into submission, they murdered his two chief councillors in his presence.

33      All these struggles had one thing in common: they were doomed. United against a common threat, the ruling class could summon greater strength than its antagonists and acted to suppress insurrection with savagery equal to the fury from below. Yet discontent had found its voice; dissent and rejection of authority for the first time in the Middle Ages became a social force. Demagogues and determined leaders, reformers and agitators came to the surface. Though all were killed, several by mobs of their own followers, the uprisings they led were the beginning of modern, conscious, class war.

34      Meanwhile, over the second half-century, the plague returned with lesser virulence at intervals of every twelve to fifteen years. It is hardly to be wondered that people of the time saw man's fate as an endless succession of evils. He must indeed be wicked and his enemy Satan finally triumphant. According to a popular belief at the end of the century, no one since the beginning of the schism had entered Paradise.

35      Pessimism was a mark of the age and the *Danse Macabre* or Dance of Death its most vivid expression. Performed at occasions of popular drama and public sermons, it was an actual dance or pantomime in which a figure from every walk of life—king, clerk, lawyer, friar, goldsmith, bailiff, and so on—confronts the loathsome corpse he must become. In the accompanying verses and illustrations which have survived, the theme repeats itself over and over: the end of all life is putrefaction and the grave; no one escapes; no matter what beauty or kingly power or poor man's misery has been the lot in life, all end alike as food for worms. Death is not treated poetically as the soul's flight to reunion with God; it is a skeleton grinning at the vanity of life.

36      Life as well as death was viewed with disgust. The vices and corruptions of the age, a low opinion of one's fellowmen, and nostalgia for the well-ordered past were the favorite themes of literary men. Even Boccaccio in his later works became ill-tempered. "All good customs fail," laments Christine di Pisan of France, "and virtues are held at little worth." Eustache Deschamps complains that "the child of today has become a ruffian. . . . People are gluttons and drunkards, haughty of heart, caring for nought, not honor nor goodness nor kindness . . ." and he ends each verse with the refrain, "Time past had virtue and righteousness but today reigns only vice." In England John Gower denounces Rome for simony, Lollards

for heresy, clergy and monks for idleness and lust, kings, nobles, and knights for self-indulgence and rapine, the law for bribery, merchants for usury and fraud, the commons for ignorance, and in general the sins of perjury, lechery, avarice, and pride as displayed in extravagant fashions.

These last did indeed, as in all distracted times, reflect a reaching   37 for the absurd, especially in the long pointed shoes which kept getting longer until the points had to be tied up around the knee, and the young men's doublets which kept getting shorter until they revealed the buttocks, to the censure of moralists and snickers of the crowd. Leaving miniskirts to the males, the ladies inexplicably adopted a fashion of gowns and posture designed to make them look pregnant.

Self-disgust, it seems to me, has reappeared in our time, not with-   38 out cause. The succession of events since 1914 has disqualified belief in moral progress, and pollution of the physical world is our bubonic plague. Like the fourteenth century, we have lost confidence in man's capacity to control his fate and even in his capacity to be good. So we have a literature of the anti-hero aimlessly wandering among the perverse, absurd, and depraved; we have porn and pop and blank canvases and anti-music designed to deafen. I am not sure whether in all this the artists are expressing contempt for their fellowman or the loud laugh that bespeaks emptiness of feeling, but whatever the message, it has a faint ring of the *Danse Macabre.*

Historians until recently have hurried over the fourteenth century   39 because like most people they prefer not to deal with failure. But it would be a mistake to imply that it was solid gloom. Seen from inside, especially from a position of privilege, it had beauties and wonders, and the ferment itself was exciting. "In these fifty years," said the renowned Comte de Foix to the chronicler Froissart in the year 1389, "there have been more feats of arms and more marvels in the world than in the three hundred years before." The Count himself, a famous huntsman, was known as Phoebus for his personal beauty and splendid court.

The streets of cities were bright with colored clothes; crimson fur-   40 lined gowns of merchants, parti-colored velvets and silks of a nobleman's retinue, in sky blue and fawn or two shades of scarlet or it might be the all-emerald liveries of the Green Count of Savoy. Street sounds were those of human voices: criers of news and official announcements, shopkeepers in their doorways and itinerant vendors crying fresh eggs, charcoal at a penny a sack, candlewicks "brighter than the stars," cakes and waffles, mushrooms, hot baths. Mountebanks entertained the public in the town square or village green with tricks and magic and trained animals. Jongleurs sang ballads of adventure in Saracen lands. After church on Sundays, laborers gathered in cookshops and taverns; burghers promenaded in their gardens or visited their vineyards outside the city walls. Church bells marked the eight times of day from Matins through Vespers, when shops closed, work ceased, silence succeeded bustle, and the darkness of unlit night descended.

41        The gaudy extravagance of noble life was awesome. Now and then its patronage brought forth works of eternal beauty like the exquisite illuminated Books of Hours commissioned by the Duc de Berry. More often it was pure ostentation and conspicuous consumption. Charles V of France owned forty-seven jeweled and golden crowns and sixty-three complete sets of chapel furnishings, including vestments, gold crucifixes, altarpieces, reliquaries, and prayer books. Jewels and cloth of gold marked every occasion and every occasion was pretext for a spectacle—a grand procession, or ceremonial welcome to a visiting prince, a tournament of entertainment with music, and dancing by the light of great torches. When Gian Galeazzo Visconti, ruler of Milan, gave a wedding banquet for his daughter, eighteen double courses were served, each of fish and meat, including trout, quail, herons, eels, sturgeon, and suckling pig spouting fire. The gifts presented after *each* course to several hundred guests included greyhounds in gem-studded velvet collars, hawks in tinkling silver bells, suits of armor, rolls of silk and brocade, garments trimmed with pearls and ermine, fully caparisoned warhorses, and twelve fat oxen. For the entry into Paris of the new Queen, Isabel of Bavaria, the entire length of the Rue St. Denis was hung with a canopy representing the firmament twinkling with stars from which sweetly singing angels descended bearing a crown, and fountains ran with wine, distributed to the people in golden cups by lovely maidens wearing caps of solid gold.

42        One wonders where all the money came from for such luxury and festivity in a time of devastation. What taxes could burned-out and destitute people pay? This is a puzzle until one remembers that the Aga Khan got to be the richest man in the world on the backs of the poorest people, and that disaster is never as pervasive as it seems from recorded accounts. It is one of the pitfalls for historians that the very fact of being on the record makes a happening appear to have been continuous and all-inclusive, whereas in reality it is more likely to have been sporadic both in time and place. Besides, persistence of the normal is usually greater than the effect of disturbance, as we know from our own times. After absorbing the daily paper and weekly magazine, one expects to face a world consisting entirely of strikes, crimes, power shortages, broken water mains, stalled trains, school shutdowns, Black Panthers, addicts, transvestites, rapists, and militant lesbians. The fact is that one can come home in the evening—on a lucky day—without having encountered more than two or three of these phenomena. This has led me to formulate Tuchman's Law, as follows: "The fact of being reported increases the *apparent* extent of a deplorable development by a factor of ten." (I snatch the figure from the air and will leave it to the quantifiers to justify.)

43        The astonishing fact is that except for Boccaccio, to whom we owe the most vivid account, the Black Death was virtually ignored by the great writers of the time. Petrarch, who was forty-four when it happened, mentions it only as the occasion for the death of Laura; Chaucer, from

what I have read, passes it over in silence; Jean Froissart, the Herodotus of his time, gives it no more than one casual paragraph, and even that second Isaiah, the author of *Piers Plowman*, who might have been expected to make it central to his theme of woe, uses it only incidentally. One could argue that in 1348 Chaucer was only eight or nine years old and Froissart ten or eleven and the unknown Langland probably of the same vintage, but that is old enough to absorb and remember a great catastrophe, especially when they lived through several returns of the plague as grown men.

Perhaps this tells us that disaster, once survived, leaves less track 44 than one supposed, or that man's instinct for living pushes it down below the surface, or simply that his recuperative powers are remarkable. Or was it just an accident of personality? Is it significant or just chance that Chaucer, the greatest writer of his age, was so uncharacteristic of it in sanguine temperament and good-humored view of his fellow creatures?

As for Froissart, never was a man more in love with his age. To him 45 it appeared as a marvelous pageant of glittering armor and the beauty of emblazoned banners fluttering in the breeze and the clear shrill call of the trumpet. Still believing, still enraptured by the chivalric ideal, he reports savagery, treachery, limitless greed, and the pitiless slaughter of the poor when driven to revolt as minor stumbles in the grand adventure of valor and honor. Yet near the end, even Froissart could not hide from himself the decay made plain by a dissolute court, venality in high places, and a knighthood that kept losing battles. In 1397, the year he turned sixty, the defeat and massacre of the flower of chivalry at the hands of the Turks in the battle of Nicopolis set the seal on the incompetence of his heroes. Lastly, the murder of a King in England shocked him deeply, not for any love of Richard II but because the act was subversive of the whole order that sustained his world. As in Watergate, the underside had rolled to the surface all too visibly. Froissart had not the heart to continue and brought his chronicle to an end.

The sad century closed with a meeting between King Charles VI of 46 France and the Emperor Wenceslaus, the one intermittently mad and the other regularly drunk. They met at Reims in 1397 to consult on means of ending the papal schism, but whenever Charles had a lucid interval, Wenceslaus was in a stupor and so the conference, proving fruitless, was called off.

It makes an artistic ending. Yet in the same year Johann Gutenberg, 47 who was to change the world, was born. In the next century appeared Joan of Arc, embodying the new spirit of nationalism, still pure like mountain water before it runs downhill; and Columbus, who opened a new hemisphere; and Copernicus, who revolutionized the concept of the earth's relation to the universe; and Michelangelo, whose sculptured visions gave man a new status; in those proud, superb, unconquered figures, the human being, not God, was captain.

48    As our century enters its final quarter, I am not persuaded, despite the signs, that the end is necessarily doom. The doomsayers work by extrapolation; they take a trend and extend it, forgetting that the doom factor sooner or later generates a coping mechanism. I have a rule for this situation too, which is absolute: you cannot extrapolate any series in which the human element intrudes; history, that is, the human narrative, never follows, and will always fool, the scientific curve. I cannot tell you what twists it will take, but I expect, that like our ancestors, we, too, will muddle through.

## CONSIDERATIONS

1. Barbara Tuchman's essay is built on a useful and classic plan—comparisons and contrasts support and illustrate a main idea or thesis. Find three or four uses of comparison in this essay. Then see whether they do, in fact, undergird the author's major idea. Notice how contrasts are used in Henry David Thoreau's Journal item of June 16, 1854.

2. As a professional historian, Tuchman verifies her facts in many kinds of research materials, although in this relatively informal essay she does not footnote her sources. Notice how she manages to acknowledge those sources and smoothly work the material into her discussion. Compare how she handles this with the technique of another historian in your text, Harvey Green, "The Radio Age 1915–1945" (page 251).

3. "Guilt, I suspect," writes Tuchman in paragraph 14, "is modern; sin is medieval." This highly compressed, neatly balanced statement is a good example of aphorism and, more important, shows us, if we stop to think, a truly economical use of language. What is the point of the distinction?

4. What do you make of "Tuchman's Law," as the author mischievously puts it in paragraph 42? Is she just having fun, or can Tuchman's Law be demonstrated today as the mass media manage our awareness of trends?

5. Tuchman claims that much of the decaying public confidence in governing institutions comes from "our nurture in that conspiracy of fables called advertising." In what specific ways would Daniel Boorstin (see "The Pseudo-Event") agree or disagree with her?

6. History makes sense, students say, when it is clearly related to present life. Is Tuchman successful in bringing the two together? Explain.

7. In paragraph 6, Tuchman points up the difficulty of knowing whether we are in the decline of one historical period or in the dawn of a new one. How do you see yourself and your generation in relation to these two choices?

*Mark Twain is the pseudonym of Samuel Clemens (1835–1910),
who wrote* Tom Sawyer *(1876),* Huckleberry Finn *(1884), and other
novels, as well as short stories, essays, and an autobiography. Born
in Missouri, he settled with his wife in Hartford, Connecticut; at
his best, he wrote out of his midwestern past.*

*Twain's humor disguised his gloom and the misanthropy that
grew in his later years. The lightness of this essay's tone only
thinly covers Twain's rage and contempt. His sense of human
littleness puts Twain's vision in the modern tradition.*

— 96 —————————————————

# MARK TWAIN
## *Was the World Made for Man?*

Alfred Russel Wallace's revival of the theory that this earth is at the
centre of the stellar universe, and is the only habitable globe, has
aroused great interest in the world.

> —Literary Digest

For ourselves we do thoroughly believe that man, as he lives just
here on this tiny earth, is in essence and possibilities the most sublime existence in all the range of non-divine being—the chief love
and delight of God.

> —Chicago "Interior" (Presb.)

I seem to be the only scientist and theologian still remaining to be 1
heard from on this important matter of whether the world was made for
man or not. I feel that it is time for me to speak.

I stand almost with the others. They believe the world was made 2
for man, I believe it likely that it was made for man; they think there is
proof, astronomical mainly, that it was made for man. I think there is evidence only, not proof, that it was made for him. It is too early, yet, to
arrange the verdict, the returns are not all in. When they are all in, I

think they will show that the world was made for man; but we must not hurry, we must patiently wait till they are all in.

3    Now as far as we have got, astronomy is on our side. Mr. Wallace has clearly shown this. He has clearly shown two things: that the world was made for man, and that the universe was made for the world—to stiddy it, you know. The astronomy part is settled, and cannot be challenged.

4    We come now to the geological part. This is the one where the evidence is not all in, yet. It is coming in, hourly, daily, coming in all the time, but naturally it comes with geological carefulness and deliberation, and we must not be impatient, we must not get excited, we must be calm, and wait. To lose our tranquility will not hurry geology; nothing hurries geology.

5    It takes a long time to prepare a world for man; such a thing is not done in a day. Some of the great scientists, carefully ciphering the evidences furnished by geology, have arrived at the conviction that our world is prodigiously old, and they may be right, but Lord Kelvin is not of their opinion. He takes a cautious, conservative view, in order to be on the safe side, and feels sure it is not so old as they think. As Lord Kelvin is the highest authority in science now living, I think we must yield to him and accept his view. He does not concede that the world is more than a hundred million years old. He believes it is that old, but not older. Lyell believed that our race was introduced into the world 31,000 years ago, Herbert Spencer makes it 32,000. Lord Kelvin agrees with Spencer.

6    Very well. According to these figures it took 99,968,000 years to prepare the world for man, impatient as the Creator doubtless was to see him and admire him. But a large enterprise like this has to be conducted warily, painstakingly, logically. It was foreseen that man would have to have the oyster. Therefore the first preparation was made for the oyster. Very well, you cannot make an oyster out of whole cloth, you must make the oyster's ancestor first. This is not done in a day. You must make a vast variety of invertebrates, to start with—belemnites, trilobites, Jebusites, Amalekites, and that sort of fry; and put them to soak in a primary sea, and wait and see what will happen. Some will be a disappointment—the belemnites, the Ammonites and such; they will be failures, they will die out and become extinct, in the course of the nineteen million years covered by the experiment, but all is not lost, for the Amalekites will fetch the homestake; they will develop gradually into encrinites, and stalactites, and blatherskites, and one thing and another as the mighty ages creep on and the Archaean and the Cambrian Periods pile their lofty crags in the primordial seas, and at last the first grand stage in the preparation of the world for man stands completed, the oyster is done. An oyster has hardly any more reasoning power than a scientist has; and so it is reasonably certain that this one jumped to the conclusion that the nineteen million years was a preparation for *him*; but that would be just like an oyster, which is the most conceited animal

there is, except man. And anyway, this one could not know, at that early date, that he was only an incident in a scheme, and that there was some more to the scheme, yet.

The oyster being achieved, the next thing to be arranged for in the       7
preparation of the world for man was fish. Fish and coal—to fry it with. So the Old Silurian seas were opened up to breed the fish in, and at the same time the great work of building Old Red Sandstone mountains eighty thousand feet high to cold-storage their fossils in was begun. This latter was quite indispensable, for there would be no end of failures again, no end of extinctions—millions of them—and it would be cheaper and less trouble to can them in the rocks than keep tally of them in a book. One does not build the coal beds and eighty thousand feet of perpendicular Old Red Sandstone in a brief time—no, it took twenty million years. In the first place, a coal bed is a slow and troublesome and tiresome thing to construct. You have to grow prodigious forests of treeferns and reeds and calamites and such things in a marshy region; then you have to sink them under out of sight and let them rot; then you have to turn the streams on them, so as to bury them under several feet of sediment, and the sediment must have time to harden and turn to rock; next you must grow another forest on top, then sink it and put on another layer of sediment and harden it; then more forest and more rock, layer upon layer, three miles deep—ah, indeed it is a sickening slow job to build a coal-measure and do it right!

So the millions of years drag on; and meantime the fish culture is       8
lazying along and frazzling out in a way to make a person tired. You have developed ten thousand kinds of fishes from the oyster; and come to look, you have raised nothing but fossils, nothing but extinctions. There is nothing left alive and progressive but a ganoid or two and perhaps half a dozen asteroids. Even the cat wouldn't eat such.

Still, it is no great matter; there is plenty of time, yet, and they will       9
develop into something tasty before man is ready for them. Even a ganoid can be depended on for that, when he is not going to be called on for sixty million years.

The Paleozoic time limit having now been reached, it was neces-       10
sary to begin the next stage in the preparation of the world for man, by opening up the Mesozoic Age and instituting some reptiles. For man would need reptiles. Not to eat, but to develop himself from. This being the most important detail of the scheme, a spacious liberality of time was set apart for it—thirty million years. What wonders followed! From the remaining ganoids and asteroids and alkaloids were developed by slow and steady and painstaking culture those stupendous saurians that used to prowl about the steamy world in those remote ages, with their snaky heads reared forty feet in the air and sixty feet of body and tail racing and thrashing after. All gone, now, alas—all extinct, except the little handful of Arkansawrians left stranded and lonely with us here upon this far-flung verge and fringe of time.

11      Yes, it took thirty million years and twenty million reptiles to get one that would stick long enough to develop into something else and let the scheme proceed to the next step.

12      Then the pterodactyl burst upon the world in all his impressive solemnity and grandeur, and all Nature recognized that the Cenozoic threshold was crossed and a new Period open for business, a new stage begun in the preparation of the globe for man. It may be that the pterodactyl thought the thirty million years had been intended as a preparation for himself, for there was nothing too foolish for a pterodactyl to imagine, but he was in error, the preparation was for man. Without doubt the pterodactyl attracted great attention, for even the least observant could see that there was the making of a bird in him. And so it turned out. Also the makings of a mammal, in time. One thing we have to say to his credit, that in the matter of picturesqueness he was the triumph of his Period; he wore wings and had teeth, and was a starchy and wonderful mixture altogether, a kind of long-distance premonitory symptom of Kipling's marine:

> 'E isn't one o' the reg'lar Line, nor 'e isn't one of the crew,
> 'E's a kind of giddy harumfrodite—soldier an' sailor too!

13      From this time onward for nearly another thirty million years the preparation moved briskly. From the pterodactyl was developed the bird; from the bird the kangaroo, from the kangaroo the other marsupials; from these the mastodon, the megatherium, the giant sloth, the Irish elk, and all that crowd that you make useful and instructive fossils out of— then came the first great Ice Sheet, and they all retreated before it and crossed over the bridge at Bering Strait and wandered around over Europe and Asia and died. All except a few, to carry on the preparation with. Six Glacial Periods with two million years between Periods chased these poor orphans up and down and about the earth, from weather to weather—from tropic swelter at the poles to Arctic frost at the equator and back again and to and fro, they never knowing what kind of weather was going to turn up next; and if ever they settled down anywhere the whole continent suddenly sank under them without the least notice and they had to trade places with the fishes and scramble off to where the seas had been, and scarcely a dry rag on them; and when there was nothing else doing a volcano would let go and fire them out from wherever they had located. They led this unsettled and irritating life for twenty-five million years, half the time afloat, half the time aground, and always wondering what it was all for, they never suspecting, of course, that it was a preparation for man and had to be done just so or it wouldn't be any proper and harmonious place for him when he arrived.

14      And at last came the monkey, and anybody could see that man wasn't far off, now. And in truth that was so. The monkey went on developing for close upon five million years, and then turned into a man— to all appearances.

Such is the history of it. Man has been here 32,000 years. That it    15
took a hundred million years to prepare the world for him is proof that
that is what it was done for. I suppose it is. I dunno. If the Eiffel Tower
were now representing the world's age, the skin of paint on the pinnacle-
knob at its summit would represent man's share of that age; and anybody
would perceive that that skin was what the tower was built for. I reckon
they would, I dunno.

## CONSIDERATIONS

1. How and when does Twain let us know what he is up to in this essay?
2. Twain urges us, as we study the history of man and the world, to be patient, to
be calm, to jump to no conclusions. Note how he uses the oyster (paragraph 6) and the
pterodactyl (paragraph 12) to strengthen his point.
3. "Was the World Made for Man?" begins with two epigraphs: quotations selected by the author and used to state or hint at the central theme or image of the piece.
To learn the uses and limitations of this literary device, select epigraphs for one or two
other essays in this book. Consult Bartlett's *Familiar Quotations* for a little assistance.
4. One characteristic of satire is the use of gross exaggeration (see Jonathan
Swift's "A Modest Proposal," page 558). Is exaggeration a feature of Twain's essay?
5. Twain uses the Eiffel Tower to help us get some idea of the length of time and
the complexity of human history. Setting aside his satirical motives for a moment, observe that Twain is doing what every good writer tries to do: he presents abstractions in
concrete terms. Try the technique yourself by inventing a concrete way of making comprehensible the distance from here to the sun.
6. Read David Quammen's "So What?" (page 511) or Wendell Berry's "A Native
Hill" (page 42). They, too, are concerned with evolution. How does the tone of Twain's
essay differ from that of either Quammen's or Berry's? What has that to do with the
writer's purposes?

*John Updike (b. 1932) grew up in Pennsylvania and went to Harvard, where he edited the humor magazine, the* Lampoon. *On a fellowship year at Oxford, Updike sold a poem to the* New Yorker *and began his long relationship with that magazine. First he worked on the staff of the* New Yorker, *contributing to "The Talk of the Town." When he quit to freelance, he continued to write stories, poems, reviews, and articles for the magazine.* The Poorhouse Fair *(1959), his first novel, appeared in the same year as his first collection of stories,* The Same Door.

*Updike has published stories, novels, poems, and miscellaneous collections:* Assorted Prose *(1965),* Picked-up Pieces *(1975), and* Hugging the Shore *(1983). Among his best novels are* The Centaur *(1963) and* Rabbit at Rest *(1990).*

*In most of Updike's fiction, his protagonists are men, and they are men with considerable interest in their bodies.*

*This essay comes from an issue of the* Michigan Quarterly Review *devoted to the male body. On page 36 is Margaret Atwood's contribution to the same issue.*

*Notice how Updike handles tone: he is serious; he is not quite serious.*

— 97 —————————————————————

# JOHN UPDIKE
## *The Disposable Rocket*

1    Inhabiting a male body is much like having a bank account; as long as it's healthy, you don't think much about it. Compared to the female body, it is a low-maintenance proposition: a shower now and then, trim the fingernails every ten days, a haircut once a month. Oh yes, shaving—scraping or buzzing away at your face every morning. Byron, in *Don Juan*, thought the repeated nuisance of shaving balanced out the periodic agony, for females, of childbirth. Women are, his lines tell us,

---

Condemn'd to child-bed, as men for their sins
Have shaving too entail'd upon their chins,—
A daily plague, which in the aggregate
   May average on the whole with parturition.

From the standpoint of reproduction, the male body is a delivery system, as the female is a mazy device for retention. Once the delivery is made, men feel a faint but distinct falling-off of interest. Yet against the enduring female heroics of birth and nurture should be set the male's superhuman frenzy to deliver his goods: he vaults walls, skips sleep, risks wallet, health, and his political future all to ram home his seed into the gut of the chosen woman. The sense of the chase lives in him as the key to life. His body is, like a delivery rocket that falls away in space, a disposable means. Men put their bodies at risk to experience the release from gravity.

When my tenancy of a male body was fairly new—of six or so years' duration—I used to jump and fall just for the joy of it. Falling—backwards, downstairs—became a specialty of mine, an attention-getting stunt I was practicing into my thirties, at suburban parties. Falling is, after all, a kind of flying, though of briefer duration than would be ideal. My impulse to hurl myself from high windows and the edges of cliffs belongs to my body, not my mind, which resists the siren call of the chasm with all its might; the interior struggle knocks the wind from my lungs and tightens my scrotum and gives any trip to Europe, with its Alps, castle parapets, and gargoyled cathedral lookouts, a flavor of nightmare. Falling, strangely, no longer figures in my dreams, as it often did when I was a boy and my subconscious was more honest with me. An airplane, that necessary evil, turns the earth into a map so quickly the brain turns aloof and calm; still, I marvel that there is no end of young men willing to become jet pilots.   2

Any accounting of male-female differences must include the male's superior recklessness, a drive not, I think, toward death, as the darker feminist cosmogonies would have it, but to test the limits, to see what the traffic will bear—a kind of mechanic's curiosity. The number of men who do lasting damage to their young bodies is striking; war and car accidents aside, secondary-school sports, with the approval of parents and the encouragement of brutish coaches, take a fearful toll of skulls and knees. We were made for combat, back in the post-simian, East African days, and the bumping, the whacking, the breathlessness, the pain-smothering adrenaline rush, form a cumbersome and unfashionable bliss, but bliss nevertheless. Take your body to the edge, and see if it flies.   3

The male sense of space must differ from that of the female, who has such interesting, active, and significant inner space. The space that interests men is outer. The fly ball high against the sky, the long pass spiraling overhead, the jet fighter like a scarcely visible pinpoint nozzle laying down its vapor trail at forty thousand feet, the gazelle haunch   4 flickering just beyond arrow-reach, the uncountable stars sprinkled on their great black wheel, the horizon, the mountaintop, the quasar—these bring portents with them, and awaken a sense of relation with the invisible, with the empty. The ideal male body is taut with lines of potential force, a diagram extending outward; the ideal female body curves around centers of repose. Of course, no one is ideal, and the sexes are somewhat androgynous subdivisions of a species: Diana the huntress is a more trendy body-type nowadays than languid, overweight Venus, and polymorphous Dionysus poses for more underwear ads than Mars. Relatively, though, men's bodies, however elegant, are designed for covering territory, for moving on.

5      An erection, too, defies gravity, flirts with it precariously. It extends the diagram of outward direction into downright detachability—objective in the case of the sperm, subjective in the case of the testicles and penis. Men's bodies, at this juncture, feel only partly theirs; a demon of sorts has been attached to their lower torsos, whose performance is erratic and whose errands seem, at times, ridiculous. It is like having a (much) smaller brother toward whom you feel both fond and impatient; if he is you, it is you in curiously simplified and ignoble form. This sense, of the male body being two of them, is acknowledged in verbal love play and erotic writing, where the penis is playfully given its own name, an individuation not even the rarest rapture grants a vagina. Here, where maleness gathers to a quintessence of itself, there can be no insincerity, there can be no hiding; for sheer nakedness, there is nothing like a hopeful phallus; its aggressive shape is indivisible from its tender-skinned vulnerability. The act of intercourse, from the point of view of a consenting female, has an element of mothering, of enwrapment, of merciful concealment, even. The male body, for this interval, is tucked out of harm's way.

6      To inhabit a male body, then, is to feel somewhat detached from it. It is not an enemy, but not entirely a friend. Our essence seems to lie not in cells and muscles but in the traces our thoughts and actions inscribe on the air. The male body skims the surface of nature's deep, wherein the blood and pain and mysterious cravings of women perpetuate the species. Participating less in nature's processes than the female body, the male body gives the impression—false—of being exempt from time. Its powers of strength and reach descend in early adolescence, along with acne and sweaty feet, and depart, in imperceptible increments, after thirty or so. It surprises me to discover, when I remove my shoes and socks, the same paper-white hairless ankles that struck me as pathetic when I observed them on my father. I felt betrayed when, in some tumble of touch football twenty years ago, I heard my tibia snap; and when, between two reading engagements in Cleveland, my appendix tried to burst; and when, the other day, not for the first time, there arose to my nostrils out of my own body the musty attic smell my grandfather's body had.

A man's body does not betray its tenant as rapidly as a woman's. 7
Never as fine and lovely, it has less distance to fall; what rugged beauty it
has is wrinkle-proof. It keeps its capability of procreation indecently
long. Unless intense athletic demands are made on it, the thing serves
well enough to sixty, which is my age now. From here on, it's chancy.
There are no breasts or ovaries to admit cancer to the male body, but the
prostate, that awkwardly located little source of seminal fluid, shows the
strain of sexual function with fits of hysterical cell replication, and all
that beer and potato chips add up in the coronary arteries. A writer,
whose physical equipment can be minimal, as long as it gets him to the
desk, the lectern, and New York City once in a while, cannot but be
grateful to his body, especially to his eyes, those tender and intricate
sites where the brain extrudes from the skull, and to his hands, which
hold the pen or tap the keyboard. His body has been, not himself exactly,
but a close pal, pot-bellied and balding like most of his other pals now. A
man and his body are like a boy and the buddy who has a driver's license
and the use of his father's car for the evening; he goes along, gratefully,
for the ride.

## CONSIDERATIONS

1. ". . . enduring female heroics . . . male's superhuman frenzy . . ." What do
phrases like these tell you about Updike's attitude toward the subject of male-female relations?

2. In addition to the paired terms in No. 1 above, what other paired differences
seem to interest Updike in his essay? What might be learned from his use of them?

3. In paragraph 5, Updike writes explicitly, if imaginatively, about male and female sexual organs. How does he avoid slipping into pornography? Or does he? See
Margaret Atwood's "Pornography" (page 30) for help in explaining your answer.

4. Margaret Atwood's "Alien Territory" (page 36) is the most obvious companion
piece in your text to read with the Updike essay. How are they alike? How are they different?

5. One strength of Updike's style is his ability to provide not one, but a series of
concrete examples to give body to his abstract statements. Experiment with his technique in your next essay.

6. Imagine Updike sitting down for a coffee with the following women, all represented by essays in this text: Virginia Woolf, Gretel Ehrlich, Michelle Cliff, and Margaret
Atwood. What would the five find they had in common? Select one of the women and
imagine her interviewing Updike. Write up the interview as though it were to appear in
your college newspaper.

*Gore Vidal (b. 1925) entered the army after graduating from Philips Exeter Academy and never attended college. He published his first novel the year he turned twenty-one. Since then, he has run for Congress and lived in Europe. Vidal's writing includes plays, essays, and, chiefly, novels, including* Julian *(1964),* Myra Breckinridge *(1968),* Burr *(1973),* Kalki *(1979),* Lincoln *(1984),* Empire *(1987), and* Live from Golgotha *(1992).*

*In 1993 he published an immense volume of his collected essays:* United States: Essays 1952–1992. *At present, he reports that he is working on his seventh and last novel out of American history,* The Golden Age, *which will cover the years 1940–1950.*

*"There is not one human problem that could not be solved," he once told an interviewer, "if people would simply do as I advise."*

— **98** ————————————————————————————

# GORE VIDAL
## *Drugs*

————————————————————————————————————

1     It is possible to stop most drug addiction in the United States within a very short time. Simply make all drugs available and sell them at cost. Label each drug with a precise description of what effect—good and bad—the drug will have on the taker. This will require heroic honesty. Don't say that marijuana is addictive or dangerous when it is neither, as millions of people know—unlike "speed," which kills most unpleasantly, or heroin, which is addictive and difficult to kick.

2     For the record, I have tried—once—almost every drug and liked none, disproving the popular Fu Manchu theory that a single whiff of opium will enslave the mind. Nevertheless many drugs are bad for certain people to take and they should be told why in a sensible way.

3     Along with exhortation and warning, it might be good for our citizens to recall (or learn for the first time) that the United States was the creation of men who believed that each man has the right to do what he wants with his own life as long as he does not interfere with his neigh-

bor's pursuit of happiness (that his neighbor's idea of happiness is perse-cuting others does confuse matters a bit).

This is a startling notion to the current generation of Americans. 4
They reflect a system of public education which has made the Bill of Rights, literally, unacceptable to a majority of high school graduates (see the annual Purdue reports) who now form the "silent majority"—a phrase which that underestimated wit Richard Nixon took from Homer who used it to describe the dead.

Now one can hear the warning rumble begin: if everyone is allowed 5
to take drugs everyone will and the GNP will decrease, the Commies will stop us from making everyone free, and we shall end up a race of Zombies, passively murmuring "groovie" to one another. Alarming thought. Yet it seems most unlikely that any reasonably sane person will become a drug addict if he knows in advance what addiction is going to be like.

Is everyone reasonably sane? No. Some people will always become 6
drug addicts just as some people will always become alcoholics, and it is just too bad. Every man, however, has the power (and should have the le-gal right) to kill himself if he chooses. But since most men don't, they won't be mainliners either. Nevertheless, forbidding people things they like or think they might enjoy only makes them want those things all the more. This psychological insight is, for some mysterious reason, perennially denied our governors.

It is a lucky thing for the American moralist that our country has 7
always existed in a kind of time-vacuum: we have no public memory of anything that happened before last Tuesday. No one in Washington today recalls what happened during the years alcohol was forbidden to the peo-ple by a Congress that thought it had a divine mission to stamp out Demon Rum—launching, in the process, the greatest crime wave in the country's history, causing thousands of deaths from bad alcohol, and cre-ating a general (and persisting) contempt among the citizenry for the laws of the United States.

The same thing is happening today. But the government has learned 8
nothing from past attempts at prohibition, not to mention repression.

Last year when the supply of Mexican marijuana was slightly cur- 9
tailed by the Feds, the pushers got the kids hooked on heroin and deaths increased dramatically, particularly in New York. Whose fault? Evil men like the Mafiosi? Permissive Dr. Spock? Wild-eyed Dr. Leary? No.

The Government of the United States was responsible for those 10
deaths. The bureaucratic machine has a vested interest in playing cops and robbers. Both the Bureau of Narcotics and the Mafia want strong laws against the sale and use of drugs because if drugs are sold at cost there would be no money in it for anyone.

If there was no money in it for the Mafia, there would be no friendly 11
playground pushers, and addicts would not commit crimes to pay for the next fix. Finally, if there was no money in it, the Bureau of Narcotics would wither away, something they are not about to do without a struggle.

12      Will anything sensible be done? Of course not. The American people are as devoted to the idea of sin and its punishment as they are to making money—and fighting drugs is nearly as big a business as pushing them. Since the combination of sin and money is irresistible (particularly to the professional politician), the situation will only grow worse.

## CONSIDERATIONS

1. One mark of the experienced arguer is the ability to anticipate and thus neutralize his opponent's rebuttal. Where does Vidal do this? How effective is his attempt?

2. Vidal's argument (paragraphs 10, 11, and 12) that "the bureaucratic machine has a vested interest in playing cops and robbers" rests on his implication that law enforcers are at least as interested in preserving their jobs as they are in preserving law and order. Does he present any evidence to support this argument? What kind of evidence could he offer? How could you support a counterargument?

3. Vidal contends that "every man . . . should have the legal right to kill himself." How far would he (or you) extend that "right"? To all varieties of suicide, for instance, including assisted suicide and euthanasia?

4. Refresh your memory of the Bill of Rights—where do you find it?—and explain why Vidal says it has become "unacceptable to a majority of high school graduates."

5. Is the slang term "groovie"—usually spelled "groovy"—still current? Linguists often study slang because it changes faster than standard language. For the same reason, geneticists study fruit flies because the quick turnover of generations allows them to investigate principles of genetics within a brief period of time. In what way(s) do changes in slang parallel changes in English in general?

6. Given Vidal's belief in freedom of the individual, how do you think he would approach the question of gun control?

7. Write a rebuttal to Vidal's argument, using current statistics and trends in drug abuse.

*Alice Walker (b. 1944) grew up in Georgia and went to Sarah Lawrence College in New York City. She first published as a poet, with* Once *and* Revolutionary Petunias, *and has added collections of short stories, a biography of Langston Hughes, and novels—notably* The Color Purple *(1982). In 1993 she published* Her Blue Body Everything We Know: Earthling Poems, 1965–1990 Complete.

*She collected her essays as* In Search of Our Mothers' Gardens, *from which we take this article originally published in 1970. Elsewhere in* A Writer's Reader *you will find the white southern writer Flannery O'Connor, whom Alice Walker mentions in this essay.*

*In prose that sounds like talk—the clearest and most forthright talk—Alice Walker begins from the experience of her own family to exemplify the southern experience for the black writer. See how her mother's story, told with a daughter's affection, allows us entrance to this famous essay.*

— 99 ———————————————————

# ALICE WALKER
## *The Black Writer and the Southern Experience*

My mother tells of an incident that happened to her in the thirties   1
during the Depression. She and my father lived in a small Georgia town
and had half a dozen children. They were sharecroppers, and food, especially flour, was almost impossible to obtain. To get flour, which was distributed by the Red Cross, one had to submit vouchers signed by a local
official. On the day my mother was to go into town for flour she received
a large box of clothes from one of my aunts who was living in the North.
The clothes were in good condition, though well worn, and my mother
needed a dress, so she immediately put on one of those from the box and
wore it into town. When she reached the distribution center and

presented her voucher she was confronted by a white woman who looked her up and down with marked anger and envy.

2    "What'd you come up here for?" the woman asked.

3    "For some flour," said my mother, presenting her voucher.

4    "Humph," said the woman, looking at her more closely and with unconcealed fury. "Anybody dressed up as good as you don't need to come here *begging* for food."

5    "I ain't begging," said my mother, "the government is giving away flour to those that need it, and I need it. I wouldn't be here if I didn't. And these clothes I'm wearing was given to me." But the woman had already turned to the next person in line, saying over her shoulder to the white man who was behind the counter with her, "The *gall* of niggers coming in here dressed better than me!" This thought seemed to make her angrier still, and my mother, pulling three of her small children behind her and crying from humiliation, walked sadly back into the street.

6    "What did you and Daddy do for flour that winter?" I asked my mother.

7    "Well," she said, "Aunt Mandy Aikens lived down the road from us and she got plenty of flour. We had a good stand of corn so we had plenty of meal. Aunt Mandy would swap me a bucket of flour for a bucket of meal. We got by all right."

8    Then she added thoughtfully, "And that old woman that turned me off so short got down so bad in the end that she was walking on *two* sticks." And I knew she was thinking, though she never said it: Here I am today, my eight children healthy and grown and three of them in college and me with hardly a sick day for years. Ain't Jesus wonderful?

9    In this small story is revealed the condition and strength of a people. Outcasts to be used and humiliated by the larger society, the Southern black sharecropper and poor farmer clung to his own kind and to a religion that had been given to pacify him as a slave but which he soon transformed into an antidote against bitterness. Depending on one another, because they had nothing and no one else, the sharecroppers often managed to come through "all right." And when I listen to my mother tell and retell this story I find that the white woman's vindictiveness is less important than Aunt Mandy's resourceful generosity or my mother's ready stand of corn. For their lives were not about that pitiful example of Southern womanhood, but about themselves.

10    What the black Southern writer inherits as a natural right is a sense of *community*. Something simple but surprisingly hard, especially these days, to come by. My mother, who is a walking history of our community, tells me that when each of her children was born the midwife accepted as payment such home-grown or homemade items as a pig, a quilt, jars of canned fruits and vegetables. But there was never any question that the midwife would come when she was needed, whatever the eventual payment for her services. I consider this each time I hear of a

hospital that refuses to admit a woman in labor unless she can hand over a substantial sum of money, cash.

Nor am I nostalgic, as a French philosopher once wrote, for lost poverty. I am nostalgic for the solidarity and sharing a modest existence can sometimes bring. We knew, I suppose, that we were poor. Somebody knew; perhaps the landowner who grudgingly paid my father three hundred dollars a year for twelve months' labor. But we never considered ourselves to be poor, unless, of course, we were deliberately humiliated. And because we never believed we were poor, and therefore worthless, we could depend on one another without shame. And always there were the Burial Societies, the Sick-and-Shut-in Societies, that sprang up out of spontaneous need. And no one seemed terribly upset that black sharecroppers were ignored by white insurance companies. It went without saying, in my mother's day, that birth and death required assistance from the community, and that the magnitude of these events was lost on outsiders.

As a college student I came to reject the Christianity of my parents, and it took me years to realize that though they had been force-fed a white man's palliative, in the form of religion, they had made it into something at once simple and noble. True, even today, they can never successfully picture a God who is not white, and that is a major cruelty, but their lives testify to a greater comprehension of the teachings of Jesus than the lives of people who sincerely believe a God *must* have a color and that there can be such a phenomenon as a "white" church.

The richness of the black writer's experience in the South can be remarkable, though some people might not think so. Once, while in college, I told a white middle-aged Northerner that I hoped to be a poet. In the nicest possible language, which still made me as mad as I've ever been, he suggested that a "farmer's daughter" might not be the stuff of which poets are made. On one level, of course, he had a point. A shack with only a dozen or so books is an unlikely place to discover a young Keats. But it is narrow thinking, indeed, to believe that a Keats is the only kind of poet one would want to grow up to be. One wants to write poetry that is understood by one's people, not by the Queen of England. Of course, should she be able to profit by it too, so much the better, but since that is not likely, catering to her tastes would be a waste of time.

For the black Southern writer, coming straight out of the country, as Wright did—Natchez and Jackson are still not as citified as they like to think they are—there is the world of comparisons; between town and country, between the ugly crowding and griminess of the cities and the spacious cleanliness (which actually seems impossible to dirty) of the country. A country person finds the city confining, like a too tight dress. And always, in one's memory, there remain all the rituals of one's growing up: the warmth and vividness of Sunday worship (never mind that you never quite believed) in a little church hidden from the road, and houses set so far back into the woods that at night it is impossible for strangers to find them. The daily dramas that evolve in such a private world are pure gold. But this view of a strictly private and hidden existence, with its triumphs, failures, grotesqueries, is not nearly as valuable to the socially conscious black Southern writer as his double vision is. For not only is he in a position to see his own world, and its close community ("Homecomings" on First Sundays, barbecues to raise money to send to Africa—one of the smaller ironies—the simplicity and eerie calm of a black funeral, where the beloved one is buried way in the middle of a wood with nothing to mark the spot but perhaps a wooden cross already coming apart), but also he is capable of knowing, with remarkably silent accuracy, the people who make up the larger world that surrounds and suppresses his own.

15     It is a credit to a writer like Ernest J. Gaines, a black writer who writes mainly about the people he grew up with in rural Louisiana, that he can write about whites and blacks exactly as he sees them and *knows* them, instead of writing of one group as a vast malignant lump and of the others as a conglomerate of perfect virtues.

16     In large measure, black Southern writers owe their clarity of vision to parents who refused to diminish themselves as human beings by succumbing to racism. Our parents seemed to know that an extreme negative emotion held against other human beings for reasons they do not control can be blinding. Blindness about other human beings, especially for a writer, is equivalent to death. Because of this blindness, which is, above all, racial, the works of many southern writers have died. Much that we read today is fast expiring.

17     My own slight attachment to William Faulkner was rudely broken by realizing, after reading statements he made in *Faulkner in the University*, that he believed whites superior morally to blacks; that whites had a duty (which at their convenience they would assume) to "bring blacks along" politically, since blacks, in Faulkner's opinion, were "not ready" yet to function properly in a democratic society. He also thought that a black man's intelligence is directly related to the amount of white blood he has.

18     For the black person coming of age in the sixties, where Martin Luther King stands against the murderers of Goodman, Chaney, and Schwerner, there appears no basis for such assumptions. Nor was there any in Garvey's day, or in Du Bois's or in Douglass's or in Nat Turner's. Nor at any other period in our history, from the very founding of the country; for it was hardly incumbent upon slaves to be slaves and saints too. Unlike Tolstoy, Faulkner was not prepared to struggle to change the structure of the society he was born in. One might concede that in his fiction he did seek to examine the reasons for its decay, but unfortunately, as I have learned while trying to teach Faulkner to black students, it is not possible, from so short a range, to separate the man from his works.

One reads Faulkner knowing that his "colored" people had to come   19
through "Mr. William's" back door, and one feels uneasy, and finally enraged that Faulkner did not burn the whole house down. When the
provincial mind starts out *and continues* on a narrow and unprotesting
course, "genius" itself must run on a track.

Flannery O'Connor at least had the conviction that "reality" is at   20
best superficial and that the puzzle of humanity is less easy to solve than
that of race. But Miss O'Connor was not so much of Georgia, as in it.
The majority of Southern writers have been too confined by prevailing
social customs to probe deeply into mysteries that the Citizens Councils
insist must never be revealed.

Perhaps my Northern brothers will not believe me when I say there   21
is a great deal of positive material I can draw from my "underprivileged"
background. But they have never lived, as I have, at the end of a long road
in a house that was faced by the edge of the world on one side and nobody for miles on the other. They have never experienced the magnificent quiet of a summer day when the heat is intense and one is so very
thirsty, as one moves across the dusty cotton fields, that one learns forever that water is the essence of all life. In the cities it cannot be so clear
to one that he is a creature of the earth, feeling the soil between the toes,
smelling the dust thrown up by the rain, loving the earth so much that
one longs to taste it and sometimes does.

Nor do I intend to romanticize the Southern black country life. I   22
can recall that I hated it, generally. The hard work in the fields, the
shabby houses, the evil greedy men who worked my father to death and
almost broke the courage of that strong woman, my mother. No, I am
simply saying that Southern black writers, like most writers, have a heritage of love and hate, but that they also have enormous richness and
beauty to draw from. And, having been placed, as Camus says, "halfway
between misery and the sun," they, too, know that "though all is not
well under the sun, history is not everything."

No one could wish for a more advantageous heritage than that be-   23
queathed to the black writer in the South: a compassion for the earth, a
trust in humanity beyond our knowledge of evil, and an abiding love of
justice. We inherit a great responsibility as well, for we must give voice
to centuries not only of silent bitterness and hate but also of neighborly
kindness and sustaining love.

## *CONSIDERATIONS*

1. In paragraph 15, Alice Walker pays tribute to another black novelist, Ernest J.
Gaines, for refusing to make his characters into stereotypes of the white villain and the
black martyr. She has trouble acknowledging the achievements of another, more famous southern novelist, William Faulkner. Why? Read paragraph 18 for the answer.

2. Read Eudora Welty's short story, "A Worn Path" (page 653), and speculate on what Walker might say about Welty's understanding of the black southern experience. Walker might also be interested in the white southern experience—see Shirley Abbott's "The Importance of Dissimulation" (page 1).

3. Is Walker sentimental in expressing the values of her poverty-stricken childhood? Find specific statements or phrases to support your answer. Compare her tone with Louise Bogan's in "Miss Cooper and Me" (page 61), Frank O'Connor's in "Christmas" (page 464), or Richard Wright's in "The Library Card" (page 679).

4. "But Miss O'Connor was not so much *of* Georgia, as *in* it," writes Walker in expressing her reservations about Flannery O'Connor's contribution. Why does she distinguish between "of" Georgia and "in" it?

5. Walker mentions several ironies in connection with the black experience in the American South. Isolate a few of these, and try to explain the nature and appeal of irony in a writer's work.

6. How does the story in paragraphs 1 through 8 help make Walker's conclusions in paragraph 23 credible?

7. Compare Walker's comments with those of another black writer such as Ralph Ellison, "On Becoming a Writer" (page 191); Shelby Steele, "I'm Black, You're White, Who's Innocent?" (page 539); or Toni Morrison, "Nobel Lecture" (page 432).

8. In paragraph 14, Walker interrupts a sentence with a rather long parenthetical phrase. Study that interruption to learn why she uses it and how carefully a writer must manage it to avoid confusing the reader.

*Eudora Welty (b. 1909) lives in her native Jackson, Mississippi.* A
Curtain of Green *(1941) was her first volume of stories. Her novels
include* Losing Battles *(1970) and* The Optimist's Daughter *(1972),
which won her a Pulitzer Prize. In 1980* The Collected Stories of
Eudora Welty *was published, and in 1984* One Writer's Beginnings,
*a reminiscence. She has also published volumes of her
photographs.*

*"A Worn Path" is one of Welty's best-known stories, about
which she writes in the essay that follows.*

# — 100

# EUDORA WELTY
## *A Worn Path*

It was December—a bright frozen day in the early morning. Far out 1
in the country there was an old Negro woman with her head tied in a red
rag, coming along a path through the pinewoods. Her name was Phoenix
Jackson. She was very old and small and she walked slowly in the dark
pine shadows, moving a little from side to side in her steps, with the balanced heaviness and lightness of a pendulum in a grandfather clock. She
carried a thin, small cane made from an umbrella, and with this she kept
tapping the frozen earth in front of her. This made a grave and persistent
noise in the still air, that seemed meditative, like the chirping of a solitary little bird.

She wore a dark striped dress reaching down to her shoetops, and an 2
equally long apron of bleached sugar sacks, with a full pocket; all neat
and tidy, but every time she took a step she might have fallen over her
shoelaces, which dragged from her unlaced shoes. She looked straight
ahead. Her eyes were blue with age. Her skin had a pattern all its own of
numberless branching wrinkles and as though a whole little tree stood in
the middle of her forehead, but a golden color ran underneath, and the
two knobs of her cheeks were illuminated by a yellow burning under the
dark. Under the red rag her hair came down on her neck in the frailest of
ringlets, still black, and with an odor like copper.

3      Now and then there was a quivering in the thicket. Old Phoenix said, "Out of my way, all you foxes, owls, beetles, jack rabbits, coons, and wild animals! . . . Keep out from under these feet, little bobwhites. . . . Keep the big wild hogs out of my path. Don't let none of those come running in my direction. I got a long way." Under her small black-freckled hand her cane, limber as a buggy whip, would switch at the brush as if to rouse up any hiding things.

4      On she went. The woods were deep and still. The sun made the pine needles almost too bright to look at, up where the wind rocked. The cones dropped as light as feathers. Down in the hollow was the mourning dove—it was not too late for him.

5      The path ran up a hill. "Seem like there is chains about my feet, time I get this far," she said, in the voice of argument old people keep to use with themselves. "Something always take a hold on this hill—pleads I should stay."

6      After she got to the top she turned and gave a full, severe look behind her where she had come. "Up through pines," she said at length. "Now down through oaks."

7      Her eyes opened their widest and she started down gently. But before she got to the bottom of the hill a bush caught her dress.

8      Her fingers were busy and intent, but her skirts were full and long, so that before she could pull them free in one place they were caught in another. It was not possible to allow the dress to tear. "I in the thorny bush," she said. "Thorns, you doing your appointed work. Never want to let folks past—no sir. Old eyes thought you was a pretty little *green* bush."

9      Finally, trembling all over, she stood free, and after a moment dared to stoop for her cane.

10     "Sun so high!" she cried, leaning back and looking, while the thick tears went over her eyes. "The time getting all gone here."

11     At the foot of this hill was a place where a log was laid across the creek.

12     "Now comes the trial," said Phoenix.

13     Putting her right foot out, she mounted the log and shut her eyes. Lifting her skirt, leveling her cane fiercely before her, like a festival figure in some parade, she began to march across. Then she opened her eyes and she was safe on the other side.

14     "I wasn't as old as I thought," she said.

15     But she sat down to rest. She spread her skirts on the bank around her and folded her hands over her knees. Up above her was a tree in a pearly cloud of mistletoe. She did not dare to close her eyes, and when a little boy brought her a little plate with a slice of marble-cake on it she spoke to him. "That would be acceptable," she said. But when she went to take it there was just her own hand in the air.

16     So she left that tree, and had to go through a barbed-wire fence. There she had to creep and crawl, spreading her knees and stretching her fingers like a baby trying to climb the steps. But she talked loudly to her-

self: she could not let her dress be torn now, so late in the day, and she could not pay for having her arm or leg sawed off if she got caught fast where she was.

At last she was safe through the fence and risen up out in the clear-     17
ing. Big dead trees, like black men with one arm, were standing in the purple stalks of the withered cotton field. There sat a buzzard.

"Who you watching?"     18

In the furrow she made her way along     19

"Glad this not the season for bulls," she said, looking sideways,     20
"and the good Lord made his snakes to curl up and sleep in the winter. A pleasure I don't see no two-headed snake coming around that tree, where it come once. It took a while to get by him, back in the summer."

She passed through the old cotton and went into a field of dead     21
corn. It whispered and shook, and was taller than her head. "Through the maze now," she said, for there was no path.

Then there was something tall, black, and skinny there, moving be-     22
fore her.

At first she took it for a man. It could have been a man dancing in     23
the field. But she stood still and listened, and it did not make a sound. It was as silent as a ghost.

"Ghost," she said sharply, "who be you the ghost of? For I have     24
heard of nary death close by."

But there was no answer, only the ragged dancing in the wind.     25

She shut her eyes, reached out her hand, and touched a sleeve. She     26
found a coat and inside that an emptiness, cold as ice.

"You scarecrow," she said. Her face lighted. "I ought to be shut up     27
for good," she said with laughter. "My senses is gone. I too old. I the old-est people I ever know. Dance, old scarecrow," she said, "while I dancing with you."

She kicked her foot over the furrow, and with mouth drawn down     28
shook her head once or twice in a little strutting way. Some husks blew down and whirled in streamers about her skirts.

Then she went on, parting her way from side to side with the cane,     29
through the whispering field. At last she came to the end, to a wagon track, where the silver grass blew between the red ruts. The quail were walking around like pullets, seeming all dainty and unseen.

"Walk pretty," she said. "This the easy place. This the easy going."     30

She followed the track, swaying through the quiet bare fields,     31
through the little strings of trees silver in their dead leaves, past cabins silver from weather, with the doors and windows boarded shut, all like old women under a spell sitting there. "I walking in their sleep," she said, nodding her head vigorously.

In a ravine she went where a spring was silently flowing through a     32
hollow log. Old Phoenix bent and drank. "Sweetgum makes the water sweet," she said, and drank more. "Nobody knows who made this well, for it was here when I was born."

33    The track crossed a swampy part where the moss hung as white as lace from every limb. "Sleep on, alligators, and blow your bubbles." Then the track went into the road.

34    Deep, deep the road went down between the high green-colored banks. Overhead the live-oaks met, and it was as dark as a cave.

35    A black dog with a lolling tongue came up out of the weeds by the ditch. She was meditating, and not ready, and when he came at her she only hit him a little with her cane. Over she went in the ditch, like a little puff of milk-weed.

36    Down there, her senses drifted away. A dream visited her, and she reached her hand up, but nothing reached down and gave her a pull. So she lay there and presently went to talking. "Old woman," she said to herself, "that black dog come up out of the weeds to stall you off, and now there he sitting on his fine tail, smiling at you."

37    A white man finally came along and found her—a hunter, a young man, with his dog on a chain.

38    "Well, Granny!" he laughed. "What are you doing there?"

39    "Lying on my back like a June-bug waiting to be turned over, mister," she said, reaching up her hand.

40    He lifted her up, gave her a swing in the air, and set her down. "Anything broken, Granny?"

41    "No, sir, them old dead weeds is springy enough," said Phoenix, when she had got her breath. "I thank you for your trouble."

42    "Where do you live, Granny?" he asked, while the two dogs were growling at each other.

43    "Away back yonder, sir, behind that ridge. You can't even see it from here."

44    "On your way home?"

45    "No, sir, I going to town."

46    "Why that's too far! That's as far as I walk when I come out myself, and I get something for my trouble." He patted the stuffed bag he carried, and there hung down a little closed claw. It as one of the bobwhites, with its beak hooked bitterly to show it was dead. "Now you go on home, Granny!"

47    "I bound to go to town, mister," said Phoenix. "The time come around."

48    He gave another laugh, filling the whole landscape. "I know you colored people! Wouldn't miss going to town to see Santa Claus!"

49    But something held Old Phoenix very still. The deep lines in her face went into a fierce and different radiation. Without warning she had seen with her own eyes a flashing nickel fall out of the man's pocket on to the ground.

50    "How old are you, Granny?" he was saying.

51    "There is no telling, mister," she said, "no telling."

52    Then she gave a little cry and clapped her hands, and said, "Git on away from here, dog! Look! Look at that dog!" She laughed as if in admi-

ration. "He ain't scared of nobody. He a big black dog." She whispered, "Sick him!"

"Watch me get rid of that cur," said the man. "Sick him, Pete!    53
Sick him!"

Phoenix heard the dogs fighting and heard the man running and    54
throwing sticks. She even heard a gunshot. But she was slowly bending forward by that time, further and further forward, the lids stretched down over her eyes, as if she were doing this in her sleep. Her chin was lowered almost to her knees. The yellow palm of her hand came out from the fold of her apron. Her fingers slid down and along the ground under the piece of money with the grace and care they would have in lifting an egg from under a sitting hen. Then she slowly straightened up, she stood erect, and the nickel was in her apron pocket. A bird flew by. Her lips moved. "God watching me the whole time. I come to stealing."

The man came back, and his own dog panted about them. "Well, I    55
scared him off that time," he said, and then he laughed and lifted his gun and pointed it at Phoenix.

She stood straight and faced him.    56

"Doesn't the gun scare you?" he said, still pointing it.    57

"No, sir, I seen plenty go off closer by, in my day, and for less what I    58
done," she said, holding utterly still.

He smiled, and shouldered the gun. "Well, Granny," he said, "you    59
must be a hundred years old, and scared of nothing. I'd give you a dime if I had any money with me. But you take my advice and stay home, and nothing will happen to you."

"I bound to go on my way, mister," said Phoenix. She inclined her    60
head in the red rag. Then they went in different directions, but she could hear the gun shooting again and again over the hill.

She walked on. The shadows hung from the oak trees to the road    61
like curtains. Then she smelled wood-smoke, and smelled the river, and she saw a steeple and the cabins on their steep steps. Dozens of little black children whirled around her. There ahead was Natchez shining. Bells were ringing. She walked on.

In the paved city it was Christmas time. There were red and green    62
electric lights strung and crisscrossed everywhere, and all turned on in the daytime. Old Phoenix would have been lost if she had not distrusted her eyesight and depended on her feet to know where to take her.

She paused quietly on the sidewalk, where people were passing by.    63
A lady came along in the crowd, carrying an armful of red-, green-, and silver-wrapped presents; she gave off perfume like the red roses in hot summer, and Phoenix stopped her.

"Please, missy, will you lace up my shoe?" She held up her foot.    64

"What do you want, Grandma?"    65

"See my shoe," said Phoenix. "Do all right for out in the country,    66
but wouldn't look right to go in a big building."

67      "Stand still then, Grandma," said the lady. She put her packages down carefully on the sidewalk beside her and laced and tied both shoes tightly.

68      "Can't lace 'em with a cane," said Phoenix. "Thank you, missy. I doesn't mind asking a nice lady to tie up my shoe when I gets out on the street."

69      Moving slowly and from side to side, she went into the stone building and into a tower of steps, where she walked up and around and around until her feet knew to stop.

70      She entered a door, and there she saw nailed up on the wall the document that had been stamped with the gold seal and framed in the gold frame which matched the dream that was hung up in her head.

71      "Here I be," she said. There was a fixed and ceremonial stiffness over her body.

72      "A charity case, I suppose," said an attendant who sat at the desk before her.

73      But Phoenix only looked above her head. There was sweat on her face; the wrinkles shone like a bright net.

74      "Speak up, Grandma" the woman said. "What's your name? We must have your history, you know. Have you been here before? What seems to be the trouble with you?"

75      Old Phoenix only gave a twitch to her face as if a fly were bothering her.

76      "Are you deaf?" cried the attendant.

77      But then the nurse came in.

78      "Oh, that's just old Aunt Phoenix," she said. "She doesn't come for herself—she has a little grandson. She makes these trips just as regular as clockwork. She lives away back off the Old Natchez Trace." She bent down. "Well, Aunt Phoenix, why don't you just take a seat? We won't keep you standing after your long trip." She pointed.

79      The old woman sat down, bolt upright in the chair.

80      "Now, how is the boy?" asked the nurse.

81      Old Phoenix did not speak.

82      "I said, how is the boy?"

83      But Phoenix only waited and stared straight ahead, her face very solemn and withdrawn into rigidity.

84      "Is his throat any better?" asked the nurse. "Aunt Phoenix, don't you hear me? Is your grandson's throat any better since the last time you came for the medicine?"

85      With her hand on her knees, the old woman waited, silent, erect, and motionless, just as if she were in armor.

86      "You mustn't take up our time this way, Aunt Phoenix," the nurse said. "Tell us quickly about your grandson, and get it over. He isn't dead, is he?"

87      At last there came a flicker and then a flame of comprehension across her face, and she spoke.

"My grandson. It was my memory had left me. There I sat and for- 88
got why I made my long trip."

"Forgot?" The nurse frowned. "After you came so far?" 89

Then Phoenix was like an old woman begging a dignified forgive- 90
ness for waking up frightened in the night. "I never did go to school—I
was too old at the Surrender," she said in a soft voice. "I'm an old woman
without an education. It was my memory fail me. My little grandson, he
is just the same, and I forgot it in the coming."

"Throat never heals, does it?" said the nurse, speaking in a loud, 91
sure voice to Old Phoenix. By now she had a card with something written on it, a little list. "Yes, Swallowed lye. When was it—January—two—
three years ago—"

Phoenix spoke unasked now. "No, missy, he not dead, he just the 92
same. Every little while his throat begin to close up again, and he not
able to swallow. He not get his breath. He not able to help himself. So
the time come around, and I go on another trip for soothing medicine."

"All right. The doctor said as long as you came to get it you could 93
have it," said the nurse. "But it's an obstinate case."

"My little grandson, he sit up there in the house all wrapped up, 94
waiting by himself," Phoenix went on. "We is the only two left in the
world. He suffer and it don't seem to put him back at all. He got a sweet
look. He going to last. He wear a little patch quilt and peep out, holding
his mouth open like a little bird. I remembers so plain now. I not going to
forget him again, no, the whole enduring time. I could tell him from all
the others in creation."

"All right." The nurse was trying to hush her now. She brought her 95
a bottle of medicine. "Charity," she said, making a check mark in a book.

Old Phoenix held the bottle close to her eyes and then carefully put 96
it into her pocket.

"I thank you," she said. 97

"It's Christmas time, Grandma," said the attendant. "Could I give 98
you a few pennies out of my purse?"

"Five pennies is a nickel," said Phoenix stiffly. 99

"Here's a nickel," said the attendant. 100

Phoenix rose carefully and held out her hand. She received the 101
nickel and then fished the other nickel out of her pocket and laid it beside
the new one. She stared at her palm closely, with her head on one side.

Then she gave a tap with her cane on the floor. 102

"This is what come to me to do," she said. "I going to the store and 103
buy my child a little windmill they sells, make out of paper. He going to
find it hard to believe there such a thing in the world. I'll march myself
back where he waiting, holding it straight up in this hand."

She lifted her free hand, gave a little nod, turned round, and walked 104
out of the doctor's office. Then her slow step began on the stairs, going
down.

## CONSIDERATIONS

1. Some features of Old Phoenix's long journey might bring to mind Everyman's difficult travel through life. Do specific passages suggest that Old Phoenix's journey is symbolic or archetypal? Is such an interpretation necessary to the enjoyment of the story?

2. Would you say that Old Phoenix is senile or that she is in excellent control of her thoughts? What evidence can you find for your answer?

3. Is the grandson alive or dead? After you answer this question, read Welty's own comments on the story in the next selection.

4. Who was the little boy with the slice of marble-cake? Why does he appear and disappear so abruptly?

5. Eudora Welty makes no comment in the story on Old Phoenix's encounter with the white man. What details of that encounter reveal something about relations between whites and blacks?

6. What do you learn of Old Phoenix's sense of morality, sense of humor, and feeling of personal worth?

7. Read Alice Walker's "The Black Writer and the Southern Experience" (page 647), and decide if Welty's characterization of Phoenix Jackson is in any way representative of a writer's inheritance of the Southern experience.

*Here is the essay Welty wrote about "A Worn Path." Note how much, in her modest manner, she tells us about fiction.*

# — 101 —

# EUDORA WELTY
## *The Point of the Story*

A story writer is more than happy to be read by students; the fact that these serious readers think and feel something in response to his work he finds life-giving. At the same time he may not always be able to reply to their specific questions in kind. I wondered if it might clarify something, for both the questioners and myself, if I set down a general reply to the question that comes to me most often in the mail, from both students and their teachers, after some classroom discussion. The unrivaled favorite is this: "Is Phoenix Jackson's grandson really *dead*?" It refers to a short story I wrote years ago called "A Worn Path," which tells of a day's journey an old woman makes on foot from deep in the country into town and into a doctor's office on behalf of her little grandson; he is at home, periodically ill, and periodically she comes for his medicine; they give it to her as usual, she receives it and starts the journey back.

I had not meant to mystify readers by withholding any fact; it is not a writer's business to tease. The story is told through Phoenix's mind as she undertakes her errand. As the author at one with the character as I tell it, I must assume that the boy is alive. As the reader, you are free to think as you like, of course: the story invites you to believe that no matter what happens, Phoenix for as long as she is able to walk and can hold to her purpose will make her journey. The *possibility* that she would keep on even if he were dead is there in her devotion and its single-minded, single-track errand. Certainly the *artistic* truth, which should be good enough for the fact, lies in Phoenix's own answer to that question. When the nurse asks, "He isn't dead, is he?" she speaks for herself: "He still the same. He going to last."

3        The grandchild is the incentive. But it is the journey, the going of the errand, that is the story, and the question is not whether the grandchild is in reality alive or dead. It doesn't affect the outcome of the story or its meaning from start to finish. But it is not the question itself that has struck me as much as the idea, almost without exception implied in the asking, that for Phoenix's grandson to be dead would somehow make the story "better."

4        It's *all right*, I want to say to the students who write to me, for things to be what they appear to be, and for words to mean what they say. It's all right, too, for words and appearances to mean more than one thing—ambiguity is a fact of life. A fiction writer's responsibility covers not only what he presents as the facts of a given story but what he chooses to stir up as their implications; in the end, these implications, too, become facts, in the larger, fictional sense. But it is not all right, not in good faith, for things not to mean what they say.

5        The grandson's plight was real and it made the truth of the story, which is the story of an errand of love carried out. If the child no longer lived, the truth would persist in the "wornness" of the path. But his being dead can't increase the truth of the story, can't affect it one way or the other. I think I signal this, because the end of the story has been reached before old Phoenix gets home again: she simply starts back. To the question "Is the grandson really dead?" I could reply that it doesn't make any difference. I could also say that I did not make him up in order to let him play a trick on Phoenix. But my best answer would be: "Phoenix is alive."

6        The origin of a story is sometimes a trustworthy clue to the author—or can provide him with the clue—to its key image; maybe in this case it will do the same for the reader. One day I saw a solitary old woman like Phoenix. She was walking; I saw her, at middle distance, in a winter country landscape, and watched her slowly make her way across my line of vision. That sight of her made me write the story. I invented an errand for her, but that only seemed a living part of the figure she was herself; what errand other than for someone else could be making her go? And her going was the first thing, her persisting in her landscape was the real thing, and the first and real were what I wanted and worked to keep. I brought her up close enough, by imagination, to describe her face, make her present to the eyes, but the full-length figure moving across the winter fields was the indelible one and the image to keep, and the perspective extending into the vanishing distance the true one to hold in mind.

7        I invented for my character as I wrote, some passing adventures—some dreams and harassments and a small triumph or two, some jolts to her pride, some flights of fancy to console her, one or two encounters to scare her, a moment that gave her cause to feel ashamed, a moment to dance and preen—for it had to be a journey, and all these things belonged to that, parts of life's uncertainty.

A narrative line is in its deeper sense, of course, the tracing out of a    8
meaning, and the real continuity of a story lies in this probing forward.
The real dramatic force of a story depends on the strength of the emotion
that has set it going. The emotional value is the measure of the reach of
the story. What gives any such content to "A Worn Path" is not its circumstances but its subject: the deep-grained habit of love.

What I hoped would come clear was that in the whole surround of    9
this story, the world it threads through, the only certain thing at all is
the worn path. The habit of love cuts through confusion and stumbles or
contrives its way out of difficulty, it remembers the way even when it
forgets, for a dumbfounded moment, its reason for being. The path is the
thing that matters.

Her victory—old Phoenix's—is when she sees the diploma in the    10
doctor's office, when she finds "nailed up on the wall the document that
had been stamped with the gold seal and framed in the gold frame, which
matched the dream that was hung up in her head." The return with the
medicine is just a matter of retracing her own footsteps. It is the part of
the journey, and of the story, that can now go without saying.

In the matter of function, old Phoenix's way might even do as a    11
sort of parallel to your way of work if you are a writer of stories. The
way to get there is the all-important, all-absorbing problem, and this
problem is your reason for undertaking this story. Your only guide, too,
is your sureness about your subject, about what this subject is. Like
Phoenix, you work all your life to find your way, through all the obstructions and the false appearances and the upsets you may have
brought on yourself, to reach a meaning—using inventions of your imagination, perhaps helped out by your dreams and bits of good luck. And finally, too, like Phoenix, you have to assume that what you are working
in aid of is life, not death.

But you would make the trip anyway—wouldn't you?—just on hope.    12

---

## CONSIDERATIONS

1. Welty says that old Phoenix's return trip is "the part of the journey, and of the
story, that can now go without saying." If you were writing this story, would you choose
a different place to end it? Would you follow Old Phoenix all the way back into the
hills? Would you show the grandson? Why?

2. How does Welty feel about writers who intentionally mystify their readers?

3. Does "A Worn Path" illustrate what Welty means when she says, "A narrative
line is in its deeper sense . . . the tracing out of a meaning"?

4. In paragraph 4, Welty touches on the "factuality" of a work of fiction. This introduces a fascinating (if maddening) question: what is the difference between fiction
and nonfiction? Pay particular attention to Welty's paragraph 6, in which she discrimi-
nates between the "real thing" and the things she "invented." Think, too, of her statement
in paragraph 4: "these implications, too, become facts, in the larger, fictional sense."

5. Another southern writer, William Faulkner, wrote a short novel, *As I Lay Dying*, that can be read as a fuller version of "A Worn Path." It, too, is based on "an errand of love," as Welty puts it. Read the novel and discuss its parallels with Welty's story.

6. Eudora Welty in this essay, Amy Tan in "In the Canon, For All the Wrong Reasons" (page 576), and Flannery O'Connor, in her letters (page 439) discuss readers' interpretations of their stories. Which of these is most/least tolerant of her readers' notions? Which of the three adds most to your understanding of the story?

*Bailey White (b. 1950) is a commentator for the NPR program* All Things Considered. *She lives in the house where she grew up. For some time, she taught first grade, but has turned to writing full-time.*

*We take this memoir—her father* did *write for film and television—from* Mama Makes Up Her Mind and Other Dangers of Southern Living *(1994). See how the most extravagant details and anecdotes gather reality as they are told deadpan, without comment.*


— **102** —————

# BAILEY WHITE
## *Porsche*

Mama and I live in one of those houses where things accumulate. 1
Something can get laid down on a table or in the seat of a broken chair and just stay there forever. There's my great-grandmother's coat she hung on a nail before she died, and an old cousin's unfinished model of the *Flying Cloud*. There's a couple of bamboo chinaberry-seed popguns from three generations back and six bottles of Maybloom Cream beginning to turn iridescent with the tops rusted on. There's a row of Mason jars with some spooky-looking mold growing inside, left over from an old dead aunt's experiments with lethal herbs, and a drop-seat viyella union suit folded up on top of the carburetor of a Model A Ford. After a while the things begin to interlock. I really don't think we could get the ship model out in one piece even if we tried.

When I was eight years old, it got to be too much for my father. I re- 2
member the day he left for good. "I can't take it anymore!" he wailed. "I'm stagnating here! That coat!" He clutched the top of his head. I looked at my great-grandmother's coat. "That coat has been hanging

there for fifty years!" And he hurled himself out of the house, jumped into his little red Porsche, and scratched off in a swirl of dust.

3     I missed my father. "Why don't we move the coat?" I asked my mother. "Then maybe he'll come back."

4     "It's not just the coat, child," she told me. I looked around. There were my great-aunt Bertie's lavender satin wedding shoes perched on the seat of my Uncle Luten's unicycle, and Uncle Ralph's walleyed, hunchbacked, one-legged stuffed turkey on the library table. She was right. Even I could see it wasn't just the coat.

5     We never saw my father again, but we heard that he had driven that Porsche all the way to Hollywood, California, and made piles of money writing scripts for TV shows. Our neighbors told us they had actually seen his name on TV. We wouldn't know. We didn't have a TV set. Where would we have put it?

6     The years went by. Twenty years, thirty years. Then one fall my father died. His fourth wife, now his widow, called us on the phone. "He left you something," she said. "It should be there in a few days."

7     And a week later it arrived. It was my father's Porsche, the same one he had left us in—a 1958 Model 356 speedster, in original condition, complete with a wild-eyed driver whose hair stood straight up on end. Mama told him, "Just park it out behind the garden with those two tractors and that thing that might have been a lawnmower."

8     But he wouldn't do it. "Lady, you're crazy. You don't know what this is." He rubbed the car's fender with his shirttail. "You don't park a car like this out with the tractors."

9     We stood around and looked at it, Mama sighed. Then she went over and started pulling a section of screen off the side porch. We built a ramp, and the man drove the car up onto the porch. We drained the oil and gas out of it, put it up on blocks, and replaced the screen.

10    Now a man who says he belongs to the Porsche Club of America calls us up almost every night hoping to buy the car. We keep telling him no, no, no. Besides, that car has been in our house almost a year now. Even if he came all the way down here, I doubt he could get to it.

## CONSIDERATIONS

1. Bailey White's light, whimsical touch glosses over what another writer might have seized on as the subject of a thoroughly dismal story. What is that subject, and what do you think would happen to the Porsche in the hands of such a gloomy writer?

2. White's story is very brief, less than 750 words, yet she takes time to give us very specific images of some of the accumulated stuff. Why do you think she resisted, with brevity in mind, the temptation to summarize and instead rendered that accumulation? Write a summary of your own—a single sentence, say, of not more than twenty-

five or thirty words—to take the place of her opening paragraph. That should help you answer the preceding question.

3. Still thinking of rendering versus summarizing, look at White's summary of the father's life in paragraphs 5 and 6. What's missing?

4. With a professional writer's eye for bringing a piece to full circle, White manages something in the last sentence of her story that should remind you of her first. Explain.

5. In paragraph 9, what does White accomplish with the two-word statement "Mama sighed"?

*E. B. White (1899–1985) was born in Mount Vernon, New York, graduated from Cornell in 1921, and joined the staff of the* **New Yorker** *in 1926. For many years, he wrote the brief essay that led off that magazine's "Talk of the Town" and edited other "Talk" segments. In 1929 White collaborated with James Thurber on a book called* **Is Sex Necessary?** *and from time to time he published collections of essays and poems, most of them taken from the* **New Yorker** *and* **Harper's.** *Some of his best-known collections are* **One Man's Meat** *(1942),* **The Second Tree from the Corner** *(1953), and* **The Points of My Compass** *(1962). He is also the author of children's books, most notably* **Stuart Little** *(1945) and* **Charlotte's Web** *(1952), and the celebrated book on prose,* **The Elements of Style** *(with William Strunk Jr., 1959).*

*In 1937 White retired from the* **New Yorker** *and moved to a farm in Maine, where he continued to write those minimal, devastating comments attached to the proofhacks and other errors printed at the ends of the* **New Yorker's** *columns. There he continued his slow, consistent writing of superb prose. The collected* **Letters of E. B. White** *(1976),* **Essays of E. B. White** *(1977), and* **Poems and Sketches of E. B. White** *(1981) have reconfirmed this country's infatuation with the versatile author. A special citation from the Pulitzer Prize Committee in 1978 celebrated the publication of White's letters.*

*White celebrated the ordinary, even something as commonplace as the middle-class summer vacation by the lake. His prose raises the ordinary to the extraordinary. See how his quiet, intense attention to detail makes that detail luminous.*

## — 103 —

# E. B. WHITE
## *Once More to the Lake*

1     One summer, along about 1904, my father rented a camp on a lake in Maine and took us all there for the month of August. We all got ring-

worm from some kittens and had to rub Pond's Extract on our arms and legs night and morning, and my father rolled over in a canoe with all his clothes on; but outside of that the vacation was a success and from then on none of us ever thought there was any place in the world like that lake in Maine. We returned summer after summer—always on August 1st for one month. I have since become a salt-water man, but sometimes in summer there are days when the restlessness of the tides and the fearful cold of the sea water and the incessant wind that blows across the afternoon and into the evening make me wish for the placidity of a lake in the woods. A few weeks ago this feeling got so strong I bought myself a couple of bass hooks and a spinner and returned to the lake where we used to go, for a week's fishing and to revisit old haunts.

I took along my son, who had never had any fresh water up his nose   2 and who had seen lily pads only from train windows. On the journey over to the lake I began to wonder what it would be like. I wondered how time would have marred this unique, this holy spot—the coves and streams, the hills that the sun set behind, the camps and the paths behind the camps. I was sure that the tarred road would have found it out and I wondered in what other ways it would be desolated. It is strange how much you can remember about places like that once you allow your mind to return into the grooves that lead back. You remember one thing, and that suddenly reminds you of another thing. I guess I remembered clearest of all the early mornings, when the lake was cool and motionless, remembered how the bedroom smelled of the lumber it was made of and of the wet woods whose scent entered through the screen. The partitions in the camp were thin and did not extend clear to the top of the rooms, and as I was always the first up I would dress softly so as not to wake the others, and sneak out into the sweet outdoors and start out in the canoe, keeping close along the shore in the long shadows of the pines. I remembered being very careful never to rub my paddle against the gunwale for fear of disturbing the stillness of the cathedral.

The lake had never been what you would call a wild lake. There   3 were cottages sprinkled around the shores, and it was in farming country although the shores of the lake were quite heavily wooded. Some of the cottages were owned by nearby farmers, and you would live at the shore and eat your meals at the farmhouse. That's what our family did. But although it wasn't wild, it was a fairly large and undisturbed lake and there were places in it which, to a child at least, seemed infinitely remote and primeval.

I was right about the tar: it led to within half a mile of the shore. But   4 when I got back there, with my boy, and we settled into a camp near a farmhouse and into the kind of summertime I had known, I could tell that it was going to be pretty much the same as it had been before—I knew it, lying in bed the first morning, smelling the bedroom, and hearing the boy sneak quietly out and go off along the shore in a boat. I began to sustain the illusion that he was I, and therefore, by simple transposition, that I was my father. This sensation persisted, kept cropping up all the time we were there. It was not an entirely new feeling, but in this setting it grew much stronger. I seemed to be living a dual existence. I would be in the middle of some simple act, I would be picking up a bait box or laying down a table fork, or I would be saying something, and suddenly it would be not I but my father who was saying the words or making the gesture. It gave me a creepy sensation.

5      We went fishing the first morning. I felt the same damp moss covering the worms in the bait can, and saw the dragonfly alight on the tip of my rod as it hovered a few inches from the surface of the water. It was the arrival of this fly that convinced me beyond any doubt that everything was as it always had been, that the years were a mirage and there had been no years. The small waves were the same, chucking the rowboat under the chin as we fished at anchor, and the boat was the same boat, the same color green and the ribs broken in the same places, and under the floor-boards the same fresh-water leavings and débris—the dead hellgrammite, the wisps of moss, the rusty discarded fishhook, the dried blood from yesterday's catch. We stared silently at the tips of our rods, at the dragonflies that came and went. I lowered the tip of mine into the water, tentatively, pensively dislodging the fly, which darted two feet away, poised, darted two feet back, and came to rest again a little farther up the rod. There had been no years between the ducking of this dragonfly and the other one—the one that was part of memory. I looked at the boy, who was silently watching his fly, and it was my hands that held his rod, my eyes watching. I felt dizzy and didn't know which rod I was at the end of.

6      We caught two bass, hauling them in briskly as though they were mackerel, pulling them over the side of the boat in a businesslike manner without any landing net, and stunning them with a blow on the back of the head. When we got back for a swim before lunch, the lake was exactly where we had left it, the same number of inches from the dock, and there was only the merest suggestion of a breeze. This seemed an utterly enchanted sea, this lake you could leave to its own devices for a few hours and come back to, and find that it had not stirred, this constant and trustworthy body of water. In the shallows, the dark, water-soaked sticks and twigs, smooth and old, were undulating in clusters on the bottom against the clean ribbed sand, and the track of the mussel was plain. A school of minnows swam by, each minnow with its small individual shadow, doubling the attendance, so clear and sharp in the sunlight. Some of the other campers were in swimming, along the shore, one of them with a cake of soap, and the water felt thin and clear and unsubstantial. Over the years there had been this person with the cake of soap, this cultist, and here he was. There had been no years.

7      Up to the farmhouse to dinner through the teeming, dusty field, the road under our sneakers was only a two-track road. The middle track was missing, the one with the marks of the hooves and splotches of dried,

flaky manure. There had always been three tracks to choose from in choosing which track to walk in; now the choice was narrowed down to two. For a moment I missed terribly the middle alternative. But the way led past the tennis court, and something about the way it lay there in the sun reassured me; the tape had loosened along the backline, the alleys were green with plantains and other weeds, and the net (installed in June and removed in September) sagged in the dry noon, and the whole place steamed with midday heat and hunger and emptiness. There was a choice of pie for dessert, and one was blueberry and one was apple, and the waitresses were the same country girls, there having been no passage of time, only the illusion of it as in a dropped curtain—the waitresses were still fifteen; their hair had been washed, that was the only difference—they had been to the movies and seen the pretty girls with the clean hair.

Summertime, oh summertime, pattern of life indelible, the fade-    8
proof lake, the woods unshatterable, the pasture with the sweetfern and the juniper forever and ever, summer without end; this was the background, and the life along the shore was the design, the cottages with their innocent and tranquil design, their tiny docks with the flagpole and the American flag floating against the white clouds in the blue sky, the little paths over the roots of the trees leading from camp to camp and the paths leading back to the outhouses and the can of lime for sprinkling, and at the souvenir counters at the store the miniature birch-bark canoes and the post cards that showed things looking a little better than they looked. This was the American family at play, escaping the city heat, wondering whether the newcomers in the camp at the head of the cove were "common" or "nice," wondering whether it was true that the people who drove up for Sunday dinner at the farmhouse were turned away because there wasn't enough chicken.

It seemed to me, as I kept remembering all this, that those times    9
and those summers had been infinitely precious and worth saving. There had been jollity and peace and goodness. The arriving (at the beginning of August) had been so big a business in itself, at the railway station the farm wagon drawn up, the first smell of the pine-laden air, the first glimpse of the smiling farmer, and the great importance of the trunks and your father's enormous authority in such matters, and the feel of the wagon under you for the long ten-mile haul, and at the top of the last long hill catching the first view of the lake after eleven months of not seeing this cherished body of water. The shouts and cries of the other campers when they saw you, and the trunks to be unpacked, to give up their rich burden. (Arriving was less exciting nowadays, when you sneaked up in your car and parked it under a tree near the camp and took out the bags and in five minutes it was all over, no fuss, no loud wonderful fuss about trunks.)

Peace and goodness and jollity. The only thing that was wrong now,    10
really, was the sound of the place, an unfamiliar nervous sound of the

outboard motors. This was the note that jarred, the one thing that would sometimes break the illusion and set the years moving. In those other summertimes all motors were inboard; and when they were at a little distance, the noise they made was a sedative, an ingredient of summer sleep. They were one-cylinder and two-cylinder engines, and some were make-and-break and some were jump-spark, but they all made a sleepy sound across the lake. The one-lungers throbbed and fluttered, and the twin-cylinder ones purred and purred and that was a quiet sound too. But now the campers all had outboards. In the daytime, in the hot mornings, these motors made a petulant, irritable sound; at night, in the still evening when the afterglow lit the water, they whined about one's ears like mosquitoes. My boy loved our rented outboard, and his great desire was to achieve singlehanded mastery over it, and authority, and he soon learned the trick of choking it a little (but not too much), and the adjustment of the needle valve. Watching him I would remember the things you could do with the old one-cylinder engine with the heavy flywheel, how you could have it eating out of your hand if you got really close to it spiritually. Motor boats in those days didn't have clutches, and you would make a landing by shutting off the motor at the proper time and coasting in with a dead rudder. But there was a way of reversing them, if you learned the trick, by cutting the switch and putting it on again exactly on the final dying revolution of the flywheel, so that it would kick back against compression and begin reversing. Approaching a dock in a strong following breeze, it was difficult to slow up sufficiently by the ordinary coasting method, and if a boy felt he had complete mastery over his motor, he was tempted to keep it running beyond its time and then reverse it a few feet from the dock. It took a cool nerve, because if you threw the switch a twentieth of a second too soon you could catch the flywheel when it still had speed enough to go up past center, and the boat would leap ahead, charging bull-fashion at the dock.

11    We had a good week at the camp. The bass were biting well and the sun shone endlessly, day after day. We would be tired at night and lie down in the accumulated heat of the little bedrooms after the long hot day and the breeze would stir almost imperceptibly outside and the smell of the swamp drift in through the rusty screens. Sleep would come easily and in the morning the red squirrel would be on the roof, tapping out his gay routine. I kept remembering everything, lying in bed in the mornings—the small steamboat that had a long rounded stern like the lip of a Ubangi, and how quietly she ran on the moonlight sails, when the older boys played their mandolins and the girls sang and we ate doughnuts dipped in sugar, and how sweet the music was on the water in the shining light, and what it had felt like to think about girls then. After breakfast we would go up to the store and the things were in the same place—the minnows in a bottle, the plugs and spinners disarranged and pawed over by the youngsters from the boys' camp, the fig newtons and the Beeman's gum. Outside, the road was tarred and cars stood in front of

the store. Inside, all was just as it had always been, except there was more Coca-Cola and not so much Moxie and root beer and birch beer and sarsaparilla. We would walk out with a bottle of pop apiece and sometimes the pop would backfire up our noses and hurt. We explored the streams, quietly, where the turtles slid off the sunny logs and dug their way into the soft bottom; and we lay on the town wharf and fed worms to the tame bass. Everywhere we went I had trouble making out which was I, the one walking at my side, the one walking in my pants.

One afternoon while we were there at that lake a thunderstorm   12
came up. It was like the revival of an old melodrama that I had seen long ago with childish awe. The second-act climax of the drama of the electrical disturbance over a lake in America had not changed in any important respect. This was the big scene, still the big scene. The whole thing was so familiar, the first feeling of oppression and heat and a general air around camp of not wanting to go very far away. In midafternoon (it was all the same) a curious darkening of the sky, and a lull in everything that had made life tick; and then the way the boats suddenly swung the other way at their moorings with the coming of a breeze out of the new quarter, and the premonitory rumble. Then the kettle drum, then the snare, then the bass drum and cymbals, then crackling light against the dark, and the gods grinning and licking their chops in the hills. Afterward the calm, the rain steadily rustling in the calm lake, the return of light and hope and spirits, and the campers running out in joy and relief to go swimming in the rain, their bright cries perpetuating the deathless joke about how they were getting simply drenched, and the children screaming with delight at the new sensation of bathing in the rain, and the joke about getting drenched linking the generations in a strong indestructible chain. And the comedian who waded in carrying an umbrella.

When the others went swimming my son said he was going in too.   13
He pulled his dripping trunks from the line where they had hung all through the shower, and wrung them out. Languidly, and with no thought of going in, I watched him, his hard little body, skinny and bare, saw him wince slightly as he pulled up around his vitals the small, soggy, icy garment. As he buckled the swollen belt suddenly my groin felt the chill of death.

## CONSIDERATIONS

1. White notes changes at the old summer place, but he is more moved by the sameness. Locate examples of his feeling of sameness, and consider how these examples contribute to his themes.

2. One of the talents of E. B. White is his ability to select tiny details and make them work for what one might call the larger cause of his essay. An example would be his use of a cake of soap at the end of paragraph 6. Jot down several other instances of this technique, and write a paragraph explaining how they work.

3. The author expresses a predictable dislike of outboard motors in paragraph 10. How, in his development of the paragraph, does he overcome the stereotypical quality of that reaction?

4. In the same way that the old woman's long trip in Eudora Welty's "A Worn Path" (page 653) could be seen to take on allegorical meanings, White's awareness of the succession of generations returning to the lake might suggest a much larger, more universal meaning than the literal account could offer. How does the author accomplish this? Point out specific passages to back up your answer.

5. To keep his account from becoming too serious, White is careful to use a rather slangy diction here and there. Find a few examples of words of that sort, and reflect on the way White uses them to control the tone of his essay. Contrast them with the diction of a sentence like that which begins paragraph 8.

6. Study paragraph 12, which is what might be called an extended metaphor, or an analogy, beginning with the second sentence. How does his figurative treatment of the thunderstorm contribute to our appreciation of the scene? Notice the characteristic E. B. White touch in the last sentence of the paragraph.

7. Has White prepared us for the last sentence of the essay? How does it change the effect of the whole essay?

*Virginia Woolf (1882–1941) is best known as a novelist. The* Voyage Out *appeared in 1915, followed by* Night and Day *(1919),* Jacob's Room *(1922),* Mrs. Dalloway *(1925),* To the Lighthouse *(1927),* Orlando *(1928),* The Waves *(1931),* The Years *(1937), and* Between the Acts, *published shortly after her death. Daughter of Sir Leslie Stephen, Victorian critic and essayist who edited the* Dictionary of National Biography, *she was educated at home and began her literary career as a critic for the* Times Literary Supplement. *She wrote essays regularly until her death; four volumes of her* Collected Essays *appeared in the United States in 1967. Her publishers issued six volumes of her collected letters, and her diary was published in 1953.*

*With her sister Vanessa, a painter; her husband Leonard Woolf, an editor and writer; and Vanessa's husband Clive Bell, an art critic, Woolf lived at the center of the Bloomsbury group— artists and intellectuals who gathered informally to talk and to amuse each other, and whose unconventional ideas and habits, when they were known, shocked the stolid British public. John Maynard Keynes, the economist, was a member of the varied group, which also included biographer Lytton Strachey, novelist E. M. Forster, and eventually expatriate American poet T. S. Eliot. With her husband, Virginia Woolf founded* The Hogarth Press, *a small firm dedicated to publishing superior works. Among its authors were Eliot and Woolf herself.*

*Virginia Woolf, a biography by her nephew, Quentin Bell, gives an intimate picture of the whole group. Of all the Bloomsbury people, Woolf was perhaps the most talented. Through most of her life, she struggled against recurring mental illness, which brought intense depression and suicidal impulses. When she was fifty-nine, she drowned herself in the River Ouse.*

*The following famous passage from* A Room of One's Own *(1929) presents a feminist argument by means of a memorable supposition.*

— **104** —————————————————

# VIRGINIA WOOLF
## *If Shakespeare Had Had a Sister*

*vocab word*

1    It is a perennial puzzle why no woman wrote a word of that extraordinary (Elizabethan) literature when every other man, it seemed was capable of song or sonnet. What were the conditions in which women lived, I asked myself; for fiction, imaginative work that is, is not dropped like a pebble upon the ground, as science may be; fiction is like a spider's web, attached ever so lightly perhaps, but still attached to life at all four corners. Often the attachment is scarcely perceptible; Shakespeare's plays, for instance, seem to hang there complete by themselves. But when the web is pulled askew, hooked up at the edge, torn in the middle, one remembers that these webs are not spun in midair by incorporeal creatures, but are the work of suffering human beings, and are attached to grossly material things, like health and money and the house we live in. . . .

2    But what I find . . . is that nothing is known about women before the eighteenth century. I have no model in my mind to turn about this way and that. Here am I asking why women did not write poetry in the Elizabethan age, and I am not sure how they were educated; whether they were taught to write; whether they had sitting-rooms to themselves; how many women had children before they were twenty-one; what, in short, they did from eight in the morning till eight at night. They had no money, evidently; according to Professor Trevelyan they were married whether they liked it or not before they were out of the nursery, at fifteen or sixteen very likely. It would have been extremely odd, even upon this showing, had one of them suddenly written the plays of Shakespeare, I concluded, and I thought of that old gentleman, who is dead now, but was a bishop, I think, who declared that it was impossible for any woman, past, present, or to come, to have the genius of Shakespeare. He wrote to the papers about it. He also told a lady who applied to him for information that cats do not as a matter of fact go to heaven, though they have, he added, souls of a sort. How much thinking those old gentlemen used to save one! How the borders of ignorance shrank back at their approach! Cats do not go to heaven. Women cannot write the plays of Shakespeare.

*salvation*

*Why did she include this?*

Be that as it may, I could not help thinking, as I looked at the works  3
of Shakespeare on the shelf, that the bishop was right at least in this; it
would have been impossible, completely and entirely, for any woman to
have written the plays of Shakespeare in the age of Shakespeare. Let me
imagine, since facts are so hard to come by, what would have happened
had Shakespeare had a wonderfully gifted sister, called Judith, let us say.
Shakespeare himself went, very probably—his mother was an heiress—to
the grammar school, where he may have learned Latin—Ovid, Virgil and
Horace—and the elements of grammar and logic. He was, it is well
known, a wild boy who poached rabbits, perhaps shot a deer, and had,
rather sooner than he should have done, to marry a woman in the neigh-
bourhood, who bore him a child rather quicker than was right. That es-
capade sent him to seek his fortune in London. He had, it seemed, a taste
for the theater; he began by holding horses at the stage door. Very soon he
got work in the theatre, became a successful actor, and lived at the hub of
the universe, meeting everybody, knowing everybody, practising his art
on the boards, exercising his wits in the streets, and even getting access to
the palace of the queen. Meanwhile his extraordinarily gifted sister, let us
suppose, remained at home. She was as adventurous, as imaginative, as
agog to see the world as he was. But she was not sent to school. She had no
chance of learning grammar and logic, let alone of reading Horace and
Virgil. She picked up a book now and then, one of her brother's perhaps,
and read a few pages. But then her parents came in and told her to mend
the stockings or mind the stew and not moon about with books and papers. They would have spoken sharply but kindly, for they were substantial people who knew the conditions of life for a woman and loved their
daughter—indeed, more likely than not she was the apple of her father's
eye. Perhaps she scribbled some pages up in an apple loft on the sly, but
was careful to hide them or set fire to them. Soon, however, before she was
out of her teens, she was to be betrothed to the son of a neighbouring wool-
stapler. She cried out that marriage was hateful to her, and for that she was
severely beaten by her father. Then he ceased to scold her. He begged her
instead not to hurt him, not to shame him in this matter of her marriage.
He would give her a chain of beads or a fine petticoat, he said; and there
were tears in his eyes. How could she disobey him? How could she break
his heart? The force of her own gift alone drove her to it. She made up a
small parcel of her belongings, let herself down by a rope one summer's
night and took the road to London. She was not seventeen. The birds that
sang in the hedge were not more musical than she was. She had the quickest fancy, a gift like her brother's, for the tune of words. Like him, she had
a taste for the theatre. She stood at the stage door; she wanted to act, she
said. Men laughed in her face. The manager—a fat, loose-lipped man—guf-
fawed. He bellowed something about poodles dancing and women acting—no woman, he said, could possibly be an actress. He hinted—you can
imagine what. She could get no training in her craft. Could she even seek
her dinner in a tavern or roam the streets at midnight? Yet her genius was

for fiction and lusted to feed abundantly upon the lives of men and women and the study of their ways. At last—for she was very young, oddly like Shakespeare the poet in her face, with the same grey eyes and rounded brows—at last Nick Greene the actor-manager took pity on her; she found herself with child by that gentleman and so—who shall measure the heat and violence of the poet's heart when caught and tangled in a woman's body?—killed herself one winter's night and lies buried at some cross-roads where the omnibuses now stop outside the Elephant and Castle.

4      That, more or less, is how the story would run, I think, if a woman in Shakespeare's day had had Shakespeare's genius. But for my part, I agree with the deceased bishop, if such he was—it is unthinkable that any woman in Shakespeare's day should have had Shakespeare's genius. For genius like Shakespeare's is not born among labouring, uneducated, servile people. It was not born in England among the Saxons and the Britons. It is not born today among the working classes. How, then, could it have been born among women whose work began, according to Professor Trevelyan, almost before they were out of the nursery, who were forced to it by their parents and held to it by all the power of law and custom?

*[margin handwritten note: Refers to question / his authority.]*

## CONSIDERATIONS

1. In paragraph 3, Woolf develops at length an imaginary sister of Shakespeare. Why does the writer call that sister Judith rather than Priscilla or Elizabeth or Megan? A quick look at Shakespeare's biography will give you the answer and alert you to a mischievous side of Woolf.

2. At the end of paragraph 2, Woolf says, "How the borders of ignorance shrank back at their approach!" Is this a straight statement, or does she mean something other than what the words say? Study the differences among the following terms, which often are used mistakenly as synonyms: sarcasm, satire, irony, wit, humor, cynicism, invective, the sardonic.

3. Woolf's essay consists of four paragraphs, one of which accounts for more than half of the composition. Can you find a justification for this disproportionately long paragraph? If you can't justify it, where would you break the paragraph into two or more? Why?

4. Concoct an imaginary biography with a purpose like Woolf's account of Judith: for example, Mozart's daughter, Napoleon's father, the brother of Jesus Christ, the Queen of Luxembourg, Tolstoy's nephew or niece.

5. ". . . for fiction . . . is not dropped like a pebble upon the ground, as science may be . . ." (paragraph 1). In what sense is science dropped like a pebble upon the ground? What is the point of this odd comparison?

6. If you were to invite three authors from this book to an informal discussion of Woolf's essay, whom would you select? Why? Make your selections on the basis of some relationship among their ideas and hers. What sort of outcome would you expect from such a conversation? Write a page of this dialog.

7. Woolf wrote in the informal idiom of an educated Englishwoman of the 1920s; there are a number of differences between her language and ours. Circle a half dozen such differences and contrast British English with American English.

*Richard Wright (1908–1960) was born on a plantation in Natchez, Mississippi. A restless and unruly child, he left home at fifteen and supported himself doing unskilled work, gradually improving his employment until he became a clerk in a post office. In this essay from his autobiography* Black Boy *(1944), he writes about an occasion that transformed his life. By chance, he became obsessed with the notion of reading H. L. Mencken, the iconoclastic editor and essayist. He schemed and plotted to borrow Mencken's books from the library, and when he succeeded, his career as a writer began.*

*Determined to be a successful writer, Richard Wright worked on the Federal Writers' Project, wrote for the* New Masses, *and finally won a prize from* Story *magazine for a short novel called* Uncle Tom's Children. *The following year he was awarded a Guggenheim Fellowship, and in 1940 he published his novel* Native Son, *which has become an American classic. In 1946 he emigrated to Paris, where he lived until his death. His later novels include* The Outsider *(1953) and* The Long Dream *(1958). In 1977 his publisher issued the second half of* Black Boy, *entitled* American Hunger. *In 1991 the Library of America published Richard Wright's* Works *in two volumes.*

— 105 ————————————————————————————

# RICHARD WRIGHT
## *The Library Card*

————————————————————————————

One morning I arrived early at work and went into the bank lobby    1
where the Negro porter was mopping. I stood at a counter and picked up
the Memphis *Commercial Appeal* and began my free reading of the
press. I came finally to the editorial page and saw an article dealing with
one H. L. Mencken. I knew by hearsay that he was the editor of the
*American Mercury*, but aside from that I knew nothing about him. The
article was a furious denunciation of Mencken, concluding with one,
hot, short sentence: Mencken is a fool.

2      I wondered what on earth this Mencken had done to call down upon him the scorn of the South. The only people I had ever heard denounced in the South were Negroes, and this man was not a Negro. Then what ideas did Mencken hold that made a newspaper like the *Commercial Appeal* castigate him publicly? Undoubtedly he must be advocating ideas that the South did not like. Were there, then, people other than Negroes who criticized the South? I knew that during the Civil War the South had hated northern whites, but I had not encountered such hate during my life. Knowing no more of Mencken than I did at that moment, I felt a vague sympathy for him. Had not the South, which had assigned me the role of a non-man, cast at him its hardest words?

3      Now, how could I find out about this Mencken? There was a huge library near the riverfront, but I knew that Negroes were not allowed to patronize its shelves any more than they were the parks and playgrounds of the city. I had gone into the library several times to get books for the white men on the job. Which of them would now help me to get books? And how could I read them without causing concern to the white men with whom I worked? I had so far been successful in hiding my thoughts and feelings from them, but I knew that I would create hostility if I went about the business of reading in a clumsy way.

4      I weighed the personalities of the men on the job. There was Don, a Jew; but I distrusted him. His position was not much better than mine and I knew that he was uneasy and insecure; he had always treated me in an offhand, bantering way that barely concealed his contempt. I was afraid to ask him to help me get books; his frantic desire to demonstrate a racial solidarity with the whites against Negroes might make him betray me.

5      Then how about the boss? No, he was a Baptist and I had the suspicion that he would not be quite able to comprehend why a black boy would want to read Mencken. There were other white men on the job whose attitudes showed clearly that they were Kluxers or sympathizers, and they were out of the question.

6      There remained only one man whose attitude did not fit into an anti-Negro category, for I had heard the white men refer to him as a "Pope lover." He was an Irish Catholic and was hated by the white Southerners. I knew that he read books, because I had got him volumes from the library several times. Since he, too, was an object of hatred, I felt that he might refuse me but would hardly betray me. I hesitated, weighing and balancing the imponderable realities.

7      One morning I paused before the Catholic fellow's desk.

8      "I want to ask you a favor," I whispered to him.

9      "What is it?"

10      "I want to read. I can't get books from the library. I wonder if you'd let me use your card?"

11      He looked at me suspiciously.

12      "My card is full most of the time," he said.

"I see," I said and waited, posing my question silently.  13

"You're not trying to get me into trouble, are you, boy?" he asked,  14
staring at me.

"Oh, no, sir."  15

"What book do you want?"  16

"A book by H. L. Mencken."  17

"Which one?"  18

"I don't know. Has he written more than one?"  19

"He has written several."  20

"I didn't know that."  21

"What makes you want to read Mencken?"  22

"Oh, I just saw his name in the newspaper," I said.  23

"It's good of you to want to read," he said. "But you ought to read  24
the right things."

I said nothing. Would he want to supervise my reading?  25

"Let me think," he said. "I'll figure out something."  26

I turned from him and he called me back. He stared at me quizzically.  27

"Richard, don't mention this to the other white men," he said.  28

"I understand," I said. "I won't say a word."  29

A few days later he called me to him.  30

"I've got a card in my wife's name," he said. "Here's mine."  31

"Thank you, sir."  32

"Do you think you can manage it?"  33

"I'll manage fine," I said.  34

"If they suspect you, you'll get in trouble," he said.  35

"I'll write the same kind of notes to the library that you wrote  36
when you sent me for books," I told him. "I'll sign your name."

He laughed.  37

"Go ahead. Let me see what you get," he said.  38

That afternoon I addressed myself to forging a note. Now, what were  39
the names of books written by H. L. Mencken? I did not know any of them.
I finally wrote what I thought would be a foolproof note: *Dear Madam:
Will you please let this nigger boy*—I used the word "nigger" to make the
librarian feel that I could not possibly be the author of the note—*have
some books by H. L. Mencken?* I forged the white man's name.

I entered the library as I had always done when on errands for  40
whites, but I felt that I would somehow slip up and betray myself. I
doffed my hat, stood a respectful distance from the desk, looked as un-
bookish as possible, and waited for the white patrons to be taken care of.
When the desk was clear of people, I still waited. The white librarian
looked at me.

"What do you want, boy?"  41

As though I did not possess the power of speech, I stepped forward  42
and simply handed her the forged note, not parting my lips.

"What books by Mencken does he want?" she asked.  43

"I don't know, ma'am," I said, avoiding her eyes.  44

45    "Who gave you this card?"

46    "Mr. Falk," I said.

47    "Where is he?"

48    "He's at work, at the M—— Optical Company," I said. "I've been in here for him before."

49    "I remember," the woman said. "But he never wrote notes like this."

50    Oh, God, she's suspicious. Perhaps she would not let me have the books? If she had turned her back at that moment, I would have ducked out the door and never gone back. Then I thought of a bold idea.

51    "You can call him up, ma'am," I said, my heart pounding.

52    "You're not using these books, are you?" she asked pointedly.

53    "Oh, no, ma'am. I can't read."

54    "I don't know what he wants by Mencken," she said under her breath.

55    I knew now that I had won; she was thinking of other things and the race question had gone out of her mind. She went to the shelves. Once or twice she looked over her shoulder at me, as though she was still doubtful. Finally she came forward with two books in her hand.

56    "I'm sending him two books," she said. "But tell Mr. Falk to come in next time, or send me the names of the books he wants. I don't know what he wants to read."

57    I said nothing. She stamped the card and handed me the books. Not daring to glance at them, I went out of the library, fearing that the woman would call me back for further questioning. A block away from the library I opened one of the books and read a title: *A Book of Prefaces.* I was nearing my nineteenth birthday and I did not know how to pronounce the word "preface." I thumbed the pages and saw strange words and strange names. I shook my head, disappointed. I looked at the other book; it was called *Prejudices.* I knew what that word meant; I had heard it all my life. And right off I was on guard against Mencken's books. Why would a man want to call a book *Prejudices*? The word was so stained with all my memories of racial hate that I could not conceive of anybody using it for a title. Perhaps I had made a mistake about Mencken? A man who had prejudices must be wrong.

58    When I showed the books to Mr. Falk, he looked at me and frowned.

59    "That librarian might telephone you," I warned him.

60    "That's all right," he said. "But when you're through reading those books, I want you to tell me what you get out of them."

61    That night in my rented room, while letting the hot water run over my can of pork and beans in the sink, I opened *A Book of Prefaces* and began to read. I was jarred and shocked by the style, the clear, clean sweeping sentences. Why did he write like that? And how did one write like that? I pictured the man as a raging demon, slashing with his pen, consumed with hate, denouncing everything American, extolling every-

thing European or German, laughing at the weaknesses of people, mocking God, authority. What was this? I stood up, trying to realize what reality lay behind the meaning of the words. . . . Yes, this man was fighting, fighting with words. He was using words as a weapon, using them as one would use a club. Could words be weapons? Well, yes, for here they were. Then, maybe, perhaps, I could use them as a weapon? No. It frightened me. I read on and what amazed me was not what he said, but how on earth anybody had the courage to say it.

Occasionally I glanced up to reassure myself that I was alone in the 62 room. Who were these men about whom Mencken was talking so passionately? Who was Anatole France? Joseph Conrad? Sinclair Lewis, Sherwood Anderson, Dostoevski, George Moore, Gustave Flaubert, Maupassant, Tolstoy, Frank Harris, Mark Twain, Thomas Hardy, Arnold Bennett, Stephen Crane, Zola, Norris, Gorky, Bergson, Ibsen, Balzac, Bernard Shaw, Dumas, Poe, Thomas Mann, O. Henry, Dreiser, H. G. Wells, Gogol, T. S. Eliot, Gide, Baudelaire, Edgar Lee Masters, Stendhal, Turgenev, Huneker, Nietzsche, and scores of others? Were these men real? Did they exist or had they existed? And how did one pronounce their names?

I ran across many words whose meanings I did not know, and I ei- 63 ther looked them up in a dictionary or, before I had a chance to do that, encountered the word in a context that made its meaning clear. But what strange world was this? I concluded the book with the conviction that I had somehow overlooked something terribly important in life. I had once tried to write, had once reveled in feeling, had let my crude imagination roam, but the impulse to dream had been slowly beaten out of me by experience. Now it surged up again and I hungered for books, new ways of looking and seeing. It was not a matter of believing or disbelieving what I read, but of feeling something new, of being affected by something that made the look of the world different.

As dawn broke I ate my pork and beans, feeling dopey, sleepy. I 64 went to work, but the mood of the book would not die; it lingered, coloring everything I saw, heard, did. I now felt that I knew what the white men were feeling. Merely because I had read a book that had spoken of how they lived and thought, I identified myself with that book. I felt vaguely guilty. Would I, filled with bookish notions, act in a manner that would make the whites dislike me?

I forged more notes and my trips to the library became frequent. 65 Reading grew into a passion. My first serious novel was Sinclair Lewis's *Main Street*. It made me see my boss, Mr. Gerald, and identify him as an American type. I would smile when I saw him lugging his golf bags into the office. I had always felt a vast distance separating me from the boss, and now I felt closer to him, though still distant. I felt now that I knew him, that I could feel the very limits of his narrow life. And this had happened because I had read a novel about a mythical man called George F. Babbitt.

66    The plots and stories in the novels did not interest me so much as the point of view revealed. I gave myself over to each novel without reserve, without trying to criticize it; it was enough for me to see and feel something different. And for me, everything was something different. Reading was like a drug, a dope. The novels created moods in which I lived for days. But I could not conquer my sense of guilt, my feeling that the white men around me knew that I was changing, that I had begun to regard them differently.

67    Whenever I brought a book to the job, I wrapped it in newspaper—a habit that was to persist for years in other cities and under other circumstances. But some of the white men pried into my packages when I was absent and they questioned me.

68    "Boy, what are you reading those books for?"

69    "Oh, I don't know, sir."

70    "That's deep stuff you're reading, boy."

71    "I'm just killing time, sir."

72    "You'll addle your brains if you don't watch out."

73    I read Dreiser's *Jennie Gerhardt* and *Sister Carrie* and they revived in me a vivid sense of my mother's suffering; I was overwhelmed. I grew silent, wondering about the life around me. It would have been impossible for me to have told anyone what I derived from these novels, for it was nothing less than a sense of life itself. All my life had shaped me for the realism, the naturalism of the modern novel, and I could not read enough of them.

74    Steeped in new moods and ideas, I bought a ream of paper and tried to write; but nothing would come, or what did come was flat beyond telling. I discovered that more than desire and feeling were necessary to write and I dropped the idea. Yet I still wondered how it was possible to know people sufficiently to write about them? Could I ever learn about life and people? To me, with my vast ignorance, my Jim Crow station in life, it seemed a task impossible of achievement. I now knew what being a Negro meant. I could endure the hunger. I had learned to live with hate. But to feel that there were feelings denied me, that the very breadth of life itself was beyond my reach, that more than anything else hurt, wounded me. I had a new hunger.

75    In buoying me up, reading also cast me down, made me see what was possible, what I had missed. My tension returned, new, terrible, bitter, surging, almost too great to be contained. I no longer *felt* that the world about me was hostile, killing; I *knew* it. A million times I asked myself what I could do to save myself, and there were no answers. I seemed forever condemned, ringed by walls.

76    I did not discuss my reading with Mr. Falk, who had lent me his library card; it would have meant talking about myself and that would have been too painful. I smiled each day, fighting desperately to maintain my old behavior, to keep my disposition seemingly sunny. But some of the white men discerned that I had begun to brood.

"Wake up there, boy!" Mr. Olin said one day.   77

"Sir!" I answered for the lack of a better word.   78

"You act like you've stolen something," he said.   79

I laughed in the way I knew he expected me to laugh, but I resolved   80
to be more conscious of myself, to watch my every act, to guard and hide
the new knowledge that was dawning within me.

If I went north, would it be possible for me to build a new life then?   81
But how could a man build a life upon vague, unformed yearnings? I
wanted to write and I did not even know the English language. I bought
English grammars and found them dull. I felt that I was getting a better
sense of the language from novels than from grammars. I read hard, dis-
carding a writer as soon as I felt that I had grasped his point of view. At
night the printed page stood before my eyes in sleep.

Mrs. Moss, my landlady, asked me one Sunday morning:   82

"Son, what is this you keep on reading?"   83

"Oh, nothing. Just novels."   84

"What you get out of 'em?"   85

"I'm just killing time," I said.   86

"I hope you know your own mind," she said in a tone which im-   87
plied that she doubted if I had a mind.

I knew of no Negroes who read the books I liked and I wondered if   88
any Negroes ever thought of them. I knew that there were Negro doctors,
lawyers, newspapermen, but I never saw any of them. When I read a
Negro newspaper I never caught the faintest echo of my preoccupation in
its pages. I felt trapped and occasionally, for a few days, I would stop
reading. But a vague hunger would come over me for books, books that
opened up new avenues of feeling and seeing, and again I would forge another note to the white librarian. Again I would read and wonder as only
the naïve and unlettered can read and wonder, feeling that I carried a secret, criminal burden about with me each day.

That winter my mother and brother came and we set up housekeep-   89
ing, buying furniture on the installment plan, being cheated and yet
knowing no way to avoid it. I began to eat warm food and to my surprise
found that regular meals enabled me to read faster. I may have lived
through many illnesses and survived them, never suspecting that I was
ill. My brother obtained a job and we began to save toward the trip north,
plotting our time, setting tentative dates for departure. I told none of the
white men on the job that I was planning to go north; I knew that the
moment they felt I was thinking of the North they would change toward
me. It would have made them feel that I did not like the life I was living,
and because my life was completely conditioned by what they said or
did, it would have been tantamount to challenging them.

I could calculate my chances for life in the South as a Negro fairly   90
clearly now.

I could fight the Southern whites by organizing with other Negroes,   91
as my grandfather had done. But I knew that I could never win that way;

there were many whites and there were but few blacks. They were strong and we were weak. Outright black rebellion could never win. If I fought openly I would die and I did not want to die. News of lynchings were frequent.

92        I could submit and live the life of a genial slave, but that was impossible. All my life had shaped me to live by my own feelings, and thoughts. I could make up to Bess and marry her and inherit the house. But that, too, would be the life of a slave; if I did that, I would crush to death something within me, and I would hate myself as much as I knew the whites already hated those who had submitted. Neither could I ever willingly present myself to be kicked, as Shorty had done. I would rather have died than do that.

93        I could drain off my restlessness by fighting with Shorty and Harrison. I had seen many Negroes solve the problem of being black by transferring their hatred of themselves to others with a black skin and fighting them. I would have to be cold to do that, and I was not cold and I could never be.

94        I could, of course, forget what I had read, thrust the whites out of my mind, forget them; and find release from anxiety and longing in sex and alcohol. But the memory of how my father had conducted himself made that course repugnant. If I did not want others to violate my life, how could I voluntarily violate it myself?

95        I had no hope whatever of being a professional man. Not only had I been so conditioned that I did not desire it, but the fulfillment of such an ambition was beyond my capabilities. Well-to-do Negroes lived in a world that was almost as alien to me as the world inhabited by whites.

96        What, then, was there? I held my life in my mind, in my consciousness each day, feeling at times that I would stumble and drop it, spill it forever. My reading had created a vast sense of distance between me and the world in which I lived and tried to make a living, and that sense of distance was increasing each day. My days and nights were one long, quiet, continuously contained dream of terror, tension, and anxiety. I wondered how long I could bear it.

## CONSIDERATIONS

1. How do you heat a can of beans if you don't have a hot plate or a stove? How is Wright's answer to this question an autobiographical fact that might affect your appreciation of his essay?

2. In paragraph 65, Wright says of himself, "Reading grew into a passion." You don't have to look too far in the lives of other writers to find similar statements about reading. Reread the first paragraph of the preface to this book, think about the importance of reading to your prospects of improving as a writer, then write a substantial paragraph on your conclusions about the relationship of reading and writing. See also Ralph Ellison's "On Becoming a Writer."

3. Compare what Wright had to endure to use the public library with your own introduction to the same institution. How do you account for the motivation Wright needed to break the barriers between him and freedom to read?

4. The word Wright uses throughout to refer to his own race is no longer widely accepted? Why? What other words have been used at other times in American history? What difference does a name make?

5. Notice how Wright uses dialog in this essay. How do you decide when to use dialog? What are its purposes? Try converting some portion of the dialog of paragraphs 8 through 38 into what is commonly called Black English. Why didn't Wright use that form of speech?

6. The authors mentioned by Wright in his essay would make a formidable reading program for anyone. If you were to lay out such a program for yourself, what titles would you include? Why?

7. In paragraph 75, Wright says, "In buoying me up, reading also cast me down." Have you had a similar experience? Think back to a particular book or story or poem that grabbed your imagination and lured you into becoming a reader. Write a personal essay about that event and any related subsequent events. Note that the negative effects of reading persisted in Wright to the point where, in his last paragraph, he wrote, "I wondered how long I could bear it." Does Wright imply that one would be better off without learning to read?

# A Rhetorical Index

The various writing patterns—argument and persuasion, description, exposition, and narration—are amply illustrated in the many essays, stories, journal entries, and poems in *A Writer's Reader*. If any classification of writing according to type is suspect—because good writers inevitably merge the types—this index offers one plausible arrangement. Anyone looking for models or examples for study and imitation may well begin here.

A word about subcategories: We index two sorts of argument—formal and implicit—because some selections are obvious attempts to defend a stated proposition, often in high style, whereas others argue indirectly, informally, or diffusely, but persuasively nonetheless. Under "Description" we index selections that primarily describe persons, places, or miscellaneous phenomena. Under "Exposition" are those selections that clearly show the various rhetorical patterns of development: cause and effect; classification; comparison, contrast, and analogy; definition; example; and process analysis. "Narration" categorizes memoirs, essays, stories, and nonfiction nonautobiographical narratives.

At the end, we list the nonessay materials in the *Reader*—journal entries, short stories, poems, and drama.

## ARGUMENT AND PERSUASION

### Formal, Overt

### Informal, Subdued, Oblique, Elliptical, Implied

## DESCRIPTION

### Abstract Conditions, Institutions, Things, Phenomena, Events, Creatures

## EXPOSITION

*Analogy. See Comparison, Contrast, Analogy*

*Cause and Effect*

*Classification, Analysis, and Division*

### Definition

### Example

### Process

## NARRATION

### Autobiography and Memoir

# A Thematic Index

697

## CONTESTS, STRUGGLES, WINS AND LOSSES

## EDUCATION, THE ACQUISITION OF WISDOM

## EPIPHANY, IMAGINATION, VISION

**FAMILIES, PARENTS, OFFSPRING**

**FREEDOM AND RESTRAINT,
OPPRESSORS AND OPPRESSED**

## HEROES, LEADERS, PERFORMERS

## HISTORY, THE POWER OF THE PAST

## HUMOR, WIT, SATIRE

## THE IMPORTANCE OF PLACE, ROOTS

## INDIVIDUALITY, PRIVACY, SOLITUDE

**PLAY, GAMES, SPORTING LIFE**

**REBELS AND CONFORMISTS**

## WORKING

## WRITING, LANGUAGE, RHETORIC, AND STYLE

## THE ARTS AND THE MEDIA